# Family–Peer Relationships:
# Modes of Linkage

# Family–Peer Relationships:
# Modes of Linkage

Edited by

**Ross D. Parke**
*University of California at Riverside*

**Gary W. Ladd**
*University of Illinois at Champaign-Urbana*

**LEA** LAWRENCE ERLBAUM ASSOCIATES, PUBLISHERS
1992  Hillsdale, New Jersey                 Hove and London

Lawrence Erlbaum Associates, Inc., Publishers
365 Broadway
Hillsdale, New Jersey 07642

**Library of Congress Cataloging-in-Publication Data**

Family-peer relationships : modes of linkage / edited by Ross D.
   Parke, Gary W. Ladd.
         p.      cm.
   Includes bibliographical references and index.
   ISBN 0-8058-0600-8. — ISBN 0-8058-0601-6 (pbk.)
   1. Parent and child.  2. Age groups.  3. Family.  I. Parke, Ross
D., 1938–       II. Ladd, Gary W., 1950–
HQ755.85.F366   1992
306.874 – dc20                                              91-46149
                                                              CIP

Printed in the United States of America
10  9  8  7  6  5  4  3  2  1

To Barbara and Nicki, who illustrate
that family and friends are closely linked.

# Contents

# Acknowledgments

A variety of individuals contributed to the successful completion of this volume. Thanks and appreciation are extended to Sondra Birch for her help with the subject index, Donnalee Peccerilli for her assistance in the preparation of the author index, and Chris Strand for typing various parts of the manuscript. Debbie Ruel, our production editor, did a marvelous job in guiding the final manuscript into production. Finally, thanks to both Nicki Crick and Barbara Tinsley for their support throughout this project.

*Ross D. Parke*
*Gary W. Ladd*

# PART ONE

# INTRODUCTION
# AND OVERVIEW

# CHAPTER ONE

# Themes and Theories: Perspectives on Processes in Family–Peer Relationships

Gary W. Ladd
*University of Illinois*

Children's experiences within the family and the peer group have occupied a position of central importance in recent research on human development. During the past two decades, important advances have been made within both fields of inquiry. For example, recent studies of family processes and parenting have produced important findings concerning the impact of adult–child relations on child socialization and development. In the field of peer relations, researchers have begun to achieve a better understanding of how agemates influence children's personalities, social behaviors, and cognitions.

Progress in research on family and peer relations has also brought about an interest in the relations or linkages between the two domains. Previously, researchers interested in family relations have studied children's peer relations primarily as a means of indexing the putative effects of targeted family processes or alterations (e.g., fathering, divorce, authoritarian vs. permissive parenting). However, more recently, researchers interested in families have broadened the scope of their theories to include the interface between family and peer relations. In particular, they have become interested in understanding *how* families influence children's peer relations and competence, and they have begun to search for the mechanisms that may be responsible for such effects.

Similar developments can be observed in past research on children's peer relations. In early studies, researchers attempted to describe the types of relationships children formed with peers and the ways in which these

3

relationships changed with age. Later, interest in the processes of relationship formation and maintenance gave rise to studies of the correlates of popularity in peer groups, and the features of friendships between pairs of children. Findings from these investigations led many investigators to conclude that children's success in peer relations was a function of their social competence, or requisite skill at initiating and maintaining social ties with agemates. Not surprisingly, this hypothesis spurred an interest in the origins of children's social competence, and a search for antecedents within the family.

## PATHWAYS BETWEEN THE FAMILY AND PEER SYSTEMS

To explore potential relations between the family and peer systems, investigators have begun to construct and evaluate models of the "pathways" through which families influence children's peer relations, and vice versa. Pathways, as conceptualized here, refer to processes that may impinge on the child in one context (e.g., family relations), and to the mechanisms or mediating variables that may be responsible for transmitting the effects of such processes to another context (e.g., peer relations). At present, the effects of families on children's peer competence are thought to travel through either "direct" or "indirect" pathways (see Parke, MacDonald, Beitel, & Bhavnagri, 1988). Activities or processes that parents engage in as a means of controlling or enhancing their children's skills and relationships with peers are viewed as direct pathways. In contrast, aspects of family life or operations that do not directly impinge on children's peer relations (e.g., parents' disciplinary or parenting styles, the marital relationship) are often construed as indirect pathways.

For many investigators, the concept of an indirect pathway also implies that the family's effect on children's peer relations is mediated through some intervening child outcome. For example, both Pettit and colleagues (e.g., Pettit, Dodge, & Brown, 1988; Pettit, Harrist, Bates, & Dodge, 1991) and Hart, Ladd, and Burleson (1990) have hypothesized that parental disciplinary styles affect children's problem-solving skills and reasoning, which, in turn, influence the quality of their peer relations. It is made clear in subsequent chapters that many other types of mediating variables are being investigated, including aspects of the child's cognitive processing, emotions and emotional regulation, mental representations of relationships, and self-efficacy.

It is also important to recognize that evidence from recent studies, including several reported in this volume, illustrates that the pathways from family to peer relations may transmit both positive and negative effects.

On the one hand, children may learn important skills or competencies within the family that can be transferred or generalized to the peer group. On the other hand, adverse family circumstances and relations may also serve as a staging area for child incompetence and maladjustment.

The concept of a pathway also implies a particular direction of effect. Contemporary research, including most of the work reported in this volume, has been based almost entirely on "family effect" models, or pathways in which the direction of effect travels from family (or parent) to child. It is important to recognize, however, that a convincing case can be made for exploring pathways that traverse the opposite direction of effect. It seems probable that the events that children encounter in the peer culture will, at times, spill over into family life, and precipitate certain reactions (perhaps some of the same processes we now view as potential causes within the family). In the long run, we may find that the greatest explanatory power is achieved with models that permit us to consider both types of pathways, or even bidirectional effects.

## Identifying and Mapping Significant Pathways

Families are complex, and many of the processes that occur in this system may directly or indirectly affect the quality of children's peer competence and relations. Therefore, progress toward an understanding of the linkages between the family and peer systems depends, in part, on the types of pathways researchers choose to investigate.

Within the past few years, researchers have targeted a broad range of family features and characteristics as possible correlates and antecedents of children's social competence. For organizational purposes, these characteristics can be grouped into three major domains (cf. Ladd, 1991): (a) indirect influences: family relations, interactions, perceptions, and environments; (b) direct influences: families as teachers and organizers; and (c) variations on family–peer relationships. Within each of these domains, investigators have developed models that are designed to represent potential pathways or linkages between the family and peer systems. It is important to consider these perspectives, both as conceptual foundations for research on family–peer relations, and as background for the content of this book.

## INDIRECT INFLUENCES: FAMILY RELATIONS, INTERACTIONS, AND ENVIRONMENTS

Relationships among family members, the cognitive and behavioral processes that evolve from family life, and the characteristics of the family environment may have an important bearing on the development of children's social skills and competence in peer relations. Generally, researchers have taken the perspective that these features of the family operate as indirect influences on children's peer relations.

*Attachment.* Many researchers view the parent–child relationship and parenting as important precursors for later social development. Research on the child's attachment status has figured prominently in this literature, and many studies have been conducted to determine whether the quality of the early parent–child relationship has important conse-quences for the child's later relationships with peers. Although perspec-tives on the attachment construct vary and have evolved over time (Ainsworth, 1973; Bowlby, 1969; Sroufe, 1983; Sroufe & Fleeson, 1986), two key propositions have served as a stimulus for research on family–peer linkages (see Cohn, Patterson, & Christopoulos, 1991). The first is that secure parent–child attachments, which may grow out of sensitive-responsive caretaking (Belsky, Rovine, & Taylor, 1984), help children to develop the autonomy and confidence needed to explore and develop relationships with others, including peers. Conversely, insecure attach-ments (i.e., insecure-avoidant or insecure-resistant patterns as identified in Ainsworth's strange situation) appear to have their origins in less sen-sitive parenting or inconsistent responsiveness from caretakers (see Ains-worth, Blehar, Waters, & Wall, 1978; Belsky, 1984; Lamb, Thompson, Gardner, & Charnov, 1985) and are thought to deprive children of the emotional and social resources needed to negotiate later relationships with peers. A second key proposition is that the attachment relationship serves as a "template" for the child's later relationships because children infer "working models," or expectations about the self and others (i.e., value of the self to others, likely responses of others to the self), from their experiences with the parent. Once internalized, these working models may affect children's behavior and success in future relationships. For example, securely attached children may develop working models that lead them to expect peers to be warm, nurturing, and responsive. As a result, they may be more likely than children with insecure attachment histories to initiate peer interactions and respond to peers' overtures in a cooperative and confident manner.

Evidence linking early attachment patterns to the quality of children's peer relations in preschool can be found in a number of recent studies. Several investigations reveal that, whereas children who are securely at-tached during the first and second years tend to be more engaging, so-ciable, and cooperative with preschool peers, children with insecure attachment histories tend to become more withdrawn or negative in this context (e.g., Easterbrooks & Lamb, 1979; Pastor, 1981; Waters, Wippman, & Sroufe, 1979). Other studies show that securely attached children, when compared to their insecurely attached counterparts, tend to display higher levels of positive affect in peer interactions (LaFreniere & Sroufe, 1985), better peer relationships (i.e., well liked by peers; LaFreniere & Sroufe, 1985; Park & Waters, 1989), and fewer behavior problems (Erickson, Sroufe, & Egeland, 1985).

Although less is known about the relation between attachment and children's peer relations in middle childhood or adolescence, there is some evidence to suggest that the potential effects of attachment status generalize beyond early childhood (see Cohn et al., 1991). Lewis and Feiring (1989) found that boys who were securely attached as infants tended to have more male friends at age 9 than did insecurely attached boys. No relation emerged, however, for girls in this sample. Other studies suggest a relation between later manifestations of attachment (i.e., attachment assessed in early to middle childhood) and children's peer competence. Similar to the findings reported by Lewis and Fiering (1989), Cohn (1990) found that boys who displayed secure attachments following kindergarten were more competent in their peer relations during Grade 1 than their insecurely attached counterparts. By comparison, insecurely attached boys were viewed by peers as less likeable and more aggressive.

Thus, there is a growing evidence of a relation between attachment and children's competence in peer relations. Further research on this pathway is needed, however, to understand the significance of working models, which are hypothesized to mediate the linkage between initial attachment relations and later peer relations. It may also be useful to parse the attachment construct into more specific relationship processes, and investigate how specific aspects of the parent–child relationship affect children's social learning and competence (cf. Eckerman & Stein, 1983; Parke et al., 1988). Another issue that remains to be addressed is the possibility that variation in attachment, and therefore its potential outcomes, are reflective of underlying or inherited child dispositions, such as sociability or temperament (cf. Lamb & Nash, 1989).

Also, most of the research on attachment relations has been conducted with mothers and children, often to the exclusion of the potential role of fathers. Findings from a recent investigation by Patterson, Kupersmidt, and Griesler (1990) suggest that children's relationships with their fathers may also play an important role in the development of peer competence. In this study, peer-rejected children reported feeling less companionship and affection from their fathers than did children in other sociometic groups (e.g., peer-neglected children). Moreover, this relation was even more apparent for peer-rejected children who were also aggressive.

***Child-Rearing Styles and Parent–Child Interaction.*** Research has shown that many of the behaviors, values, and attitudes parents display in child-rearing situations are correlated and can be combined into typologies. Drawing on models developed by Becker (1964) and Baumrind (1973), Maccoby and Martin (1983) have classified research on parenting styles along two primary dimensions: warmth (e.g., responsive vs. unresponsive) and control (e.g., demanding vs. undemanding). Four typologies emerge from this two-dimensional scheme: authoritarian (i.e., more demanding than responsive), authoritative (i.e., demanding but also responsive), indulgent (i.e., more responsive than demanding), and indifferent-uninvolved (i.e., undemanding and unresponsive).

Although there is some evidence to suggest that these typologies, or aspects of parenting styles, are associated with the quality of children's peer relations, few detailed models have been proposed to account for this linkage. However, as Putallaz and Heflin (1990) have recently observed, a number of propositions have been advanced to explain the impact of parenting styles on child behavior, and some of these pathways may help to explain how children develop competencies that transfer to peer relations. For example, parents' child-rearing styles may provide children with models for affiliative behaviors and skills, or foster expectations about relationships that generalize to the peer group. Other provisions, such as parental warmth and responsiveness, may influence children's emotional needs and thus determine their ability to trust and care about others (e.g., peers).

The research on parenting styles shows that authoritarian parenting is associated with a variety of problematic peer outcomes for children. Parents who rely on authoritarian or power-assertive styles tend to have children who are more aggressive, withdrawn, or dominated by peers (Baldwin, 1948; Baumrind, 1967; Patterson, 1982). Indulgent parenting styles, especially when permissiveness toward aggression is included in this pattern, appear to forecast children's aggressive reputations in the peer group (Olweus, 1980). In particular, this research suggests that preexisting aggressive dispositions in children may be exacerbated in families where parents fail to impose limits on children's aggressive behaviors (Olweus, 1980). Parents with indifferent or uninvolved child-rearing styles appear to monitor their children's whereabouts and peer associates less carefully, and tend to have children who become more involved in deviant and delinquent peer activities (Dishion, 1990; Patterson & Stouthamer-Loeber, 1984; Wilson, 1980). Data from at least one study also shows that children with uninvolved parents tend to be more aggressive with peers (Attili, 1989). In contrast to these child-rearing parenting styles, authoritative parenting has been associated with higher levels of social responsibility and independence in both boys and girls (Baumrind, 1967, 1971).

Parental warmth, in particular, appears to be an important correlate of children's prosocial behavior (see Brody & Shaffer, 1982; Hoffman, 1975), and recent studies suggest that the same linkage can be found in samples of English and Italian families (Attili, 1989; Hinde & Tamplin, 1983).

Unfortunately, the specific parenting processes or mechanisms that may be responsible for these outcomes have received relatively little attention in past research. Therefore, rather than study global parenting styles, some researchers have begun to observe more molecular features of parent–child interaction and investigate potential linkages between these variables and children's peer competence.

Parke and colleagues (see Parke et al., 1988; Parke et al., 1989) have proposed that children learn and develop many of the social skills that are needed in family and peer relationships during face-to-face interactions with their parents. In particular, these investigators view parent–child play as an important context for examining several processes that are hypothesized to impact the development of children's interpersonal competence. Included among these are specific parenting behaviors, such as directiveness, involvement, and the ability to elicit positive affect from the child during play. Parke and colleagues have argued that the level of directiveness parents employ may affect the way children learn how to regulate interactions with peers. Overly directive parents, for example, may prevent children from learning how to initiate, control, and maintain social interactions. Efforts to engage (e.g., sustain) the child's play interactions and elicit positive affect may help children learn how to construct interactions that peers will find rewarding. The parents' attempts to elicit and regulate affective exchanges are seen as a means of teaching children how to interpret others' emotional displays and how to understand the impact of their own affect on others (e.g., peers). For this reason, children's abilities to encode and decode emotional expressions have also been studied.

These and other hypotheses have been explored in a series of studies conducted by Parke and colleagues (see MacDonald & Parke, 1984; Parke et al., 1988; Parke et al., 1989). This work has produced a number of important findings, many of which are consistent with the pathways identified in this framework. First, there is strong evidence to suggest that the nature of parents' involvement during play is associated with children's popularity in peer groups. One such correlate is the parents' ability to sustain ongoing play bouts. Parents, and especially fathers, who were able to maintain reciprocal play interactions tended to have children who were more popular with peers. Children's peer popularity was also correlated with the extent to which parents elicited positive affect during play. Second, the parents' styles of interaction, particularly their directiveness and coerciveness within play encounters, emerged as significant correlates of children's peer status. In general, parents who controlled play interactions with directive and coercive strategies tended to have children who scored lower on measures of peer competence, acceptance, and school adjustment. This type of interaction was particularly characteristic of peer-rejected children and their fathers. In these dyads, the children were more inclined to respond to parental overtures with coercive tactics, and they had difficulty regulating their interactions and affect (i.e., they often tended to escalate out of control or withdraw from parental stimulation).

Further studies of children's emotional encoding and decoding abilities (see MacDonald, 1987; Parke et al., 1989) show that peer-rejected children are less competent than their peer-accepted counterparts both at identifying and displaying affective cues or "signals." In addition, a positive relation was found between the length of parent–child play interaction and children's abilities to correctly interpret their parents' emotional expressions. Together, these findings suggest that children's affect regulation abilities, particularly their emotional encoding and decoding skills, may be fostered in the context of parent–child play, and mediate their success in social interactions with peers.

Additional studies of the linkage between parental behaviors and children's peer relations have been conducted by Putallaz and colleagues (Putallaz, 1987; Putallaz & Heflin, 1990). Much of this work has been based on both modeling and response evocation hypotheses. More specifically, modeling is thought to be an important mechanism for the transmission of affective dispositions. For example, Putallaz suggested that the affective tone of parents' social interactions, both with the child and with other persons, is imitated by children in their social interactions with peers. In a study comparing mothers and children interacting in differing interpersonal contexts (e.g., with each other, with an age-mate), Putallaz (1987) found that: (a) agreeable mothers (i.e., mothers who elicited positive affect with their children and other mothers) tended to have children who were agreeable with peers, and (b) disagreeable mothers tended to have children who were disagreeable with peers, and (c) disagreeable children tended to have lower status among peers.

A second mechanism that Putallaz and colleagues (Putallaz & Heflin, 1990) have proposed to account for links between parent–child and child–peer relations is response evocation. According to this view, parent behaviors may also induce complementary or defensive behaviors in children that, in turn, generalize to peer interactions. Not unlike the research on parenting styles, Putallaz (1987) found that mothers who permitted less child autonomy (controlling mothers; i.e., mothers high on disagreeableness and demandingness) tended to have children who were less assertive and more self-focused in their interactions with peers. In contrast, mothers who permitted greater child autonomy tended to have children who were more assertive and agreeable with peers.

***Parents' Disciplinary Strategies.*** A number of investigators have proposed that parents' disciplinary styles may influence the nature of children's interactions with peers (for reviews, see Cohn et al., 1991; Putallaz & Heflin, 1990). Early studies (e.g., Becker, 1964; Hoffman, 1960; Zahn-Waxler, Radke-Yarrow, & King, 1979) revealed that, whereas parents who employed power-assertive techniques (e.g., commands, physical power) tended to have children who were more aggressive and domineering toward peers, parents who relied on inductive methods of discipline tended to have children with more prosocial orientations. Recent investigations conducted with preschool and grade-school children and their families have extended this work. Consistent with earlier studies, findings from many of these investigations suggest that harsh, demanding, and punitive discipline styles are associated with children's peer difficulties.

Pettit et al. (1988) have argued that many of the deviant cognitions that appear to underlie children's peer difficulties (for a review, see Dodge & Feldman, 1990; Ladd & Crick, 1989) may have their origins in the child's early family experiences, including the parents' disciplinary practices. Their research has shown that several aspects of the early family environment, including parents' discipline styles, may be related to children's competence with peers. Pettit et al. (1988) found that mothers with more restrictive disciplinary styles (i.e., based on the degree of concern, constraint, and reasoning displayed in response to hypothetical discipline situations), and those who endorsed the use of aggression, tended to have children who were less accepted and skilled among peers and more aggressive in the classroom. Moreover, the effect of early family experiences appeared to be mediated by children's interpersonal problem-solving skills. That is, coercive family environments predicted the quality of children's problem-solving skills, which, in turn, predicted their competence in peer relations. Similar findings were obtained in a subsequent study by Pettit and colleagues (Pettit et al., 1991). In this study, the effects of coercive and intrusive family interactions on children's social competence were mediated by children's social cognitions.

Additional evidence of a connection between parents' disciplinary styles and children's peer competence can be found in a study by Hart et al. (1990). These investigators hypothesized that parents' disciplinary styles (i.e., power assertion vs. induction) may teach children to expect different types of outcomes in interpersonal situations. Whereas inductive techniques focus children's attention on how their behavior affects relationships with others (i.e., relationship outcomes), power-assertive techniques focus attention on compliance with little emphasis on relationship or psychological consequences. Hart et al. further hypothesized that, once learned, these expectancies would mediate children's behavior toward peers and ultimately determine their acceptance or rejection by agemates. In fact, data gathered with kindergarten and fourth-grade samples revealed that children of power-assertive mothers tended to have outcome expectations that were more instrumentally focused than relationship-focused (i.e., concerned with getting their way in peer situations), and that children with this type of outcome expectation tended to be less accepted by peers at school.

The hypothesis that parents' disciplinary practices may have indirect effects on children's peer relations receives additional support from research conducted by Dishion (1990). Dishion proposed that parents who employed inconsistent, coercive disciplinary styles would encourage children to develop higher levels of antisocial behavior, which, in turn, would lead children to become rejected by peers. Data gathered with samples of grade-school boys and their families supported this hypothesis. Other findings revealed that the parents of rejected boys were less prone to monitor their whereabouts and social activities.

***Parental Perceptions, Attitudes, and Beliefs.***   Potential indirect pathways may also exist between parental cognitions and children's social competence. Although there is growing evidence to suggest that parents' perceptions, attitudes, and beliefs are related to children's cognitive and physical development (see Goodnow, 1988; Miller, 1988), research on how these factors may affect children's social development is at an early stage.

Most investigators who have begun to probe these pathways tend to view parental cognitions as affecting children's social competence indirectly. Often, within such models, it is hypothesized that parents' cognitions about children or child rearing cause them to engage in differing socialization practices that, in turn, produce differing child outcomes (see Ladd & Price, 1986; Rubin, Mills, & Rose-Krasnor, 1989). The possibility of reciprocal relationships has also been recognized, as in the case where children's competence (or incompetence) serves as an impetus for compensatory or remediative child-rearing strategies (see Ladd & Golter, 1988; Ladd & Price, 1986).

In a study of parents' perceptions, Ladd and Price (1986) correlated the difficulty parents ascribed to academic and social child-rearing tasks with measures of children's perceived and actual competence in corresponding domains. They hypothesized that the level of difficulty parents perceived for interpersonal socialization tasks (e.g., helping children make friends or learn social skills) would be inversely related to children's social competence. Two potentially reciprocal pathways were proposed to account for this anticipated relation. The logic of the first pathway, a "parent effects explanation," was that parents may avoid or de-emphasize "difficult" socialization tasks, and thereby reduce socialization pressure and, ultimately, child competence in such areas. The rationale for the second pathway, a "child effects explanation," was that differences in children's competence might shape parents' perceptions of the ease or difficulty of corresponding socialization tasks. For example, parents of children who have trouble talking to peers may be inclined to see this as a difficult skill to socialize.

As predicted, Ladd and Price (1986) found that parents' difficulty estimates for social tasks were inversely correlated with children's social competence. In general, stronger relations were found between parents' estimates of perceived difficulty and children's actual as opposed to perceived social competence. However, parents of children who scored high on both perceived and actual social competence tended to report lower levels of perceived difficulty for corresponding socialization tasks than did parents of children whose scores on both measures were either low or "mismatched" (e.g., high perceived but low actual competence). Unfortunately, the study's design did not permit clear inferences about the direction of effect.

Melson, Ladd, and McVey (1990) have attempted to extend this work by exploring the attributions parents employ to account for the ease or difficulty of interpersonal socialization tasks with preschoolers (e.g., helping children make friends, or gain acceptance from peers). It was anticipated that parents' attributions would differ depending on the degree of difficulty they were experiencing with their child, and that the pattern of such attributions would reflect a "positivity bias" (see Gretarrson & Gelfand, 1988). That is, parents were expected to give the child credit for socialization tasks that were perceived as "easy" and refrain from blaming the child for tasks that were perceived as "difficult." In fact, different attributional patterns were found for parents who reported greater as opposed to lesser difficulty at socializing children's peer competence. When parents were asked to choose explanations for difficult as opposed to easy hypothetical tasks, parents who were experiencing some difficulty with helping their child socially tended to endorse more reasons for difficulty and fewer attributions for ease. Consistent with the positivity bias hypothesis, these parents also attributed difficulty to parent-centered rather than child-centered causes, and to unstable rather than stable causes, particularly if the attributions chosen referred to causes internal to the child. These findings are important because they show that parents tend to take personal responsibility for difficult socialization tasks. To the extent that parents view difficulties as stemming more from themselves than the child, and more from unstable than stable causes, they may be more motivated to persist at helping the child. The positivity bias also has important implications for parents' affective reactions to difficult helping situations. Bugenthal (1989) has shown that parents react with more negative emotion if they infer that they have limited ability to deal with problematic child-rearing events. Similarly, Dix and Lochman (1989) found that parents report being less upset with their children's negative behavior if they infer that their parenting in some way contributed to their child's behavior.

In a related line of research, Rubin and colleagues (Mills & Rubin, 1990; Rubin et al., 1989) have emphasized the importance of parental beliefs in the development of children's competence. Toward this end, they have proposed an information-processing model of parenting behavior (Rubin et al., 1989). Among the types of cognitions they target for investigation are parents' beliefs about the timing of children's social development (i.e., developmental milestones), causes of social development (i.e., attributions), the importance of various forms of social development (i.e., values), and means by which these developments can be accomplished (i.e., socialization strategies).

The empirical work derived from this model has been designed to examine mothers' "proactive" and "reactive" beliefs about aspects of their children's social development and behavior. In a study conducted with preschool children and their mothers, Rubin et al. (1989) defined proactive beliefs as cognitions that underlie mothers' efforts to promote children's skilled or competent behaviors. These included beliefs about when children develop certain social skills, how such skills develop, and what should be done to facilitate skill development. Three types of skills were examined, including making friends, sharing possessions, and leading or influencing others. Results showed that mothers believed that children accomplish all three developments during the preschool years, and that they see friendship skills emerging before abilities such as sharing and leading. With the exception of sharing, mothers tended to attribute skill development to causes within the child (e.g., child's disposition) rather than to environmental sources. Sharing, in contrast, was more likely to be seen as evolving from external demands and greater parental involvement.

Relations were also found between mothers' beliefs and their preschooler's social problem-solving behaviors in the classroom. Mothers who valued the investigated social skills tended to have children who were more prosocial, assertive, and successful in their problem-solving behaviors. Similar findings emerged for mothers who viewed skill development as externally caused or controllable, and whose socialization strategies tended to be planful and devoid of power assertive or coercive tactics.

Rubin and colleagues (Mills & Rubin, 1990; Rubin et al., 1989) have also studied parents' "reactive" beliefs, or the appraisals, attributions, and anticipated socialization strategies parents construct in response to problematic child behaviors such as aggression and social withdrawal.

This work reveals that parents react to both aggression and withdrawal with concern, and tend to attribute such behaviors to transient states in the child (e.g., mood or passing stage). More forceful strategies were suggested for dealing with aggression than with withdrawal, although the types of strategies parents reported also varied with the family's socioeconomic and life circumstances.

Also included in this domain are factors such as the parents' memories of their peer experiences during childhood (see Putallaz, Costanzo, & Smith, 1991). Specifically, Putallaz et al. have argued that parents' recollections of their own childhood peer experiences may influence their parenting behavior as adults, which, in turn, may affect their children's peer relations. Within this model, parents' memories are thought to influence the types of expectations they develop for children's peer relations, and color their perceptions and interpretations of their children's experiences in this context. This "affective lens" or "strategy frame" (cf. Putallaz et al., 1991) is hypothesized to become an impetus for differential parenting behaviors and socialization practices.

Although research on this pathway is in an early stage, the available evidence is consistent with the proposed model. Studies by Putallaz et al. (1991) have shown that mothers with anxious peer memories, as opposed to those with predominantly positive or negative recollections, were more concerned about guiding their children's peer experiences. The form of these intentions, however, varied with children's gender. For boys, anxious mothers tended to focus on facilitating positive peer experiences, whereas for girls, greater emphasis was placed on avoiding negative peer experiences.

***Family Environments.*** Ecologically oriented investigators have focused attention on features of the family's social context. Cochran and Brassard (1979), for example, have proposed that qualities of the family's social network exert indirect influences on children's social development. Among the potential indirect pathways they identify are the social experiences children encounter as they participate in their parents' networks. In some cases, these experiences may have a direct bearing on children's peer relationships. For example, when the membership of parents' networks includes other families, children may be afforded greater opportunity to interact with agemates, and form their own network among peers. Although very little research has been conducted to explore this proposition, there is some evidence to suggest that preschoolers' friendships tend to be more stable when the parents of both children are acquainted with each other (Schiavo & Solomon, 1981; Schiavo, Soloman, Evers, & Cohen, 1982).

Another important ecological variable is the family's physical or geographic context. Factors such as the family's choice of neighborhoods and schools, and availability of community resources (e.g., scouts, playgrounds, etc.) may affect children's access to peers, and their opportunities to develop social skills and relationships (see Ladd & Coleman, in press; Ladd, Hart, Wadsworth, & Golter, 1988; Parke et al., 1988). As Cohn et al. (1991) have recently noted, there is some evidence to suggest that access or proximity is an important dimension in grade-school children's friendships. Although mixed, evidence from several studies conducted during the 1930s, 1940s, and 1950s showed that grade schoolers tended to be friends with children who lived near them (see DeVault, 1957; Gallagher, 1958; Potashin, 1946; Seagoe, 1939). Of course, the impact of these settings may also depend on how parents and children *manage* or utilize them. Models that address this aspect of family–peer relations are examined in greater detail within the domain of "direct" pathways.

## DIRECT INFLUENCES:
## FAMILIES AS TEACHERS AND ORGANIZERS

Parents' efforts to directly promote and manage children's experiences with peers can be conceptualized as "direct" pathways that connect the family and peer systems. Although parents may facilitate children's peer relations in many ways (see Rubin & Sloman, 1984), only a few of these potential socialization activities have been empirically investigated. Existing evidence points to four types of roles that parents may adopt as means of influencing children's peer opportunities and interactions (see Ladd & Coleman, in press; Ladd, Le Sieur, & Profilet, in press): designers, mediators, supervisors, and consultants.

First, parents may operate as "designers" of the social environment. They may choose to reside in neighborhoods that provide safe play environments and access to peers, or enroll children in child-care settings, schools, or other organized activities involving peers (see Ladd, Le Sieur, & Profilet, in press; Parke & Bhavnagri, 1989). Although no formal models have been proposed to study this pathway, there is evidence to suggest that these environmental variations are linked to the quality of children's peer relations. For example, research on the social ecology of neighborhoods (Berg & Medrich, 1980; Medrich, Roizen, Rubin, & Buckley, 1982) shows that children's opportunities to meet peers are greater when they grow up in neighborhoods with dense child populations, flat landscapes, and amenities such as sidewalks and playgrounds. These studies also show that children tend to have larger friendship networks and more spontaneous play arrangements when houses are closely spaced and have few barriers between them. In contrast, children's access to peers is more restricted in dangerous neighborhoods (Cochran & Riley, 1988) and rural settings (Medrich et al., 1982).

As "mediators," parents may influence young children's social development by arranging informal peer contacts, and by regulating their choice of play partners (see Bhavnagri, 1987; Ladd & Golter, 1988). Ladd and colleagues (Ladd & Golter, 1988; Ladd & Hart, 1991; Ladd et al., 1988) have hypothesized that by initiating play opportunities with peers, parents may facilitate children's entrance into the peer culture, and provide a context for them to develop important relationship skills (e.g., teach children how to meet peers, find playmates, and maintain relationships).

Findings from several studies conducted with preschool children lend support to this proposition. Ladd and Golter (1988) found that preschoolers whose parents initiated and arranged peer contacts, as compared to those who did not, tended to have a larger network of playmates and more consistent partners. Boys with more parent-initiated contacts were also more likely to become accepted by their classmates following their entrance into kindergarten. Similarly, studies by Lieberman (1977) and Ladd et al. (1988) show that children with regular play-group experience exhibit higher levels of social competence and school adjustment.

Parents may also act in the capacity of "supervisors" or "teachers" by monitoring children's peer interactions and offering support, instructions, or guidance. Research by Bhavnagri and Parke (1991) suggests that this type of support may be especially important for very young children, as they begin to negotiate interactions with peers. These investigators compared preschoolers' social competence with peers in conditions where their parents acted either as facilitators of the children's play or as passive observers. Comparisons of younger and older preschoolers showed that the children in the younger group were less able to maintain peer interactions on their own, and interacted more competently with peers when they received parental assistance.

Apparently, even brief bouts of parent–child interaction may prime children for interactive experiences with peers. Findings similar to those reported by Bhavnagri and Parke (1991) have been reported by Lollis (1990) in a study of the effects of mother–child interaction on toddlers post-separation behaviors. Toddlers first participated in one of two mother–child interaction conditions (i.e., extensive or minimal parent–child interaction), and were then observed with a peer in the absence of their mothers. Toddlers who had extensive interaction with their mothers played longer with the peer and displayed lower levels of distress following separation than did toddlers who were afforded only minimal interaction with their mothers.

Other studies with toddlers have been conducted in naturalistic contexts (e.g., homes), and they reveal that mothers' propensities to intervene in young children's peer-play bouts vary with the context and quality of children's interactions. Lollis and Ross (1987) conducted home observations of mothers managing toddler–peer interactions and found that mothers intervened most often during children's conflicts. Mothers were especially likely to intervene in conflicts instigated by their own children in their own homes and, in these situations, tended to employ strategies designed to balance inequities in the children's play.

Additional studies conducted with older preschool children further illustrate how parents' supervisory behaviors are related to children's peer competence. Ladd and Golter (1988) have proposed that parents may pursue more or less instructive or controlling ways to monitor their children's informal peer activities (e.g., play contacts in the home), and that more intrusive or controlling methods of supervision may be associated with lower levels of peer competence. More intrusive or "direct" styles of supervision include monitoring children's activities closely, and frequently guiding or joining their play. Such methods are hypothesized to interfere with older preschoolers' attempts to develop and deploy various interpersonal and play-management skills, such as initiating, constructing, and elaborating themes for play activities (see Mize & Ladd, 1990). In contrast, less direct forms of supervision include watching children at a distance, or sporadically checking on their activities.

Data from the Ladd and Golter (1988) investigation reveal that parents' supervisory styles during preschool were predictive of children's classroom peer acceptance in kindergarten. Compared to children whose parents employed indirect styles of supervision, those whose parents relied on direct or intrusive styles of supervision were more likely to become disliked by their kindergarten classmates. Moreover, these children were also perceived by teachers to be more hostile toward peers.

In a related line of research, Finnie and Russell (1988) have hypothesized that the content of mothers' instructional strategies may account for differences in children's competence at interpersonal tasks, such as entering a play group. To explore this proposition, Finnie and Russell observed mothers as they attempted to assist their children as they entered peers' ongoing play activities. Compared to the mothers of unpopular children, mothers of popular children tended to suggest or model more competent strategies—that is, strategies that have been shown to have a high probability of success for children in group-entry situations. In particular, the mothers of popular children encouraged children to orient to the groups' ongoing activity and employ entry behaviors that were relevant, rather than disruptive, to the focus of the activity. In a subsequent study, Russell and Finnie (1990) examined the instructions mothers gave to preschoolers both prior to (i.e., preparatory instructions) and during their attempts to enter peers' play. Here again, the findings showed that mothers of popular children tended to focus children on relevant and group-oriented entry bids.

As children grow older, however, parents may choose to play less directive roles (e.g., interpersonal "consultant") and offer assistance contingent on children's interpersonal concerns and problems (see Rubin & Sloman, 1984). Cohen (1989) found that, during middle childhood, mothers' involvement in children's peer relations tended to take several forms. Among the most common forms of maternal involvement were roles that Cohen termed *advice and support* (e.g., giving advice, talking about peer problems), *orchestration* (e.g., arranging play activities, encouraging child to invite peers to play), and *monitoring* (e.g., keeping track of child's whereabouts and play partners).

## VARIATIONS ON FAMILY–PEER RELATIONSHIPS

A number of factors may produce variations in the ways that the family and peer systems are linked. These factors may include forces that operate both outside and inside the family, and at differing levels of context. For example, at the broadest level, there may be considerable variation across cultures in the value parents place on peer relations, and in the methods they employ to socialize their children's peer relationships. Other forces may originate from daily life experiences and create pressures that disrupt or disorganize family relationships and interactions. Families may also differ internally on dimensions such as the health or pathology of its members, relationships, and interactions.

*Cultural Differences.* Little research has been conducted to determine whether there are cultural differences in pathways that link the family and peer systems. There do appear to be cultural differences in the extent to which adults rely on peers as teachers and socializers (Avgar, Bronfenbrenner, & Henderson, 1977), promote mixed-age peer interaction (Ellis, Rogoff, & Cromer, 1981), and foster values that are at odds with those found in peer groups (Bronfenbrenner, 1970). It is also conceivable that families with differing ethnic and cultural traditions may emphasize different aspects of social life as they rear their children, or permit their children to engage in different types of peer experiences and relationships.

*Divorce and Marital Discord.* The potential impact of family difficulties such as divorce and marital conflict on children's peer relations has not been well researched (cf. Grych & Fincham, 1990). However, there is considerable evidence to suggest that both of these aspects of family life affect children's psychological health and functioning (see Cummings, Iannotti, & Zahn-Waxler, 1985; Cummings, Zahn-Waxler, &

Radke-Yarrow, 1981; Emery, 1988; Grych & Fincham, 1990; Long & Forehand, 1987). Consequently, it might also be expected that family disruption and discord would be an important determinant of children's social competence and success in peer relations.

One major study of the effects of divorce on children, conducted by Hetherington and colleagues (Hetherington, Cox, & Cox, 1979), included data on children's peer relations. Families with preschool children were studied over a 2-year period following the parents' divorce, and data were gathered on the children's peer interactions and acceptance at the end of the first and second years. Comparisons between divorced and intact families showed that boys with divorced parents tended to initiate more hostile and aggressive peer interactions, and were more disliked by peers at both times of assessment. Girls from divorced and intact families did not differ significantly on these dimensions. These findings suggest that divorce is associated with early peer difficulties and that boys appear to be at greater risk for such problems than are girls.

However, recent evidence gathered with young adolescents suggests that both males and females may be at risk for impaired social competence in divorced families (Long, Forehand, Fauber, & Brody, 1987). Compared to adolescents in intact families, Long et al. found that both males and females in divorced families reported significantly lower levels of perceived social competence. Clearly, further research is needed to identify the aspects of divorce that may be relevant to children's progress in peer relations, and to explicate how these processes may influence both boys and girls.

One important factor that may underlie both family dissolution (e.g., divorce) and children's peer difficulties is marital discord (see Block, Block, & Gjerde, 1986). In fact, a recent and innovative investigation conducted by Gottman and Katz (1989) revealed that several features of the marital relationship are associated with children's peer difficulties. This investigation was based on a model linking marital discord with children's abilities to regulate affective states. Specifically, it was hypothesized that the parenting styles of maritally distressed couples would produce higher levels of physiological arousal in children that would, in turn, cause children to display higher levels of negative affect and less mature forms of peer interaction. Findings from this study, although preliminary and correlational in nature, provide some support for this model. Maritally distressed and physiologically underaroused couples were found to interact with their children in unresponsive and permissive ways. Moreover, these parental interaction styles were associated with higher levels of stress and angry-noncompliant behaviors in children which, in turn, were associated with less mature forms of play and more negative interactions with peers.

*Parental Depression.* Affective disorders in the family, such as parental depression, may also be associated with various forms of child disorder, including poor peer relations. Zahn-Waxler, Cummings, McKnew, and Radke-Yarrow (1984) suggested that if parental depression is viewed as a cause of child maladjustment, then several potential pathways deserve further investigation. Some of these pathways are based on hypotheses about the affective precursors of child maladjustment. For example, Zahn-Waxler et al. proposed that depressed parents may transmit negative emotions to the child (i.e., emotional "contagion"), may withdraw from the child in such a way as to produce insecure attachments, or may foster learned helplessness by involving the child in inescapable, traumatic interactions. Other hypotheses link child disorder to learning and biological explanations. These include the view that depressed parents are more likely to employ maladaptive socialization practices (e.g., deviant child rearing or discipline), or genetically predispose their children to disorder.

Although researchers have yet to empirically evaluate the merits of specific pathways, there is growing evidence to suggest that parental depression is related to children's competence in peer relations (see Downey & Coyne, 1990). Zahn-Waxler et al. (1984), for example, found that children with a bipolar (manic–depressive) parent had difficulty controlling aggressive behaviors and maintaining social interactions with peers. These children also displayed lower levels of prosocial behaviors, such as sharing and helping, when interacting with playmates. In addition to these antisocial tendencies, children with depressed parents appear to be at risk for social withdrawal and school adjustment problems (e.g., Baldwin, Cole, & Baldwin, 1982; Billings & Moos, 1985; Neale & Weintraub, 1975; Rolf, 1972; Weintraub, Prinz, & Neale, 1978).

*Child Abuse.* Abusive parenting constitutes another variation on the family system that may have important consequences for children's social development and peer relations. Research on linkages between abusive parenting and children's peer relations is at an early stage, and most of the available data has been gathered with small samples of toddlers and preschool children. Much of this evidence shows that abused children's peer interactions, when compared to normal peers, are characterized by higher levels of aggression and withdrawal. That is, whereas some abused children display more aggressive and antisocial patterns of behavior toward peers, others seem to avoid peers and have low rates of interaction (Mueller & Silveman, 1989). In some cases, abused children display what appear to be approach–avoidance interaction styles by alternating between aggressive and prosocial behaviors or antisocial and withdrawn behaviors (George & Main, 1979; Main & George, 1985).

Several investigators have found that abused children, and particularly those who have suffered physical abuse, are more aggressive toward peers. George and Main (1979) found that physically abused toddlers assaulted both peers and caregivers more often than nonabused children, and tended to avoid or withdraw from peers' friendly overtures. Similarly, research by Troy and Sroufe (1987) reveals that physically abused children employed more verbal aggression in their encounters with nonabused peers, and a recent study by Haskett and Kistner (1991) shows that abused children exhibited a higher proportion of negative behaviors, particularly instrumental aggression, toward peers.

There is also evidence to suggest that abused children respond to peers' overtures in maladaptive ways. Studies by Howes and colleagues (Howes & Eldrege, 1985; Howes & Espinosa, 1985) and by Main and George (1985) show that abused children are more likely to respond to peers' friendly overtures or distress with either aggression or a mixture of aggression and comforting behaviors.

Peers, it would appear, tend not to respond to the overtures of abused children, and view them as less desirable playmates. Haskett and Kistner (1991) found that interactions initiated by abused preschoolers were often ignored by nonabused children, and that abused children tended to receive lower sociometric ratings from peers.

Other forms of abuse, such as child neglect, may lead children to develop avoidant styles of interaction, or higher levels of peer withdrawal. Hoffman-Plotkin and Twentyman (1984) distinguished between children who were physically abused versus neglected and found that, whereas abused children tended to be more aggressive toward peers, neglected children tended to be more withdrawn.

Many of these findings are consistent with a model that Rubin and colleagues (Rubin, LeMare, & Lollis, 1990) have proposed to explain the origins of peer isolation and rejection. In this model, child abuse (along with other family and child factors) is an important antecedent of children's social behavior that, in turn, is an important precursor of their peer acceptance or rejection. More specifically, it is hypothesized that atypical child characteristics (e.g., difficult temperament, lower thresholds for arousal) combine with problematic parenting styles (e.g., insensitivity, abuse, neglect) to create either hostile or avoidant relationships with caregivers. Once established, the aggressive or withdrawn behavioral patterns that children exhibit in parent–child relations are carried over into their encounters with agemates, and lead to outcomes such as peer isolation or rejection.

***Economic and Life Stress.*** Investigators who do research in this domain are interested in factors that operate outside the family that may have effects on developments both within the family and in children's peer relations. Much of the research in this area is at an early stage, and has been focused largely on the potential effects of economic deprivation. Typically, researchers have relied on models of stress and coping to explicate potential relations between economic adversity and both family life and children's peer relations. Although formal models have yet to be advanced in the literature, it is commonly assumed that economic adversity operates as a stressor in family interaction and relations, and may disrupt important parenting and socialization activities. These perturbations may, in turn, have a negative impact on children's social development and their relations with peers.

Consistent with this premise, early work by Roff and colleagues (e.g., Roff, Sells, & Golden, 1972) revealed that children from families with a history of economic difficulties tended to be less popular with peers. In later studies conducted by Ladd et al. (1988), several indicators of family economic stability (i.e., dual-wage earners, higher income, stable residence) were found to be correlated with the quality of children's peer networks. Specifically, children in families with two incomes and relatively stable residences (fewer moves) tended to have larger peer networks. Children from higher income families also spent more time playing in the homes of network members than did children from lower income families. More systematic and thorough efforts to explore this question can be found in recent studies by Patterson and colleagues (e.g., Patterson, Vaden, & Kupersmidt, 1991). These investigators have shown that a range of potential stressors, including the family's economic circumstances, are related to children's peer rejection in school.

## FURTHER STEPS ALONG KEY PATHWAYS: THE PURPOSE OF THIS VOLUME

Research on family–peer relations is proceeding at a rapid pace, and important new conceptual and empirical developments are emerging in many of the aforementioned domains. The purpose of this book is to survey these developments and consider their impact on current knowledge and future research. Of particular interest are investigators' efforts to refine existing models of family–peer influences and illuminate specific pathways between the two systems.

The chapters within this volume are contributed by a distinguished group of researchers who have active research programs on family–peer relations. Collectively, the contributors represent a variety of theoretical orientations and scientific disciplines and, thus, address the book's objectives from multiple perspectives. More importantly, the authors consider a diverse set of family influences and domains, and elaborate upon some of the most promising models of indirect and direct pathways.

Overall, the book is divided into five major sections, each of which embodies a particular organizing theme or perspective on family–peer relations. These sections are entitled: "Introduction and Overview," "Indirect Influences: Family Relations, Interactions, and Environment," "Direct Influences: Families as Teachers and Organizers," "Variations on Parent–Peer Relationships," and "Epilogue and Future Directions." The following is a brief description of each section and a summary of the principal aims and contributions of the constituent chapters.

## Introduction and Overview

Background and historical perspectives are the organizing themes for this section. The aim of this chapter, and of the following one by Parke and Renshaw, is to orient the reader to the literature on family–peer relations, and to establish a foundation for the remaining chapters of the book.

Parts of the present chapter are devoted to a conceptual and empirical overview of the existing literature on family–peer relations. Within this review, I have introduced the central themes and issues around which this book is organized. Moreover, I have attempted to acquaint readers with many of the conceptual frameworks or models that have been used in past research on family–peer relations, and their empirical contributions.

In the second chapter of this section, "Family and Peer Relationships in Historical Perspective," Parke and Renshaw consider the study of family–peer relations in light of its historical context. The authors trace the origins of research on family–peer relations, and analyze the theoretical and secular trends that have brought about the current research climate. This is done by tracing important themes and concepts as they emerge in scientific and popular articles published during the late 19th and early 20th century.

## Indirect Influences: Family Relations, Interactions, and Environment

The central aim of this section is to evaluate and extend our knowledge about potential indirect linkages between the family and peer systems. Collectively, the contributors consider a number of important pathways and, in each case, they review existing research, present their own conceptual models, and evaluate the state of the art in light of evidence from ongoing research programs.

The first chapter is entitled "Predicting Peer Competence and Peer Relationships in Childhood from Early Parent–Child Relationships." In this chapter, Elicker, Englund, and Sroufe examine recent conceptual and empirical advances within the attachment field. Hypotheses about the bases and continuity of children's social competence are examined within a "developmental–organizational" perspective. That is, the authors attempt to identify critical developmental tasks that define competence at different age levels, and map the relationship abilities and patterns (e.g., working models) that children must develop before they can meet the demands of each period. Within the context of this model, the authors consider the implications of past research on attachment and peer relations, and draw upon recent longitudinal studies to illustrate how various attachment processes in infancy may allow children to succeed at friendships and peer relations during middle childhood.

In the second chapter, "Familial Contribution to Peer Competence Among Young Children: The Role of Interactive and Affective Processes," Parke, Cassidy, Burks, Carson, and Boyum consider the link between family interaction patterns and the development of children's peer competence. The authors take an historical perspective, and review progress in this domain over the last decade. The contributions of early descriptive studies and later longitudinal investigations are evaluated, along with evidence from lab-based and field studies. A central aim of this chapter is to identify not only the features of family interaction that are central to the development of peer competence, but also the mechanisms through which family interaction impacts children's competence among peers. In particular, Parke et al. explore how family interaction patterns influence the child, and how these outcomes mediate, or are transmitted to, the child's relationships with peers. Findings from the authors' own research and other recent studies are used to illustrate how the child's ability to express and regulate emotions may develop from participation in family interaction patterns, and how these processes may, in turn, mediate the quality of the child's peer relations. Based on this work, the authors evaluate future directions for theory and research on family interaction and children's peer relations.

Cooper and Cooper contribute the third chapter, entitled "Links Between Adolescents' Relationships with Their Parents and Peers: Models, Evidence, and Mechanisms." As the title suggests, the focus of this chapter is on family–peer linkages during adolescence. The authors review some of the dominant conceptual frameworks used in past research on adolescence (e.g., psychoanalytic, socialization, and cognitive theories), and illustrate how findings from recent studies have enabled researchers to revise these perspectives and propose "new" models. In keeping with this trend, Cooper and Cooper propose that the contributions peers make to adolescent development depend on the family's ability to equip children with certain types of self-competence and relational skills. This premise is explored in a series of studies in which the authors examine discourse processes as a way of understanding the family's role in promoting adolescents' negotiation skills, and the linkage between these skills and adolescents' competence within friendships. Findings from this work and from other recent studies are used to reassess past themes and establish new directions for research in this field.

"Beyond Parent–Child Relationships: Potential Links Between Family Environments and Peer Relations" is the title of the fifth chapter, written by Bryant and DeMorris. In this chapter, the authors differentiate potential family influences both in terms of relationship levels and units of analysis. Three levels of relationship are considered as possible pathways that affect children's functioning with peers. These include effects from relationships children conduct with individual family members (e.g., mother–child, father–child, or child–sibling relationships), relationships that are independent of the child but impact the child's relationships in the family (e.g., the parents' involvement in the work setting), and relationships that children observe as bystanders during family interactions (e.g., parent–sibling interactions). The authors also propose that, in order to conceptualize these relationships and understand their effects, the unit of analysis must be broadened beyond the dyad to include families as a unit, and families within groups of systems (e.g., relations between parental work and family systems). Based on this framework, Bryant and DeMorris analyze the inner and outer dynamics of the family environment and potential linkages to children's peer experiences and relationships.

In the final chapter in this section, "Societal Influences on Children's Peer Relationships," Cochran and Davila adopt a broader, societal perspective, and consider how features of the family's cultural context may impact children's peer relations. Of particular interest are the pathways that emerge between higher and lower levels of human ecology—in this case, the potential impact of societal influences on the family's social networks, and the role that networks play in shaping children's opportunities for peer companionship, learning, and intimacy. As a step toward explicating these linkages, the authors present a conceptual model and illustrate its utility with findings from a series of empirical investigations. They also weigh the merits of their perspective and findings for other areas of inquiry, and identify promising avenues for future research.

### Direct Influences: Families as Teachers and Organizers

By taking an active role in children's social lives, parents may directly affect the quality of children's peer relations and competence. However, until recently, little has been known about the methods parents employ to "manage" or influence their children's peer relations, and the effects these practices may have on children's social competence. The purpose of this section is to survey recent theory and research on this largely unexplored topic.

This section begins with a chapter entitled "Parents' Management of Children's Peer Relations: Facilitating and Supervising Children's Activities in the Peer Culture" by Ladd, Profilet, and Hart. Within this chapter, the authors propose that parents routinely act as social architects or "managers" of children's social lives and, in doing so, structure children's access to and activities with peers. Ladd et al. identify two specific forms of parental management that deserve further empirical scrutiny. These include strategies that parents use to create opportunities for young children to meet and interact with peers, and the methods they use to oversee or regulate these encounters. The authors also survey relevant empirical findings, including those generated by their own research, to determine when parents engage in these management activities, and how they may influence children's peer competence.

Lollis, Ross, and Tate contribute the second chapter in this section, entitled "Parents' Regulation of Children's Peer Interactions: Direct Influences." In this chapter, Lollis et al. conceptualize direct influences as interventions that parents intentionally perform to influence their children's peer interactions. Based on this premise, the authors propose a model of parent-based peer socialization that includes three types of interventions: parental advice-giving outside the context of peer interaction (i.e., decontextualized discussions), guidance during the course of peer interaction (i.e., directive interventions), and participation in peer interaction (i.e., interactive interventions). The authors then use this model to organize and evaluate existing research on the effects of parental interventions on children's peer interactions and relations. Findings from recent studies, including those conducted by the authors, are used to identify factors that may underlie parents' use of these strategies in differing social contexts and developmental periods.

**Variations on Family–Peer Relationships**

Another aim of this book is to examine variations in the ways that the family and peer systems relate to each other. Consistent with this objective, the chapters in this section explore how linkages between the family and peer systems differ by culture, and vary in the context of debilitating forces such as parental pathology or family stress. Within each chapter, relevant theoretical perspectives and recent empirical advances are considered.

In the first chapter of this section, "Cross-Cultural Perspectives on Family–Peer Relations," Edwards describes patterns of linkage between the family and peer systems in diverse cultures. Findings from ethnographies and cross-cultural studies are used to compare and contrast the nature of children's peer groups in different societies, and their functions relative to the family. Cultural variations in the linkages between family and peer systems are also considered in light of developmental issues, such as the age of the child. Toward this end, the author focuses on cultural variations in family–peer relations during two developmental periods, childhood and adolescence.

The topic addressed in the second chapter is "Peer Relations in Children with a Depressed Caregiver." Zahn-Waxler, Denham, Iannotti, and Cummings consider parental depression as a condition that may disrupt the development of children's social development and peer relations. As a prelude to their own research, Zahn-Waxler et al. review what is currently known about the peer relations of children with a depressed caregiver, and analyze evidence that links depressed parents' caregiving and socialization practices to children's problems in peer relations. The authors then present findings from their own studies of the peer relations of toddlers with a depressed caregiver, and evaluate the potential pathways through which affective disorders such as parental depression may place children at risk for various forms of social maladjustment.

Cicchetti, Lynch, Shonk, and Manly contribute a chapter entitled "An Organizational Perspective on Peer Relations in Maltreated Children." In this chapter, Cicchetti et al. examine how family environments that are characterized by child maltreatment may affect the development of children's peer relationships. The authors rely on an organizational perspective as a framework for understanding both the features of abusive family systems and their effects on children's social development and adjustment. Factors such as the child's attachment status, internal working models, self-perceptions, and social networks are proposed as potential mediating variables in the pathways that link maltreatment and disordered peer relations. Using these theoretical perspectives as a foundation, the authors evaluate recent empirical findings, report new evidence from their own studies, and propose future directions for research on the peer relations of maltreated children.

The final chapter in this section is "Family Economic Circumstances, Life Transitions, and Children's Peer Relations," by Patterson, Griesler, and Vaden. Within this chapter, the authors consider how ecological factors such as the family's chronic life circumstances and enduring economic conditions may affect the development of children's peer relationships during childhood. Data from the authors' recent studies are used to document potential family–peer linkages, and generate hypotheses about the pathways through which such linkages may occur. In particular, the authors focus on how individual family adversities, such as stressful life events and economic impoverishment, may combine to affect children's peer rejection in school. Based on this evidence, the authors discuss potential mediating variables and directions for future research.

## Epilogue and Future Directions

In this closing section, Parke draws upon the preceding content of the book to summarize major developments and to identify a set of unresolved issues and problems. In addition, the paradigms that have been used by the contributors to explore the relation between the family and peer systems are evaluated in terms of their utility for modeling other types of cross-system relationships.

## REFERENCES

Ainsworth, M. D. S. (1973). The development of infant–mother attachment. In B. M. Caldwell & H. N. Ricutti (Eds.), *Review of child development research* (Vol. 3, pp. 1–94). Chicago: University of Chicago Press.

Ainsworth, M. D. S., Blehar, M. S., Waters, E., & Wall, S. (1978). *Patterns of attachment: A psychological study of the strange situation.* Hillsdale, NJ: Lawrence Erlbaum Associates.

Attili, G. (1989). Social competence versus emotional security: The link between home relationships and behavior problems at school. In B. H. Schneider, G. Attili, J. Nadel, & R. P. Weissberg (Eds.), *Social competence in developmental perspective* (pp. 293–311). Dordrecht, Netherlands: Kluwer.

Avgar, A., Bronfenbrenner, U., & Henderson, C. R. (1977). Socialization practices of parents, teachers, and peers in Israel: Kibbutz, Moshav, and city. *Child Development, 48,* 1219–1227

Baldwin, A. L. (1948). Socialization and the parent–child relationship. *Child Development, 19,* 127–136.

Baldwin, A. L., Cole, R. E., & Baldwin, C. P. (1982). Parental pathology, family interaction, and the competence of the child in school. *Monographs of the Society for Research in Child Development, 47*(5, Serial No. 197).

Baumrind, D. (1967). Child care practices anteceding three patterns of preschool behavior. *Genetic Psychology Monographs, 75,* 43–88.

Baumrind, D. (1971). Current patterns of parental authority. *Developmental Psychology Monograph, 4*(1, Pt. 2).

Baumrind, D. (1973). The development of instrumental competence through socialization. In A. D. Pick (Ed.), *Minnesota Symposium on Child Psychology* (Vol. 7, pp. 3–46). Minneapolis: University of Minnesota Press.

Becker, W. C. (1964). Consequences of different kinds of parental discipline. In M. L. Hoffman & L. W. Hoffman (Eds.), *Review of child development research* (Vol. 1, pp. 169–208). New York: Russell Sage Foundation.

Belsky, J. (1984). The determinants of parenting: A process model. *Child Development, 55,* 83–96.

Belsky, J., Rovine, M., & Taylor, D. (1984). The Pennsylvania infant and family development project: III. The origins of individual differences in infant–mother attachment: Maternal and infant contributions. *Child Development, 55*, 718–728.

Berg, M., & Medrich, E. A. (1980). Children in four neighborhoods: Physical environment and its effect on play and play patterns. *Environment and Behavior, 12*, 320–348.

Bhavnagri, N. (1987). *Parents as facilitators of preschool children's peer relationships*. Unpublished doctoral dissertation, University of Illinois at Urbana-Champaign.

Bhavnagri, N., & Parke, R. D. (1991). Parents as direct facilitators of children's peer relationships: Effects of age of child and sex of parent. *Journal of Social and Personal Relationships, 8*, 423–440.

Billings, A. G., & Moos, R. H. (1985). Children of parents with unipolar depression: A controlled one-year follow-up. *Journal of Abnormal Child Psychology, 14*, 149–166.

Block, J. H., Block, J., & Gjerde, P. F. (1986). The personality of children prior to divorce: A prospective study. *Child Development, 57*, 827–840.

Bowlby, J. (1969). *Attachment and loss* (Vol. 1). New York: Basic Books.

Brody, G. H., & Shaffer, D. R. (1982). Contributions of parents and peers to children's moral socialization. *Developmental Review, 2*, 31–75.

Bronfenbrenner, U. (1970). *Two worlds of childhood: U. S. and U. S. S. R.* New York: Russell Sage Foundation.

Bugenthal, D. B. (1989, April). *Caregiver cognitions as moderators of affect in abusive families*. Paper presented at the biennial meeting of the Society for Research in Child Development, Kansas City, MO.

Cochran, M., & Brassard, J. A. (1979). Child development and personal social networks. *Child Development, 50*, 601–616.

Cochran, M., & Riley, D. (1988). Mother reports of children's personal networks: Antecedents, concomitants, and consequences. In S. Salzinger, J. Antrobus, & M. Hammer (Eds.), *Social networks of children, adolescents, and college students* (pp. 113–148). Hillsdale, NJ: Lawrence Erlbaum Associates.

Cohn, D. (1990). Child–mother attachment of 6-year-olds and social competence at school. *Child Development, 61*, 152–177.

Cohn, D., Patterson, C., & Christopoulos, C. (1991). The family and children's peer relations. *Journal of Social and Personal Relationships, 8*, 315–346.

Cohen, J. S. (1989). *Maternal involvement in children's peer relationships during middle childhood*. Unpublished doctoral dissertation, University of Waterloo, Waterloo, Ontario, Canada.

Cummings, E. M., Iannotti, R. J., & Zahn-Waxler, C. (1985). Influence of conflict between adults on the emotions and aggression of young children. *Developmental Psychology, 21*, 495–507.

Cummings, E. M., Zahn-Waxler, C., & Radke-Yarrow, M. (1981). Young children's responses to expressions of anger and affection by others in the family. *Child Development, 52*, 1274–1281.

DeVault, M. V. (1957). Classroom sociometric mutual pairs and residential proximity. *Journal of Educational Research, 50*, 605–610.

Dishion, T. (1990). The family ecology of boys' peer relations in middle childhood. *Child Development, 61*, 874–892.

Dix, T. H., & Lochman, J. (1989). *Social cognition in the mediation of negative reactions to children: A comparison of mothers of aggressive and nonaggressive boys*. Unpublished manuscript.

Dodge, K. A., & Feldman, E. (1990). Issues in social cognition and sociometric status. In S. R. Asher & J. D. Coie (Eds.), *Peer rejection in childhood* (pp. 119–155). New York: Cambridge University Press.

Downey, G., & Coyne, J. C. (1990). Children of depressed parents: An integrative review. *Psychological Bulletin, 108.* 50–76.

Easterbrooks, M. A., & Lamb, M. E. (1979). The relationship between the quality of mother–infant attachment and infant competence in initial encounters with peers. *Child Development, 50,* 380–397.

Eckerman, C. O., & Stein, M. R. (1983). The toddler's emerging interactive skills. In K. Rubin & H. Ross (Eds.), *Peer relationships and social skills in childhood* (pp. 41–72). New York: Springer-Verlag.

Ellis, S., Rogoff, B., & Cromer, C. C. (1981). Age segregation in children's social interactions. *Developmental Psychology, 17,* 399–407.

Emery, R. E. (1988). *Marriage, divorce and children's adjustment.* Beverly Hills, CA: Sage.

Erickson, M. F., Sroufe, L. A., & Egeland, B. (1985). The relationship between quality of attachment and behavior problems in a high-risk sample. In I. Bretherton & E. Waters (Eds.), Growing points in attachment theory and research. *Monographs of the Society for Research in Child Development, 50*(1 and 2, Serial No. 209).

Finnie, V., & Russell, A. (1988). Preschool children's social status and their mothers' behavior and knowledge in the supervisory role. *Developmental Psychology, 24,* 789–801.

Gallagher, J. J. (1958). Social status of children related to intelligence, propinquity, and social perception. *Elementary School Journal, 59,* 225–231.

George, C., & Main, M. (1979). Social interactions of young abused children: Approach, avoidance, and aggression. *Child Development, 50,* 306–318.

Goodnow, J. J. (1988). Parents' ideas, actions, and feelings: Models and methods from developmental and social psychology. *Child Development, 59,* 286–320.

Gottman, J. M., & Katz, L. F. (1989). Effects of marital discord on young children's peer interactions and health. *Developmental Psychology, 25,* 373–381.

Gretarrson, S. J., & Gelfand, D. (1988). Mothers' attributions regarding their children's social behavior and personality. *Development Psychology, 24,* 264–269.

Grych, J. H., & Fincham, F. (1990). Marital conflict and children's adjustment: A cognitive–contextual framework. *Psychological Bulletin, 108,* 267–290.

Hart, C. H., Ladd, G. W., & Burleson, B. R. (1990). Children's expectations of the outcomes of social strategies: Relations with sociometric status and maternal disciplinary styles. *Child Development, 61,* 127–137.

Haskett, M., & Kistner, J. A. (1991). Social interactions and peer perceptions of young physically abused children. *Child Development, 62,* 979–990.

Hetherington, E. M., Cox, M., & Cox, R. (1979). Play and social interaction in children following divorce. *Journal of Social Issues, 35,* 26–49.

Hinde, R., & Tamplin, A. (1983). Relations between mother–child interaction and behavior in preschool. *British Journal of Development Psychology, 1,* 231–257.

Hoffman, M. L. (1960). Power assertion by the parent and its impact on the child. *Child Development, 31,* 129–143.

Hoffman, M. L. (1975). Altruistic behavior and the parent–child relationship. *Journal of Personality and Social Psychology, 31,* 937–943.

Hoffman-Plotkin, D., & Twentyman, C. (1984). A multimodal assessment of behavioral and cognitive deficits in abused and neglected preschoolers. *Child Development, 55,* 794–802.

Howes, C., & Eldredge, R. (1985). Responses of abused, neglected, and nonmaltreated children to the behaviors of their peers. *Journal of Applied Developmental Psychology, 6,* 261–270.

Howes, C., & Espinosa, M. P. (1985). The consequences of child abuse for the formation of relationships with peers. *Child Abuse and Neglect, 9,* 397–404.

Ladd, G. W. (1991). Family–peer relations during childhood: Pathways to competence and pathology? *Journal of Social and Personal Relationships, 8,* 307–314.

Ladd, G. W., & Coleman, C. (in press). Young children's peer relationships: Forms, features, and functions. In B. Spodek (Ed.), *Handbook of research on the education of young children* (2nd ed.). New York: Macmillan.

Ladd, G. W., & Crick, N. R. (1989). Probing the psychological environment: Children's cognitions, perceptions, and feelings in the peer culture. In M. Maehr & C. Ames (Eds.), *Advances in motivation and achievement: Motivation enhancing environments* (Vol. 6, pp. 1–44). Greenwich, CT: JAI.

Ladd, G. W., & Golter, B. S. (1988). Parents' management of preschoolers' peer relations: Is it related to children's social competence? *Developmental Psychology, 24*, 109–117.

Ladd, G. W., & Hart, C. H. (in press). Creating informal play opportunities: Are parents' and preschoolers' initiations related to children's competence with peers? *Developmental Psychology*.

Ladd, G. W., Hart, C. H., Wadsworth, E. M., & Golter, B. S. (1988). Preschoolers' peer networks in nonschool settings: Relationship to family characteristics and school adjustment. In S. Salzinger, J. Antrobus, & M. Hammer (Eds.), *Social networks of children, adolescents, and college students* (pp. 61–92). Hillsdale, NJ: Lawrence Erlbaum Associates.

Ladd, G. W., Le Sieur, K., & Profilet, S. M. (in press). Direct parental influences on young children's peer relations. In S. Duck (Ed.), *Learning about relationships* (Vol. 2). London: Sage.

Ladd, G. W., & Price, J. M. (1986). Promoting children's cognitive and social competence: The relations between parent's perceptions of task difficulty and children's perceived and actual competence. *Child Development, 57*, 446–460.

LaFreniere, P., & Sroufe, L. A. (1985). Profiles of peer competence in the preschool: Interrelations between measures, influence of social ecology, and relation to attachment history. *Developmental Psychology, 21*, 56–69.

Lamb, M. E., Thompson, R., Gardner, W. P., & Charnov, E. (1985 ). *Infant–mother attachment: The origins and developmental significance of individual differences in strange situation behaviors*. Hillsdale, NJ: Lawrence Erlbaum Associates.

Lamb, M. E., & Nash, A. (1989). Infant–mother attachment, sociability, and peer competence. In T. J. Berndt & G. W. Ladd (Eds.), *Peer relationships in child development* (pp. 219–246). New York: Wiley.

Lewis, M., & Feiring, C. (1989). Early predictors of children's friendship. In T. J. Berndt & G. W. Ladd (Eds.), *Peer relationships in child development* (pp. 246–273). New York: Wiley.

Lieberman, A. F. (1977). Preschoolers' competence with a peer: Relations with attachment and peer experience. *Child Development, 48*, 1277–1287.

Lollis, S. (1990). Effects of maternal behavior on toddler behavior during separation. *Child Development, 61*, 99–103.

Lollis, S., & Ross, H. (1987, April). *Mothers' interventions in toddler–peer conflicts*. Paper presented at the biennial meeting of the Society for Research in Child Development, Baltimore, MD.

Long, N., & Forehand, R. (1987). The effects of parental divorce and parental conflict on children: An overview. *Developmental and Behavioral Pediatrics, 8*, 292–296.

Long, N., Forehand, R., Fauber, R., & Brody, G. (1987). Self-perceived and independently observed competence of young adolescents as a function of parental marital conflict and recent divorce. *Journal of Abnormal Child Psychology, 15*, 15–27.

Maccoby, E. E., & Martin, J. A. (1983). Socialization in the context of the family: Parent–child interaction. In P. Mussen (Series Ed.) & E. M. Hetherington (Vol. Ed.), *Handbook of child psychology: Vol. 4. Socialization, personality, and social development* (4th ed., pp. 1–102). New York: Wiley.

MacDonald, K. (1987). Parent–child physical play with rejected, neglected, and popular boys. *Developmental Psychology, 23*, 705–711.

MacDonald, K., & Parke, R. (1984). Bridging the gap: Parent–child play interaction and peer interactive competence. *Child Development, 55*, 1265–1277.

Main, M., & George, C. (1985). Response of abused and disadvantaged toddlers to distress in agemates: A study in the day-care setting. *Developmental Psychology, 21*, 407–412.

Medrich, E. A., Roizen, J. A., Rubin, V., & Buckley, S. (1982). *The serious business of growing up: A study of children's lives outside school.* Berkeley, CA: University of California Press.

Melson, G. M., Ladd, G. W., & McVey, A. (1990, April). *Parenting self-perceptions and attributions: Links to young children's social and cognitive development.* Paper presented at the annual meeting of the American Educational Research Association, Boston.

Miller, S. A. (1988). Parents' beliefs about children's cognitive development. *Child Development, 59*, 259–285.

Mills, R. S., & Rubin, K. H. (1990). Parental beliefs about problematic social behaviors in early childhood. *Child Development, 61*, 138–151.

Mize, J., & Ladd, G. W. (1990). A cognitive–social learning approach to social skill training with low-status preschool children. *Developmental Psychology, 26*, 388–397.

Mueller, E., & Silverman, N. (1989). Peer relations in maltreated children. In D. Cicchetti & V. Carlson (Eds.), *Child maltreatment: Theory and research on the causes and consequences of child abuse and neglect* (pp. 529–578). New York: Cambridge University Press.

Neale, J. M., & Weintraub, S. (1975). Children vulnerable to psychopathology: The Stoney Brook High-Risk Project. *Journal of Abnormal Child Psychology, 3*, 95–103.

Olweus, D. (1980). Familial and temperamental determinants of aggression behavior in adolescents—A causal analysis. *Developmental Psychology, 16*, 644–660.

Park, K. A., & Waters, E. (1989). Security of attachment and preschool friendships. *Child Development, 60*, 1076–1081.

Parke, R. D., & Bhavnagri, N. (1989). Parents as managers of children's peer relationships. In D. Belle (Ed.), *Children's social networks and social supports* (pp. 241–259). New York: Wiley.

Parke, R. D., MacDonald, K. B., Beitel, A., & Bhavnagri, N. (1988). The role of the family in the development of peer relationships. In R. Peters & R. J. McMahon (Eds.), *Social learning systems approaches to marriage and the family* (pp. 17–44). New York: Brunner/Mazel.

Parke, R. D., MacDonald, K., Burks, V. M., Carson, J., Bhavnagri, N., Barth, J. M., & Beitel, A. (1989). Family and peer systems: In search of linkages. In K. Kreppner & R. M. Lerner (Eds.), *Family systems and life span development* (pp. 65–92). Hillsdale, NJ: Lawrence Erlbaum Associates.

Pastor, D. L. (1981). The quality of mother–infant attachment and its relationships to toddlers' initial sociability with peers. *Developmental Psychology, 17*, 326–335.

Patterson, C. J., Kupersmidt, J. B., & Griesler, P. C. (1990). Children's perceptions of self and of relationships with others as a function of sociometric status. *Child Development, 61*, 1335–1349.

Patterson, C. J., Vaden, N. A., & Kupersmidt, J. B. (1991). Family background, recent life events, and peer rejection during childhood. *Journal of Social and Personal Relationships, 8*, 347–362.

Patterson, G. R. (1982). *The coercive family process.* Eugene, OR: Castalia Press.

Patterson, G. R., & Stouthamer-Loeber, M. (1984). The correlation of family management and delinquency. *Child Development, 55*, 1299–1307.

Pettit, G. S., Dodge, K. A., & Brown, M. (1988). Early family experience, social problem-solving patterns, and children's social competence. *Child Development, 59*, 107–120.

Pettit, G. S., Harrist, A. W., Bates, J. E., & Dodge, K. A. (1991). Family interaction, social cognition, and children's subsequent relations with peers at kindergarten. *Journal of Social and Personal Relationships, 8*, 383–402.

Potashin, R. (1946). A sociometric study of children's friendships. *Sociometry, 9*, 48–70.

Putallaz, M. (1987). Maternal behavior and children's sociometric status. *Child Development, 58*, 324–340.

Putallaz, M., Costanzo, P. R., & Smith, R. (1991). Maternal recollections of childhood peer relationships: Implications for their children's social competence. *Journal of Social and Personal Relationships, 8*, 403–422.

Putallaz, M., & Heflin, A. H. (1990). Parent–child interaction. In S. R. Asher & J. D. Coie (Eds.), *Peer rejection in childhood* (pp. 189–216). New York: Cambridge University Press.

Roff, M., Sells, S. B., & Golden, M. M. (1972). *Social adjustment and personality development in children*. Minneapolis: University of Minnesota Press.

Rolf, J. (1972). The social and academic competence of children vulnerable to schizophrenia and other behavioral pathologies. *Journal of Abnormal Psychology, 80*, 225–243.

Rubin, K. H., LeMare, L. J., & Lollis, S. (1990). Social withdrawal in childhood: Developmental pathways to peer rejection. In S. R. Asher & J. D. Coie (Eds.), *Peer rejection in childhood* (pp. 217–252). New York: Cambridge University Press.

Rubin, K.H., Mills, R. S. L., & Rose-Krasnor, L. (1989). Maternal beliefs and children's social competence. In B. Schneider, J. Nadel, G. Attili, & R. Weissberg (Eds.), *Social competence in developmental perspective* (pp. 313–331). Amsterdam: Klewer Academic Publishers.

Rubin, Z., & Sloman, J. (1984). How parents influence their children's friendships. In M. Lewis (Ed.), *Beyond the dyad* (pp. 223–250). New York: Plenum.

Russell, A., & Finnie, V. (1990). Preschool children's social status and maternal instructions to assist group entry. *Developmental Psychology, 26*, 603–611.

Seagoe, M. (1939). Factors influencing the selection of associates. *Journal of Educational Research, 27*, 32–40.

Schiavo, R. S., & Solomon, S. K. (1981, April). *The effect of summer contact on preschoolers' friendships with classmates*. Paper presented at the annual meeting of the Eastern Psychological Association, New York.

Schiavo, R. S., Solomon, S. K., Evers, C., & Cohen, W. (1982, April). *Maintenance of friendships among preschoolers*. Paper presented at the annual meeting of the Eastern Psychological Association, Baltimore.

Sroufe, L. A. (1983). Infant–caregiver attachment and patterns of adaptation in preschool: The roots of maladaptation and competence. In M. Perlmutter (Ed.), *Minnesota Symposium on Child Psychology, 16* (pp. 14–83). Minneapolis: University of Minnesota Press.

Sroufe, L. A., & Fleeson, J. (1986). Attachment and the construction of relationships. In W. Hartup & Z. Rubin (Eds.), *Relationships and development* (pp. 51–71). Hillsdale, NJ: Lawrence Erlbaum Associates.

Troy, M., & Sroufe, L. A. (1987). Victimization among preschoolers: The role of attachment and relationship history. *Journal of the American Academy of Child Psychiatry, 26*, 166–172.

Waters, E., Wippman, J., & Sroufe, L. A. (1979). Attachment, positive affect, and competence in the peer group: Two studies in construct validation. *Child Development, 50*, 821–829.

Weintraub, S., Prinz, R., & Neale, J. M. (1978). Peer evaluations of the competence of children vulnerable to psychopathology. *Journal of Abnormal Child Psychology, 4*, 461–473.

Wilson, H. (1980). Parental supervision: A neglected aspect of delinquency. *British Journal of Criminology, 20*, 203–235.

Zahn-Waxler, C., Radke-Yarrow, M., & King, R. (1979). Childrearing and children's prosocial initiations toward victims of distress. *Child Development, 50*, 319–330.

Zahn-Waxler, C., Cummings, E. M., McKnew, D. H., & Radke-Yarrow, M. (1984). Altruism, aggression, and social interactions in young children with a manic-depressive parent. *Child Development, 55*, 112–122.

# CHAPTER TWO

# Family and Peer Relationships
# in Historical Perspective

Peter D. Renshaw
*University of Queensland, Australia*

Ross D. Parke
*University of California, Riverside*

This chapter examines the relationship between the family and the peer group in an historical framework. It is structured around an analysis of specific periods: (a) the decades spanning the turn of the century, the so-called Progressive Era; (b) the decades between World Wars I and II; (c) World War II to the present. For each period, the major psychological theories are summarized, and placed in the context of the contemporary social and political concerns. The impact of these factors on the understanding of relationships between the family and the peer group is explored. The analysis suggests that at each period various social institutions were established and promoted that had a major impact on the linkages between the family and the peer group.

The chapter contributes to the recent efforts to show how the different social worlds of children interrelate, and to view childhood socialization in the context of reciprocal causalities between various social networks (Hartup, 1979). Sameroff (1983) argued that the study of child development should be conducted to account for interrelated social systems. This requires a consideration of the child, the family, the social system, and the histories of each, so that the complex network of reciprocal and multicausal influences on development can be explored. By highlighting the changing patterns of social networks, and their interrelationships over time, the historical perspective provides another, more encompassing level of analysis. Whereas such an approach implies a daunting level of complexity in the analysis, there are advantages of perspective provided by an historical approach. Networks of interrelationships are difficult to discern when an observer is positioned within the web of ongoing experiences, but by drawing back from the detail of the present, the larger patterns gradually emerge in clearer outline. Of course, one drawback of the longer view is the lack of focus on the detailed complexity of the patterns—a trade-off that may be judged as worthwhile if the historical perspective yields its own insights.

At each historical period one pattern that emerged clearly was the central place of social institutions in mediating the relationship between the family and the peer group. The social institutions originated as attempts to address the perceived social and community needs of the time. The major psychological theories of the period were used to support the initial establishment of the social institutions and the spread of their influence. For example, at the turn of the century, the social upheaval caused by immigration, industrialization, and rapid urbanization placed families under stress, and due to a lack of recreational facilities, urban children were forced to play on city streets. In response, social institutions such as urban playgrounds, publically funded kindergartens, and numerous adult-sponsored clubs, were formed. These institutions transformed the nature of the peer group by bringing it under adult influence and supervision. The institutions also transformed the relationship of the child to the family, by providing an organized social context that was designed to inculcate democratic social goals, and replace the primary socializing role of parents, at least in the case of the poor immigrant families. The institutions and the socialization goals that they endorsed were supported in a very direct way by the major developmental theory of the period—G. Stanley Hall's recapitulation theory. As this extended illustration indicates, a more complete understanding of the relationship between the family and peer group is possible from an analysis of the intersection of historical, social, and psychological influences.


## FAMILY AND PEER GROUP AT THE TURN OF THE CENTURY

### The Historical Context

*Immigration and Urbanization.*   The Progressive Era in North America, which spanned the decades around the turn of the century, was a period of rapid industrialization, and urbanization, with accompanying migration from rural communities and large-scale immigration from Europe. Against this backdrop of social upheaval, the peer group was theorized by writers such as Hall, Baldwin, and Dewey, to be a socializing force separate from the family, and able to fulfill unique functions in the development of the individual. The focus on the peer group as a socializing agent, however, was a response to the trying social conditions of the time. The influence of the peer group on children could be observed on a daily basis in the cities, as youngsters congregated into the play groups, gangs, and street-corner societies that Thrasher (1927) later studied after World War I. Howe's (1976) account of street life at the turn of the century painted it as a liberating experience for immigrant children; he wrote:

> The streets were ours. Every place else—home, school, shops belonged to the grownups. But the streets belonged to us. We would roam through the city tasting the delights of freedom, discovering possibilities far beyond the reach of our parents. The streets taught us the deceits of commerce, introduced us to the excitement of sex, schooled us in strategies of survival, and gave us our first clear idea of what life in America was really going to be like. (p. 256)

As Howe implies, the members of the play groups, gangs, and street-corner societies were not vagabonds, criminals, or homeless wanderers, but youngsters (aged anywhere from 6 to 20) of the neighborhood, "who preferred the life of the streets to the pestiferous tenements of their parents" (Kett, 1977, p. 170). Lazerson (1971) also noted that the children of the urban poor had the choice between "the tenement and the street, the former overcrowded and unsanitary, the latter corrupt and anarchic" (p. 47). Unsupervised games on the crowded city streets must have presented a picture of chaotic activity, as children in various games of marbles, stick ball, or prisoners' base, dashed about between vehicles and passers-by in pursuit of their games. Although Howe's (1976) reference was to the experience of Jewish immigrants, life on the streets was common to all the immigrant groups. Haynes, a field secretary of the Playground Association of America in Milwaukee noted in 1911 that the majority of children of immigrant families played illegally in the street, and Haynes bemoaned the lack of respect for law and order that the "foreign colonies" were allowing their children to learn (Cavallo, 1981, p. 40). Addams (1909) also noted that naive youngsters from rural communities roamed the urban streets in search of recreation. The vitality of the peer-group life on the streets, however, must be kept in perspective, as many children and adolescents worked long hours in sweat shops to help maintain the meager income of the family.

***Conflict Between Family and Peer Group.*** Growing up in the crowded urban centers of North America often meant growing away from the values and attitudes that the immigrant parents hoped to maintain in their new country. The demand for labor, the low wages, and the so-

cial alienation that accompanied the urbanization of dislocated and ethnically diverse immigrants placed the family system under great stress
(Cavallo, 1981). Severe conflicts between the generations occurred as the
youngsters began to explore their new neighborhoods, and looked at their
parents' traditional customs with more and more embarrassment. According to Howe (1976), parents were to be loved, yet kept hidden from one's
friends. Accordingly, much of the social life of the youngsters moved into
the streets. Howe (1976) described the conflict between the family and
the peer group in the following terms:

> The apartments were crowded, the streets were crowded, yet for boys and
> girls growing up in the ghetto, the apartments signified a life too well worn,
> while the streets, despite their squalor, spoke of freedom. Freedom to break
> loose from those burdens that Jewish parents had come to cherish; free-
> dom, if only for an hour or two, to be the "street bum" against whom fathers
> warned; freedom to live by the senses, a gift that had to be learned and
> fought for; freedom to sin. (p. 258)

Tyack (1974), writing of the Italian immigrants in New York at the turn
of the century, provided a similar view. He noted that the second generation was often suspended between two worlds. Their parents were the
center of their security and devotion, yet in attempting to preserve traditional customs and authority, the parents were seen as ignorant and
despotic. On the other hand, in the company of peers from the American community, the Italian youngsters felt resentful at being regarded
as inferiors. Between these worlds was the peer group where the immigrant youngster could forge a new identity in the company of others
who were trapped in the same dilemma.

## Theorists

**G. Stanley Hall.** The most influential psychologist of the period was
G. Stanley Hall, but other important theorists (for example, James Baldwin and John Dewey) who were opposed to Hall in other respects,
nonetheless provided strong support for the importance of peer groups.
Hall's recapitulation theory of development, summarized in the phrase
*ontology recapitulates phylogeny,* was not uncritically accepted, but it
had a widespread following among teachers and professional play-
workers. Hall's theory enabled these practitioners to form positive interpretations of urban youngsters' gang-like behavior, even when it was
wild, destructive, and apparently antisocial. Hall explained that such behavior was a necessary stage in the emerging history of the human race,
recurring in the developmental history of the individual. Forbush, a fol-

lower of Hall, provided the following description of the social development of children, or rather of boys; girls were perceived as remaining
under the influence of adults and expressing their gang instinct in helping others, being sociable, and exploring adult-approved interests. Forbush (1900) wrote:

> During boyhood the home shares with school the boy's time. But with the
> development of his social instincts by means of play, new acquaintance-
> ships begin to share the crevices of his time. First, he plays at home with
> a chosen companion or two, then he ventures forth to the ball field and
> the swimming hole with a larger group, finally his journeys are farther, his
> stay is longer, the group is more thoroughly organised and a mob spirit
> is apt to arise which passes from unorganised play and sportive frolic to
> barbarous and destructive deviltory, and we have, in city and country, the
> fully developed gang. (p. 313)

The pre-adolescent period (8 to 12) was perceived by Hall as particularly crucial for the expression of the social instinct. At this age children
were thought to be at the height of their independence from adults, and
to be driven to develop a life of their own outside the home circle. G.
S. Hall (1926) argued that in a natural environment the pre-adolescent
would be able to express primitive instincts that corresponded to an earlier
period of human evolution when groups formed to hunt, fish, fight, and
rove about in a predatory fashion. The problem of urban living was the
suppression of these primitive but natural instincts. The solution was to
find both direct (by visits to the forest, stream, and field) and vicarious
methods (heroic tales from literature and history) of satisfying the instincts. Burk (1897) used the theory to justify the occurrence of teasing
and bullying among children of this age:

> If these movements are the fragmentary rudiments of past combat, capture,
> and killing of prey and enemies, then they are clearly the most ancient forms
> of physical exercise, by which the organism developed. . . . These are then
> the racial forms of all exercise and for this very reason the theory is a forci-
> ble one that these movements are not only the best possible but the only
> possible forms of exercise upon which progress in physical development
> and mental development of the individual rests. (pp. 370–371)

The importance of muscular fitness and exercise, which play was intended
to promote, had more than physical health as the goal. Taut muscles and
fitness signified in G. S. Hall's (1918) view both intellectual and moral
strength.

> The muscles are nearly half the body-weight. They are the organs of the
> will . . . and if they are kept at concert pitch, the chasm between knowing
> and doing, which is often so fatal, is in a measure closed. There is no bet-

ter way of strengthening all that class of activities which we ascribe to the
will than by cultivating muscle. (1918, p. 367)

On urban playgrounds and in organized clubs, Hall believed that children
could express their primitive impulses in physical games and exercise that
would be the developmental stepping stones to intellectual and moral
strength.

*James Mark Baldwin.* As a contemporary of Hall's, Baldwin
provided a less dramatic view of children's play but one that, at the time,
strengthened the case for the importance of play and peer companionship in children's experience. Baldwin's central concern was to explain
how it was possible to build a reasonably harmonious and cohesive social group from individuals who initially were distinct and separate enti-
ties striving for survival. In the process of social learning Baldwin
emphasized the importance of play and companionship between children.
The image of the *team member* was important for Baldwin in conveying
the dialectical relationship between the individual and the society. In a
team, the individual was required to draw on personal resources of skill
and endeavor, but each individual contribution needed to be coordinated to produce the team's activity. In performing their separate team roles,
individuals were made aware of their own skills and potential, but such
self-awareness was possible only in the context of the group endeavor.
This dialectic relationship between self- and other-awareness was central
to Baldwin's developmental theory. He maintained that the process of
give-and-take in peer groups enabled the individual to attain a fully developed social perspective (see Baldwin, 1899, pp. 139–147, 287). Thus,
Baldwin's concern with how social order was possible, and what kept
individuals in harmonious relationships despite the struggle for survival,
was answered in large measure by the unique opportunities he perceived
in the peer group for play, games, and the process of "give-and-take."

*John Dewey.* A similar message regarding the importance of peer
groups and children's play was provided by Dewey. He was a friend of
Jane Addams, and saw in her settlement houses (discussed later) the possibility of creating a truly democratic community through institutions that
blurred the boundaries between everyday life and education (Davis, 1972).
Dewey thought of play among children as an ideal context for socialization because they were learning through doing, and were encountering
the social roles and activities of adult society during their play. For Dewey,
the best learning environment was one in which "community life" and
"play life" were analogous settings. He argued that schools should be
made "an embryonic community . . . , active with the types of occupa-

tions that reflect the life of the larger society" (1899, p. 27). In some urban playgrounds, play directors were influenced by Dewey's views to establish among the play group a miniature civic government with mayors, chiefs of police, and so on. Thus, the playground became a direct apprenticeship for the adult roles, to which, the play directors at least hoped, the children might aspire. Dewey's overriding concern was the creation of a democratic society through the school. He wrote in his *pedagogic creed* of 1897 that:

> . . . the only true education comes through the stimulation of the child's powers by the demands of the social situation in which he finds himself. Through these demands he is stimulated to act as a member of a unity, to emerge from his original narrowness of action and feeling, and to conceive of himself from the standpoint of the group to which he belongs. (p. 1)

Throughout Dewey's writing there are appeals to the importance of cooperation between equals, of joint planning, and common endeavor between children (Connell, 1980). These experiences of "lived democracy" were the basis of the democratic society Dewey sought to promote.

***Summary.*** The multiple theoretical voices represented by Hall, Baldwin, and Dewey converged on three notions regarding socialization within peer groups: (a) it was a necessary stage in the normal developmental sequence; (b) it was essential for life in a democracy because it gave expression to the child's emerging cooperative and egalitarian impulses; and (c) it was independent of the family—prolonged and protected care by parents was perceived as likely to stifle the normal social development of children because they had to learn to take their part in the "society of equals." These theorists, however, did not suggest that the family system and the peer system were necessarily in conflict. Rather, peer socialization was seen as independent of the family, and capable of fostering the child's social development in a manner that the family could not. Under some circumstances the peer system could come into conflict with the family. This occurred in a rather dramatic fashion in the case of immigrant families and their children at the turn of the century. Life on the city streets opened up new experiences and exposed the youngsters of immigrant families to values and attitudes that threatened the traditions of the family. Street-corner society was perceived as promoting the potentially unlawful and unsupervised expression of the social instinct, which also placed it in conflict with the values that the social reformers hoped to inculcate in the immigrant youngsters. Because the peer system was theorized to be independent of the family, and a natural social context for developing attitudes suited to a democracy, the social reformers saw it as the ideal vehicle for establishing the new American identity. It was a matter of redirecting and channeling the social instinct (expressed in peer-group affiliation) toward acceptable goals.

## Social Institutions

*Introduction.*   Prolonged efforts were made by social reformers to harness the positive potential of peer groups to form the democratic citizen—efforts by Jane Addams, who founded Settlement Houses to assist the urban poor, Elizabeth Peabody, who helped to establish the kindergarten movement, and Joseph Lee, who was prominent in the Playground Association of America, which lobbied for the establishment of playgrounds in the cities to meet the needs of urban youngsters. In addition, the public schooling system struggled throughout the Progressive Era to accommodate the diverse needs and aspirations of children from the recently arrived immigrant and rural families. Social organizations and clubs, such as the Scouts and Camp Fire Girls, were established at this time in an attempt to organize the play of children and adolescents, and to channel their social instinct to socially acceptable outlets. These organizations, however, were directed towards the middle class and it seems from their membership profiles that they effectively excluded the urban poor. A description of these social institutions follows.

*Jane Addams and the Settlement House.*   Jane Addams' mission was to rescue the so-called slum children from the unhealthy and morally pernicious streets, where they had easy access to vaudeville, burlesque, and liquor. In her book, *The Spirit of Youth and the City Streets,* Addams (1909) linked the demand for child labor to the growth of morally degrading forms of recreation. The capacity to earn money at a young age, the drudgery of the work, the lack of parental supervision, and the freedom to roam the city streets, Addams argued, made these children easy prey to the "evil-minded and unscrupulous" proprietors of dance halls and gin palaces who were able to relieve the children of their wages in quick time. Addams' solution to this crisis was to recommend the organization of recreation centers for city youngsters, so that their social needs could find an uplifting expression. At her settlement houses in the city "slums," Addams observed the effect of "sand gardens" on the play of young children, and scaled-down playgrounds on the emergence of the cooperative spirit of older children. These observations convinced her that organized recreation for the urban poor could break the cycle of petty crime and the dispiriting effects of poverty (Cavallo, 1981).

*Elizabeth Peabody and the Kindergartens.*   Peabody and her followers regarded the publically funded kindergarten as a means of gaining access to the homes of the poor, so that the parents could be educated in proper child-care practices. Laura Fisher, who was the director of Boston's public school kindergartens at the turn of the century, declared that the kindergarten drew in the children of the poor in order to elevate the home (Lazerson, 1971, p. 50). Kindergartens were promoted also because peer group experience was seen as necessary after age three, as an uninterrupted childhood in mother's "tender care" would only bolster the child's self-centeredness, which was seen as a threat to the survival of the child and society. Lazerson (1971), quoting from the lectures of Peabody in the following extract, demonstrated the extent of commitment of Peabody and her followers, to the central socializing role of the young child's "society of equals":

> After the age of three, socialization among peers and to society's mores thus became each child's central need. Here was the kindergartener's major role: it allowed the child "to take his place in the company of his equals, to learn his place in their companionship, and still later to learn wider social relations and their involved duties." In this society of equals the social instinct could be gratified and brought into equilibrium with the instinct of self-preservation. A kindergarten, Peabody wrote, "is children in society—a commonwealth or republic of children—whose laws are all part and parcel of the Higher Law alone." (p. 38)

The kindergarten movement was part of a wider interest in the study of children and their stages of development. G. Stanley Hall had published in 1883 a long article, "The Contents of Children's Minds," and a pamphlet, "The Study of Children," which marked the beginning of the child study movement (Connell, 1980). Hall's view that a child's peer companions could be a positive socializing force, particularly for instilling democratic values and behavior, was adopted eagerly by the leaders of the Playground Association of America, who lobbied vigorously for the establishment of playgrounds in poor urban environments.

***The Public School.*** Schools were regarded as harsh and unsympathetic by urban children at the turn of the century. For example, Tyack (1974) reported an account of a 1909 survey, where 500 children were asked the question, "If your father had a good job and you didn't have to work, which would you rather do—go to school or work in a factory?" Four hundred and twelve answered that they preferred the factory, because as one child said, "School is de fiercest t'ing youse kin come up against. Factories ain't no cinch, but schools is worst." It is hardly surprising that the retention rates in schools were low. Ayres (1909), in the book *Laggards in Our Schools,* suggested that the general pattern for American cities was for almost all children to stay at school until the fifth grade, only half until the eighth grade, and a mere 10% made it through high school. At this time, the high school was regarded as appropriate only for the few most able students, and although laws for compulsory attendance (usually until age 14) were passed in the majority of states, they were not enforced due to both a lack of space in the schools, and teachers' active discouragement of children from poor urban communities to remain at school (Tyack, 1974). The brief experience many immigrant youngsters had in American schools convinced them that they remained outcasts. Between the parents, who symbolized the old ways, and the school, which symbolized their exclusion from the new, was the peer group or gang. Tyack wrote of this conflict:

> A gang of adolescents often became a refuge half-way between the family and the school. Real life belied the bland civics of the textbook, which was purged of "all the crudities and unpleasantnesses of reality." The policeman at the corner was really not the "gentleman hero of peace" but a guzzling "big fat Irish bastard". . . . High truancy and drop-out rates, an average IQ score of eighty-five, negative teacher stereotypes—these were the symptoms of this conflict for the South Italian child. (1974, p. 254)

In contrast, as high school attendance became the norm for the middle class, it created a peer group within an institution that largely mirrored the values and attitudes of their families. At the turn of the century, Tyack (1974) reported that in the 13 to 16 age group, 80% of children of professionals were at school. Kett (1977) argued that high school attendance did generate extra pressure on these families because wages that a young adolescent would have been able to earn had to be foregone. Financial sacrifices were being borne by the family, which placed on students the obligation to show a high level of obedience to parents and teachers, to display self-restraint, and to strive for high achievement. Thus, middle-class adolescents may have been removed from immediate parental supervision, but they remained squarely within the influence of middle-class values. Further, as the following discussion shows, the regulation of peer-group activities by middle-class institutions was extended beyond the school through the agency of various recreational clubs.

***The Urban Playground.***    The playground movement was a significant force in the first two decades of the 20th century. Joseph Lee (1931), looking back on the playground movement on its 25th anniversary, provided a rather sober view of the movement as "a good device for keeping children (of the slums) healthy and out of mischief" (p. 13). The spread of the playground movement was impressive. Cavallo (1981) provided the following figures. In 1905, there were 24 cities operating 87 playgrounds. In 1906, when the Playground Association of America (P. A. A.) was formed, that figure had jumped to 169 playgrounds; in 1911 there were 1,543 playgrounds employing 4,132 play directors; and by 1917, at the height of its influence, there were 3,940 playgrounds affiliated with the P. A. A., spread across 481 cities, and employing almost 9,000 play directors. This represents a sizable investment of funds, largely derived from the public through city budgets.

The success of the playground movement in gaining the endorsement of public officials and generating a small army of play professionals can be explained only by acknowledging the interplay of social factors such as immigration, urban and industrial growth, the personal efforts of social reformers, and the emergence of theories in psychology that highlighted the central role of the peer group in children's growth. Play directors were given courses in psychology and sociology so that they could understand that "play is one of the means, perhaps the most important means, by which society functions" (Hetherington, 1911, p. 226).

Although the peer group was seen as the crucial socializing force, for a well-conducted playground, the guidance of a professional supervisor was thought to be essential. The professionally supervised playground was perceived as the ideal replacement for the family (Cavallo, 1981). In the city, overworked parents were thought to be unable to supervise, control, or educate their children into appropriate moral standards, and left to their own devices, children were free to roam and experience life unfettered by adult constraints (Howe, 1976). For the social reformers, the urban playground provided a venue for the expression of the child's "social instinct," but it also enabled them to be under constant surveillance, so that any discordant behaviors and attitudes could be moved toward greater conformity to social norms. The guiding principle of playground socialization was the embodiment of moral authority in the team. Systems of self-government and peer-group sanctions were instituted within a structure that mirrored "city hall" (mayors, chiefs of police, judges and juries). The playground "society" was thought of as a melting pot of ethnic diversity in which team spirit and commitment to a common American identity could be promoted in youngsters of all ethnic backgrounds. Finally, the playground, like the kindergarten (literally, child's garden), was perceived as a more natural environment—a piece of the rural landscape with its overtones of innocence, set aside to dispel the deceits of the surrounding city.

***Middle Class Clubs and Organized Groups.*** While so-called slum children were being gathered into organized playgrounds, there was a parallel movement among middle-class communities for the creation of clubs and societies dedicated to organizing the leisure activities of middle-class youngsters. These clubs were not a substitute for schools, as most middle-class children attended into the high school years. Nonetheless, there were a variety of clubs established at this time to organize and regulate children's social life. Forbush (1900, 1909) listed clubs dealing with traditional Indian culture, farm and garden work, the Boy Scouts, and the YMCA. For girls, there were similar organizations such as Camp Fire Girls and Girl Scouts. Various writers, assessing the impact of these organizations with the benefit of hindsight, were critical of their selective recruitment practices (Hollingshead, 1949; Rogers, 1939; Thomas & Thomas, 1928). The organized clubs were promoted to the general public as a means of forestalling and redirecting delinquent tendencies in children, yet as Thomas and Thomas (1928) noted with regard to scouting, "The most serious limitation of the program is that it is not adapted to the underprivileged boy, does not appeal to or receive the boy who is a behaviour problem, and practically does not touch the great mass of gang life" (p. 174).

Rogers (1939) noted that special efforts had been made toward the end of the 1930s to promote scouting in reform institutions, yet even then Rogers noted that organized groups such as the Scouts excluded the poorer sections of society. Hollingshead's (1949) study of Elmtown confirms this picture of selective bias in the recruiting practices of such organizations. Hollingshead described the social class and religious background of members of both the Scouts and the Camp Fire Girls as middle to upper-middle class and predominantly Protestant. The leaders in the Scouts in "Elmtown" were made up of men in the business and professional classes, all Protestant and interested in local politics and civic affairs. Clearly, this represented mainstream middle-class America.

The clubs were based on a mixture of beliefs, partly derived from G. Stanley Hall, that can be summarized by the phrase *muscular Christianity,* where morality was revealed more in physical courage, determination, and discipline than in piety and spirituality. Hard work, contact with nature, self-denial—in general, the rigors and innocence of a rural Christian life, rather than the sophistication and flabbiness of urban living—were the values that these clubs endorsed (Kett, 1977). The formation of adult-sponsored clubs was, in part, a protective measure to ensure that the natural instinct of youngsters did not lead them into street corner gangs. The gang instinct could be used to draw them into clubs where the values of middle-class parents were paramount—values such as self-control, physical fitness, and determination. Thus, unlike the playgrounds for the urban poor that were considered to be a replacement for the family, the clubs for the middle class were an extension of the family.

## Synthesis and Summary

The relationship between the family and the peer group during the first two decades of this century was mediated by the establishment of a range of institutions, including *kindergartens* for the preschool child, *super-*

*vised playgrounds* for older youngsters aged from 6 to late adolescence, as well as a large range of *adult-sponsored clubs* for children of all ages. The rapid expansion of these institutions at the turn of the century was based on the belief that children's natural social instinct, or gang instinct, should not be repressed, but neither should it be allowed to find unfettered expression in unsupervised street-corner societies. The positive socializing role of peer groups was seen as necessary for the normal development of even very young children (Peabody); it was regarded as the fundamental social grouping capable of giving a child the "lived experience" of democracy (Baldwin and Dewey); and in the urban environment created by rapid industrialization and immigration of ethnically diverse peoples, the peer group was promoted as the ideal replacement for the family in forming the values and attitudes of the next generation. For the middle class, the peer group was constrained within institutional structures (high schools and recreational clubs) that reinforced the core middle-class values of respect for authority, diligence, and an achievement orientation.

The notion that peer socialization in clubs and playgrounds could or should replace the direct influence of the family in industrialized cities was not accepted by all commentators at the time. For example, Dorothy Fisher in her book, *Self-Reliance* (1916), placed parents in the central role of guiding and monitoring their children's development through to early adulthood. Fisher saw parents as providing simulations and role plays of the tasks and challenges that their children would eventually face as they moved into adulthood—an early instance of a social skills program! In a carefully crafted social environment, Fisher argued, children would learn to be gradually more independent of their parents, develop social poise, and gain self-confidence. Fisher had criticized the leaders of boys' and girls' clubs for overemphasizing the importance of peer groups for the growth of independence and self-reliance (Kett, 1977). Fisher's book was widely read at the time and remained popular into the 1930s, when it was reissued (Overstreet, 1930), which indicates the high level of public support for Fisher's view that parents should be the prime socializing agents throughout childhood and adolescence.

## BETWEEN THE WARS: 1920 TO 1940

### The Historical Context

*Faith in Science.* The period between the wars began with an optimistic outlook as greater affluence enabled ordinary citizens to aspire to the ideal of the family home with sufficient space for children to play, and an automobile in the garage for excursions to the sea or into the countryside. The optimism of the times was based on a belief in the capacity of the *sciences* to solve the material and social problems of modern society. "Every Home a Laboratory," the title of an article written by the Director of the Child Development Institute at Minnesota (Anderson, 1932), conveys something of the spirit of the times. Anderson (1956) described the early 1920s as a time of great ferment in which

> . . . new sciences and new arts relating to the physical and mental development of human beings came into being. This was the period when well-baby clinics, preventive pediatrics, school health programs, child guidance clinics, mental hygiene clinics, and demonstrations in public health put in their appearance. (p. 184)

By the end of the 1920s, faith in *science* had a substantial material expression—Institutes for Child Development and Welfare had been established in universities and colleges across the country. In addition, various organizations such as the Association for Family Living (1925) and the National Council of Parent Education (1926) were established to disseminate the accumulating scientific knowledge to the general public and particularly to parents.

*Parent Education.* The need for parent education was given considerable impetus after World War I as the results of the extensive physical and mental testing of young military recruits was made public. A large number were found to have serious but correctable physical defects, many were illiterate and showed a lack of educational potential, and others were "maladjusted and inadequate persons" (Anderson, 1956, p. 184). It is not surprising, therefore, that lobbying for parent education took on the tone of a national crusade. For example, a poem distributed widely through parent–teacher associations and mothers' clubs in the 1920s instructed parents in capital letters to "Know your job!" (Braley, 1927). In popular magazines such as *Parents Magazine* (first published in 1926), parents were provided with "expert and scientific advice" to enable them to fulfill their crucial role, which was linked by the commentators to concerns of the whole nation. Clara Littledale, editor of *Parents Magazine,* wrote that there must be a

> deep realization . . . that the bringing up of children is not an isolated affair in which parents alone are concerned, but one on which the life of the nation depends. And because this is so (parents) must seek and obtain all the help that the experts can give them. (1931, p. 9)

Parents in the 1920s and 1930s thought of themselves as *modern,* as having cast off the conservative values of the previous century. They perceived themselves to have advanced ideas on sex education (simple, straightforward explanations); to have relaxed attitudes to children's clothing and cleanliness (gone were the restrictions of formal children's dress); and to assume that mothers *and* fathers would share in the care of children and participate in their interests and hobbies (Gruenberg, 1938). The reality was more conservative, however, as a survey reported by Stogdill (1936) shows. Parents reported that the best age for teaching procreation was 12, and that children's freedom to choose their own companions, books, or even their own food, should be delayed until age 16 to 18. The psychologists surveyed were considerably more liberal in granting children freedom of choice and independence at an early age. Stogdill noted that the parents seemed to feel:

> . . . that children, if left unchecked will get into harm or commit grave errors. Consequently, they rely upon parental supervision, and those institutions of the community devoted to indoctrinating children with beliefs and taboos which parents feel protect them. (p. 94)

***Parental Protectiveness and the Depression.*** The stock market crash of 1929 magnified parental preoccupation with protecting children and, if possible, delaying their independence. Parents were concerned that the Depression, which created high youth unemployment, could lead to delinquency brought on by boredom and frustration, and eventually the prospect of becoming one of the urban delinquents, criminals, or young tramps who traveled from place to place looking for work. Davis (1936), in the book *The Lost Generation,* noted that the 16 million unemployed youth (16 years and older) were an "army moving with the shuffling feet of the faithless," and Minehan (1935), in *Boy and Girl Tramps of America,* recorded his travels with thousands of young drifters, who were predominantly from poorer families but also from middle-class families caught up in the economic decline. Only a small proportion of unemployed youth actually became drifters and tramps, yet they symbolized the deep-seated insecurity that permeated society as a result of the Depression.

Hansl and Hansl (1936) asserted that the problem of the runaway youngsters must find its solution in the home, where the young must be made to feel that their place within the family could be filled by no one else. Fenton (1931), a psychologist with the California Bureau of Juvenile Research, presented a similar view, suggesting that "children go wrong" because of a range of parental faults. Delinquents, Fenton suggested, were ordinary children who lacked wholesome and intelligent care from parents. Such concerns were based partly on the writings of Healy and Bronner (1926, 1936), who suggested that crime originated in the socializing experiences of childhood and adolescence. In a study that matched delinquent and nondelinquent children from the same family, Healy and Bronner (1936) found that the delinquent child felt more discriminated against and disliked by one or both parents, and more emotionally stressed in the family. In escaping the negative home environment, the delinquent child was seen to be particularly susceptible to the influence of peers, especially the two or three close pals who were constant companions. Hartshorne and May (1928), for example, had shown that best friends had very similar scores on deception tests, which was interpreted as indicating that relationships among intimate pals exerted great influence on children for good and ill. In addition, Thrasher's study (1927) was interpreted as indicating that the neighborhood play group could change into the urban gang, which was the training ground for later criminality. Kett (1977) argued that there was only limited evidence from Thrasher's research to support such an interpretation. Nonetheless, such studies increased parental fear of allowing their children to have unsupervised social contacts with peers.

*The Family Home.* The family home was seen during the 1920–1940 period as the cure for the social ills of the times. The general public's view of delinquency was that it was the joint product of unsanitary, overcrowded, urban living conditions and a lack of commitment from mothers and fathers to their respective roles as homemakers and cooperative helper around the home (Littledale, 1937). The idealized home became a clean, safe, and controllable environment within which parents could monitor and foster the inculcation of appropriate habits in their children. The emphasis throughout the 1920s and 1930s was to assimilate as far as possible the child and the peer group into the home environment. An idyllic vision of the family home as a center for children's friends to visit and relax was captured by Tompkins (1928), who advised parents to make their house a home:

> Young people, especially, are gregarious creatures. The intermingling of ideas, the society of others, are necessary to their growth and development. They must have friends, and if the little spot which they have learned to regard as home is a home in the real sense of the word, naturally they will bring their associates to that home. Is yours a home—or just a house? . . . Does Sally have a crowd of young people on the porch in the evening singing while someone strums on a ukelele? Or is she always out in the evening? Does junior spend every moment he can at the movies? (p. 13)

The anxious questions at the end of the quotation reveal the parents' worry about the perceived dangers of the movie theaters, the dance halls, jazz clubs, and the easy access to automobiles. The *home,* with space for entertaining and a playground in the backyard, became the bulwark against such dangers.

For preschoolers and younger elementary school children, parents were exhorted to let children bring their friends to play in the backyard (Bacmeister, 1935; Batchelden, 1935; Blatz, 1933; Hartwell, 1934; Hill, 1932; Kranz, 1928; Strain, 1937a, 1937b; Woody, 1936). The image of the backyard playground provides a compelling contrast with the urban playgrounds of the early 1900s, which were public facilities for the neighborhood children. The backyard playground of the 1920s and 1930s represented, in contrast, families closing around their children. Play with peers was still seen as vital, but could and should be pursued within the safe and supervised confines of the home and the backyard. The promotion of backyard playgrounds engendered a new business in playground equipment, as well as advice on how to construct backyard playgrounds inexpensively (see Woody, 1936).

For older children and adolescents, the ideal home was a kind of clubhouse—a place to rendezvous prior to excursions, a center for entertainment, and a workshop for the pursuit of hobbies (Gay, 1934; F. Hall, 1936; Harding, 1937; Miller, 1936; Oram, 1934; Thurow, 1935). Mothers were urged by writers in *Parents Magazine* to "let the gang get supper" (Gay, 1934), and in general to make the home a site for informal and relaxed entertaining so that adolescents would invite their friends. It was the parents' task, especially the mothers', to provide the appropriate environment in which such relaxed entertaining could occur.

Fathers were urged to establish home-based hobbies, such as woodwork and radio for their sons (and occasionally for their daughters). Hobbies were seen as the expression of a boy's real interests, so that close father–son companionship around hobbies could provide a father with "insight into the boy's tendencies" and could "uncover many a secret of a boy's nature" so that his future career and education could be planned more effectively (Felix, 1931, p. 26, 79). Fathers were advised, also, that wholesome hobbies could be used to redirect the bad influences of "the gang." Holcombe (1933), discussing the gang age (which he placed from 9 to 14 years), suggested that if the gang was having a bad effect, it must be brought under the home influence. Holcombe, in a revealing paragraph, provided the following rationale for redirecting the gang urge:

Since the gang urge plays such an important role in the character development of the normal boy, its sublimation should be the first aim of every parent. Do not stifle the gang urge—foster it and direct its growth. Before your astonished eyes, your son's outlook will broaden, his popularity with other boys will increase, and his sense of social justice will be materially strengthened. (p. 6)

The adult role, as Holcombe saw it, was to gain control over the boy's urges and to direct them to desirable ends. In this specific case, Holcombe was able to interest his son and the gang in amateur radio and thereby replace the "sinister Jesse James Secret Society." In summary, the home properly managed by caring parents seemed to hold the key to meeting the child's need for companionship and supervision from the cradle to young adulthood.

***Parents as Pals.***    The foregoing example illustrates a particular view of parenting, namely, *the parent as pal,* which was promoted in the 1920s and 1930s in *Parents Magazine.* James West (1927), a leader in the Scouting movement, had advised fathers to be a *pal* to their sons, to become part of their peer group, and to participate actively in their hobbies and adventures. Perhaps with a touch of journalistic exaggeration, he urged fathers to be "a boy yourself" and "to travel the road with your son" (pp. 13–14) in a childlike frame of mind, so that close companionship could be developed with the son and his friends. Groves (1926) had introduced the *parent as pal* view of parenting when he suggested that a sympathetic understanding should exist between children and their parents. He counseled fathers to deliberately arrange companionship with their children (sons and daughters) in order to build mutual affection, loyalty, and understanding. Groves was concerned to balance the potentially exclusive influence of mothers on children by highlighting the father's role as a nonauthoritarian companion for the child. West employed the *pal* notion to illustrate how fathers could participate in their children's peer-group activities in order to continue the parental role of supervisor and guide. Only by intimate participation could a parent "make the most of concrete instances" to bend the "character and habits" of a child toward appropriate standards (1927, p. 14). Other writers in this era (Kaufman, 1928, 1929; Scotford, 1934) were more skeptical about the ideal of *parental palship,* because it seemed an invasion of the realm of children. The critics argued that children should be allowed to live their own lives and make their own mistakes; in effect, to learn from firsthand experience.

The *pal* concept provides one window into the thinking of writers in the 1920s and 1930s regarding the relationship of the family system to the peer system. It demonstrates the attempt to reconcile two convictions about the peer group: (a) that association with peers is necessary for children in order to give expression to their social needs and social instinct; and (b) that the behavior and attitudes of peer companions have a powerful influence on the child's development. The *pal* concept reconciled parents' desires to respect the natural patterns of child development, with their concern to maintain a constant if nonauthoritarian surveillance of the child so that the correct habits could be inculcated.

*Summary.* The period between the wars began optimistically. There was an expectation of material security; the Henry Ford revolution was beginning to mobilize ordinary families and extend their recreational options; and social policy was being influenced by a belief in the capacity of *science* to solve the material and social problems of the community. The "testing" preoccupation, which had begun during World War I, revealed a higher incidence of physical and psychological "deficiencies" in the youth population than anticipated. Partly in response to such information, Child Development and Welfare Institutes were established across the country in the expectation that the systematic application of the scientific method could overcome the problems. In addition, expert parenting was thought to prevent or reduce physical and psychological "defects," and so organizations were established for the education of parents (e.g., the National Council of Parent Education, 1926). Popular publications such as *Parents Magazine* disseminated the latest research findings in a form that was accessible to the educated middle class. The depression of the early 1930s dented the initial optimism and increased the anxiety of parents regarding their children's employment prospects, the possibility of them being led into delinquency, or becoming one of the thousands of drifters and tramps moving around the country. In this historical context, the family *home* was promoted as a safe haven where children and adolescents could fulfill their need for social companionship under the supervision and guidance of parents. In order to reconcile their supervisory role with their role of being understanding and caring, parents were urged to become part of the child's peer group by joining in its activities, or enticing the group to participate in home-based hobbies.

## Theorists

*Watson.* The psychological theory that dominated the period was behaviorism, and with its emphasis on objective scientific methods and habit training, the theory was particularly well attuned to the dual concerns of parents to control and supervise their children's social contacts, and at the same time follow scientific ideas of child rearing. The behaviorist theory of habits was basic to Watson's child psychology and Thorndike's educational psychology. Littledale, in 1946, reflecting on the previous 20 years of advice to parents, noted that Dr. John B. Watson had been the prophet in the field, and she provided the following summary of the accepted parenting style of the era:

> Habit training—that was the word! It should begin as soon as the child was born. The idea was that if you caught him early enough and trained and

trained, allowing no deviations from the ideal but everlastingly hauled him up in the way he should go, why, you would never have any trouble at all. How could you, if you did the right thing every minute? (p. 127)

Building habits was seen as the necessary antidote to the unpredictable life that awaited young people as they moved from the family into the larger society. A well-formed habit enabled the child to respond according to parental expectations in any environment because the response had been stamped in through repeated performances. A pertinent example of such thinking can be found in Snyder and Snyder's (1929) "Correcting Behaviour Problems Through Play." They advised parents that good habits could be taught through play, and that rightly selected toys would help. Childhood activities such as play, therefore, were seen not in Hall's terms as the natural expression of the social instinct, but as a training ground for the constant and consistent formation of good habits.

Watson proposed a controlled, aloof, and unemotional style of child training that, untempered by common-sense adaptations, seemed somewhat bizarre. The rigorous child-training procedures were perceived even by his wife as radical. In the article, "I am the Mother of a Behaviorist's Sons" (R. Watson, 1930), she provided a generally positive account of behaviorism, as it was applied in the Watson family, but she also had reservations, as shown by the following quotation:

> In some respects, I bow to the great wisdom in the science of behaviorism, and in others I am rebellious. One grave reason why I am a very bad mother, behavioristically speaking, is because I am still somewhat on the side of the children. I am afraid the scientists tackled me too late in life to wholly recondition me . . . I cannot restrain my affection for the children completely. (p. 67)

The restraint on affection was an attempt by J. B. Watson to make child rearing a completely objective process; an attempt to raise a generation of children whose behavior was controlled by the contingencies in the environment. Affection and emotion were regarded as too unpredictable to have a place in such a dispassionate scientific endeavor. In this regard, Bertrand Russell (1930) had written a tongue-in-cheek but critical critique ("Are Parents Bad for Children?") in which he told parents not to let Watson frighten them; it was perfectly safe to love ones' children; he wrote:

> Freud, it was who first terrified parents with the idea that there is something sinful dark and disastrous in the affection of children for their parents. Watson who disagrees with Freud about almost everything, nevertheless agrees with him about this; he apparently considers it a very unwise decree of nature that children have to have mothers. (p. 18)

Habit training was proposed as the technique for all aspects of development, from learning sleeping patterns, toilet training, and tidiness to acquiring character traits and morality. However, the publication of "Studies in Service and Self-Control" by Hartshorne, May, and Maller (1929), challenged the assumption that character habits could be stamped into a child, because they found that displays of honesty, helpfulness, and self-control varied for individual children from one situation to another. The challenge posed by the research was recognized at the time (see G. Watson, 1930); it seemed particularly troublesome that neither differences in religious training nor intelligence increased the consistency with which children were honest or self-controlled.

Another challenge to habit theory was the increasing concern with children's emotional development, which can be traced to the growing influence of Freud and, to a lesser extent, to the continuing influence of Hall, who had highlighted children's natural impulses and the necessity to build on their interests and needs. Littledale (1946) suggested that there had been a slow movement away from an overrigid, overconscientious, mechanistic approach to the rearing of children in the 1920s, to a more relaxed and sympathetic acceptance of children's drives and urges, "including the violence of a child's feelings" (p. 135).

Although the radical message in Watson's behaviorism was tempered by common-sense adjustments, it had a profound influence nonetheless, because it suggested to parents the need to exercise pervasive control throughout children's development to ensure that they formed the correct habits. Parents were being urged to extend their guiding influence beyond the boundaries of the home and into the peer-group activities of children.

***Gesell.***   Where the behaviorists were busy *training* the child, Gesell took up the mantle of Hall to suggest that the central task of parenting was to *understand* the individual and the laws of growth. His maturational stage theory elaborated the recapitulation theory of Hall by systematically measuring, year by year, numerous aspects of children's interests, behavior, and personality. Gesell accepted Hall's notion that the growth of the child and the history of the human race were reciprocal keys. He described the human mind as *evolving* in the history of the race, and *growing* in each individual. The essence of Gesell's approach is contained in the following quotation by Gesell and Ilg (1943):

> The process of maturing remains essentially the same throughout the whole life cycle. It is a process of developmental morphogenesis. It is a constant building up and interweaving of an infinitude of patterns and sub-patterns, always subject to the mechanisms of developmental physiology. These

mechanisms are so lawful and so fundamental that children of similar chronological age are in general most comparable with respect to their emotional characteristics. The intellectual prodigy capable of fifth grade work at the age of six is at heart more like a child of six than a child of eleven. This fact suggests that the make-up of personality depends upon instinctive and innate factors which are so ancient and deep-seated that they cannot with impunity be transcended, even in a highly sophisticated culture. (pp. 36–37)

The influence of Hall is clear, also, in Gesell's description of the preadolescent gang and organized clubs. Prior to age eight, Gesell characterized children as dependent on adults, whereas at preadolescence they showed a positive lack of interest in adults, and began to form peer groups with hierarchies and competition for leadership, which "viewed in the deep perspective of the pre-history of the race, . . . is suggestive of a culminating stage of human evolution when . . . the young of our species once shifted for themselves independently of further parental aid" (Gesell & Ilg, 1943, pp. 254–255). At adolescence, Gesell believed that indifference to adults changed back to sensitivity, and a need to seek out adult models to emulate. When *Youth: The Years from Ten to Sixteen,* was published (Gesell, Ilg, & Ames, 1956), Gesell painted the adolescent as somewhat more peer oriented, capable of peer friendships, and responsive to group pressure, but there was no suggestion that the peer culture, or *The Adolescent Society* as Coleman (1961) called it, was the principal influence on behavior (Connell, 1980).

Gesell's growth model of development influenced research such as that conducted by Parten (1932) on the stages of play. Parten justified her study of very young children as an attempt to reveal the spontaneous and socially unaffected reactions of children. Complex social factors were regarded as "noise" that normally clouded the underlying developmental patterns. The genetic (developmental) approach to the study of social phenomenon, Parten insisted, reduced the likely impact of multiple social factors and therefore could help to uncover the underlying uniformities. The study by Murphy (1937) of children's sympathetic behavior was framed initially by similar concerns: Are children inherently cooperative and helpful, or antagonistic and competitive? Murphy concluded that children were influenced greatly by the patterns of sympathetic and antagonistic behavior that the culture presented, and she rejected the implications of the growth model as an adequate explanation for her observations.

The influence of social agents, according to Gesell, should be to preserve and foster the child's unfolding potentialities, and he recommended a *developmental* style of parenting, which was one of three approaches he derived from Lewin, Lippett, and White (1939). The *authoritarian* approach was typified (according to Gesell) by the behaviorists, who emphasized imposition of adult culture on the child. The *laissez faire* doctrine was typified by the free-market economy (discredited by the 1929 crash), in which intelligent guidance was ruled out. The *developmental* approach took the child's inherent nature as the point of departure, but included intelligent adult guidance based on an understanding of the laws of the growth process. Lewin did not agree with Gesell's growth model, and he sought to demonstrate that individual attitudes and behavior were a function of forces created by social and environmental factors. It is significant that Gesell renamed the *democratic* leadership style of Lewin et al. (1939), *developmental* parenting. A political and social category (democracy) was transformed into an individual and biologically derived category (developmental). When Gesell discussed *democracy* in childrearing (Gesell & Ilg, 1943, p. 10), he focused on respect for the individuality of each person, but did not mention the sense of common purpose, cooperation, group solidarity, and the emergence of individuality from social relationships—issues that were basic to the writing of Lewin as well as to the theorists of the Progressive Era such as Dewey, Baldwin, and Cooley. This individualistic view is another instance of Gesell's preoccupation with an unfolding growth process. Such a theory did not assist researchers to explore reciprocal connections between family and peer group, nor to place the process of socialization in cultural and historical perspective. It did provide support, however, for the parent education movement of the 1920–1940 period, because it promoted the view that in essence parenting was a process of *understanding* the real child (sometimes hidden beneath confusing appearances), and providing intelligent guidance that was compatible with each unfolding period of growth.

***Lewin and Field Theory.*** The basis of Lewin's theory was Gestalt psychology, which originated just prior to World War I and made three central claims: first, learning should be regarded as a purposive activity that was motivated by the learner's goals; second, learning was the result of grasping the whole pattern of an activity rather than proceeding in a piecemeal fashion; and third, human behavior could only be understood if it was studied in a field of social and environmental forces in which the individual was striving to find an effective adaptation (Connell, 1980). Lewin argued that the characteristics of *human relationships* were central in the development of personality, and his studies from the 1930s demonstrated how such claims could be researched successfully; the most influential was the Lewin et al. (1939) experimental study of group climates mentioned earlier. The study illustrates Lewin's dual approach of maintaining as natural a setting as possible, but using experimental manipulation in order to reveal the conditions that influence group processes.

Lewin's studies had widespread influence for a number of reasons. First, the issue of democratic versus totalitarian forms of control had been central to American researchers since the early decades of the century, when Dewey and the urban reformists wrestled with the problem of how democratic institutions could arise and be maintained in the face of rapid social change. These concerns were heightened in the 1930s as a result of the depression, and uncertainty about the survival of democracy as totalitarian governments came to power in Europe. Second, the 1930s was an era of innovation and experimentation in the study of social development (Renshaw, 1981). In particular, the use of sophisticated observational techniques and experimental methods had been employed by Jack (1934) and Page (1936) to describe and change the ascendant (outgoing, assertive) and submissive behavior of particular children. Harold Anderson (1937) criticized these studies for failing to distinguish between forms of ascendance that were compatible with respect for the individual (integrative), versus those forms that ignored the rights of the individual in gaining ascendance (dominative). This line of research foreshadowed Lewin's research in the United States both in the use of experimental intervention and in the conceptual distinction between behavioral styles consistent with a democracy (integrative), or a totalitarian regime (authoritarian and dominative). Lewin brought a new perspective to the issue by highlighting the effects of group forces (leadership styles) on all individuals rather than focusing on the personality traits of individuals.

## Social Institutions

*Introduction.*    Protective guidance and pervasive monitoring well into the teenage years was the goal of parents during the late 1920s and in the 1930s. Parental influence in the peer group was made possible by many educational and recreational institutions, which enabled parents to choose an option compatible with their attitudes and values. Schools, camps, and clubs extended the influence of the family (particularly the middle-class family) beyond the boundaries of the home, and into the everyday settings of the child where they interacted with peers.

*Nursery Schools and Kindergartens.*    Lazerson (1971) attributed the decline in public support for kindergartens over the first two decades of the century as due to tight city budgets, and the undermining of the rationale used by social reformers to advocate their establishment. They had emphasized the role of the kindergarten in compensating for the home experiences of the child, and in educating poor urban mothers in proper child-care practices. The reality, however, was that cities with the greatest need had few kindergartens, and those that were available had difficulty attracting the children of the poor (Lazerson, 1971, p. 63). In addition, the social reformers saw the kindergarten as weaning children away from the effects of maternal overprotection. Fisher (1916), in her influential writing on parenting, however, had criticized the overemphasis given to peer-group socialization. For a variety of practical and substantive reasons, therefore, educational facilities for the preschooler declined. It seems that the situation did not change during the 1920s and 1930s. The White House Conference on Child Health and Protection (Anderson, 1936) reported that only 5% of the preschool population attended nursery school, and that only 30% of 5-year-olds were in kindergartens. These children were overwhelmingly from the higher socioeconomic groups. Peer contacts did occur during the preschool period, however, as indicated by the survey results: Over half of the 1-year-olds had "played" away from home, and 80% of the 4-year-olds had done so. About half of the preschoolers were reported to have a favorite playmate. These data indicate that mothers arranged play opportunities at home for their children in the absence of a nursery school or kindergarten. The opportunity for arranging peer contacts varied greatly between rural families and those in towns or cities. Baldwin, Fillmore, and Hadley (1930), in their detailed study of farm families, found that young farm children lacked companionship, toys, and play equipment, and demonstrated little competence in starting and maintaining games with their peers when play opportunities arose.

*High Schools.* O'Donnell (1937) suggested that the choice of school was the most important decision faced by parents "anxious to surround . . . children with the influences which will draw out . . . the very best in them" (p. 27). Prior to World War I, many youngsters left school at an early age to avoid the harsh discipline and to seek work in order to supplement the income of the family. After the war, however, there was a steady rise in the retention rates at high schools. Child labor was made illegal in almost all states, and the laws that made attendance at high school compulsory until age 16 were enforced more vigorously. Tyack (1974) recorded the soaring enrollment and graduation numbers of high school students from 1920 to 1940. For those aged from 14 to 17 the percentage at school increased from 61.6% in 1920, to 73.1% in 1930, to 79.4% in 1940. Although the actual percentage of 17-year-olds who were high school graduates was substantially less (respectively, 16.8%, 29%, 50.8%), the pattern of growth was similar. The increasing rate of retention and graduation kept the younger adolescent off the streets, and provided a peer-group context in schools that allayed parental anxieties about delin-

quency. In *Middletown,* described by Lynd and Lynd (1929), the high
school had become the center of the social life of the adolescent. The
Lynds wrote,

> The high school, with its athletics, clubs, sororities and fraternities, dances
> and parties, and other 'extracurricular activities,' is a fairly complete cos-
> mos in itself, and about this city within a city the social life of the inter-
> mediate generation centers. (p. 211)

The adults in Middletown strongly supported the social life of schools,
and although contacts between the generations was frequent, it was likely
to occur at a school-sponsored social or sporting event. Hollingshead
(1949) collected data in Elmtown in 1941–1942, and he demonstrated
the many ways that schools operated in accord with the concerns of the
middle class: regulating children's social activities, selecting their social
companions, forming their aspirations, and organizing their leisure activities.

***Organized Summer Camps.***    The growing availability of organized
summer camps also overcame the need of anxious parents to monitor
their children's summer activities (Huebner, 1936). Camping was drawing over a million boys and girls by the summer of 1931, and the benefit
of camping in rural settings near lakes and forests was perceived to be
both ruggedly romantic (drawing the child back to Mother Nature) and
socially educative (Hamilton, 1931; Mason, 1933). As Mason (1933) wrote:

> Contact, association, is the educating and civilizing factor in life, and here-
> in lies perhaps the greatest contributions of organized camping. Boys and
> girls need many many contacts with boys and girls of their own age, and
> with men and women. They need new and varying human contacts . . .
> New associations push the horizons farther back, broaden the vision, tone,
> shape, and humanize the personality. (p. 22–23)

The camp experience was perceived as an appropriate and gentle
means of weaning children from emotional dependence on parents, and
of providing them with the opportunity to learn "how to adjust" to other
people (see also Gulick, 1935; Huebner, 1936). Parents exercised considerable control in this weaning process because they could pick and
choose between a large number of camps in order to find an appropriate
one. Each edition of *Parents Magazine,* for example, contained pages
of advertisements for different summer camps. Rogers (1939), in discussing the use of summer camps as a therapeutic treatment for children with
behavior problems, noted that difficulties often arose when children of
diverse social classes were mixed in one camp. This was uncommon,

however, as parents were able to choose camps consistent with their incomes and values, thereby maintaining pervasive proxy parental influence on children's peer relationships.

*Scouting and Organized Clubs.* In addition, organizations such as the Boy Scouts, Girl Scouts, and Camp Fire Girls grew in membership during the depression years, which was interpreted at the time as a response to "social chaos" (Schain, 1933). As was noted previously, the Scouts were a middle-class organization that, in practice, effectively excluded children from poorer sections of the community. Hollingshead (1949) summarized the reasons middle-class parents sent youngsters to these special institutions as a belief that the children were acquiring " 'citizenship,' 'leadership' or 'character,' which would keep the boy or girl from being tempted by the 'pleasures of adult life' " (p. 149). In the social institutions of schools, camps, and clubs, therefore, middle-class communities extended their protective umbrella in an attempt to shield adolescents from the contradictions and conflicts of the adult world.

*Urban Recreation Facilities.* The provision of adequate recreational facilities remained a problem for the urban poor. Financial support for playgrounds declined after the war, and complaints about the lack of facilities were common from urban youngsters. Bell (1938) completed an extensive survey of youth during the mid-1930s in which he asked youngsters to assess the recreational programs in their communities. Their verbatim responses suggested a good deal of repression by police and exclusion from facilities by public officials. The following quotes are taken from Bell's (1938) report:

> "Cops should not run us away from wharves when it's the only place we can swim."
> "They have school grounds right across from us, but they won't let us play there."
> "Can't play in the streets . . . won't allow us to play in school yard . . . police run us out every time."
> "Kids here have no place to play except the streets, and the cops get you for that." (p. 184)

These comments reflect not only the objective situation, as there were few recreational outlets for poor youngsters in the cities, but a sense of social alienation from those that were actually available. Bell (1938) remarked that even in communities with good facilities (for example, a library, clinic, gymnasium, and public park grouped around the school), the main complaint of the youngsters was the lack of social and sports centers, apparently because they perceived the available facilities as unwelcoming.

## Synthesis and Summary

Between World War I and World War II the role of parents in supervising and guiding children's growth and learning was reemphasized. Parents were advised to oversee the child's peer-group activity, either by participating directly in the peer group, enticing the peer group into the family home for relaxation and recreation, or by carefully selecting schools, clubs, and summer camps that offered experiences consistent with parental attitudes and values. In this way, the institutions provided proxy parental supervision.

The overriding preoccupation with supervision and monitoring seems to have been the result of the dominant psychological theories of the era, as well as the threat (perceived and actual) to social stability and order posed by the Depression. The habit theory of Watson and the growth theory of Gesell both influenced the concepts of parenting promoted during the period. Watson's view that social habits were stamped into the child from repeated practice implied that parents should provide a consistent, controlled environment, and constant vigilance if children were to learn the correct habits. The practical advice given to parents suggested, for example, that play could be a training ground for the formation of social habits, and that friends should be chosen carefully to prevent children from learning undesirable habits from their peers. The impact of habit theory challenged the assumption of the progressive theorists that the peer group offered unique socializing experiences. The peer group became simply another context where "good" or "bad" habits could be learned.

Gesell's theory, as an extension of Hall's recapitulation theory, promoted the view that there was a period in the child's growth, the preadolescent stage, where preoccupation with peer-group activity would supplant the orientation towards adults. At this stage, the parent should not suppress the gang instinct, but as Holcombe (1933) advised, guide and direct the gang instinct toward socially desirable goals. The influence of Gesell and Hall can be discerned also in the advice West (1927) offered fathers, who were urged to participate in their children's peer groups. The gang instinct must be allowed freedom of expression, but the learning outcomes of the experience could be enhanced by on-the-spot guidance by the wise father. Felix (1931) likewise supported the companionship of parents and children because through such close association a parent might discover the hidden needs and abilities of the child. This reflects Gesell's image of the ideal parent as an *understanding guide* of the child's unfolding growth towards maturity. Hall's notion of the peer group stage as a reenactment of an earlier phase of human civilization remained part of Gesell's theory, but in the context of the 1920s and 1930s, more emphasis was given to the extension of parental guidance into the peer group, rather than trusting the laws of growth to guarantee positive socialization outcomes for the child and society.

## WORLD WAR II TO PRESENT

### The 1940–1950 Period: The Historical Context

The impact of World War II on children and families was very marked (Stolz, 1954; see Modell, 1989, and Tuttle, 1992, for recent reviews of this issue). Two themes predominate. First, there was a large increase in interest in the effects of father absence on children's social relationships, especially their sex role development. These studies suggest that father absence modified the sex role patterns, especially of boys. Boys raised without fathers were less masculine (Bach, 1946; Sears, Pintler, & Sears, 1946) or else exhibited compensatory hypermasculinity and aggressiveness (Biller, 1971). These studies both reflect and anticipate the rising impact of Freudian theory on studies of social development. These early studies did not stimulate much direct investigation of the active role of the father in children's peer relationships; in part because of the continued emphasis on the centrality of the maternal role in childrearing and children's development (for critiques of these early studies see Herzog & Sudia, 1970; Shinn, 1978).

The second issue involved the high rate of maternal employment outside the home during wartime. During the war the female labor force grew by 57% (Tuttle, 1992) and "constituted a part of the wartime experience of half or more of the adult women" (Hartmann, 1982, p. 31). In turn, this probably led to an increase in children in out-of-home care, which would have increased the opportunities for peer contact. However, a very incomplete picture is available not only of the types of child-care arrangements, but (also) of the impact of out-of-home child care on children's development during this period (Tuttle, 1992).

Moreover, the effects of any single factor such as father absence or maternal employment are difficult to evaluate in view of the host of other changes such as family migration, improvements in the economic climate, and the rising birth rate that were associated with wartime. Detailed study of the impact of the multiple changes in family organization and functioning on peer relationships remains to be undertaken. The research that was conducted on the family–peer linkage issue was valuable, but did not recognize how the special circumstances of wartime altered findings. Instead the impact of the war is reflected in the politically motivated work of Lewin on group climates (Lewin et al., 1939), which in turn influenced subsequent work on the effects of family organization on children's social behavior (e.g., Baldwin, 1949; Baumrind, 1967).

## The 1940–1950 Period: Theorists

In the 1940s, there were studies by Baldwin of the effects of democratic home climates on the personality development of young children (Baldwin, 1948, 1949; Baldwin, Kalhorn, & Breese, 1945). Measures of democratic home climates were derived from the Fels Parent Behavior Rating Scales, and measures of the child's personality development were derived from ratings of behavior in the nursery school or school. Baldwin (1949) reported that there were three consequences of being raised in a democratic home: (a) children are socially active and outgoing, and display both dominative and friendly types of behavior with peers (a clear reference to Anderson's distinction); (b) they are popular with other children; and (c) they show higher intellectual curiosity, originality, and constructiveness. Baldwin reported (Baldwin, Kalhorn, & Breese, 1945) that by the time the children from democratic homes had entered school, they were leaders and popular with their peers because of their friendliness rather than their dominative behavior. The democratic home was described as providing the child with a serene and emotionally secure personality that enabled a successful adjustment to school.

Other research conducted in the 1940s and 1950s in general supported Baldwin's research. Mummery (1954), in reviewing the literature from that period, used Jack's (1934) notion of ascendance (assertiveness) to summarize the consistent findings. What types of homes make for assertive children? Mummery suggested the following types: homes that permit freedom; encourage exploration; provide assistance in acquiring skills; provide explanations for regulations; include children in decision making; and allow the children to face normal risks and responsibilities. What types of homes produce acceptable forms of assertiveness, that is, integrative rather than dominative assertiveness? Mummery indicated that there is less consistency in the findings here, but the general pattern is families that are happy, accepting, affectionate, and with a democratic type of control tend to produce children who are cooperative and considerate in their own behavior. In contrast, coerciveness and an autocratic style of discipline were associated with dominative behavior by children. Mummery proposed that the explanatory process for the development of assertiveness may be the level of self-confidence that the home engenders in the child. With regard to the learning of integrative behavior, Mummery proposed that the democratic home: (a) enables the child to take the perspective of the other and to work towards a mutual goal; (b) provides many models (examples) of the integrative methods of interacting with others; and (c) provides direct guidance and training in integrative behavior, such as that illustrated in Chittenden's (1942) experimental study to increase cooperative forms of assertion. These suggestions foreshadowed the social skill intervention programs of the 1970s and 1980s. Mummery appears to have anticipated the notion of the parent as a direct and an indirect influence on the child's peer relationships as well (Parke, MacDonald, Beitel, & Bhavnagri, 1988).

## The 1950–1970 Period: Historical Context

During the 1950s and 1960s the popular framing of the family–peer linkage issue was in terms of "parents versus peers." As Youniss and Smollar (1989) argued, "peers were given responsibility for almost all of adolescents' problem behaviors. Authors of popular articles, policymakers in federal agencies such as the FBI, and social scientists began to generate the notion that the peer culture counteracts the positive effects that 12 or so years of rearing in the home had cultivated . . . the term *peers* suddenly took on a negative connotation" (p. 308).

A variety of factors may have contributed to this climate of intergenerational suspicion, including the increase in TV availability and the universality of high school experience, which, in turn, led to an increased mixing of class and racial groups (Gilbert, 1986; cited by Youniss & Smollar, 1989). In spite of this climate, little evidence supports this pessimistic view of family–peer relationships. In fact, the vast majority of studies support the view that there is a high level of agreement between the attitudes and values of parents and peers (e.g., Douvan & Adelson, 1966; Kandel & Lesser, 1972). However, the unrest during the 1960s surrounding the protests over the Vietnam War added face validity to this view. (For a useful discussion of how family–child relationships are shaped by changing societal circumstances during this period, see Riesman's [1953] classic volume, *The Lonely Crowd.*)

The majority of discussion of this period has focused on the adolescent–family relationship and much less attention has been devoted to younger children's relationships with peers and families. A useful starting point for such an analysis would be the rise in popularity of organized sports for younger children and the role that parents play in relation to these activities (see Fine & West, 1979, for a review of the rise of Little League, for example). Interestingly, these shifts in the organization of children's activities had little impact on either the research agenda or in stimulating new research on family–peer relationships, in spite of the fact that these organized activities represent an interesting example of family management of children's peer relationships (Parke & Bhavnagri, 1989).

## The 1950–1970 Period: Theorists

Two research traditions can be distinguished. First, as we noted previously, in response to the popular framing of the era in terms of intergenerational conflict and a clash of parental and peer attitudes, there was considerable research on these issues, especially as with adolescents (Bronfenbrenner, 1970; Douvan & Adelson, 1966). This work was heavily influential by social psychological theories of attitude formation, psychoanalytic theory, and sociological viewpoints, but was less influenced by the dominant theories of child development of the era. However, these studies were useful in leading to the current reformulation of adolescents' parent and peer relationships in terms of continuity and mutual influence rather than in conflictual terms (Cooper & Ayers-Lopez, 1985; Cooper & Cooper, this volume).

Within mainstream child development, the period from 1950 to 1963 was dominated by a second tradition, namely the theoretical writings of Robert Sears and his colleagues. This framework cast Freudian theory in Hullian learning theory terms (Sears, 1951). In turn this permitted traditional Freudian hypotheses concerning the importance of different child-rearing practices to be empirically tested. Evaluation of the impact of different types of feeding (bottle vs. breast), severity of weaning, and the timing of toilet training on children's social development was undertaken in a series of large-scale interview studies (see Sears, Maccoby, & Levin, 1957; Sears, Rau, & Alpert, 1965; Sears, Whiting, Nowlis, & Sears, 1953). The focus on family factors was consistent with the Freudian roots of these investigators. In turn, they selected dependent measures such as dependency, aggression, sex typing, and conscience development that were suggested by Freudian theory. In this era, the family was viewed as the major socialization agency by social scientists, and peers were relatively neglected as a central socialization agency or even as a context in which to measure the impact of family childrearing variables. There were several notable exceptions, especially studies that focused on children's behavior in nursery school contexts. For example, Sears et al. (1953) examined the impact of parental childrearing styles on children's attention-seeking behavior and aggression in nursery school. However, there was little use of direct measures of children's peer relationships in terms of either sociometric measures or teacher ratings, nor was there any interest in peer group formation or organization during the Sears era. It was clearly a family-dominated period, with little interest in either other agents of socialization or in the links between different socialization forces.

The major shift in theory that served to bring the issue of peer relationships and families back to a more central place on the research agenda was the publication of Bandura and Walters' (1963) seminal volume

"Social Learning and Personality Development." Instead of the reliance on Freudian and Hullian learning theory that had characterized the Sears era, these theorists emphasized imitation and modeling as key components for the acquisition, maintenance, and modification of social behavior. Moreover, it was assumed that a range of agents—families, peers, and TV—were all potentially important in the socialization process. Peers as well as adults were found to play important roles as models and reinforcers of social behavior (Bandura & Walters, 1963; Hartup, 1964; Hartup & Coates, 1967; Wahler, 1967; Walters, Parke, & Cane, 1965), and these demonstrations set the stage for the return of peer group work to center stage in the research arena. However, these earlier studies were more concerned with demonstrating that peers could function as agents of modeling or reinforcement than they were in the exploration of the familial origins of peer relationships.

In addition to the renewed interest in peers as socialization agents that was stimulated by social learning theory, a series of advances in the conceptualization and measurement of peer relationships provided a strong foundation for the reemergence of research on this topic. First, the reintroduction of observational methods that had been popular in peers research in the 1930s (e.g., Jack, 1934; Goodenough, 1931; see Renshaw, 1981, for a review) was a major advance (e.g., Charlesworth & Hartup, 1967; Eckerman, Wheatley, & Kutz, 1975). Second, rekindled interest in sociometric methods that again can be traced to the 1930s (Moreno, 1934) were evident during this period as well (Hartup, Glazer, & Charlesworth, 1967; McCandless & Marshall, 1957; Moore & Updegraff, 1964). Together, this combined resurgence of interest in observational methods and sociometric assessments set the stage for the rapid advances in the study of peer relationships that occurred during the 1970s and has continued unabated to the present. Although this resurgence of interest in peers was welcome, few of these mainstream studies of peers in the 1960s and 1970s focused on the antecedents of variations in peer competence in general or the role of the family in particular.

Other work on the family side began to probe more directly the impact of families on children's social competence. Some empirical studies of family disciplinary style, especially the work of Diana Baumrind (1967), provided evidence of how family experience relates to peer adaptation. Specifically, her now classic work of the effects of authoritative, authoritarian, and permissive parental styles on children's social adaptation to peers was an early indication of the links between family and peer systems. However, the focus of this work was largely family-oriented, and the peer measures were viewed as ways of capturing the impact of these variations in family childrearing style. It stimulated little direct interest in the family–peer linkage question per se.

## 1970–Present: Historical Context

The reemergence of interest in the links between peer and family systems has origins in the secular sphere as well as in scientific arenas. A variety of shifts in the 1970s clearly contributed to this interest. The advent of the women's liberation movement and the rise in women's employment outside the home were important factors. Between 1970 and 1982 there was a major increase in the percentage of women who had children and who also were employed.

In 1970, 32% of women with children under 5 years of age were in the labor force and by 1982, 49.9% were employed. Similarly for mothers of older children, 51.5% had jobs outside the home in 1970 and this percentage was 65.8% by 1982. This, in turn, led to a rise in the number of children who were enrolled in some type of day-care arrangement. By 1985, approximately two thirds of children under age 5 whose mothers worked received care for some portion of time each week from individuals other than their parents, grandparents, and siblings (Hayes, Palmer, & Zaslow, 1990).

Nearly 46% of the children in this age group with working mothers were cared for outside their own home, either in the home of a nonrelative caregiver or in an organized child-care facility. Of relevance is the fact that these children were afforded opportunities for contact with agemates at younger ages and in a more sustained fashion than in earlier eras. Cross-cultural exceptions, such as the Israeli kibbutz, have provided such arrangements for decades, but the proportion of children involved was much less (Rabin, 1958).

Although it is unclear the extent to which these shifts influenced current interest in this topic, it undoubtedly made research easier to execute due to the ready access to toddlers and young children in these centers. Additionally, although many scientists often claim otherwise, there are clear ties between social concerns and values and our selection of scientific problems. In the 1970s and 1980s there was an increasing awareness of social policy issues and of the need to explore the implications of theory for policy, practice, and intervention. An example of one form that this issue has assumed is the controversy concerning the timing of maternal reentry into the labor force after the birth of a child on both the development of attachment and, by implication, in the later adjustment of the child (see Belsky, 1988; Clarke-Stewart, 1989).

## 1970–Present: Theorists

The contemporary framing of the family–peer issue has its roots not only in shifts in the secular arena but also in research and theory. First, the work of Harry Harlow with rhesus monkeys served to highlight the importance of both family and peer systems for adequate social development; ironically, Harlow viewed these systems as independent, although his classic studies of maternal social deprivation clearly suggested that reduced social contact produced later social maladaptation to peers (Harlow, 1969). The studies suggest the importance of links between early family environment and later adaptation to peers.

A second related strand was, of course, the rise of interest in Bowlby's ethologically oriented theory of attachment (Bowlby, 1969). As indicated elsewhere (Elicker, Egeland, & Sroufe, this volume; Sroufe & Fleeson, 1986), this theory provided a clear theoretical basis for focusing on the family as a formative experience that, in turn, would affect children's relationships with others outside the family.

A third influence was Bronfenbrenner's (1979) volume *The Ecology of Human Development,* which provided the field with a view of the family as embedded in a variety of social contexts, including peer contexts. This volume offered a framework for conceptualizing links across levels of interaction and settings and clearly underscored the interdependent nature of the family and the peer group. Although not focused on family–peer relationships per se, the volume appeared at a time when the field was prepared for this type of thinking. These emerging themes were well captured by Hartup's (1979) call for the specific study of the links between family and peer systems. His articulation of the alternative pathways including parent–child interaction and parental management provided a research agenda that is clearly being addressed in the chapters of this volume.

## CONCLUSION

This chapter has offered an overview of how the relationships between families and peers have been dually influenced by both theory and contemporary social and political concerns. Our analysis should be viewed less as a final statement than as an invitation to consider the value of historical analyses in developmental psychological inquiry. Not only do different historical contexts dictate, in part, the importance of an issue, but they also play a major role in the framing of the research agenda (Elder, Modell, & Parke, 1992). The lingering question that remains to be addressed in future collaborative efforts between developmentalists and historians is the extent to which the basic processes and mechanisms of family–peer linkage are similar across different historical periods. It is conceivable that the processes remain constant, but the degree of influence that families exert fluctuates, or the proportion of families exhibiting one or another type of facilitative or disruptive environment may shift. For example, during the Great Depression, there was a high rate of family conflict and a redistribution of power relationships between older adolescents and their parents. Whereas families under severe economic stress function differently, recent work has shown that similar processes, such as coercive interaction patterns (Patterson, 1981), can account for negative outcomes in children's behavior in the 1930s and the 1970s. Alternatively, it could be argued that the processes or mechanisms by which families influence peer relationships, in fact, shift across historical time. Parents' direct face-to-face influence on their children's peer relationships may be higher in eras where most mothers are full-time caregivers. In contrast, in times of high maternal employment where decisions about out-of-home care, for example, are more salient, parental management strategies may play a relatively more important role in shaping children's peer relationships. The disentanglement of the role of historical context in altering the impact of basic processes is a challenge for the future.

## ACKNOWLEDGMENT

Preparation of this chapter and the research reported here were supported in part by National Science Foundation Grant 8919391 to Ross D. Parke.

## REFERENCES

Addams, J. (1909). *The spirit of youth and the city streets.* New York: Macmillan.

Anderson, H. H. (1937). Domination and integration in the social behavior of young children in an experimental play situation. *Genetic Psychology Monographs, 19,* 343–408.

Anderson, J. E. (1932, October). Every home a laboratory. *Parents Magazine,* p. 9.

Anderson, J. E. (1936). *The young child in the home: A survey of three thousand American families.* New York: Appleton-Century.

Anderson, J. E. (1956). Child development: An historical perspective. *Child Development, 27,* 181–196.

Ayres, L. P. (1909). *Laggards in our schools: A study of retardation and elimination in city school systems.* New York: Charities Publication Committee.

Bach, G. R. (1946). Father fantasies and sex typing in father-separated children. *Child Development, 17,* 63–80.

Bacmeister, R. W. (1935, December). Your child needs friends. *Parents Magazine,* pp. 18–19, 60–62.

Baldwin, A. L. (1948). Socialization and the parent–child relationship. *Child Development, 19,* 127–136.

Baldwin, A. L. (1949). The effect of the home environment on nursery school behavior. *Child Development, 20,* 49–61.

Baldwin, A. L., Kalhorn, J., & Breese, F. H. (1945). Patterns of parent behavior. *Psychological Monographs, 58,* 1–73.

Baldwin, B. T., Fillmore, E. A., & Hadley, L. (1930). *Farm children.* New York: Appleton.

Baldwin, J. M. (1899). *Social and ethnical interpretation in mental development: A study in social psychology.* New York: Macmillan.

Bandura, A., & Walters, R. H. (1963). *Social learning and personality development.* New York: Holt, Rinehart, & Winston.

Batchelden, G. E. (1935, June). Play in your backyard. *Parents Magazine,* pp. 39, 89.

Baumrind, D. (1967). Child-care practices anteceding three patterns of preschool behavior. *Genetic Psychology Monographs, 4*(1, Pt. 2).

Bell, H. M. (1938). *Youth tell their story.* Washington, DC: American Council on Education.

Belsky, J. (1988). The "effects" of infant day care reconsidered. *Early Childhood Research Quarterly, 3,* 235–272.

Biller, H. (1971). *Father, child, and sex roles.* Lexington, MA: Heath.

Blatz, W. E. (1933, February). Your child's choice of friends. *Parents Magazine,* pp. 22–23, pp. 58–60.

Bowlby, J. (1969). *Attachment and loss: Vol. 1. Attachment.* New York: Basic Books.

Braley, B. (1927, November). Parents, know your job! *Parents Magazine,* p. 26.

Bronfenbrenner, U. (1970). *Two worlds of childhood.* New York: Russell Sage.

Bronfenbrenner, U. (1979). *The ecology of human development.* Cambridge, MA: Harvard University Press.

Burk, F. (1897). Teasing and bullying. *Pedagogical Seminary, 4,* 336–371.

Cavallo, D. (1981). *Muscles and morals: Organized playgrounds and urban reform, 1880–1920.* Philadelphia: University of Pennsylvania Press.

Charlesworth, R., & Hartup, W. W. (1967). Positive social reinforcement in the nursery school group. *Child Development, 38,* 993–1002.

Chittenden, G. F. (1942). An experimental study in measuring and modifying assertive behavior in young children. *Monographs of the Society for Research in Child Development, 7*(1, Serial No. 31).

Clarke-Stewart, K. A. (1989). Infant day care: Maligned or malignant? *American Psychologist, 44,* 266–274.

Coleman, J. (1961). *The adolescent society.* New York: Free Press.

Connell, W. F. (1980). *A history of education in the twentieth century world.* Canberra: Curriculum Development Centre.

Cooper, C. R., & Ayers-Lopez, S. (1985). Family and peer systems in early adolescence: New models of the role of relationships in development. *Journal of Early Adolescence, 5,* 9–21.

Davis, A. F. (1972). Introduction. In J. Addams, *The spirit of youth and the city streets,* (pp. i–xxx). Urbana, IL: University of Illinois Press.

Davis, M. (1936). *The lost generation.* New York: Macmillan.

Dewey, J. (1899). *School and society.* Chicago: Chicago University Press.

Douvan, E., & Adelson, J. (1966). *The adolescent experience.* New York: Wiley.

Eckerman, C. O., Wheatley, J. L., & Kutz, S. L. (1975). The growth of social play with peers during the second year of life. *Developmental Psychology, 11,* 42–49.

Elder, G. H., Jr., Modell, J., & Parke, R. D. (Eds.). (1992). *Children in time and place.* New York: Cambridge University Press.

Felix, E. H. (1931, March). Share your boy's hobby. *Parents Magazine,* pp. 26, 78–79.

Fenton, J. C. (1931, June). Why children go wrong. *Parents Magazine,* pp. 22–23, 48–50.

Fine, G. A., & West, C. S. (1979). Do little leagues work: Player satisfaction with organized preadolescent baseball programs. *Minnesota Journal of Health, Physical Education, and Recreation, 7,* 4–6.

Fisher, D. C. (1916). *Self-reliance.* Indianapolis, IN: Merrill.

Forbush, W. B. (1900). The social pedagogy of boyhood. *Pedagogical Seminary, 7,* 307–346.

Forbush, W. B. (1909). Boys clubs. *Pedagogical Seminary, 16,* 337–343.

Gay, L. (1934, May). Let the gang get supper. *Parents Magazine,* pp. 38, 42, 44.

Gesell, A., & Ilg, F. L. (1943). *Infant and child in the culture of today.* New York: Harper.

Gesell, A., Ilg, F. L., & Ames, L. B. (1956). *Youth: The years from ten to sixteen.* London: Hamish Hamilton.

Goodenough, F. L. (1931). *Anger in young children.* Minneapolis: University of Minnesota Press.

Groves, E. R. (1926, October). Inside tips for father. *Parents Magazine,* pp. 12–14.

Gruenberg, S. M. (1938, January). Parents then and now. *Parents Magazine,* pp. 14–15, 40, 42.

Gulick, H. F. (1935). What camp offers your child. *Parents Magazine,* 10(4), 22–23, 50.

Hall, F. (1936, September). For fathers only. *Parents Magazine,* p. 92.

Hall, G. S. (1918). Morale in war and after. *Psychological Bulletin, 15,* 367.

Hall, G. S. (1926). *Youth: Its education regimen and hygiene.* New York: Appleton.

Hamilton, A. E. (1931). Is America camp crazy? *Parents Magazine, 8*(3), 11.

Hansl, E., & Hansl, B. (1936, July). Why children run away. *Parents Magazine,* pp. 18–19, 73.

Harding, A. M. (1937, September). For fathers only. *Parents Magazine,* p. 16.

Harlow, H. F. (1969). Age-mate or peer affectional system. In D. Lehrman, R. Hinde, & E. Shaw (Eds.), *Advances in the study of behavior* (Vol 2, pp. 139–157). New York: Academic Press.

Hartmann, S. M. (1982). *American women in the 1940s: The home front and beyond.* Boston: Twayne.

Hartshorne, H., & May, M. (1928). *Studies in deceit.* New York: Macmillan.

Hartshorne, H., May, M., & Maller, J. (1929). *Studies in service and self-control.* New York: Macmillan.

Hartup, W. W. (1964). Friendship status and the effectiveness of peers as reinforcing agents. *Journal of Experimental Child Psychology, 1,* 154–162.

Hartup, W. W. (1979). The social worlds of childhood. *American Psychologist, 34,* 944–950.

Hartup, W. W., & Coates, B. (1967). Imitation of a peer as a function of reinforcement from the peer group and rewardingness of the model. *Child Development, 38,* 1003–1016.

Hartup, W. W., Glazer, J. A., Charlesworth, R. (1967). Peer reinforcement and sociometric status. *Child Development, 38,* 1017–1024.

Hartwell, S. (1934, November). Are you helping your child to make friend? *Parents Magazine,* pp. 20–21, 54–56, 60.

Hayes, C. D., Palmer, J. L., & Zaslow, M. J. (Eds.). (1990). *Who cares for America's children? Child-care policy for the 1990s.* Washington, DC: National Academy Press.

Healy, W., & Bronner, A. F. (1926). *Delinquents and criminals: Their making and unmaking.* New York: Macmillan.

Healy, W., & Bronner, A. F. (1936). *New light on delinquency and its treatment.* New Haven: Yale University Press.

Herzog, E., & Sudia, C. (1970). *Boys in fatherless families.* Washington, DC: Department of Health, Education, & Welfare.

Hetherington, G. (1911). Playground directors—Sources from which they may be obtained. *Playground, 5,* 225.

Hill, M. (1932, March). Your child and other children. *Parents Magazine,* pp. 18–20, 51.

Holcombe, B. (1933, September). For fathers only. *Parents Magazine,* p. 6.

Hollingshead, A. B. (1949). *Elmtown's youth: The impact of social classes on adolescents.* New York: Wiley.

Howe, I. (1976). *World of our fathers.* New York: Simon & Schuster.

Huebner, H. A. (1936, April). Camp as a father sees it. *Parents Magazine,* pp. 32, 42.

Jack, L. M. (1934). An experimental study of ascendant behavior in preschool children. *University of Iowa Studies in Child Welfare, 9,* 9–65.

Kandel, D., & Lesser, G. S. (1972). *Youth in two worlds: U.S. & Denmark.* San Francisco: Jossey-Bass.

Kaufman, H. L. (1928, April). This pal idea. *Parents Magazine,* pp. 20–21, 53.

Kaufman, H. L. (1929, August). Should we hand-pick our children's friends? *Parents Magazine,* pp. 16–17, 46.

Kett, J. F. (1977). *Rites of passage: Adolescence in America, 1970 to the present.* New York: Basic Books.

Kranz, L. L. (1928, July). Come play in our yard. *Parents Magazine,* p. 20–21.

Lazerson, M. (1971). *Origins of the urban school: Public education in Massachusetts 1870–1915*. Cambridge, MA: Harvard University Press.

Lee, J. (1931, July). Children and tomorrow's leisure. *Parents Magazine*, p. 13.

Lewin, K., Lippitt, R., & White, R. R. (1939). Patterns of aggressive behavior in experimentally produced "social climates." *Journal of Social Psychology, 10,* 271–299.

Littledale, C. S. (1931, January). After the conference, what? *Parents Magazine*, p. 9.

Littledale, C. S. (1937, November). The home behind the child. *Parents Magazine*, p. 11.

Littledale, C. S. (1946, October). Then and now. *Parents Magazine*, pp. 18–19, 127–136.

Lynd, R. S., & Lynd, H. M. (1929). *Middletown: A study in American culture*. New York: Harcourt Brace.

Mason, B. S. (1933). Five things to require of a camp. *Parents Magazine, 8*(5), 22–23, 53.

McCandless, B. R., & Marshall, H. R. (1957). A picture of sociometric technique for preschool children and its relation to teacher judgments of friendship. *Child Development, 28,* 139–148.

Miller, R. H. (1936, December). For fathers only. *Parents Magazine*, p. 40.

Minehan, T. (1935, March). Boys and girls on the march. *Parents Magazine*, pp. 14–15, 70–72.

Modell, J. (1989). *Into one's own: From youth to adulthood in the United States 1920–1975*. Berkeley, CA: University of California Press.

Moore, S. G., & Updegraff, R. (1964). Sociometric status of preschool children as related to the age, sex, nurturance-giving, and dependence. *Child Development, 35,* 519–524.

Moreno, J. L. (1934). *Who will survive? A new approach to the problem of human interrelations*. Washington, DC: Nervous and Mental Disease Publishing.

Mummery, D. V. (1954). Family backgrounds of assertive and non-assertive children. *Child Development, 25,* 63–80.

Murphy, L. B. (1937). *Social behavior and child psychology: An exploratory study of some roots of sympathy*. New York: Columbia University Press.

O'Donnell, F. F. (1937). The school shapes the child. *Parents Magazine, 12*(7), 27, 42.

Oram, G. (1934, April). Entertaining high-school heroes. *Parents Magazine*, pp. 33, 76–77.

Overstreet. (1930, October). Review of *Self-Reliance* by D. C. Fisher. *Parents Magazine*, p. 62.

Page, M. L. (1936). The modification of ascendant behavior in preschool children. *University of Iowa Studies in Child Welfare, 12,* 7–69.

Parke, R. D., MacDonald, K. B., Beitel, A., & Bhavnagri, N. (1988). The role of the family in the development of peer relationships. In R. Peters & R. J. McMahon (Eds.), *Social learning and systems approaches to marriage and the family* (pp. 17–44). New York: Bruner/Mazel.

Parke, R. D., & Bhavnagri, N. (1989). Parents as managers of children's peer relationships. In D. Belle (Ed.), *Children's social networks and social supports* (pp. 241–259). New York: Wiley.

Parten, M. B. (1932). Social participation among preschool children. *Journal of Abnormal and Social Psychology, 27,* 243–269.

Patterson, G. R. (1981). *Coercive family processes*. Eugene, OR: Castilia Press.

Rabin, A. I. (1958). Behavior research in collective settlements in Israel: Six infants and children under conditions of "intermittent" mothering in the kibbutz. *American Journal of Orthopsychiatry, 28,* 577–584.

Renshaw, P. D. (1981). The roots of peer interaction research: A historical analysis of the 1930s. In S. Asher & J. Gottman (Eds.), *The development of children's friendships*, (pp. 1–25). New York: Cambridge University Press.

Riesman, D. (1953). *The lonely crowd*. Garden City, NY: Doubleday.

Rogers, C. R. (1939). *The clinical treatment of the problem child*. Cambridge, MA: Riverside Press.

Russell, B. (1930, May). Are parents bad for children? *Parents Magazine*, pp. 18–19, 69.

Sameroff, A. J. (1983). Developmental systems: Contexts and evolution. In P. H. Mussen (Ed.), *Manual of child psychology* (Vol 1, pp. 237–294). New York: Wiley.

Schain, J. (1933, March). The Girl Scouts come of age. *Parents Magazine,* p. 11.

Scotford, J. R. (1934, November). For fathers only. *Parents Magazine,* p. 10.

Sears, R. R. (1951). A theoretical framework for personality and social behavior. *American Psychologist, 6,* 476–483.

Sears, R. R., Maccoby, E. E., & Levin, H. (1957). *Patterns of child rearing.* Evanston, IL: Row, Peterson.

Sears, R. R., Pintler, M. H., & Sears, P. S. (1946). The effect of father separation on preschool children's doll play aggression. *Child Development, 17,* 219–243.

Sears, R. R., Rau, L., & Alpert, R. (1965). *Identification and child rearing.* Stanford, CA: Stanford University Press.

Sears, R. R., Whiting, J. W. M., Nowlis, V., & Sears, P. S. (1953). Some child-rearing antecedents of aggression and dependency in young children. *Genetic Psychology Monographs, 47,* 135–234.

Shinn, M. (1978). Father absence and children's cognitive development. *Psychological Bulletin, 85,* 295–324.

Snyder, A. M., & Snyder, M. A. (1929, October). Correcting behavior problems through play. *Parents Magazine,* pp. 16, 55.

Sroufe, L. A., & Fleeson, J. (1986). Attachment and the construction of relationships. In W. Hartup & Z. Rubin (Eds.), *Relationships and development* (pp. 51–72). Hillsdale, NJ: Lawrence Erlbaum Associates.

Stogdill, R. M. (1936, February). Let your child grow up. *Parents Magazine,* pp. 15, 94.

Stolz, L. M. (1954). *Father relations of war-born children.* Stanford, CA: Stanford University Press.

Strain, F. B. (1937, January). Children need friends. *Parents Magazine,* pp. 18–20, 172.

Strain, F. B. (1937, May). When play goes wrong. *Parents Magazine,* pp. 24–25, 62–63.

Thomas, W. D., & Thomas, D. (1928). *The child in America.* New York: Knopf.

Tompkins, J. (1928, September). Are your children's friends welcome? *Parents Magazine,* pp. 13, 53.

Thrasher, F. M. (1927). *The gang: A study of 1,313 gangs in Chicago.* Chicago: University of Chicago Press.

Thurow, M. B. (1935, June). Succeeding as a family. *Parents Magazine,* pp. 24–25.

Tuttle, W. M. (1992). Historical changes and human development: The care of America's home front children during the Second World War. In G. H. Elder, J. Modell, & R. Parke (Eds.), *Children in time and place.* New York: Cambridge University Press.

Tyack, D. B. (1974). The one best system: A history of American urban education. Cambridge, MA: Harvard University Press.

Wahler, R. G. (1967). Child–child interaction in five field settings: Some experimental analyses. *Journal of Experimental Child Psychology, 5,* 278–293.

Walters, R. H., Parke, R. D., & Cane, V. A. (1965). Timing of punishment and the observation of consequences to others as determinants of response inhibition. *Journal of Experimental Child Psychology, 2,* 10–30.

Watson, R. (1930, May). Review of "Studies in service and self-control" by H. Hartshorne, M. May, and J. Maller. *Parents Magazine,* p. 74.

Watson, R. (1930, December). I am the mother of a behaviorist's son. *Parents Magazine,* pp. 16–18, 67.

West, J. (1927, January). Building family friendships. *Parents Magazine,* pp. 13–14.

Woody, R. J. (1936, April). You can make a playground. *Parents Magazine,* pp. 33, 85.

Youniss, J., & Smollar, J. (1989). Adolescents' interpersonal relationships in social context. In J. Berndt & G. Ladd (Eds.), *Peer relationships in child development* (pp. 300–316). New York: Wiley.

# PART TWO

# INDIRECT INFLUENCES: FAMILY RELATIONS, INTERACTIONS, AND ENVIRONMENTS

# CHAPTER THREE

# Predicting Peer Competence and Peer Relationships in Childhood from Early Parent–Child Relationships

James Elicker
*University of Wisconsin—Green Bay*

Michelle Englund
L. Alan Sroufe
*University of Minnesota*

Observations of Amy at 12 months of age with her mother, Susan, revealed a well-coordinated pair. Susan was attentive to her daughter's activities as she explored the environment of a playroom. She responded with an encouraging word or a smile, for instance, as Amy exclaimed and pointed to a newly discovered toy. She was reassuring when Amy was momentarily distracted by the sudden movement of the camera's self-focusing lens. Susan seemed content to watch Amy's explorations, rather than join in or direct them. There was a smooth, relaxed interchange between the two as Amy picked up each toy, examined it, mouthed or shook it, and occasionally looked over her shoulder to smile at Susan and display a new discovery.

Ten years later, at age 11, Amy was observed with a small group of peers at a summer day camp. There was an excited, happy tone to the four girls' activity as they made preparations to open a "craft store" to barter some of the bracelets and necklaces they had been making at camp over the past few days. Amy surprised her friends when she revealed a small bag of necklaces she had made at home the night before. She explained she had been thinking about it at home and decided that the store would "look better if there were lots of things to display." The other girls agreed that more merchandise would make the shop look more attractive. As they quickly scooped up their belongings in joyous response to a camp counselor's call to prepare for swimming, they all agreed to take some yarn and beads home with them that night, so that they could make even more items to display on the next day of camp. Walking toward the lockers to get their swimming gear, Amy noticed that Clarissa did not have any yarn and offered to share some of hers. Clarissa gratefully accepted the yarn, put it in her locker, and the two girls rushed to catch up with the rest of the group, now on its way to the pool.

What are the developmental threads that connect Amy's social relations across 10 years' time, in these vastly different contexts? Is her enjoyment of constructive play with her camp friends, and her popularity and leadership with them, in some sense an outcome of the secure, well-coordinated relationship she had with her parent as an infant? Did Susan's emotional responsiveness and encouragement of Amy's early strivings for autonomy provide a foundation for Amy's later empathy and self-confidence with her friends?

In this chapter we consider these questions in light of recent theory and research concerned with the quality of relationships formed between infants and their primary caregivers, and then examine the implications these first relationships have for social development during early and middle childhood. First, we review the use of social competence as a developmental–organizational theoretical construct. Second, we discuss the changing expression of competence in social relations through the first decade of life—infancy, early childhood, and middle childhood. We identify the critical developmental tasks of each phase, the favorable resolution of which indicates a high level of competence. We outline the implications of this developmental–organizational perspective for the assessment of social competence. Third, we briefly review previous research examining the relationship between attachment in infancy and peer competence in early childhood. We then present results of our recently completed longitudinal study of the association between attachment in infancy and friendship and peer competence in middle childhood. Finally, we discuss the nature of "developmental pathways" and processes that might account for the remarkable continuity in social development through childhood that we and others have observed.

## SOCIAL COMPETENCE AS AN ORGANIZATIONAL/RELATIONSHIP CONSTRUCT

A developmental perspective on social competence has several ramifications (e.g., Sroufe, 1979; Sroufe & Waters, 1977; Waters & Sroufe, 1983). Rather than defining competence in terms of discrete social skills or specific traits or capacities, this perspective emphasizes the broad, integrative aspects of social adaptation. Competence is viewed with respect to the individual's adaptation to age-appropriate developmental issues. Children develop coherent patterns of adaptation as the result of their successive adjustments to the social environment, in the service of changing physiological and psychological needs.

Competence at any age can be determined by the extent to which the child is able to "make effective use of personal and environmental resources to achieve a good developmental outcome" (Waters & Sroufe, 1983, p. 81). Good developmental outcomes are those that lead to healthy adaptations during the phases that follow, or at least do not limit or foreclose on subsequent developmental change. Successful short-term adaptation is important, but equally important are the long-term implications of a child's cumulative proximate social adjustments.

A central hypothesis drawn from this view of social competence is that different kinds or qualities of adaptation at each phase of development have predictable implications for the preparedness of the individual to meet the challenges that follow. In order to test this hypothesis of continuity across time, the salient developmental issues for each phase of development must be identified. It is the child's adaptation with respect to these important, age-related issues that will predict the quality of adaptation in the next phase. Because salient issues change as the child matures, methods of assessment and contexts for observation must also change. These basic principles for understanding and assessing social competence will be reflected in the discussion of the development of social competence that follows.

Another important advance in research on social competence is centered on the study of relationships. In particular, some researchers now emphasize the definition and assessment of *relationships* as an important level of analysis (Hinde, 1979; Sroufe & Fleeson, 1986). Relationships are not simply the sum of each member's characteristics; rather, they are determined by unique patterning and qualities of the dyadic interaction that endure over time. Thus, attachment relationships between infants and caregivers refer to the particular quality of reciprocal coordination and dyadic affect regulation achieved by the pair. Each attachment relationship is unique. The same infant may have strikingly different relationships with two parents (Main & Weston, 1981), and the same parent may have quite different attachments with two siblings (Ward, Vaughn, & Robb, 1988). Similarly, peer friendships have unique qualities (Gottman, 1983), and bully–victim relationships among children depend on two developmental histories (Troy & Sroufe, 1987). For example, children prone to be victimized will not look like victims in relationships with supportive partners. Victimization is a relationship, not an individual characteristic.

For decades, theorists have discussed the reciprocal relation between individuals and relationships (Baldwin, 1911; Mead, 1934; Sroufe, 1989,

Sroufe & Fleeson, 1986). Individuals are the products of relationships, yet relationships are constructed by individuals. Infant–caregiver attachments are viewed as prototype relationship experiences. They also are the product of the pair's interactive history (see Sroufe, 1985, for a review), as well as the caregiver's developmental history (Main, Kaplan, & Cassidy, 1985; Morris, 1980; Ricks, 1985), and they exercise a formative influence on the young child's developing personality (Cassidy, 1988; Sroufe, 1989).

An argument we develop in this chapter is that as an early index of competence, in the developmental sense just outlined, the quality of the infant–caregiver relationship is a broad band assessment of the organizational and integrative capacity of the pair, keyed to the salient issues of infancy: affect regulation; exploration and mastery of the environment; and the origins of social reciprocity. One needs only to assume that such assessments at the level of the relationship are suitable for forecasting the later competence of the individual as he or she enters new relationships. This is a plausible assumption and also is open to empirical test.

At least three specific reasons may be cited as to why an effective, secure attachment relationship in infancy should promote later peer competence (i.e., good developmental outcomes, as required to validate attachment as an index of competence). First, a secure attachment relationship with the caregiver, based on a history of availability and responsiveness, should lead to *positive social expectations.* Because of the caregiver's key role in comforting and other aspects of affect regulation, the "other" will be valued and positively appraised. In Bowlby's (1973) terms, the child will have developed an internal working model of self and others that will guide him or her toward positive interactions with others. The child will expect it to be worthwhile to be with others. Second, the child will have learned the rudiments of *reciprocity,* or give and take. Moreover, we assume that by participating in a relationship with an empathic, responsive caregiver, the child not only learns how to receive care (and count on aid from others) but learns the very nature of empathic relating (Sroufe & Fleeson, 1986). Later, in more symmetrical relationships (such as peer relationships), this child will know how to respond empathically when the other is in need. Finally, through a history of responsive care and support for autonomy within the relationship, the child develops a *sense of self-worth and efficacy* ("I have an impact on the world"). Just as the other is positively appraised and valued, so is the self considered worthy of respect and care. Such basic feelings underlie the child's self-confidence, curiosity, enthusiasm, and positive affect, all characteristics that are attractive to peers. In the following sections we present data from a number of studies that support these propositions.

It is important to note that from the organizational-relationship perspective, there is nothing to preclude the possibility of change in development. Bowlby's notion of *working* models explicitly includes the possibility that patterns of feelings, expectations, thoughts, and behaviors can change with experience. However, we expect that relationship patterns established during infancy will often forecast stable patterns of personal and social adaptation for the individual throughout childhood.

## ASSESSING SOCIAL COMPETENCE DURING INFANCY AND CHILDHOOD

Assessment principles derived from the organizational perspective have been elaborated in previous writings (see Sroufe, 1979; Waters & Sroufe, 1983). Briefly stated, the quality of a child's resolution of the salient adaptational issues of each developmental phase constitutes competence. *Attachment* in infancy; *individuation* in the toddler period; *peer relations* and *self-regulation* in the preschool period; and *agency, friendship,* and *successful functioning in the peer group* in middle childhood, are hypothesized to be the important tasks for each developmental phase (see Table 3.1). Successful resolution of the issues of each phase constitutes social competence in that phase and provides a foundation for meeting the challenges of the next phase. The empirical validation of this developmental hypothesis depends on demonstrating longitudinal continuity in adaptational patterns, with respect to these issues.

TABLE 3.1.
Salient Developmental Issues

| Developmental Phase | Issues | Caregiver role |
|---|---|---|
| Infant | Physiological/tension regulation; Establishing effective attachment relationship | Sensitive, predictable care; Responsive availability |
| Toddler | Exploration/mastery; Individuation | Secure base; Firm support |
| Pre-schooler | Impulse management; Sex-role identification; Peer relations | Clear roles and values; Flexible management |
| Middle Childhood | Self-confidence/constructiveness; Peer group membership; Close friendship | Open communication; Acceptance; Supportive monitoring |

Assessment of competence varies with the phase of development. Competence in infancy is defined in terms of the quality of the infant's primary caregiving relationship. As Ainsworth has stated, the infant can be competent only to the extent that the caregiver is responsive (Ainsworth, Blehar, Waters, & Wall, 1978). But the infant can indeed be competent within an effective caregiving system. Such competence will be revealed in the infant's engagement and mastery of the environment, in the capacity to use the caregiver as a base for exploration, and, in general, in the smooth dyadic regulation of affect. This includes being able to be readily comforted by the caregiver when stressed and the sharing of positive affect with the caregiver.

By preschool age, competence continues to have important social referents, but it is a concept that can be applied meaningfully to the individual child. The competent preschooler is actively engaged in the world of peers. He or she also has achieved a notable level of self-reliance and self-management. Now, competent children first seek to master challenges and problems using their own resources. They are not so dependent on adult guidance and supervision to find meaningful activities, to contain impulses, to follow rules, or to avoid prohibited behavior. Still, they are effective in using adults as resources when their own capacities are exceeded, or when disappointment, sadness, or other strong emotions are beyond a level they can manage.

By the school years, competent children are much more autonomous. Not only do they cope with challenges, but challenges are embraced as children stretch their capacities to the limit, not so much in fantasy play, but in terms of real-world problems. In Erikson's (1963) terms, they are *industrious*. They are agentic and self-organized. Equally impressive advances occur in the social world. Loyal friendships emerge (Sullivan's "chumships"), which are based on mutuality and reciprocity. Moreover, complex norms governing interactions with same- and opposite-gender peers are internalized, and the competent child develops the capacity to deal with the complexities of combining group and individual relationships.

Other important principles of assessment of social competence from the organizational–relationship perspective concern the required level of observation and analysis. Rather than discrete behaviors or capacities (which vary dramatically across time and context), we have emphasized broad band measures representing the *quality* of adaptation over time and across contexts (e.g., Q-sorts, behavior composites, and integrative ratings or rankings). Two children may exhibit distinctly different discrete behaviors and behavioral strategies, yet be comparably competent in terms of adaptation to their respective social environments. This is not only because diverse social environments or developmental changes present different challenges and opportunities, but (also) because there can be multiple pathways to adaptive success (see Sroufe & Jacobvitz, 1989). Discrete measures, such as social participation or sharing, are used to provide concurrent validity for the broad band competence measures, or in follow up analyses to examine specific aspects of overall competence.

Additional assessment strategies compatible with the organizational perspective include: emphasis on naturalistic observation, rather than on highly structured laboratory tasks, especially in the early stages of research; emphasis on situations in which there is a clear need for the individual to coordinate affect, cognition, and behavior; and special attention to situations that tax the adaptive capacity of the individual. These strategies have been discussed in detail by Waters and Sroufe (1983).

The value of this developmental approach for the study of individual differences in the development of social competence has been demonstrated in several programs of longitudinal research, to be reviewed in the next section. These studies constitute a growing body of evidence for the importance of the quality of the primary caregiving relationship as a predictor of competence in early childhood, when peer relationships are first constructed. Following our review of these early childhood studies, we detail for the first time results of recently completed research examining the association between quality of attachment in infancy and social competence 10 years later, in middle childhood. It is during middle childhood and early adolescence that peer relationships assume pivotal importance in terms of children's salient social activities and motivations, as a key outcome of previous social development, and as an important predictor of subsequent social adaptation in adolescence and adulthood.

## ATTACHMENT AND EARLY SOCIAL COMPETENCE

There is now considerable research providing evidence for developmental continuity between quality of infant–caregiver attachment relationships and outcomes in early childhood. In this section, we review studies based on assessment of quality of attachment, using the Strange Situation (Ainsworth et al., 1978) as a predictive measure for social competence in early childhood. We first summarize the results of studies employing broad band outcome measures of competence in early childhood and then review findings produced by more focused preschool measures, those we consider important constituents of overall social competence in early childhood.

### Attachment and Broad Measures of Peer Competence in Early Childhood

The most striking demonstrations of developmental continuity produced in longitudinal attachment research have been with respect to broad, integrative measures of social competence. These "broad band" assessments include teacher or observer assessments based on extensive periods of observation and/or interaction. They also include composites of more discrete behavioral measures.

*Early Social Responsiveness.* Evidence for differences in early peer competence associated with quality of infant attachment was provided by Pastor (1981). An investigation of sociability within a 30-minute play session with a peer playmate showed that toddlers who were securely attached at 18 months exhibited higher overall sociability than those who had been anxiously attached. Securely attached toddlers also oriented more positively both to peers and to their mothers, present at the periphery of the play session. In addition, Pastor found that mothers of securely attached children were more supportive, responsive, and appropriately directive with their children, an indication of continuity in the quality of the mother–child relationship from 18 months to 22 months.

Main and her colleagues (Main, 1983; Main & Weston, 1981) also found significant associations between quality of attachment with parents and social responsiveness with others. In one study, 12-month-old infants who were securely attached were rated higher on a scale of "relatedness" (including behavioral and emotional responsiveness, interest, and positive affectivity) when observed in a play session with a friendly adult stranger (Main & Weston, 1981). In addition, 12 out of 21 nonsecure infants exhibited unusual "conflict behaviors" during the play session (e.g., inappropriate affect, odd gestures or vocalizations.) Only 1 out of 23 secure infants displayed such conflict behaviors. In a later study of the association between attachment at 12 months and social play with an adult at 21 months (Main, 1983), more secure children than insecure children were classified as "playful." In all of these studies of early social responsiveness, mothers were present as their children interacted with others. Thus, the differences in sociability and competence that were found can be considered reflective of stable qualities of the mother–child dyad, as well as early competence in the child.

*Preschool Social Competence.* Whereas studies of early sociability show impressive continuity from attachment in infancy, stronger evidence comes from studies in which preschool children were observed in settings away from their parents. Waters, Wippman, and Sroufe (1979) assessed competence in a sample of middle class 3½-year-olds in the preschool classroom. Using Q-sort methodology (Block, 1961), each child was described by observers blind to attachment history, after 5 weeks of observation. The observers placed 72 descriptive items into nine categories, ranging from most characteristic to least characteristic. Scores for peer competence were calculated by summing the scores for 12 items, independently selected to characterize the socially competent child. Children who had been securely attached as 15-month-old infants received significantly higher peer competence scores than those who had been anxiously attached (72.8 vs. 49.6, $p < .01$).

In a separate, somewhat older sample of middle class children (mean age = 5½ yrs), Arend, Gove, and Sroufe (1979) found that securely attached infants received significantly higher preschool ego-resiliency scores than did anxiously attached infants, as assessed by teachers' California Child Q-sorts. Ego-resiliency, after Block and Block (1980), was defined as "the ability to respond flexibly, persistently, and resourcefully, especially in problem situations" (p. 48). Resiliency scores for this study were derived by correlating each child's Q-sort scores with a criterion sort for a hypothetical ego-resilient child. When based on observations made over the course of at least 8 months in a preschool or kindergarten setting, this measure is properly considered an indicator of competence.

These significant associations between infant attachment and peer competence/ego resiliency were replicated in a third, high-risk sample by Sroufe and his colleagues (LaFreniere & Sroufe, 1985; Sroufe, 1983). In these studies, children (mean age = 4 years) were extensively observed over 12 to 20 weeks in the laboratory preschool at the University of Minnesota. As with previous studies, teachers and observers were blind to children's attachment histories or any other developmental information about the children. On several global measures of social competence, preschoolers who had been securely attached as infants received significantly higher scores than those with anxious attachment histories. As in the Arend et al. (1979) study, teacher Q-sorts for ego-resiliency for children with secure attachment histories were consistently correlated with the ego-resiliency criterion sort ($M = +.50$), whereas the correlations for children with anxious attachment histories were more often small or negative $M = -.13, p < .01$). Teacher rankings and ratings revealed similar striking differences. Children with secure attachment histories were ranked or rated higher on measures of emotional health and self-esteem, social competence, agency, and positive affect, and lower on measures of dependency and negative affect (Sroufe, 1983).

More support for the prediction of continuity between infant–parent relationships and early peer competence has come from two other studies in which researchers used a more discrete, behavioral approach to assess peer competence in preschool-age children. Lieberman (1977) used behavior-composite measures of peer competence based on observations of 3-year-olds in a play session with a same-gender peer. Quality of parent–child attachment was measured by constructing composites based on home observations and a Strange Situation assessment, both completed at age 3. Four out of five measures of peer competence were found to be significantly related to one attachment security composite (low home anxiety). Responsiveness with peers was also associated with less "excessive mother-centeredness" in the Strange Situation. Even when previous peer experience was partialled from the analyses, attachment security proved to be associated significantly with peer reciprocity and an absence of negative behavior in the peer play session.

Suess (1987), reporting studies with a longitudinal sample in West Germany, also showed a link between quality of attachment at 12 and 18 months and behavioral competence in a preschool setting at 5½ years. This study provides yet another picture of competent peer play and self-management by children with a history of secure attachment. Coders used observational and child interview data to categorize the preschool subjects as high or low in competence (including quality of play, conflict resolution, occurrence of problem behaviors, and social perceptions.) Most children who had been securely attached with their mothers as infants were classified as high on competence (17 out of 18), whereas more than 50% of the anxiously attached children (primarily anxious-avoidant) were placed in the low competence category (10 out of 17).

Finally, Erickson, Sroufe, and Egeland (1985) assessed agency (confidence, assertiveness), dependency, and peer social skills in 96 children attending preschools or child-care centers, including the 40 children described previously in the Minnesota Preschool Study (Sroufe, 1983). Observers completed rating scales after watching children on at least two occasions in a variety of teacher-directed and free-play activities. Infants who had been classified anxious-resistant *(C)* were found to be less agentic in the preschool setting than secure *(B)* or anxious-avoidant *(A)* infants. Anxiously attached subjects (both avoidant and resistant) also had lower social skill with preschool peers than those who had been securely attached.

Summarizing this review of studies investigating associations between security of attachment in the second year and broad measures of social adaptation at ages 12 months to 6 years, relations between primary relationships in infancy and social competence in early childhood have been consistently found. Using a variety of assessment strategies, researchers have shown that attachment security forecasts later peer competence and individual qualities of ego-resilience and self-confidence in peer group contexts. Further evidence for the predictive power of attachment is provided by studies of more specific constituents of competence: affectivity; empathy; reciprocity/conflict resolution; social understanding; and self-esteem. We review these studies in the following section.

## Attachment and Components of Peer Competence in Early Childhood

In addition to broad band measures of peer competence, attachment researchers have investigated qualities or behaviors in young children that can be considered components or constituents of social competence. If, in addition to predicting overall social competence, security of attachment at 12 or 18 months also predicts such preschool capacities as positive affect, empathy, interpersonal understanding, and positive self-esteem, the validity of the broad competence assessments is strengthened. Further, we can gain a more differentiated picture of the development of various aspects of social competence. Studies by a number of investigators have revealed such longitudinal associations.

*Affectivity.* Young children who have secure attachments with their parents as infants later display more positive affect in their interactions with their parents, and with peers and teachers in the preschool. In the Minnesota Preschool study (LaFreniere & Sroufe, 1985; Sroufe, 1983; Sroufe, Schork, Motti, Lawroski, & LaFreniere, 1985) teacher ratings and $Q$-sort measures of positive affect distinguished securely attached youngsters from those who had been anxiously attached, as did an affect checklist completed by classroom observers. Securely attached children displayed less overall negative affect, they less often responded negatively to other children's social initiations, they more often initiated encounters with positive affect, and they more often responded with positive affect to the overtures of others.

Other studies examining social affectivity have had similar results, using various affect measures. Waters et al. (1979) found that positive affective sharing was more characteristic of securely attached infants at 18 and 24 months, when observed with mothers in free-play situations. Lieberman (1979) found that 3-year-old children with secure attachment (low home anxiety) displayed more positive reciprocity and fewer negative behaviors with peer playmates.

*Empathy.* A child who receives responsive, empathic care in infancy may be more able to relate to and respond empathically to peers in early childhood (Sroufe & Fleeson, 1986). The relation between attachment in infancy and empathy with preschool peers has been examined in two studies with the Minnesota sample. In the first study (Sroufe, 1983), empathy was assessed using teacher $Q$-sorts. The secure group received the highest scores on an empathy $Q$-sort mega item, the anxious-resistant group received intermediate scores, and the anxious-avoidant group was seen as least empathic. This finding, which conforms closely to the predictions of organizational-attachment theory, was confirmed in a second study of the same sample of children (Kestenbaum, Farber, & Sroufe, 1989), using an independent measure of empathy. Observers viewed 50 days of classroom videotape to find situations in which a child was overtly distressed, and other children were close enough in proximity to respond. Coder ratings of children's responses to these events revealed that children with secure attachment histories more often responded empathically than children having anxious-avoidant histories. Again, the anxious-resistant group had intermediate empathy scores. The study produced another interesting result. Children in the anxious-avoidant group were far more likely to respond in an "anti-empathic" manner (i.e., showing inappropriate affect or behavior) than were the other groups.

*Reciprocity/Conflict Resolution.*    Another presumed component of peer competence in early childhood is the capacity to engage effectively in the give and take of balanced interactions with peers (e.g., Howes, 1987). A related ability is that of successfully resolving conflicts as they arise, in order to maintain this reciprocity. Two studies provide evidence that infants who were securely attached display more reciprocity and deal more capably with conflict in their later interactions with preschool peers. Lieberman's (1977) behavior composite for "reciprocal interaction" in play sessions included instances of sharing, effective requests, social initiations, and subtracted nonsocial behaviors. Security of attachment proved to be significantly and positively related to this measure of peer reciprocity.

Suess (1987) categorized preschool children on the basis of observed quality of play in the preschool (including initiations, concentration, low conflict) and conflict resolution (number of conflicts, negotiation, types of resolutions and reactions). Children who had been securely attached as infants were more likely to be placed in the "good" quality play group and the "competent" conflict resolution group than were those who had been anxiously attached.

*Quality of "Friendships."*    Not only are those with secure attachment histories more competent with peers, their relationships with particular salient peers have more of the characteristics of mutual friendships. In the Minnesota Preschool Project, assigned pairs of children were observed as they participated in 14–20 play sessions. A major finding was a significant difference between global ratings of positive mutual emotional commitment shown by dyads with and without a member with a history of avoidant attachment. "Avoidant" dyads also showed more hostility and distance (Pancake, 1985; Sroufe, 1988).

More recently, Park and Waters (1989), using contemporaneous Q-sort assessments of attachment, found that secure–secure friendship pairs were more harmonious, less controlling, more responsive, and happier than secure–insecure pairs. The latter measures were based on observations of 1-hour free play sessions of children and their "best friends."

Pancake (1985) observed the interactions of play pairs of preschoolers from the Minnesota sample over several weeks. The pairs were composed of children having various combinations of attachment histories. Observers rating videotapes of the play sessions noted higher sensitivity in the interactions of pairs having at least one securely attached child, compared to pairs composed of anxiously attached children.

***Interpersonal Understanding.***    Bowlby (1973) proposed that infants and young children construct mental representations of their primary relationships: "internal working models." These mental models are thought by contemporary attachment theorists to be generalized, often subconscious, representations that are both cognitive and affective in nature (e.g., Bretherton, 1985). Internal working models are also thought to guide attitudes, expectations, and evaluations regarding the formation and maintenance of relationships beyond the parent–child dyad, including early peer relationships (Sroufe & Fleeson, 1986).

Whereas most studies examining internal working models have focused on representations of parent–child relationships (e.g., Bretherton, Ridgeway, & Cassidy, 1990; Main et al., 1985) some investigators have recently undertaken studies of interpersonal cognition or representations with respect to peers. Rosenberg (1984) observed the fantasy play of 4½-year-olds. Comparing children who had been securely or anxiously attached as infants, she found that those in the anxious group were less likely to incorporate people into their play themes and that their fantasized resolutions for misfortunes or interpersonal conflicts were less likely to be positive. These results suggest that young children who had been anxiously attached may be less interested in interpersonal relationships, may value them less highly, or may expect negative outcomes in relationships, whereas those who were securely attached may regard relationships more positively.

Suess (1987) provided evidence that preschool children with different attachment histories may develop distinctive cognitive biases with respect to peer interactions. This study includes cartoon-based interviews in which subjects were asked to judge the intentions of children involved in various hypothetical mishaps with peers. Suess found that the securely attached children usually made realistic attributions or displayed a bias toward attributing benevolent intentions. Subjects with anxious-avoidant attachment, however, revealed more unrealistic or hostile/negative biases in their attributions of intention. These studies provide preliminary evidence that the quality of attachment in infancy may have direct or indirect influences on later general mental representations that are applied to challenges in peer relations.

*Self-Esteem.* Although not always considered an aspect of social competence, a child's appraisal of self is likely intertwined with early experiences in primary relationships. Bowlby (1973) proposed that feelings of self-worth and efficacy originate through early sensitive care and support for autonomy. Thus, secure attachment in infancy may provide a foundation for positive orientations toward both others and the self in early childhood (Sroufe & Fleeson, 1986). Research evidence accumulated thus far supports this notion.

In the Minnesota preschool study (Sroufe, 1983), teachers assessed children's self-esteem over 12–20 weeks using Waters' self-esteem $Q$-sort criterion, ratings, and rankings. On all three measures, those who had been securely attached as infants scored higher than the anxiously attached groups. In another study, Cassidy (1988) used more direct measures of self-esteem with 6-year-olds and a concurrent measure of attachment with mothers. She found a consistent pattern of open, flexible responses to self-evaluation questions by securely attached children, and either deprecating or defensive, "perfect" self-evaluations by those who had been categorized as insecurely attached.

To summarize, we have reviewed prospective longitudinal and concurrent investigations of the relationships between quality of parent–child attachment and constituents of peer competence. As was the case with broader measures of social competence, we find clear evidence for continuity over as much as 4 years of dramatic developmental change, in strikingly different social contexts. Can these stable continuities, apparently originating in the child's first caregiving relationships, be discerned beyond early childhood? Our most recently completed research, reported in the section that follows, is the first investigation of the relation between attachment in infancy and peer competence and peer relationships in middle childhood.

## THE MINNESOTA SUMMER CAMP PROJECT

In order to study the association of attachment history and the social adaptation of 11-year-olds, we recruited children from the Minnesota Mother–Child Project sample for summer day camps, held in 3 consecutive years.

Each camp hosted a separate group of subjects and lasted 4 weeks, with children attending 5 days per week, 4 hours each day. Children were transported to and from camp to encourage consistent attendance. They were observed daily by both the camp program staff and a team of observers, all blind to attachment classifications or any other specific information about the children and their families.

## Subjects

For each year's camp, 16 children were selected from the longitudinal sample of the Mother–Child Project, a 12-year study of children at risk for child abuse, developmental and social adjustment problems, and subject to frequent life stress. One child in the third camp returned to his out-of-state home after 5 days, leaving 47 subjects for the study.

The original Mother–Child sample ($N = 267$) had been recruited through the Minneapolis Public Health Center clinics, during the mothers' third trimester of pregnancy. All children were first-born. Mother–child dyads were observed at regular intervals from birth through 42 months, and child- and mother-assessments continued through the school years. Previous studies, some reviewed in earlier sections of this chapter, have focused on social–emotional and personality functioning, life-event changes, and adaptation of the children to school. (See Egeland & Kreutzer, 1991; Pianta, Egeland, & Sroufe, in press; Renkin, Egeland, Marvinney, Sroufe, & Manglesdorf, 1989; Sroufe, 1983).

Assessments of the quality of mother–child attachment, using the standard Strange Situation procedure (Ainsworth et al., 1978), had been completed at 12 and 18 months. The Strange Situation assessments resulted in each mother–child dyad being classified as: secure (B), characterized by use of the caregiver as a secure base for exploring the environment and by actively seeking and being readily comforted upon reunion with the caregiver when distressed (or active greeting if not distressed); anxious-resistant (C), wary, with poverty of exploration, mixing contact seeking with contact resistance upon reunion, with much distress and difficulty settling; or anxious-avoidant (A), showing little preference for the caregiver over strangers and active avoidance of the caregiver upon reunion following a brief separation. Where 12- and 18-month assessments were inconsistent (12 cases), a 24-month dyadic assessment was used to resolve the discrepancy, so that each child ultimately was given just one classification.

Children for each camp were selected on the basis of several criteria: attachment classification (approximately equal numbers of secure and anxious children in each camp, with representation of both anxious-resistant and anxious-avoidant attachments within each group); participation in the preschool study at age 4 (children who had been observed in the preschool project [Sroufe, 1983] were given preference); gender (equal numbers of boys and girls in each camp); and age (oldest subjects in the sample participated in the first year, youngest in the third year). The mean age of the subjects at the time of camp participation, across all 3 camps, was 10 years, 11 months (range = 9 years, 7 months to 11 years, 8 months; SD = 7 months).

In the first camp there were nine children with secure (B) attachment histories, four with anxious-resistant (C) histories, and three with anxious-avoidant (A) histories. In the second camp there were eight children with B histories, two with C histories, and six with A histories. In the third camp there were eight children with B histories, three with C histories, and four with A histories. Table 3.2 summarizes the composition of the sample in terms of age, gender, and attachment history.

Attachment groups did not differ significantly in terms of age, ethnicity, or intelligence as measured by the WISC in third grade (see Table 3.2). Of the 25 children with secure attachment, 16 were Caucasian and 9 were Black or of mixed ethnicity. Of the 22 with anxious attachment, 15 were Caucasian and 7 were Black or of mixed ethnicity.

## Camp Routine

Children were transported daily by van between home and camp. Attendance was consistent (M = 18.3 days, SD = 1.8). The daily program of activities was varied and interesting, including group meetings, singing, snacks and lunch, swimming, art and craft projects, outdoor games, and sports. Weekly day trips were taken to recreation parks, and one overnight campout was held at the camp facility, located on the university campus. Observations took place during all of these activities.

TABLE 3.2.
Sample Characteristics. Gender, Mean Age,
and Mean 3rd Grade WISC Scores

|  | Secure (B) | Anxious-Resistant (C) | Anxious-Avoidant (A) | Total |
|---|---|---|---|---|
| Number of Females | 13 | 5 | 6 | 24 |
| Number of Males | 12 | 5 | 6 | 23 |
| Total | 25 | 10 | 12 | 47 |
| Age (yrs; mo.)[1] | 10;11 | 10;8 | 11;2 | 10;11 |
| (SD, mo.) | (7.0) | (8.6) | (3.8) | (7.0) |
| IQ (WISC, 3rd grade)[1] | 110 | 103 | 117 | 110 |
| (SD) | (14.3) | (19.7) | (5.5) | (15.0) |

[1]ANOVA using the three attachment groups and gender as independent factors revealed no significant differences for either age or IQ.

Many of the camp activities involved all of the children as a group, but there were also frequent opportunities for children to choose among two or more activities, and to select their companions for a particular activity. Each year's camp counselor staff was composed of five master's-level graduate students and one or two advanced undergraduate assistants, all experienced in working with school-aged children.

## CAMP MEASURES OF PEER COMPETENCE AND FRIENDSHIP

In keeping with the integrative approach underlying this research and the assessment strategy taken in the earlier preschool studies (e.g., Sroufe, 1983), a wide variety of social competence data at various levels of abstraction was collected. At the broadest, most integrative level, camp counselors made qualitative ratings, rankings, and nominations at the end of each camp, based on their experience with the children throughout the 1-month camp session. At a more discrete level, child–child and child–adult associations were time sampled by observers. Also, individual interviews with the children were conducted during the last week of each camp. All counselors and observers contributing data were blind to attachment histories, or any other information about the children prior to the camp sessions.

### Counselor Data

Camp counselors had extensive opportunities to observe and get to know each child in a variety of camp contexts. As with teachers in the Preschool Project, counselors were considered to be our primary data source. We expected that the counselors' broad assessments of children's social functioning and friendships would be corroborated by the more discrete observational data.

At the conclusion of each camp, counselors rank-ordered the children on dimensions of emotional health/self-esteem, self-confidence, and social competence. Rankings were based on paragraphs describing each construct. Ratings of agency, social skill with peers, and dependency were made using 7-point scales. Both rating and ranking measures were originally developed for preschool teacher assessments and were modified to be age-appropriate for these school-age assessments. Counselors were also asked to independently list all of the friendship pairs that had developed and been maintained during each camp session.

## Observation of Child Associations

Extensive observations of social participation were completed during each camp session. Using a child-sampling procedure, observation teams repeatedly noted the number and identity of each child's companions and the nature of contacts with adult camp counselors. Instances of isolation were also noted. During daily group meetings ("circle times"), maps were charted of the children's and counselors' seating patterns.

## Child Interviews

During the last week of each camp, two individual interviews were conducted to provide insight into each child's perspective on his or her camp experience, camp relationships, and some aspects of interpersonal understanding. The first interview, lasting 10 minutes, focused on friendship and included a sociometric assessment. Children were asked if they had made friends during the camp, the names of their friends, and how they liked each other child of the same gender. The second interview, lasting approximately 20 minutes, focused on the child's understanding of the thoughts and feelings of peers and group processes during a recent team activity.

## SUMMER CAMP RESULTS

### Broad Measures of Competence

An average of 10 years after first being observed in the Strange Situation, children who had been classified as securely attached infants were consistently ranked higher by camp counselors on broad band measures of competence than were children who had been classified as anxiously attached. Children with secure attachment histories ranked higher on social competence when camp counselors ordered all children according to overall effectiveness in the peer group. Combining the results of all three camps, 16 children with secure histories ranked in the top half of children in their camp sessions, and only nine ranked below the midpoint. Conversely, only 8 out of 22 children with anxious attachment in infancy ranked above the midpoint in their camp groups. In each camp, the top three children in social competence rankings had been securely attached as infants. The mean rank position (out of 16) for secure children was 6, versus a mean rank of 10 for anxiously attached children. ($F = 13.01$, $p = .001$.)

On two other broad measures of adjustment, counselor rankings for emotional health/self-esteem and self-confidence, children with secure attachment histories also were consistently ranked higher than those with anxious attachment. ($F = 8.99$, $p = .004$, and $F = 12.76$, $p = .001$, respectively.) In addition, children with anxious attachment histories were rated as more dependent upon adults by the counselors (mean ratings = 4.25 vs. 3.12 on a 7-point scale, $p = .003$).

Overall, camp counselors without prior information about the camp subjects saw those with secure attachment histories as more self-assured, emotionally healthy, and competent. Results from additional measures, reported in the sections that follow, validate the counselors' broad competence judgments and provide a more differentiated picture of the social competence of 10- and 11-year-olds in the summer camp context.

## Social Participation

Observer teams, also blind to attachment history and other child information prior to the camps, provided a source of data independent of the counselor judgments and more discrete than the measures discussed thus far. The question addressed by study of the social participation data, collected extensively throughout the three camp sessions, concerned the sociability of preadolescent children who had either secure or anxious attachments in infancy. We expected that children with secure histories would be more involved and more sociable with peers. Our hypothesis was confirmed by these observational data.

One team observed children's associations with peers and adults throughout the 20-day camp sessions. The mean numbers of observations per child in each camp were 127, 172, and 241, respectively. Children who had secure attachments were found to spend a significantly greater portion of their time with peers ($F = 6.84$, $p = .01$) and significantly less time with adults only ($F = 4.09$, $p = .05$) or in isolation ($F = 6.32$, $p = .02$). (See Table 3.3.) In addition, those with secure attachment histories were observed more often in groups of three or more children than those with anxious histories (38% vs. 27%, $F = 6.73$, $p = .01$). Thus, it may be that those with early secure attachments develop a greater affinity for, or facility with, peer group activity during the school years.

Although these group differences in social participation are statistically significant, the magnitude of the differences may seem moderate. This is because involvement with the peer group is a normative activity for children in middle childhood. All children, regardless of attachment history or level of competence, were often involved in activities with other children. However, the higher level of peer participation and less frequent isolation or adult interaction of children with secure attachment

TABLE 3.3.
Mean Proportion of Social Participation Observations with Peers,
with Adult Only, and Isolated, as a Function of Attachment History

|         | Peers | Adult Only | Isolated |
|---------|-------|------------|----------|
| Secure  | 74%   | 14%        | 12%      |
| Anxious | 61%   | 22%        | 17%      |

histories are congruent with the counselor assessments of peer competence, dependency, and overall adjustment. Taken together, the observational social participation data and broad band competence results
suggested to us that there may be important differences in some of the
skills children bring to their relations with peers, or in the quality of peer
relationships. We explored these aspects of peer competence further.

## Social Skill with Peers

*Counselor Ratings.*   At the conclusion of each camp session, counselors rated each child's level of social skill with peers, including ability
to interact with peers, sociability, popularity, and prosocial interaction
techniques. The mean rating for children with secure attachment histories were 4.5, just above the midpoint on the 7-point scale. Children with
anxious histories received a mean rating of 3.4, somewhat below the midpoint ($F$ = 8.97, $p$ = .005).

Social skill ratings were then correlated with independently observed
peer participation, reported previously. These two measures were found
to be significantly associated ($r$ = .63, $p$ < .001). Further, the proportion of time a child spent with adults and no peers was inversely correlated with counselor-rated social skill ($r$ = – .41, $p$ = .002), indicating
that counselors may have considered those children who spent more time
with them less socially adept with peers, or perhaps that counselors directed more attention to those who were perceived as less skillful with peers.
Observed isolation showed a strong inverse relationship with rated social skill ($r$ = – .60, $p$ = .001), suggesting that being alone in a situation
like summer camp may be an important indicator of low social ability.

*Interpersonal Understanding.* Another possible aspect of social
skill with peers is the child's level and quality of social understanding,
perhaps influenced by internal working models originally formed in the
context of attachment relationships in infancy. Elicker (1989) investigated the relation of attachment history to measures of interpersonal understanding obtained in the context of interviews focused on films of
recent camp activities. Preliminary results are based on data from the first
two camps ($N$ = 31).

First, children with anxious-avoidant (A) histories showed low levels of interpersonal sensitivity in their inferences about the thoughts and feelings of others in their peer group. Children with secure (B) and anxious-resistant (C) attachment histories showed similar, higher levels of interpersonal sensitivity. Second, children with secure attachment histories were more likely to display positive biases in evaluating the performance of their own peer group versus a standard reference group, whereas children with anxious histories (both C and A) displayed more negative biases in their evaluations. Taken together, these results suggest the possibility that children with resistant (C) histories are not deficient in their level of understanding of others' internal states, but may have negative biases or anxieties with regard to peer relations. Such ambivalence may interfere with competent functioning. Those with avoidant (A) histories may have both lower interpersonal understanding and more negative social-evaluative biases. This possibility is supported by the results of the Suess (1987) preschool study reported earlier, in which most of the anxiously attached subjects were the avoidant (A) type.

***Cross-gender Behavior.*** Quality of interaction between boys and girls in the summer camps, a probable aspect of social competence in middle childhood, has been the focus of an investigation by Sroufe, Bennett, Englund, Urban, and Shulman (1992). Socially competent children of this age should know and follow explicit and implicit rules regarding gender boundary relations and behavior (Thorne, 1986). Therefore, we expected such boundary behavior to be related to measures of peer competence. In general, a high level of cross-gender interaction was expected to be associated with lower peer competence. This prediction was supported by the camp data. Significant inverse correlations were found between frequency of dyadic interaction with members of the opposite gender and social skill with peers ratings ($r = -.33, p = .01$), and with sociometric status ($r = -.30, p = .02$). In addition, children with anxious attachment in infancy engaged in cross-gender interaction more frequently than those with secure attachment histories ($F = 4.82, p = .03$). They also more often sat next to opposite gender children during large group "circle times" ($p < .02$).

## Friendship

A primary objective of the summer camp study was to explore the longitudinal association between quality of attachment in infancy and friendship formation in middle childhood. As discussed earlier, we believe the formation of close friendships is an important developmental task of middle childhood and should also be a predictable outcome of earlier relationship experiences. The inclination and ability to form friendships with same-age peers is thus a key aspect of social competence at this phase of development.

We expected that children who had experienced a secure relationship with their primary caregivers in infancy, when compared to those who had anxious primary relationships, would be more likely to form camp friendships. Further, we predicted that the children with secure histories would be attracted to others with secure histories, and that the quality of their friendships would be characterized by openness, trust, coordination, and complexity of activity. Data from several camp measures, independently obtained, supported these predictions.

With respect to the prevalence of friendship formation, counselor friendship pair nominations at the end of each camp provided evidence that children with secure histories are more likely to form friendships. Nineteen of the 25 children with secure attachment (76%) were seen by counselors as having made at least one friend during the 4-week camp session. Eleven out of 22 (50%) of the children with anxious histories were perceived to have formed friendships ($\chi^2$ = 3.33, $p$ < .10).

Stronger, independent corroboration of these results was obtained by using a network affinity friendship measure (adapted from Ladd, 1983). This friendship measure combined observations of observed child–child associations with children's sociometric friendship nominations. "Friends" in this case were those who had nominated the child as a friend in the interview *and* had been observed in association with the child in at least 20% of social participation observations. Again, children with secure attachment were more likely to form friendships by this criterion than were those with anxious attachment (76% vs. 45%; $\chi^2$ = 4.86, $p$ < .05.)

Children who had been securely attached as infants were expected to find a friend or friends within the camp group and spend a large proportion of time with that individual. This prediction was supported by the observer social participation data. A friend-association score was obtained for each child by determining the proportion of time spent with the most frequent play partner. Children with secure attachment histories had higher friend associations than did children with anxious attachment histories (39% vs. 25%; $F$ = 9.23, $p$ = .004).

Other significant findings concern the composition of friendship pairs. We expected that in addition to forming camp friendships more often, children with secure histories would be likely to form relationships with peers who also had secure attachments in infancy. We reasoned that these secure children would be mutually attracted by their social competence and by an interest in forming challenging peer relationships. Further, such competent pairs might be more successful at maintaining a friendship over a 4-week time period.

These predictions were supported by both the counselor friendship nominations and the seating chart assessments. Assuming friendships are likely only with same-gender peers, there were 40 potential secure–secure pairings in the 3 camp groups, 91 potential mixed-attachment pairings, and 37 possible anxious–anxious pairings. Counselors actually nominated a total of 24 friendship pairs: 12 secure–secure pairs (30% of the possible secure–secure friendship pairs); 9 mixed pairs (10% of the possible mixed pairs); and 3 anxious–anxious pairs (8% of the possible anxious–anxious pairs.) Thus, secure–secure pairs were more likely to form than the other combinations ($\chi^2 = 15.12$; $p < .005$). In the seating chart assessment of friendship, observers mapped the arrangement of all individuals at each group meeting ("circle time") when children and counselors assembled for songs, announcements, or group games. Analyses of the seating charts showed that children more often sat next to others with the same, rather than different, attachment histories ($p = .02$). Clearly, children with secure attachment histories are more likely to form friendships, and they are attracted to other securely attached peers when establishing friendships.

## DISCUSSION

Findings from the Minnesota preschool and summer camp studies and the results of other longitudinal attachment research provide clear evidence that the quality of caregiver–infant relationships is an important predictor of peer relationships and peer competence throughout childhood. Such continuities in adaptation persist, despite dramatic developmental transformations and imperfect methods of assessment, across strikingly different social contexts. Whereas the security of the attachment relationship in infancy has been shown to be a function of the responsiveness and sensitivity of the caregiver during the first year, correlates of secure attachment are seen 10 years later in the self-confidence and competent social functioning of the preadolescent child in his or her peer group, away from direct parental influence. Perhaps the most notable aspect of these cross-age relationships is that the attachment predictor is not best conceptualized as an assessment of the infant, but rather as an assessment of the infant–caregiver relationship, nested in the total context of the family relationship. Thus, not sociability or infant interactive competence with peers, but early relationship history is seen as the context for the emergence of the social self (Sroufe, 1989).

How are we to understand such remarkable developmental continuity? Certainly, the parent–infant relationship does not directly produce or cause differences in competence 10 years later. However, there does appear to be considerable stability in the "major pathways" (Sroufe & Jacobvitz, 1989) or broad developmental patterns followed by many children between infancy and adolescence. Such stabilities cannot be adequately explained, we believe, solely by inherited temperamental differences among children, nor solely by stability in the care and support offered by parents throughout childhood (Sroufe, Egeland, & Kreutzer, 1990). Temperamental differences in infancy have not distinguished securely attached from anxiously attached infants at 12 months (Sroufe, 1985; Vaughn, Lafever, Seifer, & Barglow, 1989). Moreover, in preschool and middle childhood, children who displayed qualitatively different attachment behaviors in the Strange Situation as infants (anxious-avoidant and anxious-resistant) appear quite similar with respect to their difficulty adapting to the peer group. For example, anxious-avoidant attachment has been ascribed by others to "bold" temperament (e.g., Kagan, 1984). We have found, however, that avoidant attachment is significantly associated with high dependency toward preschool teachers and camp counselors, much as is anxious-resistant attachment. Securely attached infants, on the other hand, who are more likely to seek contact with their caregivers when distressed, later become self-confident and independent preschoolers and preadolescents.

There are three explanations we suggest for the continuity found in social adaptation between infancy and middle childhood. They are probably all important to some extent, and not mutually exclusive. First, presence or absence of continuity in care undoubtedly contributes significantly to stability and change in individual social and personality development. Our own research has shown such associations (Erickson et al., 1985; Matas, Arend, & Sroufe, 1978; Vaughn, Egeland, Waters, & Sroufe, 1979). Parents who care for their infants in a sensitive and responsive manner, encouraging autonomy or closeness as sought by the child, develop secure attachment relationships with their infants. These same parents are likely to provide the support and guidance their children need as they move on to the challenges of school and relationships with teachers and peers. Such continuity in parental behavior between 6 and 42 months has been demonstrated in the Minnesota sample (Pianta, Sroufe, & Egeland, 1989), and Lieberman (1977) showed that mothers of securely attached 3-year-olds explicitly encouraged and supported peer relationships. Some continuity in parental support is undoubtedly essential for continued successful social adaptation.

The second mechanism for developmental continuity in social adaptation and quality of relationships is the child's elicitation of feedback from others, which supports his or her particular adaptive style. Our research provides clear and varied evidence for this proposition. Children's relationships with their preschool teachers are predictable from the quality of their relationships with their parents as infants (Motti, 1986, reported in Sroufe & Fleeson, 1988). Children with the same attachment histories were found to elicit similar affective and behavioral responses from two different preschool teachers, but reactions of teachers were quite distinctive across the attachment groups. Teachers showed age-appropriate maturity demands, high expectations, and warm regard toward those with histories of secure attachment. They were warm toward those with histories of anxious-resistant attachment, but also controlling and unduly nurturant (infantilizing). They showed controllingness and low expectations for compliance toward those with histories of anxious-avoidant attachment, and additionally, anger and low warmth. Thus, children often elicit reactions from teachers that may perpetuate previous maladaptive patterns of adaptation. In their relationships with peers, children with a history of vulnerability (anxious-resistant or anxious-avoidant attachment) were prone to victimization in the preschool, and the children doing the victimizing had anxious-avoidant histories (Troy & Sroufe, 1987). In many cases, victims repeatedly reinitiated contact that resulted in their being exploited. This pattern of victimization did not occur when anxious-resistant children were paired with securely attached peers, who were supportive of them. Further evidence for the child's role in eliciting responses from others congruent with previous relationships is found in the prevalence and quality of secure–secure friendship pairs in the summer camps, described earlier. On one hand, we have documented patterns that lead children to be accepted, rejected, or neglected by the peer group in preschool, and on the other hand, children who are able to form reciprocal, supportive friendships with competent partners in preadolescence. Such experiences would further consolidate adaptational patterns brought to these contexts.

The issues here call for replication and for more research at the level of process. At present we have largely anecdotal evidence concerning what children do to elicit differential responses from teachers and peers. It seems that nursery school teachers are drawn to nurture and support those children that seem needy, easily frustrated, and obviously dependent, and who show their vulnerability in direct ways (those with anxious-resistant histories); yet they are put off by the equally needy anxious-avoidant children, whose defiance and aggression toward others communicate an apparent self-sufficiency or lack of interest in social support. Members of the first group are easy targets for bullies, because they are so easily upset and disorganized by aggressive encounters, whereas the latter group is disliked and viewed as "mean" by the more competent children with secure histories. We need much more information both about the details of behavioral interaction among such children over time and about the developing beliefs and cognitive styles of these children.

The third explanation for the adaptational continuity we have observed lies in Bowlby's notion of internal working models. Are early relationship experiences mentally represented in such a way that they are generalized and influence expectations, feelings, and behavior in other relationships throughout childhood, and perhaps throughout one's entire life? (See Bretherton, 1985.) Initial investigations have shown associations between quality of attachment and various representations of parent–child relationships (e.g., Main et al., 1985; Rosenberg, 1984), cognitive biases toward peers and peer interaction, and inferences about the internal states of peers (Elicker, 1989; Suess, 1987). Again, there is need for further research. We are only beginning to examine the complexities of family influences on the child's internal working models. Preliminary work suggests, for example, that when attachment relationships to mother and to father differ, it is the relationship with mother that is more predictive of social competence, at least in infancy (Main & Weston, 1981). Recent studies (Main et al., 1985; Owen & Henderson, 1989; Suess, 1987) suggest that this difference in predictability favoring the mother may persist to age 5. Will this change at later ages? Do relationships with mothers and fathers predict better to different outcomes? And how does this interact with the child's gender? Moreover, when do children begin observing the nature of the spousal relationship, and how do relationship patterns among adults in the household influence working models of relationships as the child develops? Obviously, all of these influences will combine in a complex way.

In the Minnesota project we are currently gathering assessments of family functioning (age 13 years), which allow us to compare the relative influences of prior and contemporaneous parental support and to examine the impact of changing family structure. Also, extensive individual interviews are being conducted to help us learn more about the current mental models of children with different early relationship histories and various levels of current social competence. We hope to be able to bridge the gap between work on individual differences in social-cognitive style and skills (e.g., Dodge, 1986) and our own research on developmental history.

These studies will increase our understanding of processes involved in the maintenance of stable patterns in social development. We do not expect, however, that a simple, unitary explanation will emerge. The processes that produce and channel the streams of experience we call collectively "development" are complex. They operate at multiple levels: the individual, the dyadic relationship, and the family system. Whereas description of processes in individuals is an important preliminary goal, it will also ultimately be enlightening to discover more general principles governing stability and change in the relationships and family systems that these individual processes combine to produce.

## ACKNOWLEDGMENTS

Support for the summer camp research reported in this chapter was provided to James Elicker by a Spencer Foundation Dissertation Year Fellowship and to L. Alan Sroufe by a grant from the National Institute of Mental Health, MH-40864. The authors gratefully acknowledge the hard work and dedication of the Minnesota summer camp staff and observers. Our greatest gratitude, however, is to the campers themselves, who for the past 12 years have shared glimpses of their lives with us, illuminating some of the intricate pathways of childhood development.

## REFERENCES

Ainsworth, M., Blehar, M., Waters, E., & Wall, S. (1978). *Patterns of attachment: A psychological study of the Strange Situation.* Hillsdale, NJ: Lawrence Erlbaum Associates.

Arend, R., Gove, F., & Sroufe, L. A. (1979). Continuity of individual adaptation from infancy to kindergarten: A predictive study of ego-resiliency and curiosity in preschoolers. *Child Development, 50,* 950–959.

Baldwin, J. M. (1911). *The individual and society.* Boston: Goreham.

Block, J. (1961). *The Q-sort method in personality assessment and psychiatric research.* Springfield, IL: Thomas.

Block, J. H., & Block, J. (1980). The role of ego-control and ego-resiliency in the organization of behavior. In W. A. Collins (Ed.), *Minnesota symposium of child psychology* (Vol. 13, pp. 39–101). Hillsdale, NJ: Lawrence Erlbaum Associates.

Bowlby, J. (1973). *Attachment and loss: Vol. 2. Separation.* New York: Basic.

Bretherton, I. (1985). Attachment theory: Retrospect and prospect. In I. Bretherton & E. Waters (Eds.), Growing points of attachment theory and research. *Monographs of the Society for Research in Child Development, 50*(1–2, Serial No. 209).

Bretherton, I., Ridgeway, D., & Cassidy, J. (1990). Assessing internal working models of the attachment relationship: An attachment story completion task for 3-year-olds? In M. Greenberg, D. Cicchetti, & E. M. Cummings (Eds.), *Attachment during the preschool years: Theory, research and intervention* (pp. 273–308). Chicago: University of Chicago Press.

Cassidy, J. (1988). Child–mother attachment and the self in 6-year-olds. *Child Development, 59,* 121–134.

Dodge, K. A., Pettit, G. S., McCluskey, C. L., & Brown, M. M. (1986). Social competence in children. *Monographs of the Society for Research in Child Development, 51*(2, Serial No. 213).

Egeland, B., & Kreutzer, T. (1991). A longitudinal study of the effects of maternal stress and protective factors on the development of high risk children. In A. Greene, E. Cummings, & K. Karraker (Eds.), *Life-span developmental psychology: Perspectives on stress and coping* (pp. 61–84). Hillsdale, NJ: Lawrence Erlbaum Associates.

Elicker, J. (1989, April). *The role of attachment in children's understanding of peer relationships in middle childhood.* Paper presented at the Biennial Meeting of the Society for Research in Child Development, Kansas City, MO.

Erickson, M. F., Sroufe, L. A., & Egeland, B. (1985). The relationship between quality of attachment and behavior problems in preschool in a high-risk sample. In I. Bretherton & E. Waters (Eds.), Growing points of attachment theory and research. *Monographs of the Society for Research in Child Development, 50*(1–2, Serial No. 209).

Erikson, E. H. (1963). *Childhood and society* (2nd ed.). New York: Norton.

Gottman, J. M. (1983). How children become friends. *Monographs of the Society for Research in Child Development, 48*(2, Serial No. 201).

Hinde, R. A. (1979). *Towards understanding relationships.* London: Academic Press.

Howes, C. (1987). Peer interaction of young children. *Monographs of the Society for Research in Child Development, 48*(2, Serial No. 201).

Kagan, J. (1984). *The nature of the child.* New York: Basic.

Kestenbaum, R., Farber, E., & Sroufe, L. A. (1989). Individual differences in empathy among preschoolers: Relation to attachment history. In N. Eisenberg (Ed.), *Empathy and related emotional responses.* San Francisco: Jossey-Bass.

Ladd, G. (1983). Social networks of popular, average, and rejected children in school settings. *Merrill-Palmer Quarterly, 29*(3), 283–307.

LaFreniere, P., & Sroufe, L. A. (1985). Profiles of peer competence in the preschool: Interrelations between measures, influence of social ecology, and relation to attachment history. *Developmental Psychology, 21*(1), 56–69.

Lieberman, A. F. (1977). Preschoolers' competence with a peer: Relations with attachment and peer experience. *Child Development, 48,* 1277–1287.

Main, M. (1983). Exploration, play, and cognitive functioning related to infant–mother attachment. *Infant Behavior and Development, 6,* 167–174.

Main, M., Kaplan, N., & Cassidy, J. (1985). Security in infancy, childhood, and adulthood: A move to the level of representation. In I. Bretherton & E. Waters (Eds.), Growing points of attachment theory and research. *Monographs of the Society for Research in Child Development, 50*(1–2, Serial No. 209).

Main, M., & Weston, D. R. (1981). The quality of the toddler's relationship to mother and to father: Related to conflict behavior and the readiness to establish new relationships. *Child Development, 52,* 932–940.

Matas, L., Arend, R., & Sroufe, L. A. (1978). Continuity of adaptation in the second year of life: The relationship between quality of attachment and later competence. *Child Development, 49,* 547–556.

Mead, G. H. (1934). *Mind, self, and society.* Chicago: University of Chicago Press.

Morris, D. (1980). *Infant attachment and problem solving in the toddler: Relations to mother's family history.* Unpublished doctoral dissertation, University of Minnesota.

Motti, F. (1986). *Relationships of preschool teachers with children of varying developmental histories.* Unpublished doctoral dissertation, University of Minnesota.

Owen, M. T., & Henderson, V. K. (1989, April). *Relations between child-care qualities and child behavior at age 4: Do parent–child interactions play a role?* Paper presented at the Biennial Meeting of the Society for Research in Child Development, Kansas City, MO.

Pancake, V. R. (1985, April). *Continuity between mother–infant attachment and ongoing dyadic peer relationships in preschool.* Paper presented at the Biennial Meeting of the Society for Research in Child Development, Toronto.

Park, K. A., & Waters, E. (1989). Security of attachment and preschool friendships. *Child Development, 60*(5), 1076–1081.

Pastor, D. L. (1981). The quality of mother–infant attachment and its relationship to toddlers' sociability with peers. *Developmental Psychology, 17*(3), 326–335.

Pianta, R. C., Egeland, B., & Sroufe, L. A. (in press). Maternal stress and children's development: Prediction of school outcomes and identification of protective factors. In J. Rolf, A. Masten, D. Cicchetti, K., Neuchterlein, & S. Weintraub (Eds.), *Risk and protective factors in the development of psychopathology.* Cambridge, MA: Harvard University Press.

Pianta, R. C., Sroufe, L. A., & Egeland, B. (1989). Continuity and discontinuity in maternal sensitivity at 6, 24, and 42 months in a high risk sample. *Child Development, 60,* 481–487.

Renkin, B., Egeland, B., Marvinney, D., Sroufe, L. A., & Manglesdorf, S. (1989). Early childhood antecedents of aggression and passive-withdrawal in early elementary school. *Journal of Personality, 57,* 257–282.

Ricks, M. (1985). The social transmission of parental behavior: Attachment across generations. In I. Bretherton & E. Waters (Eds.), Growing points of attachment theory and research. *Monographs of the Society for Research in Child Development, 50*(1–2, Serial No. 209).

Rosenberg, D. M. (1984). *The quality and content of preschool fantasy play: Correlates in concurrent social-personality function and early mother–child attachment relationships.* Unpublished doctoral dissertation, University of Minnesota.

Sroufe, L. A., (1979). The coherence of individual development: Early care, attachment, and subsequent developmental issues. *American Psychologist, 34*(10), 834–841.

Sroufe, L. A. (1983). Infant–caregiver attachment and patterns of adaptation in preschool: The roots of maladaptation and competence. In M. Perlmutter (Ed.), *Minnesota symposia on child psychology* (Vol. 16, pp. 41–81). Hillsdale, NJ: Lawrence Erlbaum Associates.

Sroufe, L. A. (1985). Attachment classification from the perspective of infant–caregiver relationships and infant temperament. *Child Development, 56,* 1–14.

Sroufe, L. A. (1988). The role of infant–caregiver attachment in development. In J. Belsky & T. Nezworski (Eds.), *Clinical implications of attachment,* (pp. 18–38). Hillsdale, NJ: Lawrence Erlbaum Associates.

Sroufe, L. A. (1989). Relationships, self, and individual adaptation. In A. J. Sameroff & R. N. Emde (Eds.), *Relationship disturbances in early childhood: A developmental approach* (pp. 70–96). New York: Basic.

Sroufe, L. A., Bennett, C., Englund, M., Urban, J., & Shulman, S. (1992). *The significance of gender boundaries in preadolescence: Antecedents and correlates of individual differences in boundary violation and maintenance.* Unpublished manuscript.

Sroufe, L. A., Egeland, B., & Kreutzer, T. (1990). The fate of early experience following developmental change: Longitudinal approaches to individual adaptation in childhood. *Child Development, 61,* 1363–1373.

Sroufe, L. A., & Fleeson, J. (1986). Attachment and the construction of relationships. In W. Hartup & Z. Rubin (Eds.), *Relationships and development* (pp. 51–71). Hillsdale, NJ: Lawrence Erlbaum Associates.

Sroufe, L. A., & Fleeson, J. (1988). The coherence of family relationships. In R. Hinde & J. Stevenson-Hinde (Eds.), *Relationships within families* (pp. 57–71). Oxford: Oxford University Press.

Sroufe, L. A., & Jacobvitz, D. (1989). Diverging pathways, developmental transformations, multiple etiologies and the problem of continuity in development. *Human Development, 32,* 96–103.

Sroufe, L. A., Schork, E., Motti, F., Lawroski, N., & LaFreniere, P. (1985). The role of affect in social competence. In C. Izard, J. Kagan, & R. Zajonc (Eds.), *Emotions, cognition, and behavior* (pp. 289–319). NY: Cambridge University Press.

Sroufe, L. A., & Waters, E. (1977). Attachment as an organizational construct. *Child Development, 48,* 1184–1199.

Suess, G. J. (1987). *Auswirkungen frükindlicher Bindungserfahrungen auf die Kompetenz im Kindergarten* [Consequences of early attachment experiences on competence in preschool]. Unpublished doctoral dissertation, Universität Regensburg, Regensburg, Germany.

Thorne, B. (1986). Girls and boys together . . . but mostly apart: Gender arrangements in elementary schools. In W. Hartup & Z. Rubin (Eds.), *Relationships and development* (pp. 167–184). Hillsdale, NJ: Lawrence Erlbaum Associates.

Troy, M., & Sroufe, L. A. (1987). Victimization among preschoolers: The role of attachment relationship history. *Journal of the American Academy of Child Psychiatry, 26,* 166–172.

Vaughn, B., Egeland, B., Waters, E., & Sroufe, L. A. (1979). Individual differences in infant–mother attachment at 12 and 18 months: Stability and change in families under stress. *Child Development, 50,* 971–975.

Vaughn, B. E., Lafever, G. B., Seifer, R., & Barglow, P. (1989). Attachment behavior, attachment security, and temperament during infancy. *Child Development, 60,* 728–737.

Ward, M. J., Vaughn, B., & Robb, M. (1988). Attachment and adaptation in siblings: The role of the mother in cross-sibling consistency. *Child Development, 59,* 643–651.

Waters, E., & Sroufe, L. A. (1983). Social competence as a developmental construct. *Developmental Review, 3,* 79–97.

Waters, E., Wippman, J., & Sroufe, L. A. (1979). Attachment, positive affect, and competence in the peer group: Two studies in construct validation. *Child Development, 50,* 821–829.

# CHAPTER FOUR

# Familial Contribution to Peer Competence Among Young Children: The Role of Interactive and Affective Processes

Ross D. Parke
*University of California, Riverside*

Jude Cassidy
*Pennsylvania State University*

Virginia M. Burks
*Vanderbilt University*

James L. Carson
Lisa Boyum
*University of Illinois*

In recent years, considerable progress has been made in our understanding of the relationships between the family and the peer group. No longer are these two sets of social systems viewed as independent, but instead they are conceptualized as mutually interdependent (Hartup, 1979; Rubin & Sloman, 1984). Moreover, it is recognized that these two systems are linked in multiple ways. In earlier presentations, we have outlined three alternative pathways that serve to link family and peer systems; these links are not mutually exclusive and may play different roles at different developmental points across development (Parke, MacDonald, Beitel, & Bhavnagri, 1988; Parke, MacDonald, Burks, Carson, Bhavnagri, Barth, & Beitel, 1989).

Briefly, parents are viewed as functioning not only as interactive partners influencing their children's peer relations through their child rearing practices and interactive styles, but also in a second role as a direct instructor or educator. In this role, parents may explicitly set out to educate their children concerning appropriate ways of negotiating the peer system. They may serve as coaches as they provide advice, support, and directions about the most helpful and successful strategies for managing peer relationships. They may act as supervisors of peer play in which their child is a participant; they may directly assist their children in maintaining play with other children (see Lollis & Ross, this volume; Parke & Bhavnagri, 1989, for reviews). In a third role, parents function as managers of their children's social lives (Hartup, 1979; Parke, 1978). Parents serve as providers of opportunities for social contact with extrafamilial social partners (see Ladd, Hart, & Muth, this volume; Parke & Bhavnagri, 1989, for reviews).

Our focus in this chapter is on the first parental role. This role of parent as interactive partner is the most common and well-researched manner in which parents influence their children's peer relationships. It is assumed that the social skills or social expectations acquired in the context of this familial relationship, in turn, impact the relationship with a child's peers. Two research traditions can be distinguished. First, in the attachment tradition, the focus has been on the impact of early infant–parent attachment on social adaptation in the peer group (see Sroufe & Fleeson, 1986, and Elicker, Egeland, & Sroufe, this volume, for reviews). The second tradition is illustrated by studies of the relations between particular styles of childrearing (Baumrind, 1973; Hoffman, 1960) or parent–child interaction (see Parke et al., 1988, 1989; Puttalaz, & Heflin, 1990, for reviews) and children's social competence. In both traditions, there is clear evidence that the quality of the parent–child relationship is linked with variations in the quality of children's peer relationships. The impact or carry over effects are often indirect, as the parent's goal is not explicitly to modify or enhance children's relationships with extrafamilial social partners such as peers.

The goal of this chapter is to review and evaluate recent research that has examined the link between parent–child interaction patterns and peer competence. This research has progressed through several phases over the last decade. In the first phase, studies were designed to demonstrate that variations in patterns of parent–child interaction were, in fact, related to peer outcomes. The aim of these studies was a careful description of the specific types of parent–child interaction that, in turn, would be most predictive of variations in peer outcomes. More recently, a second phase of this research has begun, namely the search for mediating processes that, in turn, can account for the observed relations between these two systems. It is proposed that emotional regulatory mechanisms play a central role as mediators between the family and peer contexts. An exploration of both of these phases of research in this area is undertaken in this chapter.

## PHASE I. PARENT–CHILD INTERACTION AND PEER COMPETENCE: DESCRIPTIVE EVIDENCE

This first phase of research provides a detailed description of the ways in which parent–child interaction patterns relate to children's peer group interaction. This research is based on the assumption that face-to-face interaction may provide opportunities to learn, rehearse, and refine social skills that are common to successful social interaction with peers. Two sets of evidence are reviewed in this section: first, data concerning stylistic differences in the parent–child interactions of children of varying levels of sociometric acceptance; second, descriptive findings concerning the nature of the affect that characterizes the parent–child interactions of children of different levels of peer social competence.

## Parent–Child Interaction Styles and Peer Competence

In this section, cross-sectional and longitudinal data concerning parent–child interactive styles is reviewed.

*Cross-Sectional Evidence.*   Several recent studies have examined this issue using a variety of interactive contexts. In general, these studies follow a similar two-step paradigm. In one phase, parents and children are observed in interaction with their children, while separate and independent measures of peer competence are collected as well. In turn, the relationship between variations in the parent–child interaction and peer outcome is examined. Typically, game-like or play contexts have been utilized in these studies.

In the initial descriptive studies, the two classic dimensions that have characterized parent–child interaction for several decades, warmth and control, emerge as common themes. Puttalaz (1987), in a study of first graders, examined mother–child interaction in a word naming game and related patterns of mother–child interactions with observations of pairs of unacquainted peers. Independent assessments of children's sociometric status were available as well. Several features of mother–child interaction were related to children's sociometric status. The extent to which mothers behaved in an agreeable manner and exhibited positive affect was related positively to sociometric status, and disagreeableness was negatively related to this index of peer acceptance. In other words, the mothers of high status children interacted in a more positive and agreeable manner with their children and were found to be more concerned with both their own feelings as well as those of their children. In contrast, mothers of lower status children exhibited more negative and controlling behavior with their children than did mothers of higher status children. In short, the dual themes of warmth and control characterize the interaction differences of mothers and children of higher and lower sociometric status.

A similar pattern of results has emerged in the studies of MacDonald, Parke, and their colleagues. This research employed a two-step paradigm. In the first phase, mothers and fathers on separate occasions were videotaped interacting with their 3- to 5-year-old children. In all studies, a

10-minute period in which parents were specifically instructed to play physically with their children is included. Parents are given examples such as tickling, tumbling, or wrestling. In the second phase, measures of peer interactive competence were secured. These have varied across studies and include: (a) teacher assessments, (b) sociometric ratings, and (c) observations of peer–peer interaction.

In our initial study (MacDonald & Parke, 1984), 3- to 5-year-old boys and girls were observed interacting during free and physical play with their mothers and fathers in their homes. A variety of measures of verbal and physical behavior were derived from videotape of these play interactions, including: number of 10-second periods of parent–child physical play, verbal interchanges, directive statements, and ratings of children's positive affect. As a measure of peer status, teacher rankings of children's popularity were secured (see MacDonald & Parke, 1984, for details and other measures). Our results indicated that popular boys have mother and fathers who are engaging and elicit positive affect during play, mothers who are verbally stimulating, and fathers who are low in directiveness but physically playful. Girls whose teachers rated them as popular have physically playful and affect-eliciting but nondirective fathers, and directive mothers.

Work by Burks, Carson, and Parke (1987) utilizing a molecular coding strategy and measures of sociometric status confirmed our earlier work and extended our understanding of familial antecedents of peer interactive competence. Popular and rejected 4- to 5-year-old boys and girls were observed interacting with their mothers and fathers on separate occasions for a 10-minute physical play session in a lab playroom. Dyads of popular children and their parents had play bouts of longer duration and played for a larger proportion of the time than dyads of rejected children and their parents. Initiation strategies varied by sociometric status. Popular parent–child dyads used noncoercive initiation tactics, such as questions, whereas dyads involving rejected children and their parents used more coercive tactics, such as suggestions and directives. Similarly, responses to initiations differed across the status groups. Dyads involving a rejected child were more likely to respond negatively than dyads involving a popular child. The consistency of these findings with those from studies of parental disciplinary styles increases our confidence in the ecological validity of the laboratory-based findings. For instance, children of mothers with power assertive disciplinary styles have been found to be less accepted by peers than have children of mothers with inductive disciplinary styles (Hart, Ladd, & Burleson, 1990).

Other data (Gottman & Fainsilber-Katz, 1989) provide further support for this parental profile. In an examination of the parent–child interaction, these investigators found that a parenting style characterized as cold, unresponsive, angry, and low in limit setting and structuring leads to higher levels of anger and noncompliance, as well as high levels of stress-related hormones. Children from such homes tend to play at a lower level with peers, display more negative peer interaction, and have poorer physical health. Maritally distressed couples were more likely to exhibit this parenting style—a finding consistent with other work (see Grych & Fincham, 1990, for a review of the impact of marital interaction on children's social adaptation).

One limitation of the studies reviewed in this section is their reliance on concurrent assessments of both parent–child interaction and peer competence. The nature of this cross-sectional approach limits the extent to which the direction effects can be assessed as well as the long-term impact of familial effects on later adjustment to peers.

*Short-Term Longitudinal Evidence.*    Recent evidence suggests that both the ability of the parent–child dyad to maintain physical play and the style of parent–child interaction not only are concurrent correlates of children's peer behavior, but also are related to children's later adjustment after the transition to school (Barth & Parke, 1991). In this study, the relation between parent–child interaction and children's social adjustment as they make the transition to elementary school was examined. Children who were entering kindergarten were observed in physical play sessions separately with their mothers and fathers, 1 to 2 months prior to school entrance. Social adjustment in the school setting was assessed through parent ratings, teacher reports, and interviews with the children 2 weeks after school began and at the end of the first school semester.

Both mother–child and father–child interaction predicted subsequent school social adaptation. First, the amount of time that the parent and child spent in sustained play interaction was a significant predictor. For mothers, this "length of bout" measure was positively associated with teachers' ratings (Schaefer, Edgerton, & Aaronson, 1978) of a child's consideration of others and negatively related with teachers' ratings of dependence, both at 2 weeks after school entry and again at the end of the semester. Similarly, there was a positive relation between the extent to which there was sustained parent–child interaction and children's attitudes toward school; children's attitudes were measured by a scale, the "One Child's Day" (Barth, 1988), which asks children to evaluate specific events that occur in a typical school day on a 3-point scale. For example, children were asked how much they liked getting ready for school, arriving at school, and playing with other children during free time. In addition, the children's positive attitudes toward school were associated with low ratings of loneliness (Barth, 1988) after the beginning of school and with low teacher hostility ratings at the end of the semester. For fathers, time in play bouts was associated with parents' ratings of home behavior after the onset of school. Each parent independently completed the Home Behavior Questionnaire (HBQ), which assessed a child's interaction with adults and other children at home, school concerns, and physical signs of stress related to health, appetite, and sleep patterns. Parents completed the questionnaire for several days at the onset of school and at the end of the semester. (Favorable ratings on the HBQ were correlated with independent observations of frequent positive social interaction and infrequent nonsocial bystander behavior in the classroom.) Children whose time in play bouts with fathers was higher received higher parental ratings of their home behaviors in the 2-week period after school onset.

In addition to the quantity or amount of interaction, style of interaction was an important correlate of children's social adjustment. In contrast to earlier studies, in which independent measures of parent or child behaviors were examined, a dyadic measure of parent–child interaction style was obtained by use of a principal components analysis for mother–child and father–child interactions. Mother–child dyads in which the child was highly directive and unwilling to accept maternal input were related to poor social adjustment, as indexed by high hostility and low consideration ratings from teachers. In addition, these children reported higher levels of loneliness after the initial onset of school. Mother–child dyads characterized by a dominant mother and an uncooperative, resistant child were related to teacher ratings of dependency after the onset of school and higher ratings of hostility at the end of the semester. Similarly, father–child dyads characterized by a pattern of parent control and child resistance were also correlated with poor social adjustment in both home and school settings. Immediately after school entrance, this interaction style was associated with children's reports of loneliness and parents' reports of behavior problems at home. By the end of the semester, this style was negatively correlated with teachers' reports of consideration. Finally, nondirective dyads in which fathers use an indirect style of interaction (e.g., high reliance on questions and low reliance on directives) was consistently related to favorable home behaviors at the onset of school and at the end of the semester and with reports of low hostility from the teacher at the end of the semester.

Taken together, these results support past research that shows controlling and directive parenting styles and noncompliant demanding child behaviors are negatively related to social adjustment in school settings (Campbell, Breaux, Ewing, & Szumoski, 1985) and peer sociometric assessments (Puttalaz, 1987). Most importantly, these data suggest that earlier observed parent–child interaction patterns have value in predicting later social adjustment in school and peer contexts. Although the Barth and Parke (1991) study does not imply a causal relationship between parent–child interaction and later behavior in peer contexts, it suggests the plausibility of this direction of effect, in view of the fact that parent–child interaction was observed prior to the school measures.

To summarize, the studies in this section suggest that both the ability to maintain social interaction and the style of social interchanges in families of children of varying levels of social acceptance are clearly different. Many of the patterns found in parent–child play are similar to patterns of peer interactions. Peer interactions with popular children generally involve more engaged activities that are of longer duration than interactions involving rejected children. Similarly, popular children tend to be less controlling and more willing to adapt to the activities of the group, whereas rejected children tend to be assertive and directive when they interact with peers (Asher & Coie, 1990; Dodge, 1983). The similarities between family and peer settings suggest that children may be generalizing the interactive lessons acquired in the family to peer contexts.

## Parent–Child Affect and Peer Competence

This section examines in more detail the nature of the affect that characterizes families of children of varying levels of sociometric status. Two issues are examined, namely, family expressiveness and the nature of affect displays during the course of parent–child interaction.

### *Family Expressiveness and Children's Social Competence.*
First, we examine the relationship between the degree to which families express emotion in the course of everyday interactions and their children's social competence.

To assess the relation between family emotional expressiveness in home contexts and peer social acceptance was the goal of a recent study by Cassidy and Parke (1989). As in our prior studies, a two-step procedure was used in which sociometric and behavioral ratings were collected from peers and teachers. An independent measure of family expressiveness, Halberstadt's (1984) Family Expressiveness Questionnaire (FEQ) was secured for the parents of the 5- to 6-year-old children in the study. The FEQ measures the extent to which family members typically express emotions in common situations in the home. Although this scale was originally developed for use with college students, Cassidy and Parke adapted it for use with parents. Their adapted scale revealed similar subscales and high internal reliability. Briefly, positive and negative expressiveness factors were found. Positive expressiveness includes such items as "praising someone for good work," "demonstrating admiration," "telling family members how happy you are," or "expressing gratitude for a favor." Negative expressiveness refers to items such as "expressing anger at someone's carelessness," "showing how upset you are after a bad day," "expressing dissatisfaction with someone else's behavior." Mothers and fathers each completed the questionnaire separately.

*Mothers'* total expressiveness, mothers' positive expressiveness, and mothers' negative expressiveness were all positively correlated with *girls'* peer acceptance, but not with *boys'* peer acceptance. Conversely, *fathers'* total expressiveness and fathers' negative expressiveness were positively correlated with *boys'* acceptance, but not with girls' acceptance. Fathers' positive expressiveness was not related to boys' acceptance, but was related to girls' acceptance.

Parents' emotional expressiveness was also significantly correlated with peer and teacher behavior measures. Greater maternal total expressiveness was associated, for boys, with less shyness. Greater maternal total expressiveness was associated, for girls, with greater prosocial behavior and with less disruptiveness. A congruent pattern of results emerged in relation to maternal positive and negative expressiveness. A different pattern emerged in relation to paternal emotional expressiveness. Greater paternal total expressiveness was associated, for boys, with less aggression, less shyness, and more prosocial behavior. For girls, greater paternal total expressiveness was associated with less aggression, more prosocial behavior, and less disruptiveness. A congruent pattern of results emerged in relation to paternal positive and negative expressiveness, with one exception: a positive correlation between fathers' negative expressiveness and girls' shyness.

These findings reveal connections between parental emotional expressiveness within the family context and children's social competence. Greater self-reported parental expressiveness is associated with children's greater competence with peers as assessed by sociometric and behavior measures. More specifically, both mothers' and fathers' expressiveness may relate to prosocial and shy behavior. The more expressive the parent, the more prosocial and less shy the child. The only finding incongruent with the pattern of results is a positive correlation between fathers' negative expressiveness and shyness in girls. It is not clear why this relation emerged; given the otherwise clear pattern of results, overemphasis of this incongruity is not warranted. In relation to aggression, fathers' expressiveness alone was relevant. The *more* expressive the father, the *less* aggressive the child. This finding meshes with previous research that suggests that fathers may play a particularly important role in helping children learn to modulate aggression (Bandura & Walters, 1959; Eron, Walder, & Lefkowitz, 1971), and underscores the notion that parents of different sexes may influence specific but different aspects of their children's social behavior.

A limitation of this study should be noted, namely the reliance on parental reports as the only measure of expressiveness in the home. Fortunately, some observation-based studies are available and in general support these findings.

These observational studies suggest that it is not only the degree of expressiveness, but the ways in which emotional displays are responded to by other family members that is important in the socialization of social competence in children. Observations of parents' responses to emotional distress of their children underscores the important role that emotional socialization plays in the emergence of peer competence. Roberts and Strayer (1987) measured the social competence of preschool children using teacher ratings of peer competence, ego strength, and purposiveness. To assess parent–child interaction, home observations, parent self-reports, and child interviews were undertaken. The extent to which parents encourage expression of upset (e.g., value and permit emotional expression), although focusing on compliance (in agonistic situations), or on problem solving in non-agonistic situations (don't deny distress or attempt to suppress expression and value or teach emotional control), was nonlinearly related to competence. Similarly, a self-report measure of the extent to which "Father Encourages Emotional Expression" was related to competence in an inverted U-shaped fashion, indicating that moderate levels of responsiveness to upset were associated with higher levels of competence. Maternal self-reports of encouragement of emotional expression were not related to child competence. These data are consistent with earlier theoretical views that suggest that learning to manage moderate levels of negative affect is a skill that is important for management of social relationships (Sroufe, 1979). Similarly it is consistent with other data. For example, Zahn-Waxler, Radke-Yarrow, and King (1979) found that parents who responded positively to their children's upset had children who responded positively to upset in others and were more often prosocial in their behavior. At the other extreme, Main and George (1985) reported that toddlers who are abused by their parents become emotionally distressed by their peers' emotional upset and attack them verbally and physically.

Whereas the studies suggest that family expressiveness is a significant correlate of children's peer relationships, there is a need for a more differentiated definition of expressiveness in which individual components or dimensions such as intensity, duration appropriateness, clarity, and frequency are examined separately and in combination to better determine the aspects of this construct that accounts for its impact on children.

***Further Specification of the Nature of Affect Expressions.***    In this section, we examine more closely the nature of the affect accompanying parent–child interaction patterns as a function of children's sociometric status. Does the quality of affect within parent–child interaction differ across dyads of sociometrically popular and rejected children and their parents? Studies conducted in both the laboratory and in the home are examined to determine if the type of affect displayed by children and their parents varies as a function of peer sociometric status.

Across a number of studies (MacDonald, 1987; MacDonald & Parke, 1984) it is clear that the quality of affect exhibited during the interaction of popular children and their parents differs from the quality of affect displayed during the interactions of rejected children and their parents. Consistently, higher levels of positive affect were found for children in the popular dyads than in the rejected dyads. This is evident not only for the children, but for the parents as well (Burks et al., 1987). In these studies, ratings of positive and negative ratings were made by observers either for the entire period or for selected time-sampled intervals. Little information is available from these studies concerning specific types of emotional displays beyond their negative or positive valence.

In an effort to learn more about the nature of the specific emotional cues exhibited by children of differing sociometric status and their parents, Carson (1991) has recently examined the frequency with which parents and children use different categories of emotional expressions during parent–child play. To achieve this goal, a new play paradigm was required, because naturally occurring physical play does not permit detailed videotaping of the emotional expressions of the partners. A hand game was developed that was physically arousing and stimulating but required the participants to remain seated during the course of the game. The game required one partner to "grab" the outstretched hands of the other player before the person withdrew his or her hands. Participants were told that they may switch "grabber" and "grabbee" roles at any time. This game is physically stimulating and has been found to be affect-eliciting in previous work done in our lab. Because children and parents remain seated in their chairs, it is possible to obtain high-quality videotape records of their facial expressions throughout the interaction. To permit face-to-face interaction, the child was placed on an elevated stool, while the parent was seated on a normal-sized chair. Data have revealed status differences in the frequency with which some types of emotional cues are displayed during the course of parent–child physical play. Popular children were found to show more happiness and laughter, whereas rejected children showed more neutral affect. The parents of popular children were more likely to use affect-laden guidance (e.g., they would remind children of the game rules while expressing positive affect) during the course of the game, and were more likely to be apologetic. Parents of rejected children showed more anger as well as more neutral affect. In addition, the level of anger shown by fathers and their rejected children was positively correlated, which suggested that father and child may be engaged in reciprocal displays of anger. This pattern of positive correlations between maternal anger and either popular or rejected children's anger was not evident for mothers, nor did fathers show this pattern with their popular offspring. We are hopeful that sequential analyses of these data will also show significant status-related differences in the ways in which emotional cues may have an impact on the course of parent–child interaction.

Similar evidence based on home observations of a relationship between peer acceptance and the type of affective expressions exhibited during the course of parent–child interaction comes from a recent study by Boyum (1991). In this work, kindergarten children of varying levels of peer acceptance—as indexed by sociometric ratings by their classmates—and their parents were videotaped at home during a family dinnertime. The affective expressions of mothers, fathers, and children were scored during 30-second intervals throughout the dinnertime period. Boyum found negative correlations between the level of a variety of father negative affect expressions, including anger, disgust, and anxiety, and their kindergarten children's sociometric studies. There were no significant correlations found for mothers. Just as Carson (1991) found in laboratory parent–child interaction, paternal negative affect is associated with lower levels of peer acceptance.

These findings concerning the heightened degree of negative affect on the part of parents of less socially accepted children have several implications. First, children may transfer some of the negative affect that is learned in the course of parent–child interaction to interactions with peers; in turn, this may account for the higher level of negative affect and aggression found among some rejected children. Second, other evidence (Lindahl, 1991; Lindahl & Markman, 1990) suggests that high levels of negative affect on the part of mothers is associated with less ability to manage their negative emotions and higher levels of negative affect on the part of their children. In summary, children may be learning to display *specific patterns of emotions* during parent–child interaction that, in turn, may be utilized during peer–peer interaction.

## PHASE II. IN SEARCH OF MEDIATING PROCESSES: AFFECT MANAGEMENT SKILLS

In this section, we begin to explore possible factors that serve as mediators between parent–child interaction and peer outcomes. As noted earlier, children of differing sociometric status vary in terms of the specific affective displays that they develop as well as in the nature of the level of expressiveness characteristic of their daily lives. However, children learn more than specific types of affects or general levels of expressiveness in the family. We argue that a cluster of processes associated with the understanding and regulation of affective displays that are subsumed under the rubric of *affect management skills* are acquired during the course of parent–child interaction and, in turn, are available to the child during the course of peer–peer interaction. It is assumed that these affect management skills are general skills that are not specific to particular emotions. Moreover, it is assumed that these affect management skills play a central mediating role in accounting for the links between parent–child interaction and peer outcomes. Three aspects of this cluster of skills are examined. First, we examine evidence that indicates that successful peer adaptation requires the ability to recognize others' emotional expressions and produce clear and appropriate emotional displays (Beitel & Parke, 1986; Edwards, Manstead, & MacDonald, 1984; Field & Walden, 1982). Second, we present evidence that children's cognitive understanding of the causes and consequences of emotion is a further contributor to peer competence. Third, some (e.g., Parker & Gottman, 1989) have argued that the main task of the developmental period of early childhood (3 to 7 years of age) is to learn to manage emotional arousal in social interaction contexts. As we illustrate in the following, it is our contention that these emotional management skills are learned, in part, in the context of parent–child play. Figure 4.1 summarizes our model and the mediating role of these emotional management skills in linking the family and peer systems.

## Emotional Encoding and Decoding Skills

***Emotional Encoding and Decoding and Peer Acceptance.***   One set of skills relevant to successful peer interaction that may partly be acquired in the context of parent–child play, especially arousing physical play, is the ability to clearly encode emotional signals and to decode others' emotional signals. To determine the role that the ability to decode affect cues may play in mediating peer relationships, we (Beitel & Parke, 1985) asked 3- and 4-year-old children to correctly identify facial expressions depicting the following emotional states: happy, sad, scared, angry, and neutral. Consistent with prior work (Field & Walden, 1982) there were significant positive relations between emotional decoding ability and various measures of children's peer status.

Other recent evidence suggests that the detection of a relation between emotional recognition ability and peer acceptance may depend on the type of emotional stimuli used. In one study, (Denham, McKinley, Couchoud, & Holt, 1990), the investigators found no link between chil-

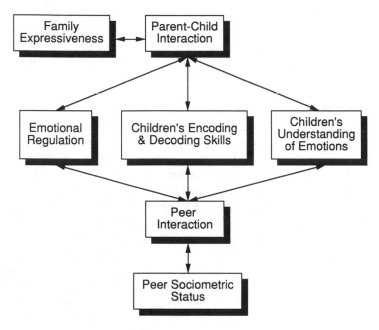

FIG. 4.1.  Parent–child interaction and peer sociometric status: emotional mediators.

dren's ability to identify prototypical expressions of happy, sad, angry, afraid, and peer relations. Combined with the modest relations found in earlier studies, it suggests that simply the ability to identify emotions may be important, but the use of prototypical stimuli of emotional expressions may produce ceiling effects that, in turn, may obscure the potential relationships. A better strategy may be to use a range of stimuli ranging from prototypic to poorer examples of the particular emotion. Children who can identify subtle versions of the emotion may in fact be the more competent and hence be more highly accepted. In support of this argument, Dodge (1986) has shown that aggressive children show a hostile attribution bias only in response to an ambiguous provocation situation. By following a similar strategy in the emotional recognition research, clearer progress may be evident.

This evidence suggests that one component of peer acceptance may be a child's ability to correctly identify the emotional states of other children. It is assumed that this emotional identification skill would permit a child to more adequately regulate social interactions with other children; in turn, this could contribute to greater acceptance by peers. Carson, Burks, and Parke (1987) extended earlier work by examining how sociometric status is related to emotional production and recognition skills within the family. In Carson et al.'s paradigm, parents and children were asked to identify each other's facial expressions (happy, sad, mad, scared, surprised, neutral, and disgusted). There were no sociometric status-related differences in parents' ability to recognize the faces of their children or in children's abilities to recognize their parents' faces. This suggests that within the family, children and parents, regardless of sociometric status, can recognize each other's facial expressions.

However, emotional expressions exchanged within the family might not be clear to individuals outside of the family. Some families may utilize idiosyncratic affect cues that are not recognizable in interactions outside of the family. Their communications may reflect a "familycentric" bias. In support of this possibility, we found that there was a significant sociometric status difference in undergraduates' ability to accurately decode the children's facial expressions. The undergraduates were better able to recognize the facial expressions of the popular children than those of the rejected children. There were no status differences in the recognition of the facial expressions of parents. This suggests that the emotional production skills of popular children are greater than those of rejected children, because rejected children's facial expressions are not as well-recognized outside the family. Other evidence suggests that emotional encoding is linked with children's social status as well. Buck (1975), for instance, has found positive relations between children's ability to encode emotional expressions and children's popularity with peers.

These studies provide support for the links between children's emotional encoding and decoding skills and children's sociometric status. Next, the question of the role of parent–child play in the development of emotional encoding and decoding skills is considered.

***Emotional Encoding and Decoding and Parent–Child Interaction.***    The aim of this phase of our project was to assess the relations between affect decoding ability and parent–child interaction. Support for these links comes from another recent study (Muth, Burks, Carson, & Parke, 1988). Using the same facial production game described earlier, 4- and 5-year-old popular and rejected children were asked to identify facial expressions of different emotions produced by their mothers and fathers. In support of the expected link between parent–child and decoding ability, we found positive relations between the length of the parent–child play bouts and the child's ability to correctly identify both maternal and paternal emotional expressions.

To evaluate the relations between parent–child play and encoding ability, undergraduate recognition of children's emotional productions was correlated with the length of parent–child play bouts (see Burks et al., 1987). Children who had longer play bouts produced expressions that were more easily identified by undergraduate raters. These data support the link between parent–child play engagement (as assessed by the length of the play bouts) and children's ability to accurately produce emotional expressions.

***Emotional Encoding and Decoding: Evidence from Abusive Families.*** Research on abusive families provide further support for the importance of emotional encoding and decoding in accounting for variations in peer competence. Camras and her colleagues (Camras, Grow, & Ribordy, 1983; Camras et al., 1988) found that abused children perform more poorly on affect identification tasks (Camras et al., 1988) and also produce less-clear facial expressions than control children (Camras et al., 1988). The potential influence of parents in accounting for these child deficits in encoding and decoding skills is further supported by the finding of a positive relationship between children's ability to identify facial expressions and mothers' ability to pose facial expressions (Camras et al., 1988).

Moreover, there is evidence of parental deficiencies in both emotional encoding and decoding skills among abusive parents. When abusive mothers and control mothers were shown slides of babies producing pain, surprise, joy, interest, fear, and anger expressions, Kropp and Haynes (1987) found that abusive mothers had fewer correct identifications overall and were more likely to identify negative emotional signals as positive. Other evidence (Camras et al., 1988) suggests that abusive mothers of preschoolers exhibited encoding deficits. Their facial expressions were less easily identified by objective observers than those of control mothers.

To complete our argument it is necessary to briefly examine differences in social competence between abusive and nonabusive children (see Cichetti et al., this volume). Several investigators have found marked differences in the social skills and peer acceptance of abused children in comparison to their nonabused counterparts. In general, abused children are rated by peers (Cichetti et al., this volume), teachers (Camras et al., 1983), and observers (Cichetti et al., this volume; George & Main, 1979; Main & George, 1985), as less socially competent than nonabused children.

A plausible interpretation of this pattern of findings would be that parental deficits in encoding and decoding skills, in turn, promote similar deficiencies among their children. One consequence of these skill deficits may be an inability to function as well in social interactions with peers.

***Beyond Static Models: The Need for a Dynamic Interactive Approach.*** Together, these findings provide support for the importance of parent–child play as a potential context for either learning and/or for refining and rehearsing emotional encoding and decoding skills—a set

of skills that, in turn, appears to play a role in the successful management of peer social relationships. Our hypothesis is not a static one, but
a dynamic one, and a more adequate test involves an examination of the
extent to which the child is able to adequately decode emotional signals
of an interactive partner. Establishment of covariation among these factors represents only one further step in the evaluation of this hypothesis. Our assumption is that the ability may be acquired in the context of
parent–child play interaction, especially father–child interaction, which
in turn may generalize to other social encounters including peer–peer
exchanges. This requires further analysis of the interactive exchanges between parents and children during play, with specific attention to the
extent to which children recognize and respond appropriately to the emotional signals of the parent-play partner. Similarly, children's ability to
utilize emotional signals to regulate social interaction can be assessed by
examining the degree to which parents recognize and respond to their
children's emotional cues during the course of play interaction.

## Emotional Understanding

In order to develop a more comprehensive model of the role of affect
in the emergence of peer competence, we have recently examined other
aspects of this issue. Successful peer interaction requires not only the ability to recognize and produce emotions, but (also) requires a social understanding of the cause of emotions, of the meaning of emotions, of the
responses appropriate to others' emotional displays, and of one's own
emotion-related experiences. Recently, Cassidy and Parke (1991) evaluated this hypothesized role of emotional understanding in a study of 5-
and 6-year-old children. Based on interviews with the children about their
understanding of emotions, they found that greater peer acceptance was
associated with greater ability to identify emotions, greater acknowledgment of experiencing emotion, greater ability to describe appropriate
causes of emotions, greater understanding that at least in some circumstances expression is acceptable, and greater expectations that they and
their parents would respond appropriately to the display of emotions.
The composite variable tapping understanding of emotions across domains was also significantly correlated with peer acceptance. Children's
emotional understanding also was correlated significantly with peer and
teacher behavior measures. Total understanding was negatively correlated
with peer reports of shyness, and positively correlated with both peer
and teacher reports of prosocial behavior, respectively. Notably, children's emotional understanding was not correlated with ratings of aggression.

Similar evidence was recently reported (Denham et al., 1990). These investigators examined the relations between children's knowledge of emotional situations and peer assessments of likability. To assess this aspect of emotional understanding, 3- to 4-year-old children were presented with a series of vignettes and asked to indicate their understanding of the type of emotion that the situation would elicit by affixing one of four emotions to a puppet's face. Emotional situational knowledge was related to peer likability scores. Moreover, understanding of anger and fear situations were each related to likability, while confusing sad and happy to a lesser extent anger from happy and/or sadness was negatively related to likability. "Such errors could make interaction difficult and for that reason lead to peers' dislike" (Denham et al., 1990, p. 1150). Gnepp, McKee, and Domanic (1987) found a relation between sociometric status and the ability to make personal inferences among 8-year-old children. Children who are better able to understand other people's appraisals of emotional situations are more highly accepted by their peers. Perhaps, "an understanding of other people's appraisals makes one more desirable as a friend" (Gnepp et al., 1987, p. 286). These findings are consistent with other research that suggests connections between other components of social understanding and peer relations (Asher & Renshaw, 1981; Dodge, Pettit, McClaskey, & Brown, 1986; Hart et al., 1990).

***Relations Among Familial Factors, Emotional Understanding, and Peer Competence.***    Evidence that provides a direct assessment of the relationships between parent–child interaction, emotional understanding, and peer competence is not available. However, recent work by Cassidy, Parke, Butovsky and Braungart (in press) suggests that children's emotional understanding may influence the link between family and peer systems. This would be consistent with the evidence provided for emotional decoding and encoding as possible mediating processes.

In support of this argument, Cassidy et al. (in press) recently examined the relationships among parental expressiveness, children's understanding of emotion, and children's peer acceptance. In this case, no direct measure of parent–child interaction was available and, instead, parental expressiveness was used as the family-based variable in this study. Parental expressiveness was assessed in two ways. First, Halberstadt's (1986) Family Expressiveness Questionnaire (described earlier) was used to tap parental emotional expressiveness in the home. A second measure of parental expressiveness was based on observations of parental emotion elicited while their children played a laboratory game. The game "Beat the Buzzer" involved tossing rings on a peg before the buzzer sounded. The buzzer was timed so that all children won half of the trials and failed half the trials. This structure provided an opportunity to observe parental positive (e.g., happiness, joy, excitement) and negative (e.g., sadness, disappointment) emotions. Understanding of emotions was tapped with a composite measure, described earlier, involving identification of the emotion, acknowledgment of experiencing the emotion, provision of scenarios for appropriate circumstances under which the emotion might be elicited, comfort in expression of emotions, and expectations of appropriate responses to others' expression of emotions.

Different patterns of results emerged for mothers and for fathers. For mothers, there was a significant relationship between self-reported expressiveness in the home and children's peer acceptance. Further analyses revealed that this relation was influenced by children's emotional understanding. For instance, a child with low family expressiveness might have better peer relations than would otherwise be expected due to relatively greater understanding of emotions. For fathers, both self-reports of paternal expressiveness in the home as well as observed expressiveness during game play in the laboratory predicted children's peer acceptance. In both cases, more expressive fathers had children who were more accepted by their peers. In addition, emotional understanding influenced the association between paternal expressiveness during the game and children's peer acceptance. However, in contrast to the maternal model, children's understanding of emotions did not influence the connection between fathers' expressiveness in the home and peer acceptance. Perhaps these reflect differences in the contexts and styles of interaction between mothers and fathers. Fathers are more likely to engage in playful interactions with their children and therefore the laboratory game context may have better reflected the types of settings in which fathers are both emotionally expressive and, in turn, provide their children opportunities to understand their own emotional displays. Mothers, on the other hand, engage their children in a wider range of contexts in the home and the home-based measure may have better captured their influence than the more restricted game setting in the lab. These findings underscore the importance of examining a range of contexts for assessing the impact of parent–child interaction on peer relationships.

The important implication of this study is the support that it provides for the role of emotional understanding as an influence on the link between family and peer systems. The overall pattern is consistent with earlier findings concerning the mediating roles that emotional decoding and encoding are assumed to play as well. More detailed measures of parent–child interaction in home and lab would be helpful in order to determine the ways by which children argue emotional understanding in family contexts. It will also be important for later research to begin to articulate the relative importance of these various processes (e.g., encoding, decoding, emotional understanding) in mediating between family and peer contexts, as well as the degree of interrelationship among these measures.

In summary, these studies suggest that various aspects of emotional development—encoding, decoding, and cognitive understanding—play an important role in accounting for variations in peer competence. Our argument is that these aspects of emotion may be learned in the context of family interaction and serve as mediators between the family and peer systems. Accumulating support for this view suggests that this is a promising direction for future research.

## Regulation of Affect

Children need not only learn to encode, decode, and gain a social understanding of emotions, but they need to learn to regulate their emotions as well. A number of theorists (Kopp, 1989; Maccoby, 1980) have suggested that the ability to regulate both emotional experience and expression is an important developmental task especially for infants and young children (Gottman & Fainsilber-Katz, 1989; Parker & Gottman, 1989; Sroufe, Schork, Motti, Lawroski, & LaFreniere, 1984; Stern, 1977, 1985). Recently, Fainsilber-Katz and Gottman (in press) argued for the importance of emotional regulation for children's social development as follows:

> We believe that when a child is flooded (Ekman, 1984) by affect and is unable to regulate his or her emotions, the flooded affect is disorganizing to the child in terms of disrupting the child's ability to focus attention and to become organized for coordinated action in the service of an objective. The resulting deficits in attention processes and the disorganization of goal-related activity in the child who cannot regulate his or her emotions may be an important step in the development of more severe behavior problems. (p. 15–16)

In support of their claim, Fainsilber-Katz & Gottman (in press) presented some preliminary data that is consistent with this general theoretical stance. Specifically, these investigators found that children who showed a great deal of anger during parent–child interaction also had low vagal tone. Prior work (Porges, McCabe, & Yongue, 1982) suggests that a low score in this psychophysiological index is associated with difficulties in focusing attention and coordinating actions. As Fainsilber-Katz and Gottman note, "these same children may not be able to regulate strong affect when it arises, leaving them victims of their own emotional worlds" (p. 22). The higher levels of aggression (Coie, 1990; Pelligrini, 1990) that are characteristic of a subset of sociometrically rejected children may in part be due to their inability to regulate negative affect states. Further support for this view comes from Pelligrini (1990), who found that peer rough-and-tumble play among popular and rejected children led to different outcomes. In the case of popular children, peer rough-and-tumble play led to games with rules and very seldom resulted in aggression, whereas in the case of rejected children, this type of play led to aggression nearly 30% of the time.

How do families contribute to emotional regulation? It is our view that the ability to regulate affect may be learned during parent–child play. This assumption has led us to focus our studies largely on parent–child physical play, because this type of play involves the regulation of affectively arousing stimulation. Parent–child physical play requires complex and subtle ability on the part of the parent to help keep stimulation within an optimal range. Overstimulation of the child by the parent and approach–withdrawal behaviors on the part of the child are common, and both parent and child may be seen as regulating the child's affect displays during these bouts.

MacDonald (1987) has evaluated directly the ways in which these arousal regulatory strategies are utilized by parents of children of different sociometric statuses during parent–child play. As in our other studies, participants were 3- to 5-year-old children, but in this investigation only boys were included. Children were selected on the basis of their sociometric status using the Coie, Dodge, and Coppotelli (1982) method with 12 rejected, 12 popular, and in this case, 12 neglected children were included as well. Twenty-minute videotaped observations of parent–child interaction were made in the home (10 minutes of free play and 10 minutes of physical play). Mother–son and father–son sessions were conducted on separate home visits. Results consistent with previous work (Burks et al., 1987; MacDonald & Parke, 1984; Putallaz, 1987) emerged: popular children engaged in higher levels of physical play and expressed more positive affect than rejected children, especially during the physical play sessions. Moreover, parents tend to be more directive with rejected children.

Despite the indication that popular children engage in more physical play and show more positive affect than rejected children, the data indicated that the play sessions of rejected children were characterized by more overstimulation and avoidance of stimulation than was the case with popular children and their parents. The interactions of the rejected children were characterized by alternatively approaching the source of stimulation and then withdrawing from stimulation. Moreover, the rejected children were characterized by higher levels of overstimulation (i.e., child became overaroused during physical play and screamed or showed a negative affective response to stimulation). Findings that the rejected children were characterized by higher levels of overstimulation than popular children and that stimulation often coincided with expressions of overstimulation on the part of the child, suggest that withdrawal from stimulation was motivated by the child being overstimulated. This, in turn, may account for the reduced amount of positive affect in the sessions of the rejected children in comparison to their popular counterparts. These findings underscore the regulation of affectively arousing stimulation as an important social process.

The differences that were found in the regulation of arousal in the dyads of parents with popular and rejected children may, in fact, be evident in peer–peer interactions as well. If this hypothesis is correct, deficits in arousal-regulating ability may be another factor associated with the lowered acceptance of rejected children. Although the current work cannot confirm that this skill is learned in parent–child interactive contexts, it is a viable possibility and provides a further clue concerning potential ways that parents may contribute to children's differing social competence with their peers.

Further evidence suggests that marital quality may affect parent–child interaction patterns that, in turn, are related to poor emotion regulation among children. In their work, Fainsilber-Katz and Gottman (in press) found that in families in which wives were withdrawn during marital interaction, both parents were negative listeners (i.e., they made negative facial expressions, or withdrew from interactions) during parent–child interaction. In turn, this pattern of parent–child interaction was associated with anger and low vagal tone in 5-year-old children—a pattern that may bode poorly for later peer interactions. Together, these findings underscore the role of emotional regulation as a potential mediator between family and peer contexts.

## UNRESOLVED ISSUES AND FUTURE DIRECTIONS

As this chapter has indicated, family and peer systems are related in a variety of ways, but a wide range of issues remain to be addressed in future studies.

First, our focus in this chapter has been on the role of emotional processes, such as encoding, decoding, understanding, and regulation as mediators between family and peer systems. This emphasis on emotional processes is, in part, a corrective to earlier cognitive accounts of parent–peer relationships (Pettit, Dodge, & Brown, 1988) and peer relationships (Dodge et al., 1986). It is clear that both cognitive and emotional processes play important and overlapping roles in accounting for the relationships between family and peer systems. (See Dodge, 1991, for a useful discussion of the relationship between emotion and cognition.) One of the challenges for future research is to explore the mutual influences of cognitive and emotional processes in this domain.

Second, a variety of other affect management strategies need to be examined, especially the role of children's knowledge of and ability to utilize cultural display rules governing the expression of emotion (Ekman & Friesen, 1975). Although evidence is accumulating concerning developmental shifts in children's understanding of these rules (Saarni, 1988; Saarni & Crowley, 1990), less is known about the socialization of these rules through parent–child interaction. Even less is known about ways in which display rules might differ between family and peer systems and how children acquire and cope with these differences. Consider, for example, the display of anger in the family and peer contexts. Directing intense anger displays at parents is likely to be considered very inappropriate in nearly all situations, whereas intense anger displays directed at peers may, under some circumstances, be considered appropriate and may actually be valued in some groups.

Third, it is important to consider these affect management strategies in combination rather than singly in future studies. In fact, there may be individual differences across children in the particular strategies that they employ to manage emotion-laden social encounters in both family and peer settings. By greater utilization of a multimeasure approach in which a range of management strategies are assessed in a single study for the same subjects, both of these limitations of prior research could be, in part, overcome.

Fourth, the issue of direction of effects remains unresolved. It is implicitly assumed in our studies that the direction of influence can plausibly flow from the family to the peer group. Whereas this assumption is valid in the experimental studies of parental management (e.g., Bhavnagri & Parke, 1991), it is not clear that this assumption holds under naturalistic nonexperimental conditions. Perhaps, incompetent children elicit more parental managerial intervention—a prediction that finds some support from a recent study by Ladd and Golter (1988). Moreover, our correlational studies of parent–child interaction must clearly be interpreted with even greater caution in terms of the directionality issue. It is reasonable to assume that socially skilled children, in turn, elicit more sustained and appropriate forms of social play interaction from their parents. A variety of strategies could be employed to examine the directionality issue. One strategy involves the assessment of shifts in parental interactive strategies or parental management techniques across different children of varying social skill. Changes in parental behavior would support the active role of the child in shaping the nature of parental input and more clearly establish the plausibility of a model in which the direction of effect flowed from child to parent. Similarly, the monitoring of shifts in child behavior as a function of the social skill of the adult interactive partner would underscore the plausibility of a model in which the direction of influence flowed from parent to child. These nonexperimental strategies that capitalize on known social skill capabilities of children and adults could be complemented by experimental approaches as well, in which either adult or child behavior is systematically modified through training or instruction to assess the impact on the partner's behavior. These strategies alone are not sufficient to attribute causality; they will indicate the plausibility of alternative models, but not the necessary conditions for the acquisition and maintenance of peer social skills under naturalistic conditions. To achieve this goal, longitudinal studies of the emergence of both social systems—families and peers—are necessary.

Fifth, a developmental analysis of these issues is clearly needed. As other research suggests (Grotevant & Cooper, 1986; Krappman, 1989), the direction of influence between parent and child is not balanced across development, as issues of autonomy become of more central importance to the child and adolescent. Even fundamental descriptive data concerning the ways in which different interactive strategies or managerial processes shift across development are lacking at this point. More importantly, the ways in which the family strategies relate to peer relational competence at different points in the child's development merit investigation.

Sixth, do the nature of the mediating processes change across development as well? Perhaps the regulation of emotional arousal is more critical for infants and young children (Kopp, 1989), and more cognitively based processes, such as emotional understanding, play a more central role later in development.

Seventh, a major concern is our limited understanding of the generalizability of the processes that have been discussed. This issue takes a variety of forms. For example, do variations in family structure impact on children's peer relationships? Although we have made significant progress in tracking single-parent versus two-parent families (Hetherington, 1989), the range of family forms and their impact is only beginning to be appreciated. In recent years, sociologists and epidemiologists have made us increasingly aware of the variety of family forms and household arrangements that exist in our own society (Cherlin, 1981). Even less is known about how variations in ethnicity, race, and class impact on how families orient their children for peer–peer interactions. Consider the pioneering work of Madsen (e.g., Madsen & Shapira, 1970) on how cooperative and competitive attitudes vary among Anglo- and Mexican-American families. Mexican-American children were found to be more cooperative than their more competition-oriented Anglo peers. What implications do Asian-American family values of self-control in matters of emotional expression, aggression, and self-assertion (Suzuki, 1980) have for peer relationships?

These variations across ethnic lines represent important opportunities, not only to explore the universality of processes and mechanisms of family–peer linkages, but they (also) provide naturally-occurring variations in the relative salience of certain key determinants such as interactive style or emotional expressiveness. As we become aware of our cultural diversity, it becomes important that we begin to make a serious commitment to an exploration of this diversity, both theoretically and through systematic empirical inquiry. The search for a balance between processes that are universal and processes that are unique to particular cultural, racial, or ethnic groups represents one of our greatest challenges for the future.

Eighth, just as we cannot restrict ourselves to one type of family, we should not restrict ourselves to a description of only one type of peer relationship. We have focused on children's degree of acceptance by their peers as assessed by sociometric indices. However, family processes may not affect all aspects of children's peer relationships in the same way. In addition to individual measures, dyadic and group levels of analysis merit consideration as well. Dyadic relationships include friendships, work, or play partners. Groups vary in terms of their size, goals, activities, and organization, and children's behavior in group settings may be affected by different sets of familial factors, rather than by individual or dyadic aspects. To date, we know little about the familial antecedents of these different types of children's peer relationships.

Finally, as is clear from other chapters in this volume, parent–child interaction is only one avenue through which parents influence their children's peer relationships. Parents function both as coaches who directly teach social skills and as managers of opportunities for social contact with other children. We need to develop family profiles in recognition of the fact that different families may utilize different combinations of strategies. For example, do parents who are low in one domain (e.g., direct face-to-face interaction) compensate by increasing their investment in opportunities that they provide to their children for social interaction with other children? What are the implications for children's peer relationships of selecting different combinations? Perhaps a variety of combinations all yield different but still satisfactory outcomes as assessed by the social adaptation of their children. Development often follows multiple pathways to achieve similar goals.

In conclusion, we have illustrated some of the ways in which the family and peer systems are related. Together, the studies described here provide support for a contextual view of social relationships in which different social systems function in an interdependent fashion rather than as isolated and separate influences on the developing child. Future research needs to address the links between the family and other systems and institutions in order to determine the uniqueness or generality of the kinds of relationships established between the family and peer systems. By following this strategy, the groundwork for a more general theory of how families relate to other social systems will begin to emerge.

## ACKNOWLEDGMENT

Preparation of this chapter and the research reported here were supported in part by National Science Foundation Grant 8919391 to Ross D. Parke.

## REFERENCES

Asher, S. R., & Coie, J. D., (Eds.). (1990). *Peer rejection in childhood.* New York: Cambridge University Press.

Asher, S. R., & Renshaw, P. D. (1981). Children without friends: Social knowledge and social skill training. In S. R. Asher & J. M. Gottman (Eds.), *The development of children's friendships* (pp. 273–296). New York: Cambridge University Press.

Bandura, A., & Walters, R. H. (1959). *Adolescent aggression.* New York: Ronald Press.

Barth, J. (1988). *Transition to school.* Unpublished doctoral dissertation, University of Illinois at Urbana-Champaign.

Barth, J. M., & Parke, R. D. (in press). Parent–child relationship influences on children's transition to school. *Merrill Palmer Quarterly.*

Baumrind, D. (1973). The development of instrumental competence through socialization. In A. D. Pick (Ed.), *Minnesota symposia on child psychology* (Vol. 7). Minneapolis: University of Minnesota Press.

Beitel, A., & Parke, R. (1986). *Relationships between preschoolers' sociometric factors and emotional decoding ability.* Unpublished manuscript, University of Illinois, Urbana.

Bhavnagri, N., & Parke, R. D. (1991). Parents as direct facilitators of children's peer relationships: Effects of age of child and sex of parent. *Journal of Personal and Social Relationships, 8,* 541–549.

Boyum, L. (1991, April). *Family emotional expressiveness: A possible antecedent of children's social competence.* Poster presented at the Biennial Meeting for the Society for Research in Child Development, Seattle, WA.

Buck, R. (1975). Nonverbal communication of affect in children. *Journal of Personality and Social Psychology, 31,* 644–653.

Burks, V.M., Carson, J. L., & Parke, R. D. (1987). *Parent–child interactional styles of popular and rejected children.* Unpublished manuscript, University of Illinois, Urbana.

Campbell, S. B., Breaux, A. M., Ewing, L. J., & Szumoski, E. K. (1985). A 1-year follow-up study of parent-referred hyperactive preschool children. *Journal of the American Academy of Child and Adolescent Psychiatry, 23*(3), 243–249.

Camras, L. A., Grow, J. G., & Ribordy, S. C. (1983). Recognition of emotional expression by abused children. *Journal of Clinical Child Psychology, 12,* 325–328.

Camras, L. A., Ribordy, S., Hill, J., Martino, S., Spaccarelli, S., & Stefani, R. (1988). Recognition and posing of emotional expressions by abused children and their mothers. *Developmental Psychology, 24,* 776–781.

Carson, J. L. (April, 1991). *In search of mediating processes: Emotional cues as links between family and peer systems.* Poster presented at the Biennial Meeting for the Society for Research in Child Development, Seattle, WA.

Carson, J. L., Burks, V. M., & Parke, R. D. (1987). *Emotional encoding and decoding skills of parents and children of varying sociometric status.* Unpublished manuscript, University of Illinois, Urbana.

Cassidy, J., & Parke, R. D. (April, 1989). *Family expressiveness and children's social competence.* Symposium presented at the Biennial Meeting of the Society for Research in Child Development, Kansas City, MO.

Cassidy, J., & Parke, R. D. (April, 1991). *Children's emotional understanding and peer relations.* Symposium presented at the Biennial Meeting of the Society for Research in Child Development, Seattle, WA.

Cassidy, J., Parke, R. D., Butovsky, L., & Braungart, J. (in press). Family–peer connections: The roles of emotional expressiveness within the family and children's understanding of emotions. *Child Development.*

Cherlin, A. (1981). Trends in United States men's and women's sex-role attitudes—1972 to 1978. *American Sociological Review, 46,* 453–460.

Coie, J. (1990). Toward a theory of peer rejection. In S. Asher & J. Coie (Eds.), *Peer rejection in childhood* (pp. 365–401). New York: Cambridge University Press.

Coie, J. D., Dodge, K. A., & Coppotelli, H. (1982). Dimensions and types of social status: A cross-age perspective. *Developmental Psychology, 18,* 557–570.

Denham, S., McKinley, M., Couchoud, E. A., & Holt, R. (1990). Emotional and behavioral predictors of preschool peer ratings. *Child Development, 61,* 1145–1152.

Dodge, K. A. (1983). Behavioral antecedents of peer social status. *Child Development, 54,* 1386–1399.

Dodge, K. A. (1986). A social information-processing model of social competence in children. In M. Perlmutter (Ed.), *Minnesota symposia on child psychology* (Vol. 18, pp. 77–126). Minneapolis: University of Minnesota Press.

Dodge, K. A. (1991). Emotion and social information processing. In J. Garber & K. Dodge (Eds.), *Emotion regulation* (pp. 159–181). New York: Cambridge University Press.

Dodge, K. A., Pettit, G. S., McClaskey, C. L., & Brown, M. (1986). Social competence in children. *Monographs of the Society for Research in Child Development, 51*(2, Serial No. 213).

Edwards, R., Manstead, A. S. R., & MacDonald, C. J. (1984). The relationship between children's sociometric status and ability to recognize facial expressions of emotion. *European Journal of Social Psychology, 14,* 235–238.

Ekman, P. (1984). Expression and the nature of emotion. In K. P. Scherer & P. Ekman (Eds.), *Approaches to emotion* (pp. 1–17). Hillsdale, NJ: Lawrence Erlbaum Associates.

Ekman, P., & Friesen, W. V. (1975). *Unmasking the face.* Englewood Cliffs, NJ: Prentice-Hall.

Eron, L. D., Walder, L. O., & Lefkowitz, M. M. (1971). *Learning of aggression in children.* Boston: Little, Brown.

Fainsilber-Katz, L., & Gottman, J. M. (in press). Marital relationships and children's social-emotional adjustment. In R. Parke & S. Kellam (Eds.), *Exploring family relationships with other social contexts.* Hillsdale, NJ: Lawrence Erlbaum Associates.

Field, T. M., & Walden, T. A. (1982). Production and discrimination of facial expressions by preschool children. *Child Development, 53,* 1299–1311.

George, C., & Main, M. B. (1979). Social interactions of young abused children: Approach, avoidance, and aggression. *Child Development, 50,* 306–318.

Gnepp, J., McKee, E., & Domanic, J. A. (1987). Children's understanding of situational information to infer emotion: Understanding emotionally equivocal situations. *Developmental Psychology, 23,* 114–123.

Gottman, J. M., & Fainsilber-Katz, L. F. (1989). Effects of marital discord on young children's peer interaction and health. *Developmental Psychology, 25,* 373–381.

Grotevant, H. D., & Cooper, C. R. (1986). Individuation in family relationships: A perspective on individual differences in the development of identity and role-taking skills in adolescence. *Human Development, 29,* 82–100.

Grych, J. H., & Fincham, F. D. (1990). Marital conflict and children's adjustment: A cognitive–contextual framework. *Psychological Bulletin, 108,* 267–290.

Halberstadt, A. G. (1984). Family expression of emotion. In C. Z. Malatesta & C. E. Izard (Eds.), *Emotion in adult development* (pp. 235–252). Beverly Hills, CA: Sage.

Halberstadt, A. G. (1986). Family socialization of emotional expression and nonverbal communication styles and skills. *Journal of Personality and Social Psychology, 51,* 827–836.

Hart, C. H., Ladd, G. W., & Burleson, B. R. (1990). Children's expectations of the outcomes of social strategies: Relations with sociometric status and maternal disciplinary styles. *Child Development, 61,* 127–137.

Hartup, W. W. (1979). The social worlds of childhood. *American Psychologist, 34,* 944–950.

Hetherington, E. M. (1989). Coping with family transitions: Winners, losers and survivors. *Child Development, 60,* 1–14.

Hoffman, M. L. (1960). Power assertion by the parent and its impact on the child. *Child Development, 31,* 129–143.

Kopp, C. B. (1989). Regulation of distress and negative emotions: A developmental view. *Developmental Psychology, 25,* 343–354.

Krappman, L. (1989). Family relationships and peer relationships in middle childhood: An exploratory study of the associations between children's integration into the social network of peers and family development. In K. Kreppner & R. Lerner (Eds.), *Family systems and life-span development* (pp. 93–104). Hillsdale, NJ: Lawrence Erlbaum Associates.

Kropp, J. P., & Haynes, O. M. (1987). Abusive and nonabusive mothers' ability to identify general and specific emotion signals of infants. *Child Development, 58,* 187–190.

Ladd, G. W., & Golter, B. S. (1988). Parents' initiation and monitoring of children's peer contacts: Predictive of children's peer relations in nonschool and school settings? *Developmental Psychology, 24,* 109–117.

Lindahl, K. M. (April, 1991). *Negative affect regulation in premarital, marital, and parent–child interactions: A longitudinal view.* Poster presented at the Biennial Meeting for the Society for Research in Child Development, Seattle, WA.

Lindahl, K. M., & Markman, H. J. (1990). Communication and negative affect regulation in the family. In E. Blechman (Ed.), *Emotions and the family* (pp. 99–115). Hillsdale, NJ: Lawrence Erlbaum Associates.

Maccoby, E. E. (1980). *Social development: Psychological growth and the parent–child relationship.* New York: Harcourt Brace Jovanovich.

MacDonald, K. (1987). Parent–child physical play with rejected, neglected, and popular boys. *Developmental Psychology, 23,* 705–711.

MacDonald, K., & Parke, R. D. (1984). Bridging the gap: Parent–child play interaction and peer interactive competence. *Child Development, 55,* 1265–1277.

Madsen, M. S., & Shapira, A. (1970). Cooperative and competitive behavior of urban Afro-American, Anglo-American, Mexican-American, and Mexican village children. *Developmental Psychology, 3,* 16–20.

Main, M. B., & George, C. (1985). Responses of abused and disadvantaged toddlers to distress in agemates: A study in the day-care setting. *Developmental Psychology, 21,* 407–412.

Muth, S., Burks, V., Carson, J., & Parke, R. D. (1988). *Peer competence: Parent–child interaction and emotional communication skills.* Unpublished manuscript, University of Illinois at Champaign-Urbana.

Parke, R. D. (1978). Children's home environments: Social and cognitive effects. In I. Altman & J. F. Wohlwill (Eds.), *Children and the environment* (pp. 33–81). New York: Plenum.

Parke, R. D., & Bhavnagri, N. P. (1989). Parents as managers of children's peer relationships. In D. Belle (Ed.), *Children's social networks and social supports* (pp. 241–259). New York: Wiley.

Parke, R. D., MacDonald, K., Beitel, A., & Bhavnagri, N. (1988). The role of the family in the development of peer relationships. In R. Peters & R. J. McMahon (Eds.), *Social learning and systems approaches to marriage and the family* (pp. 17–44). New York: Brunner/Mazel.

Parke, R. D., MacDonald, K., Burks, V., Carson, J., Bhavnagri, N., Barth, J., & Beitel, A. (1989). Family and peer systems: In search of the linkages. In K. Kreppner & R. M. Lerner (Eds.), *Family systems and life–span development* (pp. 65–92). Hillsdale, NJ: Lawrence Erlbaum Associates.

Parker, J. G., & Gottman, J. M. (1989). Social and emotional development in a relational context: Friendship interaction from early childhood to adolescence. In T. Berndt & G. Ladd (Eds.), *Peer relationships in child development* (pp. 95–131). New York: Wiley.

Pelligrini, A. (1989). Elementary school children's rough and tumble play. *Early Childhood Research Quarterly, 4,* 245–260.

Pettit, G. S., Dodge, K. A., & Brown, M. M. (1988). Early family experience, social problem-solving patterns, and children's social competence. *Child Development, 59,* 107–120.

Porges, S. W., McCabe, P. M., & Yongue, B. G. (1982). Respiratory-heart rate interactions: Psychophysiological implications for pathophysiology and behavior. In J. Cacioppo & R. Petty (Eds.), *Perspectives in cardiovascular psychophysiology* (pp. 223–264). New York: Guilford Press.

Putallaz, M. (1987). Maternal behavior and sociometric status. *Child Development, 58,* 324–340.

Putallaz, M., & Heflin, A. H. (1990). Parent–child interaction. In S. R. Asher & J. Coie (Eds.), *Peer rejection in childhood* (pp. 189–216). New York: Cambridge University Press.

Roberts, W., & Strayer, J. (1987). Parents' responses to the emotional distress of their children: Relations with children's competence. *Developmental Psychology, 23,* 415–422.

Rubin, Z., & Sloman, J. (1984). How parents influence their children's friendships. In M. Lewis (Ed.), *Beyond the dyad.* New York: Plenum.

Saarni, C. (1988). Emotional competence: How emotions and relationships become integrated. In R. Thompson (Ed.), Sociometric development. *Nebraska Symposium on Motivation* (Vol. 36, 131–198). Lincoln, NE: University of Nebraska Press.

Saarni, C., & Crowley, M. (1990). The development of emotion regulation: Effects on emotional state and expression. In E. Blechman (Ed.), *Emotions and the family: For better or worse* (pp. 53–73). Hillsdale, NJ: Lawrence Erlbaum Associates.

Schaefer, E. S., Edgerton, M., & Aaronson, M. (1978). *Classroom behavior inventory.* Unpublished form, University of North Carolina at Chapel Hill.

Sroufe, L. A. (1979). The coherence of individual development: Early care, attachment, and subsequent developmental issues. *American Psychologist, 34,* 731–746.

Sroufe, L. A., & Fleeson, J. (1986). Attachment and the construction of relationships. In W. W. Hartup & Z. Rubin (Eds.), *Relationships and development* (pp. 51–72). Hillsdale, NJ: Lawrence Erlbaum Associates.

Sroufe, L. A., Schork, E., Motti, F., Lawroski, N., & LaFreniere, P. (1984). The role of affect in social competence. In C. Izard, J. Kagan, & R. Zajonc (Eds.), *Emotions, cognition and behavior.* New York: Cambridge University Press.

Stern, D. (1977). *The first relationship.* Cambridge, MA: Harvard University Press.

Stern, D. (1985). *The interpersonal world of the infant.* New York: Basic Books.

Suzuki, H. H. (1980). The Asian-American family. In M. Fantine & R. Cardenas (Eds.), *Parenting in a multicultural society.* New York: Congman.

Zahn-Waxler, C., Radke-Yarrow, M., & King, R. A. (1979). Child rearing and children's prosocial initiations toward victims of distress. *Child Development, 50,* 319–330.

# CHAPTER FIVE

# Links Between Adolescents' Relationships with Their Parents and Peers: Models, Evidence, and Mechanisms

Catherine R. Cooper
*University of California at Santa Cruz*

Robert G. Cooper, Jr.
*San Jose State University*

Two opposite views of adolescents' peer relationships recur in popular and scholarly writing. One holds that "peers are bad": they foster undesirable qualities—at least in the eyes of middle-class adults—such as aggression, early sexual involvement, and drug use. Evidence for this view can be found in reports that peers influence adolescents' decisions to begin drinking and offer the context, especially in the absence of parental supervision, for predelinquent or delinquent acts (Downs, 1985; Snyder, Dishion, & Patterson, 1986). The opposite view that "peers are good" stems from the work of Sullivan (1953) and Piaget (1932), who portrayed peer relationships as providing both the setting and the means for adolescents to develop a mature sense of self (Youniss & Smollar, 1985). These definitions of adolescents' relationships with peers as either threats or benefits have in turn framed the linkages between adolescents' families and peers as competitive, compensatory, or complementary.

In recent years, a burst of new work on adolescent development, marked by the founding of new scholarly journals and professional societies, has transformed these traditionally polarized views. Our chapter begins with an overview of three classic models of family–peer linkages in adolescence: psychoanalytic, socialization, and cognitive; then shows how recent conceptual and empirical work from each perspective has enriched our understanding of the mechanisms that account for these linkages. In this section we bring our own findings to bear on these issues. Finally, we conclude with an orientation to what we see as important directions for future work.

We argue that the benefits of peer relationships, perhaps more so in adolescence than earlier in development, are most accessible to those with family experiences that equip them to establish and maintain friendships. Such emotional, cognitive, and relational capacities involve self-esteem, perspective taking, and problem solving, as well as interpersonal skills of planning and conflict negotiation. Conversely, we argue that difficulties in adolescents' peer relationships can be traced to societal, family, and parental issues that funnel adolescents into contexts that at least appear to merit the "peers are bad" characterization.

## THREE EARLY MODELS OF FAMILY–PEER RELATIONS IN ADOLESCENCE

Until recently, three models have dominated discussions of the linkages between family and peer relationships in adolescence: psychoanalytic, socialization, and cognitive. The characterization of adolescents' development by each model has lent either a globally positive or negative cast to adolescent peer relationships and thus oriented how family experience is seen as affecting them.

### Psychoanalytic Models: Peers as Necessary Compensation for Parents

Psychoanalytic models portray maturity in terms of three concepts: conflict, emancipation, and autonomy. In classic writings (A. Freud, 1966), adolescence is a time of internal conflict between the dependency of childhood and the drive for autonomy, created when puberty triggers a regression of rational ego functions and a resurgence of childhood Oedipal feelings. Somewhat paradoxically, peer relationships are seen as offering a safe context for developing this autonomy and detachment from parents.

Here maturity is defined in terms of severing parent–adolescent ties. To resolve what Blos (1979) called the "second individuation" crisis (the first occurring in toddlerhood), adolescents need to move away from parents into peer relations, replacing parents as important objects. However, because parents are viewed as so important in psychoanalytic accounts of development, peers are seen as merely a reflection of the parent–child relationship (Youniss & Smollar, 1985).

Even so, because of the strength of these inner needs, psychoanalytic writers have considered adolescence to be the most intense period for the development of friendships, in which the:

> . . . adolescent does not choose friendship, but is driven into it . . . Erotic and aggressive drives toward family members become so intense that the

youngster must have a neutral arena in which to work them out; he [sic] is in the process of breaking (or recasting) his ties to the family and desperately needs the support, approval, and security, as well as the norms, of a peer group. He is discovering, and trying to interpret and control, a changed body, and with it, new and frightening impulses, and so requires both the example and communion of peers. He is about to crystallize an identity, and for this needs others of his generation to act as models, mirrors, helpers, testers, foils. (Douvan & Adelson, 1966, p. 197)

## Socialization Models:
## Peers as Competing with Parents

A more negative view of adolescent friendships emerges from sociological research on parent and peer reference groups. This view casts parents as the critical molders and guides of their children's development as they provide continuity in societal norms (Brittain, 1963; Kahn, 1989). Because the adolescent's task is seen as conforming to these parental models, peers become a source of cross-pressures between two mutually exclusive sets of values. Typical of this approach is a concern with peer conformity in a tug-of-war between the "two worlds of childhood" (Bronfenbrenner, 1970).

Early sociological accounts portrayed the adolescent as a member of this distinct and cohesive peer culture, ". . . 'cut off' from the rest of society, forced inward toward his own age group, made to carry out his whole social life with others his own age. With his fellows he comes to constitute a small society, one that has most of its important interactions within itself, and maintains only a few threads of connection with the outside adult society" (Coleman, 1961, p. 39). Norms of the peer culture are portrayed as framed in rebellion against adult values of self-restraint and achievement (Kahn, 1989).

One corollary of this model is that if adults do not know about, monitor, or restrain adolescents' activities, then adolescents will be drawn by default into an alien peer culture. A related view of peers and parents as mutually exclusive "worlds" underlies contentions that if children's behavioral styles with parents and peers differ, they constitute entirely different streams of socialization. For example, Maynard (1985) contended that because children argue so much more frequently with their peers than parents, they must learn to argue from peers.

## Cognitive Models:
## Peers as Unique and Complementary to Parents

In a positive vein, cognitive developmental theories have long held that peer relationships make unique contributions to development. For example, Piaget (1932) emphasized the distinctive rather than compensatory or competitive nature of children's experiences with peers vis-à-vis parents. He proposed that during their play with one another, children confront discrepancies from their own thinking and experience cognitive disequilibrium, which in turn stimulates further growth. Piaget saw peer interaction as optimal for development because children are less likely to accept one another's positions by virtue of their authority and thus more likely to integrate their perspectives through negotiation. Both Piaget (1932) and Sullivan (1953) viewed peer relationships as uniquely egalitarian in contrast to the more asymmetrical and unilateral authority of adults. This similarity in status provides unique advantages, described in cognitive terms by Piaget and in terms of intimacy for Sullivan (Youniss & Smollar, 1985).

## NEW MODELS OF FAMILY–PEER LINKAGES IN ADOLESCENCE

Although early psychoanalytic, socialization, and cognitive models of the linkages between adolescents' parent and peer relationships centered on compensation, competition, and structural differences, recent work has focused on patterns of continuity and mutual influence between them (Cooper & Ayers-Lopez, 1985). This reframing of basic questions has been stimulated by evidence that often contradicts or qualifies earlier theories (Kahn, 1989). Then too, enriched accounts of family, societal, and cultural contexts of socialization and cognitive developmental research have depicted family and peer relationships as well as the mechanisms of interconnectedness between them in more differentiated terms. We now consider how these traditional perspectives on family–peer linkages have each been enriched by recent research.

### New Perspectives on Relationships

Recent findings shed doubt on the emphasis by early psychoanalytic and socialization theories on the "two worlds" model that framed parent–adolescent relationships as inherently conflictual. Cross-national studies have revealed that adolescents largely agree with parents about life goals concerning education and work as well as moral values and standards (Kandel & Lesser, 1982). In contrast with "storm and stress" accounts based on clinical interviews, observational and self-report studies of normal adolescents and their families in the United States have shown that overt conflicts are in fact quite infrequent and typically involve, in Hill's apt terms, "garbage and galoshes," or mundane matters (Hill & Holmbeck, 1986). The significance of such matters may vary as a function of the beholder (Smetana, 1988), as conflicts that seem mundane to parents may signify "jurisdictional" issues of great salience to adolescents. Finally, current work distinguishes between functional and dysfunctional family conflicts, depending on whether conflict occurs in the context of family cohesion and mutual respect (Cooper, 1988).

***Adolescents' Relationships with Parents: Emancipation Versus Mutuality.*** Some scholars still gauge adolescents' development in terms of separation and autonomy, and argue that "detachment" best describes adolescents' goals to "stamp out" their parents' influence on them (Schafer, 1973). But other neopsychoanalytic scholars see adolescents as neither abandoning nor disowning their parents as they mature. Rather, they find a *rapprochement* by gaining confidence in their individuality in the context of parental support (White, Speisman, & Costos, 1983). As one young woman put it, "Rather than having to leave, you can stay, be different, and still be loved" (Josselson, 1987, p. 20). Another 18-year-old reflected, "I am not afraid to do something against (my father's) will, . . . (but) I talk to him more" (Youniss & Smollar, 1985, p. 162). As parents grant more freedom in recognition of their adolescents' growing abilities, adolescents show more individuality while still seeking their parents' advice. A critical impetus for this continuing cohesion is that adolescents feel greater needs for parental guidance as they near adulthood.

Behavioral evidence for this increasing autonomy in the context of cohesion is illustrated by an observational study of negotiation patterns of families with sixth- and twelfth-grade adolescents (Cooper & Carlson, 1990; Cooper et al., 1990). Parents of younger adolescents were more likely to prompt their children's suggestions, whereas older adolescents expressed their ideas more often without prompting. In turn, older adolescents elicited their parents' suggestions and provided compromises during disagreements; thus, older adolescents were more able to express individuality while also providing connectedness. Such behavioral evidence indicates that the rapprochement of later adolescence is achieved through adolescents as well as parents contributing both autonomy and closeness.

***Adolescents' Friendships: Potential and Risk.*** Close friendships offer benefits that differ from those of popularity within the larger peer group (Berndt & Ladd, 1989). From early childhood to adulthood, friends can share the gratifications of play, but by middle childhood, friends can also provide emotional reassurance in the face of stresses at home and school, cognitively rich explanations of social and physical problems, and a place to learn to express and resolve conflicts (Nelson & Aboud, 1985).

By adolescence, new cognitive and emotional abilities allow adolescents the tolerance to relish friends who differ from them, in contrast to the more rigid categorical bases of acceptance and rejection in middle childhood that are often marked by sexist and racist tones. Adolescents view friendships as embodying more flexible principles of fairness through negotiation than they did in middle childhood, when simple reciprocation of positive, negative, or neutral actions is more typical (Youniss & Smollar, 1985). Adolescent friendships can also offer safe settings for candid exploration of identity and intimacy issues, often through gossip and sharing secrets (Fine, 1986; Gottman & Parker, 1986). These new capacities are first more typical in same-gender friendships but become evident in opposite-gender friendships by tenth grade (Sharabany, Gershoni, & Hoffman, 1981). From a study of adolescents' reports of their activities and moods with families and peers, Csikszentmihalyi and Larson (1984) concluded that "time with friends is the best part of adolescents' daily lives . . . for boys and girls, upper-middle-class and lower-middle-class adolescents . . . friends are a context of leisure and talk, enjoyment and freedom" (p. 159–160).

Despite this rosy picture of the potential benefits of friendships, many adolescents do not have close friends. They do not have relationships that offer an "arena of comfort" in the face of the multiple stresses of pubertal development, school transition, and family breakup or relocation (Simmons & Blyth, 1987), perhaps because they lack the skills to initiate and maintain them (Cooper & Ayers-Lopez, 1985). Then too, adolescents' time with friends is not always beneficial, and can stimulate escalating patterns of rowdiness. As Csikszentmihalyi and Larson (1984) noted, such

> . . . normless behavior sometimes resulting from peer interactions reflects a lack of skills, an inability to deal with its openness . . . Teens who cannot enjoy playing basketball turn to breaking windows; teens who can't cope with losses turn to cocaine; teens who have nothing to say to a friend turn to more risky sexual involvement. The skills of friendship require more than the courage to provide the group with deviation-limiting negative feedback; they are skills of mutually defining a set of boundaries, staying within them—and simultaneously having a good time. (p. 175)

In summary, friendships offer the potential benefits of support, exploration of identity and intimacy, and alternative modes for expressing emotions and resolving conflicts, but the risks of poor peer relationships range from missing these benefits to participating in deviation-amplifying interactions. We now examine the pathways by which adolescents move into peer relationships that offer these advantages or risks.

*Family–Peer Linkages: Continuity Versus Compensation.*
Links between family and peer relations are typically construed in two
ways. *Continuity* models, including attachment, object relations, and social learning approaches, argue that family patterns are re-enacted in peer
relationships, whereas *compensatory* models hold that if family relationships are inadequate, adolescents can find with peers the experiences they
need for psychosocial well-being (Berndt & Ladd, 1989). Most evidence
bearing on these issues is based on adolescents' own accounts of both
relationships. Typical findings are that adolescents who describe themselves as securely attached to their parents also view their relationships
with peers as trusting (Armsden & Greenberg, 1982), or that adolescent
girls who see their families as highly cohesive also report having more
mutually-chosen girlfriends (Bell, Cornwell, & Bell, 1988).

*Linkages between Negotiation Skills in Family and Peer Rela-
tionships.* Over the last decade, we have conducted a series of studies
concerning the development of peer relational competence from early
childhood to adolescence, using methodologies ranging from naturalistic observations of spontaneous behavior in classrooms to structured observations, training studies, and self-reports from children, parents, and
teachers (e.g., Cooper, 1980; Cooper, Ayers-Lopez, & Marquis, 1982;
Cooper & Cooper, 1984; Cooper, Marquis, & Edward, 1986). A surprising finding of our work on peer learning was that even in schools dedicated to cooperative learning, children's access to the expertise and help
of peers depended on their discourse and relational skills, especially those
involved in negotiation. Even with dedicated teachers, many children
failed to access these benefits. From this work, we turned our attention
to tracing possible family origins of these dramatic and consequential
differences in children and adolescents' peer competence.

In this chapter, we describe two studies linking family experience to
adolescents' peer relational competence (Cooper & Carlson, 1989; Cooper, Grotevant, & Ayers-Lopez, 1992). This program of research has focused on the interplay between *individuality and connectedness* in the
ongoing mutual regulation involved in relationships (Cooper, Grotevant,
& Condon, 1983; Grotevant & Cooper, 1986). At the core of our model
is the proposition that central to all relationships is the transactive interplay of individuality and connectedness, which functions as an important mechanism for both individual and relational development.
Individuality refers to processes that reflect the distinctiveness of the self;
in language, it is seen in self-assertions and disagreements with others.
Connectedness involves processes that link the self to others, seen in expressions of acknowledgment, respect for, and responsiveness to others.
A second proposition is that children's and adolescents' experiences in

family relationships regarding the interplay of individuality and connectedness affect attitudes, expectations, and skills in self and relational functioning within and beyond the family. This model differs from accounts of parent–adolescent relationships, which are framed in terms of unilateral constructs such as dominance and control, which consider conflict as inherently negative, and which cast maturity in terms of adolescents' separation, autonomy, and distance.

We have pursued these questions with early adolescents in sixth grade and with high school seniors. Individuality and connectedness are assessed in face-to-face interaction so that we can observe these transactive processes in real time. Adolescents and their families are observed in their home in a task designed to enhance family members' potential for exhibiting both individuality and connectedness by asking them to plan the day-by-day itinerary of a fictitious vacation, given two weeks and unlimited funds. This task allows but does not, of course, ensure them the chance to express and coordinate their points of view, and creates a high density of negotiations in a short period of time. The interactions are audiotaped, transcribed, and coded for expressions of individuality, including self-assertions and disagreements, as well as connectedness, including agreements, acknowledgments, and compromise (Condon, Cooper, & Grotevant, 1984).

Our work with high school seniors (Cooper, Grotevant, & Ayers-Lopez, 1992) traced carryover from family to peer interaction at individual and relational levels of analysis. We found consistency in adolescents' individuality across the two settings, as well as links from family patterns of parental connectedness and adolescent individuality to adolescents' peer negotiation patterns.

In a subsequent study of younger adolescents (Cooper & Carlson, 1989), we examined links between family and peer negotiation patterns in early adolescence. We were interested first in how *average* patterns of expressing individuality and connectedness that adolescents experience in their families would compare with their negotiations with close friends, and second, whether *individual differences* in adolescents' peer negotiations could be predicted by family patterns. According to the individuality and connectedness model, the average patterns of negotiation in family and peer relationships might differ, but individual differences in peer friendships should be predicted from family patterns. Besides participating in the family interaction task at home with their parents, each adolescent and his or her closest friend of the same gender also participated at their school in an analogous task in which they planned a weekend together given unlimited funds and parental permission. Transcripts from both tasks were coded in terms of utterances operationalizing individuality and connectedness.

Two key findings were evident. First, on the average, adolescents' negotiations with their friends were markedly more contentious than with their parents. Both boys and girls expressed more disagreements with friends and more connectedness with their parents (based on proportional analyses). In both family and peer negotiations, boys expressed more disagreements than girls, and girls more connectedness than boys. These findings are consistent with Piaget's views that egalitarian peer relationships allow conflict to be more freely expressed than within more asymmetrical parental relationships (Youniss & Smollar, 1985).

Despite these average differences between family and peer negotiation patterns, can individual differences in adolescents' negotiations with their friends be predicted by family patterns? Our data provide support for the continuity model. At the individual level, we found that adolescents who expressed more disagreements and assertions in family negotiations were more contentious with their friends. At the relational level, adolescents who coordinated their own views with those of their friends tended to experience distinctive patterns of family negotiation. These patterns were marked by collaborative strategies which were notable for their use of reasoning rather than unilateral conflict negotiation strategies. This parallels our earlier findings that such highly engaged negotiation styles, involving parental expressions of individuality as well as connectedness, typify families of high-self-esteem adolescents (Cooper & Carlson, 1989). It also highlights the significance of cognitive qualities of family relational experience for adolescents' competence with peers, a topic discussed later in this chapter.

The following examples contrast the family and peer negotiations of two early adolescent girls, both with high levels of verbal ability as measured by the WISC-R vocabulary subtest, but one scoring high and one low on Harter's (1985) measure of global self-esteem (Cooper & Carlson, 1988). The marked differences in the two families' responses to their daughters' expressions of individuality are paralleled in the daughters' interactions with their respective friends. The parents of a daughter with low perceived competence (whom we call Valerie) used questions to elicit suggestions from her, but phrased them in such a way as to constrain the ideas she could offer. When Valerie offered ideas different from those the father was pursuing, he ignored them:

**Valerie:** See, I haven't been to Italy and Scandinavia.

**Mother:** We've been a lot to Italy but I don't think you remember it.

**Valerie:** I want to go there again; we studied that . . . or in Greece or those two places 'cause we studied that, and I. . . .

**Father:** How about France? You could use your French.

**Valerie:** I don't have any French, Dad . . . Yeah, let's go to all the Scandinavian countries that we missed, you know. What places did we miss?

**Mother:** There are a lot of them . . . O.K., give me some ideas.

**Father:** Let's fly . . . we'll fly in to Amsterdam. How's that?

Over the course of this discussion, Valerie spoke less and less frequently.

In planning a weekend with her closest friend, Valerie appeared to carry over her family patterns. She did not allow a single suggestion made by her friend to be incorporated into their plans:

**Friend:** No, let me see . . . oh, if they have a concert that night . . .

**Valerie:** Where would they have a concert? No, let's go watch a play.

**Friend:** Yeah, we'll watch a play at a theater.

**Valerie:** No, uh. . . .

**Friend:** At the theater we'll go watch a play and go have a gourmet dinner. And also on Saturday, we can go to see the Eiffel Tower.

**Valerie:** No, we'll do that Sunday.

A contrast is provided by the family dialogue of an adolescent with high self-esteem whom we call Anne:

**Father:** Well, you get in these rubber rafts and you go down the river starting at the far western end of the park and it takes you through all the canyons; there are several canyons in there. Remember that one canyon that we saw?

**Anne:** Yeah. Well, could we take like a shorter trip?

**Father:** Yeah, you can take shorter trips.

**Anne:** How long are those?

**Father:** I think they have just day trips . . . one-day trips. Would you like to do that?

**Anne:** Yeah, I guess.

**Father:** That might be best the first time. . . .

**Anne:** 'Cause I haven't ever been in a raft.

**Father:** Six days is a lot of time on the river.

**Anne:** Okay, five.

**Father:** Okay.

In this family, suggestions elicited from Anne were legitimized, and, moreover, when disagreement inevitably followed, Anne's father responded to the substance of her ideas. In contrast to the first example, over the course of this discussion Anne expressed both individuality (suggestions and disagreements) and connectedness with increasing frequency. In negotiating with her friend, Anne expressed her own views, supporting them when challenged, and was responsive to those of her friend. Their plans were developed collaboratively, with suggestions from each being incorporated into the final decisions:

**Anne:** I want a party; I really do. How about a slumber party on Saturday night?

**Friend:** What about Friday?

**Anne:** No, because that's when they are going to leave. We won't have much time to get it all set up. Like Saturday afternoon we could get all the stuff we're gonna set up for them and then Saturday night we could have the party.

**Friend:** (laughs) I think we should see a movie on Friday night.

**Anne:** Yeah!

**Friend:** And then on Saturday we plan the party or get everything set. . . .

**Anne:** Call everybody.

Thus, our findings replicate classic contrasts between adolescents' egalitarian interactions with friends and their more asymmetrical patterns with parents. But our findings also suggest that strengths in family relationships are associated with competence in friendships, and that key mediators include self-esteem and conflict resolution skills that are likely to play a central role in the maintenance of close peer relationships.

***Can Peer Experiences Compensate for Family Difficulties?*** Some writers have seen family conflict as driving adolescents to seek relief in harmonious peer experiences (Iacovetta, 1975), whereas others have viewed family conflict as augering difficulties with peers as well (Patterson, DeBaryshe, & Ramsey, 1989). In a study involving over 800 adolescents in ninth through twelfth grades, Kahn (1989) found both continuity and compensation—or at least attempts at it—between adolescents' perceptions of family and close same-sex friendships. First, adolescents who had friendships in which they could be supportive solved problems by negotiating compromises. Those who felt confident enough to take distinctive stances also saw their families as supporting them and encourag-

ing their independence, such as by allowing them a voice in family decision making. These findings are consistent with work of Josselson, Greenberger, and McConochie (1977) that found that adolescents whose families
supported their independence were more resistant to peer pressure for
conformity and more likely to explore issues of self-definition with
friends.

In potentially compensatory patterns, adolescents who saw their families as low in cohesion described themselves as involved in supportive
friendships. Compared with adolescents who felt that they provided more
or equal amounts of support as their friends, those who saw their friends
as providing more support than they did were more likely to view their
families as low in cohesion. Adolescents who saw their families as non-
cohesive also said they listened to their friends but would relinquish their
own views if friends held different opinions. Thus, adolescents may *seek*
compensation for difficulties with their families but not have the skills
to sustain the relationships in which it may be available.

The continuity/compensation issue was also investigated with regard
to school achievement by Steinberg and Brown (1989) with a sample of
ninth- through twelfth-grade adolescents who were heterogeneous with
regard to social class and ethnicity. Overall, findings indicate support for
the continuity model, with 70% of adolescents who viewed their families as highly supportive of their school achievement also regarding peers
as supportive. Compensatory patterns are relatively rare, with fewer than
3% of adolescents reporting unsupportive parents but supportive friends,
although the reverse is more common. Although this study did not address the actual mechanisms by which such support is negotiated, the
processes by which both additive and compensatory patterns operate certainly merit further investigation.

Finally, doubts about the compensatory role of peer relationships have
emerged from concern about the effects of marital discord on adolescent
functioning. Hertz-Lazarowitz, Rosenberg, and Guttman (1989) posited
that children who "witness drastic changes in the love, trust, and care
between their parents . . . may learn that interpersonal relations mean
exploitation, quarrels, hate, and conflict, and may therefore avoid establishing such relations" (p. 2), rather than compensate for the lack of parental closeness by seeking closer ties with peers. Fifth- and sixth-grade Israeli
adolescents from divorced and intact families completed Sharabany's
(1974) Intimacy Scale. As a group, those from divorced families reported lower intimacy towards their fathers (but not their mothers), yet did
not report higher intimacy with either their mothers or with friends. They
also reported fewer friends besides a best friend than adolescents from
intact families. Similarly, Gold and his colleagues also found no evidence
that adolescents from single-parent families exhibited compensatory pat-

terns either with peers or siblings (Gold & Yanov, 1985; Luker, Gold, & Buerger, 1988).

## New Perspectives on Socialization:
## Family, Gender, and Culture

Whereas early work on socialization portrayed the "worlds" of peers and families as distinct and uniform, recent research has addressed three issues that bear upon contextual variability in both family and peer experience. These include the nature and effects of parental monitoring of adolescents' activities with peers, the role of gender in family and peer relationships, and culturally transmitted values in these relationships.

*Parental Monitoring of Adolescents' Activities with Peers.*  As adolescents spend more time away from home with peers than younger children, parental monitoring of their activities assumes greater significance (see Ladd, this volume). Poor parental monitoring of adolescent boys has been found to be more highly predictive of their delinquency than any other measure of family management practices (Patterson et al., 1989).

Although parental monitoring is receiving increased research attention, disagreement exists as to its causal role in adolescent competence or difficulties with peers. Suggesting that monitoring may be an indicator of other family relational conditions, Steinberg (1986) reported that latchkey adolescents "whose parents know their whereabouts and those who have been raised authoritatively are less susceptible to peer influence than their peers, even if their afternoons are spent in contexts in which adult supervision is lax and susceptibility to peer pressure is generally high" (p. 438).

Similarly, Patterson and his colleagues traced the origins of adolescents' antisocial behavior to early family experiences, including harsh, inconsistent discipline, and little positive involvement or supervision (Patterson et al., 1989). These practices are seen as teaching children an antisocial behavioral repertoire, in which coercive patterns of parent–child and sibling interactions both shape antisocial behavior and fail to reward prosocial skills. Displaying such aggressive behaviors at school, these adolescents are rejected by their more competent peers, fail to achieve academically, and fall into membership in deviant peer groups, who in turn provide both the values as well as the opportunities for engaging in antisocial behavior.

*The Role of Gender in Adolescents' Family and Peer Relationships.*  Although some gender differences in family and peer relationships persist from early and middle childhood into adolescence, their extent and interpretation are now under considerable debate (Collins & Russell, 1991). When interviewed about their parents, both adolescent males and adolescent females view their fathers as more emotionally distant and encouraging of autonomy and their mothers as more communicative, disclosing, and encouraging of connectedness (Youniss & Smollar, 1985). However, in our observations of families of early adolescents, although fathers expressed more individuality and mothers more connectedness, we also found that mothers of sons expressed more individuality than mothers of daughters, and fathers of daughters expressed more connectedness than fathers of sons (Cooper & Carlson, 1988). These findings suggest that some gender differences may be properties of relationships as much as of individuals.

Further, although gender differences in peer relational patterns occur as an average pattern, within-group variability appears linked to key competencies. For example, in our interviews with young adolescents, girls' reports of conflicts with close friends are more likely to involve betrayal of secrets (although this is the most common conflict for both genders), whereas boys are more likely to report conflicts over friends pressuring them to do things (Spradling, Ayers-Lopez, Carlson, & Cooper, 1989). In our observations of these adolescents interacting with their friends of the same gender, the girls expressed more agreements, acknowledgments, and requests for information, whereas boys expressed more commands and disagreements and were more likely to give than request information (Cooper & Carlson, 1989).

However, differences *within* each gender group in adolescents' peer relational patterns are associated with differences in their perceptions of self-competence. For example, when adolescents in our study were asked how they would behave in a hypothetical dilemma involving a friend pressuring them to drink beer, adolescents who described resisting pressure to drink without alienating their friends held more positive expectations for their friends' reactions and higher perceptions of their own general social competence (Spradling, Loera, Carlson, & Cooper, 1989).

***Cultural Perspectives on Family and Peer Relationships.***   Developmental scholars are increasingly concerned with how both individual development and social processes are embedded in culturally organized practices, activities, and patterns of mutual regulation (Rogoff, 1990). Not surprisingly, patterns of family–peer linkages vary across cultures. For example, in cultures in which parents expect boys to take care of younger siblings, they are observed to engage in more prosocial behavior with peers (Whiting & Edwards, 1988).

Increasingly, new work traces these cultural and ethnic traditions concerning family and peer relationships and reveals how they are powerful yet dynamic, changing in the process of immigration, acculturation, economic mobility, and political transformations. Recent work on cultures in transition to modernity illustrates that much of the "social capital" of adaptive knowledge that parents offer their children remains valuable, but because each generation faces a rapidly changing world, parents must share socializing functions with peers and teachers (Youniss, 1988). In an interview study of Israeli Arab adolescents from Moslem and Christian families, Seginer (1989) found that older sisters act as socializing agents by offering advice and information that is available neither from parents nor friends; their younger sisters see them as "sources of information, consultants and confidantes in matters pertaining to school, future plans, social relations and romantic dreams, and clothes" (p. 150). In contrast, the younger sisters consulted with friends only about current social events, friends, and clothes, with mothers about pubertal changes, and with fathers about permission, money for school trips, and discussions of political issues. Seginer concluded that Arab adolescent girls sought from their older sisters advice that American adolescents seek from parents and friends.

We have long been concerned that our own work on the links between family individuality and connectedness and adolescent competence has been limited to European-American, middle-class families. In new work conducted in northern California, Chinese-American, Filipino-American, Vietnamese-American, and Hispanic-American adolescents (of whom a very high proportion were themselves immigrants) and European-American adolescents were asked about expressions of individuality and connectedness with their fathers, mothers, siblings, and peers, as well as about familistic values concerning norms of support and reliance on the advice of family members (Cooper, Baker, Polichar, & Welsh, 1991). Adolescents from the three Asian-American groups expressed high levels of familistic values but lower comfort in actually expressing and negotiating ideas with their parents, especially their fathers, with whom their relationships were quite formal. Within-group differences in expressing individuality and connectedness with friends was predicted by such patterns with mothers and siblings but not with fathers. Thus, recent views of parents and adolescents as renegotiating asymmetrical patterns of parent–child regulation toward peer-like mutuality appear to be better descriptions of European-American families than more recent immigrants from Asia and Mexico, for whom more formal relationships with mothers and especially fathers appear more common. We anticipate that this work will enrich our understanding of the interplay between developmental and cultural perspectives on individuality and connectedness in family–peer linkages.

## New Cognitive Perspectives

In addition to new perspectives from relational and societal themes of family, gender, and culture, a third major resource for reconceptualizing family–peer linkages in adolescence can be drawn from recent work in cognitive development. Adolescents' more advanced conceptual skills allow them both to learn and generalize new kinds of understanding about self and relational capacities (Harter, 1990; Keating, 1990; Savin-Williams & Berndt, 1989). In this section we address how new models of the role of social interaction in cognitive development derived from those proposed by Vygotsky (1978) suggest mechanisms of linkages between family and peer experience, and how these linkages can also be seen in part as a consequence of transfer of skills and knowledge from one realm to the other.

***Parental Scaffolding of Adolescents' Cognitive and Relational Development.***    Although Piaget discussed the contribution of the *process* of peer interaction to cognitive development, Vygotsky accorded a more central role to the *content* of social interaction in the process of cognitive change, arguing that development consisted of internalizing the activities, goals, and tools that exist in the culture during interactions with others. In this view, the content of social interaction becomes an intrinsic part of cognitive development. Vygotsky saw interactions with more knowledgeable peers or adults who can guide the child as especially beneficial (Rogoff, 1990).

Although neither Piaget nor Vygotsky addressed linkages from one relational context to another, we can build on their work to understand the cognitive nature of parents' contribution to children's competence with peers and how it changes from childhood to adolescence. With younger children, optimal conditions for learning might be hypothesized as involving direct "scaffolding" by family members (Rogoff, 1990). However, as adolescents' cognitive abilities approach those of their parents, their parents in turn become increasingly removed from and hence less expert about the contexts in which their adolescents function with peers. Consequently, parents' contributions may be defined more as monitoring and fostering of their adolescents' exploration than as direct management (see Ladd, this volume).

However, rather than becoming more indirect, we might conceptualize the kind of scaffolding that parents of adolescents could provide as more abstract. This scaffolding might help adolescents analyze social structure and process and select among alternative behaviors in such contexts. If this view has value, we need further specification of what scaffolding parents might provide, the contexts for which it is useful, and the skills adolescents would need to benefit from it in different contexts.

*Factors Limiting or Enhancing Transfer Between Family and Peer Experience.* Cognitive developmentalists have sought to understand when a cognitive skill learned in one context will or will not generalize to another one. The concepts of *modularity* and *domain* in cognitive psychology may be useful in considering the transfer between parent–child and peer relationships because they involve explicit claims about limitations in the range of application of some cognitive processes (Fodor, 1985). In cognitive psychology, modularity refers to the lack of interpenetrability of two cognitive processes. For example, even if a viewer measures the two lines of the Muller-Lyer illusion and "knows" they are equally long, this knowledge does not penetrate the perceptual process and eliminate the illusion. Gardner (1985) has argued that modularity is intrinsic to cognitive processing and applied it to a range of different aspects of intelligence.

Whereas modularity is seen as an innate characteristic of the cognitive system, the related concept of *domain* is used to describe developmentally emergent or constructed subdivisions of knowledge (Campbell & Bickhard, 1986) and appears more appropriate for the present discussion. For our purposes, separate domains in family and peer relationships would be indicated if processes used in one were not used in the other. Adolescents' construction of boundaries both between and within family and peer contexts is indicated by their feeling more comfortable discussing sexuality and drugs with their mothers than their fathers and more comfortable with same- than opposite-gender friends (Cooper et al., 1991). Such findings suggest that links between family and peer relationships depend centrally on whether adolescents construe them as two separate domains or as different contexts within the same domain.

*The Specific versus General Nature of What Is Learned.* In discussing transfer, it is useful to differentiate along a dimension from very general to very specific skills and characteristics. For example, having positive self-esteem might be considered a general characteristic, whereas the skill of restating another person's case before countering with one's own in an argument is more specific. In examining links between family and peer relationships, we would expect to find transfer of both general skills and characteristics and quite specific ones. Newell (1979) pointed out that specific skills are used infrequently because they are appropriate in only a limited number of circumstances, yet are very powerful because when used appropriately they greatly increase the probability of success. On the other hand, general skills can be used in a wide range of circumstances but may contribute only modestly to the chance of success.

This analysis suggests that the research design of the study used to ex-

amine the links between family and peer settings could dramatically influence whether general or specific skill transfer is found. Naturalistic
observational studies of family and peer interaction are more likely to
reveal transfer of weaker general skills such as supportiveness, because
they have the broadest range of appropriate application, whereas studies
that constrain participants to solve very similar problems in family and
peer contexts, such as with negotiation tasks, are more likely to provide
evidence for the transfer of specific skills involved in conflict resolution
(Cooper & Carlson, 1989). Further, when interviewed, adolescents may
not report transfer from family to peer contexts because the most salient
characteristics of any particular situation are those that are most powerful and therefore most specialized for that situation. General characteristics such as positive self-esteem or verbal fluency may be less salient
exactly because they are more pervasive.

Transferring specific skills to new contexts may be more difficult.
Brown, Bransford, Ferrara, and Campione (1983) pointed out that analyz-
ing the appropriateness of large numbers of specific skills or approaches
to tasks places great demands on the executive control system. Even college students frequently fail to generalize a specific problem-solving strategy unless they are provided with "hints" (Gick & Holyoak, 1980). Brown
et al. (1983) suggested that one major problem in transfer across problem-
solving contexts is recognizing the underlying similarity between
problems. Because this may also occur between family and peer contexts,
transfer of specific skills may be less likely without guidance from others
such as parents, teachers, or other mentors.

Brown's (1989) analysis of learning and transfer of causal reasoning
and problem-solving skills in young children provides a cogent analogue
for both general and specific components of the family–peer links question. Conceiving of transfer as learning underlying causal properties rather
than similarity of surface characteristics, Brown found that transfer was
enhanced by focusing children's attention on explicating causal rules, a
practice that fosters differentiated causal structures, and by providing
repeated experiences with tasks in which success was possible and relatively likely. Extending this line of reasoning, we might predict that family experiences facilitating transfer of adaptive skills to peer relationships
would help adolescents' causal understanding of relational patterns, such
as how to resolve conflicts.

Developmental changes in the mechanisms of family–peer linkages can
be described at different levels. First, adolescents are able to transfer more
abstract causal rules. Whereas younger children generalize specific rules
of the form, "When someone does X, do Y," as in "If a friend is angry
with you, give them something," socially competent adolescents learn
rules such as, "When a friend is angry with you, it is more helpful to listen

and express understanding than to offer instrumental solutions.'' The higher levels of cognitive functioning that support such analyses might be described either within the Piagetian framework of formal operations or with the information-processing construct of the development of expertise (Anderson, 1983). Although the explanatory mechanisms are not well understood, it is well documented that adolescents are much better than younger children at understanding causal relationships within abstract problems, and so would be more likely to understand principles of trust, loyalty, betrayal, and contrition (Youniss & Smollar, 1985). Adolescents who do not understand such underlying systems would be expected to transfer particular behaviors to situations that "looked" similar to that in which they were first learned, such as by giving a gift to mollify a friend after having seen such behavior between parents.

The foregoing analysis leads to several testable hypotheses that we are now investigating in current work: First, relational capacities that parents can offer become more relevant to adolescents as their peer relationships become more adultlike, so that transfer of such capacities is more likely in later than early adolescence. Second, within any age cohort, if parents engage in egalitarian relationships with their adolescents, relational skills learned in the family are more useful with peers. Finally, family–peer transfer of complex skills is more likely among parents who conceive of linkages between these domains and help establish them with explicit metacognitive scaffolding, and among adolescents who also engage in metacognitive causal thinking about such linkages.

In summary, we have argued that issues of transfer in cognitive development are particularly important to family–peer links; that cognitive growth influences adolescents' ability to make links between family and peer contexts, and their ability to make such links, in turn, has important implications for the course of cognitive development; and family experiences influence both the real and perceived similarity on which transfer depends. Hence, any position that characterizes transfer between family and peers only in terms of specific skills or characteristics will inevitably be inadequate. Models that enjoy support in the long run will take into account developmental changes and the processes and contexts that foster effective links between family and peer contexts.

## CLOSING COMMENTS

In closing, we emphasize the importance of focusing research concerning family and peer relationships on issues of diversity, especially with regard to gender, ethnicity, social class, culture, and family structure. Most studies reviewed in this chapter include only European-American, middle-class, two-parent families, and some only males or females. Recent research has shown how family–peer linkages vary with age, who is considered family (parents, sibling, biological or fictive kin), and what dimensions are assessed in both family life (perceptions of family relationships, parental monitoring, communication patterns) and peer life (conformity, delinquency, rejection, friendships, romantic relationships).

Enriched accounts of family, societal, and cultural factors in socialization and the postPiagetian era in cognitive research offer more sophisticated accounts of the mechanisms of connection between family and peer relationships. Discourse analyses provide insight about transactive relational patterns of which individuals may not be aware and hence able to report, and survey methods are critical for assessing generalizability over the diverse populations with whom we are especially concerned on issues of linkages among families, peers, schools, and the workplace.

We are just beginning to understand at the psychological level the variability of values concerning individuality and connectedness and the roles of men, women, and children in family and peer relationships, as well as how economic, political, and historical forces offer or restrict the opportunities of families, children, and adolescents. One way to gauge the significance of our ignorance is with new work demonstrating that some behaviors once unequivocally designated with the "peers are bad" rubric, including adolescent pregnancy, school dropout, and gang affiliation, are now being reinterpreted as adaptive behaviors developed in response to the challenges of poverty, war, and urban crime (Burton, 1990; Ogbu, 1987; Spencer & Dornbusch, 1990). Bringing issues of diversity into mainstream developmental theory will enrich our accounts of intragroup variability and provide a more complete normative-developmental picture.

## ACKNOWLEDGMENTS

We gratefully acknowledge the many thoughtful readings and insightful comments of Margarita Azmitia and the bibliographic assistance of Carolyn Cherry and Dina Polinchar. Research reported in this chapter was supported by grants from the National Institute of Education, National Institute of Child Health and Human Development, Hogg Foundation for Mental Health, the Spencer Foundation, University Research Institute of the University of Texas at Austin, and the University of California at Santa Cruz Faculty Research Grant program.

## REFERENCES

Anderson, J. R. (1983). Acquisition of cognitive skill. *Psychological Review, 89,* 369–406.

Armsden, G. C., & Greenberg, M. T. (1982). The inventory of parent and peer attachment: Individual differences and their relationship to psychological well-being in adolescence. *Journal of Youth and Adolescence, 16,* 427–454.

Bell, L. G., Cornwell, C. S., & Bell, D. C. (1988). Peer relationships of adolescent daughters: A reflection of family relationship patterns. *Family Relations, 37,* 171–174.

Berndt, T. J., & Ladd, G. W. (1989). *Peer relationships in child development.* New York: Wiley.

Blos, P. (1979). *The adolescent passage: Developmental issues.* New York: International University Press.

Brittain, C. V. (1963). Adolescent choices and parent-peer cross pressures. *American Sociological Review, 28,* 385–391.

Bronfenbrenner, U. (1970). *Two worlds of childhood.* New York: Russell Sage.

Brown, A. (1989, Fall). "Learning to learn revisited" of "Kelp keeps everyone happy." *American Psychological Association Division 7 Newsletter.*

Brown, A. L., Bransford, J. D., Ferrara, R. A., & Campione, J. C. (1983). Learning, remembering, and understanding. In J. H. Flavell & E. M. Markman (Eds.), *Handbook of child psychology: Vol. 3. Cognitive development* (pp. 77–166). New York: Wiley.

Burton, L. M. (1990). Teenage childbearing as an alternative life-course strategy in multigeneration Black families. *Human Nature, 1,* 123–138.

Campbell, R. L., & Bickhard, M. H. (1986). *Knowing levels and developmental stages.* New York: Karger.

Coleman, J. S. (1961). *The adolescent society.* New York: Free Press.

Collins, W. A., & Russell, G. (1991). Mother–child and father–child relationships in middle childhood and adolescence: A developmental analysis. *Developmental Review, 11,* 99–136.

Condon, S. M., Cooper, C. R., & Grotevant, H. D. (1984). Manual for the analysis of family discourse. *Psychological Documents, 14,* (MS. No. 2616).

Cooper, C. R. (1980). The development of collaborative problem solving among preschool children. *Developmental Psychology, 16,* 433–440.

Cooper, C. R. (1988). Commentary: The role of conflict in adolescent–parent relationships. In M. Gunnar & A. Collins (Eds.), *The Minnesota Symposium in Child Psychology* (pp. 181–187). Hillsdale, NJ: Lawrence Erlbaum Associates.

Cooper, C. R., & Ayers-Lopez, S. (1985). Family and peer systems in early adolescence: new models of the role of relationships in development. *Journal of Early Adolescence, 5,* 9–21.

Cooper, C. R., Ayers-Lopez, S., & Marquis, A. (1982). Children's discourse during peer learning in experimental and naturalistic situations. *Discourse Processes, 5,* 177–191.

Cooper, C. R., Baker, H., Polichar, D., & Welsh, M. (1991). *Ethnic perspectives on individuality and connectedness in adolescents' relationships with family and peers.* Paper presented at the meetings of the International Society for the Study of Behavioral Development, Minneapolis, Minnesota.

Cooper, C. R., & Carlson, C. I. (1988). *Individuality and connectedness in family relationships during early adolescence: Gender differences and predictors of self-esteem.* Paper presented at the meeting of the Society for Research in Adolescence, Alexandria, VA.

Cooper, C. R., & Carlson, C. I. (1989). *Individuation in family and peer relations in adolescence.* Paper presented at the meeting of the International Society for the Study of Behavioral Development, Jyvaskyla, Finland.

Cooper, C. R., & Carlson, C. I. (1990). *Shifts in family discourse from early to late adolescence: Age and gender patterns.* Paper presented at the National Institute of Mental Health Family Research Consortium, Monterey, California.

Cooper, C. R., Carlson, C. I., Koch, P., Keller, J., Spradling, V., Houchins, S., & Grotevant, H. D. (1990). *Shifts in family discourse from early to late adolescence: Age and gender patterns.* Paper presented at the meeting of the NIMH Family Research Consortium, Monterey, CA.

Cooper, C. R., & Cooper, R. R. (1984). Skill in peer learning discourse: What develops? In S. Kuczaj (Ed.), *Children's discourse* (pp. 77–97). New York: Springer-Verlag.

Cooper, C. R., Grotevant, H. D. & Ayers-Lopez, S. (1992). *Links between patterns of negotiation in adolescents' family and peer interaction.* Manuscript submitted for publication.

Cooper, C. R., Grotevant, H. D., & Condon, S. M. (1983). Individuality and connectedness in the family as a context for adolescent identity formation and role taking skill. In H. D. Grotevant & C. R. Cooper (Eds.), *Adolescent development in the family: New directions in child development* (pp. 43–59). San Francisco: Jossey-Bass.

Cooper, C. R., Marquis, A., & Edward, D. (1986). Four perspectives on peer learning among school children. In E. C. Mueller & C. R. Cooper (Eds.), *Process and outcome in peer relationships* (pp. 269–300). New York: Academic Press.

Csikszentmihalyi, M., & Larson, R. (1984). *Being adolescent: Conflict and growth in the teenage years.* New York: Basic Books.

Douvan, E., & Adelson, J. (1966). *The adolescent experience.* New York: Wiley.

Downs, W. R. (1985). Using panel data to examine sex differences in causal relationships among adolescent alcohol use, norms, and peer alcohol use. *Journal of Youth and Adolescence, 14,* 469–486.

Fine, G. A. (1986). The social organization of adolescent gossip: the rhetoric of moral evaluation. In J. Cook-Gumperz, W. A. Corsaro, & J. Streek (Eds.), *Children's worlds and children's language* (pp. 405–424). Berlin: De Gruyter.

Fodor, J. A. (1985). Precis of the modularity of mind. *The Behavioral and Brain Sciences, 8,* 1–42.

Freud, A. (1966). Instinctual anxiety during puberty. *The writings of Anna Freud: The ego and the mechanisms of defense.* New York: International Universities Press.

Gardner, G. (1985). *Frames of mind: The theory of multiple intelligences.* New York: Basic Books.

Gick, M. L., & Holyoak, K. J. (1980). Analogical problem solving. *Cognitive Psychology, 12,* 306–355.

Gold, M., & Yanov, D. S. (1985). Mothers, daughters, and girlfriends. *Journal of Personality and Social Psychology, 49,* 654–659.

Gottman, J. M., & Parker, S. (Eds.). (1986). *Conversations of friends: Speculations on affective development.* Cambridge: Cambridge University Press.

Grotevant, H. D., & Cooper, C. R. (1986). Individuation in family relationships: A perspective on individual differences in the development of identity and role taking in adolescence. *Human Development, 29,* 82–100.

Harter, S. (1985). *The self-perception profile for adolescents.* Unpublished manuscript, University of Denver.

Harter, S. (1990). Self and identity development. In S. S. Feldman & G. R. Elliott (Eds.), *At the threshold: The developing adolescent* (pp. 352–387). Cambridge, MA: Harvard University Press.

Hertz-Lazarowitz, R. L., Rosenberg, M., & Guttman, J. (1989). Children of divorce and their intimate relationships. *Youth and Society, 21,* 85–104.

Hill, J. P., & Holmbeck, G. N. (1986). Attachment and autonomy during adolescence. *Annals of Child Development, 3,* 145–189.

Iacovetta, R. G. (1975). Adolescent-adult interaction and peer group involvement. *Adolescence, 10,* 327–336.

Josselson, R. (1987). *Finding herself: Pathways to identity development in women.* San Francisco: Jossey-Bass.

Josselson, R., Greenberger, E., & McConochie, D. (1977). Phenomenological aspects of psychosocial maturity in adolescence. *Journal of Youth and Adolescence, 6,* 145–167.

Kahn, C. M. (1989). *Family relationships and friendships in adolescence: Continuities and discontinuities.* Unpublished doctoral dissertation, Catholic University of America, Washington, DC.

Kandel, D., & Lesser, G. S. (1982). *Youth in two worlds.* San Francisco: Jossey-Bass.

Keating, D. (1990). Adolescent thinking. In S. S. Feldman & G. R. Elliot (Eds.), *At the threshold: The developing adolescent* (pp. 54–90). Cambridge: Cambridge University Press.

Luker, R., Gold, M., & Buerger, V. (1988). *Affection, emulation, and control in adolescent relationships with parents and friends: A developmental approach.* Unpublished manuscript, University of Michigan.

Maynard, D. W. (1985). On the functions of social conflict among children. *American Sociological Review, 50,* 207–223.

Nelson, J., & Aboud, F. E. (1985). The resolution of social conflict between friends. *Child Development, 56,* 1009–1017.

Newell, A. (1979). One final word. In D. T. Tuma & F. Reif (Eds.), *Problem solving and education: Issues in teaching and research* (pp. 175–192). Hillsdale, NJ: Lawrence Erlbaum Associates.

Ogbu, J. U. (1987). Variability in minority school performance: A problem in search of an explanation. *Anthropology and Education Quarterly, 18,* 312–334.

Patterson, G. R., DeBaryshe, B. D., & Ramsey, E. (1989). Developmental perspective on antisocial behavior. *American Psychologist, 44,* 329–335.

Piaget, J. (1932). *The moral judgment of the child.* London: Routledge & Kegan Paul.

Rogoff, B. (1990). *Apprenticeship in thinking: Cognitive development in social context.* New York: Oxford University Press.

Savin-Williams, R. C., & Berndt, T. J. (1989). Friendship in adolescence. In S. S. Feldman & G. R. Elliot (Eds.), *At the threshold: The developing adolescent* (pp. 277–307). Cambridge: Cambridge University Press.

Schafer, R. (1973). Concepts of self and identity and the experience of separation-individuation in adolescence. *Psychoanalytic Quarterly, 42,* 42–59.

Seginer, R. (1989). *Adolescent sisters: the relationship between younger and older sisters among Israeli Arabs.* Paper presented at the meeting of the International Society for the Study of Behavioral Development, Jyvaskyla, Finland.

Sharabany, R. (1974). The development of capacity for altruism as a function of object relations development and vicissitudes. In E. Staub, D. Bart-Tal, J. Karylowski, & J. Reykowski (Eds.), *Development and maintenance of prosocial behavior* (pp. 201–224). New York: Plenum.

Sharabany, R., Gershoni, R. & Hoffman, J. E. (1981). Girlfriend, boyfriend: Age and sex differences in intimate friendship. *Developmental Psychology, 17,* 800–808.

Simmons, R. G., & Blyth, D. A. (1987). *Moving into adolescence: The impact of pubertal change and school context.* New York: Aldine de Gruyter.

Smetana, J. G. (1988). Adolescents' and parents' conceptions of parental authority. *Child Development, 59,* 321–335.

Snyder, J., Dishion, T. J., & Patterson, G. R. (1986). Determinants and consequences of associating with deviant peers during preadolescence and adolescence. *Journal of Early Adolescence, 6,* 23.

Spencer, M. B., & Dornbusch, S. M. (1990). Challenges in studying minority youth. In S. S. Feldman & G. R. Elliott (Eds.), *At the threshold: The developing adolescent* (pp. 123–146). Cambridge, MA: Harvard University Press.

Spradling, V. Y., Ayers-Lopez, S. J., Carlson, C. I., & Cooper, C. R. (1989). *Conflict between friends during early adolescence: sources, strategies, and outcomes.* Paper presented at the meeting of the American Psychological Association, New Orleans.

Spradling, V. Y., Loera, L. L., Carlson, C. I., & Cooper, C. R. (1989). *Sixth graders' expressed attitudes toward alcohol use and expected peer responses.* Paper presented at the meetings of the Texas Psychological Association, Houston.

Steinberg, L. (1986). Latchkey children and susceptability to peer pressure: An ecological analysis. *Developmental Psychology, 22,* 435–439.

Steinberg, L., & Brown, B. B. (1989). *Beyond the classroom: parental and peer influences on high school achievement.* Paper presented at the meetings of the American Educational Research Association.

Sullivan, H. S. (1953). *The interpersonal theory of psychiatry.* New York: Norton.

Vygotsky, L. S. (1978). *Mind in society: the development of higher psychological processes* (M. Cole, V. John-Steiner, S. Scribner, & E. Souberman, Eds. & Trans.). Cambridge, MA: Harvard University Press.

White, K. M., Speisman, J. C., & Costos, D. (1983). Young adults and their parents: Individuation to matuality. In H. D. Grotevant & C. R. Cooper (Eds.), *Adolescent development in the family: New directions for child development* (pp. 61–76). San Francisco: Jossey-Bass.

Whiting, B. B., & Edwards, C. P. (1988). *Children of different worlds.* Cambridge, MA: Harvard University Press.

Youniss, J., & Smollar, J. (1985). *Adolescent relations with mothers, fathers, and friends.* Chicago: University of Chicago Press.

Youniss, J. (1988). Mutuality in parent–adolescent relationships: Social capital for impending adulthood. In *Youth and America's Future.* New York: William T. Grant Foundation Commission on Work, Family, and Citizenship.

# CHAPTER SIX

# Beyond Parent–Child Relationships: Potential Links Between Family Environments and Peer Relations

Brenda K. Bryant
Kristine A. DeMorris
*University of California, Davis*

American families in the ideal are cooperative units, headed by two parents with two or more children (Davis, 1983), that function to protect their members from danger, to ensure an adequate food supply, to provide children with the opportunity to learn the skills of their culture, and to share leisure time together. In addition to these general task functions of a family group, group maintenance skills and attitudes are required to keep the social functioning of the family unit oriented toward achieving these tasks. The relevance of family functioning for children's functioning with peers is seen in how families operate to achieve the requirements for the family's group maintenance and task functions.

Families are typically biologically defined groups of individuals who share a common household unless difficulties preclude such arrangements. Very practically, a family consists of at least one adult, generally referred to as a "parent" and at least one child. When they are working as they "are supposed to," families share resources to secure food, clothing, household goods, transportation to places of work, school, and entertainment. In other words, families are social units designed to work and play together. Furthermore, they function within a larger social context consisting of formal and informal social structures. Parental work place, schools, neighbors, and peer relations in part characterize this larger social framework in which family life is functionally embedded. Both the group goals of the family unit and the social context in which the family is embedded affect the child's functioning with others, including peers.

Because of the repetition of daily sequences in family life, and because such fundamental needs of the individuals are addressed in family units, the family serves as a potent arena for influence on the child's functioning, both at home and "abroad."

In this chapter, we explore three levels of influences through which families influence children's functioning with peers. First, there are the direct influences of specific dyadic relationships that occur between children and individual family members (e.g., the mother–child relationships; father–child relationships; and specific sibling relationships). Second, there are indirect influences beginning both within and outside the family setting but that impact on children's relations with other family members (e.g., mother–father marital relation can affect parent–child functioning; the employment status and conditions of mother can affect parent–child functioning). Third, there are participant observation effects or child bystander/witness effects (e.g., observing husband–wife interactions, sibling interactions, or parent–sibling relations). How we view family influences on child development will dictate the unit of analysis we choose to study. Dyadic interaction (e.g., mother–child interaction) has historically been the preferred unit of analysis. As we widen our perspective on potential influences to child development, we begin to broaden our unit of analysis to triads, families as a unit, or groups of systems (such as parental work and family systems). This chapter begins to consider these various types of influences and units of analysis as they relate to family life in relation to children's peer relations. The organization of this chapter is based on the functions and needs of the family as a cooperative unit:

1. Families provide protection.
2. Families are economic units.
   a. Availability of economic resources.
   b. Economic production impacts on physical availability of parents.
   c. Economic production impacts on emotional availability of parents.
3. Families maintain households.
4. Families are caretaking units: stress buffering as part of caretaking.
5. The sibling component to complex family functioning.
   a. The myth of family relationships as basically dyadic in nature.
   b. Siblings' further impact on family functioning.
6. Family units require relationship maintenance.
   a. Quality of marital relationships and marital conflict resolution.
   b. Family/sibling conflict management.
7. Families manage leisure time.

## Families Provide Protection: The American Concern with Violence

Although American parents have the desire to make their children feel secure and self-confident, the realities of competition, violence, and family breakup in the United States puts some constraints on what families can effect (Zill, in press). More than half the children in this study of a representative sample of American children reported feeling afraid when their parents argue, and families' experiences with violence are not limited to those perpetrated by family members. Children and their families experience violence in their neighborhoods, and this is particularly true of children growing up in the United States as compared to children growing up in France or Japan (Zill, in press).

Zill (in press) reported that some 20% of American school children live in neighborhoods where, according to their parents, there are problematic persons such as drunks, drug addicts, or tough older kids, and more than 15% assess their neighborhoods to have a "crime problem." Furthermore, one third of the school-aged children (aged 7–11) report that they've been threatened with a beating and 13% say they have actually been beaten up. Youngsters from rural communities experience less of this violence, but children in urban and suburban areas do not differ. One reason for this lack of difference may be that mothers living in high-risk inner city environments are more likely than other mothers to accompany their school-age children outside to supervise their play (Zill, in press). Safe neighborhoods, those relatively free of traffic dangers and relatively free of dangerous characters, also affect the extent to which school-aged children are free to go out alone or without adult chaperonage (Moore & Young, 1978), and girls are especially affected (i.e., restricted) by these parental perceptions of danger in the neighborhood. Thus, family functioning is affected when parents must contend with the perceived safety of their neighborhoods; this perception affects the way in which peers are allowed to meet and interact with one another.

The image of the ideal place to raise a child typically includes single-family-style dwellings, suburban shelter from crime and noise, and access to ("safe") people of one's kind. Are single-family-style dwellings really more conducive to developing peer relations? Can residing in an apartment dwelling really interfere with children's peer relations? There is some evidence that the answer to both these questions is yes. Seventy-five percent of the mothers in low-rise complexes indicated that they let their children out to play alone, but only 35% of the mothers in the high-rise complex permitted their children to play outdoors alone (Marcus, 1974). Similar findings are reported by others (Littlewood & Sale, 1972; Newman, 1972). Opportunities for peer interaction become limited as parental accessibility to supervise their children becomes more restrictive, and enforced, continuous contact between parents and their children in these conditions may produce parental irritability and tensions within the household, which in turn may impact negatively on the child and his or her relationship with others (Parke, 1978).

Perceived danger external to the family dwelling can impact on peer relations in two ways: (a) it can influence the extent of access to peers, and (b) it can influence the nature of peer interactions when directly overseen by adults. Research focused on the impact of the presence of parents/adults on peer relations is needed.

## Families are Economic Units

Economic resources for food, shelter, and clothing are fundamental to sustaining a family. How and to what extent families obtain economic resources have an indirect influence on children's peer relations. This position is consistent with the view that parents' world of work and family life are interrelated environments (Kanter, 1977; Kline & Cowan, 1988). Parental employment impacts not only on availability of economic resources but also on the physical availability of parents to directly supervise children, and the emotional availability and well-being that parents bring to their interactions with their children, their spouses, and their children's friends. Family functioning is directly impacted by conditions of parental employment, which thus, at least, indirectly influences children's peer relations. Although parents' investments in work do not preclude an investment in parenting (Greenberger & Goldberg, 1989), the costs and benefits of parental employment in relation to children's peer relations appear to vary by family and circumstance.

*Availability of Economic Resources.* The manner in which parents gain economic resources for the family is related to their social status, and children's reputations outside the family are partially derived from the social position of their family (Elder, 1974). Income viability affects status in varying ways, including such things as clothing choices and housing options. To the extent that economic resources contribute to a child's physical attractiveness, his status among peers is likely to be improved, as Roff, Sells, and Golden (1972) found a clear link between physical attractiveness and positive peer evaluations, and this may be especially true for adolescent girls (Elder, 1974). Social status can mediate between economic resources and peer relations in other ways also.

In particular, children from economically deprived families have been found to prefer the company of friends and to seek the advice of peers more than do children from nondeprived families (Elder, 1974). This need for group inclusion is also thought to make them both more emotionally vulnerable to the reactions of their peers and more sensitive to their peers.

The consequences of this increased sensitivity may also benefit the child in his or her peer relations by spurring ambitions to achieve those social skills valued by peers (e.g., leadership). Indeed, Elder (1974) found that although economically deprived children displayed these internal reactions, the perceptions of their peers as well as those of adult observers revealed their actual social skills and social acceptance in the context of a progressive school system in a societal economic depression remained unaffected. Thus, the motivational basis for peer success may be different for children from economically deprived families in comparison with children from economically advantaged families.

More than minimal economic viability for some families means that children have greater access to educational materials at home, educational excursions to the library and museums, and other experiences that provide children with understanding the wider world than that represented by their home neighborhoods. Economic resources also provide access to organized group lessons with one's peers and peer activities requiring money for equipment, travel, and lessons. In other words, parents' work and families' use of leisure time are interrelated. Whereas most children, regardless of family economic status, have enough opportunity for social exchanges and hobbies, this is least true for children of economically deprived, working-class children (Elder, 1974). The extent to which information, skills, and attitudes experienced in leisure activities are useful in peer relations is a complex matter not typically considered in developmental literature. The extent to which persons learn to participate in leisure activities is likely to influence whom they meet by virtue of common interests and skills. In addition, leisure time spent furthering academic success is not irrelevant to peer relations, as academic success is positively related to peer acceptance.

Financial enhancement can also be used to move to a "better" neighborhood in which children may attend a school that has a higher level of achievement. In turn, children may develop friendships with more talented and achievement-oriented peers who can benefit (from the parent's point of view) from a higher, less worrisome cadre of peers, as peers have been found particularly influential with respect to achievement aspirations (Berndt, 1983; Johnson, 1981; Kandel, 1978). The developmental impact of educational aspirations on subsequent career choices and resulting opportunities for peer relations in adulthood merits further attention.

Given that financial problems are a leading cause of marital disputes (Elder, 1974; Komarovsky, 1962), improved economic viability for some families can reduce these disputes and, in turn, contribute to better relationships between parents and children and between children and peers (Berndt, 1983). The process by which the quality of the parent–child relationship and marital conflict links to children's peer relations is discussed in a later section.

Economic resources appear to impact most directly on the contexts in which children encounter peers and indirectly mediates the impact on peer relations through children's perception of their social worth and desires, as well as through the impact of family dynamics influenced by family economic concerns. The evidence regarding popularity with one's peers suggests that economic viability, per se, need not interfere with this aspect of peer functioning, especially for males.

***Economic Production Impacts on Physical Availability of Parents.*** When mothers go to work, issues of child care become paramount. One of the immediate family management issues has to do with the supervision and care of children during the mother's working hours (cf. chapters by Ladd and Ross, this volume). Substitute parental care generally comes in the form of other relatives or some formal day care/after school arrangement.

Employment of both parents is associated with school-age children exploring their neighborhoods more fully without the presence of parents (but, presumably, often in company with peers and often with distal parental supervision, including prior parental permission) than is the case for children with one parent unemployed and at home (Hart, 1978). Some of these children with both parents employed outside the home appear to suffer from lack of adult supervision, and this impacts in some instances directly on the child's relationships with peers. Children and adolescents in grades 5 through 9 who report home after school are not significantly more susceptible to peer pressure than children who are supervised by their parents at home during after-school hours (Steinberg, 1986). However, the same cannot be said of children who are further removed from adult supervision. More specifically, children and adolescents who are home alone are less susceptible to peer pressure than are those who are at a friend's house after school, and those who are at a friend's house are even less susceptible than those who describe themselves as "hanging out." Furthermore, Steinberg documents that latchkey children whose parents know their whereabouts and those who have been raised authoritatively are less susceptible to peer influence than their peers are, even if their afternoons are spent in contexts in which adult supervision is lax and susceptibility to peer pressure is generally high.

Parental employment (i.e., both parents employed) does appear to influence both the extent to which children get exposed to casual contacts with peers and the meaning these relationships have for social–emotional functioning. With respect to extent of exposure to casual peer relationships, Bryant (1989b) found that older children (i.e., age 10) whose parents both worked full-time reported knowing and interacting with more peers than was true of the children whose mothers were unemployed or employed part-time. The opposite was true of younger children (age 7) who tended to know and interact with fewer peers when both their parents worked full-time. Why this occurred is not clear, but the findings suggest that younger children are more constrained in expanding their peer acquaintances whereas older children are freer to do so, relative to children whose mothers are not fully employed.

Traditionally, our concern with respect to children in relation to parental employment has been that, because of the employed mothers' increased unavailability, children of employed mothers will not have all their needs met. Relatively unexamined is the possibility that children with unemployed mothers will not have all their developmental requirements met either. Perhaps it would be more useful to consider the differences in the types of needs that characterize children whose mothers work and those whose mothers don't work. Bryant (1989b), using a family systems approach, considered this perspective in terms of a lifelong duality of human needs that vary across individuals according to, among other factors, age and maternal employment: (a) needs for support (e.g., need for adult support in the form of supervision when one is young), and (b) needs for autonomy (e.g., need for opportunity for distal supervision from one's parents when one is engaged with peers during middle childhood). Thus, children with full-time employed mothers may have special requirements for adult support, and children with mothers who are unemployed may have special requirements for autonomy from close adult supervision.

Consistent with this formulation, Bryant (1989b) found that the relationship between having various kinds of experiences with peers differs according to a child's experience of their mother vis-à-vis employment status. Among 10-year-olds, Bryant found that children of full-time working mothers showed a negative relationship between amount of informal peer involvement and social-perspective taking, whereas there was a positive association for those children whose mothers were not employed. The following interpretation was given this set of findings: Among the 10-year-old children with moms presumably at home in fairly constant direct supervision of their children, social functioning was "benefited" by having some "free" time with their peer friends (autonomy from direct adult supervision). On the other hand, 10-year-olds who lacked steady adult supervision from their moms did not "benefit" but "suffered" from increased "free" time off with their peers. Consistent with this need for direct adult support and supervision, involvement in formal organizations with adult-structured activities, such as scouts and sports teams, was negatively linked to social-perspective taking skill among children whose mothers were unemployed, but positively linked to this skill among children whose mothers were employed full-time. These findings suggest how differing systems of ongoing adult availability for supervision due to maternal availability mediate the impact of other adult and peer relations on child development. Neither knowing simply whether mothers work full-time nor knowing the extent to which children participate in particular formal child-oriented organizations will inform us as to what social skills children are acquiring.

### *Economic Production Impacts on Emotional Availability of Parents.*    Employment can impact on the well-being of both men and women. Employment frequently contributes to physical, emotional, and financial well-being of women (Burden, 1986). Working women are healthier, show more self-acceptance, greater satisfaction with life, freedom from emotional disturbance, fewer physical symptoms, greater longevity, and increased marital satisfaction than to various comparison groups of nonworking women (Belle, 1982; Hofferth & Moore, 1979; Hoffman & Nye, 1974; Kanter, 1977). Where family conditions are highly problematic, employment in some cases helps women cope with these difficulties. Paid work has also been found to be an important basis for some women to enhance their response to coping with the challenge of a major life disruption caused by divorce (Wolkind & Rutter, 1985). Finally, employment has also been found to be an important factor enabling women to leave and stay away from abusive relationships (Burden, 1986; Strube & Barbour, 1984). Employment affects many facets of adult well-being.

Family economic resources can affect mental health status of family members. Job loss has been found particularly deleterious on men's self-evaluation and family relationships (Hoffman, 1984; Kline & Cowan, 1988; Patterson, 1983). A field study of low-income mothers found the lack of financial resources and the uncertainty about their financial situation to be the single stressor area most strongly associated with maternal depression ($r = .59$) (Belle, Longfellow, & Makovsky, 1982). It should not be surprising that working for pay can benefit the mental health of family members—directly for the parents who find relief from major financial concern and reduced risk for depression, and indirectly by children whose daily interactions with their parents are linked with the emotional availability of their parents.

To what extent is parental well-being linked to the quality of children's relations with peers? Children with at least one parent with a mental health problem have been found to have more difficulties in their relationships with peers than do children of mentally well parents (Rolf, 1976; Weintraub, Neale, & Liebert, 1975). Fathers' stresses at work appear to have a deleterious impact on children's functioning with others through the connection of paternal depression (Daniels & Moos, 1988). Emotional well-being impacts on a parent's emotional availability to their children. The impact of parental depression, in particular, on parenting behavior, seems best characterized as unresponsiveness to children's dependency bids and reduced levels of parental initiation of nurturant interactions with their offspring (Belle et al., 1982). Depressed mothers were more likely to use angry, dominating styles when interacting with their children and were less likely to be attentive, responsive, and warm. Distortion of relationships rather than weak interpersonal bonds seems central to the link between problematic parent–child relationships and peer relations (Rutter, 1981). (See the Zahn-Waxler chapter in this volume on depressed mothers and peer relationships.)

Working does not always enhance mental health, however. For women, the fact of employment, her marital status, and support and stress within both the family and work settings are related to their mental well-being (Golding, 1989). Although Golding found that being married and being employed were associated with decreased depression, stress and support in either the work setting or the family setting were associated with depressive symptoms, even when marital status and employment status were held constant. Historical factors of family life in conjunction with current employment status are linked to functioning as well. In a study of working women following divorce, women coming from marriages with a dominant decision-making husband were more likely in post-divorce times to have a negative reaction to breadwinning in contrast to women coming from more egalitarian or women decision-focused marriages (Fassinger, 1989). Working conditions can also be linked to the level of home stress and mental health of mothers. In this vein, Fernandez (1985) found that the level of stress at home was related to having a supervisor who was not supportive about the employee's child-care needs. Single mothers, often overburdened by the absolute number of tasks required by parenting, including income production and household maintenance (Hetherington, Cox, & Cox, 1978; Weiss, 1979), frequently give up personal care activities, including rest and recreation (Burden, 1986; Sanik & Mauldin, 1986). Consistent with this, Burden (1986) found that single female parents were more prone to depression and decreased life satisfaction than other adults, and this decreased well-being was attributed to high job–family role strain, the result of most single women parents spending an average of 75 hours per week trying to balance both job and family responsibilities with little financial or emotional assistance.

Stage of development of children appears to affect the relationship between the effects of employment on maternal well-being (Kline & Cowan, 1988). There is greater strain between work and family roles among women with children under the age of 6 than there is for women with older children (Kelly & Voydanoff, 1985). Mothers of young children also report both greater positive and negative spillover of family to work life than either fathers or mothers with older children (Crouter, 1984). In contrast to the strain of employment and mothering of a young child, employment is likely to enhance the psychological well-being of single mothers with adolescents. Maternal employment among single mothers has been linked to adolescents' greater positive subjective experiences during times spent with their mothers (Duckett & Richards, 1989). To the extent that parent–child relations impact both directly and indirectly on childrens' peer relations, the psychological benefits of employment for parents are valuable to consider, as are the conditions impinging on the relationship between parental employment and children's experiences in the home and outside the home. Further investigation is warranted regarding under what conditions parents are responsive to their children's bids for contact with peers, as well as the mechanisms by which distorted relationships with parents affect peer relations.

### Families Maintain Households

Families require maintenance of households. Households need to be cleaned, meals need to be prepared, and clothes need to be washed. Children's experiences with responsibility for household maintenance varies. First-borns in one-parent homes (homes most likely to have an externally employed mother) are also more likely to have more responsibility for household chores than their counterparts in two-parent homes (Medrich, Roizen, Rubin, & Buckley, 1982). The same is true for girls in economically deprived families as well (Elder, 1974). Whether or not mothers work impacts on who engages in this household maintenance. Although husbands of employed women spend little or no more time in housework than do husbands of nonemployed women (Fox & Nickols, 1983; Spitze, 1988), children's participation in household chores, especially babysitting, is more likely to occur in families with a working mother (Hayes & Kamerman, 1983). The relationship between these responsible children and their parent(s) is surely critical to the children's experience of added responsibility. There is cross-cultural data to suggest that this increased responsibility with respect to child care is linked to being more helpful in their relationships with others, including peers (Whiting &

Whiting, 1975), although sheer increased involvement in other household maintenance does not appear so linked (Elder, 1974). Do children who grow up being responsible for others develop models of relationships that are defined in terms of caretaking? Not addressed in the research literature is an examination of the kinds of roles children take on with their peers in terms of providing caretaking. Given the caretaking nature of household maintenance, the caretaking role component possible in peer relations would be one way to approach looking at the link between household maintenance experiences in relation to the development of relationships with peers.

## Families Are Caretaking Units: Stress Buffering as Part of Caretaking

Caretaking means addressing the needs of others, and as such, families are stress-buffering units. Families are thought to mitigate stress of family members, in part because they define and address stressful situations of its individuals as familial concerns rather than individual concerns (Barbarin, 1983). They do this because they define themselves as a cooperative unit. Not all individuals under all familial circumstances live up to this ideal, however.

Family support in times of stress appears to be a critical time for the family to react in a cooperative fashion and whether or not families "come together" in times of stress has implications for children's peer relations. Patterson (1981) found that children who are aggressive with peers were living in families that differed from families without an aggressive child with respect to how crises involving child discipline were handled in a family setting. Fathers who actively entered into the disciplining when mothers were being ineffective (i.e., during periods of crisis involving child discipline) had children who were unaggressive with peers. Fathers of aggressive children, on the other hand, were likely to remain uninvolved with a crisis involving the mother–child dyad. In this instance, when the family fails to function as a cooperative unit (e.g., mother and father united in establishing a consistent limit with a child), the quality of a child's relation with others, including peers, suffers.

More generally, it appears that to the extent children's stress experiences are aided, children are predisposed to respond prosocially to peers. The evidence for this is correlational in nature and is discussed in terms of children's expressions of empathic arousal. Bryant (1987) found that it is not general ongoing parental support but rather mothers' apparent expressive support in situations specifically stressful to children that is conducive to the development of empathy. Consistent with this data she also found that children from large families who turned to grand-parents as well as older children (aged 10 as compared to age 7) who turned to pets for intimate talks in response to stress more than their respective counterparts reported greater empathy on a measure that is loaded most heavily with situations describing predicaments of peers. Thus, as parents are less available in times of stress as is thought to be the case in large as compared to small families and when parents view that there is less need for the aid (as may be true as their children age), the availability of extended family members for stress buffering appears relevant for children's increased sensitivity to the emotional needs of their peers.

Other instances of family stress result from externally derived sources of stress and familial support involving extended family members. The relevance of a cooperative family system that includes grandparents and other extended relatives has been particularly studied in the context of the American Black extended-family system (Wilson, 1989). The family system headed by a single parent (as Black families often are) has been found to be particularly aided by extended familial support, and this aid has been found to be linked to lower rates of deviant activities with peers as well as the teenage mothers having more involvement with peers, ap-parently relatively positive in nature (Wilson, 1989).

It is proposed that the experience of parental support and warmth is not experienced in isolation of others. When parents are not available to help, effectively respond, or sensitively respond to their children, as at times all parents are not, are there others who step in to help, and does the extra help affect the child's experience of mother and the skills and predispositions they take to their interaction with others, including peers? It appears to these reviewers that the answer is yes, and, when we widen our vision beyond the dyad of parent–child relations, we be-gin to see how this occurs.

## The Sibling Component
## to Complex Family Functioning

*The Myth of Family Relationships as Basically Dyadic in Na-ture.*    Although many children now live part of their childhood in one-parent homes, and an increasing number of children have no siblings, children in the United States still typically live with two parents and have at least one sibling (Veenhoven & Verkuyten, 1989). Despite this reality, we have a research literature that, for the most part, operates as though this were not the case. Everyday parent–child interactions are not ac-curately portrayed as pure dyadic interchanges. Virtually all of the liter-ature on the influences of parenting are suspect in this regard, as there is good reason to believe that dyadic "findings" carry with them the un-revealed phenomena of how parenting behavior directed towards one family member impinges on others, who in turn respond toward the child of interest or are "objects" of child observation with concomitant "wit-ness/bystander" effects. Bryant and Crockenberg (1980), in observing mother–sibling triads, found that the effect of a mother's behavior on her children's social interaction with one another depended in part on how she treated each child relative to her sister. Dunn and Munn (1985) also demonstrated that children responded to comments spoken direct-ly to themselves as well as to those made by one family member to another. Similarly, "sibling effects" must be considered in relation to parent–child functioning, as the two subsystems are not independent. In other words, dyadic interactions within the family will influence and/ or be influenced by whoever else is present.

What appears to be a parental caretaking effect or what appears to be independent sibling caretaking effects may actually reflect a coordinat-ed system of relationships among family members (including parents and siblings). Research designs and analyses have typically not addressed chil-dren's social development in this manner, so we have very little data-base to consider. Consider the following example linking children's experiences in the family with their predisposition toward accepting in-dividual differences among peers of their same age (Bryant, 1989a). In this example, Bryant started with the traditional direct dyadic parent–child or sibling–child relations vis-à-vis the child's attitudes toward peers, and then followed up with a more complex analysis of indirect effects within the family system to begin to understand the family process by which the apparent direct effects were obtained.

Acceptance of individual differences was defined as allowing close physical proximity to a range of peers, including children known to be relatively negatively evaluated by their peers (Bryant, 1982a). Caretak-ing experiences of children's mothers, fathers, and siblings were assessed by a modified version of the Cornell Parent Behavior Inventory (De-vereux, Bronfenbrenner, & Rodgers, 1969). (See Bryant, 1989a, for a more complete description.)

The simplest indication that what parents and siblings do are in part interdependent is the direct correlation between sibling and parental caretaking along comparable factors. Punishment was the only factor com-parable across all caretakers (mothers, fathers, brothers, and sisters). The extent of punishment children reported their mothers giving to them was correlated to that administered by older siblings, $r(166) = .39, p < .001$, whereas no significant correlation was found between fathers and older siblings in this regard (Bryant, 1989a). Mothers and older siblings shared a concern factor in common, and older sibling demonstrations of concern were also comparably related to mothers' expressions of concern. Sibling relationships, then, are in part moderated by the relationship that children have with their mothers or, conversely, mother–child relationships are in part moderated by the relationship that siblings have. In this sense, family relationships are not accurately described in terms of mere dyadic exchanges.

Siblings' and parents' relationships with children can be similarly moderated by other categories of behavior, not simply by the same prototype of behavior. To consider these possible moderating effects, Bryant (1989a) followed up complex (three-way interaction effects) findings pertaining to sibling behavior in predicting children's acceptance of individual differences in peers and used Minuchin's (1974) family system's concepts of enmeshed and disengaged family systems to organize an interpretation of these indirect family influences on peer relations. In Minuchin's system, members of "healthy" families know they are connected but have a good sense of separateness as individuals as well. According to this approach, supplementarity of sibling and parental functioning in which both a parent and a sibling coordinate the giving of support (to enmesh the child) or giving of punishment (to disengage the child) would lead to family enmeshment and family disengagement, respectively. Both enmeshment and disengagement in the family system is considered to impact unfavorably on children's social development.

Table 6.1 presents the three-way interaction effects based on sibling dyadic relationships and then includes the follow-up analyses that consider more complex family functioning. Congruent with an image of enmeshed family functioning, sibling nurturance and supportive challenge, when paired with parental concern or support, were related to children's reduced acceptance of individual differences among peers. Similarly, and congruent with an image of disengaged family functioning, sibling punishment (boundary setting behavior), when paired with paternal punishment (also boundary setting behavior), was related to reduced acceptance of individual differences among peers.

Not only do these follow-up analyses of complex interactions help clarify how context (such as family size) and individual differences (such as age of child) operate in socializing children, they also define conditions under which the family system may be the more revealing unit of analysis. In the last example, neither sibling punishment nor paternal punishment alone was sufficient to "effect" lower acceptance of individual differences among peers. A system of punishment within the family involving both the father and older sibling was required to impact on children's functioning vis-à-vis acceptance of individual differences among peers. Until we begin to recognize, both in research designs and in analytic strategies, that much of sibling relations and parenting occurs not

TABLE 6.1
Sibling Effects Within the Context of Family Functioning

---

*Sibling Three-Way Interaction #1—Sibling nurturance × sex of child × family size*

---

*Description of interaction:* Among females in large families, experiences of older sibling nurturance was associated with lowered acceptance of individual differences of peers.

*Family system follow-up analysis:* Sibling nurturance interacted with maternal concern, sex of the child, and family size. The correlation between sibling nurturance and maternal concern was $r(40) = .39$, $p < .05$ for girls in large families but negligible for girls in small families and for all boys.

*Sibling Three-Way Interaction #2—Sibling Supportive Challenge × family size × sex*

---

*of older sibling*

*Description of interaction:* For children in large families with older brothers, sibling supportive challenge was associated with lowered acceptance of individual differences of peers.

*Family system follow-up analysis:* Sibling challenge tended to interact with both maternal and paternal support in conjunction with family size and sex of sibling. In each case, the highest obtained correlation between sibling challenge and parental support (maternal and paternal) was found for the group of children in large families with older brothers, $r(40) = .61$, $p < .001$, and $r(40) = .43$, $p < .01$, respectively.

*Sibling Three-Way Interaction #3—Sibling punishment × age × sex of sibling effect*

---

*Description of interaction:* Amoong 10-year-olds with older sisters, sibling punishment was related to lesser acceptance of individual differences.

*Family system follow-up analysis:* Sibling punishment tended to interact with both maternal and paternal punishment in conjunction with age of child and sex of child's older sibling. Among 10-year-olds with older sisters, the correlation between sibling and paternal punishment is $r(46) = .55$, $p < .001$.

---

in isolation of each other as our research literature predominantly implies but rather in concert with other family members, we will not be clear how dyadic relations (neither parent–child nor sibling relations) operate within larger social systems to affect children's social development.

**Siblings' Further Impact on Family Functioning.**  Siblings are also thought to have more direct effect on each other. Siblings are thought to set and maintain standards, provide models to emulate and advice to consider, enact complementary and reciprocal roles in relation to one another through which they develop and practice social skills, and, as children get older, serve as confidantes in times of emotional stress (e.g., breakups with steady dates, menarche, pregnancy scares) (Lamb, 1982; Mendelson, Aboud, & Lanthier, 1990). Consistent with this formulation, kindergartners who were popular with their peers experienced their siblings as providing reciprocal and complementary roles (Mendelson et al., 1990). The evidence suggests that there are many qualifications to this idea of transfer of skills across situations; this is reviewed later and in the section on management of sibling conflict.

In addition to roles learned, siblings frequently introduce aspects of culture outside the family to other siblings within the family. Sometimes siblings import friends, unique language, styles of dress, and games into the family system. They introduce to parents the needs for new rules or adjustments vis-à-vis peers and others outside the family. At other times, children take their siblings to places beyond the family dwelling. Younger siblings are often able to go out further in their neighborhoods without being directly supervised by a parent because older siblings (usually sisters) provide supervision (Hart, 1978). Thus, range restrictions imposed on first-borns are generally not imposed on later-borns, because parents think that the older siblings can chaperone the younger ones and because parents change and relax their ideas regarding the need for control over later-borns (Hart, 1978). Exceptions to this seem to occur for children of single parents and last-born children for whom parents exert greater control (Holt, 1975). In other words, siblings are companions who link one another to larger social worlds, including that of peers.

Although considerable research has linked a child's sibling status characterized by birth order, same-gender or mixed-gender sibling pairs, and age interval between siblings to indices of social functioning and personality functioning, the actual documentation of behavioral consistencies in thoughts, feelings, or behaviors between sibling relations and peer relations per se is very limited. Cross-situational consistency of behavior has been found for certain children with respect to consistency of their behavior interacting with their siblings and their peers. Preschool children who were more aggressive with their siblings were also more aggressive with their peers (Berndt & Bulleit, 1985). Likewise, children who were often unoccupied or onlookers at home were similarly withdrawn with peers at school.

The exploration of similarities and differences in peer and sibling interactions is incomplete. Abramovitch, Corter, Pepler, and Stanhope (1986) found great reciprocity among siblings with respect to displays of agonism. The same was true for older peers (roughly 8 years old) but not younger peers (i.e., roughly 5 years old). At the same time, it has been documented that children who play a subordinate role to an older sibling can play a dominant role with a peer, and vice versa (Abramovitch et al., 1986; Gump, Schoggen, & Redl, 1963). Are similarities across relations sometimes not found because the content of behavioral episodes (e.g., episodes of conflict) is not adequately differentiated? Do we fail to find consistency of behavior across relations at times because we do not consider the quality of relations between social participants? Indeed, Dunn and Kendrick (1982) found that older siblings who have an affectionate relationship with their new sibling are also more likely to use questions in their speech with this sibling, a conversational model apparently reflecting a desire to engage the baby in reciprocal exchange. Do we fail to find consistency at times also because we look for the same exact behaviors rather than the same type of behavior (e.g., passive, covert aggression is not equated with active, overt aggression)? Also to be considered is that the frequency of particular contents of conflict, the conflict resolution strategies employed,and the relationship repair strategies all apparently differ between siblings and peers (Raffaelli, 1989). Thus, we need to examine if, when a child has the same type (content comparability) disagreement with a peer as with a sibling, the conflict resolution strategies employed are the same or different across settings. Future research needs to consider the nature of the existing relationship between siblings and peers and the content of conflict in relation to reactions to potentially differing types of conflict responses, to further determine when strategies learned with siblings do and do not transfer to those with peers. People can and do learn that others operate according to varying norms of behavior. Thus, it may be that cross-situational transfer works mostly in choice of friendship, perhaps replicating satisfactory sibling relationships, and that the cross-situational transfer also works best among strangers with same relative characteristics such as age and gender.

Also, peers are generally defined as agemates and presumed different from siblings on this basis. Age and relative age is clearly an important variable that influences children's dyadic interactions. This is seen in sibling dyads where the older sibling is found repeatedly to be more dominant than the younger siblings (Abramovitch et al., 1986; Berndt & Bulleit, 1985). It also appears that younger siblings are more likely to imitate both siblings and peers than are older siblings (Abramovitch et al., 1986), so that cross-situational consistency may come in the form of attitudes and responses to others behavior, not in the form of repeating specific behaviors that are exhibited at home in a peer setting.

Age or relative age is not the only basis to consider peer status, and this may be particularly true in peer relations that are viewed as "same age." Physical prowess among boys is one possible relevant standard for defining peer status among boys because boys are especially prone to disputes about power. Whereas relative age may be a salient aspect of developmental status among siblings, a different dimension such as physical prowess or academic status may be more relevant in children's assessment of their status and rights in peer relations. This idea is consistent with the findings that there is greater consistency between behavior with peers and behavior with siblings when the siblings are very close in age (Berndt & Bulleit, 1985).

Finally, there is evidence that children are quite conscience of various context variables (such as, at whose home are you playing) that influence their social behavior with peers (Abramovitch et al., 1986). Given this, we cannot assume that sibling interactions are uniform across settings or uniform with interactions among peers, irrespective of context also. Greater attention to context factors that are linked to roles assumed in both sibling and peer relations is needed.

## Family Units Require Relationship Maintenance

*Quality of Marital Relationships and Marital Conflict.* Children in families where marriages are described by their parents as unhappy are more likely to have gotten into a fight at school in the previous week than are those children from homes housing happy marriages (Zill, in press). Disturbed relationships between parents put the child at risk for antisocial behavior (Rutter, 1981). What makes this link between the quality of the marital relationship and children's peer relations? Decreased marital satisfaction is associated with both increased conflict and poorer parent–child relations (Brody, Pillegrini, & Siegal, 1986; Goldberg & Easterbrooks, 1984; Johnson & Lobitz, 1974), and it is these two components of family functioning that most clearly appear to impact on children's relationships with their peers.

Marital conflict—if not used as a signal that the status quo is no longer acceptable, resulting in the emergence of new norms that revitalize the marriage—results in dissatisfied marriage partners and nonproductive, if not destructive, conflict (Deutsch, 1973). Ongoing interparental conflict and anger appear to be important influences on children's emotional and social development, particularly antisocial and anxious behavior (Cummings & Cummings, 1988; Grych & Fincham, in press). It appears that parents who successfully resolve their conflicts provide positive modeling of problem solving, which leads to children's reduced levels of distress in response to conflict, thereby increasing both social competence and relatively mature coping skills in response to conflict (Grych & Fincham, in press). At all ages (ages 4- to 9-year-olds), unresolved anger was reported by children as more negative and brought on more hostile emotional reactions than did resolved anger (Cummings, Vogel, & Cummings, 1987). Given the importance of conflict and its resolution for effective cooperative group functioning in both family and peer group contexts (Johnson & Johnson, 1989), the links between parental conflict resolution and the development of children's conflict resolution skills warrants attention.

In addition to how marital conflict is resolved, interparental conflict varies according to frequency, intensity, the extent to which it is overt or covert, and content. Children who have been exposed to more frequent conflict are more reactive when other conflict occurs (Cummings, Iannotti, & Zahn-Waxler, 1985; Cummings, Zahn-Waxler, & Radke-Yarrow, 1981), presumably including being more reactive to conflict with peers. With respect to frequency of marital conflict, the more topics a child's mother (or father) reports arguing about, the more likely the child reports being anxious in response to parental conflict, exemplified by their increased fear of parental arguments (Zill, in press). More frequent marital conflict that is open to children's view (i.e., overt conflict) is also associated with increased behavior problems (Johnston, Gonzalez, & Campbell, 1987; Long, Forehand, Fauber, & Brody, 1987; Long, Slater, Forehand, & Fauber, 1988; Porter & O'Leary, 1980; Wierson, Forehand, & McCombs, 1988), particularly represented by aggressiveness towards peers (Cummings et al., 1985). Intense marital conflict (i.e., conflict involving physical aggression) is more upsetting to children than mild marital conflict (Grych & Fincham, in press). Likewise, varying content of conflict has been found to differentially affect children's responses to it, with interparental conflict involving matters directly concerning the child and the marital relationship thought to be more arousing and damaging to the child's functioning both in the family and with peers (Grych & Fincham, in press).

Marital conflict specifically, and marital dissatisfaction in general, may lead to children's behavioral problems because it leads to a deterioration in parent–child relations (Grych & Fincham, in press; Hess & Camera, 1979; Jouriles, Barling, & O'Leary, 1987; O'Leary & Emery, 1984; Peterson & Zill, 1986). In particular, there are some data that suggest that within the context of teaching functions, maritally distressed couples are physiologically underaroused and have a parenting style that is cold, unresponsive, angry, and low in limit setting and structuring; conditions in turn related to relatively negative peer interactions for children from these families (Gottman & Katz, 1989). It is also suggested that family conflict often leads to direct parental maltreatment of children, and such maltreatment also tends to go along with reduced access to persons in the neighborhood, including peers (cf. chapter 12, this volume; Lewis & Schaeffer, 1981). Hostility, aggression, and disengagement found in interspousal relations appears linked to reduced levels of peer interaction (Gottman & Katz, 1989) and behavioral problems in childrens' peer relations (Gottman & Katz, 1989; Grych & Fincham, in press).

In addition, parental conflict creates a context that includes background anger as a family stressor. Children can make adaptive or maladaptive responses to this kind of stressor. What happens during the observation of background anger has been found to be different from what happens following the child's observation of angered disputes. Heightened emotionality is observed during exposure to background anger, whereas increased aggressiveness in play is more characteristically observed after exposure to anger (Cummings & Cummings, 1988). It is important to note that direct imitation of the parents' actual expressions of anger is not as characteristic of this aftereffect as is children's increased level of physical aggression with peers in ways that are more characteristic of aggression among peers. For example, increased hitting, biting, pushing, and taking each other's toys was characteristic of preschoolers' response to the observation of adult anger. Direct modeling of behavior is not apparently exported from observations of parental conflict but rather heightened emotionality, heightened vigilance for cues that may lead to anger and dissatisfaction, reduced level of peer play to maintain vigilance, are coupled with trouble regulating anger once it arises (Gottman & Katz, 1989), and seen as aggressiveness in response to others of equal or less power status in terms consistent with the behavioral norms of children.

Thus, aggression is not the only response to angry home environments. Interpersonal distancing seems to be another consequence of dissatisfied marital relationships. To this end, Dickstein and Parke (1988) found that marital dissatisfaction was related to children actively seeking their fathers less for emotional and/or instrumental information to help appraise an ambiguous situation. Television viewing may be another source of interpersonal distancing. Withdrawn vigilance is another form of interpersonal distancing. Alternatively, actively seeking out peers can serve to distance children from ongoing parental conflict. The extent to which all these forms of interpersonal distancing form the basis for future interpersonal distancing from peers warrants scrutiny.

Finally, it is not merely the absence of marital conflict and stress that can impact on the maintenance of the family's functioning. Warm and supportive marital relations appear to serve children well in their relations to other children. Warm, supportive marriages that also provide their children with warmth and support may serve as buffers to a range of stresses, including the stress of marital conflict (Emery, 1982; Rutter, 1979). Both the stresses that are a natural part of peer relations as well as family relations may be moderated by the nature of the marital relationship and the related parent–child relations. The positive provision of support of spouses to one another as it impacts on children's provision of support to others, including peers, as well as the impact of stress on children experiencing families with vital, supportive marital relations, merits further research.

*Family/Sibling Conflict Management.* Empirical studies suggest that popular children (i.e., children who are sociable, outgoing, helpful with peers, relatively unaggressive, well-adjusted, above average in school achievement; see Hartup, 1983) come from families that are cohesive and lacking in tension (Berndt, 1983). This kind of formulation is easily taken to infer that conflict is problematic. To the contrary, conflict is a normal part of interpersonal relations and thought to be helpful to normal, healthy interpersonal functioning and development (Dunn & Munn, 1987; Johnson & Johnson, 1989; Piaget, 1965). Learning to understand family members and the rules of families is of major interest to children (Dunn & Munn, 1985). Dunn and Munn (1985), in fact, demonstrated the centrality of conflict in even the young child's daily experiences at home and, based on the content of the conflicts, suggested that children make use of conflict to develop an understanding of the rules of their social worlds. The use of reasoned arguments has been found critical in aiding children to delineate and resolve conflict with peers (Eisenberg & Garvey, 1981), siblings, and parents (Dunn & Munn, 1987).

A family that is predominantly cooperative in orientation will encourage the discussion of difficulties that family members are having, and these discussions will enhance an appreciation of other family members as distinct individuals with unique and shared needs to reduce family dissatisfaction, disruption, and aggression (Johnson & Johnson, 1989). They will, in other words, focus on developing effective communication around efficient problem-solving activities. Consistent with this, there is research that indicates that parents who encourage cooperative behavior and nonaggressive solutions to interpersonal difficulties are more successful in promoting positive social interaction among their children if they also have a warm relationship with their children and use discipline that is neither aggressive in nature or is a result of losing control (Rutter & Cox, 1985). The ongoing context of interpersonal relations as conflict and problem solving appears of central importance.

The assumption that siblings provide a ground for practicing conflict disputes with peers needs empirical verification. To the extent that affective reactions, routines, expectations, jokes, games, sanctions, and prohibitions are the same in peer-based settings, and to the extent that children care about their relations with others, these experiences at home would be expected to extend. To the extent that they differ, the reworking of conflict manifestations and resolution would be expected to modify over time in interaction with one's peers.

Such proposed modification of children's social adeptness is shown within family life (Dunn & Munn, 1985). Over the second year of life, toddlers become increasingly adept at getting mother to provide them with help when they are in conflict with a sibling in two ways: (a) by explicitly formulating the sibling's transgression, and (b) by refraining from further aggravating the sibling conflict. Such modes for managing conflict with peers seem viable with teachers in peer-based settings, but we do not have clear data on this matter. What is clear is that the family context provides an important milieu for explicitly learning social rules and, when families include more than one child, siblings bring experiences that will do two things: first, the content of conflict will focus on rights and possessions and, second, conflict will involve children early on with practicing justification of rights and behaviors that will result in more favorable adult intervention in their behalf.

Strategies for conflict are thought to vary according to sibling status, with first-borns using high-power persuasive techniques on their younger siblings and last-borns using more low-power persuasion (Sutton-Smith & Rosenberg, 1968). Bragg, Ostrowski, and Finley (1973) found that this phenomenon had more to do with the relative age of participants in an interchange rather than sibling ordinal position per se. Miller and Maruyama (1976), as well as Sells and Roff (1964), provided data that are consistent with the view that later-borns, especially later-born girls, use more low-power strategies for negotiating with peers in that later-born children were more popular with peers than first-borns, and later-borns were described as more social and friendly and less demanding of peers. To date, actual observations of younger siblings with older siblings do not give a picture of younger siblings being particularly accommodating and tolerant of the older siblings, as was suggested by Miller and Maruyama (1976). It does appear, however, that younger siblings participate in dyadic interchanges in which they experience less power and more demands for subservient behavior toward older siblings (especially girls with older sisters) (Bryant, 1982b). This may be a situation in which skills of negotiation are learned, but behavior exhibited in interaction with older siblings does not always appear to transfer directly to situations with peers. Conflict resolution skills may well be learned as lessons practiced and rehearsed in sibling relations, but they may be performed in more final skilled form among peers (Bryant, 1982b). Empirical data are still needed to resolve these questions.

Families handle conflict in varying ways (Dunn & Munn, 1985). Families in which there is an aggressive child, aggressive both at home and at school, have been found to lack methods of resolving conflict once it arises so that conflict leads to persistent tension and dissatisfaction (Rutter & Cox, 1985). One important component missing in families with an aggressive child is fathers coming in to support their wives to effect a follow-through on establishing parental control when their wives are having difficulty in this regard (Patterson, 1981). Crisis management is at best a family affair and appears to be a critical "moment" with important impact on subsequent interpersonal relations both in the home and outside.

## Families Manage Leisure Time

Another aspect of maintenance of familial relations has to do with how families manage leisure time together. Whether or not families are able to organize leisure time together and how they do so varies across families. Leisure is viewed by some as a luxury they cannot afford. For example, concern about supervision of their children's care can lead parents to arrange their work schedules so that one parent works one shift and the other parent a different shift, thus enabling one parent to be home with their children (Mott, Mann, McLoughlin, & Warwick, 1965). One result of this arrangement means that the parent working the shift that enables him or her to be home after school with the children is stuck with the job of delivering most of the disciplining of the children. This stress together with little shared time with spouse can produce conflicts over what to do with the shared time. In other words, an attempt to have time with children may lead a parent to accept a night shift job, but this solution often leads to tension between mothers and fathers. Lack of adequate shared leisure time may at times be costly to the marital couple maintaining a mutually supportive relationship, with the unfortunate consequences on children's peer relations discussed earlier.

At home, toys and games often provide content to leisure time interactions in the family. Children receive toys, often from before birth at a baby shower. Parents and family friends can influence this aspect of the home environment by influencing the kind and amount of social interaction as well as the skills of playing with objects by determining the types of toys (isolate or social toys that require two or more participants) that they make available (Parke, 1978). These toys are powerful stimuli for interpersonal interaction and play a role in sibling interaction (Lamb, 1978). Children are more likely to play with toys when in the presence of members of the peer generation than when the mother alone is present (Rubenstein & Howes, 1976). The way in which recreation proceeds also differs according to whether or not a parent or peer is present. When recreation involves toys, infants first regard the use that the older sibling makes of the toys and then takes the toys from the older sibling (Lamb, 1978). In contrast, parents provide a more formal, planned didactic exchange around toys. How these leisure-time activities in the home setting provide children with game/play skills or social capital in their exchanges with peers warrants examination.

Television may well be the most popular family "toy" or leisure-time activity. Television is especially important to consider given the amount of time families make use of it. Preschoolers average 27 hours per week, school-age children average 26 hours, and teens average 23 hours per week of television viewing (A. C. Nielsen Company, 1982). Since television has been introduced, children spend more time at home (Belson, 1959), visit other children less, and spend less time outdoors, especially younger children (Himmelweit, Oppenheim, & Vince, 1958). Informal, unorganized activities are more affected by television viewing than is participation in formally organized sports.

Children who spend most of their free time with TV report the least amount of play with other children after school (Hoffman, 1971). Television viewing has also resulted in children spending less time in outdoor and indoor play as well as in household tasks (Maccoby, 1951). Although maternal unavailability due to working outside the home and father's absence from the home are related to greater television viewing among adolescents (Brown, Childers, Bauman, & Koch, 1990), maternal work status does not have the same implications for television viewing among preschool children (Pinon, Huston, & Wright, 1989), probably because of their need for direct adult supervision during periods of maternal working. Regardless of how much a child watches television, the pervasiveness of television in American culture also means that there is a reduced number of children outdoors for play, even if a family eliminates or restricts the use of television in their own home. Neighboring among both child and adult generations, or peer relations at all ages, appears to be affected by pervasive involvement with the television.

On the other hand, not all aspects of television viewing limit peer interaction. Television provides topics of conversations among family members (LoScuito, 1972; Lyle & Hoffman, 1972), among teachers and students (Goodman, 1983), and among peers on the playground (Goodman, 1983). Television content can be a source of peer pressure as children are seen adopting gestures, styles, and phrases of favorite television characters (Goodman, 1983).

Other aspects of leisure time and how families manage this activity appear particularly relevant for how families provide ongoing maintenance of feelings of well-being among family members and the role that leisure time might play in reducing levels of stress, influencing social goals and strategies, impacting on social rules in the family, and affect crisis management. In contrast to angry backgrounds, what are the effects of joyful backgrounds in the family? To the extent that effective cooperative groups are aided by generating fun as well as work, the value of studying family leisure time in relation to social development is warranted. When children report their leisure activities with pleasure, does this attract peers to enter into their social worlds? Because peers are expected to provide fun for one another, this consideration of family leisure time is additionally important. A complex of family factors, including types of toys, availability of peers and siblings in the family setting, parental participation, and the affective outcome associated with leisure-time activities, must have a differential impact on the kinds of interpersonal experiences, skills, and motivations for other experiences children acquire in this process.

## Conclusions

If we keep in mind that playing with other children is the most time-consuming activity of the school-age child's waking hours, surpassed only by going to school and watching television (Zill, in press), the way in which family experiences link children with their peers is all the more important. The examination of children's experiences "Beyond Parent–Child Relationships" has emphasized that children's experiences with parents do not occur in isolation of other individuals (e.g., siblings) or other systems (e.g., neighborhood/work environments). Family life is not accurately reduced to matters of dyadic parent–child or sibling interaction because children experience parents and siblings as part of a cooperatively organized group (which varies in the degree to which it functions as such). These cooperative units have subsystems (e.g., marriage partners), but much of each subsystem impacts on all family members, including those members who are not in the subsystem. More research is needed on the marital relations and sibling relations and the differential impact of direct and indirect effects on peers.

Consistent with this, how needs in families are met and how the needs of various family members impact on children's development of peer relations need greater attention. Parents' needs for money and self-esteem is related to their work life and in turn impact on family relations as well as on relations outside the nuclear family, and these dynamics involve the children and their peers. How work arrangements impact on parents' physical and emotional availability to their children and who is available when the parent(s) is (are) not available in times of children's needs must translate into children's social functioning with others.

In addition to opportunities to work and play with peers, children may bring varying motives (i.e., social goals) and skills to their transactions with peers. Needs for approval as compared to needs for information from peers differentiate the quality of peer relations. Why children seek out peers, at times in lieu of siblings, for particular reasons needs greater consideration. Skills needed in both family and peer systems involve negotiation, conflict resolution, caregiving, and pleasuring. These skills are in part acquired in dynamic, complex social systems called nuclear families, extended families, and neighborhoods. Although it is easier to study components of these systems such as dyads, much of the meaning of dyadic interchange is lost when we do not see the interplay of a dyad with other family members and social systems.

Finally, the research literature to date does not offer a clear developmental view of the impact of family system on peer relations. Are certain aspects of family functioning or extrafamilial functioning more salient and powerful in influencing peer relations at some stages of a child's development over others? Are some developmental trajectories of peer relations arrested or changed due to how family systems change and develop?

Parental tensions in systems outside the parent–child dyad (e.g., perceived dangerous community, economic and/or work pressures, ongoing marital conflict and dissatisfaction) impact on family processing in direct and indirect ways. How these family events inhibit, sensitize, or redirect children's attention to certain experiences (e.g., conflict) within their experiences with peers warrants our research attention.

## ACKNOWLEDGMENT

Special acknowledgment is given to Michel Djakovic and Ross Parke for their critical feedback on earlier drafts of this chapter.

## REFERENCES

Abramovitch, R., Corter, C., Pepler, D. J., & Stanhope, L. (1986). Sibling and peer interaction: A final follow-up and a comparison. *Child Development, 57*, 217–229.

A. C. Nielsen Company. (1982). *Nielsen report on television*. Northbrook, IL: Author.

Barbarin, O. (1983). Coping with ecological transitions by Black families: A psychosocial model. *Journal of Community Psychology, 11*, 308–311.

Belle, D. (Ed.) (1982). *Lives in stress: Women and depression*. Beverly Hills: Sage.

Belle, D., Longfellow, C., & Makovsky, V. P. (1982). Stress, depression, and the mother–child relationship: Report of a field study. *International Journal of Sociology of the Family, 12*, 251–263.

Belson, W. A. (1959). *Television and the family*. London: British Broadcasting Corporation.

Berndt, T. (1983). Peer relationships in children of working parents: A theoretical analysis and some conclusions. In C. D. Hayes and S. B. Kamerman (Eds.), *Children of working parents: Experiences and outcomes* (pp. 13–43). Washington, DC: National Academy Press.

Berndt, T. J., & Bulleit, T. N. (1985). Effects of sibling relationships on preschoolers' behavior at home and at school. *Developmental Psychology, 21*(5), 761–767.

Bragg, B. W. E., Ostrowski, M. V., & Finley, G. E. (1973). The effects of birth order and age of target on use of persuasive techniques. *Child Development, 44*, 351–354.

Brody, G. H., Pillegrini, A. D., & Siegal, I. E. (1986). Marital quality and mother–child and father–child interactions with school-aged children. *Developmental Psychology, 22*, 291–296.

Brown, J. D., Childers, K. W., Bauman, K. E., & Koch, G. G. (1990). The influence of new media and family structure on young adolescents' television and radio use. *Communication Research, 17*(1), 65–82.

Bryant, B. (1982a). An index of empathy for children and adolescents. *Child Development,* *53,* 413–425.

Bryant, B. (1982b). Sibling relationships in middle childhood. In M. E. Lamb & B. Sutton-Smith (Eds.), *Sibling relationships: Their nature and significance across the lifespan* (pp. 87–122). Hillsdale, NJ: Lawrence Erlbaum Associates.

Bryant, B. (1987). Mental health, temperament, family, and friends: Perspectives on children's empathy and social perspective taking. In N. Eisenberg & J. Strayer (Eds.), *Empathy and its development* (pp. 245–270). New York: Cambridge University Press.

Bryant, B. (1989a). The child's perspective of sibling caretaking and its relevance to understanding social-emotional functioning and development. In P. Zukow (Ed.), *Sibling interactions across cultures* (pp. 143–164). New York: Springer-Verlag.

Bryant, B. (1989b). The need for support in relation to the need for autonomy. In D. Belle (Ed.), *Children's social networks and social supports* (pp. 332–351). New York: Wiley.

Bryant, B., & Crockenberg, S. (1980). Correlates and dimensions of prosocial behavior: A study of female siblings with their mothers. *Child Development, 51,* 529–544.

Burden, D. S. (1986). Single parents and the work setting: The impact of multiple job and homelife responsibilities. *Family Relations, 35,* 37–43.

Crouter, A. C. (1984). Spillover from family to work: The neglected side of the work–family interface. *Human Relations, 37,* 425–442.

Cummings, E. M., & Cummings, J. L. (1988). A process-oriented approach to children's coping with adults' angry behavior. *Developmental Review, 8,* 296–321.

Cummings, E. M., Iannotti, R. J., & Zahn-Waxler, C. (1985). Influence of conflict between adults on the emotions and aggression of young children. *Developmental Psychology, 21,* 495–507.

Cummings, E. M., Vogel, D., & Cummings, J. S. (1987). Children's responses to different forms of expression of anger between adults. Cited in E. M. Cummings & J. L. Cummings, A process-oriented approach to children's coping with adults' angry behavior. *Developmental Review, 8,* 296–321.

Cummings, E. M., Zahn-Waxler, C., & Radke-Yarrow, M. (1981). Young children's responses to expressions of anger and affection by others in the family. *Child Development, 52,* 1274–1281.

Daniels, D., & Moos, R. H. (1988). Exosystem influences on family and child functioning. In E. Goldsmith (Ed.), Work and family: Theory, research, and applications [Special issue]. *Journal of Social Behavior and Personality, 3*(4), 113–133.

Davis, J. A. (1983). *General social surveys, 1972–1983: Cumulative codebook.* Chicago: National Opinion Research Center.

Deutsch, M. (1973). *The resolution of conflict.* New Haven, CT: Yale University Press.

Devereux, E. C., Bronfenbrenner, U., & Rodgers, R. R. (1969). Child-rearing in England and the United States: A cross-national comparison. *Journal of Marriage and Family, 31,* 257–270.

Dickstein, S., & Parke, R. D. (1988). Social referencing in infancy: A glance at fathers and marriage. *Child Development, 59,* 506–511.

Duckett, E., & Richards, M. (1989). *Maternal employment and young adolescents' daily experience in single-mother families.* Paper presented at the Biennial Meeting of the Society for Research on Child Development, Kansas City, Missouri.

Dunn, J., & Kendrick. C. (1982). *Siblings: Love, envy, and understanding:* Cambridge, MA: Harvard University Press.

Dunn, J., & Munn, P. (1985). Becoming a family member: Family conflict and the development of social understanding in the second year. *Child Development, 56,* 480–492.

Dunn, J., & Munn, P. (1987). Development of justification in disputes with mother and sibling. *Developmental Psychology, 23*(6), 791–798.

Eisenberg, A. R., & Garvey, C. (1981). Children's use of verbal strategies in resolving conflicts. *Discourse Processes, 4,* 149–170.

Elder, G. H., Jr. (1974). *Children of the Great Depression: Social change in life experience.* Chicago: University of Chicago Press.

Emery, R. E. (1982). Interparental conflict and the children of discord and divorce. *Psychological Bulletin, 92,* 310–330.

Fassinger, P. A. (1989). Becoming the breadwinner: Single mothers' reactions to changes in their paid work lives. *Family Relations, 38,* 404–411.

Fernandez, J. (1985). *Child care and corporate productivity: Resolving family/work conflict.* New York: Lexington Books, D. C. Heath.

Fox, K. D., & Nickols, S. Y. (1983). The time crunch: Wife's employment and family work. *Journal of Family Issues, 4,* 61–82.

Goldberg, W. A., & Easterbrooks, M. A. (1984). Role of marital quality in toddler development. *Developmental Psychology, 20,* 504–514.

Golding, J. M. (1989). Role occupancy and role-specific stress and social support as predictors of depression. *Basic and Applied Social Psychology, 10*(2), 173–195.

Goodman, I. F. (1983). Televisions' role in family interaction. *Journal of Family Issues, 4*(2), 405–424.

Gottman, J. M., & Katz, L. F. (1989). Effects of marital discord on young children's peer interaction and health. *Developmental Psychology, 25*(3), 1–9.

Greenberger, E., & Goldberg, W. (1989). Work, parenting, and the socialization of children. *Developmental Psychology, 25*(1), 22–35.

Grych, J. H., & Fincham, F. D. (in press). Marital conflict and children's adjustment: A cognitive–contextual framework. *Psychological Bulletin.*

Gump, P., Schoggen, P., & Redl, F. (1963). The behavior of the same child in different milieu. In R. Barker (Ed.), *The stream of behavior* (pp. 169–202). New York: Appleton-Century-Crofts.

Hart, R. (1978). *Children's sense of place.* New York: Halstead.

Hartup, W. (1983). Peer relations. In E. M. Hetherington (Ed.), *Carmichael's manual of child psychology* (4th ed., pp. 103–196). New York: Wiley.

Hayes, C., & Kamerman, S. B. (1983). *Children of working parents: Experiences and outcomes.* Washington, DC: National Academy Press.

Hess, R. D., & Camera, K. A. (1979). Postdivorce family relationships as mediating factors in the consequences of divorce for children. *Journal of Social Issues, 35,* 79–98.

Hetherington, M., Cox, M., & Cox, R. (1978). The aftermath of divorce. In J. H. Stevens, Jr. & M. Mathews (Eds.), *Mother-child, father-child relationships* (pp. 398–439). Washington, DC: National Association for the Education of Young Children.

Himmelweit, H. T., Oppenheim, A. N., & Vince, P. (1958). *Television and the child.* New York: Oxford University Press.

Hofferth, S. L., & Moore, K. A. (1979). Women's employment and marriage. In R. E. Smith, (Ed.), *The subtle revolution: Women at work* (pp. 141–155). Washington, DC: The Urban Institute.

Hoffman, L. W. (1971). Deviation amplifying processes in natural groups. In J. Haley (Ed.), *Changing families* (pp. 91–131). New York: Grune & Stratton.

Hoffman, L. W. (1984). Work, family, and the socialization of the child. In R. Parke (Ed.), *Review of child development research* (Vol. 7, pp. 223–282). Chicago: University of Chicago Press.

Hoffman, L. W., & Nye, F. I. (1974). *Working mothers.* San Francisco: Jossey-Bass.

Holt, J. (1975). *Escape from childhood: The needs and rights of children.* Baltimore: Penguin Books.

Johnson, D. W. (1981). Social psychology. In F. Farley & N. Gordon (Eds.), *Educational psychology* (pp. 43–67). Berkeley, CA: National Society for the Study of Education.

Johnson, D. W., & Johnson, R. T. (1989). *Cooperation and competition: Theory and research.* Edina, MN: Interaction.

Johnson, S. M., & Lobitz, G. K. (1974). The personal and marital adjustment of parents as related to observed child deviance and parenting behaviors. *Journal of Abnormal Child Psychology, 2*, 193–207.

Johnston, J. R., Gonzalez, R., & Campbell, L. E. (1987). Ongoing postdivorce conflict and child disturbance. *Journal of Abnormal Child Psychology, 15*, 497–509.

Jouriles, E. N., Barling, J., & O'Leary, K. D. (1987). Predicting child behavior problems in maritally violent families. *Journal of Abnormal Child Psychology, 15*, 165–173.

Kandel, D. B. (1978). Homophily, selection, and socialization and adolescent friendships. *American Journal of Sociology, 84*, 427–436.

Kanter, R. (1977). *Work and family in the United States: A critical review and agenda for research and policy*. New York: Russell Sage.

Kelly, R. F., & Voydanoff, P. (1985). Work/family role strain among employed parents. *Family Relations, 34*, 367–374.

Komarovsky, M. (1962). *Blue-collar marriage*. New York: Random House.

Kline, M. & Cowan, P. A. (1988). Re-thinking the connections among "work" and "family" and well-being. In E. Goldsmith (Ed.), Work and family: Theory, research, and applications [special issue]. *Journal of Social Behavior and Personality, 3*(4), 61–90.

Lamb, M. (1978). Interactions between 18-month-olds and their preschool-aged siblings. *Child Development, 49*, 51–59.

Lamb, M. (Ed.). (1982). *Nontraditional families: Parenting and child development*. Hillsdale, NJ: Lawrence Erlbaum Associates.

Lewis, M. L., & Schaeffer, S. (1981). Peer behavior and mother–infant interaction. In M. L. Lewis & S. Schaeffer (Eds.), *The uncommon child* (pp. 93–223). New York: Plenum.

Littlewood, J., & Sale, R. (1972). Children at play: A look at where they play and what they do on housing estates. As cited in R. Parke (1978). Children's home environments: Social and cognition effects. In I. Altman & J. F. Wohlwill (Eds.), *Children and the environment* (pp. 33–81). New York: Plenum.

Long, N., Forehand R., Fauber, R., & Brody, G. (1987). Self-perceived and independently observed competence of young adolescents as a function of parental marital conflict and recent divorce. *Journal of Abnormal Child Psychology, 15*, 15–27.

Long, N., Slater, E., Forehand, R., & Fauber, R. (1988). Continued high or reduced interparental conflict following divorce: Relation to young adolescent adjustment. *Journal of Consulting and Clinical Psychology, 56*, 467–469.

LoScuito, L. (1972). A national inventory of television viewing behavior. In E. Rubinstein, G. Comstock, & J. Murray (Eds.), *Television and social behavior* (Vol. 4, pp. 43–67). Washington, DC: Government Printing Office.

Lyle, J., & Hoffman, H. R. (1972). Children's use of television and other media. In E. Rubinstein, G. Comstock, & J. Murray (Eds.), *Television and social behavior* (Vol. 4, pp. 129–256). Washington, DC: Government Printing Office.

Maccoby, E. (1951). Television: Its impact on school children. *Public Opinion Quarterly, 15*, 421–444.

Marcus, C. C. (1974). Children's play behavior in a low rise inner-city housing development. In D. Carson (Ed.), *Man–environment interactions: Evaluation and applications* (Vol. 12, pp. 197–211). Milwaukee, WI: Environmental Design Research Association.

Medrich, E. A., Roizen, J. A., Rubin, V., & Buckley, S. (1982). *The serious business of growing up: A study of children's lives outside school*. Berkeley: University of California Press.

Mendelson, M. J., Aboud, F. E., & Lanthier, R. (1990, August). *Sibling relationships and popularity in kindergarten*. Poster presented at the meeting of American Psychological Association, Boston.

Miller, N., & Maruyama, G. (1976). Ordinal position and peer popularity. *Journal of Personality and Social Psychology, 33*, 123–131.

Minuchin, S. (1974). *Families and family therapy*. Cambridge, MA: Harvard University Press.

Moore, R., & Young, D. (1978). Childhood outdoors: Toward a social ecology of the landscape. In J. Altman & J. Wohlwill (Eds.), *Children and the environment* (pp. 83–130). New York: Plenum Press.

Mott, P., Mann, F., McLoghlin, Q., & Warwick, D. (1965). *Shift work: The social, psychological, and physical consequences*. Ann Arbor: University of Michigan Press.

Newman, O. (1972). *Defensible space*. New York: Macmillan.

O'Leary, K. D., & Emery, R. E. (1984). Marital discord and child behavior problems. In M. D. Levine & P. Satz (Eds.), *Developmental variation and dysfunction* (pp. 345–364). New York: Academic Press.

Parke, R. (1978). Children's home environments: Social and cognitive effects. In I. Altman & J. F. Wohlwill (Eds.), *Children and the environment* (pp. 33–81). New York: Plenum.

Patterson, G. R. (1981). Mothers: The unacknowledged victims. *Monographs of the Society for Research in Child Development, 46*, (Whole No. 5).

Patterson, G. (1983). Stress: A change agent for family process. In N. Garmezy & M. Rutter (Eds.), *Stress, coping, and development in children* (pp. 235–264). New York: McGraw-Hill.

Peterson, J. L., & Zill, N. (1986). Marital disruption, parent–child relationships, and behavior problems in children. *Journal of Marriage and the Family, 48*, 295–307.

Piaget, J. (1965). *The moral judgment of the child*. New York: Free Press.

Pinon, M. F., Huston, A. C., & Wright, J. C. (1989). Family ecology and child characteristics that predict young children's educational television viewing. *Child Development, 60*, 846–856.

Porter, B., & O'Leary, K. D. (1980). Marital discord and childhood behavior problems. *Journal of Abnormal Child Psychology, 8*, 287–295.

Raffaelli, M. (1989, April). *Conflict with siblings and friends in late childhood and early adolescence*. Paper presented at the Biennial Meeting of the Society for Research in Child Development, Kansas City, MO.

Roff, M., Sells, S. B., & Golden, M. M. (1972). *Social adjustment and personality development in children*. Minneapolis, MN: University of Minnesota Press.

Rolf, J. (1976). Peer status and the directionality of symptomatic behavior. *American Journal of Orthopsychiatry, 46*, 74–87.

Rubenstein, J. L., & Howes, C. (1976). The effects of peers on toddler interaction with mothers and toys. *Child Development, 47*, 597–605.

Rutter, M. (1979). Maternal deprivation, 1972–1978: New findings, new concepts, new approaches. *Child Development, 50*, 283–305.

Rutter, M. (1981). *Maternal deprivation reassessed*. (2nd ed.). New York: Penguin Books.

Rutter, M., & Cox, A. (1985). Other family influences. In M. Rutter & L. Hersov (Eds.), *Child and adolescent psychiatry: Modern approaches* (2nd ed., pp. 58–81). Boston, MA: Blackwell Scientific.

Sanik, M. M., & Mauldin, T. (1986). Single versus two-parent families: A comparison of mothers' time. *Family Relations, 35*, 53–56.

Sells, S. B., & Roff, M. (1964). Peer acceptance–rejection and birth order. *Psychology in the Schools, 1*, 156–162.

Spitze, G. (1988). Women's employment and family relations: A review. *Journal of Marriage and the Family, 50*, 595–618.

Steinberg, L. (1986). Latchkey children and susceptibility to peer pressure: An ecological analysis. *Developmental Psychology, 22*(4), 433–439.

Strube, M., & Barbour, L. (1984). Factors related to the decision to leave a relationship. *Journal of Marriage and Family, 46*, 837–844.

Sutton-Smith, B., & Rosenberg, B. (1968). Sibling consensus on power tactics. *Journal of Genetic Psychology, 112*, 63–72.

Veenhoven, R., & Verkuyten, M. (1989). The well-being of only children. *Adolescence, 24*(93), 155–166.

Weintraub, S., Neale, J. M., & Liebert, D. E. (1975). Teacher ratings of children vulnerable to psychopathology. *American Journal of Orthopsychiatry, 45*, 839–845.

Weiss, R. (1979). *Going it alone: The family life and social situation of the single parent.* New York: Basic Books.

Wierson, M., Forehand, R., & McCombs, A. (1988). The relationship of early adolescent functioning to parent-reported and adolescent-perceived interparental conflict. *Journal of Abnormal Child Psychology, 16*, 707–718.

Whiting, B. B., & Whiting, J. W. M. (1975). *Children of six cultures.* Cambridge, MA: Harvard University Press.

Wilson, M. (1989). Child development in the context of the Black extended family. *American Psychologist, 44*(2), 380–385.

Wolkind, S., & Rutter, M. (1985). Separation, loss, and family relationships. In M. Rutter & L. Hersov (Eds.), *Child and adolescent psychiatry: Modern approaches* (pp. 34–57). Palo Alto, CA: Blackwell Scientific.

Zill, N. (in press). *Learning to listen to children.* New York: Cambridge University Press.

# CHAPTER SEVEN

# Societal Influences
# on Children's Peer Relationships

Moncrieff Cochran
Virginia Davila
*Cornell University*

The purpose of this chapter is to suggest some of the ways that the influences of the larger society are transmitted to children, to set some of
the parameters for peer relations, and in turn affect the access children
and adolescents have to opportunities for companionship, for the learning of important social skills, and for the satisfaction of intimacy needs.
We are challenging the reader to look beyond personality characteristics, the parent–child dyad, and family dynamics for explanations of
differences in peer relationships, and the impacts of those relationships
on development. Four studies are presented as a starting point, to illustrate the links in a conceptual chain connecting macrolevel factors with
networks, peer relations, and peer-related social outcomes. Then we introduce and discuss briefly a conceptual model for understanding how
society affects the development of networks, and how network characteristics in turn affect human development. Following introduction of
the model, we draw on the work of others to justify a basic assumption
underlying our own research; that peer relations have significance for
development in childhood and adolescence. The remainder of the chapter is devoted to presentation and discussion of findings from the Cornell Family Matters Project; findings that lead us to propose that the
structure of society shapes peer relations, and that parents' networks provide one of the primary means by which these societal influences reach
the developing child.

What evidence exists that might induce the reader to venture further

191

into a chapter on societal influences, in a book that focuses primarily on linkages between family and peer systems? The previous research linking features of society with social networks, and networks with peer-related outcomes, is sparse, but we have found four studies that we hope, when taken together, are tantalizing enough to pique the reader's interest. These studies are summarized in the following, as a prelude to introduction of an overall model and presentation of data gathered through the Cornell Family Matters Project.

## Society, Networks, and Peer-Related Outcomes

The most comprehensive published accounts to date of studies linking parents' social networks with childrearing patterns and effects on children have been conducted in Australia. Homel, Burns, and Goodnow (1987) set out to better understand "the influence upon children of their parents' links with community, friends, neighbors, and kin" (p. 339). They interviewed the fathers, mothers, and 9- to 11-year-old children in 305 families from areas in Sydney defined as high, medium, and low according to the number of social risk indicators contained in each area. Information about the "family" network was gathered from one or the other parent (alternating), yielding data about the frequency, location, and dependability of relations with neighbors, friends, and relatives, and about affiliation with community organizations. Data collected from the children included information about their happiness, negative emotions, social skills, friendship networks, and school adjustment. Especially relevant to the peer relations focus of this book were the measures of social skills and child's networks. Social skills were assessed by mothers, who rated their children in terms of ability to get along with others the same age, and how considerate the child was toward others. The children themselves provided various kinds of information about friendships, including how many children they played with regularly, whether they liked most children in their class, and whether they had a best friend.

The authors reported two primary clusters of findings. First, a number of child variables were related to the presence/absence or the number of dependable adult friends in the family network: happiness with the family, negative emotions, peer-related social skills, extensiveness and diversity of friendship networks, and school adjustment. Also important were local friendship networks and ties to community organizations. The family friends who made a difference were nonkin, as distinguished from the kinfolk in the networks. One especially interesting detail in the larger array of findings pertains to the relationship between the friendship networks of family and child. Where the parents reported the presence of just one dependable friend, the child was likely to report friendship with one or two children or membership in a small clique. Children whose parents reported a number of dependable friends themselves tended to describe peer contact with a number of equally liked friends.

Complicating interpretation of the findings presented is the fact that the number of "social risk" factors found in the family's residential area also bore a strong relationship to the child's friendship network and social skill outcomes. The authors presented neighborhood risk and family networks as "alternative models" for understanding the development of child characteristics and behavior; they did not use their statistical methods in an attempt to sort out the causal relations that might exist among all three ecological domains.[1] Homel et al. (1987) did, however, point out that neighborhood risk can exert effects independent of parental networks, saying that "The children of even the best-connected parents would be likely to be affected by constant moves, or by their friends constantly moving, or by a hostile neighborhood atmosphere" (p. 176). They also noted the need in future research for more detailed consideration of links between parental networks and other demographic variables.

Another Australian has completed a study of parent networks and childrearing that, although connecting fewer ecological levels than the work of Homel et al. (1987), provides a more differentiated picture of relations between the macro and midrange forces affecting the child. John Cotterell (1986) was interested in the influences on childrearing of the father's workplace, the mother's social network, and the community itself. With 96 married mothers recruited from four rural towns in inland Australia, he compared the personal networks and childrearing milieus provided by those whose husbands were regularly present with those whose partner's jobs routinely required periods of absence from home. The groups were further stratified by community type: rural versus mining towns. Characteristics of the childrearing environment were measured with the Caldwell HOME inventory, and the quality of maternal expectations and beliefs was assessed with the Parent as a Teacher (PAAT) inventory. When the "quality of childrearing" variables were analyzed by father's presence/absence and by mother's amount of informational support from the network, the characteristics of the father's work exerted independent influence on only two of the variables, whereas the effects of support were statistically significant for six of the seven childrearing measures. In order to assess the separate and joint contributions of the three environmental dimensions, Cotterell (1986) entered them all with the childrearing variables in a regression equation; in his own words:

---

[1]See Cochran and Bø (1989) for an example of this approach to the relationship between neighborhood risk and personal networks.

Between 40% and 60% of the variance explained in the full model could
be attributed to the factors of father absence, community characteristics,
and mother's informational support. Of the three factors, the support factor had the greatest prominence in terms of its power to add significantly
to the variance in the measures of child-rearing quality. (p. 369)

Cotterell was careful to point out the danger of assuming that these
three environmental forces—general character of the community, father's
work situation, and mother's network support—operate independently
and at the same level of influence. He suggested that "the chain of influence of father's work is connected to maternal behavior via the patterns of social relationships established by the mother" (p. 371). His
evidence indicates that the wives of absentee husbands had smaller networks, and that these women had a more limited range of settings available for contacting network members.

Cottrell's work is especially useful for distinguishing among what Bronfenbrenner (1989) called *exosystem influences*, as mediated by the
mother's social network, on her childrearing attitudes and behavior. He
did not make the link to developmentally salient outcomes in the child,
and the childrearing variables he used were more tuned to cognitive than
social development. Another researcher, Brenda Bryant, has completed
an exciting study of relationships between sources of social support and
socioemotional functioning during middle childhood. Her work coun-
terbalances the strengths and limitations of Cotterell's study, providing
insight into the link to outcomes but only hinting at possible ties to macrolevel forces. Bryant (1985) carried out a cross-sectional comparison of
7 and 10-year-old children, assessing their resources of support (rather
than those of their parents) at home and in the neighborhood, and ad-
ministering several measures of social-emotional functioning. Some of
the factors generated with these measures are pertinent for development
of peer relations; social perspective taking, attitudes toward competition,
empathy, acceptance of help, and acceptance of individual differences.

Bryant found that there was a positive relationship between the support variables and socioemotional functioning for the 10-year-olds but
not for the 7-year-olds. She offered three possible interpretations of this
age-related difference. First, she said, it may be that 10-year-olds are able
to make use of available resources in ways that are beyond the reach of
7-year-olds. A second possibility is that there is a "sleeper" effect at work:
supports already operating with the 7-year-olds don't show up in behavior
until 3 years later. Bryant's third interpretation was that a certain amount
of parental distancing in middle childhood may nudge the 10-year-olds
from the parental nest, thereby giving other supports more salience. An
implication of this third interpretation is that network resources may be
most useful in circumstances where the child is experiencing some

"press" to acquire social support. It is worth noting in this regard that the notion of "press" has become important to those studying the mobilization of social support by adults (Eckenrode & Gore, 1981). It is also of interest in the Bryant study that the social responses to this (hypothesized) press were gender-differentiated in ways that conform with what others have written about the nature of male and female social relationships.[2] For boys, extensive, casual involvement with adults was linked to positive outcomes, whereas for girls the positive link was with intensive, intimate involvement.

None of the children in Bryant's sample were growing up in impoverished conditions, and all benefited from some socioeconomic benefits and the advantages of location in the ethnic majority. Despite rather little variation in the sample by length of residence or type of community, Bryant (1985) did find that:

> In sum, the extent of a child's network of support is weakly tempered in some respects by the length of a child's residence at a particular address (especially with respect to involvement with the parent generation) and in a limited way by the type of community (e.g., with respect to support sources requiring adult sanction) represented in this study of non-metropolitan and rural communities. (p. 75)

She suggested that these factors might play a larger role in mediating the child's support during middle childhood in studies that contain a wider range of communities. To the extent that communities differ by family income, parents' educational attainment, race, and family structure, it is reasonable to extend Bryant's suggestion about the impacts of community differences on network supports to include systematic consideration of these structural factors.

The studies by Homel, Burns, and Goodnow, and by Cotterell focused on the social supports provided to parents, whereas Bryant interviewed children about the sources of support they themselves were experiencing. What is the relationship between the social networks of parents and those of their children? Anne Tietjen (1985) was the first researcher to study this question empirically. Her sample consisted of 72 Swedish mothers and their 8- and 9-year-old children. Mothers and children were interviewed separately. Tietjen found similarities between the networks of mothers and their daughters that were not apparent for mothers and sons, and she proposed modeling, teaching, and the provision of opportunities for interaction as the processes that might account for such commonalities. In so doing she suggested a set of network-building processes that would rather neatly explain the gender-differentiated findings of

---

[2]See Gilligan (1982) on the development of moral thought, and Blyth, Hill, and Thiel (1982) on the significant others of young adolescents.

Bryant reported earlier. If girls model the networking behavior of their mothers, and boys that of their fathers, and if the network ties of mothers are more intense than those of fathers, then the Bryant data showing girls with intensive and boys with extensive involvement in social relationships would follow.

Tietjen's early research in Sweden has helped us appreciate how much the social supports available to parents condition those available to young children. Since then she has studied support systems for childrearing and the development of child competence in Papua New Guinea (Tietjen, 1986). In a recent chapter (Tietjen, 1989) she used 8-year-old girls from Sweden and Papua New Guinea as case study examples to illustrate "an ecological model for understanding the role of social support systems in the development of context-appropriate competence in children . . ." (p. 45). In her model, cultural and ideological beliefs shape the economic, social, and political roles of a given ecological context, and so determine what skills and abilities define the nature of competence in that context. Tietjen used data from larger subject pools in the two countries to demonstrate that "The collectivist orientation of the Maisin and the more individualistic orientation of the Swedes are already evident in the social networks and interaction patterns of children" (p. 63).

What linkages have been established or suggested by these four studies that might illuminate the ways the influences of the larger society are transmitted to children to set the parameters for peer relations? First, links are made between the forces structuring the larger society and the networks of both parents and children. Culture, level of urbanization, community type, social risk factors, and employment characteristics are identified by one or another of these researchers as factors possibly affecting the breadth or depth of parents' or children's networks. Second, evidence is presented for relationships between the networks of parents and those of their children. Anne Tietjen has examined this link most closely, and posited the causal direction primarily from parent to child, but Homel, Burns, and Goodnow also report similarities between the network characteristics of parents and their children. Third, there is the link between children's networks and their peer relationships, made explicit by Bryant in relation to her sample of 10-year-olds. It is also apparent from her study that the salience of this relationship is mediated by a characteristic of the children themselves: their chronological age.

## The Personal Network: Its Development and Its Effects on Development

In order to make a case for the proposition that the influences of the larger society are played out in peer relations, a model is needed that contains a chain of social relations made up of the three links just identified, and including the active involvement of the developing child in the network-building process. The model presented in Fig. 7.1 is taken from a book by Cochran, Larner, Riley, Gunnarsson, and Henderson (1990), in which the network-related findings from the Cornell Family Matters Project are presented in considerable detail. Here we introduce the model, as an aide to orientation of the reader, before summarizing some of the findings.

The focus in this schematic is on the parent's network, but the basic model could be applied as well to development of the network of the child. This model incorporates the forces constraining or shaping network development, the factors stimulating individual initiatives at network-building, the network itself, and reference to the resultant developmental processes and outcomes for both parent and child.

It is very important to project the dynamic qualities of the processes driving the model. Most of the potential for network change comes from the right side; shifts in developmental stage, level of knowledge and skill, and personal identity all affect the amount and direction of social initiatives. Initiatives themselves can take two forms: the selection of network members from the pool of individuals available to the parent and maintenance activities undertaken within the existing network.

Use is made in the model of the idea of a "pool of eligibles" as a way of distinguishing between the people actually available for inclusion in the network and those selected as members. The pool of eligibles consists of those people to whom the person has access for *potential* inclusion in the network. Use of this concept permits us to define the constraints on the left side of the model as establishing the boundaries

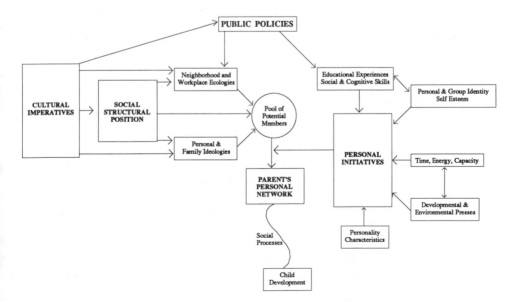

FIG. 7.1. Development of the personal network: A model.

for the size and content of the pool, while at the same time providing the individual with a role in building a network from that pool.

Determining the pool of potential network members are a more stable set of factors on the left side of the model. Cultural imperatives are the values and beliefs guiding a society (Ogbu, 1981). Social structural position is defined in a given society by how resources like education, work, and income are allocated according to race, gender, ethnic background, and type of family. In general, for instance, network size increases with increases in the educational level of parents and in family income (Cochran et al., 1990; Fischer, 1982).

In selecting the term *constraints* to characterize the factors included on the left side of the model, we have chosen the terminology of Claude Fischer and other sociologists doing networks research. (Fischer, 1982; Wellman, 1979). To us this term connotes restraint on individual action. We and others have identified a number of ways in which individuals and families are restrained from establishing social relations that are crucial to their development, some of which are presented later in this chapter, yet we also recognize that many of the constraints by societies placed on individual behavior are positive; for example, limits placed on violence against children and spouses, and on the right of parents to relinquish responsibility for financial support of their children.

This is a good place to interject a point that may not be obvious to readers unfamiliar with the basic elements comprising personal networks, who still may be wondering why networks are receiving attention in a book of family–peer relationships. Network members play different roles for the person anchoring the network; perhaps the most generic of those roles is kinship. Fischer (1982) presented data indicating that 30%–50% of the membership in the networks of his respondents were kinfolk. In our Family Matters data, where all the respondents were parents with young children, relatives made up 40%–60% of those parents' networks, and 31%–55% of the networks of their children. Thus, for both parents and children, a large proportion of the network is "family" in the broader sense of that term. Equally importantly, significant numbers of network members are not "family," and so can provide a bridge from the family to the society at large.

Where in the model presented in Fig. 7.1 should the reader look to find the chain of social relations proposed earlier, linking larger social forces, parents' networks, childrens' networks, and child peer relations? The first link can be found on the left side of the model, as indicated by the arrows from cultural imperatives and social-structural position to the pool of membership potential available to the developing person—in this case the parent. The second link, between parents' networks and those of their children, is included in the social processes connecting the parent's network with child development, shown at the bottom of the model.[3] The third link, connecting the characteristics of parents' and children's networks with the nature of the children's peer relations, is also captured in the processes connecting the parent's networks with the child's development.

We use these links to structure the remaining sections of the chapter, in which findings that bear on each link are presented from our own research. However, because the Family Matters Project was carried out as a large-scale attempt to better understand the ecology of *human development*, we set the stage with a short review of the findings and theory generated by others especially interested in how development might be affected by peer relations.

## Peer Relations and Child Development

In the contents of the box in Fig. 7.1 labeled "Child Development," we have included basic trust, self-appraisal, network-building skills, tolerance, respect for differences, openness to others, empathy, and respect for others (Cochran et al., 1990). These are not developmental outcomes measured in our own research; they have been extracted instead from the research of others. They serve as the basis for a pair of assumptions, in support of which we offer no new evidence. These assumptions are presented to emphasize that the central concern in this chapter is not with the nature of peer interaction, or with the developmental outcomes flowing from those interactions. Our primary interest, when presenting the Family Matters data, is with the extent to which children have **access to the opportunity to engage in or observe such interactions in the first place**.

Our first and most basic assumption is that peer relationships have significance for development in childhood and adolescence, and, indeed, at all stages in the life course. Three contributions made by peer relations to development are of special interest, because of our network orientation. The first is the *opportunity provided by peers to learn and practice social skills*. Peer relations provide children with interaction opportunities that are qualitatively different from interactions with parents and other adults (Sullivan, 1953). Peers tend to "tell it like it is," providing the child with an opportunity to learn about his "true" self. Rubin (1980) noted the importance of social comparison, comparing oneself with similar others in order to evaluate oneself and develop a sense of one's personal identity. Rubin has also noted the opportunity that peers

---

[3]Chapter 14 of Cochran et al. (1990) provides a more comprehensive articulation of the social processes linking parents' networks and child development, and some of the developmental outcomes postulated in the literature.

provide to learn perspective taking, communication, conflict resolution, engagement, and empathy skills. Hartup (1983) suggested that peer relations with co-equals are important for effective communication skills, modulation of aggression, sexual socialization, and formation of moral values.

Peers also provide *companionship*. Weiss (1974) distinguished two types of loneliness: emotional isolation (lack of an attachment figure or primary relationship), and a lack of friends (social isolation). Weiss reasoned that both types of relationships are necessary. Peers appear to reduce social isolation: In an empirical study of fifth- and sixth-grade children's perceptions of their own social networks, Furman and Buhrmeister (1985) found that friends were most commonly cited as the principal source of companionship. Rubin (1980) has further hypothesized that friends provide children with a sense of group belongingness. According to him, this sense of belonging is very important for young children, often leading to a sense of felt security. Berndt (1982), referencing others, argued that peer relations also contribute to a sense of security in pre- and early adolescents, by reducing anxieties associated with developmental changes.

Later on in development, peers provide *satisfaction for intimacy needs* Furman and Buhrmeister (1985) also reported that peers were the greatest source of intimacy for the children in their sample. The authors predicted that as these children enter adolescence, this feature of friendship will continue to increase in importance. Some support for this hypothesis has come again from Rubin (1980), who described the second, more mature stage of children's conceptualizations of friendships as characterized by intimate and mutual sharing.

Our second assumption is that the processes involved in peer interactions have different meanings and serve different functions at different stages in development. For instance, Parker and Gottman (1989) presented a model of friendship and social and emotional development in which friendship serves differing functions in early childhood, middle childhood, and adolescence. In early childhood, friendship organizes behavior in face of the arousal caused by social amusement and play. In middle childhood, increasing expectations regarding peer relations require that friendships provide knowledge of behavioral norms, and skills for self-presentation. Parker and Gottman postulated that in adolescence friendships help young people explore the ''Who am I?'' and ''Who will I become?'' questions, and integrate logic with emotion.

## The Family Matters Project

In the rest of this chapter we rely heavily on findings from a 3-year longitudinal study of stresses and support in the lives of parents with preschool children, conducted by the International Group for Comparative Human Ecology.[4] Most of the analyses referred to have been carried out by the American team at Cornell University, where the research project has been called "Family Matters." Within the overall research project, our purpose with the mapping of parents' networks was to better understand the ways that communities in urban, Western, industrialized societies support the childrearing process through *informal* social relations, and how families with differing characteristics might be more or less supported in such ways, due to the structure of American society. We mapped the networks of children in the follow-up phase of the research, when they were 6 years old, to test the hypothesis that one consequence of differences in parents' networks is parallel differences in the network resources available to their children.

*Sample.*   Here in the United States a stratified random sampling procedure was employed at the levels of both neighborhood and family. Eighteen neighborhoods were selected from a possible 57 neighborhoods in an upstate New York metropolitan area, using classification by family income level and ethnic/racial composition. Within-neighborhood families with 3-year-old children were identified through door-to-door canvas and selected within eight subgroups defined by race, family structure, and gender of child. This process produced an initial sample consisting of 286 families with 3-year-olds, 34% of which were single-parent in family structure. The amounts of schooling reported by the parents in these families and their family incomes mirrored the 1979 national averages. Twenty-seven percent of the original sample was African-American. Three years later, we were able to reinterview 80% of the parents in these families, in a follow-up sample with the same distribution by race and family structure. At both data points extensive information was gathered about family background and parents' social networks. During the follow-up we also gathered data from the mothers about their 6 year-old children's personal networks, and from teachers about those children's social behavior and performance in school.[5]

*Parent Network Interview.*   This interview was designed to generate a multifaceted picture of the parent's social world. Each parent was

---

[4]The five countries that participated in this research group were West Germany, Israel, Sweden, the United States, and Wales. Scientific leadership was provided by Rudolf Shouval (Israel), Bengt-Erik Andersson and Lars Gunnarsson (Sweden), Jill Lewis and Ronald Davie (Wales), and Urie Bronfenbrenner, Moncrieff Cochran, William Cross, Jr., and Charles R. Henderson, Jr. (USA). The members of this group worked cooperatively on concepts, instruments, research methods, and cross-cultural comparison of data related to the ecology of families with young children.

[5]For more detail about the methods used in this series of studies, see Cochran and Henderson (1986), and Cochran et al. (1990, chapters 2 and 3).

asked for a list of those people outside the household who "are important to you in one way or another," thinking first of neighbors, followed
by relatives, organizational friends, work- or schoolmates, and finally,
all others. The parent then indicated with whom on this list she or he
participated in each of nine interpersonal exchanges, including child-
related assistance, borrowing, financial support, work-related support,
and emotional support. Finally, information was gathered for each network member on age, family life stage, geographic proximity, frequency
of contact, and duration of the relationship.

   *Child Network Interview.*   Each of the 225 mothers participating
in the follow-up phase of the study was interviewed about her 6-year-
old's social ties. The mothers were told that the purpose of the interview was to generate a list of adults and children who the child "cares
about, or sees a couple of times a month." The interviewer asked first
about adults. After obtaining a list of adults and recording their role relationship with the child, (uncle, neighbor, etc.), information was collected about the kinds of things each adult did with the child. A similar list
was made of children that the child "knows or plays with," not count-
ing siblings. Then for every network member information was gathered
about frequency of contact, race, and gender.
   Having produced this background on the Family Matters research
project, we are ready now to introduce data from the project related to
links in the proposed chain introduced earlier, connecting society with
peer relations via networks. We begin at the most microlevel in the chain,
with the relationship between the child's network and his or her relationships with peers.

## Children's Networks and Peer Relationships

How much overlap is there between the child's network membership and
his or her peer group? It is important when talking about peer relationships to distinguish the concept of friend from the more inclusive peer
concept. Ladd (1989) pointed out that children's relationships with peers
include acquaintance, classmate, and teammate, as well as friend. Furman and Robbins (1985) distinguished close friendships, containing affection, intimacy, and reliable alliance, from more general peer relations,
the contents of which are limited to instrumental aid, nurturance, companionship, and enhancement of worth. Bukowski and Hoza (1989) argued that friendship is dyadic in nature, involving bilateral judgments
that reflect both liking and loyalty or intimacy.
   Children's personal networks are made up of people with whom the
child is in regular contact, and include but may not be limited to people

the child cares about (Cochran & Riley, 1988; Feiring & Lewis, 1989). These networks contain both children and adults. Of the children, some are peers (about the same age) and others are not (much older and much younger children). Many of the peers in the network are friends, as previously defined, but some are not. When referring to network data in this chapter, we use the terms *peers* and *child network members* interchangeably, because no more discrete differentiation can be made with the data. We do this while recognizing that a few of the children included in these networks probably do not function as peers, because (although still children) they are substantially older or younger than the children whose networks they inhabit.

Thus the peers in the children's networks we describe include both friends, as previously defined, and acquaintances. However, the full range of peers available to children is clearly not included in their networks. Many classmates and teammates are excluded because they are not perceived by the respondent, in this case the mother, to have a sustained dyadic relationship with the child.

As indicated earlier in the chapter, and in the findings of other researchers, the peers that are contained in the child's network are both relatives and nonrelatives (Cochran & Riley, 1988; Lewis & Feiring, 1989; Teitjen, 1982). Peer relatives may have differing ascribed relationships with the child, ranging from sibling to distant cousin (Lewis & Feiring, 1989). Nonkin peers in the network also have a number of distinguishing characteristics. Especially important for building the chain linking societal structural factors with peer relations is an understanding of the settings from which these nonkin peers are drawn. Some of these settings are examined empirically later in the chapter.

In summary, then, children's networks contain varying numbers of peers, and these peers vary in their personal and role characteristics. Children also have experiences with peers who are not included in their networks. Thus, conclusions about the constraints on children's networks imposed by societal factors should not necessarily be drawn for the entire range of peer relations.

## Parents' Networks and Those of Their Children

One major source of membership in the child's network is the networks of his or her parents. We referred earlier to the work of Anne Tietjen (1985), who found significant relationships between the characteristics of mothers' social networks and those of their children in a sample of Swedish mothers and their children. The link between child and parent networks is important because, if established, it can help explain how societal factors constraining development of the parent's network translate into constraints on the peer relations available to the child. We examined the overlap between mothers' and childrens' networks in our Family Matters sample. The results are shown in Table 7.1 as percent of the child's network overlapping with that of the mother.

The data in Table 7.1 show that 30%–44% of the child's network was also included in the mother's network. The data also indicate that the overlap is primarily accounted for by adults. This is because the mothers very rarely included children as members of their own networks.

The reader may be wondering what this network overlap has to do with peer relations, if what is coming to children from their parents' networks is adult membership. The Family Matters network data indicate that many of the peers in the networks of younger children come to them through adults in the networks of their parents. This is especially true with relatives, of course; one has peer cousins who are the children of uncles and aunts. But nonkin adult membership also provides playmates to young children. The point is that the factors constraining parents in the development of their networks affect the peer membership in the networks of their children in part by limiting the numbers of adults available to provide children as potential peers.

## Social-Structural Forces and the Networks of Parents

If the parents' network membership is an indirect source of potential peers for young children, then the factors determining the size and composition of parents' networks become salient as factors also influencing children's peer relations. In our studies of mothers' networks, not only in the U. S. sample but also in Sweden, Wales, and West Germany, we paid particular attention to the parents' levels of educational attainment, their family incomes, and the types of jobs in which they were employed. Like Fischer (1982), we found that educational attainment was the best single predictor of the size and richness of the parents' personal network. In addressing the question of just *how* educational level has these effects

TABLE 7.1
Percent Overlap of Child's and Mother's Networks

|  | Black | | White | |
|---|---|---|---|---|
|  | *One Parent* | *Two Parent* | *One Parent* | *Two Parent* |
| Total child network | 30 | 33 | 44 | 39 |
| Kin adults | 68 | 75 | 83 | 85 |
| Nonkin adults | 51 | 46 | 57 | 51 |

nts on the peer relations available to the child. We ex-
ip between mothers' and childrens' networks in our
~is sample. The results are shown in Table 7.1 as percent of
...ild's network overlapping with that of the mother.

The data in Table 7.1 show that 30%–44% of the child's network was
also included in the mother's network. The data also indicate that the
overlap is primarily accounted for by adults. This is because the mothers
very rarely included children as members of their own networks.

The reader may be wondering what this network overlap has to do
with peer relations, if what is coming to children from their parents' networks is adult membership. The Family Matters network data indicate
that many of the peers in the networks of younger children come to them
through adults in the networks of their parents. This is especially true
with relatives, of course; one has peer cousins who are the children of
uncles and aunts. But nonkin adult membership also provides playmates
to young children. The point is that the factors constraining parents in
the development of their networks affect the peer membership in the networks of their children in part by limiting the numbers of adults available to provide children as potential peers.

## Social-Structural Forces
## and the Networks of Parents

If the parents' network membership is an indirect source of potential peers
for young children, then the factors determining the size and composition of parents' networks become salient as factors also influencing children's peer relations. In our studies of mothers' networks, not only in
the U. S. sample but also in Sweden, Wales, and West Germany, we paid
particular attention to the parents' levels of educational attainment, their
family incomes, and the types of jobs in which they were employed. Like
Fischer (1982), we found that educational attainment was the best single
predictor of the size and richness of the parents' personal network. In
addressing the question of just *how* educational level has these effects

TABLE 7.1
Percent Overlap of Child's and Mother's Networks

|  | Black | | White | |
| --- | --- | --- | --- | --- |
|  | *One Parent* | *Two Parent* | *One Parent* | *Two Parent* |
| Total child network | 30 | 33 | 44 | 39 |
| Kin adults | 68 | 75 | 83 | 85 |
| Nonkin adults | 51 | 46 | 57 | 51 |

the child cares about (Cochran & Riley, 1988; Feiring & Lewis, 1989). These networks contain both children and adults. Of the children, some are peers (about the same age) and others are not (much older and much younger children). Many of the peers in the network are friends, as previously defined, but some are not. When referring to network data in this chapter, we use the terms *peers* and *child network members* interchangeably, because no more discrete differentiation can be made with the data. We do this while recognizing that a few of the children included in these networks probably do not function as peers, because (although still children) they are substantially older or younger than the children whose networks they inhabit.

Thus the peers in the children's networks we describe include both friends, as previously defined, and acquaintances. However, the full range of peers available to children is clearly not included in their networks. Many classmates and teammates are excluded because they are not perceived by the respondent, in this case the mother, to have a sustained dyadic relationship with the child.

As indicated earlier in the chapter, and in the findings of other researchers, the peers that are contained in the child's network are both relatives and nonrelatives (Cochran & Riley, 1988; Lewis & Feiring, 1989; Teitjen, 1982). Peer relatives may have differing ascribed relationships with the child, ranging from sibling to distant cousin (Lewis & Feiring, 1989). Nonkin peers in the network also have a number of distinguishing characteristics. Especially important for building the chain linking societal structural factors with peer relations is an understanding of the settings from which these nonkin peers are drawn. Some of these settings are examined empirically later in the chapter.

In summary, then, children's networks contain varying numbers of peers, and these peers vary in their personal and role characteristics. Children also have experiences with peers who are not included in their networks. Thus, conclusions about the constraints on children's networks imposed by societal factors should not necessarily be drawn for the entire range of peer relations.

## Parents' Networks and Those of Their Children

One major source of membership in the child's network is the networks of his or her parents. We referred earlier to the work of Anne Tietjen (1985), who found significant relationships between the characteristics of mothers' social networks and those of their children in a sample of Swedish mothers and their children. The link between child and parent networks is important because, if established, it can help explain how societal factors constraining development of the parent's network trans-on social relations, it is useful to note that, in all four of the countries represented in our research, a positive correlation was found between level of educational attainment and both work force attachment and job classification. We found, in turn, that employment produced network membership and that the size of work-related membership increased with hours worked per week. Furthermore, we learned that at the level of network support there was a substantial difference in size in favor of women living in families characterized by white collar occupations. This pattern was remarkably consistent across cultures, indicating that the effect of job classification on the social relations of parents operated at least somewhat independent of the effect of culture.

## Neighborhoods and Schools
## as Other Linking Mechanisms

Greater educational attainment can be linked to workplace attachment and to jobs that encourage network building. This link provided by the parent's network, between peers in the child's network and constraining factors at the level of society, is only one of three such mechanisms that we hypothesize transmits the constraints imposed by social structure to the peer relations of the child. Educational attainment beyond the high school diploma usually leads to a job providing income well above the poverty level, and so permits residence in a safe, well-maintained neighborhood. Thus, another link with educational attainment involves the neighborhood as a context for social relations. That is, schooling can operate through neighborhood of residence to stimulate or constrain social ties. In her earlier work, Joyce Epstein (1986) called attention to how the process of friendship selection changes over the life course. She described the ways that patterns of interaction are affected by school, neighborhood, and work environments, affecting (among other things) the proportion of cross-race and cross-gender friendships. More recently, Epstein (1989) has expanded this analysis of friendship selection to include the question of proximity. She pointed out that home, community, and school establish the boundaries that place children in more or less proximity with one another. Parke and Bhavnagri (1989) identified parents as primary mediators of opportunities for social contact. They identified, as factors mediating decisions and activities, choice of neighborhood to live in, provision of access to child-centered activities, and the arranging of access to other children to permit informal contacts. Lewis and Feiring (1989), referencing Parke and Bhavnagri, suggested that "accessibility and density of children available rather than psychological, dynamic factors may be responsible for size of friendship network" (p. 258).

We paid particular attention to the settings referred to by Epstein and by Park and Bhavnagri in gathering data about the 225 6-year-old children in our Family Matters sample. Their mothers reported that these children had six or seven children under age 12 in their networks (excluding siblings). Table 7.2 shows how these children were distributed among relatives, neighbors, and schoolmates.

We compared the network sizes in these four subgroups using analysis of covariance, including the mother's educational level as a covariate (Cochran & Riley, 1988). The strongest relationship with the number of nonrelatives in the networks of these children was found with the number of years of schooling acquired by their mothers ($F$ for covariate Mo. Ed. $= 18.99$; $p < .001$). The impact of the mother's educational level was also evident for differences in schoolmates ($F = 8.80$; $p < .01$) and children in the neighborhood ($F = 4.35$; $p < .05$).

It is clear from Table 7.2 that both the neighborhood and the school served as sources of nonkin peers in these children's networks, and that these settings were more productive for some children than for others. Size means in the table that were significantly different by $t$ test ($p < .05$), even after controlling for mother's education, are shown with superscripted letters ($a$ different from $b$). The neighborhood appears to be especially unproductive as a source of peers for Black children living in one-parent families. The school emerges as a much more socially generative setting for White children in two-parent families than for their one-parent counterparts or for Black children, regardless of family structure.

What are we to make of these differences in child network membership by social address (Bronfenbrenner, 1989) and setting? Schooling, especially in higher education, provides mothers with increased likelihood of employment outside the home, which in turn provides potential for network building that can also provide sources of peers for the children. We believe that education beyond high school also is likely to produce a generalized feeling of self-confidence that provides impetus to social involvement in contexts with high potential for network building (work-

TABLE 7.2
Number of Children in the Child's Social Network

|  | Black | | White | |
|---|---|---|---|---|
|  | One Parent | Two Parent | One Parent | Two Parent |
| Relatives | $2.6^b$ | 1.4 | $0.7^a$ | $1.7^b$ |
| Nonrelatives | $3.3^a$ | 4.3 | 4.5 | $5.5^b$ |
| Neighbors | $1.3^a$ | 2.2 | 2.5 | $2.9^b$ |
| Schoolmates | $.3^a$ | $.7^a$ | $.9^a$ | $2.3^b$ |

Note: Means that are significantly different ($p < .05$) by $t$ test, after adjustment for mother's education, are indicated by subscripted letters ($b > a$).

place, neighborhood). Again, such involvement can "spin off" network membership to the child.

We pointed out earlier that further education also leads to more highly paid work, which in turn makes it possible to live in a "decent" neighborhood. The Black, single-parent families in our Family Matters sample lived in the city's poorest neighborhoods, in housing and physical surroundings of markedly lower quality than those experienced by the families in the other three subgroups. Drawing from in-depth interviews and ethnographic observations, our colleague Heather Weiss (1982) described these parents' insights into life under those conditions:

> In the low-income areas, parents' concern about the safety of the neighborhood is accompanied by a set of worries about the negative influence of other children and adults in the environment. The parents worry about their children picking up bad habits and language, their early exposure to sex and violence, physical harm from drunks or gangs of teenagers, and the bad influence of other children who they feel are allowed to "run wild." (These) other children . . . are not seen as a resource but as a source of bad influence and corruption. As a result, the parents frequently restrict their children to the home and try to limit their access to other nearby adults and children. "Almost everyone here keeps their kids to themselves; they don't let their children play with other children, or at least they try to prevent it," one low-income mother reported. (pp. 4.7–4.8)

In contrast, parents in moderate- and middle-income neighborhoods talked about neighboring children and adults as a source of stimulation and support. They felt comfortable allowing their children the run of the block, knowing that neighbors would keep an eye on them. These differences in perceptions of neighbors provide a plausible explanation for the differences in neighboring patterns reflected in Table 7.2.

As a setting for network building, the school was really only productive for children in the most mainstream families, those White families containing two parents. How do schools encourage or discourage the building of friendships between classmates? One way is to serve families in a local catchment area, so that relationships initiated at school can be strengthened through neighborhood contact. Some of the Black children in our study were not attending neighborhood schools, and the schools they were attending contained relatively few other Black children. The combination of geographic distance from home and being racially different may have made the consolidation out of school of friendships initiated in the classroom difficult. Many of the low-income parents, regardless of race, had no reliable private transportation, and so were not able to chauffeur their children to the homes of schoolmates in the way that is so much a part of middle-class life. Time is also a commodity in short supply for most of the single parents; many of them were working long hours at relatively low pay, and simply couldn't take the time to help their children capitalize on friendships made at school.

The data linking neighborhood and school to peers in the child's network are only suggestive. They permit nothing more than a hypothesis that the neighborhood and school settings, like the parents' networks, mediate the effects of the factors structuring society—educational attainment, family income, job classification—on the opportunities for peer interaction available to young children.

As they grow older children become increasingly mobile, and increasingly less dependent on their parents for access to peers. However, evidence from another networks study in which the senior author played a collaborative role indicates that parents' socioeconomic status continues to strongly predict the size of the peer network well into adolescence. In a study of the networks and behavior of ninety-two 16-year-old Norwegian boys, Cochran and Bø (1989) found that the socioeconomic status of their fathers was significantly associated with the number of nonkin peers in the boys' networks (Pearson correlation = .37; $p < .001$). What are the processes that produce larger numbers of peers for those adolescent boys with better-educated fathers working in higher prestige occupations? We know that the networks of higher SES parents contain many more nonkin than do those of less-advantaged parents. It is possible that children growing up around large numbers of their parents' unrelated friends develop skills in interacting with such people, and expectations for themselves regarding the building of such friendship ties beyond kinship. The idea is that the processes by which socioeconomic status is translated into peer relations change over developmental time, from the direct provision of opportunity through the neighborhood, school, and parents' network (early and middle childhood) to the indirect influence provided by models in the parents' networks (late childhood and adolescence).

## Race as a Factor Structuring American Society

We alluded earlier to the question of what it means for peer relations to be a Black child in a predominantly White school. One area of development affected by peer relations is tolerance for differences, and social access to children of other races would provide the opportunity to develop accepting attitudes and skills in interacting with people from different backgrounds and life experiences. In order to examine the potential that children's networks provide for experience with peers of different races, we documented the number of cross-race relationships contained in the networks of our 225 study children. The results are shown in Table 7.3.[6]

---

[6]The Ns in Tables 7.2 and 7.3 are slightly different, because of the removal of 6 children in which child and parent were of different races. Therefore, the data in the two tables are not comparable.

TABLE 7.3
Cross-Race Peer Relationships in the Child Social Network

|  | Black | | White | |
| --- | --- | --- | --- | --- |
|  | One Parent | Two Parent | One Parent | Two Parent |
| Number of Opposite-Race Children | 0.9 | 1.0[b] | 0.4 | 0.3[a] |
| % of All Children in the Network | 14 | 18 | 10 | 05 |

Size means significantly different by $t$ test ($p < .05$) after controlling for mother's education are shown with superscripted letters ($a$ vs. $b$).

The reader can see from Table 7.3 that, on average, children in the four subgroups have no more than a single peer of another race, and that even in the case of that subgroup, the cross-race relationship constitutes less than 20% of the children in those networks. It is also clear from the table that Black children are significantly more likely than White children to have regular interaction with a peer of another race.

We have identified respect for differences as an important outcome developing through peer interaction. Development of such respect is to a substantial degree contingent on the opportunity to interact with different kinds of people throughout childhood and adolescence; in this case, people of different races. William Cross (1990) hypothesized that these kinds of differences in the social worlds of Black and White children should lead to differences in racial preference. A same race preference would be expected for White children as a group, and a split preference for Black children. He went on to note that these are in fact the patterns documented in the racial-preference literature.

Given the overlap between the networks of children and those of their parents documented earlier, it is reasonable to predict that patterns of cross-race peer relations in children are also to some degree a reflection of those developed by their parents. Cross (1990) examined the cross-race relationships in the networks of our Syracuse, New York Family Matters parents, and found that 41% of married and 21% of single Black mothers reported at least one opposite race friend, whereas for Whites the equivalent percentages were only 11% (married) and 16% (single). The pattern of these percentages mirrors the patterns seen in the child network data, again suggesting that parents' networks are one mechanism through which social-structural constraints are transmitted into the child's social world.

## Productive Areas for Future Research

Discussing the major influences on the selection of friends, Epstein (1989) said:

It is no longer feasible to study or explain the selection of friends with attention only to psychological constructs and child development terms. It is also necessary to give attention to the designs of the school, classroom, family, and other environments in which peer relations and the selection and influence of friends take place. (p. 183)

The networks data gathered through the Family Matters Project provide added support for Epstein's claim. However, the chain we have tried to forge in this chapter extends farther than the one she proposed. Our evidence suggests that neighborhoods, schools, and even parents' networks, are to some degree simply the processes by which the dominant beliefs of a society—about economic opportunity, racial equality, and educational opportunity—are translated into the social opportunities available to children and adolescents. Weighing the dynamics of the model presented in Fig. 7.1 as a whole, based on the evidence available to date, we are struck by the dominance of the constraints on free choice imposed on American parents and children, and especially on those who are socioeconomically disadvantaged, by the structural forces arrayed on the model's left-hand side. Claude Fischer (1982) said early in his book, *To Dwell Among Friends*, that "In general, we each construct our own networks" (p. 4). Our findings, taken as a whole, indicate first that it is inappropriate to generalize across ecological niches, and second that the networks of the poor and undereducated parents and children (who make up 20%–25% of all families in the United States) are largely constructed for them by their life circumstances.

What kinds of studies would further illuminate our understanding of how societal factors shape peer relations? The evidence that the range of opportunities for peer interaction available to children is affected by where they are positioned in the social structure is quite strong. Although these findings need to be further replicated and elaborated, our recommendations for future research center on the questions of *how social-structural factors are transmitted*, and *what can be done*, through modifications in the environment, *to interrupt transmission of socially and culturally disadvantageous peer relations*. We agree with Epstein (1989) that there are "important environmental effects on the selection of friends" (p. 180). Insight into the mechanisms and processes of transmission could come from small-scale studies using ethnographic methods to: (a) describe how neighborhoods and schools differ in opportunities provided for peer friendship; (b) document the impacts of differential opportunity on the peer networks of the children in those settings; and (c) examine whether and how setting differences might be related to resource allocation at the community level. A better understanding of how to change the settings children frequent in order to generate a richer array of opportunities for the development of peer relations will require research combining the systematic modification of neighborhood and school settings with careful documentation of peer relations before and then after the intervention. An important element in such studies will be description not only of *what* environmental changes were made, but also *how those changes had their impacts* on relationships between peers in those environments.

It is important to conclude with some reference to the key beliefs shaping our cultural responses; racism, intolerance for differences, and the conviction that the poor in this country are to blame for their poverty. These beliefs in turn shape the neighborhoods, schools, and other settings in which our children become socialized, so clearly intervention strategies must be played out in policies located there. But we are also convinced that serious attention must be paid to beliefs themselves, which if unaddressed will continue to thwart attempts to modify local settings in the interest of richer peer relations.

## REFERENCES

Berndt, T. (1982). The features and effects of friendship in early adolescence. *Child Development, 53*, 1447–1460.

Blyth, D., Hill, J., & Thiel, K. (1982). Early adolescents' significant others: Grade and gender differences in perceived relationships with familial and nonfamilial adults and young people. *Journal of Youth and Adolescence, 11* (6), pp. 425–450.

Bronfenbrenner, U. (1989). Ecological systems theory. In R. Vasta (Ed.) *Annals of Child Development* (Vol. 6, pp. 185–246). Greenwich, CT: JAI Press.

Bryant, B. (1985). The neighborhood walk: Sources of support in middle childhood. *Monographs of the Society for Research in Child Development, 50*, (3, Serial No. 210).

Bukowski, W., & Hoza, B. (1989). Popularity and friendship: Issues in theory, measurement, and outcome. In T. Berndt & G. Ladd (Eds.), *Peer relationships in child development* (pp. 15–45). New York: Wiley.

Cochran, M., & Bø, I. (1989). The social networks, family involvement, and pro- and antisocial behavior of adolescent males in Norway. *Journal of Youth and Adolescence, 18*(4), 377–398.

Cochran, M., & Henderson, C. (1986). *Family matters: An evaluation of the parental empowerment process*. Unpublished manuscript, Cornell University, Ithaca, NY.

Cochran, M., Larner, M., Riley, D., Gunnarsson, L., & Henderson, C., Jr. (1990). *Extending families: The social networks of parents and their children*. Cambridge, England, and New York: Cambridge University Press.

Cochran, M. M., & Riley, D. (1988). Mother reports of children's personal networks: Antecedents, concomitants, and consequences. In S. Salzinger, M. Hammer, & J. Antrobus (Eds.), *Social networks of children, youth, and young adults*, (pp. 113–147). Hillsdale, NJ: Lawrence Erlbaum Associates.

Cotterell, J. (1986). Work and community influences on the quality of childrearing. *Child Development, 57*, 362–374.

Cross, W. (1990). Social networks, race, and ethnicity. In M. Cochran, M. Larner, D. Riley, L. Gunnarsson & C. Henderson, Jr., (Eds.), *Extending families: The social networks of parents and their children* (pp. 67–85). Cambridge, England and New York: Cambridge University Press.

Eckenrode, J., & Gore, S. (1981). Stressful events and social support: The significance of context. In B. Gottlieb (Ed.), *Social networks and social support* (pp. 43–68). Beverly Hills: Sage.

Epstein, J. (1986). Friendship selection: Developmental and environmental influences. In E. Mueller & C. Cooper (Eds.), *Process and outcome in peer relationships* (pp. 129–160). New York: Academic Press.

Epstein, J. (1989). The selection of friends: Changes across the grades and in different school environments. In T. Berndt & G. Ladd (Eds.), *Peer relationships in child development* (pp. 158–187). New York: Wiley.

Feiring, C., & Lewis, M. (1989). The social networks of girls and boys from early through middle childhood. In D. Belle (Ed.), *Children's social networks and social support*, (pp. 119–150). New York: Wiley.

Fischer, C. (1982). *To dwell among friends: Personal networks in town and city.* Chicago: University of Chicago Press.

Furman, W., & Buhrmeister, D. (1985). Children's perceptions of the personal relationships in their social networks. *Developmental Psychology, 21*, 1016–1024.

Furman, W., & Robbins, P. (1985). What's the point? Issues in the selection of treatment objectives. In B. Schneider, K. Rubin, & J. Ledington (Eds.), *Children's peer relations: Issues in assessment and intervention* (pp. 41–54). New York: Springer-Verlag.

Gilligan, C. (1982). *In a different voice: Psychological theory and women's development.* Cambridge, MA: Harvard University Press.

Hartup, W. (1983). Peer relations. In E. M. Hetherington (Ed.) and P. H. Mussen (Series Ed.) *Handbook of social psychology: Vol. 4. Socialization, personality, and social development* (pp. 130–170). London: Methuen.

Homel, R., Burns, A., & Goodnow, J. (1987). Parental social networks and child development. *Journal of Social and Personal Relationships, 4*, 159–177.

Ladd, G. (1989). Toward a further understanding of peer relationships and their contributions to child development. In T. Berndt & G. Ladd (Eds.), *Peer relationships in child development* (pp. 1–12). New York: Wiley.

Lewis, M., & Feiring, C. (1989). Early predictors of school friendship. In T. Berndt & G. Ladd (Eds.), *Peer relationships in child development* (pp. 246–273). New York: Wiley.

Ogbu, J. (1981). Origins of human competence: A cultural–ecological perspective. *Child Development, 52*, 413–429.

Parke, R., & Bhavnagri, N. (1989). Parents as managers of children's peer relationships. In D. Belle (Ed.), *Children's social networks and social support* (pp. 241–259). New York: Wiley.

Parker, J., & Gottman, J. (1989). Social and emotional development in a relational context: Friendship interaction from early childhood to adolescence. In T. Berndt & G. Ladd (Eds.), *Peer relationships in child development* (pp. 95–132). New York: Wiley.

Rubin, Z. (1980). *Children's friendships.* Cambridge, MA: Harvard University Press.

Sullivan, H. S. (1953). *The interpersonal theory of psychiatry.* New York: Norton.

Tietjen, A. (1985). Relationships between the social networks of Swedish mothers and their children. *International Journal of Behavioral Development, 8*, 195–216.

Tietjen, A. (1986). Prosocial reasoning among children and adults in a Papua New Guinea society. *Developmental Psychology, 22*, 861–868.

Tietjen, A. (1989). The ecology of children's social support networks. In D. Belle (Ed.), *Children's social networks and social support* (pp. 37–69). New York: Wiley.

Weiss, H. (1982). Neighborhoods as contexts for child development. In *The ecology of urban family life*, a summary report to the National Institute of Education, Cornell University, Ithaca, NY.

Weiss, R. (1974). The provisions of social relationships. In Z. Rubin (Ed.), *Doing unto others* (pp. 122–140). Englewood Cliffs, NJ: Prentice-Hall.

Wellman, B. (1979). The community question: The intimate networks of East Yorkers. *American Journal of Sociology, 84*, 1201–1231.

# PART THREE

# DIRECT INFLUENCES

# CHAPTER EIGHT

# Parents' Management of Children's Peer Relations: Facilitating and Supervising Children's Activities in the Peer Culture

Gary W. Ladd
*University of Illinois—Urbana Champaign*

Susan Muth Profilet
*University of Illinois—Urbana Champaign*

Craig H. Hart
*Louisiana State University*

The search for linkages between the family and peer systems has been complicated not only by the fact that many aspects of parent–child relations may be related to children's peer relations, but also by the fact that events within either system can be viewed as causal (i.e., cause–effect relations may be bidirectional). In light of these complexities, it is essential for researchers to develop conceptual frameworks that can be used to identify and test propositions about the operation and outcomes of key family–peer processes. Although past research has been driven largely by empirical speculation, Parke and colleagues (1988) have recently proposed a framework that may help to identify key linkages between the family and peer systems.

Parke et al. (1988) suggested that there are two alternative pathways through which the family may influence children's peer relations. The first of these pathways is termed a *direct* avenue and consists of parental acts that are performed as a means of selecting, modifying, or structuring the child's physical and/or social environment in order to enhance peer relationships. Direct influences would include such activities as a parent's efforts to organize features of the social milieu (e.g., play settings and locations), access to play partners and types of playmates, and planning or supervision of children's activities and interactions with peers. Aspects of parenting and the parent–child relationship that occur for other purposes (i.e., not explicitly to foster competence with peers), are part of the second pathway, termed the "indirect" avenue. Indirect influences may include such factors as the parent's attempts to develop a harmonious relationship with the child, or the parent's typical style of interacting with the child during play, or other socialization activities (e.g., discipline).

The major aims of this chapter are to identify potential direct pathways that link parenting and young children's peer relations, and to consider the possible functions these socialization activities serve in the development of preschoolers' social competence and peer relationships. Our efforts to identify these avenues and chart their potential functions are organized around the concept of *parental management*. For young children, this term refers to parents' attempts to plan, regulate, and modify children's social environments, interactions, and relationships with peers. Included among such activities would be the parents' efforts to select or design features of the social milieu (e.g., play settings and locations), mediate or control access to play partners and types of playmates, and engage in planning or supervision of children's activities and interactions with peers. In particular, we attempt to address the following key questions: (a) Do parents act as managers or social architects of their children's peer relations?; (b) What types of management activities do parents employ to help their children develop and maintain social ties in the peer culture?; and (c) What functions might different management activities serve in the socialization of children's peer relations and social competence? After exploring these issues, we consider some of the strengths and shortcomings of past research on parental management, and identify issues and avenues for further investigation.

## DO PARENTS MANAGE
## THEIR CHILDREN'S PEER RELATIONS?

Before we ask the question of how parents manage children's peer relations, and with what possible consequences, it is useful to consider whether these activities actually occur in real-world families. Is it the case that parents engage in peer-oriented managerial activities, or are we falling prey to an interesting but false premise? Perhaps parents see their children's roles in the peer culture as the responsibility of other socialization agents (e.g., teachers). Or perhaps they view children's social lives as a domain that should be private and free of parental interventions, and prefer that children negotiate tasks such as friendship making and playmate selection by themselves. Were this the case, the socialization activities that we refer to as *parental management* might not be very prevalent in children's lives or very influential in their development.

We are inclined to think that most parents do take an active role in their children's social lives and perform various managerial activities in this domain. Both logic and findings from recent empirical investigations support this conclusion. A decade ago, Hartup (1979) argued that parents of young children routinely act as social managers, and by doing so, foster ties with agemates outside the family. His view was as follows: "Parents manage the social lives of their children directly. Mothers and fathers consciously determine the timing and circumstances under which their offspring will have contact with individuals outside the nuclear family" (p. 949).

However, not all of what parents do as managers of their children's peer relations may fall within the domain of planful, intentional activities. Much of what parents do in this area of child socialization may be accomplished rather unintentionally as a reaction to children's behavior and social circumstances. In fact, Rubin and Sloman (1984) argued that the business of childrearing is such that parents often act as managers of their children's social lives whether they intend to or not. As they put it, "Even parents who have no specific intention of influencing their child's friendships can hardly avoid doing so, through the settings they choose to live in, their reactions to the child's social behavior, and the values they convey through their own relationships with others" (pp. 223–224).

Thus, as portrayed in recent literature, parents' management of children's peer relations can be seen as a common, if not inescapable, aspect of parent–child relations and socialization. Moreover, as a concept, management seems to encompass planful activities that originate with the parent (e.g., conscious, intentional attempts by the parent to foster a child's peer relationships), as well as more spontaneous activities that parents perform as a response to the child, or other external demands (e.g., responding to a child's request to play with neighborhood peers, discouraging the child's involvement with undesirable play partners).

A small but growing body of empirical evidence from field-based investigations also suggests that parents routinely manage various aspects of their children's peer relations. Ladd and colleagues (Ladd, 1988; Ladd & Golter, 1988; Ladd, Hart, Wadsworth, & Golter, 1988; Ladd & Price, 1987) have employed both telephone interviews and mail questionnaires to gather information about parents' efforts to manage preschool children's peer relations in the home, neighborhood, and community. In a short-term longitudinal study of early school transitions, Ladd and Price

(1987) found that 83% of 130 parents in a kindergarten sample regularly transported their child to one or more community settings to participate in activities involving peers (e.g., the community pool, library, organized playgroups, etc.).

Ladd and Golter (1988) gathered data on preschool children's peer relations in the home and neighborhood for a sample of 58 middle-class families. These investigators found that approximately half the parents in the sample regularly arranged opportunities for peers to play with their child, and nearly all of the parents provided some form of supervision for peer-play sessions that took place in their homes. Although these findings suggest that the management of children's peer relations is a common parental activity, it may not be one that is equally shared by mothers and fathers in two-parent families. Findings from the Ladd and Golter study revealed that mothers, more often than fathers, were responsible for arranging and supervising their children's contacts with peers. In fact, of the sampled peer-play activities that were parent initiated, fully 82% were arranged by mothers. Moreover, when these peer-play activities occurred in the subject's (parents') homes, mothers were the only parent present to supervise the children in 67% of the peer-play activities sampled.

Research by Bhavnagri and Parke (1991) also suggests that parents actively manage their children's peer relations. In this study, mothers of 2- through 6-year-old children were interviewed and asked to report potential management activities. Results indicated that parents often arranged opportunities for their children to play with peers, and supervised their activities. The data also revealed that these functions were performed more often by mothers than fathers, and by the parents of younger as opposed to older preschoolers.

Parents' managerial activities were also investigated for a sample of younger preschoolers (ages 23 to 40 months) by Ladd et al. (1988). Included among the parental behaviors studied were the extent to which they arranged activities with peers and bought toys that were intended to facilitate children's social interactions with peers. The authors found that, depending on children's ages, parents' perceived involvement in these planning functions was predictive of the amount of time children spent playing in peers' homes. Apparently, even at early ages, some parents create opportunities for their children to socialize with peers, and the children within these families tend to have greater exposure to play settings outside the home.

In summary, it would appear that many parents do attempt to manage their children's peer relations. Moreover, in the sections that follow, we consider evidence to suggest that the roles parents play as managers may have an important bearing on children's social development.

## PARENTS AS MANAGERS OF CHILDREN'S
## PEER RELATIONS: EXPLORING POTENTIAL
## FORMS AND FUNCTIONS

We have chosen to employ the "manager" metaphor when discussing parents' involvement in their child's social development because it connotes a broad range of roles that parents may play as socializers in this domain, and it allows the parent to be viewed as both a proactive (i.e., planful or strategic) socializer and reactive (i.e., responding to perceived behavior or needs in the child) participant in this process. Due to a paucity of descriptive research, we currently know very little about the range of activities that parents engage in as managers of their children's peer relations. Perhaps more importantly, we know even less about the possible functions that various management roles or activities may serve in children's development. Insights into the possible functions that parental management activities may serve for children are further complicated by the fact that relations between the variables that have been investigated on each side of the parent–child equation may be bidirectional. As is true in most types of research on relationships, it is not difficult to conceive of either partner as a "cause" of the other's behavior or development. Much of what parents do to promote children's peer relationships may be a "response" to the child and his or her social circumstances, and much of what children think and do in the context of peer relations may be a result of their parents' efforts to prepare them for this social system.

In light of these constraints, our objectives for this portion of the chapter are to consider two forms of parental management that have received the most empirical attention in recent years. We also restrict our coverage of the life span to young children, focusing primarily on families with preschool- and primary-age children. Specifically, we consider parents' efforts to facilitate young children's activities in the peer culture and their efforts to supervise young children's social interactions during peer-play encounters or activities. In addition to defining and describing these forms of management, we rely on available research findings to speculate about their potential origins (e.g., casual locus and direction) and possible functions in child socialization and development (e.g., impact on children's social competence and peer relationships).

### Creating Opportunities for Peer Interaction
### and Relationships

Access to peers is a critical resource for children's social development—exposure to agemates provides children with a context for social interaction, relationship formation, and a variety of other interpersonal experiences that are essential for the growth of interpersonal competence (see Berndt & Ladd, 1989). It is likely, however, that the means through which children achieve access to peers, and the contexts in which these encounters occur (e.g., durations, locations, types of companions, etc.) change with age. Whereas very young children are entirely dependent on their parents to meet peers or assemble agemates for play, older children become more autonomous at managing their social lives, and begin to negotiate issues such as play locations, companions, and durations with parents. Thus, it is important to recognize that the forms of management parents may employ to facilitate children's access to peers, and the potential functions these activities may serve, change over the course of the child development.

One of the most common ways that parents of young children attempt to influence their development or control their behavior is by manipulating the surrounding environment. Thus, it would not be surprising to find that parents rely on various forms of environmental management to create opportunities for children to meet and interact with peers. Differences in this type of peer management and its potential impact upon children might be attributed both to the methods parents use to facilitate children's access to social settings, and to the types of contexts they arrange or choose as potential "staging areas" for peer relations. In the sections that follow, we attempt to discriminate between the roles that parents play as facilitators of children's peer relations in "formal" and "informal" social contexts. Formal contexts are defined as social systems that lie outside the bounds of the immediate family and tend to be sponsored or controlled by adults. Examples of formal contexts would include child-care centers or schools and various community settings and organizations, such as the library, pool, or church. Informal contexts, as we use the term, refer to smaller social settings that are largely under the parents' control and purview, such as a play group conducted in a child's home or children's after-school play activities in the neighborhood.

## Formal Opportunities: Parents as Facilitators of Peer Relations in School and Community Settings

There are many social systems that lie outside the bounds of the immediate family that can provide, along with other types of socialization experiences, a context for children to meet, interact, and form relationships with peers. We consider two such settings, the child-care center or school, and the community, and attempt to delineate some of the ways that parents influence children's access to and participation in these settings. We also consider the potential functions of these experiences; in particular, the possible ways that children's experiences in these contexts may affect the course of their social development and competence.

### Provision of Child Care and Preschool Experience.

A major way in which parents influence children's early social environments is by enrolling them in child-care or preschool programs. However, parents' reasons for placing children in child-care or preschool programs may vary and, thus, reflect differing socialization or "management" aims. For many parents, the provision of child-care or preschool experience may be motivated primarily by economic or employment concerns, and be viewed as a source of custodial care. Parents such as these may be more likely to enroll their children in full-day child-care programs. Other parents may see half- or full-day preschool programs as a place to enhance their child's scholastic readiness and preparation for the academic demands of grade school. Still other parents may enroll their child in preschool settings to foster early social development (e.g., to provide exposure to peers). Rubin and Sloman (1984), for example, argued that socialization concerns are one of the main reasons why parents place their children in preschool and child care. Results of a recent study conducted by Rescorla (1989) support this contention, in that virtually all of the 371 parents surveyed endorsed the importance of preschool social experiences, but were divided in their opinions about the value of early academic instruction. Similarly, Bhavnagri & Parke (1991) found that most parents view provisions for children's social development as a priority in their selection of preschool programs. It is also possible that parents who mainly intend to foster their child's peer relations choose different types of child-care arrangements or preschool programs than those who seek primarily custodial care or academic enrichment. Unfortunately, we currently know of no data that might help to shed light on these issues and potential relations.

In fact, our present state of knowledge forces us to think about the possible effects of early child-care and school experience in broader terms. Risking this imprecision, we employ the following proposition as a basis for our speculations: Although parents' reasons for placing children in this type of setting may vary, a general consequence is that children are exposed to a variety of peers at an early age. In essence, we are suggesting that the provision of early child care or schooling, no matter what the parents' reasons for initiating it, may provide children with access to peers, and create opportunities for social interaction and relationships with agemates.

Our speculations about the possible social opportunities and effects of preschool and child-care experience are drawn from research conducted on children's early peer relations in these settings. One conclusion we may infer from this literature is that children's participation in early child-care or preschool environments does foster access, interaction, and relationships with agemates. Research findings reveal that, on the average, children who are enrolled in preschool and day-care programs become more involved and sociable with peers over time. For example, Finkelstein, Dent, Gallacher, and Ramey (1978) found that, for toddlers who regularly attended day-care settings, the frequency of teacher–child interaction tended to decline and the frequency of child–peer interaction tended to increase over time. There is also evidence to suggest that interaction between children and their peers begins at a very early age in day-care and preschool contexts. Howes (1988) found that complementary and reciprocal play emerged among 1-year-olds, and various forms of social pretend play were present in the interactions of 2-year-olds. In an earlier study, Howes (1983) also found that, beyond momentary interactions, some toddlers and preschoolers in child-care settings also developed lasting relationships with peers. In fact, Howes (1988) found that many of children's friendships in child care (between 50% and 70% of those observed) were stable over a 1-year-period, and some (10% of those observed) were stable as long as 2 years.

Another inference that we may draw from this literature is that children's peer experiences in child-care and preschool environments has an effect on their social development and competence. Although there is some evidence to suggest that children who attend child care for prolonged periods tend to become more aggressive (Haskins, 1985; Schwartz, Strickland, & Krolick, 1974), there is also a growing body of evidence to suggest that exposure to day care enhances children's sociability and interpersonal competence. Supporting evidence for this conclusion can be found in a number of investigations, although few of the existing studies permit strong causal interpretations.

Mueller and Brenner (1977) observed male toddlers who were participants in teacher-supervised play groups several mornings per week and found that boys who became more acquainted with peers developed more sophisticated forms of play and social interaction than did boys who were less acquainted with peers. A more extensive and recent analysis, conducted by Howes (1988), shows that toddlers who spent considerable time in child care (e.g., 1 year or more) with the same group of peers tended to develop more competent forms of social interaction. Moreover, children who began preschool at earlier ages tended to have less difficulty with peers (as rated by teachers) than those who began at later ages. However, in light of these findings, it is interesting to note that Ladd and Golter (1988) found no relationship between the amount of time children spent in preschool and their later social competence in grade school classrooms (although Ladd and Price, 1987, did find that the length of prior preschool experience forecasted lower levels of anxious behavior in the early weeks of school). Perhaps, as is suggested in the following section, it is more the quality of children's early social experiences in preschool (e.g., friendship formation and maintenance) than the sheer amount of time they spend in these settings that foreshadows later social competence.

The potential functions of children's friendships in child-care and school settings have been studied by gathering data on both stability and change in these relationships. Howes (1983) found that toddlers and preschoolers who possessed stable or "maintained" friendships in child care also tended to develop more complex and sophisticated forms of social interaction and play. Conversely, children who lost friends due to moves and other transitions tended to be less socially skilled and less accepted by peers than were children who kept their friends, suggesting that peers can become important "attachment" figures or sources of emotional support for young children. Similar findings have been reported by Ladd and colleagues from research conducted on early school transitions. Ladd and Price (1987) found that children who began grade school with familiar classmates tended to develop more favorable attitudes toward school attendance. Further investigation of this finding, reported by Ladd (1990), revealed that the presence and maintenance of old friends among classmates, and the formation of new friends, was predictive of children's school adjustment as they moved from preschool to kindergarten.

There is also some evidence to suggest that the quality of the child-care environment is related to children's social development. Vandell and colleagues (Vandell, Henderson, & Wilson, 1988) have shown that children who attend higher quality day care programs tend to have more friendly and less antisocial interactions with peers. These children were also perceived as better adjusted in school (e.g., happier, more socially competent, and less shy) than were children attending lower quality programs. More recently, Howes (1990) found that family background is associated with the quality of child-care settings parents choose, and that this factor, along with the quality of children's child-care experience, may forecast children's social adjustment.

Taken together, these findings suggest that there may be important social benefits to children's participation in child-care and preschool environments. Some of the factors that may enhance or inhibit these benefits include family background, the age at which children enter preschool or child care, the familiarity of the peer groups in these settings, the types of relationships children form with peers, and the stability of these relationships over time and social settings. Some of these factors, especially those related to the placement of children in child care or preschool, and choice over the type of program or curriculum, are subject to parental control and may, therefore, represent aspects of parental peer management.

### *Involvement in Community-Based Peer Activities.* Opportunities for children to relate with peers can also be found in a variety of community settings, and parents' involvement in these settings may help children develop social connections beyond the more immediate contexts of home and neighborhood. In charting various types of community settings, Bryant (1985) distinguished between two types of adult-sponsored contexts that may provide children with important social opportunities. The first type of adult-sponsored community setting includes organizations that provide structured activities for children, many of which require involvement with peers. Examples of this type of setting would include organizations such as Little League, Boy Scouts and Girl Scouts, 4-H clubs, and the like. Bryant investigated children's involvement in structured community settings along with numerous other aspects of social support. Although her research points to some important developmental changes in children's use of these settings, she found little evidence to suggest that they make important contributions to children's social and emotional development. Specifically, she found that children's involvement in structured community settings tends to increase with age—older school-age children (i.e., 10-year-olds) were found to be more involved in these types of settings than were younger school-age children (i.e., 7-year-olds). However, the level of children's involvement in structured community settings bore little relationship to their social-emotional functioning, as indexed on a variety of adjustment measures.

A second type of community setting includes formal, adult-sponsored organizations that provide children with unstructured activities, such as community pools, parks, school yards, and libraries. In these settings, children are afforded largely unstructured opportunities to meet and relate with peers. For example, parents may allow children to accompany them as they pursue recreational, educational, or health-related activities, such as routine visits to a community pool, library, or park. Because other parents pursue these activities, and bring their children, these contexts serve as a place for children to meet and interact with peers.

In contrast to the first type of setting, formal organizations within the community that provide unstructured activities for children may provide important socialization activities that, in turn, influence children's social development and adjustment. In a study of children's neighborhood and community supports, Bryant (1985) found that involvement in unstructured community settings was predictive of some aspects of children's social-emotional functioning. In particular, participation in formally sponsored organizations with unstructured activities was predictive of children's perspective-taking skills, especially among older children (i.e., 10- as opposed to 7-year-olds). Bryant's interpretation of this finding was that certain environmental settings, particularly those that allow children a role in structuring their own activities, may provide many of the resources needed for self- and social development (e.g., mastery, control, autonomy).

Findings similar to those reported by Bryant (1985) were obtained with a much younger sample of children in a study of the transition from preschool to kindergarten (Ladd & Price, 1987). These investigators found that preschoolers who participated in a larger number of formal community settings with opportunities for unstructured interactions with peers displayed lower levels of school avoidance following kindergarten entrance. This finding led Ladd and Price to conclude that regular contact with agemates in many community settings may foster coping skills for novel peer situations, such as the types of settings children encounter during school transitions.

### Informal Opportunities: Parents' Roles in Fostering Peer Relations in the Home and Neighborhood

Much of what parents do as managers of children's peer relations occurs on a day-to-day basis as they oversee and respond to children's activities in the home and neighborhood. Within these contexts, parents may create opportunities for children to meet and relate with peers in a variety of ways. For example, parents may directly initiate social encounters as a means of helping a child meet peers or find play partners (e.g., inviting a peer to the house, sponsoring an in-home play group), or they may rely on less direct methods to influence the social settings and activities that are available for children to pursue (e.g., choosing to live in a neighborhood with many potential playmates).

*Initiating Peer Contacts.* One way that parents may choose to facilitate children's early peer relations is by acting as a mediator, and arranging opportunities for their child to meet and play with other children. Some parents may "sponsor" informal peer contacts as part of early socialization, perhaps as a means of helping young children forge a transition from the family to the peer culture. Other parents may tend to pursue or refrain from this type of peer management based on their perception of specific child characteristics, or attributes they perceive in potential playmates. Parents of sociable children, for example, may see less need to arrange children's social contacts, whereas parents of shy or aggressive children may do so to compensate for their child's lack of peer involvement or social skills. Still other parents may rely on this type of strategy to control the types of peers their children are exposed to, or to facilitate ties with particular agemates (e.g., potential classmates, a child belonging to a friend of the family).

Researchers who have explored this aspect of peer management find that many, but not all parents actively initiate peer contacts for their preschool-aged children. Working with a sample of 58 middle class families, Ladd and Golter (1988) used a series of telephone interviews to record parents' efforts to arrange play contacts for their preschool children. The interviews were conducted during preschool, several months prior to the time the children entered kindergarten in local grade schools. Results indicated that slightly more than half of the parents in the sample (51%) had not initiated any of their children's peer contacts during the sampled intervals. Although the remaining parents in the sample did arrange some of their children's social opportunities, the degree to which they engaged in this activity varied greatly, with some parents initiating as few as 6% and others arranging all (100%) of the children's recorded peer contacts (the median for this distribution was 33%).

There is also some evidence to suggest that parents tend to be more involved in arranging play opportunities and peer contacts for younger as compared to older children. Bhavnagri and Parke (1991) interviewed the mothers of 2- through 6-year-old children, and found that parent-initiated play invitations were more prevalent among the toddlers than the $3^1/_2$- to 6-year-olds in the sample. The older children in the sample were found to initiate more of their own peer contacts, and to receive a larger number of overtures from friends.

Although parents' efforts to arrange children's peer contacts appear to vary with the age of the child, gender differences in this regard have not been found. In fact, the data gathered by both Bhavnagri and Parke (1991) and Ladd and Golter (1988) suggest that parents are equally facilitative of boys' and girls' peer contacts. However, the fact that parents do not differentiate by gender in their efforts to promote children's peer relations does not necessarily mean that the informal social experiences of boys and girls are comparable. In fact, Bryant (1985) found that 7- and 10-year-old boys tended to develop more informal, unsponsored meeting places in their neighborhoods and communities than did girls of the same ages. Moreover, age differences were found for males in her sample, such that the younger grade school boys tended to report a greater number of informal meeting places than did the older boys. This age difference was attributed, in part, to the fact that older boys become more involved in formal settings and meeting places.

The impact of parents' initiations on children's development is difficult to gauge due to the design problems and constraints that currently plague investigators. The available evidence pertaining to this question is largely correlational and does not support clear, causal inferences. However, the existing evidence does point to a relationship between early parental initiation and children's social competence. Ladd and Golter (1988), for example, examined differences in children's peer relations and social competence in families where parents performed high versus low levels of peer initiation. The aspects of peer relations that were measured included concurrent indices of children's neighborhood social contacts in preschool, and measures of their social behavior and peer status later in kindergarten. Children of parents who tended to arrange peer contacts more frequently had a larger range of playmates, and more frequent play companions (i.e., consistent partners across play contacts) in the neighborhood. Boys from these families, but not girls, also tended to become better liked and less rejected by their classmates following entrance into kindergarten.

Ladd et al. (1988) conducted a similar study with younger preschool children, assessing parents' peer management activities prior to the time their child was enrolled in a preschool classroom. These data showed that parents' involvement in facilitating children's peer relations (e.g., initiating contacts, purchasing toys for social applications) was related to the time children spent in playing in peer's homes. One inference that is consistent with this finding is that parental facilitation helped to expand children's ties with peers outside the family.

Additional evidence pertaining to this question can be found in a study conducted by Krappman (1986) with a sample of German children ranging from 10 to 12 years of age. Krappman found that parents who took an active role in stimulating and arranging their children's peer relations tended to have offspring who developed closer and more stable ties with agemates. These children also tended to form peer relationships that had fewer difficulties and problems.

Finally, it is also important to consider the possibility that the context itself may be an important contributor to children's social development. Whether directly sponsored by the parent or not, informal contexts may provide children with greater autonomy and control over their social experiences, which, in turn, may foster higher levels of social learning and development. Bryant's (1985) findings provide some support for this premise. She found that, among smaller families, children who developed more informal unsponsored meeting places tended to become more tolerant and accepting of peers.

Thus, at present, there are findings from several investigations indicating that parents' efforts to arrange informal social experiences are associated with children's social competence. Further research is needed to understand the processes that account for this relation, and to establish the potential direction of effect.

***Arranging Informal Play Groups.*** It may also be important to distinguish between parents' efforts to involve children in individual or sporadic peer contacts, and the arrangements they make for children to participate in larger, more consistent peer contexts, such as play groups. Much of children's contact with peers occurs in schools or other "group-oriented" settings, and the skills children need to succeed in this type of milieu may not be learned entirely in dyadic or short-term relationships.

In a study of early attachment relations with preschool children and their parents, Lieberman (1977) used home interviews to assess children's experience with peers. Although Lieberman attempted to differentiate between children's experience in peer dyads and groups, the resulting indices were combined to form a single measure of peer experience. Results indicated that children with histories of greater peer experience were more competent in later, laboratory-based observations of their interactions with peers. These differences were found primarily in the quality of children's verbal exchanges and, thus, suggest that the facilitation of children's peer experience (including involvement in play groups) may augment early communicative competence.

Clearer evidence of a potential relation between children's play group experience and their social competence and adjustment is found in the study conducted by Ladd et al. (1988). In this study, the investigators measured a number of features of preschoolers' social milieus and networks, including the number of play groups participated in by each child. Prior to children's entrance into preschool, parents were asked to define play groups by indicating on a list containing the names of all of their child's peer companions, those with whom their child consistently interacted in groups of three or more. These scores, reflecting the number of play groups in which children regularly participated, were then used to predict children's social and school adjustment in preschool classrooms. Specifically, teachers were asked to provide ratings of children's classroom peer status, social competence, and school adjustment. Results indicated that the relation between prior play group experience and later social and school adjustment differed, depending on the age of the child. Specifically, the number of play groups and teacher's perceptions of classroom adjustment were negatively related for younger preschoolers (ages 23–40 months), but positively correlated for older preschoolers (ages 41–55 months). Among older preschoolers, a larger number of play groups also forecasted higher levels of social visibility among classmates on a peer sociometric. These data suggest that, among older preschoolers, the experiences provided in multiple play groups (e.g., the skills children learn while negotiating these contexts) are related to their social and school adjustment in the classroom.

*Choice of Neighborhoods.* As Bryant (1985) pointed out, "children are the primary consumers of residential neighborhoods" (p. 14), and much of their time is spent pursuing activities in this context (Moore & Young, 1978). Moreover, the neighborhood, or the interpersonal environment surrounding the family's residence, can be seen as an important setting for young children's peer relations. According to Garbarino and Gilliam (1980, quoted in Bryant, 1985), the neighborhood is one of the most important contexts for the socialization of young children, and it provides a wide array of social opportunities. Young children may meet peers and play together on sidewalks, schoolyards, playgrounds, and vacant lots (Moore & Young, 1978). Neighborhood travels may also result in visits to other children's homes, and contact with other social agents systems (e.g., a friend's siblings, another family's policies regarding play and social interaction).

Factors such as the parents' choice of neighborhoods, and their policies regarding neighborhood activities, represent another form of peer management and may have an important bearing on children's social opportunities and experiences. Parents often seek to control the location of their residence, and in doing so may consider features such as cost of living, distance from the workplace, access to schools, and type of community. They may also weigh features of the surrounding interpersonal environment that may add to or detract from the quality of life for themselves and their children.

There are a number of ways that the location of the family's residence may affect children's social opportunities. For example, locations that are physically isolated or difficult to access may restrict children's social mobility and contacts. Studies by Medrich and colleagues (Berg & Medrich, 1980; Medrich, Roizen, Rubin, & Buckley, 1982) with 11- and 12-year-olds suggest that children who live in geographically "flat" locations have more opportunity for peer contact than do children who reside in "hilly" locations. Also, van Vliet (1981) found that children living in urban neighborhoods, which often had higher levels of child density, tended to have more friends than children living in suburban neighborhoods. Generalizing from these findings, it also seems likely that children who live in diverse urban neighborhoods will have a larger number of locations for meeting and interacting with peers than those who live in isolated rural settings. Data on children's neighborhood preferences, also gathered by Medrich and colleagues, provide some support for this idea. They used open- and closed-format questions to probe children's "out-of-school life," and found that they tended to prefer neighborhoods that were situated near commercial areas because they were perceived to have a variety of settings (e.g., school yards, shopping areas, parks) that could support peer activities.

Other dimensions of neighborhoods, such as their interpersonal composition and climate, may also affect children's social opportunities. For example, it seems likely that children who reside in neighborhoods dominated by adults may have more difficulty finding and keeping playmates than children who live in neighborhoods populated largely by families with children. In fact, additional findings from studies conducted by Medrich and colleagues (Berg & Medrich, 1980; Medrich et al., 1982) reveal that children's friendships tended to be more sparse and formal in areas where the child population was smaller or less dense. The investigators attribute this finding partly to the fact that, under these conditions, children's play contacts and arrangements become a more complex and time-consuming activity for parents. One could also imagine how these circumstances might alter the types of encounters children have with peers, especially if parents' involvement in logistics such as planning and transportation afforded children less autonomy and privacy in the conduct of their peer activities and relationships.

## Monitoring and Supervising
## Children's Peer Activities and Interactions

In addition to providing access to peers, parents may also contribute to children's social development by attempting to oversee and regulate their activities and interactions with agemates. In general, we refer to this type of activity as parental "supervision." However, it is important to recognize that parents' supervisory behavior may vary along dimensions such as proximity (e.g., parents' presence or absence in the child's social setting) and awareness (e.g., parents' knowledge about the child's social activities).

In this article, the term *supervision* is used to describe the parent's behavior in proximal settings, or situations in which the parent, child, and peer(s) are in the same general location. In contrast, the term *monitoring* is used to describe variations in the parents' policies toward and awareness of children's social activities in distal locations (i.e., situations in which the parent is not present).

In addition to individual differences in parents, it is assumed that factors such as the age or gender of the child may also have an effect on the forms and styles of supervision employed by parents. As children grow older, parents may change their supervisory styles to fit new socialization aims, or to compensate for gains in children's autonomy and mobility. Similarly, parents may adapt their styles of supervision to conform to specific gender-role expectations, or differential premises about male and female socialization.

## Parents' Supervision of Children's Peer Relations

Parents may act as supervisors of children's peer activities for a variety of reasons. For many parents, the primary aim of supervision is to anticipate and protect children from environmental and interpersonal hazards. However, supervision may well serve other purposes, such as the socialization of children's competence with agemates. That is, in addition to ensuring children's safety, parents may supervise children's social encounters as a means of teaching them how to relate successfully with peers.

As supervisors, parents may differ in the level and type of involvement they have in children's social activities. For example, parents may choose roles that afford low versus high levels of involvement in children's peer activities (e.g., occasional onlooker vs. observant bystander vs. active participant in the children's activities) and offer differing degrees of guidance and structure before, during, and after play sessions with peers. In part, these differences may be a function of children's ages. Older children, for example, may need less guidance and corrective feedback than their younger counterparts and, therefore, receive less parental supervision. However, it is also likely that individual differences in parents' supervisory styles at a given age level contribute to the quality of children's peer experiences and affect their social learning and development.

*Lab-Based Studies of Parental Supervision.* Recent studies of parental supervision have been conducted in both field (e.g., home) and laboratory settings. Using lab-based paradigms, Bhavnagri and Parke (1985; 1991) have explored parents' facilitation of children's social competence during play sessions with peers, and the relation between specific supervisory strategies and children's social performance. Specifically, Bhavnagri and Parke (1985) observed toddlers in dyads during a series of four play segments. The segments were organized as follows: During the first segment the two children played alone. Thereafter, each of the children's mothers took turns supervising their play during alternate 10-minute periods. In the final segment, the toddlers played again without maternal supervision. Mothers and children's behaviors were videotaped during each segment, and rated by independent coders on five global rating scales. The findings indicated that toddlers' social competence ratings were higher when they played in the mother's presence than when they interacted alone with a peer, and that some forms of maternal supervisory behaviors correlated positively with the child's peer competence. Specifically, mothers' attempts to help children initiate and maintain interactions, and their responsiveness, synchrony, and level of positive affect during children's play, correlated positively with children's peer competence.

In a subsequent laboratory study, Bhavnagri and Parke (1991) examined the supervisory behaviors of both mothers and fathers, and expanded the sample to include children from ages 2 through 6. They found that children's peer competence increased in the presence of fathers as well as mothers, and that gains attributable to parental facilitation were stronger but less enduring among younger children (2- to 3½-year-olds) than among older children (3½- to 6-year-olds). More specifically, although both younger and older children increased their levels of interaction in the presence of a parent, only the older children were able to maintain these gains in the parent's absence. Findings for specific supervisory behaviors revealed that parents' attempts to foster peer interactions bore more of a relation to older than younger children's competence. Younger children, in contrast, appeared to benefit most from direct and continuing forms of parental supervision (e.g., teaching specific skills, such as turn taking). Based on these findings, Bhavnagri and Parke concluded that younger children may need more supervisory assistance from adults to maintain their interactions with peers.

Mothers' attempts to supervise their preschoolers were also explored in a group-entry paradigm employed by Finnie and Russell (1988). In this study, mothers were instructed to offer as much or as little assistance as they deemed necessary while their children attempted to enter a play session with two peers. Mothers' supervisory behaviors during this period were observed and subsequently coded into a series of categories reflecting the type of involvement they pursued with their child during the play session (e.g., codes such as "avoidance of the supervisory role" and "power assertive discipline" were used). Results indicated that mothers differed greatly in both their level of involvement (e.g., some joined the play, others watched closely, and some remained aloof), and in the types of behaviors they used to help their child gain entry to the peers' activities. For example, mothers of children judged to have high sociometric status encouraged them to adopt the peers' frame of reference and encouraged them to enter without disrupting the peers' ongoing activities. Mothers of low sociometric status children, in contrast, tended to disrupt the peers' activities, and employed more intrusive, hostile tactics as a means of helping their child gain entry.

***Field-Based Studies.***   Additional findings pertaining to parental supervision can be found in recent field studies. In studies conducted by Ladd and colleagues (Ladd & Golter, 1988; Ladd et al., 1988), telephone interviews and mail questionnaires were employed to gather data about parents' efforts to initiate and supervise children's peer contacts at home. Ladd and Golter (1988) found that nearly all parents provided some form of supervision for peer-play sessions that took place in their homes. Differences were found, however, in the style of supervision reported by parents, and these differences were predictive of children's peer competence and school adjustment. Specifically, children of parents who tended to use direct (i.e., intrusive, controlling) as opposed to indirect (i.e., unintrusive) styles of supervision tended to be less well liked and more rejected by classmates in school, and were also viewed as hostile and disruptive by their teachers.

There is also some data on the types of child behaviors parents respond to when supervising children's peer interactions. Using home-based observations, Lollis and Ross (1987) recorded mothers' interventions as they supervised toddlers' peer-play bouts. Perhaps not surprisingly, mothers intervened in toddler's conflicts more than in any other type of peer–peer activity. Often, such interventions produced more equitable outcomes for the children (e.g., increased sharing, fairer distribution of play materials). Mothers also tended to address their interventions to their own child, as opposed to the peer, and were less likely to intervene when they were supervising children in a peer's home as opposed to their own. These and other issues await further investigation.

### Parents' Monitoring and Peer Relations Policies

The need for direct and continuous supervision of children's social activities becomes less necessary and possible as they grow older. As children become more mobile and autonomous, a growing proportion of their social activities cannot be directly observed by their parents. Patterson and Stouthamer-Loeber (1984), for example, have shown that the number of hours children spend in unsupervised activities increases dramatically during middle childhood and early adolescence. As a consequence, parents must rely on more indirect forms of supervision (i.e., monitoring, rules and policies about social activities) as a means of guiding and regulating children's social activities. For most parents, this shift from direct to indirect forms of supervision is no doubt predicated upon careful assessments of the child's capacity to engage in self-supervision and demonstrated ability to act within prescribed social rules and regulations. However, differences in parents, children, and family circumstances may influence the timing and success of this process, and pave the way for different types of interpersonal and child outcomes.

***Monitoring: Parents' Knowledge and Awareness of Children's Peer Activities.*** Monitoring refers to the parents' awareness and knowledge about the child's whereabouts (e.g., play locations), companions (e.g., identity and types of peer partners), and activities (e.g., what the child and peers are doing together). Research on the role of parental monitoring in children's social development is scarce; most of what we know about this form of supervision comes from investigations designed to probe the origins of juvenile delinquency during adolescence. For example, Wilson (1980) interviewed the parents of 10- and 11-year-old boys in Great Britain, and asked them to describe their supervisory practices. Parents were questioned about their sons' activities, amount of time spent outdoors, and family rules about curfew. Based on these measures, the families were divided into categories representing three levels of monitoring (i.e., "strict," "intermediate," or "lax"). Results revealed that inner-city families were more lax in their monitoring, and that parents who engaged in less monitoring, regardless of their strata, tended to have sons with higher levels of delinquency.

The results of a study by Patterson and Stouthamer-Loeber (1984) also suggest a link between parental monitoring and delinquency. These investigators interviewed boys from three age groups (fourth, seventh, and tenth graders) and their mothers. To assemble a composite measure of monitoring, children were asked about their whereabouts and the amount of information they shared with parents, and mothers were asked about the importance of supervision and their awareness of their sons' activities. Among other variables, parental monitoring was found to be one of the best predictors of both police contacts and juvenile delinquency. Moreover, parental monitoring was the only measure that discriminated between moderate and severe offenders.

With few exceptions, these and other studies tend to show that parents of delinquent youth are less aware of their children's whereabouts, peer companions, and social activities (see McCord, 1979; Patterson & Stouthamer-Loeber, 1984; Steinberg, 1986; Wilson, 1980). Much of this literature also points to a link between parental monitoring and family conflict and disruption. In general, lower levels of parental monitoring are found in families undergoing various forms of stress and disruption (McCord, 1979). Although these findings suggest that parental monitoring may play an important role in the origins and maintenance of juvenile conduct disorders (which can be construed as one index of social competence), they do not help us understand how monitoring may be related to other developments in the social domain, including children's peer relations. Moreover, past work on parental monitoring has been conducted primarily with adolescent samples, and we know little about the use of monitoring with younger children.

One exception is a recent study by Crouter, MacDermid, McHale, and Perry-Jenkins (1990), in which the investigators explored the linkage between parental monitoring and grade school children's school performance. In this study, monitoring was defined as the parents' knowledge about children's daily experiences, and was assessed through a series of evening telephone interviews, much like those employed by Ladd and Golter (1988). The investigators found that boys who were less well monitored by their parents tended to receive lower grades than children who were monitored more closely. Moreover, in dual-earner families, boys who were not well monitored tended to view themselves as engaging in more negative forms of behavior.

To the best of our knowledge, Ladd and Golter (1988) were the first investigators to explore the potential linkage between parental monitoring and children's competence in peer relations. Using a telephone log interview methodology, these investigators asked parents of preschool children to report the type of supervision they employed for each of their child's sampled peer contacts. The parents' supervisory behavior during each reported peer play period was coded into one of three categories (i.e., "direct," "indirect," or "unmonitored"), to reflect the parents' level of involvement with their child during play sessions. Direct supervision occurred when parents "maintained a presence or participated in the children's activity," and indirect supervision occurred when parents "tended to oversee and were aware of the children's activity, but were not consistently present or involved in it" (p. 111). Thus, as presently defined, what Ladd and Golter coded as indirect supervision can be seen as a form of parental monitoring.

Based on their tendency to employ each of these supervisory styles, the parents in the sample were classified into two "types"; those whose supervision was primarily direct, and those whose supervision was largely indirect. Very few of preschoolers' peer contacts were coded as "unmonitored," and so none of the parents in this sample were assigned to this category.

Findings from this study include a positive relation between parental monitoring and children's competence in classroom peer relations. Parents who were less involved in their children's peer activities, as indexed by their use of indirect supervision (i.e., monitoring rather than direct supervision), tended to have children who were less hostile toward peers in school, and better accepted and less rejected by classmates. In contrast, children of parents who employed more direct forms of supervision received higher ratings for classroom aggression and were less accepted and more rejected by their classmates. One explanation for these findings is that direct forms of parental supervision interfere with child's autonomy and control within peer situations. This type of parental interference may essentially restrict the child's attempts to negotiate and manage their own social encounters and relationships, and keep them from mastering and generalizing peer-related social skills. It is also possible, however, that the parents' supervisory style is the result of the child's behavior. Thus, it is possible that children who are more aggressive and "difficult" tend to elicit more parental control, including more direct forms of supervision. Further research is needed to disentangle the potential direction of effect, and to investigate the forms of monitoring parents employ with a wider range of age groups.

***Parent's Policies for Neighborhood Peer Relations.*** As we have argued in previous sections, the parents' choice of a residence or neighborhood determines, in part,the type of social milieu that surrounds the child. However, once a family has settled into a particular neighborhood, the parents' policies about children's neighborhood activities may have an important bearing on children's peer relations in this context.

It seems likely that parents' policies are partially dependent on the age of the child. Parents may grant school-age children greater autonomy and freedom of movement in the neighborhood than they allow toddlers and preschoolers (Levin, 1951, quoted in Bryant, 1985). Bhavnagri (1987), for example, interviewed mothers of preschool children between the ages of 2 and 6, and found that older preschoolers tended to have more unsupervised access to neighborhood companions and facilities than did their younger counterparts. Older children also played outdoors with friends more than younger children did, and had a larger number of playmates in the neighborhood. Similarly, among preschoolers ranging in age from 32 to 70 months, Ladd (1988) found that the size of the peer network and membership in different play groups increased with age.

In addition to age, the child's gender may also influence parents' policies about neighborhood activities. Hart (1978) found that, during middle childhood, boys were more likely than girls to travel greater distances from home without seeking parental permission. Moreover, parents appear to supervise the outdoor activities of girls more closely than those of boys (Landy, 1959, quoted in Bryant, 1985).

Parents' perceptions of the neighborhood may also affect the types of policies they devise for children. In studies reported by Medrich and colleagues (Berg & Medrich, 1980; Medrich et al., 1982), factors such as traffic volume, crime rate, and perceived dangerousness of the neighborhood (i.e., parents' perceptions), were found to be negatively associated with the frequency of children's neighborhood peer contacts and activities. Thus, it would appear that neighborhood safety is an important consideration to parents, and may influence the degree to which they permit children to play or otherwise participate in this context. Seemingly, higher levels of traffic, crime, and perceived dangerousness cause parents to restrict children's activities in the neighborhood, potentially limiting their contacts and social experiences with peers (see also Ladd et al., 1988).

## RESEARCH ON PARENTAL MANAGEMENT: CONTEMPORARY STATUS AND FUTURE DIRECTIONS

Thus far, researchers interested in parents' management of children's peer relations have tended to pursue descriptive and correlational aims. Much of the research conducted thus far has been designed to describe parents' management practices, and to determine whether these behaviors are related to developments in children's social competence and peer relations. An examination of both lines of evidence, however, suggests that a great deal remains to be learned about the features and potential effects of parents' management in the social domain.

### Research on the Forms and Features of Parents' Management

Previous research motivated by descriptive aims suggests that many parents do attempt to manage their children's peer relations, both by arranging peer contacts and by monitoring and supervising their social activities. Beyond this, however, many descriptive issues remain to be addressed. For example, additional work is needed to provide detailed descriptions of the various management activities parents actually employ in natural settings. For example, although we know that some parents arrange contacts for their children, we know very little about *how* they do this. It is possible that some parents exercise considerable control over this activity, perhaps making the arrangements themselves, deciding what the children will do, where and how long they can play, and so forth. Other parents may accomplish the same task more indirectly, by involving the child in each step of the process. The consequence may be that one style (possibly the latter?) fosters greater interpersonal mastery and autonomy in the child. Attempts to expand and refine naturalistic data collecting and recording methods will further this aim, and help to provide a richer and more ecologically valid account of parents' typical management styles and practices. Data such as these will foster clearer conceptualizations of the various management constructs, help us to delineate meaningful forms and features, and aid in the generation of hypotheses about the potential functions of these practices.

It will also be important to determine whether other types of socialization agents act as managers of children's peer relations, and whether their behaviors complement or work at cross-purposes with the parents' practices. It is quite possible that other important persons facilitate children's access to peers, establish social policies, and supervise play periods. For example, as children grow older, they may arrange many of their own play activities with peers. Also, siblings may introduce children to their friends, or siblings of their friends, and babysitters or grandparents may assume responsibility for management practices when parents are absent. Moreover, although we may infer from existing data that mothers tend to engage in this type of activity more than fathers, we know very little about what fathers do when they play this role.

In addition, we know very little about the frequency with which parents engage in various types of management activities, and whether the incidence of this behavior varies according to important contextual factors such as family demographics (e.g., SES, single parents, dual- vs. single-earner families, ethnicity), geographic settings (e.g., urban vs. rural locations), and climatic conditions (e.g., winter vs. summer weather). Also, researchers have largely ignored the role that specific peer situations or tasks may play in shaping parents' supervisory activities. Most investigators have not attempted to gather information on these factors, or have employed data collection periods that are too limited to allow analysis of contextual and temporal variations.

Although some investigators have included children from multiple ages in their samples, most have not. Consequently, we know very little about how parents may adapt or change their management practices over time. Equally lacking are data on parents' management practices with important subsamples of children, such as those at risk for later interpersonal problems and conduct disorders (e.g., aggressive, withdrawn, and rejected children). It is conceivable that parents' management practices may affect (or be affected by) these anticipated social trajectories. Ultimately, it would be of value to determine whether parents' management efforts serve to mitigate or exacerbate these risks.

In relation to what we know about parents' efforts to arrange and supervise children's peer contacts, we know very little about monitoring practices and policies concerning children's peer relations outside the home. What types of rules do parents teach their children about social relations outside the family, and how do they regulate child behavior in distant social settings? It seems likely that parents create policies that govern play locations (e.g., how far a child can travel from home), partners (e.g., peers a child is and isn't allowed to play with), activities (e.g., what can be done with peers), materials (e.g., types of toys available or permitted), and times (e.g., when and how long play with peer is permitted). Conceivably, all of these factors may have some bearing on the child's social experiences and development.

## The Role of Parental Management in Children's Social Development

In view of past research, it is reasonable to conclude that parents' management of peer relations is associated with children's social development and competence. There is preliminary evidence to suggest that parents do provide opportunities for children to meet and interact with peers by sending them to child care and preschool, by involving them with peers in informal play groups and community settings, and by selecting neighborhoods and developing policies for children's extrafamilial contacts with peers. Some of this evidence also suggests that children's participation in these social settings is related to the development of their social skills and to the diversity and quality of their relationships with peers.

Linkages have also been found between parental supervision and children's social competence, although the direction of these findings has been mixed. Among younger children (i.e., toddlers), direct forms of parental supervision have been associated with higher levels of peer interaction and competence. Conversely, among older preschoolers, similar forms of supervision have been related to lower levels of peer competence. Perhaps the potential contribution of parental supervision changes as children grow older—practices that are beneficial to young children may outlive their usefulness with older children, or even begin to restrict their social experiences and development. Supervision, like other forms of social support, may either enhance or interfere with development depending on its form, timing, and "fit" with the child.

Beyond these rather general conclusions, however, much remains to be learned about the nature of the linkage between parents' peer management and children's social development. In particular, greater effort should be devoted to understanding the potential direction(s) of effect between parental management and children's social competence. As research in other domains of parent–child relations has shown, parents and children affect each other in reciprocal ways (e.g., Bell, 1979; Bell & Chapman, 1986; Keller & Bell, 1979). In this domain, it is possible to view parents' management practices as both a cause of children's social development and as a response to the social characteristics of the child. For example, in relation to findings pertaining to parents' supervisory behaviors, Ladd and Golter (1988) concluded that:

> Children who display higher levels of social competence may be granted more independence from their parents than those who manifest interpersonal difficulties. In other words, parents may see children who are more active, disruptive, and aggressive as less autonomous and more in need of close scrutiny and direct supervision. Conversely, it may be that parents' early monitoring styles have an effect on children's ability to relate to peers. . . . (p. 116)

Clearly, questions concerning the causal priority and direction of these variables call for innovative and creative research designs and analyses. By employing longitudinal rather than cross-sectional designs, researchers can measure both parent and child variables at two or more times of measurement and, using cross-lag, regression, path analysis, LISREL, or other statistical tools, explore models in which each variable serves as a potential antecedent (or consequence) of the other(s). Another avenue for clarifying causal influence might be achieved by dividing samples of children into subgroups representing different, relatively stable forms of social adjustment (e.g., average vs. aggressive, rejected children). Within each subgroup, individual differences in parents' management styles could be identified and used to forecast child outcomes at later points in time. For example, if parents of aggressive children were found to manage their peer relations in different ways (e.g., some create opportunities for constructive peer interaction and others supervise in ways that inhibit aggression but fail to foster competent forms of peer interaction), it might be possible to predict which children would become better adjusted over time. A similar but stronger design could be achieved by manipulating the management variable (e.g., randomly assigning parents of aggressive children to different management-training conditions).

There is also a need to develop stronger theoretical perspectives or working models that can be used to guide empirical investigation and aid in the interpretation of results. In addition to distinguishing between various forms of peer management, there is a need to understand how these practices affect children's social lives and experiences (e.g., the functions of specific forms of management), and vice versa. This calls for considerable conceptual work and, in particular, the development of working models or a logic that can explain how certain forms of management impact children's social lives, and produce specific interpersonal outcomes.

Finally, investigators interested in parental management have not explored the cognitions and motivations that underlie parents' actions. In one sense, it is not possible to fully comprehend parents' management styles without also understanding their perceptions, goals, strategies, and so on. For example, a parent who does not intervene in a quarrel between two children may do so either out of choice or lack of awareness. On the one hand, the parent may deliberately refrain from intervening because she wants the child to learn or practice skills for resolving fights with peers. On the other hand, the parent may not intervene because he is not monitoring the children's interactions.

A variety of cognitive and motivational factors may impinge on parents' management practices and, thus, warrant further research attention. For heuristic purposes, we have attempted to delineate some of these factors and chart their potential links to parental management and children's social behavior, within the model shown in Fig. 8.1. Within this "circular" model, factors such as the parents' socialization history (see Putallaz, 1989; Putallaz, Costanzo, & Smith, 1991) and their current cognitions are viewed as important antecedents of their management behavior. For example, as Putallaz and colleagues have suggested, parents' memories

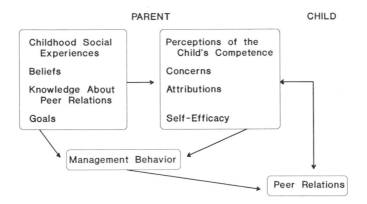

FIG. 8.1. Potential relations between parent's cognitions, management behavior, and children's peer relations.

of their own childhood peer experiences may influence their current socialization perspectives and practices, including their management aims and behaviors. In fact, these investigators have shown that mothers with positive peer memories perceive their children as more socially competent, and that the children of mothers with anxious/lonely memories tend to become well-accepted by peers.

In addition to these historical factors, other types of parental cognitions may operate contemporaneously with their management practices, and function as motivational influences. Investigators such as Rubin, Mills, and Rose-Krasnor (1989) have emphasized the potential importance of parental beliefs and attributions, and have shown that mothers' beliefs are related to their methods of teaching children social skills and their strategies for handling problematic social behaviors. Beyond these factors, we would speculate that parents' knowledge and goals (intentions) may contribute to their management activities. Parents who know very little about child development, or about peer relations in particular, may underestimate the importance of agemates or be less involved and competent at managing children's social experiences. Parents may also pursue different management objectives as a function of the outcomes they value in the social domain. Some, for example, may place more importance on leadership and assertive behaviors, whereas others may emphasize the development of expressive behaviors. Pertaining to this point, Rubin et al. (1989) found that mothers who emphasized the importance of social skills tended to have children who displayed higher levels of social competence.

It also seems likely that the parents' perceptions of the child, and his or her functioning in the social domain (depicted as feedback loops from child behavior in the proposed model) may be an important impetus for their management activities. As Ladd and Golter (1988) have suggested, parents who see their child as less willing and interested in peer relations (e.g., shy or withdrawn) may be more inclined to foster peer contacts and nurture social interactions. These same perceptions may give rise to other cognitions, such as concerns and attributions, that affect parents' management efforts. Perceptions that result in concern (i.e., recognition that a problem exists) may motivate managerial strategies aimed at solving child's interpersonal problems. Attributions about the locus and stability of the perceived problems may determine the targets of parents' interventions (e.g., themselves, their child, the peer group), and influence the degree to which they perceive themselves as able to resolve the child's problems (e.g., parents may feel less efficacious or more helplessness if they attribute their child's difficulties to temperamental or genetic causes). As Ladd and Price (1986) have shown, parents' self-efficacy at peer-related socialization tasks (e.g., their confidence at tasks such as helping children make friends) is closely tied to their child's performance in the peer culture.

## EXPANDING RESEARCH ON PARENTAL MANAGEMENT: NEW DIRECTIONS AND FINDINGS

As can be seen in the preceding review, much remains to be learned about parents' roles as facilitators of young children's peer relations and competence. One important objective within our own research program has been to gather further evidence on the role that parents play as facilitators or mediators of children's peer relationships and play opportunities. A second objective has been to shed light on the potential antecedents of parents' involvement or participation in these roles—that is, the factors that may motivate or discourage parents from acting as facilitators of children's informal play contacts with peers.

### Initiating Informal Peer Contacts: Contributions of Parents and Children

Ladd and Hart (in press) recently conducted an investigation of the frequency with which parents and children initiate informal play opportunities with peers. Past findings from our own research and that of other investigators has taught us that parents differ in the frequency with which they initiate informal peer contacts for preschoolers (Bhavnagri & Parke, 1991; Ladd & Golter, 1988). However, we also know that parents are not the only persons who are involved in this aspect of the child's social life. Starting in preschool, children begin to initiate their own peer contacts and receive play invitations from persons outside the family (Bhavnagri & Parke, 1991).

Thus, the opportunities children have to relate with peers in informal play settings, and the contributions that these experiences make to their overall social competence, may depend not only on the frequency of their parents' initiations but also on those performed by the child (and others). In view of this, an initial aim of this investigation was to gather data on the frequency with which preschoolers' informal peer-play opportunities were initiated by parents, children, and peers. A second aim of this investigation was to determine the relative importance of parent and child initiations as predictors of preschoolers' social competence. Specifically, we sought to determine whether the frequency of initiations performed by parents, children, or the combined initiations of both parties predicted preschoolers' peer competence in informal and classroom settings.

The sample for this study consisted of 83 preschool children (35 boys, 48 girls) and their families, all of whom resided in a moderate-sized southern community. The children were enrolled in one of four center-based preschools, and were between 42 and 67 months of age at the outset of the study. Consent was obtained from 74% of the families who were invited to participate, and 83% of the children came from two-parent families.

Assessments of parents' initiation practices and children's peer relations and behavior were conducted during both the winter and spring months of the school year, and were separated by a 6–8-week interval. On each assessment occasion, one of six trained interviewers conducted a series of eight telephone interviews with each parent (a total of 16 interviews were conducted with each family). Each interview was conducted on a separate day, with the constraint that 5 weekdays and 3 weekend days be sampled over a 3–4-week period. Interviewers employed a standardized interview and recording protocol, and parents were asked to recount all of their child's social activities and relevant aspects of their own behavior on an hour-by-hour basis for each sampled day.

During each of these calls, the interviewers recorded the amount of time children spent in preschool or child care and made a log of all reported peer contacts. Peer contacts were defined as activities that children performed with one or more peers in an informal, nonschool setting (e.g., child's home, peer's home, neighborhood). For each reported peer contact, interviewers documented the duration (in minutes), location (e.g., child's house), and a description of the participating peers (e.g., name, sex, age). Data from these sources were summed across each of the eight interviews conducted at both times of assessment to create several measures of children's informal peer relations, including: *contact frequency* (i.e., number of reported peer contacts), *contact duration* (i.e., mean length of contacts in minutes), *range of partners* (i.e., number of different playmates), and *number of frequent play companions* (i.e., number of playmates present in 25% or more of the child's contacts). An estimate of time spent in child care was created by summing the number of hours and minutes recorded across the 8 days sampled in each of the two assessment intervals.

For each reported contact, several interview questions were used to ascertain who had initiated the play opportunity and what roles (if any) the parent and child had played in the initiation process. Parents were also asked to complete a demographic questionnaire, and this measure yielded information on family size and SES, as well as parents' ages, occupations, income, years of education, and employment.

Classroom observations and sociometric ratings were used to assess children's social competence in child care settings. Using a coding scheme developed by Ladd (see Ladd & Price, 1987), trained observers recorded children's social and nonsocial behaviors during free-play periods on the playground. Children were observed in a predetermined random order, and their behaviors were reliably coded (Kappas > .84) into 1 of 11 behavioral codes (i.e., social conversation, cooperative play, arguing, rough play, aggression, solitary play, parallel play, onlooking, unoccupied, teacher, and transition), and 1 of 5 anxiety codes (i.e., immobile, rocking, shuffling, sucking hair or fingers, and automanipulation). Scores for categories that were highly correlated were summed to create behavioral composites, including: prosocial (cooperative play + social conversation), antisocial (arguing + aggression), nonsocial (onlooking + unoccupied), and anxious behavior (sum of all five anxiety codes).

A picture sociometric rating and nomination procedure (see Ladd & Golter, 1988) was used to assess children's peer status among classmates at each time of assessment. Measures of peer liking and disliking were created by summing the number of positive and negative nominations each child received, respectively, from all classmates. These scores were standardized by classrooms and then subtracted to create a measure of social preference (*Z* positive minus *Z* negative nominations).

***How Often Do Parents, Children, and Peers Initiate Informal Play Opportunities with Peers?*** The frequency of children's peer contacts, summed across all 16 interview occasions, is shown by age, sex, and type of initiator in Table 8.1. On average, children arranged 2.26 peer contacts during the sampled period—slightly fewer than were arranged by their parents (*M* = 2.47) and slightly more that were initiated by peers (*M* = 1.84). The total number of informal peer contacts children

TABLE 8.1
Average Number of Informal Peer-Play Opportunities Initiated
by Parents, Children, and Peers

|  | Age | | Gender | | |
|  | Younger | Older | Males | Females | Full Sample |
|---|---|---|---|---|---|
| Sponsor: | | | | | |
| Parents | | | | | |
| M | 2.68 | 2.25 | 2.69 | 2.31 | 2.47 |
| SD | (2.18) | (1.46) | (1.45) | (2.09) | (1.85) |
| Children | | | | | |
| M | 1.89 | 2.61 | 2.56 | 2.04 | 2.26 |
| SD | (1.84) | (2.56) | (2.66) | (1.90) | (2.20) |
| Peers | | | | | |
| M | 1.61 | 2.08 | 1.81 | 1.87 | 1.84 |
| SD | (1.66) | (2.07) | (1.89) | (1.91) | (1.89) |
| Total Contacts | | | | | |
| M | 8.50 | 10.28 | 10.50 | 8.62 | 9.40 |
| SD | (4.34) | (5.61) | (5.95) | (4.23) | (5.06) |

Note: Standard deviations are shown in parentheses.

participated in over the 16 interview occasions averaged 9.62, with a range of 0 to 21.

As suggested by the means reported in Table 8.1, differences in the average number of contacts arranged by parents, children, or peers were small, and they proved to be statistically nonsignificant. Furthermore, an age × sex MANOVA performed on the frequencies attributable to parents, children, and peers produced no significant effects. The number of initiations performed by parents, children, or peers did not differ substantially for boys and girls or for older and younger preschoolers. Although the total number of peer contacts (regardless of sponsorship) was somewhat larger for older preschoolers and boys, these differences approached but did not achieve statistical significance ($p < .10$).

***Are Features of Children's Informal Peer Networks Related to the Frequency with Which Parents and Children Arrange Play Opportunities?*** When we examined qualities of children's nonschool peer relations, such as their range of partners, contact durations, and number of frequent play companions, significant sex and age differences emerged for the range of partners measure. An age × sex MANOVA, which was performed on these three measures, revealed that older children's peer contacts encompassed a larger range of partners than did their younger counterparts, and that boys had significantly higher scores on this same measure than did girls. Findings for the remaining two measures were not significant.

Further analyses revealed that the range of children's peer contacts was positively correlated with the frequency of both parents' and children's initiations. That is, parents who arranged a larger number of informal play contacts tended to have children with a larger range of playmates ($r = .28$, $p < .05$), and a similar relation was found between the number of initiations performed by children and the size of their playmate networks ($r = .29$, $p < .05$). In order to determine the relative importance of parent and child initiations, we performed a hierarchical regression analysis in which these two variables (and their interaction) were entered after controlling for the amount of time children spent in child care and their age and gender. Consistent with an additive model, the interaction term failed to achieve significance, but scores for the frequency of parent and child initiations each accounted significant and nonoverlapping proportions of variance in the range of partner scores. Thus, the number of different play partners children develop in informal settings appears to depend on the extent to which both parents and children initiate play opportunities in this context.

### Are the Frequencies of Parents' and Children's Peer Initiations Related to Children's Social Competence in School?

We also found evidence of a relation between the frequency with which parents and children initiate informal peer contacts and children's social competence in school. However, in contrast to the prior findings, differential relationships emerged between these two family variables and the various measures of children's classroom competence. Perhaps not surprisingly, we found that children who initiated a larger number of peer contacts outside of school tended to be better liked by their peers in preschool classrooms. These children also tended to display fewer anxious behaviors at school.

Parent initiations, in contrast, predicted the level of prosocial and nonsocial behavior children exhibited in classrooms and, among boys, acceptance by classmates. Parents who frequently initiated informal peer-play opportunities tended to have children who were more prosocial toward peers and spent less time engaging in onlooking and unoccupied behaviors. For boys, but not girls, parents' initiations were predictive of higher levels of classroom peer acceptance.

These findings clearly illustrate that parents are not the only persons who initiate informal play activities with peers. Rather, it would appear that many young children express a desire to spend time with peers and thus become the impetus for parents' efforts to arrange informal play opportunities. Moreover, it would also appear that young children are often recipients of play opportunities that are initiated (or reciprocated) by peers.

The present findings also suggest that there is a link between the frequency of parents' and children's social initiations and the type of peer companionship children experience in nonschool settings. More specifically, parents and children's initiations were positively correlated with the size of children's informal peer networks. Children in families where initiations were performed more frequently, either by themselves or their parents, tended to associate with a larger range of play companions. Although the design of this study precludes strong causal inferences, these findings are consistent with the following two perspectives. One is that parents who frequently initiate play opportunities also encourage children to play extensively, perhaps as a means of increasing children's experience with different types of playmates. Another is that children who are highly motivated to seek peer companionship also tend to form a larger range of peer relationships.

Finally, if parents' initiations are viewed as a strategy designed to socialize children's peer relationships and skills, then children who are frequently exposed to these opportunities might be expected to display higher levels of social competence in peer-oriented settings, such as classrooms or playgrounds. Consistent with this interpretation, we found that parents who often initiated peer contacts tended to have children who interacted in prosocial ways with peers and spent less time in unconstructive solitary behaviors on the playground. In particular, these children were observed to spend less time engaging in "tuned out" behaviors and were less likely to act as passive bystanders, watching classmates from the periphery of their activities. Moreover, the frequency of parents' initiations predicted higher levels of prosocial behavior in the classroom and, among boys, greater peer acceptance. The latter finding is consistent with prior evidence linking the frequency of parents' initiations with early peer acceptance among boys (Ladd & Golter, 1988).

These findings must also be considered in light of the apparent role that children play as initiators of their own social contacts with peers. Children who take an active role in arranging informal peer activities were found to be less anxious in classroom settings and better liked by their preschool classmates. These findings may be attributable to variation in children's social maturity or independence or, alternatively, to differences stemming from their temperaments or learning experiences within the family. On the one hand, socially precocious children, by virtue of their greater maturity, may be better equipped not only to initiate more of their own play opportunities but also to negotiate the uncertainties and interpersonal demands of preschool classrooms. On the other hand, the frequency with which children initiate toward peers in nonschool settings may stem from other influences, such as parents' efforts to interest children in peers and the strategies they use to nurture children's social overtures. Skills at social initiation, once acquired, may generalize to classroom settings, and make children more comfortable and engaging play partners for their classmates. Unfortunately, the validity of these explanations cannot be fully tested within the correlational framework of the present study. Further research is needed to explore these possibilities.

## Potential Antecedents of Parents Involvement

A second aim of our research was to assess the relationship between parents' perceptions of their children's progress in peer relations and their management behaviors. These aims were addressed in two related studies (Le Sieur, Profilet, & Ladd, 1992; Profilet & Ladd, 1992) conducted with a sample of 62 preschool children (34 girls and 28 boys; ages 43 months to 72 months) and their mothers and teachers. Interviewers visited families in their homes and employed questionnaires to gather data about mothers' perceptions of their children's progress in peer relations, concerns, and policies pertaining to children's informal peer relations. School data were obtained by asking teachers to rate each child's social behavior and peer relations in the classroom.

Progress perceptions, as conceived in this study, refer to mothers' views of their child's progress in social skills and peer relations, as compared to other children of the same age. Progress perceptions were assessed with a 20-item parent-report measure. Mothers rated their perceptions of their child's progress for each behavior on a 7-point scale ranging from "behind" to "ahead" of agemates. Psychometric analyses revealed that scores on this scale were internally consistent (alpha = .95) and stable ($r$ over 2 months = .89).

Parental concerns were defined as the degree of concern or worry mothers have about their children's peer relations and social behaviors and were assessed with a 20-item scale. Mothers rated their degree of concern on a 7-point scale ranging from "not concerned" to "very concerned." Psychometric analyses revealed that scores on this scale were internally consistent (alpha = .97) and stable ($r$ over 2 months = .76).

Measures of parents' policies for informal peer relations were obtained by asking mothers to rate a series of items including: (a) how often they encourage their child to get together with a friend or playmate (7-point scale ranging from "less than once a month" to "every day"), (b) the degree to which play contacts are typically sponsored by mother versus child (7-point scale ranging from "usually mother's idea" to "usually child's idea''), and (c) the degree to which mother versus child determines what the children will do together (7-point scale ranging from ''parent decides'' to ''child and/or playmate decides'').

With the parents' permission, teachers were asked to complete the Preschool and Kindergarten Teacher Rating scale, developed for this study. This instrument consists of 81 items, including many items selected from instruments such as the Preschool Behavior Questionnaire (PBQ) (Behar, 1977) and a number of new and revised items. Factor analysis of this scale produced four factors, and inspection of item loadings and content allowed us to create four reliable (alphas > .87) subscales termed *antisocial*, *asocial*, *prosocial*, and *outgoing* behavior.

*Do Mothers and Teachers View Children's Social Competence in Similar Ways?* To address this question, scores for mothers' progress perceptions and teachers' behavior ratings were correlated. Results indicated that mothers' progress perceptions were positively correlated ($r = .48$, $p < .001$) with teacher ratings of sociable behavior, but negatively related to teacher ratings of asocial behavior ($r = -.37$, $p < .01$). Thus, children who were perceived by their mothers as progressing successfully in peer relations tended to be seen by their teachers in similar ways (i.e., as more sociable and less asocial).

*Are Mothers' Perceptions of Children's Progress Related to Their Concerns?* Correlational analyses revealed that mothers' progress perceptions and concerns were negatively related ($r = -.26$, $p < .05$). In addition, to compare mothers with differing concerns, a median split on the concerns measure was used to divide the sample into two groups (i.e., mothers with higher versus lower concerns), and a one-way ANOVA (groups: concerned versus unconcerned) was used to examine differences in mothers' progress perceptions. Results indicated that the progress ratings of concerned mothers were significantly lower than those of unconcerned mothers, $F(1,60) = 10.21$, $p < .01$. Thus, mothers who tended to view their children as delayed in peer relations also reported higher levels of concern.

*Are Parents' Progress Perceptions Related to Their Management Behaviors?* To compare mothers with differing progress perceptions, a median split on the progress measure was used to divide the sample into two groups (i.e., mothers with higher versus lower perceptions of their child's progress in peer relations). One-way ANOVAs (groups: higher versus low progress) were used to explore differences in mothers' ratings of the frequency with which they encourage children to arrange play activities with peers and the degree to which they allow children to choose their own activities during play sessions with peers. Results indicated that mothers who viewed their children as "ahead" in peer relations more often encouraged their child to play with peers than did mothers who were inclined to see their child as behind, $F(1,60) = 4.92$, $p < .01$. In addition, mothers with higher progress perceptions tended to rate their children as having more control over their own play activities, $F(1,60) = 4.47$, $p < .05$.

Although preliminary, these findings suggest that parents' assessments of their children's early social abilities are related to the way they manage their children's peer relations. Reliable individual differences were found in mother's progress perceptions, and these differences converged with teachers' ratings of children's social competence in preschool classrooms. More importantly, mothers who tended to see their children as socially mature were less worried about their children's peer relations and more encouraging of their children's participation in informal peer relations (i.e., play activities in the home and neighborhood). These mothers also tended to see themselves as providing children with greater control over their own peer-play activities.

## CONCLUSION

In summary, there is growing evidence to suggest that parent's management practices are related to children's peer relations. Preliminary studies of parent's attempts to manage their children's peer relations have been conducted in both lab and field settings, and have produced findings that are consistent with the "direct" linkage hypothesis (see Parke & Bhavnagri, in press; Parke et al. 1988). However, much remains to be learned about the nature of this linkage. In particular, we still know very little about the types of individuals who engage in this aspect of children's socialization, nor are we well informed about the frequency with which various socialization agents perform these functions. Because previous investigators have relied primarily on observer's ratings and parents' self-reports of their management activities, we know very little about the behaviors parents actually employ in these situations. There is also a need to chart parent's management styles with children who are at risk for adjustment problems (e.g., behaviorally aggressive and withdrawn children), as well as with "normal" samples. Also, researchers have largely ignored the role that specific peer situations or tasks play in shaping parents' management activities.

To date, parental management has been studied primarily by asking parents to act as facilitators of children's free play in the laboratory, or to report their practices for undefined situations that occur in their homes. No attempt has been made to determine whether parents' management styles differ across cultural or family contexts, geographic locations, climatic conditions, and social situations. We also do not know whether the behaviors parents display in the lab are consistent with those they employ in their homes. Finally, it will be important for investigators to explore parents' motivations for their management practices. Among the factors that may warrant further research attention are parents' social memories and histories, knowledge of peer relations, interpersonal goals, self-perceptions, and their perceptions of the child.

## REFERENCES

Bell, R. Q. (1979). Parent, child, and reciprocal influences. *American Psychologist, 34*, 821–826.

Bell, R. Q., & Chapman, M. (1986). Child effects in studies using experimental or brief longitudinal approaches to socialization. *Developmental Psychology, 22*, 595–603.

Berg, M., & Medrich, E. A. (1980). Children in four neighborhoods: Physical environment and its effects on play and play patterns. *Environment and Behavior, 12*, 320–348.

Berndt, T., & Ladd, G. W. (1989). *Peer relationships in child development*. New York: Wiley.

Bhavnagri, N., & Parke, R. D. (1985, April). *Parents as facilitators of preschool peer interaction*. Paper presented at the Biennial Meeting of the Society for Research in Child Development, Toronto.

Bhavnagri, N. & Parke, R. D. (1991). *Parents as facilitators of preschool children's peer relationships: Effects of age of child and sex of parent. Journal of Social and Personal Relationships, 8*, 423–440.

Bryant, B. (1985). The neighborhood walk: Sources of support in middle childhood. *Monographs of the Society for Research in Child Development, 50*(3, Serial No. 210).

Crouter, A., McDermid, S., McHale, S., & Perry-Jenkins, M. (1990). Parental monitoring and perceptions of children's school performance and conduct in dual- and single-earner families. *Developmental Psychology, 26*, 649–657.

Finkelstein, N. W., Dent, C., Gallacher, K., & Ramey, C. T. (1978). Social behavior of infants and toddlers in a day-care environment. *Developmental Psychology, 14*, 257–262.

Finnie, V., & Russell, A. (1988). Preschool children's social status and their mothers' behavior and knowledge in the supervisory role. *Developmental Psychology, 24*, 789–801.

Garbarino, J., & Gilliam, G. (1980). *Understanding abusive families*. Lexington, MA: Lexington Books.

Hart, R. (1978). *Children's sense of place*. New York: Halstead.

Hartup, W. W. (1979). The social worlds of childhood. *American Psychologist, 34*, 944–950.

Haskins, R. (1985). Public school aggression among children with varying day-care experience. *Child Development, 56*, 689–703.

Howes, C. (1983). Patterns of friendship. *Child Development, 54*, 1041–1053.

Howes, C. (1988). Peer interaction of young children. *Monographs of the Society for Research in Child Development, 53*,(1, Serial No. 217).

Howes, C. (1990). Can the age of entry into childcare and the quality of childcare predict adjustment to kindergarten? *Developmental Psychology, 26*, 292–303.

Keller, B. B., & Bell, R. Q. (1979). Child effects on adult's method of eliciting altruistic behavior. *Child Development, 50*, 1004–1009.

Krappman, L. (1986, December). *Family relationships and peer relationships in middle childhood: An explanatory study of the association between children's integration into the social network of peers and family development*. Paper presented at the Family Systems and Life-Span Development Conference at the Max Planck Institute, Berlin, FRG.

Ladd, G. W. (1988). Friendship and peer status during early and middle childhood. *Developmental and Behavioral Pediatrics, 9*, 229–238.

Ladd, G. W. (1990). Having friends, keeping friends, making friends, and being liked by peers in the classroom: Predictors of children's early school adjustment? *Child Development, 61*, 312–331.

Ladd, G. W., & Golter, B. S. (1988). Parents' management of preschoolers' peer relations: Is it related to children's social competence? *Developmental Psychology, 24*, 109–117.

Ladd, G. W., & Hart, C. H. (in press). Creating informal play opportunities: Are parents' and preschoolers' initiations related to children's competence with peers? *Developmental Psychology*.

Ladd, G. W., Hart, C. H., Wadsworth, E. M., & Golter, B. S. (1988). Preschoolers' peer network in nonschool settings: Relationship to family characteristics and school adjustment. In S. Salzinger, J. Antrobus, & M. Hammer (Eds.), *Social networks of children, adolescents, and college students* (pp. 61–92). Hillsdale, NJ: Lawrence Erlbaum Associates.

Ladd, G. W., & Price, J. M. (1986). Promoting children's cognitive and social competence: The relations between parent's perceptions of task difficulty and children's perceived and actual competence. *Child Development, 57*, 446–460.

Ladd, G. W., & Price, J. M. (1987). Predicting children's social and school adjustment following the transition from preschool to kindergarten. *Child Development, 58*, 1168–1189.

Landy, D. (1959). *Tropical childhood*. Chapel Hill: University of North Carolina Press.

Le Sieur, K. D., Profilet, S. M., & Ladd, G. W. (1992, April). *Arranging preschool children's peer contacts: A look at parent/child contributions and gender effects*. Paper presented at the Annual Meeting of the American Educational Research Association, San Francisco, CA.

Lewin, K. (1951). *Field theory in social science: Selected theoretical papers*. New York: Harper & Row.

Lieberman, A. F. (1977). Preschoolers' competence with a peer: Relations with attachment and peer experience. *Child Development, 48*, 1277–1287.

Lollis, S., & Ross, H. (1987, April). *Mother's interventions in toddler–peer conflicts*. Paper presented at the Biennial Meeting of the Society for Research in Child Development, Baltimore, MD.

McCord, J. (1979). Some childrearing antecedents of criminal behavior in adult men. *Journal of Personality and Social Psychology, 9*, 1477–1486.

Medrich, E. A., Roizen, J. A., Rubin, V., & Buckley, S. (1982). *The serious business of growing up: A study of children's lives outside school*. Berkeley: University of California Press.

Moore, R., & Young, D. (1978). Children outdoors: Toward a social ecology of the landscape. In I. Altman & J. F. Wohlwill (Eds.), *Children and the environment* (pp. 83–130). New York: Plenum.

Mueller, E., & Brenner, J. (1977). The origins of social skills and interaction among playgroup toddlers. *Child Development, 48*, 854–861.

Parke, R. D., & Bhavnagri, N. P. (1989). Parents as managers of children's peer relationships. In D. Belle (Ed.), *Children's social networks and social supports* (pp. 241–259). New York: Wiley.

Parke, R. D., MacDonald, K. B., Beitel, A. & Bhavnagri, N. (1988). The role of the family in the development of peer relationships. In R. Peters & J. McMahon (Eds.), Social learning systems approaches to marriage and the family (pp. 17–44). New York: Brunner Mazel.

Patterson, G. R., & Stouthamer-Loeber, M. (1984). The correlation of family management and delinquency. *Child Development, 55,* 1299–1307.

Profilet, S. M., & Ladd, G. W. (April, 1992). *Mothers' perceptions and concerns about their preschool children's progress in peer relations.* Paper presented at the Annual Meeting of the American Educational Research Association, San Francisco, CA.

Putallaz, M. (1989, April). *Linkages between family and peer systems.* Paper presented at the Biennial Meeting of the Society for Research in Child Development, Kansas City, MO.

Putallaz, M., Costanzo, P. R., & Smith, R. (1991). Maternal recollections of childhood peer relationships: Implications for their children's social competence. *Journal of Social and Personal Relationships, 8,* 403–422.

Rescorla, L. (1989, April). *Academic experiences for preschool children: An investigation of parental attitudes.* Paper presented at the Biennial Meeting of the Society for Research in Child Development, Kansas City, MO.

Rubin, K. H., Mills, R. S. L., & Rose-Krasnor, L. (1989). Maternal beliefs and children's competence. In B. Schneider, G. Attili, J. Nadel, & R. Weissberg (Eds.), *Social competence in developmental perspective* (313–331). Amsterdam: Klewer Academic.

Rubin, A., & Sloman, J. (1984). How parents influence their children's friendships. In M. Lewis (Ed.), *Beyond the dyad* (pp. 223–250). New York: Plenum.

Schwartz, C., Strickland, R., & Krolick, G. (1974). Infant day care: Behavioral effects at preschool age. *Developmental Psychology, 10,* 502–506.

Steinberg, L. (1986). Latchkey children and susceptibility to peer pressure: An ecological analysis. *Developmental Psychology, 22,* 433–439.

Wilson, H. (1980). Parental supervision: A neglected aspect of delinquency. *British Journal of Criminology, 20,* 203–235.

Vandell, D. L., Henderson, V. K., & Wilson, K. S. (1988). A longitudinal study of children with day-care experiences of varying quality. *Child Development, 59,* 1286–1292.

vanVliet, W. C. (1981). The environmental context of children's friendships: An empirical and conceptual examination of the role of child density. In A. E. Osterberg, C. P. Tiernan, & R. A. Findlay (Eds.), *Proceedings from the 12th Annual Conference of the Environmental Design Research Association* (pp. 216–224). Washington, DC: EDRA.

# CHAPTER NINE

# Parents' Regulation of Children's Peer Interactions: Direct Influences

Susan P. Lollis
*University of Guelph*

Hildy S. Ross
*University of Waterloo*

Ellen Tate
*University of Waterloo*

Traditionally, the social lives of children have been studied in their separate social spheres, namely the parent–child social system or the peer–child social system. Few researchers have studied situations in which both spheres are operational and therefore overlap in influence, or situations in which one system might influence the other system (for reviews see Hartup, 1979, 1983, 1989; Radke-Yarrow, Zahn-Waxler, & Chapman, 1983). Nonetheless, children do not live separate lives within different spheres; mutual influences exist across domains defined by psychological study. Of those researchers who have actually considered the influence of the two social systems on each other, the majority have looked at the indirect influence that parents have on their children's relationships with peers. Indirect influences are those that are mediated by intervening agents or stages. The influence of parents on peer relationships is considered to be indirect when the impact is mediated by the parent–child relationship (Parke & Bhavnagri, 1988; Parke, MacDonald, Beitel, & Bhavnagri, 1988; Rubin & Sloman, 1984). In establishing a positive parent–child relationship, parents do not explicitly intend to enhance their children's relationships with peers; such effects are by-products of other goals. The parent–child attachment relationship and the parent–child interactive relationship have been assessed for their influence on peer relationships (for attachment studies see Bowlby, 1973; Bretherton & Waters, 1985; Easterbrooks & Lamb, 1979; Lieberman, 1977; Sroufe, 1983; Sroufe & Fleeson, 1986, this volume; for examples of interactive studies see MacDonald

& Parke, 1984; Putallaz, 1987). These researchers posit that children learn what to expect and how to interact in peer relationships through the quality of attachment and interactive behavior that has been shared with the parent. However, the "lessons" that children learn from their parents may not be completely transferable to peers because children must also learn to expect differences between peers and parents and to interact differently with peers than they do with parents.

Recently, a small handful of researchers has begun to investigate the role that parents play in directly and intentionally influencing their children's peer interactions by way of discussing, coaching, supervising, and intervening in peer interactions (Finnie & Russell, 1988; Ladd & Golter, 1988; Levitt, Weber, Clarke, & McDonnell, 1985; Lollis & Ross, 1987; Lollis, Ross & Tate, 1988; Nash, 1989; Parke & Bhavnagri, 1988; Parke et al., 1988; Ross, Tesla, Kenyon, & Lollis, 1990). These direct means of influencing peer relationships are the focus of this chapter. We review what is known about the direct methods that parents use to transmit social knowledge concerning peer relations to their children. We particularly emphasize the type of parental regulation that occurs in actual ongoing peer interactions. Accordingly, in this chapter we (a) present a model of different methods of parental socialization of peer interaction, (b) review the current research on parental intervention in relation to this model, and (c) recommend areas for further research to increase our understanding of the parental influence.

## MODEL FOR PARENTAL SOCIALIZATION
## OF PEER INTERACTION

As we have reviewed the work on parent's regulation of peer interactions, we have distinguished the structural characteristics of parents' direct attempts to influence their children's interactions. Three forms of parental intervention are distinguished.

First, parents can influence peer interaction when their children are removed from the actual situation by discussing and giving advice on interaction. Such advice occurs outside of the context of peer interaction. Parents may prepare children for an upcoming peer interaction by discussing hypothetical situations that might actually occur. For example, a parent or child might bring up the possibility that a particular peer may interact in a particular manner. (For example, Child: "Mary is going to tease me about the mistake I made in dance class," or, Parent: "What should you do if John wants to fight?") The parent might discuss the possible options in reacting to the upcoming interaction and thus influence the actual event of the interaction. In addition to this preparation for possible interaction, the parent might also review an interaction after the event to bring understanding to a past event and to prepare for similar events that may occur in the future. Here, the child or parent may recall an event and bring it up for discussion or interpretation at a later date. (For example, Child: "Why did Kerry laugh when I hurt myself?," or, Parent: "Why do you think that Adrian always takes the crayon you want to use?")

Parental advice and comment offered outside of the context of peer interaction might be more reasoned and dispassionate than that offered while interaction is ongoing, but when parents act outside of the context of peer interaction, children must find the appropriate time and place for the application of parental input. The child is the linchpin in the system. One experiment indicates that the issue of application is not trivial (Ross, 1982). Toddlers were taught a set of simple games by an experimenter immediately prior to their encounters with agemates. However, when the children played with their peers they did not use the games that they had learned. Like others who had not had the advantage of adult tutoring, they invented new games to play with their peers.

Moreover, in this type of intervention parents rarely have an opportunity to evaluate the effectiveness of their counsel or their children's skill in its application. Socialization techniques must therefore be of the type most likely to elicit compliance over the long term, such as reasoning and explanation that help the child to understand relationships between people and the specific situations in which to use certain behavior (Kuczynski, 1984).

In addition to offering specific advice, parental comments outside of the peer context could help to create attitudes and orientations to others. Parents and children may gossip about the child's friends (For example, Child: "He's often mean, isn't he?" or, Parent: "That was an awfully nice thing for her to do. She must really like you."), or they may comment on other children more generally (For example, Child: "Day camp is a lot of fun with so many friends to play with."). Children's attributions concerning self and others could be crystallized in explicit discussions with parents (Grusec & Dix, 1986).

There are many labels that might be attached to this type of regulation; we prefer *decontextualized discussion* to characterize the cool and reasoned advice that parents might offer when they have the time to consider what is best. However, we hasten to add that we have found no literature that examines parent–child discussions of peer relationships outside of the interactive context. The best approximation that we may have in the psychological literature of the advice that parents might offer in a decontextualized manner may be the responses that parents give to questionnaires including vignettes describing peer interaction. Similarly, we consider that proactive discussions across a variety of domains are frequent parent–child exchanges that have been virtually ignored in the literature on parent–child relations. Our own experience, and the fact that people often offer one another social advice, makes such interaction a logical and likely possibility.

A second way in which parents might influence their children's peer interactions is by directing or giving advice while the interaction is occurring. They can give advice when the child is within the actual interaction (For example, Parent: "Give that toy back right now."). Here the parent would have potentially the most influence in the turn by turn interactions of the child with the peer. Advice offered in context occurs in the presence of the child's peer and sometimes in the presence of other people such as the peer's mother and therefore has to take into account this more complex social situation. Such parental intervention is more likely to be reactive in that the ongoing interaction between the children will determine when and how parents intervene. Parental intervention will also be timed closely to the events it must influence. The parent's goal is more likely to be short-term compliance by the child, and so suggestions could often be offered without explanation, and accompanied by emotional appeals (Kuczynski, 1984; Zahn-Waxler, Radke-Yarrow, & King, 1979). Parents can assess the situation, the child's and the peer's behavior, the child's reactions to parental demands, and the effectiveness of the advice. In fact, parents and children might often differ in their interpretations of the ongoing interaction and parents might sometimes force their view on their children. In any case, parental advice in the context of ongoing interaction is likely to be quite different in character and effect from advice offered either before or after encounters with peers. We have begun to label this type of within-context regulation as *directive intervention*. Most studies of parents' direct influence on peer relationships involve directive intervention.

A third means of direct influence occurs when parents actually become part of the exchange that occurs between children, thus easing the way for the children's interactions and at the same time inadvertently modeling friendly and appropriate behavior toward others. We label this type of interaction *interactive intervention*. Parents may become part of a game, organizing the interactions among three participants and prolonging the fun (For example, Parent: "You throw to Jamie, Jamie throws to me, and I'll throw to you," or, Parent: "Well she just passed *Go* so she gets $200."). Parents might introduce themselves, along with their child, to young new neighbors and begin the conversation that breaks the ice between the children. In this way, a parent interacts with both children and does not rely on just changing the behavior of his or her own child in order to improve the quality of peer relationships. The parent attempts to *scaffold* the interactive behavior of the children, much in the same way that mothers have been described as scaffolding the games children play with them (Ratner & Bruner, 1978). Interactive interventions may be more subtle, but influential nevertheless on children's peer relations, enabling children to overcome potential conflicts or breakdowns in interaction that parents can foresee and mediate. Some of the studies we review include parental interactive interventions in peer relationships.

Thus, three forms of interventions may be distinguished from one another on a number of bases. Parental interventions differ in (a) the context in which socialization takes place, including such factors as the physical and temporal removal of parents from the peer situation; (b) parental goals for immediate behavioral change or for longer term understanding; and (c) parental strategies of reasoning about, directing, or interacting in situations of child peer interchange. As noted previously, there is, to our knowledge, no research concerning decontextualized discussions between parents and children about peer relationships. Thus, our review of the literature focuses on research in the other two areas. However, we must keep in mind that most of the socialization literature does not address the issue of socialization for peer relationships.

## EFFECT OF PARENTS' IMMEDIATE INTERVENTION INTO CHILD–PEER INTERACTION

### Interactive Intervention

Ross Parke and Navaz Bhavnagri have worked with interactive intervention (Bhavnagri, 1987; Bhavnagri & Parke, 1985; Parke & Bhavnagri, 1988; Parke et al., 1988). They have found consistently that children are more socially competent with a peer when parents help the children play together. In one laboratory study (Bhavnagri & Parke, 1985), the competence of 24-month-old toddlers in interaction with an unfamiliar playmate was assessed under two conditions, with and without assistance from their mothers. Pairs of children were first allowed to play unaided by their mothers for 5 minutes, next were helped to play together by one and then the other mother for 10 minutes each, and last were left to play unassisted for an additional 5 minutes. Ratings were made on a 5-point scale of the children's behavior. The length of play bouts, the children's overall social competence, as well as their ability to take turns, to sustain interaction, to cooperate, to agree on an activity, to respond, and to behave altruistically were rated significantly higher during the sessions when their mothers assisted in play than when their mothers were more passive. Inasmuch as children's play was scored lower on all these qualities both before and after the periods of maternal assistance, increased familiarity with the peer was unlikely to account for the changes observed over time. However, these findings also indicate that effects of maternal intervention were short-lived; they did not persist even to the minutes immediately following maternal involvement.

Ratings of children's behavior were also correlated with 5-point ratings made of the mothers' behaviors to specify which maternal strategies were most effective in facilitating peer interaction. General factors such as the mother's overall supervisory competence, ability to promote social skills and to express affect, as well as more specific factors such as the mother's ability to initiate and sustain interaction, to be responsive to changes in the peer interaction, to interact in a synchronous manner, and to express positive affect were significantly and positively associated with peer competence.

A second study by Navaz Bhavnagri (1987) replicates and extends the findings of Bhavnagri and Parke (1985) to older children. In this study, the effects of both mother and father separately were observed in the laboratory setting as they helped their children play with a peer. Children in this study ranged in age from 2 to 6 years. The findings indicated, as in the previous study, that assistance by the parents enhanced the quality of the children's play, particularly assistance in sustaining interaction. However, two additional findings specific to this study were reported. First, fathers were as skilled as mothers in promoting peer interaction. Second, specific assistance from parents related to initiation of and turn-taking in peer interaction differentially influenced younger children (2 to $3^1/_2$ years of age as compared with those slightly older, $3^1/_2$ to 6 years of age). The rated competence of parents in initiation of peer interaction was related to older children's peer play whereas parents' competence in promoting turn-taking was positively related to younger children's peer play. The authors observed that older children appear to need assistance in initiating peer interaction but are able to maintain levels of interaction throughout the entire laboratory sequence after the parents' initial assistance, whereas younger children appear to need more sustained and continuing support to maintain their levels of interaction.

We have placed these studies within the category of interactive intervention. Little information is provided about the specific details of parental intervention beyond a description of the rating scales of general categories of parental ability. We have, therefore, inferred that the "helping" that parents engaged in was more of an interactive than directive type. It may be that parents gave directions to their children about how to initiate and maintain interaction rather than becoming a part of the peer exchange in the role of a play partner. Beyond this, we are concerned that many of the parental ratings reported were constructed around the parent's success in facilitating peer interaction; therefore, the high correlations found between parental and child competence may simply mirror a common source of variance. Further work that differentiates the two would be necessary as work in this area progresses.

A second researcher, Alison Nash (1989), has focused on peer relations of slightly younger children (14-month-olds) and has differentiated the effects of interactive and directive intervention from mothers. Her design was a reversal of that used by Bhavnagri and Parke (1985) and Bhavnagri (1987) in that over three 10-minute trials, mothers were asked first to encourage interaction between their children, then to fill out a detailed questionnaire that fully occupied their time, and finally to encourage interaction between the children once again. In this study, children generally remained near one another for a longer period of time, interacted more often with one another, and engaged in longer bouts of interaction when their mothers were busy than when their mothers encouraged interaction, a seeming reversal of Parke's and Bhavnagri's findings. A more detailed look at the data, however, suggests some agreement in that interactive rather than directive intervention was more effective in encouraging peer interaction. Nash evaluated the immediate effectiveness of maternal interventions. Overall, adult interventions were not highly successful in fostering interaction between the peers. Interventions made when children were not yet interacting were successful only 33% of the time, whereas those made when peer interaction was proceeding resulted in continuing interaction only 44% of the time. However, Nash noted that the two major types of parental interventions differed in their effectiveness. Most interventions consisted of verbal directions, similar to our conceptualizations of directive intervention. These produced new interaction or sustained ongoing interaction 21% and 30% of the time respectively. On the other hand, parental interventions that involved objects, such as parents positioning or holding objects so the children could play, and manipulating or exchanging objects between the children, succeeded in eliciting interaction 59% of the time and in sustaining interaction 80% of the time. These latter types of interventions appear to be similar to what we have termed interactive intervention. In explaining her findings, and especially in explaining the divergence between these and other findings, Nash referred to the relative youth of her subjects. Although most of the parents' interventions were verbal, the hallmark of peer interaction in children as young as 14 months is that they are able to interact nonverbally without a common language. Nonverbal and interactive techniques were more helpful than interventions that involved language. Nash pointed out that this may soon change once children begin to master language and integrate it with other peer behavior. Research on other types of maternal interventions have also indicated a shift from physical to verbal modalities as children increase in age from 15 to 44 months of age (Kuc-zynski, Kochanska, Radke-Yarrow, & Girnuis-Brown, 1987). Parke and Bhavnagri's and Nash's results suggest, however, that at least in the early preschool years, interactive behavior may still be useful in fostering peer interaction.

These studies establish that parents can influence the ongoing interaction between their children, and that the quality of parental intervention is related to the quality of play between the children. Parents used interactive intervention to guide their children in accomplishing a goal imposed by the researchers "to help the children play together." Moreover, parental strategies had a short-term impact on achieving the goal of the research, immediate increased interaction of the children, but did not appear to have a persisting influence on peer relations.

We have also investigated the influence of different styles of mother assistance on social relations of toddlers ranging in age from 15 to 18 months (Lollis, 1990). Pairs of unacquainted children and their mothers met in a laboratory playroom for an 8-minute play session prior to one of the mothers departing from the play room for a 4-minute period. During the play period, mothers who were to leave their children for a brief period were instructed to interact extensively or minimally with their children in the environment or were given no instructions except to interact normally. An analysis of the two instructed groups is particularly relevant. Mothers who were instructed to interact minimally in this study were asked to refrain from initiating interaction or engaging in play with their children, and to remain seated in their chairs for the duration of the session, but were allowed to respond in their usual manner to their children's solicitations for interaction. Mothers who were instructed to interact extensively became play partners in the peer environment. These mothers were asked to begin interaction with their children by choosing toys that might be of interest, engaging the children in play, and then responding to their children's interests as the session continued. Both of these groups refrained from mentioning their impending departure until a cue was given and then both groups announced their departures in the same manner before leaving the play room. Then the interactions of these mothers with their children were assessed on two factors, whether or not the interaction was solicited by the child and whether the intervention carried information about the physical or social environment. Mothers in the instructed extensive group provided their children with more unsolicited information about the physical and social environment than did the mothers in the instructed minimal group. These differences, however, had little effect on the level of peer interaction that the children engaged in during the preseparation time period.

During the separation period, the amount of time the separated children were mutually engaged with the peer was related to type of mater-

nal pre-separation interaction. Children with mothers who were instructed to interact extensively spent reliably more time playing with their playmates in their mothers' absences than did the children whose mothers
had interacted with them minimally. These children also frowned, fussed,
and/or cried less than those in the minimal interaction group. Although
this study failed to display the immediate impact of maternal behavior
on peer interaction, it is the first evidence of any persistence of influence
of maternal intervention; the results reflect the utility of interactive intervention in orienting children to the social environment.

## Directive Intervention

There is also a body of research accumulating that is concerned with the
effects of parents' directive interventions on children's peer relations.
One of the first such studies was reported by Mary Levitt and colleagues
(Levitt, Weber, Clark, & McDonnell, 1985). These researchers placed two
toddler-aged children (29–36 months) in a playroom, one on each side
of a wooden open-lattice barrier that divided the room down the center.
All toys were placed on one side of the barrier within one child's reach
for 5 minutes and then placed on the other side of the barrier within reach
of the other child for another 5 minutes. Mothers were instructed to
refrain from intervening in the children's activities during each 5-minute
session except to encourage one child to give a toy to the other child
if the child had not shared spontaneously by 4 minutes into the session.
Over a 4-minute period, none of the children spontaneously shared with
the peer; however, 65% of the children shared in response to their
mothers' pleas after 4 minutes had elapsed. The success of the interventions by some mothers in motivating their children to share had implications for later interactions between the children during a second 5-minute
session. Sharing in the second session by the previously bereft toddler
reciprocated the sharing received in the first session; almost without exception, those whose partners had shared toys with them, offered toys
to the peer, and those whose partners had not shared, despite the mothers'
urgings, did not share. Thus, mothers who succeeded in inducing their
own children to share also inadvertently benefited their children through
the mechanism of reciprocity.

Victoria Finnie and Alan Russell (1988) studied the relation between
parental intervention and the social status of preschool children 4 to 5
years of age. Children whose social status fell in the top or bottom 10%
of their class were chosen for this study. In a laboratory setting, mothers
were asked to help their children become acquainted with peers by joining in the ongoing block play between two same-age, same-gender chil-

dren, and by completing a floor puzzle with the two children. Maternal actions were then directly observed.

This study had the advantage of including good behavioral measures of what mothers do within this context to encourage peer interaction. Finnie and Russell (1988) identified seven basic behavioral categories (observation, avoidance of supervisor role, active but less skillful strategies, active and more skillful strategies, verbal instruction, positive discipline, and power assertive discipline), each composed of numerous actions or strategies on the part of the parent. Only one strategy (plays interactively by joining play as equal) out of 14 composing the "active and more skillful" category and one out of four in the "active but less skillful" category could clearly be interpreted as similar to our concept of interactive intervention; therefore, most of the strategies studied in this research were directive in nature. Finnie and Russell found that mothers of children in both the top and bottom social status groups most frequently used "active and more skillful strategies." Furthermore, these interventions conceptually resembled or encouraged strategies that have been shown to be successful for children who wish to enter a group of two interacting peers (Putallaz, 1987). Active skillful strategies included encouraging both their own children and the others to (a) cooperate, (b) communicate, (c) participate in the activity, (d) validate, and (e) support one another. Interventions were relevant to the ongoing activity and served to stop inappropriate group behavior. Mothers also frequently just observed the group play or used positive discipline (reinforcement for accomplishment, reasoning, and reactions to conflict and aggression that gently stopped or redirected such behavior). Less-skillful strategies (disrupting ongoing interaction and redirecting behavior to some new activity) were less frequent than more-skillful strategies; power assertive discipline was less frequent than positive discipline; avoidance (ignoring the children, talking exclusively to one of them, allowing conflict) was observed less often than active strategies; and verbal coaching of own child ("say hello," "tell them your name," "ask if you can play," etc.) occurred almost exclusively early in the session.

However, interesting differences were found in this study. Despite the fact that active skillful strategies outnumbered negative, less skillful ones by a factor of 20 to 1, the former strategies were used more often by the mothers of high-social status children, and the latter were used more by mothers of low-social status children. Mothers of low-status children were also more likely to avoid any attempts at intervention, especially early in the session. Strategies also varied according to the context of play (block or puzzle). "Observation" was used less in puzzle play and "active more skillful strategies" and "positive discipline" was used more in puzzle play. The authors suggest that the different types of play afforded the mothers different roles for involvement.

This study is the first of two that we review (see also Ladd & Golter, 1988) that focused on the relationship between maternal intervention strategies and children's general social status or peer popularity, an association that is very different from the relationship that we have been focusing on up to this point, namely that between maternal intervention and immediate changes in peer play. Whereas other studies measured the short-term outcome in specific dyads and focused on the interaction of two children, Finnie and Russell (1988) evaluated the relation between maternal strategies and generalized social status within a classroom. Nevertheless, Finnie and Russell's results seem somewhat consonant with the other laboratory studies involving directive intervention; directive maternal intervention with older children was associated with more skillful social interaction (or at least higher social status). Therefore, directive intervention was frequent and useful for children 4 and 5 years of age.

However, children who are generally very popular with their peer group use strategies to enter a group that are different from children who are generally rejected (Putailaz, 1987). Finnie and Russell (1988) considered the possible impact of the children's ongoing behavior on the way in which parents intervened and suggested that the children's behavior may have made it possible for their mothers to react in different ways.

We must consider, however, that in the laboratory studies that we have reviewed, parents had an assigned goal of helping the children to interact. Furthermore, in most laboratory studies the children are unacquainted with the peers with whom they are to interact. Both these factors may be important contextual factors in determining the nature of parental intervention.

Unlike the previous researchers, Gary Ladd and Beckie Golter (1988) have reported a negative relation between the directness of maternal supervision and the popularity and social competence of their preschool and kindergarten-aged subjects. Ladd and Golter's project included longitudinal assessments of how frequently children played with peers outside of school settings, how parents supervised such peer contacts, how children interacted with peers in school, and how peers and teachers rated the children. Few parents did not supervise their children's peer encounters at all. The majority either directly monitored their children's play with peers by maintaining a presence and often participating in the play, or indirectly monitored the play by being aware of the children's activities without being consistently present, leaving the children to play more on their own. In this study, the parents' specific strategies for directly and indirectly monitoring their children's peer play were not evaluated. Consequently, we have little knowledge of the actual behaviors that the parents used when intervening in play. However, Ladd and Golter assessed the effect of the parents' level of monitoring. Level of parental supervision was not related to observations made of children's actual behavior in school but it was related to peer and teacher-rated social status. Children whose parents monitored them directly received fewer positive nominations, more negative nominations, and lower group acceptance from peers, and were assessed as hostile and aggressive by their teachers when compared with children whose parents monitored them indirectly.

The authors presented two likely interpretations of this relationship between parental supervision and child social competence. Like Finnie and Russell (1988), these researchers considered the impact of the children's behavior on the parents. "It may be the case that children who display higher levels of social competence are granted more independence from their parents than those who manifest interpersonal difficulties" (p. 116). Children with interpersonal difficulties may be hostile with peers at home, or their past behavior may make parents wary of unsupervised peer play. Alternatively, parental styles may influence children's experience with and abilities to play independently with peers. That is, intrusive parents may structure and guide interaction, and their children may be at a loss to manage peer interaction without parental structure. Thus parental control may "inhibit children's ability to master independently and generalize peer-related social skills" (p. 116). The authors called for more research to resolve these uncertainties.

In addition, close monitoring of children's behavior in kindergarten seems inappropriate for the age and stage of the child especially when we consider the apparent effectiveness of interactive intervention for earlier work reviewed when children were of a younger age. The previous research was with 24- to 36-month-old toddlers, a sample that was considerably younger than Ladd and Golter's (1988). Interactive intervention might be considered a technique that is more appropriate and perhaps more effective with younger children. Or, as many of the researchers we have reviewed have suggested, certain types of interventions are more useful for older children than others. However, we need to know more about the context and content of parental interventions before we can make this statement with confidence. The following questions come to mind. What type of interactions are the children engaged in when parents supervise them closely? What is the history of interaction of the peer pair? What goals do parents have in intervening in their children's peer relations and what strategies do they use to meet these goals? Do parents get involved in play at the outset, and provide structure in initiating or maintaining ongoing interaction, or do they mainly intervene when children are in conflict? Such information would also help us resolve the apparent discrepancy between Ladd's and Golter's results and those presented earlier.

It is likely that context and goal differences are important characteristics of parental intervention. Mothers in the laboratory context intervened with the specific goal of helping their children to play together, to share, to get involved in the environment; parents who closely supervise play in their own homes may be more likely to be intervening in conflict situations to help children resolve their disputes and to restore harmonious, peaceful interaction. Parents observed by Ladd and Golter (1988) were largely reactive to the quality of their children's interactions with peers. We know that relations found in laboratory studies resulted from experimentally imposed goals of the parents.

The work that has been reviewed thus far, with the possible exception of Ladd and Golter (1988), has been concerned with parents' encouragement of and responses to their children's attempts to be prosocial. Young children, however, also engage in "antisocial" behaviors. Included in this category of behaviors would be actions such as protesting a peer's previous action when it had no harmful intent, hitting a peer, and taking an object from a peer. Hay (1984) estimated that preschoolers engage in conflicts with their peers approximately 8 times per hour. This rate would allow parents ample opportunity to socialize with reference to their children's conflict. Furthermore, it is reported that the majority of conflicts that preschoolers engage in are settled by the children themselves without adult intervention (Shantz, 1987). It is likely that the context for data gathering has influenced the occurrence of adult intervention. For example, some of the data that Shantz summarized was collected in toddler and preschool programs where the adult-to-child ratio would be much higher than the home environment, a factor that could decrease the frequency of adult intervention per child (Bakeman & Brownlee, 1982). Other data referred to by Shantz was collected in a laboratory setting where mothers were instructed *not* to intervene in their children's interactions (Hay & Ross, 1982), another factor that most likely decreased maternal intervention. Very little observational data exists that relates children's peer conflicts with parental behavior in the home.

The two studies that do examine parental intervention in conflict focus on issues of moral development. Judith Smetana (1989) compared the responses of mothers to the moral and conventional transgressions of 2- and 3-year-olds in their own homes. Smetana compared the type of responses mothers made in relation to the type of transgression committed when the children were alone with their mothers and when the children were engaged in play with their peers.

The findings concerning mothers' responses to moral transgressions are most relevant to our focus in this chapter. Moral transgressions were defined as acts against another that had consequences for the rights and welfare of the peer and included object conflicts (i.e., attempts to take away a toy in another's possession or not sharing a toy) and aggression (hitting, kicking, biting, pulling hair, punching, or otherwise intentionally harming another). Only the moral transgressions of the children that were responded to by their mothers were considered for analysis. Smetana outlined, in some detail, the strategies used for the responses that mothers made to their children's transgressions. All these responses were directive in nature. The response categories included statements that:

1. Provided a rationale for a rule or behavior.
2. Made perspective-taking requests.
3. Noted rights or fairness.
4. Indicated that sanctions or punishment would be used.
5. Indicated that the behavior created disorder.
6. Specified a rule governing the action.
7. Commanded the child to cease the act.

Smetana found that moral transgressions were more frequent than conventional transgressions during the peer sessions and that the type of moral transgression committed was evenly split between the two categories, object conflicts and aggression. On the whole, mothers in conjunction with children (primarily the victims of the transgressions) were more likely to respond to 2-year-olds' rather than 3-year-olds' moral transgressions. When the nature of the response was examined in light of the type of transgression, it was found that mothers of children in both age groups were more likely to use strategies that were perspective-taking requests and evaluations of rights in response to moral rather than conventional transgressions.

In our own prior work we focused on maternal interventions in the object conflicts of 20- and 30-month-old peers (Ross, et al., 1990). Children were observed in pairs that met 18 times, alternating homes so that the children met equally often in each child's home. Both mothers were present during each 40-minute play session. Mothers were asked to behave naturally, but not to play with the children. Observers dictated a running record of the children's interactions and the mothers' interventions on audiotape. We found that each mother directed her interventions almost exclusively to her own child, but that her interventions overwhelmingly favored the peer. Mothers supported their own children only 10% of the time, but interestingly such support was offered more often to boys than to girls. We examined the context and content of maternal interventions to see if mothers endorsed principles of justice that might resolve the dispute fairly. That is, we asked whether mothers consistently ruled that the owner of an object was entitled to the object. Alternatively, we also asked if prior possession was the basis for entitlement. We found that mothers were inconsistent in their endorsement of either principle; they supported owners only 45% of the time and non-owners 55% of the time; they supported possessors 56% of the time and requesters 44% of the time. Thus neither principle was a consistent determinant of the mothers' rulings. What did happen was slightly more complex. When the mother's own child was the owner of the toy, then rights of ownership were seldom supported; when the other child owned the toy, then the entitlement of owners was strongly enforced. Similarly, the rights of the possessor were enforced only when it was the other child who had the toy first. Moreover, mothers could offer reasons to support either side of an argument. They could support the owners by stating "it's the other child's toy," or the non-owner by reminding their children that the other didn't have one like that to play with at home. A possessor is entitled because "she had it first," and a requester is supported "because you've had it long enough and he deserves a turn." It appeared to us that mothers were not attempting to teach principles of entitlement when they intervened in their children's conflicts. Rather, we felt they were responding to more immediate goals to keep the peace by urging their own children to yield to the peer in order to restore harmony between the children.

This first analysis focused only on object conflicts between the children. In this chapter, we broaden the scope considerably so that the nature of mothers' interventions in conflict can be compared with those in other interactive contexts. When our audiotapes were transcribed, four types of interactive sequences were identified. These were games, pretence, conflicts, and contingent interactions. Due to the low occurrence of pretence sequences, we have combined games and pretence into one category of nonliteral play for the purpose of the analyses reported in this chapter.

We were interested in the purpose or the goal that each mother appeared to have in her interventions in each sequence and the strategies that she used to achieve her goal. We conceptualized mothers, a priori, as having a specific goal in each sequence, but carrying out the goal through the use of various strategies; thus, there are more strategies than goals. When we consider the joint occurrence of goals and strategies, each strategy is associated with the overall goal that mothers had within a given sequence. We were only concerned with overt goals and strategies and did not code the absence of intervention even in situations when it appeared that the mother was consciously refraining from intervening for a certain purpose.

Five goals were identified through consideration of the transcripts and relevant parental socialization literature:

1. Emotionally **support** children in their interaction by means of comfort and reassurance.
2. Convey **basic principles** of interpersonal interaction by referring to manners or general rules of conduct.
3. **Structure** interaction by suggesting definite roles or drawing attention to features of the interaction.
4. **Discourage** behavior by not allowing the interaction to progress in its present manner.
5. **Distribute** property among children engaged in an interaction.

As well, eight strategies for achieving the various goals were identified:

1. Provide physical guidance through positive and negative **nonverbal** interventions.
2. **Reason**.
3. Restate aspects of the situation to **clarify** the interaction.
4. Suggest **alternative** behavior or activities.
5. **Command**.
6. **Interject** in an unelaborated manner (e.g., Hey, calling the child's name).
7. **Evaluate** the quality of the child's behavior or character.
8. **Bargain** or **threaten**.

Most of these strategies were consistent with the socialization literature. However, the reason and clarify strategies varied slightly. Whereas most researchers have included clarify within the reason category, we chose to separate the two based on whether or not a reason was explicitly stated, using such words as "because," "since," or "if." Clarifying statements merely made observations on the situation and the child would have to independently infer that the comment justified the request.

We found that overall the children engaged in nearly 30,000 (29,504) interactive sequences. Mothers intervened nearly 10,000 times (9,872) in their children's peer interactions, accounting for .33 interventions per sequence overall, regardless of type of sequence (Table 9.1). Many more interventions occurred overall in conflicts than in nonliteral play or contingent interaction. When maternal intervention was considered as a proportion of the number of sequences of a given type, .61 interventions were made per conflict sequence, whereas proportionally fewer interventions were made per nonliteral play and contingent interaction sequences (.42 and .14, respectively). As reported earlier, 82% of all interventions were addressed to the mothers' own children (Lollis & Ross,

## TABLE 9.1
Strategies that Mothers Used Presented by Goal and Interactive Sequence

| | Nonliteral | | | | | Conflict | | | | | Contingent | | | | | Total |
|---|---|---|---|---|---|---|---|---|---|---|---|---|---|---|---|---|
| | Sup | Bas | Str | Dis | Dist | Sup | Bas | Str | Dis | Dist | Sup | Bas | Str | Dis | Dist | |
| Nonverbal | 1 | 0 | 82 | 11 | 14 | 6 | 54 | 86 | 174 | 624 | 1 | 0 | 51 | 14 | 45 | 1163 |
| Reason | 1 | 2 | 20 | 15 | 1 | 6 | 46 | 54 | 90 | 109 | 4 | 7 | 23 | 16 | 20 | 414 |
| Clarify | 5 | 3 | 285 | 27 | 23 | 41 | 149 | 370 | 188 | 824 | 16 | 82 | 513 | 61 | 145 | 2732 |
| Alternative | 0 | 2 | 8 | 6 | 4 | 8 | 18 | 57 | 40 | 381 | 1 | 1 | 10 | 6 | 20 | 562 |
| Command | 4 | 22 | 413 | 95 | 30 | 30 | 374 | 413 | 558 | 1140 | 11 | 134 | 611 | 96 | 215 | 4146 |
| Interject | 0 | 0 | 2 | 10 | 0 | 7 | 5 | 11 | 268 | 106 | 0 | 0 | 7 | 14 | 2 | 432 |
| Evaluative | 5 | 4 | 7 | 2 | 0 | 17 | 58 | 12 | 59 | 31 | 32 | 16 | 28 | 4 | 3 | 278 |
| Bargain | 0 | 0 | 5 | 2 | 0 | 0 | 19 | 3 | 24 | 81 | 0 | 1 | 2 | 5 | 3 | 145 |
| Total | 16 | 33 | 822 | 168 | 72 | 115 | 723 | 1006 | 1401 | 3296 | 65 | 241 | 1245 | 216 | 453 | 9872 |
| | | | | | 1111 | | | | | 6541 | | | | | 2220 | |

*Note.* Sup = Support, Bas = Basic Principles, Str = Structure, Dis = Discourage, Dist = Distribute.

1987). As well, within conflicts, mothers intervened more often when their own children were initiators of conflicts, $F(1,4) = 22.34, p < .01$, but only in their own homes, $F(1,50) = 18.21, p < .001$ (own child, own home = 1.99; other child, own home = 1.16; own child, other home = 1.03; other child, other home = .82). Mothers' interventions were also found to change the proportion of winning to greater equality between the children, $F(1,4) = 14.41, p < .025$. Children who were typically victorious without mothers' interventions won less often when mothers intervened (proportion won without maternal intervention = .62; proportion won with maternal intervention = .54).

First, we decided to look within each sequence to see which goals and strategies were used most frequently. The three types of sequences were similar across the analyses. Significant goal effects were found for all three of sequence types. For nonliteral play and contingent interaction, mothers used the goal of providing structure most frequently ($F[4,39] = 17.17$, $p < .000$ and $F[4,39] = 3.91, p < .017$, respectively), whereas distributing property, used twice as much as the second most frequent goal of discouraging interaction, was the major goal in conflicts, $F(4,39) = 8.9$, $p < .000$. Significant strategy effects were also found for all three types of sequences. For each of the sequences, the most frequent strategy was command followed by clarify (nonliteral play, $F[7,63] = 13.19, p < .000$; conflict, $F[7,63] = 8.03, p < .000$; contingent interaction, $F[7,63] = 15.7, p < .000$).

Beyond these findings for nonliteral play and contingent interaction, age effects for both goals and strategies conveyed the information that mothers used a significantly higher number of goals and strategies with their 30-month-olds than with their 20-month-olds. For conflict and contingent interaction, significant sex differences for goals and strategies showed that more goals and strategies were directed to male than female children. This finding was not an artifact of overall differences in the number of sequences in which male and female children engaged because no such differences were found (Ross & Lollis, 1989). In contingent interaction, goal and age effects were supplanted by a goal × age effect, $F(4,39) = 3.41, p < .017$, and strategy and age main effects were replaced by a strategy × age effect, $F(7,63) = 3.83, p < .004$. The goal of structuring the interaction increased significantly in use from 20 to 30 months of age. The two strategies of command and clarify increased significantly in use from our younger group to our older group.

In order to understand the important associations between the variables in our study, we turned to multiway frequency analysis (Tabachnick & Fidell, 1989). We constructed a multiway frequency table and through loglinear analysis of this matrix sought to identify those associations between the variables that were important in reproducing the observed frequencies. Simple models were compared with more complex models (i.e., those involving higher order associations between variables) to determine if the more complex models improved the overall ability to predict the data. Usually, this process of comparing simple models with more complex models is continued until a model is found that does not differ significantly from the observed data. However, our data set with nearly 10,000 observations was extremely powerful in rejecting the null hypothesis. Therefore, we did not apply the usual statistical standards but tentatively accepted a model that included all of the factors that strongly contributed to the utility of the model.

We began with a model that included only the main effects goal (GOAL), strategy (STR), sequence type (SEQ), age (AGE), and gender (SEX) (Table 9.2). This model allowed differences in the frequencies of the levels of all factors, but included no interactions or relationships among factors. This model failed to provide a good fit to the data (likelihood ratio $X^2$ (464) = 7008, $p$ = 4E-32). We next added each two-way interaction to this model to see which among them improved the fit of the model. Four interactions improved the model's fit considerably; these were GOAL × SEQ where the improvement in likelihood $X^2$ was 2615 with 8 $df$; GOAL × STR where improvement in $X^2$ was 1798 with 28 $df$; STR × SEQ where improvement in $X^2$ was 693 with 14 $df$; and STR × AGE where improvement in $X^2$ was 423 with 7 $df$ (Table 9.2). Thus, interactions between the factors indicated led to models with a substantial improvement in fit to the observed data. These results are generally consistent with the ANOVA results previously reported.

To interpret these factors, we examined the simple two-way chi-square tables for the factors involved and report those instances where $z > 2.0$

TABLE 9.2
Log-Linear Models

| Model | df | $X^2$ | $p <$ | $\Delta df$ | $\Delta X^2$ |
|---|---|---|---|---|---|
| All First-Order Effects | 464 | 7008 | 4E-32 | | |
| Goal × SEQ | 456 | 4393 | 4E-32 | 8 | 2615 |
| Goal × STR | 436 | 5211 | 4E-32 | 28 | 1797 |
| STR × SEQ | 450 | 6315 | 4E-32 | 14 | 693 |
| STR × AGE | 457 | 6585 | 4E-32 | 7 | 423 |
| All First- and Second-Order | | | | | |
| Effects | 387 | 1169 | 4E-32 | | |
| SEQ × AGE × SEX | 385 | 829 | 4E-27 | 2 | 340 |
| GOAL × AGE × SEX | 383 | 950 | 4E-32 | 4 | 219 |
| GOAL × STR × SEQ | 341 | 1020 | 4E-32 | 46 | 149 |
| All First-, Second-, and | | | | | |
| Above-Third-Order Effects | 335 | 595 | 8E-16 | | |

[$z$ = adjusted residual calculated as observed-expected/$\sqrt{}$expected, $z >$ 2.0, $p < .05$].

1. *GOAL* × *SEQ*. Mothers intervened to provide structure for children engaged in nonliteral play and contingent activity and to distribute resources, discourage behavior, and teach basic principles within conflicts.

2. *GOAL* × *STR*. Evaluative statements were used to support interactions. Commands and evaluative statements were used to teach basic principles. Commands and clarifying statements were used to interest children in interaction or to structure play. Interjections and reasoning were used to discourage behavior; nonverbal means, suggestions of alternatives, and bargaining or threatening were used when mothers wished to distribute property.

3. *STR* × *SEQ*. Mothers used simple commands and clarifying statements within nonliteral play and contingent interactions. They used nonverbal means, suggestions of alternatives, and unclear interjections during conflicts.

4. *STR* × *AGE*. Nonverbal interventions occurred more with younger children; clarifying statements and reasoning more with older children.

Next, we examined the model that contained all main effects and all two-way interactions among the variables. The fit of this model was necessarily better than that of previous ones, because it included all factors from prior models but still left substantial room for improvement (likelihood ratio $X^2[387]$ = 1169, $p <$ 4E-32). This model was therefore used as a baseline for evaluation of the next stage in the hierarchy, the three-way interactions. The inclusion of separate three-way interactions each led to an improvement in fit with observed frequencies. The ones that accounted for the most change from the baseline two-way interaction were: SEQ × AGE × SEX where improvement in likelihood $X^2$ was 340 with 2 *df*, GOAL × AGE × SEX where improvement in likelihood $X^2$ was 220 with 4 *df*, and GOAL × STR × SEQ where improvement in likelihood $X^2$ was 149 with 46 *df*.

As with the two-way interactions, these three-way interactions were interpreted in light of chi-square analyses.

1. *SEQ* × *AGE* × *SEX*. Mothers of younger girls and older boys were more likely to intervene in games; mothers of younger boys intervened more in conflict; and mothers of older boys intervened more in contingent interaction.

2. *GOAL* × *AGE* × *SEX*. Mothers used structuring more with older males than with younger males. As well, mothers discouraged younger males and older females more and made more requests for redistribution of younger males and younger females.

3. *GOAL* × *STR* × *SEQ*. There were associations between certain goals and strategies, regardless of the sequence type when we compared the matrices of the three different types of sequences. In all three types of sequences, emotional support was achieved by evaluative comments; basic principles of interaction were taught by commands and evaluative statements; structuring was achieved by using clarifying statements; discouraging behavior was associated with the use of reasoning and interjections; and distributing property was associated with nonverbal means and suggestions for alternative behavior.

For sequences that included nonliteral play only, there was an absence of an association that was present in the other two types of sequences; teaching basic rules of interaction through commands was not found for nonliteral play. In Contingent Interactions, mothers discouraged behavior by using the bargaining or threatening strategy. Within Conflict sequences mothers emotionally supported their children through clarifying statements; they taught basic principles of interaction by reasoning; they discouraged behavior by using evaluative comments; and they distributed goods by bargaining and threatening their children.

Next, we examined the model that contained all main effects, all two-way interactions, and the three three-way interactions just discussed. The fit of this model did not reach significance, (likelihood ratio $X^2[335] = 595, p < 8E-16$). After assessing this last model, we decided to stop testing models because we were approaching the saturated model. In addition, we found that each additional three-way interaction and the four-way interactions added very little to the explanatory power of the model. We also felt that we had to be cautious in interpreting the significance level of models as our data violated the assumption of independence (that each data point come from independent subjects). One major effect of this violation is to make the tests more powerful than they should be, in rejecting the hypothesis that the model provides a good fit for the observed data. Another major effect of the violation results in the problem of clustering; the fact that some relations in the data may be a result of certain subjects. Bakeman and Gottman (1986) suggested that if the intervention is regarded as the unit of interest and if one does not generalize to children beyond the data set, then the analyses can be used to explore relations within the data to provide hypotheses for further study. We have proceeded to interpret the data as far as we felt comfortable in order to provide hypotheses based on a large data set.

## CONCLUSION AND FUTURE DIRECTIONS
## FOR RESEARCH

Most parents have the general desire to encourage and support their children's peer relationships. There are many ways in which parents can carry out this task. We have suggested that there are three types of direct parental intervention into children's peer interactions: decontextualized, interactive, and directive. Each of the studies reviewed in this chapter was chosen as an investigation of the influence of direct parental intervention into peer interaction. As the small number of articles attests, there is a scarcity of work investigating parents' direct interventions in children's peer interactions.

We have found in our review that several factors influence the goals that parents have and the strategies they use when intervening in their children's peer interactions. These factors include the age of the child, the gender of the child, and the context of interaction.

The parental role in direct intervention with young children appeared to be particularly prevalent when children were preschool age or younger, and to change markedly as children grew older (Bhvagnagri & Parke, 1985). Differences, however, were even noted in the preschool years. Parents appeared to use interactive intervention more frequently with younger children and to use directive intervention more frequently with older children. We found more frequent directive intervention with older children. In particular, in contingent interaction the goal of structuring the interaction and strategies of command and clarify increased with age. We also found that nonverbal interventions occurred more with younger children and clarifying and reasoning more with older children. This finding parallels the finding in the child compliance literature that mothers' responses changed over time with their toddlers and preschoolers from physical to verbal (Kuczynski, Kochanska, Radke-Yarrow, & Girnius-Brown, 1987). The influence of the age of the child was also noted in the content of the intervention. Smetana (1989) reported that maternal responses to moral transgressions decreased as the child's age increased from 24 to 36 months of age. Additionally, mothers responded to 2-year-olds' conventional transgressions with peers with statements of rules, and to 3-year-olds' conventional transgressions with sanctions, suggesting that by the age of 3 children were expected to understand and remember familial conventional rules. With older children, beyond the preschool years, the role of the parent may actually involve more discussion and consultation rather than prompting or directing behavior within the child–peer interaction (Finnie & Russell, 1988; Ladd & Golter, 1988). However, as we have stated earlier, we have found no literature in which "decontextualized discussion" has been considered as one of the means of parents influencing their children's peer relations. We can only speculate that as children develop into middle childhood and adolescence, parents progressively take on a less-immediate role in their children's peer relations and may be found more frequently intervening in a decontextualized manner.

Few of the studies reviewed here found differences in parental intervention associated with the gender of the child. Ross et al. (1990) found that when children fought over toys, mothers supported the entitlement of their sons more than their daughters. Smetana (1989) found that mothers' responses to their daughters' moral transgressions focused on the consequences of the act for others' rights and welfare whereas their responses to their sons' moral transgressions used social control strategies. In the analyses that we report in this chapter, we have found that more goals and strategies were used overall with male children than female children in conflict and contingent interaction sequences, and that this difference could not be attributed to a difference in the rate of occurrence of conflict or contingent interactions for male and female children.

Beyond age and gender of the child, there is accumulating evidence that parents have different goals and choose different strategies for their interventions according to the different social problems that their children face with peers. Smetana (1989) found that mothers responded to moral transgressions of children with requests for the children to take the victim's perspective, and with evaluations of the rights and welfare of the other, whereas mothers respond to conventional transgressions with statements focusing on the social disorder the act created and commands for regulation of behavior. Our own work also has displayed that mothers' goals for their interventions and the strategies they used varied according to the type of interaction in which their children were engaged with peers. As mentioned previously, the goal of teaching basic principles occurred proportionally more often in conflict and contingent interaction, providing structure occurred proportionally more in nonliteral play and contingent interaction, and discouraging behavior and distributing property were found proportionally more in conflict. The strategies of offering alternatives and making interjections were used proportionally more in conflict, whereas commands were used in nonliteral play and contingent interaction, and bargaining was used proportionally more in nonliteral play and conflict.

These findings of the influence of interactive context on directive intervention generally corroborate findings in interview studies. Finnie and Russell (1988) found, in a companion study to that previously reviewed, that parents' reported that they varied their strategies according to social situations that included initiating contact with peers, achieving entry into a group after a rebuff, resolving conflict, and helping a friend. Furthermore, Grusec and Kuczynski (1980) found that disciplinary strategies were determined by the social problem. When mothers were presented with several taped conversations between parents and children in which the children were disobedient, mothers reported that in situations in which the child either physically or psychologically hurt a peer they would use power-assertive techniques or withdraw privileges.

In the current research we found that mothers were sensitive to the interactive context of their children's play. The principle contrast is between conflict and more positive sequences of nonliteral play or contingent interaction. Reasonably, mothers sought to redistribute resources or to discourage behavior when their children fought, but to interest children in and structure their play when they interacted peacefully. Although commands and clarifying statements were frequent strategies of intervention in all kinds of sequences, they were most prevalent in nonliteral play and contingent interaction where together they accounted for over 80% of maternal strategies. Within conflict, 38% of interventions were commands and 24% were clarifying statements, whereas other, less frequently used strategies such as nonverbal strategies (14%), suggestions of alternatives (8%), unclear interjections (6%), and bargaining (2%) were used more often in conflict than elsewhere. Thus, although the major maternal strategies were consistent regardless of the nature of the children's play, conflict evoked a greater variety of maternal techniques.

We also found strong relations between the goals mothers had for their interventions and the strategies that they chose to implement these goals. Here, also, the influence of interactive context was evident. Although some of the relations between goals and strategies were found in all three types of sequences, some of the relations were distinctive to specific contexts. That is, maternal intervention in nonliteral play did not display the association between teaching basic rules of interaction and commands that the other two types of sequences displayed. Furthermore, only in contingent interactions was the association between discouraging behavior and bargaining found. And, it was conflict sequences that again displayed the most variety of association; emotional support was associated with clarifying statements, teaching basic principles with reasoning, discouraging behavior with evaluative comments, and distributing goods with bargaining or threatening.

Little is known about the process by which parents become directly involved in children's peer interactions. Most research requests intervention from parents or considers only the sequences in which parents actually intervene. However, we do know that parents do not directly intervene in all of their children's peer interactions and that their propensity to intervene is not the same across all types of sequences (Lollis & Ross, 1987). It is rare for research to consider the antecedents and consequences of parental intervention into peer interaction. We suggest that research begin to include much more of the actual environment of the interactive sequence, what happens before the parent intervenes and what happens as a consequence of the intervention. This type of analysis has occurred more frequently in parent–child and child–peer research (e.g., Zahn-Waxler & Chapman, 1982). Of course, this model could be expanded to include more than the three-step interchange suggested so that parent–child negotiation processes within the context of peer interaction could be explored in order to demonstrate processes of mutual influences.

We began this chapter by suggesting that direct parental intervention influences children's peer interactions. Some of the work reviewed in this chapter attests to this influence. However, in our own work, and in the work of others reviewed here, the reverse direction of influence has been investigated: The interactions in which the children engaged were interpreted as the context that influenced their parents' interventions. This difference in perception of influence is, of course, the question of bidirectionality of effect. Researchers seem to have focused a priori on one influence or the other. Both spheres of influence, the children's and the parents', have been shown to be functioning when parents intervene in children's peer interactions, but rarely are mutual effects examined within the same study. Research that investigates situations in which there is direct parental intervention into peer interaction could be improved by focusing on the environment that the child creates for the parent as well as on the environment that the parent creates for the child.

## ACKNOWLEDGMENTS

This research was supported by a Canada Research Fellowship and a Social Sciences and Humanities Research Council of Canada research grant to Susan Lollis, and a Social Sciences and Humanities Research Council of Canada research grant to Hildy Ross. An earlier version of this manuscript was presented at the Seventh International Conference on Infant Studies, Montreal, Quebec, Canada, April 1990. The observational data used in this study were also the basis of a Social Relations Analysis of relationships between the children (Ross & Lollis, 1989). We would like to thank the mothers and children who participated in this study as well as Maria Fellato, Mary Lynn Hagen, Nora Lackie, Karen Sinden, and Susan Williams, who observed the families.

## REFERENCES

Bakeman, R., & Brownlee, J. R. (1982). Social rules governing object conflicts in toddlers and preschoolers. In K. H. Rubin and H. S. Ross (Eds.), *Peer relationships and social skills in childhood* (pp. 99–111). New York: Springer-Verlag.

Bakeman, R., & Gottman, J. M. (1986). *Observing interaction: An introduction to sequential analysis.* New York: Cambridge University Press.

Bhavnagri, N. (1987). *Parents as facilitators of preschool children's peer relationships.* Unpublished doctoral dissertation, University of Illinois at Champaign-Urbana.

Bhavnagri, N., & Parke, R. (1985). *Parents as facilitators of preschool peer interaction.* Paper presented at the Biennial Meeting of the Society for Research in Child Development, Toronto.

Bowlby, J. (1973). *Attachment and loss: Vol. 2. Separation.* New York: Basic.

Bretherton, I., & Waters, E. (1985). Growing points of attachment theory and research. *Monographs of the Society for Research in Child Development, 50*(1–2, Serial No. 209).

Easterbrooks, M. A., & Lamb, M. E. (1979). The relationships between quality of infant–mother attachment and infant competence in initial encounters with peers. *Child Development, 50,* 380–387.

Finnie, V., & Russell, A. (1988). Preschool children's social status and their mothers' behavior and knowledge in the supervisory role. *Developmental Psychology, 24,* 789–801.

Grusec, J. E., & Dix, T. (1986). The socialization of altruism. In C. Zahn-Waxler, E. M. Cummings, & R. Iannotti (Eds.), *Altruism and aggression* (pp. 218–237). Cambridge: Cambridge University Press.

Grusec, J. E., & Kuczynski, L. (1980). Direction of effect in socialization: A comparison of the parent's versus the child's behavior as determinants of disciplinary techniques. *Developmental Psychology, 16,* 1–9.

Hartup, W. W. (1979). The social worlds of childhood. *American Psychologist, 34,* 944–950.

Hartup, W. W. (1983). Peer relations. In P. H. Mussen (Ed.), *Handbook of child psychology: Vol. 4. Socialization, personality, and social development* (pp. 103–196). New York: Wiley.

Hartup, W. W. (1989). Social relationships and their developmental significance. *American Psychologist, 44*(2), 120–126.

Hay, D. F. (1984). Social conflict in early childhood. In G. Whitehurst (Ed.), *Annals of child development* (Vol. 1, pp. 1–44). Greenwich, CT: JAI.

Hay, D. F., & Ross, H. S. (1982). The social nature of early conflict. *Child Development, 53,* 105–113.

Kuczynski, L. (1984). Socialization goals and mother–child interaction: Strategies for long-term and short-term compliance. *Developmental Psychology, 20,* 1061–1073.

Kuczynski, L., Kochanska, G., Radke-Yarrow, M., & Girnius-Brown, O. (1987). A developmental interpretation of young children's noncompliance. *Developmental Psychology, 23,* 799–806.

Ladd, G. W., & Golter, B. S. (1988). Parents' management of preschooler's peer relations: Is it related to children's social competence? *Developmental Psychology, 24,* 109–117.

Levitt, M. J., Weber, R. A., Clark, M. C., & McDonnell, P. (1985). Reciprocity of exchange in toddler sharing behavior. *Developmental Psychology, 21,* 122–123.

Lieberman, A. F. (1977). Preschoolers' competence with a peer: Relations with attachment and peer experience. *Child Development, 48,* 1277–1287.

Lollis, S. P. (1990). Maternal influence on children's separation behavior. *Child Development, 61,* 99–103.

Lollis, S. P., & Ross, H. S. (1987, April). *Mothers' interventions in toddler–peer conflicts.* Poster presented at the Biennial Meeting of the Society for Research in Child Development, Baltimore, MD.

Lollis, S., Ross, H., & Tate, E. (1988, April). *Maternal interventions in toddler peer conflict: Goals and strategies.* Poster presented at the International Conference on Infant Studies, Washington, DC.

MacDonald, K., & Parke, R. D. (1984). Bridging the gap: Parent–child play interaction and peer interactive competence. *Child Development, 55*, 1265–1277.

Nash, A. (1989). *The role of adults in infant–peer interactions.* Poster presented at the Biennial Meeting of the Society for Research in Child Development, Kansas City, MO.

Parke, R. D., & Bhavnagri, N. P. (1988). Parents as managers of children's peer relationships. In D. Belle (Ed.), *Children's social networks and social supports* (pp. 241–259). New York: Wiley.

Parke, R. D., MacDonald, K. B., Beitel, A., & Bhavnagri, N. (1988). The role of the family in the development of peer relationships. In R. DeV. Peters & R. J. McMahan (Eds.), *Marriages and families: Behavioral treatments and processes.* New York: Brunner-Mazel.

Putallaz, M. (1987). Maternal behavior and children's sociometric status. *Child Development, 58*, 324–340.

Radke-Yarrow, M., Zahn-Waxler, C., & Chapman, M. (1983). Children's prosocial dispositions and behavior. In P. H. Mussen (Ed.), *Handbook of child psychology: Vol. 4. Socialization, personality, and social development* (pp. 469–545). New York: Wiley.

Ratner, N., & Bruner, J. S. (1978). Games, social exchange, and the acquisition of language. *Journal of Child Language, 5*, 1–15.

Ross, H. S. (1982). The establishment of social games amongst toddlers. *Developmental Psychology, 18*, 509–518.

Ross, H. S., & Lollis, S. P. (1989). A social relations analysis of toddler peer relationships. *Child Development, 60*, 1082–1091.

Ross, H., Tesla, C., Kenyon, B., & Lollis, S. (1990). Maternal intervention in toddler peer conflict: The socialization of principles of justice. *Developmental Psychology, 26*, 994–1003.

Rubin, Z., & Sloman, J. (1984). How parents influence their children's friendships. In M. Lewis (Ed.), *Beyond the dyad* (pp. 223–250). New York: Plenum Press.

Shantz, C. U. (1987). Conflicts between children. *Child Development, 58*, 283–305.

Smetana, J. (1989). Toddlers' social interaction in the context of moral and conventional transgressions in the home. *Developmental Psychology, 25*, 499–508.

Sroufe, L. A. (1983). Infant–caregiver attachment and patterns of adaptation in preschool: The roots of maladaptation and competence. In M. Perlmutter (Ed.), *Minnesota symposium on child psychology* (Vol. 16, pp. 41–91). Hillsdale, NJ: Lawrence Erlbaum Associates.

Sroufe, L. A., & Fleeson, J. (1986). Attachment and the construction of relationships. In W. Hartup & Z. Rubin (Eds.), *Relationships and development* (pp. 51–71). Hillsdale, NJ: Lawrence Erlbaum Associates.

Tabachnick, B. G., & Fidell, L. S. (1989). *Using multivariate statistics.* New York: Harper & Row.

Zahn-Waxler, C., & Chapman, M. (1982). Immediate antecedents of caretakers' methods of discipline. *Child Psychiatry and Human Development, 12*, 179–192.

Zahn-Waxler, C., Radke-Yarrow, M., & King, R. A. (1979). Childrearing and children's prosocial initiations toward victims of distress. *Child Development, 50*, 319–330.

# PART FOUR

# VARIATIONS ON FAMILY–PEER RELATIONSHIPS

# CHAPTER TEN

# Cross-Cultural Perspectives on Family–Peer Relations

Carolyn Pope Edwards
*University of Kentucky*

Cross-cultural and anthropological studies are important for developmental psychology because they provide a unique kind of window on the process of human development. They offer the best evidence we can find for determining what are the transhuman universals, as well as the manifold cultural variations, for any given area of growth and development. When one examines what we know about human behavior around the world, especially when focusing on infants and children, one cannot but see evidence for the psychic unity of mankind, the postulate that all human beings obey the same psychological laws and think in ways that are ultimately understandable, or "commensurable," one to another. Yet, at the same time, cultural specificities—though difficult to precisely define and to quantify—challenge us to construct valid generalizations about the effects of environment on child development by determining how to assess the most significant dimensions of children's developmental niches worldwide.

Accordingly, this chapter considers the linkages between family and peer relations in diverse cultures, with an especial focus on middle-level, subsistence-based communities. The first section of this paper addresses the peer relations of adolescents. The focus is on the formal groups created when initiation ceremonies enlist youth into special cohorts, such as the age groups of East Africa and the military cults of New Guinea. These peer groups are fascinating in part because they are so different from the self-constituted gangs, cliques, and clubs of adolescents in Western soci-

285

ety. The data demonstrate how differently human societies can experience adolescent peer relations and structure the transition between childhood and adulthood in the service of different socialization goals.

The second section of the paper considers the peer groups—play groups—of children. The study of children's play groups, in particular their gender, age, and kinship composition, has been an emergent subject in recent ethnographic research. The data allow for cross-cultural comparison in terms of age of access to nonfamily agemates. It is shown how age of access to peer relations is strongly related to cultural differences simultaneously affecting the family. The socializing functions of childhood peer relations are considered by examining both the culturally universal and specific elements. The universal is seen by contrasting the generic profile of social behavior found in peer relations with the profile typically elicited in the two other common contexts of child social relations, the child caretaking context and the multi-age family play group. In contrast, culturally specific scripts can be seen in how different cultural systems attempt to modify the generic ("elicited") behaviors of peer interaction and modulate, channel, attenuate, or emphasize various behaviors typically found in childhood peer relations worldwide.

## ADOLESCENT INITIATION AND FORMAL PEER GROUPS

The oldest and most complete cross-cultural literature on peer groups in the preindustrial world concerns the adolescent. Adolescent peer groups became an important feature of human culture when societies attained what is called the "middle level" of socioeconomic complexity, characterized by food production through subsistence agriculture or animal husbandry. Prior to that point, for perhaps 90% of the total period of human evolution, simpler and less dense societies based on food collection ("hunting and gathering") prevailed. The food-collection economy cannot, except in extremely favorable ecologies, support the necessary density of population for adolescents to come together in peer groups (Hartley, 1963; Konner, 1975). But when middle-level tribal societies became dominant throughout the preliterate world, in Africa, Asia, and Melanesia, adolescent peer groups finally not only emerged but even became a focal element of collective life and sentiment. This is seen in the great rituals of adolescent initiation—a subject of fascination to ethnographers since the earliest days of anthropology. Through word, photograph, and most recently, film and video, these elaborate and complex adolescent rites have been extensively documented and studied. Today, however, all this is changing: The introduction of Western education has transformed the lives of young people and challenged their traditional concern for position in extended family, lineage, or clan with a new emphasis on individual achievement and salaried employment. Many of the old adolescent institutions are fast disappearing.

But at their heyday, adolescent initiation rites and formal peer groups were conspicuous and central to the cultural group as a whole as well as to individual participants. The ceremonies may sometimes have been harsh and severe (by contemporary standards), calling for painful tests and ordeals and abrupt separations from family and childhood home, yet they were also majestic and replete with evocative symbolism to dignify the momentous changes in identity and status that a child experienced in becoming an adult.

Adolescent initiation rites, as we see, thus concern the family in two ways: (a) as a system for detaching the initiate from his or her particular family of origin and helping the youth resolve certain psychological issues created by early childhood experience; and (b) as a system of recruiting young people from different family units into their society's most important nonfamilial collectives. Adolescent customs in preliterate societies function to socialize young people into culturally appropriate styles of sexuality, dominance, and aggression, and they serve social-organizational goals by creating affective and political ties that cut across family, lineage, and clan, and act as necessary complements to kin groups in enhancing alternative social bonds (Ericksen, 1989b).

Three examples of adolescent initiation rites and peer groups are described in the following. It is important to note that elaborated, collective rituals were more common for boys than for girls. They were particularly characteristic of warrior societies (e.g., throughout sub-Saharan Africa and Highland New Guinea) that emphasized gender differentiation in men's and women's work, leisure, and sometimes even eating and sleeping arrangements. These were also societies that tended to emphasize the solidarity of males in corporate units called "fraternal interest groups" (Young, 1965); these were groups of men of a particular consanguineal kin group who had the right to act together—using force if necessary—to defend their interests and resolve disputes.

The initiation rites were shared by all the children in a group of the specified sex and age. With most of their childhood experience located in the extended-family compound or homestead, these children may not have even known one another beforehand, but through the initiation experiences they became a reference group for the rest of their lives. The rites, by uniformly transforming the entire group of initiates to the very same new (adolescent or adult) status, served to express and enhance social cohesion and to minimize distinctions based on wealth or social rank. Thus, the rites were not only a customary way to regulate the passage to a new life stage and status, but also a process to bring together and create a new association of people.

Beatrice and John Whiting (1991) provide a comparative description of adolescence in the preliterate world, emphasizing the place and significance of initiation rites in the total context of the emotional and physical changes of the adolescent years. Initiation rites for girls, they note, are most commonly individual rather than collective affairs, taking place at the time of menarche and symbolically announcing and celebrating a girl's changing reproductive status and readiness for marriage (Brown, 1963, 1981). These individual rites are not relevant to our present concern with family–peer relationships, because they do not involve peer groups or institutions. However, in a few societies, there were found elaborated, collective rites for girls, as well as painful ordeals and group instruction in sexuality (see Ericksen, 1989a). These societies were a subset of the many more common cases also featuring elaborated rites for boys. The ethnographic literature on preliterate Africa, New Guinea, and Australia provides rich detail.

One example is the Kikuyu of Kenya, a tribal society that in precolonial times had a highly developed age-set, age-grade system. This cultural form, widespread throughout East Africa, derived originally from Ethiopia (Bernardi, 1985; Ericksen, 1989b; Spencer, 1976). Among the Kikuyu (Kenyatta, 1932/1965; J. Whiting, 1981; Worthman & Whiting, 1987), initiation rites for both sexes were highlighted by instruction in sexuality by same-sex adults (not the parents) and by operations considered necessary to "correct" the genitals and render asexual children capable of mature heterosexual intercourse. Male circumcision (slitting of the prepuce) removed the "female" portion of the penis; female clitoridectomy (excision of the tip of the clitoris) removed the "male" portion of the girl's organs. The initiation ceremonies, which took place when the boy was between 16 and 18 and the girl between 10 and 14 years of age, also marked the entry into a sequence of formal statuses and roles that continued throughout life. Each "age grade" was a recognized position in the tribal structure, with well-defined rights and duties. For Kikuyu women, the age grades were maidens (girls eligible for marriage), young wives (married women without children), mothers, and mothers of circumcised sons. For men, the age grades included junior warriors, senior warriors, junior elders, senior elders, and ritual elders. At initiation, then, each boy or girl became a member of a life-long cohort ("age set") consisting of all the individuals of one's gender who were initiated that year; the rites were supposed to make the initiates feel and become like siblings to one another, and the chief function of the age sets was mutual aid. Each age set was also given a unique name, derived from some noteworthy event of the year, and these names became important for tribal history and chronology. John Whiting (1981) remarked that whenever he meets an older Kikuyu man, that man is always much more interested in establishing Whiting's age, relative to the Kikuyu age sets, than in identifying Whiting's occupation and home country.

The Kikuyu age groups were an especially significant focus of the person's life during adolescence. The initiated boy (junior warrior) immediately joined the regiment of bachelors composed of all boys in the local area initiated over a 9-year period. They were trained in the art of war by the senior warriors, and they acted together to defend their ridge and scout out new lands to relieve population pressure. The initiated girls (maidens) were allowed and encouraged to engage in a controlled form of limited (interfemoral) sex with all the bachelor boys. This sexual life among the boy and girl peer groups both provided a method of mate selection and served to consolidate the larger kinship (clan) groups on the ridge—an essential function in a society without a hierarchical political system (Worthman & Whiting, 1987).

The older age grades similarly served critical political and leadership roles for Kikuyu society. For instance, the women's council of mothers was responsible for ensuring that the local women properly carried out rituals at female initiation, and at birth, marriage, and death. The men's council of senior elders was responsible for settling disputes, performing transvillage rituals, and debating political issues. The age-group system clearly functioned in Kikuyu and other East African societies to counteract centrifugal forces engendered by interlineage rivalries and land disputes (see Spencer, 1976). They lent society a gerontocratic cast but prevented the formation of stratification based on wealth or numbers within lineages or clans, as tended to occur in West Africa.

An example of a West African society with male initiation and secret societies is the Afikpo of Nigeria (Ottenberg, 1988). Men's solidarity groups (based on kinship descent) were strongly developed, but those for women were much less important. For boys, at age 4 or 5, a stressful event occurred: they were moved into a compound where they slept until marriage, eating food brought to them by their mothers. At age 5 or 6, with the help of male peers or their fathers, they also joined a boys' secret society. There were three age levels of these organizations in the village (for boys aged about 5–10, 10–15, and 15–20). The boys moved up the stages individually as they were ready (or as their fathers wished). Each society was led by its older boys who taught the younger ones its rules and taboos. The boys' activities emulated those of the men, including masquerades, mock aggression toward girls, wrestling, and other sports contests. From the third stage, boys were first circumcised and then initiated, at different times and ages, into the village men's secret society. The secret societies, like the East African age sets, controlled the important leadership functions (political and religious) but were different in including all the men of a village. Thus, the secret societies united men of potentially competing lineages into a broader community.

As a third example of a society with elaborate male initiation, the Sambia of the Eastern Highlands of Papua New Guinea were a fierce warrior tribe practicing endemic warfare until the 1960s (Herdt, 1982, 1987). They glorified aggression in men and through a series of physical ordeals and rituals, taught and reinforced avoidance and antagonism toward women. Initiation consisted of six cycles of ceremonies, the first three collective, the second three individual, stretching from a boy's middle childhood through his early 20s. The first rite positioned every man in an age set for life and created agemate ties throughout the valley. The initiation system also inducted males into a military club (or cult) that Herdt calls the most colorful and powerful institution of society. The age groups were like military ranks, akin to soldiers, lieutenants, and generals.

At the first ceremony, boys aged 7 to 10 years were forcibly removed from their families (never to see their mothers again until adulthood). They were subjected to terror and pain in the form of stinging nettles and nosebleeding, and they were inducted into the forced oral homosexuality believed necessary to promote their physical growth. Subsequent initiations contained repetitions of many of these elements. Up until the time of the early 1960s, when warfare was ended by colonial authorities, each year's initiation ceremonies culminated in an intertribal raid, at which the third-stage initiates got their first opportunity to prove themselves as warriors. Ultimately, at the fourth to sixth stages of the initiation cycle, men were ritually prepared to leave behind roles of bachelorhood and homosexuality and turn to marriage and heterosexuality. Most of the men expected to engage in warfare throughout their lives; the fiercest and most successful fighters became warlords, the highest prestige role in Sambia.

Initiation rites (especially for males) have been the subject of long and intense theoretical debate in anthropology. The debate centers on the question: Why do some societies but not others stage initiation rites? What are the critical features that covary with their presence or absence?

The polarity of the debate was framed by the psychological theory of John Whiting (Whiting, 1990; Whiting, Kluckhohn, & Anthony, 1958) versus the sociological theory of Frank Young (1965). Whiting theorized that male initiation is a cultural system for resolving gender-identity conflict, engendered in the normal individual who grows up in a society in which power and prestige are vested in males, but early family experience creates a strong primary feminine identification in children of both sexes. The theory is supported by the evidence that rites occur much more frequently where tropical climate and poor health conditions, coupled with polygynous family patterns, lead to infant care practices involving close, continuous physical contact between mother and baby—and little involvement by fathers in child care. The infant is carried on the mother's back or hip by day and monopolizes her company in bed at night, while the father sleeps in his own hut or with another wife. The young child comes to see the mother as center of the universe and controller of all desirable resources. Yet as the boy grows older, he observes that men are forcefully dominant (including over women). The resulting gender identity conflict must somehow be resolved; herein lies the need for initiation ceremonies involving forcible separation from mother and siblings, collective instruction in adult male roles, and painful tests (such as hazing or circumcision). Indeed, these rites are often defined in native terms as the death of the boy as a "woman-child" and rebirth as an "adult man."

Young (1965) argued that the rites can be adequately accounted for without considering early family experience, but instead by only considering social structure. He considered them a way to induct boys into corporate groups based on patrilineal clans, the organizing system of society.

It is interesting to note that both theories explain male initiation rites in terms of the family; early family experience, in one case, versus adult male sodalities based on kinship, in the other. Moreover, it is fair to say that today most anthropologists, especially psychologically minded ones, accept the validity of both theories and see them as nonconflictual (e.g., Barry & Schlegel, 1980; Ottenberg, 1988). There has been a convergence on an integrated perspective, in which boys' collective rites are thought to perform two critical psychological functions: (a) resolving gender-identity concerns; and (b) creating a male sodality in which boys can assume and practice masculine roles (aggression, dominance, and sexuality).

Yet how would the parallel initiation rites for girls, such as in Kikuyu land, fit into such a theory? Whiting (in press) and Brown (1981) believed that those cultural conditions—power and prestige vested in men, control over the young child's world vested in women—that create cross-gender envy and gender identity conflict in boys, also do so in girls. Indeed, the same family and social conditions exist in many African communities today; for example, recent research shows that contemporary Nigerian girls do envy masculine prerogatives (Hollos & Leis, 1989). Adolescent rites for both sexes, then, can involve physical ordeal and collective instruction to transmit the symbolic message, "You are a man (or) a woman. Whatever part of you was feminine (or) masculine (the opposite sex), is now gone. It is good to be part of our gender group and assume its ways of thinking, feeling, and acting. Henceforth, you will be, and want to be, a man (or) a woman of our society."

To summarize, then, collective initiation and subsequent peer experiences serve to wean the child's dependency on mother and siblings and induct him or her into an age group, military club, or secret society. In middle-level societies around the world, formal male peer relations appear to have the same central themes: aggression, dominance, and sexuality. Evidently, these are scripts for which children cannot be well prepared in the family nest of childhood. There, instead, as we detail in the next section, children tend to engage in child–child interactions that best prepare them for scripts of nurturance and prosocial responsibility.

## CHILDREN'S PLAY GROUPS
## IN COMPARATIVE PERSPECTIVE

The importance of early peer relations for social and cognitive development has been an increasing subject of recent research. As part of this study, psychologists have called for better and more comprehensive comparative data on both primate and human groups in different niches. In that way, the significance of peer relations can be understood in the broadest evolutionary and transcultural perspective.

In the following section of this chapter, comparative data is used to analyze the mediating links between family and childhood peer relations. Two issues are addressed: (a) cultural variations in children's age of access to peer interaction (where peers are defined as nonfamily children close in age to the self); and (b) cultural universalities and variations in the customary profile of that peer interaction, including how it differs from the other main kinds of childhood social relations (in child caretaking and multi-age play group contexts). Age of access is important to study because peer interaction provides such different socializing experiences from the other kinds of cross-age, family-centered child interaction.

### Age of Access to Peer Relations

Melvin Konner (1975) has written a classic statement on peer relations among infants and juveniles in the primate order and in human hunter–gatherer societies. He argued that for most primate species, interaction with nonkin peers are neither typical nor important. Instead, two other kinds of infant and juvenile interaction are much more predominant: (a) caretaking ("alloparental") behavior of a younger animal by an older one, usually a close relative; and (b) play relations among siblings, half-siblings, and cousins in a multi-age, family play group.

In his own observations of human behavior in the foraging !Kung San of the Kalahari Desert, Konner found that of the three types of childhood social relations, only the multi-age play group was seen, and it was ubiquitous. Among the !Kung, dwelling in small bands, children's play groups typically consisted of all the children available—often six to eight children, boys and girls, ranging in age from infancy through adolescence. (Or children divided themselves into two or three smaller groups with correspondingly narrower age range.) The activities of the group included the following: observation and imitation of adult subsistence activity; "pretend" subsistence play; rough-and-tumble play; sex play; and always, protection, care, and teaching of infants and children by older children.

Edward Mueller and Elizabeth Tingley (1989) echoed Konner's thesis by arguing that childhood peer relations are best understood as a recent product of our *cultural* evolution, rather than an ancient result of our *biological* evolution. They claim that because peer relations have no biologically determined survival function, they are more flexible, more open to the effects of learning and environment than some other systems of behavior (for example, the mother–child attachment system).

That peer relations are a recent product of cultural evolution can be clearly seen in the cross-cultural data on age of access to peer relations. Contrasting family life in subsistence-based, middle-level societies versus complex societies with social classes, occupational specialization, and participation in the world economy, one sees a general shift toward younger and younger ages for the time children begin to participate in peer relations. This conclusion, plus an understanding of the proximate variables involved, emerges from our recent research on children's social environments and behavior (Whiting & Edwards, 1988). Three independent factors influence children's opportunities for interaction with nonfamily agemates: (a) settlement pattern (the density and clustering of families in space); (b) reproductive strategies (number and spacing of children); and (c) educational goals and institutions (affecting age at which children first attend school and/or preschool).

> Of course, the organization of people in space and the social structure of households and neighborhoods govern the availability of child companions. As long as children are confined to the immediate environs of the home, their main companions are their siblings, half-siblings, and courtyard cousins. In places where children have more autonomy to explore the neighborhood, or where communal play areas or schools bring together large groups of children, children have more contact with nonrelatives and more opportunity to divide themselves into sex- and age-segregated play groups. (Whiting & Edwards, 1988, p. 77)

To illustrate the sweeping magnitude of these differences in the company that children keep, we consider some of the conclusions presented in *Children of Different Worlds: The Formation of Social Behavior*

Whiting & Edwards, 1988). This study is based on data collected by ourselves and 10 collaborators, as well as reanalyzed data from the Six Cultures study. The total sample includes 12 communities (studied 1954 to
1975), in which the behavior of children aged 2–10 years was observed
and recorded in running records format. These communities are located
in Kenya (five communities), north India (two communities), Liberia,
Okinawa, Mexico, Philippines, and the United States (one community
each). Nine were primarily agricultural; a generation or two previously,
the inhabitants had produced all of their subsistence (through farming
and raising animals), but already by the time of study they had become
tied into the national economy of their countries and dependent on some
of the products of the industrial world. The farmers sold some of their
produce to get cash in order to purchase goods, pay taxes, and (in Kenya)
pay school fees. The other samples consisted of urban communities,
where men worked as wage earners, entrepreneurs, or professionals.

Settlement pattern also varied, affecting the physical and social isolation of household units. In three of the Kenyan communities (Kokwet,
Kisa, Nyansongo), families lived on large farms ranging in size from 2
to 20 acres. In Ngeca, Kenya, some families lived in a village settlement
and some on small farm homesteads. In the other communities, all houses
were clustered into the following four kinds of settlements: hamlets
(Tarong, Philippines); villages (Taira, Okinawa; Kien-taa, Liberia); sections
of towns (Juxtlahuaca, Mexico; Khalapur, India; Orchard Town, New England); and urban areas (Bhubaneswar, India; Kariobangi, Kenya).

Not only settlement pattern but also household size and availability
of kinfolk varied greatly between the 12 communities. For example, the
polygynous Kenyan households included as many as eight separate dwelling units. In many samples, families had kinfolk living on contiguous land.
Most isolated from kin were the families from Orchard Town (USA), Taira
(Okinawa), Kariobangi (housing estate in Nairobi, Kenya), and Bhubaneswar (north India). In terms of family size, the smallest families were found
in Orchard Town (with an average of three children per family) and the
largest in Kenya and north India (where 7 to 10 children were not
unusual).

In addition to the running-record data on 12 communities, a different
kind of observational data is available on six samples (studied 1967–1975).
There, the routine settings, activities, and interactants of children aged
5–7 years were recorded through spot observations. These communities
are located in Kenya (three communities), Guatemala, Peru, and the United States (California).

Across all of the sample communities, sizable differences were found
in the normative profiles of children's social interaction. These turn out
to be predictable in terms of objective features of culture (household com-

position, number and spacing of children, rules of residence and marriage, daily routines of men, women, and children, including their work and leisure) and subjective features (beliefs about the nature of infants and children, differences between boys and girls, and ideal behavior for each age group).

In spite of the cultural variations, obvious similarities in children's social and behavioral capabilities were also seen when looking at children of a given age grade. Accordingly, four major age grades were defined (following Margaret Mead's insightful descriptions): the *lap child* (aged 0 to 2.5 years); the *knee child* (aged 2.6 to 3.5 years); the *yard child* (aged 3.6 to 5.5 years); and the *community child* (aged 5.6 to 10.5 years). Obviously, these grades roughly correspond to the terminology we use in North America: infant, toddler, preschool child, and latency child.

These age groups proved extremely useful for summarizing both cultural specificities and similarities in children's opportunities for peer relations.

*Lap children* in all of the sample communities lived in a bounded space centered on the emotional and physical presence of the mother and other people who shared intimate space with her or took over the caregiving role when she delegated it. In many of the samples, lap children interacted with siblings and other child kin. For example, in Kenya, mothers had the heaviest workloads and relied on their elder children for help with child care, housework, and subsistence activity. Thus, the number and spacing of children, the amount of work mothers had to do on top of child care, and the number of adult relatives nearby to help her, all predicted lap children's amount of contact with kinsmen of different ages. But interaction with nonfamily agemates was rare for the lap children in our samples.

*Knee children* were ambulatory and competent to move into a larger physical and social space, though still an area monitored constantly by caretakers or supervising older children. In all of our sample communities (except Orchard Town, USA), knee children were expected to be much less dependent on mothers than before (see Edwards, 1989). They spent much of their day "tagging along" in the multi-age play group of siblings, half-siblings, and kinfolk who lived on their own or adjacent compounds.

Knee children tended to make most contact with peers from more distant homes as a result of their mothers' patterns of movement and sociability. Knee children were part of the maternal orbit, with little independent opportunity for peer relations. For example, in Kokwet (Kenya), mothers often took their youngest children with them on visits around the community (Harkness & Super, 1985). Even in Orchard Town, mothers (observed in the 1950s) did not organize play groups for toddlers. Across communities, the knee children with the most opportunity to observe and make at least casual contact with peers were those from settlements with the greatest density of people and where women had most freedom of movement (for shopping, visiting, etc.). The Rajput mothers of Khalapur were restricted by rules of *purdah* to their compounds, for example, whereas the mothers of Orchard Town took children on many errands about town.

*Yard children* were the first age grade to have independent access to the entire house and yard or homestead area. They could freely explore these areas and, if bold, venture out to explore other areas considered safe. At this age, cultural differences in children's autonomy and access to peer relations became more salient. In communities where neighbors were not kinfolk and households consisted of single nuclear families, yard children were most confined. For example, in Orchard Town, neighbors were rarely kin and, moreover, did not consider themselves responsible for the safety and discipline of one another's children. Roads with traffic posed real danger. Parents had to make plans in order for their children to play with anyone other than a sibling. Thus, in 65% of the observations of Orchard Town girls aged 4–5, and 55% of the observations of boys, children were found in the company of kinfolk only. Similarly in Kariobangi (the low-income housing estate in Nairobi), families came from many different ethnic and language groups from all over Kenya. They felt like strangers to one another and worried that their children would fight. They restricted their yard children's freedom of movement and contact with peers.

Yard children also had little autonomy in the rural Kenyan communities. They spent the majority of their time on the family homestead where they played in a large, multi-age play group composed of relatives. Parents preferred to keep their children on family land because they mistrusted nonrelatives. They feared that conflict would lead to "poisoning" by witchcraft. In 81% of the observations of 4–5-year-old girls in Nyansongo, Kenya, and 71% of boys, children were found in the presence of relatives only.

However, in most of the communities with clustered housing and public areas, yard children had much greater opportunity to interact with peers. For instance, in the Old Town section of Bhubaneswar, India, yard children played in the streets with nonrelatives. In the compact village of Taira, Okinawa, yard children had most autonomy of all. Yards were small, houses were open, and children felt free to wander throughout the village. As they played in large groups, they were monitored by the adults living nearby, who kept a watchful eye and felt responsible to act in lieu of parents when the need arose. In only 8% of the observations of 4–5-year-old Taira girls, and 14% of boys, were children found in the presence of relatives only.

*Community children* had greatly expanded social horizons. They were generally allowed to journey farther from home than before, sometimes because they were "directed" to perform errands or chores, and sometimes in "undirected" free play. The comparison of children aged 6–10 with those aged 3–6 shows the older group having the higher percentage of observations away from their own house, yard, or immediate neighborhood in all six cultures. Settlement pattern makes a difference, however: The highest levels of distant-from-home observations are found in the 6–10-year-olds from the denser settlements of Orchard Town, Taira, and Khalapur, where school-aged children (boys only in Khalapur!) had most freedom for undirected peer relations. In Orchard Town, for example, once children were of school age, they were allowed to walk to and from school, visit friends along their way, and attend club meetings or other social activities permitted by their parents. But the same trend is seen in all the communities. For instance, in the rural community of Kokwet, Kenya, one fourth of the interaction between 6–9-year-olds was between children of distant homesteads. This figure contrasts with 12% for 3–6-year-olds, typically confined to play in their own and adjacent homesteads (Harkness & Super, 1985).

In addition to the greater autonomy coming from increased cognitive and social capabilities, community children's lives were also transformed by school. School is a revolutioning force in modernizing societies by bringing children into regular contact with large groups of nonkinsmen. Of all our sample communities, only Nyansongo (studied in the 1950s), still had a majority of community children not in school. Thus, in 65% of the observations of Nyansongo girls aged 6–10, and 68% of boys, children were found in the presence of relatives only, compared with—at the other extreme—Orchard Town, where the respective figures were 4% (girls) and 2% (boys), or Taira, with 6% (girls) and 8% (boys).

## Changes in Access to Peers for Young Children in Modern Society

Given how school as an institution has transformed the social lives of community-aged children around the world by providing access to peer relations, it is interesting to think about the comparable effects of child care and nursery school on knee and yard children in contemporary society. For example, in North America and northern Europe today, women have become essential contributors to family income. The increasing use of preschools, organized play groups, and child-care arrangements has brought the age of access to peer relations down near the beginning of life.

The effect of these changes is evident in a study recently conducted among 38 families living in or near the small town of Amherst in western Massachusetts (for complete description of methodology see Edwards, Logue, Loehr, & Roth, 1986, 1987). The children were infants and toddlers aged 2 to 30 months, and half attended a high-quality, university-based infant/toddler program for 15–20 hours per week. The other half also had mothers who were working or studying at least half-time, but these children were cared for in home-based arrangements (by fathers, family day-care providers, babysitters, etc.). Spot observations were conducted in morning, afternoon, and evening time periods, 7 days a week, over 8 months, providing a detailed picture of the ecology of the children's lives. Initial interviews had revealed that most parents, whether they used center- or home-based supplementary care, strongly valued early peer contacts for children. Almost all parents saw some kind of peer experience especially beneficial (or even necessary) at the toddler age.

The sample of infants and toddlers was observed a total of 1,232 times (with 25.8% of the center-care children's observations collected at the center). For both groups, contact with other children was substantial. Observations were coded in terms of whether a *family, regularly seen,* or *strange* child was present (where a family-child was defined as a sibling, half-sibling, or step-sibling; a regularly-seen child was a regular playmate from play group or day care, or in a few cases, a child cousin seen regularly; and a strange child was any other nonfamily child). For the center-care group, peers were the most frequent kind of child companion: A regularly-seen child was present in 28.2% of observations. In fact, some of these observations took place during home time, when parents got day care "friends" together. A family-child was present in 16.9% of the center-children's observations, and a stranger in 3%. For the home-care group, the respective figures were 21.7% (family-children), 9.3% (regularly seen), and 4.8% (strange children). Combining groups of center- and home-care children gives a total of 19.2% (237) observations with family-children present; 18.9% (233) with regularly-seen children; and 3.8% (47) with strange children. Life experience for this sample of contemporary American lap children, then, resembles that of yard children in the cross-cultural observations.

In summary, ethnographic and observational evidence suggest how family differences at the transcultural level relate to children's age of access to peer relations. Within each family, of course, individual parents make the decisions and set the rules that influence the company their children keep, but these choices occur in a larger cultural context that circumscribes parents' decisions and rules and influences them in ways of which they cannot be fully conscious.

## Gender Preference and Segregation

Interestingly, the cross-cultural finding of greatest access to peers at the community age grade is paralleled by a crescendo in preference for same-gender companionship and interaction. This gender-typed affiliation strongly colors the quality of peer interaction during middle childhood.

The tendency for both boys and girls to prefer and associate more frequently with their own gender is a well-documented phenomenon in the psychological literature from North America (LaFreniere, Strayer, & Gauthier, 1984; Maccoby, 1988; Thorne, 1986). Our data indicate this phenomenon to be cross-culturally universal and robust. It is based, we believe, on yard and community children's desire to construct gender-identity and self-knowledge through reciprocal interaction with children similar to themselves (Edwards, in press).

> In interaction with same-sex children who are close in age, a child can compare her appearance, behavior, and likes and dislikes with those of the companion. These experiences teach understanding of the self, as well as understanding of the behavior of others who are perceived as similar in salient attributes of gender. (Whiting & Edwards, 1988, pp. 231–232)

In North American studies, the same-gender preference first seems to appear sometime after age 2, when both girls and boys associate most closely and direct most interaction toward same-gender peers, if they have a choice. By middle childhood, most children select same-gender playmates as their best friends, and especially when in groups of agemates (with adults absent or in a different interactional space), they segregate themselves by gender. They may even exclude children of the other gender, as for example, in playground activity and cafeteria seating in school.

This emerging preference at middle childhood for same-gender relationships also appears in all of our cross-cultural samples, even in communities where most of children's early experience involves multi-age, kin-based interaction. The most detailed analysis of children's companions, from infancy through middle childhood, is found in Martha Wenger's (1983, 1989) study, conducted in Kaloleni in the Coastal Province of Kenya. Using the methodology of spot observations, Wenger collected data in large polygynous households ranging in size from 6 to 36 members, and containing an average of six children. She found a dramatic increase with age in percentage of observations (excluding those with adults present) in which only one gender group was found together in "interactional space." At age 2–3, girls' scores were 32%, boys' 22%. At age 4–5, girls' scores were 33%, boys' 41%. At age 6–7, girls' scores were 52%, boys' 55%, and at age 8–11, girls' scores dropped to 48% (they were heavily involved in infant caretaking), whereas boys' rose to 70%. The older children had much more freedom to leave their homestead in search of companions.

The same-gender preference is, if anything, even more evident when one controls for the age of children's companions. That is, examining the composition of groups where all the children are close in age, one obtains even higher scores for single gender groupings. In Wenger's data, for example, 92% (girls) and 95% (boys) of the 8–11-year-olds' observations with same-age children were gender-segregated, and similar findings are seen in Harkness and Super's (1985) Kokwet observations, as well as other data (see Whiting & Edwards, 1988, chapters 2 and 6). The Six Cultures observations indicate the influence of availability on same-gender companionship. The yard children who lived in nucleated settlements (Taira and Khalapur), or who were sent in single-gender groups to do chores (Nyansongo), had the highest percentage of same-gender interaction. Moreover, for both yard- and community-ages, nonsibling interaction included much more cross-gender interaction than did sibling interaction.

Thus, the cross-cultural data strongly suggest that when children have the opportunity to seek out children like themselves in age, they are especially attracted to their own gender group. Perhaps, if attraction to same-gender children is motivated by the desire for self-discovery, then agemates are the best mirrors. They most likely resemble the child in abilities and activity preferences, leading to very different possibilities for play (e.g., competitive games) than are usually seen in the multi-age family play group. Or, from another point of view, perhaps when children interact with relatives in a multi-age play group, their motivation to avoid the opposite sex is diminished by emotional closeness—intimacy derived from the chronological depth of relationships.

## Peer Relations as a Context for Personality Development

Such considerations lead us, finally, to the point of what difference it makes whether or not children of a given age and culture have access to peer relations. Can general statements be made about childhood peer relations as a socialization context, in contrast to other kinds of contexts more prevalent in traditional societies?

In answer, we have theorized (Whiting & Edwards, 1988) that different child–child contexts are characterized by quite different normative profiles of social interaction. This occurs because the gender, age, and kinship relationship of social partners influences what kinds of behaviors are elicited. Stated briefly:

> We are convinced that generic, transcultural behaviors can be identified in dyadic interaction and discussed in terms of the distinctive eliciting power of certain categories of individuals who are the companions of children. The responses that these individuals elicit appear to be easily learned and to resist modification. (p. 266)

This conclusion was reached by comparing the normative profiles of interaction within each dyadic context across cultural communities. The evidence is clear for a general transcultural universality in the way children respond to different categories of social partners. We label these similarities *generic* or *prepared responses,* to acknowledge their possible source in biobehavioral systems related to human evolution and survival. We believe (based on close examination of the observations) that the generic behaviors tend to surface whenever certain kinds of social partners interact, and that they are difficult to extinguish, but that their specific form is strongly influenced by learning processes that modulate, channel, attenuate, or amplify them in culturally appropriate directions.

The significance of all this for personality development, we hypothesize, is that children's social motivations and skills may be strongly influenced by the type of social partners with whom they have most opportunity to interact. That is, children may come to prefer those kinds of interpersonal behaviors that they most frequently practice; they may develop interpersonal motives, habits, and skills through frequent interaction that then transfer to other contexts. In fact, we found some evidence that nurturant behaviors heavily practiced in caretaking contexts do transfer to the peer context: comparing 6–10-year-olds in terms of their relative nurturance to peers, it was found that girls from Tarong, Nyansongo, and Juxtlahuace, and boys from Tarong, scored highest, and these were the same groups who also had the most interaction with lap children (see Whiting & Edwards, 1988, p. 264). This finding is particularly interesting because it suggests that behavior practiced within the family generalizes to a social relationship outside the family. Could it be that by focusing children's early social interests on lap children that parents are not only influencing their children's age of access to peer relations but also indirectly affecting the behavioral expectations their children will eventually bring to peer relations (i.e., a heightened capacity for nurturance)? However, all of this remains speculative; the hypothesis of long-term personality influences cannot be proved or disproved on the basis of our observational data and remains for future investigation. Here, therefore, I only describe the different profiles found in child–

child interaction and argue that peer interaction elicits a distinctive profile and is a different kind of socializing context from cross-age family
relations.

Lap children, unquestionably, elicit nurturance, from all ages and both
sexes. (Nurturance is defined as positive, helping, and supportive behaviors offered to an individual who is perceived by the actor to be in
a state of need.) Across all of the sample communities, a high proportion
of social acts to lap children consists of nurturance, higher than to any
other age grade. People in all of the samples show similarity in the way
they tend to offer food, touch, and soothing voice to calm crying babies,
and offer smiles, tickles, and other kinds of friendly overtures to get a
happy response. Aggression is usually inhibited (except by the youngest
children who cannot control themselves when tired or frustrated). The
cultural communities do differ in their typical *styles* of expressing nurturance; for example, in preference for face-to-face interaction, verbal
stimulation, and use of various nonverbal techniques (touch, gestures,
ways of holding). Nevertheless, a transcultural behavior system of nurturance is readily and reliably recognizable as the salient category of behavior elicited by lap children. When caring for them, older children
receive consistent opportunity to acquire and practice skills of nurturance: reading the infant's cues, meeting its needs, gaining positive responsiveness, and inhibiting aggressive impulses.

Knee children, now possessed of language and independent locomo-
tion, elicit dominance—some egoistic dominance (intended to control),
but even more prosocial dominance (intended to protect, socialize, or
involve the child in socially useful activity). Knee children also still elicit
nurturance (ranking second only to lap children in proportion of nurturance received from child actors 4–10 years of age). But their emerging
mobility, speech, and desire to be included in everything also make them
the targets of much more dominance than before. In all of the sample
communities except Orchard Town, busy adults call on older children
to monitor the movements of knee children and keep them from wan-
dering off, getting left behind, falling into open cookfires, or getting into
mischief or danger of other kinds. Furthermore, knee children are considered needy of, and legitimate targets for, suggestions and reprimands
intended to teach them the basic rules of hygiene, respect, and propriety
to help them become acceptable members of the group. The details of
the teaching process and content of the rules differ from one community to the next (and from one family to the next), but nevertheless the
transcultural similarities in the basic process are striking. Thus, the company of knee children provides opportunities to learn responsibility and
prosocial dominance, whether one is acting as the official child nurse
(in a caretaking context) or merely asserting authority as an older mem-

ber of a play group containing knee children (in the multi-age play group context).

Not only toddlers but all children younger than the self (excluding infants) elicit dominance and authority behavior. In all of the samples, bigger and older children respond to others younger and smaller than themselves by establishing dominance over them in a style defined as culturally appropriate. Accordingly, a pecking order of size and strength consistently emerges in multi-age groups, certainly in the multi-age play group of siblings, half-siblings, and courtyard cousins found in most of our samples. Again, of course, culture modulates the patterns. In the Kenyan communities where older siblings are given authority over younger ones, age dominance is expected and supported. However, this power is limited by the fact that older children are reprimanded or punished for hurting an infant. Moreover, they soon learn that their younger siblings are not pawns and are much more compliant when commands are reasonable and concern things that serve the home or family (Edwards, 1986). Thus, many of the older Kenyan children are seen exercising authority in the approved "maternal" manner, that is, through prosocial rather than egoistic dominance. For instance, an older child annoyed by a younger one might send him off to do a useful errand rather than simply ordering him to go away. In the North American community of Orchard Town, however, a very different pattern is seen. There a strong egalitarian ideology prevails. Parents see themselves as the only people who can discipline and assign chores. They try (not always successfully) to suppress the dominance elicited by cross-age relations and to treat their children as status equals. They support the rights and assertiveness of younger children and interfere with the "bossiness" of older ones. Parents spend a great deal of time holding court to children's disputes and listening to defenses and accusations before adjudicating. Children are taught to negotiate and resolve every conflict on the merits of the case, in a legalistic style.

Children older than the self elicit watching, imitation, and dependency behavior. Not surprisingly, this profile can be most clearly seen in our sample communities where mothers bear heavy workloads and use their elder children as mother surrogates. Young children are often seen approaching older siblings rather than mothers for aid and comfort. For instance, in Ngecha, Kenya, a comparison was made of the behavior of 31 2- and 3-year-old children with their mothers versus their adjacent older siblings (usually aged 4 to 5). Dependency behaviors were high to both categories (where dependency is defined as the seeking of tangible or emotional resources, such as food, toys, physical contact, comfort, attention, instrumental help, permission, information). Some behaviors were as high or higher to the older siblings than to the mothers: "sitting by," "following after," "imitates," "clearly seeks sociability," "inquires," "watches." Other behaviors were higher to the mothers: "seeks food," "seeks attention or approval," "seeks help or comfort," "seeks permission" (Edwards & Whiting, in press). Even though there was visible rivalry between adjacent siblings, knee, yard, and community children spent many hours together, and the younger children appeared highly motivated to tag along, intently observe, and emulate the older ones in both play and task behaviors. Thus, in the multi-age family group, in the company of older children, younger children have the opportunity to learn behaviors that let them learn from, and get their needs met by, family members other than their mothers.

Finally, we come to the peer relation. Our evidence suggests that children similar to the self (in size, age, and gender) elicit a high proportion of both affiliation (sociability) and conflict and challenge behavior. The data come exclusively from observations of community-age children (6–10-years-old) because peer interaction was not frequent enough at the younger age grades. Moreover, the analysis had to be limited to same-gender interaction because the amount of cross-gender interaction was too infrequent to allow for cross-cultural comparison. For girls, in all but one community, the most frequent category of behavior in same-gender peer interaction was sociability (defined as behavior, such as chatting, greeting, singing together, whose judged intent is friendly interaction). The behavior that ranked second varied by cultural community: nurturance in the three communities where girls were most involved in child caretaking; miscellaneous aggression or dominance more frequent in the others. For boys, sociability ranked first in four of the communities, whereas various forms of testing behavior (egoistic dominance, rough-and-tumble play, or miscellaneous aggression) ranked first in the others. For boys in particular, peer interaction was characterized by frequent tussling, social comparison, and jockeying for dominance, sometimes in the context of competitive games, sometimes not. We constructed a new category of behavior called "challenging," to include verbal challenges (insulting, threatening, boasting, taunting, warning, comparing the self, and inciting to competition) and physical challenges (all sorts of physical testing and rough-and-tumble play). True assaulting (attempts to physically hurt another) were rare, especially among girls.

It is evident from the observations that peer interaction is exciting and pleasurable to children. Part of the excitement and pleasure seems to arise precisely from the fact that the dominance hierarchy is not set. Constant moments of comparison and challenge arise because children have not spent years growing up together with relative competence long ago established. Instead, relatively novel to one another, and similar in size, strength, and verbal ability, they have similar cognitive and social agendum that make competition and comparison particularly interesting and motivating to all concerned. In summary, and given the fact that most peer interaction in middle childhood is gender-segregated, we can conclude that peer relations provide opportunities for learning about the self (the gendered self) through reciprocal interaction and social testing and comparison.

In light of this description of the eliciting quality of peer interaction, it is easy to see why childhood peer relations would be discouraged in traditional, kin-based societies such as Kenya. Parents feared the inherent potential for competition and conflict; they did not want their children to fight with outsiders and engender spiteful relations or become vulnerable to aggression and sorcery. Moreover, as their children did not attend school, they had no need for them to early acquire skills of affiliating, negotiating, and competing with nonfamily agemates. Today, of course, the situation is changing as literacy becomes a valued skill and parents hope some of their children will succeed in school and break into the modern sector of the economy. They seek education for their children and encourage in them new character traits they see as related to school success (cleverness, confidence, ability to put the self forward, inquisitiveness) rather than the traditional traits of respect, generosity, and obedience (Beatrice Whiting, in preparation).

Such a situation as faces Kenya today has long prevailed in the industrialized societies of the West. Indeed today, among middle-class urban and suburban groups in Europe, North America, and Asia as well, families experience increasing separation from kin networks and isolation in the community. This, together with the relation of economic success to achievement values and verbal and symbolic skills, results in a desire by many parents to put young children in preschool or child care where they can "make friends" and develop cognitive and social skills that will get them ready for primary school.

## Comparative Studies of Parental Expectations for Young Children

This modern constellation of parental values and childrearing practices involves interesting corresponding changes in parental beliefs about child development (cf. Goodnow & Collins, 1990). Three recent comparative studies, using the same methodology, document the nature of parents' beliefs by assessing when (i.e., the age at which) children are expected by mothers to develop specific developmental skills and competencies. The instrument involves many items reflective of skills for early social relations with peers. Together, the three studies show that mothers in certain groups expect early mastery of verbal assertiveness and social skills with peers, whereas mothers in other groups look equally (or more) toward development of competencies for family harmony and group cohesion.

The findings from the three studies are presented together in Table 10.1. Mothers of preschool children were asked to say, for each item in the set, whether children were expected to show mastery of it "before age 4," "between ages 4 to 6," or "after age 6." Hess, Kashiwagi, Azuma, Price, and Dickson (1980) developed the original 38-item questionnaire and administered it to 67 mothers from San Francisco, California, and to 57 mothers from Tokyo and Sapporo, Japan. For the analysis, the researchers grouped the items on conceptual grounds into seven categories: emotional maturity, compliance, politeness, independence, school-related skills, social skills with peers, and verbal assertiveness (with five items not clustered, see Table 10.1). Higher scores represent *earlier* expectations, and mothers' scores were compared by *t* tests. In Table 10.1, the two leftmost columns present the Hess et al. (1980) results. The Tokyo and Sapporo mothers, relative to the San Francisco Bay mothers, show earlier expectations for emotional self-control, compliance with adult authority, and courtesy in interaction with adults. The San Francisco Bay mothers, in contrast, have the earlier expectations for social skills with peers (e.g., showing sympathy, taking initiative, negotiating, standing up for their rights) and verbal skills (seeking information, stating own needs, explaining ideas), all clearly related to getting along and getting ahead with one's peers and teachers at preschool.

Goodnow, Cashmore, Cotton, and Knight (1984) used 32 items of the same instrument with 81 mothers from Sydney, Australia. One group ("Anglo") was born in Australia; the other were immigrants from Lebanon. Both groups contained a child about to enter primary school. The Lebanese-Australian mothers valued early school entry but only 14% had sent their children to preschool, in contrast to 82% of the Anglo-Australians. In Table 10.1, the middle two columns provide the findings. The Anglo-Australian mothers had significantly earlier expectations than the Lebanese-Australians on 18 items. The domains of sharpest difference relate to the social skills with peers and verbal assertiveness.

Last, my colleagues and I recently used the instrument to study mothers and fathers of preschool children, as well as preschool and infant/toddler teachers, in two small cities in the United States and Italy that have extensive early childhood programs (Edwards & Gandini, in preparation; but see Edwards & Gandini, 1989, for description of the communities and results from a comparable earlier study using our own instrument). We added four items to the Hess questionnaire and administered it in questionnaire format (rather than printing the items on separate cards for sorting, as the earlier investigators had done).

### TABLE 10.1
Mothers' Expectations for Mastery of Developmental Tasks, in Six Cultural Communities

| Items | Tokyo, Sapporo (n = 57) | San Fran.[b] (n = 67) | Anglo-Austr. (n = 38) | Leban.-Austr.[c] (n = 43) | Pistoia Italy (n = 30) | Amherst Mass.[a] (n = 30) |
|---|---|---|---|---|---|---|
| | | | Mean Ratings[a] | | | |
| **Emotional Maturity** | **2.49** | **2.08***** | | | **1.80** | **2.12**** |
| 1. Does not cry easily | 2.67 | 1.69*** | 1.66 | 1.95 | 1.86 | 2.00 |
| 2. Can get over anger by self | 2.34 | 1.97*** | 1.93 | 1.38*** | 1.93 | 2.20 |
| 3. Stands disappointment without crying | 2.07 | 1.91 | 1.83 | 1.65 | 1.37 | 1.93** |
| 4. Does not use baby-talk | 2.07 | 1.91 | 2.66 | 2.76 | 2.07 | 2.33 |
| **Compliance** | **2.16** | **1.96**** | | | **2.00** | **2.34***** |
| 5. Comes or answers when called | 2.66 | 2.21*** | 1.79 | 1.13*** | 2.68 | 2.67 |
| 6. Does not do things forbidden by parents | 2.40 | 2.09** | | | 1.93 | 2.31* |
| 7. Stops misbehaving when told | 2.57 | 2.33 | 2.28 | 1.57*** | 1.97 | 2.34* |
| 8. Does task immediately when told | 1.86 | 1.66 | | | 2.00 | 2.38* |
| 9. Gives up reading or TV to help mother | 1.33 | 1.54 | 1.59 | 1.51 | 1.50 | 1.87 |
| **Politeness** | **2.49** | **2.30** | | | **2.25** | **2.52*** |
| 10. Greets family courteously, "good morning" | 2.90 | 2.22 | 2.69 | 2.38 | 2.33 | 2.37 |
| 11. Uses polite forms, "please," to adults | 2.08 | 2.37 | 2.76 | 2.73 | 2.17 | 2.67*** |
| **Independence** | **2.02** | **1.86***** | | | **1.62** | **1.72*** |
| 12. Stays home alone for an hour or so | 1.78 | 1.04*** | 1.10 | 1.05 | 1.07 | 1.03 |
| 13. Takes care of own clothes | 2.17 | 1.87** | 1.55 | 1.35 | 1.27 | 1.23 |
| 14. Makes phone calls without help | 1.41 | 1.21 | 1.14 | 1.21 | 1.67 | 1.47 |
| 15. Sits at table and eats without help | 2.95 | 2.76** | 2.79 | 2.59 | 2.70 | 2.77 |
| 16. Does regular household tasks | 2.03 | 1.97 | 2.07 | 1.32*** | 1.17 | 1.48* |
| 17. Spends own money carefully | 1.07 | 1.09 | | | 1.03 | 1.10 |
| 18. Can entertain self alone | 2.74 | 2.78 | 2.72 | 1.78*** | 2.70 | 2.90 |
| 19. Plays outside without adult supervision | 1.98 | 2.19 | 2.38 | 1.40*** | 1.30 | 1.80** |

*(Continued)*

TABLE 10.1
(Continued)

|  | Mean Ratings[a] | | | | | |
|---|---|---|---|---|---|---|
| Items | Tokyo, Sapporo (n = 57) | San Fran.[b] (n = 67) | Anglo-Austr. (n = 38) | Leban.-Austr.[c] (n = 43) | Pistoia Italy (n = 30) | Amherst Mass.[d] (n = 30) |
| **School-related skills** | **1.24** | **1.35** | | | **1.29** | **1.52\*** |
| 20. Can tell time up to quarter hour | 1.34 | 1.40 | | | 1.40 | 1.41 |
| 21. Read aloud a 30-page picture book | 1.17 | 1.27 | | | 1.37 | 1.63 |
| 22. Look up things in picture encyclopedia | 1.21 | 1.39 | | | 1.10 | 1.50\*\* |
| **Social skills** | **1.86** | **2.18** | | | **2.04** | **2.43\*\*\*** |
| 23. Waits for turn in games | 2.31 | 2.12 | 1.97 | 1.89 | 2.07 | 2.37\* |
| 24. Shares toys with other children | 2.62 | 2.72 | 2.72 | 1.73\*\*\* | 2.14 | 2.57\*\* |
| 25. Sympathetic to feelings of children | 1.86 | 2.13\*\* | 1.79 | 1.22\*\*\* | 1.93 | 2.63\*\*\* |
| 26. Resolves disagreements without fighting | 1.41 | 1.70\*\* | 1.45 | 1.11\*\*\* | 1.53 | 2.07\*\* |
| 27. Gets own way by persuading friends | 1.40 | 1.94\*\*\* | 1.97 | 1.30\*\*\* | 2.17 | 2.33 |
| 28. Takes initiative in playing with others | 1.59 | 2.48\*\*\* | 2.24 | 1.73\*\*\* | 2.45 | 2.63 |
| **Verbal assertiveness** | **1.73** | **2.18\*\*\*** | | | **2.20** | **2.46\*\*** |
| 29. Answers a question clearly | 2.10 | 1.98 | 2.14 | 1.46\*\*\* | 2.17 | 2.47 |
| 30. States own preference when asked | 1.72 | 2.25\*\*\* | 2.00 | 1.30\*\*\* | 2.30 | 2.87\*\*\* |
| 31. Asks for explanation when in doubt | 1.71 | 2.30\*\*\* | 2.21 | 1.38\*\*\* | 2.47 | 2.40 |
| 32. Can explain why s/he thinks so | 1.48 | 2.09\*\*\* | 1.76 | 1.32\*\*\* | 1.80 | 2.67\*\* |
| 33. Stands up for own rights with others | 1.62 | 2.27\*\*\* | 2.10 | 1.24\*\*\* | 2.27 | 2.30 |

(Continued)

## TABLE 10.1
### *(Continued)*

| Items | Mean Ratings[a] | | | | | |
|---|---|---|---|---|---|---|
| | Tokyo, Sapporo[b] (n = 57) | San Fran.[b] (n = 67) | Anglo- Austr. (n = 38) | Leban.- Austr.[c] (n = 43) | Pistoia Italy (n = 30) | Amherst Mass.[d] (n = 30) |
| Items not in any of the above clusters | | | | | | |
| 34. Uses pointed scissors w/o supervision | 2.00 | 1.54*** | 1.52 | 1.11*** | 1.40 | 1.60 |
| 35. Keeps feet off furniture | 2.74 | 2.30*** | 2.31 | 2.05 | 2.27 | 2.03 |
| 36. Disagrees w/o biting or throwing | 2.43 | 2.34 | 2.38 | 1.92*** | 2.33 | 2.69* |
| 37. Answers the telephone properly | 1.52 | 1.49 | 2.10 | 1.98 | 1.97 | 2.03 |
| 38. Resolves quarrels without adult help | 1.52 | 1.73 | 1.52 | 1.46 | 1.43 | 1.60 |
| Items added by Edwards et al.[d] | | | | | | |
| 39. Sleeps entire night in own bed w/o getting up | | | | | 2.63 | 2.86 |
| 40. Gets completely dressed without help | | | | | 1.86 | 2.33*** |
| 41. Helps a peer when help is needed | | | | | 1.93 | 2.40** |
| 42. Doesn't interrupt mother when she is talking to someone else | | | | | 1.27 | 1.27 |

[a]The items are from Hess, Kashiwagi, Azuma, Price, and Dickson (1980), and the means are based on scale 1 = age 6 or above; 2 = age 4 to 6; 3 = younger than age 4.

[b]Data on Tokyo & Sapporo, Japan, and San Francisco, California from Hess et al. (1980).

[c]Data on Sydney, Australia (native Anglo. versus Lebanese-immigrants) are from Goodnow, Cashmore, Cotton, and Knight (1984).

[d]Data on Pistoia, Italy, and Amherst, Massachusetts, were collected in 1987–1989 by Donatella Giovannini, Lella Gandini, John Nimmo, Hind Mari, Minaz Bhumani, and myself.

The parents were from a range of socioeconomic backgrounds, but mostly middle class; all had a child attending a preschool or child-care center. We asked parents to indicate "when you think children usually acquire the capacity to do each of the skills." The results, analyzed as before, are displayed in the rightmost two columns of Table 10.1. The Amherst, Massachusetts (USA) mothers show significantly earlier expectations than do the Pistoia, Tuscany (Italy) mothers on almost half the original 38 items. The most pronounced differences are in the areas of social skills with peers, compliance with adults, and verbal assertiveness. (Note that two skills not formally clustered with peer social skills, but clearly related, also show significantly earlier expectations in Amherst: "disagrees without biting or throwing" and "helps a peer when help is needed.") Inspecting the results closely, it is evident that the Pistoia mothers actually have quite early expectations for social skills with peers and verbal assertiveness; their mean scores are comparable to the San Francisco and Anglo-Australian samples. Although these Italian mothers value the closeness of the extended family, they also want their children to get along with nonfamily agemates and acquire symbolic skills needed for school success. But the Amherst sample is simply even farther along on these dimensions and has, in general, the earliest social and verbal expectations of any group. (But note: we used a slightly different methodology, so the within-study comparisons are most important.)

Taken together, these three studies suggest that there are important cultural and subcultural differences in parents' expectations for when children acquire certain social and verbal competencies relevant to getting along and competing with schoolmates. Indeed, we should not be surprised to find varying cultural scripts for childhood peer relations. Different communities, with their varying values and conditions of daily life, would be expected to have evolved their own customary styles for modulating, channeling, attenuating, or emphasizing the normative behaviors elicited in the peer context.

Unfortunately, very little literature is available for addressing this issue. Mueller and Tingley (1989) described values and goals for peer relations in various societies, based on a close reading of several studies (including our own). Their Soviet material suggests that the essential purpose of peer relations is gaining self-knowledge through social comparison: "Am I as good as, better than, or inferior to this specific peer in $X$?" The Japanese material discloses childrearing practices aimed at letting children build group cohesion by disciplining one another without adult intervention. The British families value "independence," letting children learn to stand up for themselves and manage peer aggression autonomously. Though Mueller and Tingley stressed the diversity of these cultural goals, nevertheless it is evident that all relate to the themes of interpersonal affiliation, comparison, aggression, and conflict resolution, as in our cross-cultural material.

Another recent study is even more illuminating here because the data were collected for a focused comparison and the theoretical framework links the peer setting (preschool) to the wider cultural context (particularly to historical values and contemporary societal needs and stress points). This is Tobin, Wu, and Davidson's (1989) study of preschool education in Japan, China, and the United States, using videotapes as a basis for extensive discussion with cultural "insiders" and "outsiders" about the goals and processes of preschool education.

Descriptive material in the book suggests how each of the three cultures has its own script for peer interaction. Different patterns can be seen for responding to the elicited profile of peer interaction. For example, the pulling apart of the sexes is not resisted in Japan; rather, differentiation (aggression in boys, nurturance toward younger children in girls) is expected and supported. Furthermore, children's tendencies to compare themselves to others and compete (for resources, and against one another) are treated very differently in the three cultures. For example, Japanese educators strive to downplay individual comparison and establish cohesion by use of whole-group activities, school uniforms, and group symbols to foster identification. They tend not to intervene in children's disputes (even when one child is bullying another) in order to let children learn on their own how to function as members of their peer group. The Chinese educators dislike the "chaos" and "disorder" that this can produce and practice more teacher discipline and mass control. On the other hand, their notions of groupism do not preclude certain displays of competition and individual achievement: Young children with musical or dramatic talent are routinely presented as featured performers in preschool productions. The American teachers prize individual differences and free choice above all else. They seek to minimize competition by providing much teacher attention to both satisfy and appease individual striving. In terms of conflict management, their method is to assist children in learning to "use words" to express their feelings and resolve their conflicts in a legalistic style. For example, in a way completely unlike the other two cultures, they teach children to take votes and establish their own class rules to handle some of the disputes that arise in the classroom.

In spite of these differences in teaching goals and methods between educators in Japan, China, and the United States, nevertheless the three societies are similar in looking to preschool education for help in socializing young children and alleviating pressures and needs facing the contemporary family. "In all three cultures preschool is playing an increasingly important role as a focus where parents' and society's different aspirations and concerns for children meet, compete, and are resolved" (Tobin, Wu, & Davidson, p. 204).

These pressures arise from falling birthrate and small family size (emptying the nuclear family of playmates for young children); weakened kin networks (leaving working mothers without surrogates for child care); urbanization (depriving children of safe places to play in the neighborhood); and changing values of parents regarding education (leading to early expectations for social and symbolic skills associated with school success). These factors, plus the contemporary family's inability to produce the kind of mature, cooperative adult needed by each society (whether in Japan, China, or the United States), have led each society to use preschools more and more as institutions designed to support and assist the family in its tasks of socialization.

## SUMMARY AND CONCLUSION

Adolescent peer institutions emerged to serve specialized socializing functions in middle-level societies, those dependent on food collection through subsistence agriculture or animal husbandry. Adolescent peer institutions are a socializing context for learning cultural scripts concerning sexuality, dominance, and aggression (the former for both males and females, the latter two especially for males training for warrior roles). It appears that in many traditional societies, at adolescence peer institutions "step in," as it were, to help parents accomplish certain socializing tasks that the family itself cannot well perform but which everyone knows must be done. These tasks include helping the adolescents receive coaching and practice in full-blown sexuality (heterosexual and/or homosexual modes); renounce cross-gender identifications, yearnings, and behavior; construct alliances and trusting relationships with same-gender persons from outside the family; and (for males) receive training and practice in fighting and group defense. Indeed, the comparative evidence is remarkably clear and consistent in indicating the following two things about middle-level societies: (a) other adults besides parents instruct and induct adolescents into sexuality; and (b) the family context of early childhood is not the place young males acquire the complex patterns of motivations and behaviors for intergroup aggression. Instead, severe and dramatic experiences associated with initiation serve to shatter boys' emotional dependence on their mothers and siblings and separate and seclude them with nonfamily agemates for specialized training in adult masculine behavior.

What about childhood peer relations? The comparative evidence suggests that childhood peer relations are primarily a context for play, in contrast to the more specialized kinds of learning and disciplined preparation for adult roles found in the formal adolescent institutions of middle-level societies. Moreover, childhood peer relations in middle-level societies are not formalized; rather, they take place at middle childhood as any of three changes take place:

1. Children gain increased autonomy to venture farther from the immediate vicinity of home.
2. Children are sent to do errands or chores that take them away from the house.
3. Children attend school where they meet nonfamily agemates and have opportunity to make friends to play with on the playground or after school.

School has truly revolutionized children's social lives by causing them to spend less and less time in the traditional socializing contexts of the child caretaking relationship and the multi-age playgroup.

The revolution is continuing. Today in many industrialized societies around the world, children go in increasingly greater numbers and at increasingly younger ages to their first organized peer setting. It is interesting to note that, as a result, peer relations for the youngest children in contemporary complex societies, like those for adolescents in traditional middle-level societies, are often formalized. That is, they are not the informal product of neighborhood children or schoolmates playing, relatively unsupervised by adults, in home, neighborhood, or schoolyard. They are, instead, the organized product of parents' intention and selection of a peer setting where children will be supervised (often by a trained adult) in modes of playing and interacting beneficial for school success.

Even in formal preschool settings, however, there are universal themes of childhood peer play that show many similarities to the themes of adolescent peer relations. Everywhere these universal peer agendum are acted out on a stage where the play is written in language and symbols shaped by history (cultural tradition) and by everyday patterns of family life—household composition, number and spacing of children, rules of residence and marriage, and daily routines of men, women, and children, including their work and leisure activities. For both ages, then, peer relations elicit concerns about relative status (comparison, competition, testing). Peer relations elicit problems of management of aggression (including rules about how, when, where, whom, and why to fight). Finally, maleness or femaleness is a basic theme, though for adolescents the issue is sexuality (with whom and how to have sex), whereas for children the issue is gender (gender identity, knowledge, and preferences). These issues of maleness or femaleness seem to cause boys and girls in all cultural communities to spend much of their discretionary time in the company of their own gender peers, perhaps because these are ideal partners for learning about the self (the gendered self). Indeed, the evident pleasure and excitement in peer relations everywhere is surely a feature of great importance. From a comparative perspective, this desire to affiliate with others like the self from outside one's family—what Mueller and Tingley (1989) call "peer hunger"—is the force that powers children out from the comfort of kinship relations. Children and adolescents persist in attempts to affiliate and attach with peers even in the face of what can be seen as the inherently greater difficulty of peer relations; that is, the proportionately lesser amounts of nurturance and prosocial responsibility elicited, and the proportionately greater amounts of dominance and aggression (verbal and physical). Cultural factors determine the details of what parents want from their offspring's peer relations, but there is comparability around the world in the generic behaviors children and adolescents bring to peer interaction.

Family life conditions, values, and goals for children, then, set the occasions and provide the scripts for peer relations during adolescence, middle, and early childhood. In comparative perspective, peer relations are an annex to the family as a complementary socializing context called in when and as necessary to help children pursue their developmental agendum and learn required skills for physical survival, reproductive success, and economic well-being in their own society.

## REFERENCES

Barry, H. B., III, & Schlegal, A. (1980). Early childhood precursors of adolescent initiation ceremonies. *Ethos, 8,* 132–145.

Bernardi, B. (1985). *Age class systems* (D. I. Kertzer, Trans.). London: Cambridge University Press.

Brown, J. K. (1963). A cross-cultural study of female initiation rites. *American Anthropologist, 65,* 837–853.

Brown, J. K. (1981). Cross-cultural perspectives on the female life cycle. In R. H. Munroe, R. L. Munroe, & B. B. Whiting (Eds.), *Handbook of cross-cultural human development* (pp. 581–610). New York: Garland Press.

Edwards, C. P. (1986). Another style of competence: The caretaking child. In A. Fogel & G. Melson (Eds.), *The origins of nurturance* (pp. 95–121). Hillsdale, NJ: Lawrence Erlbaum Associates.

Edwards, C. P. (1989). The transition from infancy to early childhood: A difficult transition and a difficult theory. In V. R. Bricker & G. H. Gossen (Eds.), *Ethnographic encounters in southern Mesoamerica: Essays in honor of Evon Zartman Vogt, Jr.* (pp. 167–175). Austin, TX: University of Texas Press.

Edwards, C. P. (in press). Behavioral sex differences in children of diverse cultures: The case of nurturance to infants. In M. Pereira & L. Fairbanks (Eds.), *Juveniles—Comparative socioecology.* New York: Oxford University Press.

Edwards, C. P., & Gandini, L. (1989). Teachers' expectations about the timing of developmental skills: A cross-cultural study. *Young Children, 44*(4), 15–19.

Edwards, C. P., & Gandini, L. (in preparation). Developmental expectations of mothers, fathers, and preschool teachers in two cultural communities. In S. Harkness, C. Super, & R. New (Eds.), *Parental ethnotheories: Their sociocultural origins and developmental consequences*. New York: Guilford Press.

Edwards, C. P., Logue, M. E., Loehr, S., & Roth, S. (1986). The influence of model group care on parent–child interaction at home. *Early Childhood Research Quarterly, 1*, 317–332.

Edwards, C. P., Logue, M. E., Loehr, S., & Roth, S. (1987). The effects of day-care participation on parent–infant interaction at home. *American Journal of Orthopsychiatry, 57*, 33–36.

Edwards, C. P., & Whiting, B. B. (in press). "Mother, older sibling, and me": The overlapping roles of caretakers and companions in the social world of 2–3-year-olds in Ngeca, Kenya. In K. MacDonald (Ed.), *Parents and children playing*. Albany: SUNY.

Ericksen, K. P. (1989a). Female genital mutilations in Africa. *Behavior Science Research, 23*, 182–204.

Ericksen, K. P. (1989b). Male and female age organizations and secret societies in Africa. *Behavior Science Research, 23*, 234–264.

Goodnow, J. J., Cashmore, J., Cotton, S., & Knight, R. (1984). Mothers' developmental timetables in two cultural groups. *International Journal of Psychology, 19*, 193–205.

Goodnow, J. J., & Collins, W. A. (1990). *Development according to parents: The nature, sources, and consequences of parents' ideas*. Hillsdale, NJ: Lawrence Erlbaum Associates.

Harkness, S., & Super, C. (1985). The cultural context of gender segregation in children's peer groups. *Child Development, 56*, 219–224.

Hartley, J. (1963). *Adolescent youths in peer groups: A cross-cultural study*. Unpublished doctoral dissertation, Harvard University.

Herdt, G. H. (1982). Sambia nosebleeding rites and male proximity to women. *Ethos, 18*(3), 189–231.

Herdt, G. H. (1987). *The Sambia: Ritual and gender in New Guinea*. New York: Holt, Rinehart, & Winston.

Hess, R. D., Kashiwagi, K., Azuma, H., Price, G. G., & Dickson, W. P. (1980). Maternal expectations for mastery of developmental tasks in Japan and the United States. *International Journal of Psychology, 15*, 259–271.

Hollos, M., & Leis, P. E. (1989). *Becoming Nigerian in Ijo society*. New Brunswick, NJ: Rutgers University Press.

Kenyatta, J. (1965). *Facing Mt. Kenya: The tribal life of the Gikuyu*. New York: Random House. (Originally published 1932)

Konner, M. (1975). Relations among infants and juveniles in comparative perspective. In M. Lewis & L. A. Rosenblum (Eds.), *Friendship and peer relations* (pp. 99–129). New York: Wiley.

LaFreniere, P., Strayer, F. F., & Gauthier, R. (1984). The emergence of same-sex preferences among preschool peers: A developmental perspective. *Child Development, 55*, 1958–1965.

Maccoby, E. E. (1988). Gender as a social category. *Developmental Psychology, 24*, 755–765.

Mueller, E., & Tingley, E. (1989, May). *Cross-cultural perspectives on early peer relationships: Universal processes and group care*. Paper presented at a meeting on socioemotional relationships in day care and nursery schools, Arezzo, Italy.

Ottenberg, S. (1988). Oedipus, gender, and social solidarity: A case study of male childhood and initiation. *Ethos, 16*(3), 326–352.

Spencer, P. (1976). Opposing streams and the gerontocratic ladder: Two models of age organization in East Africa. *Man, 11*, 153–175.

Thorne, B. (1986). Boys and girls together, but mostly apart. In W. W. Hartup & Z. Rubin (Eds.), *Relationship and development* (pp. 167–184). Hillsdale, NJ: Lawrence Erlbaum Associates.

Tobin, J. J., Wu, D. Y. H., & Davidson, D. H. (1989). *Preschool in three cultures: Japan, China, and the United States.* New Haven, CT: Yale University Press.

Wenger, M. (1983). *Gender role socialization in an East African community: Social interaction between 2- to 3-year-olds and older children in social ecological perspective.* Unpublished doctoral dissertation, Harvard Graduate School of Education.

Wenger, M. (1989). Work, play, and social relationships among children in a Giriama community. In B. Belle (Ed.), *Children's social networks and social supports* (pp. 91–118). New York: Wiley.

Whiting, B. B., & Edwards, C. P. (1988). *Children of different worlds: The formation of social behavior.* Cambridge, MA: Harvard University Press.

Whiting, B. B., & Whiting, J. W. M. (1991). Adolescence in the preindustrial world. In R. M. Lerner, A. C. Peterson, & J. Brooks-Gunn (Eds.), *The encyclopedia of adolescence* (pp. 814–829). New York: Garland.

Whiting, J. W. M. (1981). Aging and becoming an elder: A cross-cultural comparison. In J. G. March (Ed.), *Aging* (pp. 83–90). New York: Academic Press.

Whiting, J. W. M. (1990). Adolescent rituals and identity conflicts. In J. Stigler, R. A. Shweder, & G. Herdt (Eds.), *Cultural psychology* (pp. 357–365). New York: Cambridge University Press.

Whiting, J. W. M., Kluckhohn, R., & Anthony, A. (1958). The function of male initiation rites at puberty. In E. E. Maccoby, T. S. Newcomb, & E. L. Hartley (Eds.), *Readings in social psychology* (pp. 359–370). New York: Holt, Rinehart, & Winston.

Worthman, C. M., & Whiting, J. W. M. (1987). Social change in adolescent sexual behavior, mate selection, and premarital pregnancy rates in a Kikuyu community. *Ethos, 15*(2), 145–165.

Young, F. W. (1965). *Initiation ceremonies: A cross-cultural study of status dramatization.* New York: Bobbs-Merrill.

# CHAPTER ELEVEN

# Peer Relations in Children with a Depressed Caregiver

Carolyn Zahn-Waxler
*National Institute of Mental Health*

Susanne Denham
*George Mason University*

Ronald J. Iannotti
*Georgetown University*

E. Mark Cummings
*University of West Virginia*

According to Piaget (1932/1965), moral character and social skills evolve primarily through children's emerging understanding of mutual exchange and practice of reciprocity in peer interactions. The capacity to negotiate rather than aggress or withdraw from conflict was presumed difficult to learn in the parent–child relationship because of the hierarchical structure inherent in the family system and the unilateral power wielded by the authority figure. Problematic peer relations are now known to reflect more than poor social skills and inadequate conscience development; often they portend later behavior problems and psychopathology. Until recently there has been little interest in family factors that may contribute both to strengths and problems in child's peer relations (Hartup, 1979).

During the past decade, there has been a substantial increase in conceptual and empirical work on linkages between family and peer systems (MacDonald & Parke, 1984; Parke & Bhavnagri, 1989; Parke & Ladd, this volume; Rubin & Sloman, 1984). Moreover, there is recognition that reciprocity is not learned exclusively from peers. Research on interactions between infants and their mothers provides evidence for components of reciprocity such as turn-taking, mutual regard, and coordinated social interchanges. Despite differences in the relative "power" of parent and child, these studies document ways in which children may come to feel like valued partners in a social relationship, even in the first years of life. These coordinated exchanges may be precursors for later reciprocal peer interactions, essential elements of social competence.

Research on socialization experiences within the family (caregivers as disciplinarians, educators, models, nurturers), documents enormous variation in parents' potential for constructive and destructive shaping of children's social-emotional development. The power and authority of the parent are conveyed in markedly different ways. Discipline practices range, for example, from harsh, punitive, and abusive, to respectful and firm, to lax and erratic. Children will move into the world of peers from quite different backgrounds with regard to experiences with reciprocity and control. When a child enters the peer culture, he or she enters a world of inequality. Opportunities for give-and-take in relationships indeed exist and provide important learning opportunities. But dominance hierarchies are inevitably present and children struggle to find a niche. Aggression, victimization, and exclusion from social groups are not uncommon. It is important to consider the role that parents play in facilitating, impeding, or undermining children's relationships with other children as they become part of a larger social world in which parental protection is no longer fully assured, or indeed even appropriate.

In this chapter we first review research on aspects of parenting that predict children's social competence and quality of peer relations. We then consider parental depression as a condition that may disrupt children's developing social relations, both within and outside the family setting. The literature on peer relations of offspring of depressed parents is examined, followed by a review of research on socialization practices of well and depressed caregivers that may have implications for peer relations. We then summarize our own research on early disturbances in reciprocal, coordinated social interactions between peers, as indexed by aggressive behavior in toddlers of depressed and well mothers. The role of both child behaviors and maternal childrearing practices during these early peer interactions in predicting later problem behaviors is described.

Clinical depression in adults is characterized by prolonged episodes of sadness and inability to experience pleasure. There are different types of depression, and symptoms are varied. Physical symptoms include disturbances in activity, sleep, and eating patterns. Affective and cognitive symptoms include, for example, passivity, irritability and hostility, pessimism, confusion, helplessness, worthlessness, self-blame and pervasive guilt, in addition to the dysphoria that defines the disorder. Chronic exposure and attachment to a caregiver experiencing these difficulties is an obvious risk condition for children in their developing social relations.

## Parental Influence on Children's Peer Interactions: Direct and Indirect Effects

Families are embedded in other sets of social systems, including formal and informal social networks, as well as kin, peer, and friendship groups. Parke and Bhavnagri (1989) have provided a conceptual model for examining empirically some of the linkages between family and peer systems. They distinguish between direct and indirect paths of family influence. In the case of *indirect* influences, it is not the parents' explicit goal to modify, enhance, or disrupt the child's relationships with other children. Rather, effects occur as indirect by-products (e.g., the parents' particular childrearing and disciplinary style; the quality of the parents' interpersonal relationship with their child, often indexed by the type of attachment relationship). In the case of *direct* influences, the parents' intent is to select, modify, organize, or structure the physical and/or social environment in order to influence (typically enhance) the child's peer relationships. Parents function, in this role, as managers and organizers of their children's social lives. They arrange opportunities for peer interaction, and directly monitor and supervise these activities.

Rubin and Sloman (1984) have described direct and indirect ways in which parents may facilitate friendship patterns in their offspring. These include: (a) setting the stage (choice of neighborhood, school or day-care setting, parents' own friendship patterns), (b) arranging social contacts, (c) providing advice about choices of friends and how to interact, (d) providing models of social relationships, and (e) providing a secure home base that should inspire confidence and readiness to explore peer relationships (see also Elicker & Sroufe, this volume; Waters, Wippman, & Sroufe, 1979).

Recent studies have documented both positive and negative dimensions of caregiving that may indirectly influence children's developing peer relations. Parents who use power assertion more than inductive discipline, who are unsociable, and are less accepting and more harsh, are likely to have children who are unpopular and disliked by peers (see summary by Putallaz, 1987). Mothers' endorsement of aggression and biased expectations predict lowered social competence in their preschool children's peer relations (Pettit, Dodge, & Brown, 1988). Mothers of first-grade children with low social status were observed to be less positive, less focused on feelings, and more disagreeable and demanding when interacting with their children than mothers of high status children. These maternal behaviors predicted similar patterns in their children's peer interactions, suggesting that children acquire some of their social behavior repertoire through interaction with their mothers (Putallaz, 1987). In longitudinal research (Van Lieshout, 1987), children's cooperation with peers in kindergarten could be traced back to their cooperative interchanges in the first year of life and to their mothers' responsiveness. Murray, Webb, and Andrews (1983) reported that mothers who had satisfying contacts in the community had socially competent children.

Parenting practices that are directly targeted toward influencing children's social relations and peer competence also have been studied (Parke & Bhavnagri, 1989; see also Lollis, Ross, & Tate, this volume). Parke and Bhavnagri (1989) examined direct influences in laboratory observations of mothers with their 2-year-olds during peer interactions. Maternal difficulties in (a) supervising, initiating, and sustaining peer interaction, and in (b) maintaining responsiveness, synchrony, and positive affect during peer interactions, were associated with children's lack of social competence with the playmates. Booth, Rose-Krasnor, and Rubin (1989) reported that children who had mothers whose peer management strategies were less child centered and less jointly focused on both children, were both insecurely attached to the mother and lacking in social competence in peer interactions. Extensive home observations (Lollis & Ross, 1987) have revealed that maternal interventions in toddlers' peer interactions result in greater equality (i.e., more equal sharing of resources). Ladd and Golter (1988) found that children of parents who tended to arrange peer contacts had a larger range of playmates and more frequent play companions outside of school than children whose parents were less active in initiating peer play for their children.

## Peer Relations of Children of Depressed Parents

Several characteristics of parenting thus may contribute, directly and indirectly, to problems in children's peer relations. Examples include the following: coercive, inconsistent discipline; unsociability and unresponsiveness; difficulty initiating and sustaining social interaction; heightened negative affect and diminished positive affect; insecure relationships with children. We later review research indicating that several of these dimensions are particularly likely to characterize depressed caregivers.

Forehand and McCombs (1988) concluded that depression ranks foremost among parental characteristics associated with poor functioning in children and adolescents. Offspring of depressed parents are at risk for developing affective disorders and related emotional problems (see reviews by Beardslee, Bemporad, Keller, & Klerman, 1983; Downey & Coyne, 1990; Forehand, McCombs, & Brody, 1987; Zuckerman & Beardslee, 1987). Although a heritability component is indicated by both adoption and twin studies (e.g., Cadoret, 1978), environmental processes also may play a role in intergenerational transmission of affective problems (Radke-Yarrow & Kuczynski, 1983). One approach to understanding the early etiology of these problems is to study parenting patterns of depressed caregivers that contribute to poor peer relations and, possibly, later psychiatric problems. Recent work by Blechman, McEnroe, Carella, and Audette (1986) indicates a connection between children's lack of social competence with peers and the development of depression, by the late elementary school years. In 3- to 6-year-old children (Campbell, 1987) persistence (vs. improvement) of problem behaviors over time was characteristic of children who had difficulties with their peers.

Teachers and peers judge school-age children of depressed parents to have inadequate peer relations and difficulty getting along in the classroom, relative to controls (Billings & Moos, 1985; Grunebaum, Cohler, Kaufman, & Gallant, 1978; Neale & Weintraub, 1975; Weintraub, Neale, & Liebert, 1975; Weintraub, Prinz, & Neale, 1978). These problems in social competence can take either an internalizing (e.g., withdrawal) or externalizing (e.g., teasing and tormenting other classmates) form of expression. Popularity with peers as judged by teachers is low in elementary school-age children of depressed mothers (Goodman, Lynch, Brogan, Fielding, 1991). Interactions of 2- and 5-year-olds observed with familiar peers (Denham & Zahn-Waxler, 1989) were suggestive of lowered social competence in children of depressed mothers. A small group of 2-year-olds of manic-depressive parents who showed poor social skills when interacting with peers were likely to have psychiatric diagnoses by age 6 (Zahn-Waxler, Cummings, McKnew, & Radke-Yarrow, 1984; Zahn-Waxler et al., 1988).

Attentional problems and social-cognitive vulnerabilities also have been identified in children of depressed parents, which may make it difficult to sustain smoothly coordinated interactions. They sometimes show more negative self-concept, less positive self-schemas, and more negative attributional styles (i.e., self-blame for bad things that happen). These negative attributional styles have, in turn, been linked to depressive orientations (e.g., Jaenicke et al., 1987; Seligman et al., 1984). Cumulatively, several studies indicate that problems in social competence and self-concept are more common in children of depressed than well mothers.

## Socialization Patterns of Depressed Caregivers

We focus on representative studies of different aspects of parenting that might be expected to differ in depressed and nondepressed caregivers. These include modeling (of affect and social skills), parent–child attachment patterns, nurturance and responsivity of the caregiver, the affective climate of the home, and discipline and control practices. Because these dimensions of parenting have not been examined in the context of children's peer interactions in these studies, they represent possible *indirect* influences. Persistent disturbances in any of these aspects of socialization may compromise the development of smoothly coordinated, reciprocal social exchanges, in which the needs of self and other are optimally balanced.

In a 1980 review, Orvaschel, Weissman, and Kidd concluded that examination of the homes of children with a depressed parent revealed disruptive, hostile, and rejecting environments. At this time, the research available was based mainly on retrospective methods and questionnaire data. In the past decade, observational studies have been conducted as well. Consistent with Orvaschel's conclusion, depressed parents continue to be described as conflictual, inconsistent, ineffective, and emotionally constrained (Davenport, Zahn-Waxler, Adland, & Mayfield, 1984; Goodman & Brumley, 1990; Gordon et al., 1989; Grunebaum et al., 1978; Radke-Yarrow, Richters, & Wilson, 1988). Goodman and Brumley (1990) indicated that depressed caregivers are disproportionately more likely to manifest qualities of parenting associated with problems in children's cognitive, social, and emotional development (as summarized in a review by Maccoby & Martin, 1983). We consider next, in greater detail, these different aspects of depressed parenting that may impact, indirectly, on children's developing peer relations and integration into a larger social community.

***Modeling of Affect and Social Skills.***    Depression has been linked both to affective and social skills deficits in adults. Persons with affective disorders often provide less than optimal models of socially competent behavior. They are unskilled in interactions with strangers (e.g., in maintaining eye contact, in verbal production, in responsiveness to others' communications, and in speaking with animation; Gotlib, 1982; Hinchliffe, Hooper, & Roberts, 1978; Libet & Lewinsohn, 1973). In interpersonal situations they tend to communicate self-devaluation, sadness, and helplessness (Hokanson, Sacco, Blumberg, & Landrum, 1980); and their conversations are often self-focused and negatively toned (Jacobson & Anderson, 1982). Depressed individuals also elicit negative reactions from those with whom they interact (see review by Gotlib & Hooley, 1988). Difficulties are especially pronounced in close relationships, particularly with children and spouses (Gotlib & Hooley, 1988; Weissman & Paykel, 1974).

***Parent–Child Attachment Patterns.***    Depressed persons often have problems based on earlier experiences with separation and loss. As caregivers, these issues may become enacted in relationships with their own children, for example, problems in allowing children to develop relationships with others that reflect increased autonomy. Their children begin to play with other children during the toddler years. The normative independence strivings often accompanied by opposition, aggression, and temper tantrums may present special difficulties for many of the caregivers in this critical transition period. If secure attachment is one prerequisite of social competence with peers, then children of depressed parents are at risk. Maternal depression has been associated with insecure attachments in young offspring (Cicchetti & Aber, 1986; Radke-Yarrow, Cummings, Kuczynski, & Chapman, 1985; Zahn-Waxler, Chapman, & Cummings, 1984).

Insecure attachments in children are likely to evolve out of earlier difficulties in achieving mutually satisfying reciprocal interactions. Whereas quality of attachment is typically assessed via the *child's* response to separation, attachment is a dyadic construct, and hence it is relevant to consider it as a dimension of parenting. Secure attachment, moreover, has often been linked to maternal sensitivity and responsiveness. Depressed caregivers are frequently withdrawn and unresponsive in their social interactions with infants (Field, 1984; Tronick & Gianino, 1986). Infants express frustration, distress, and helplessness ("giving up" in the interaction when mothers fail to respond contingently and engage in coordinated interchanges). Depressed mothers appear to have difficulty establishing early prelanguage "dialogues" or protoconversations that may provide the initial base for mutuality and reciprocity (Trevarthen, 1989).

Protoconversations are intersubjective exchanges during face-to-face interactions in which infant and mother engage in nonverbal "dialogue." Early maternal responsiveness to the infant's emotional expressions acknowledges the infant's efforts to communicate and provides perhaps the earliest opportunity for give-and-take, back and forth, in social interaction. Later in the first year of life this pattern gives way to other forms in which the practice of games establishes the coordinated understanding in attending, intending, and feeling. These early forms of "cooperative awareness" begin to create a world of shared meanings, empathic understanding, and appropriate linking of one's own emotions with those of others. This emotional linking between caregiver and child is viewed as a basic controlling system for later stages of development that underlies dynamic engagements and friendships.

Whereas Trevarthen (1989) argued that this system is universal and unlearned, there are clearly individual differences in the achievement of cooperative awareness during the early years. Moreover, the capacity to take turns in the context of mutually well-regulated mother–infant interaction has been found to predict later reciprocal peer interactions (Vandell & Wilson, 1987). These investigators proposed that the ability to take turns and maintain smoothly coordinated social interchanges in early parent–child interaction provides a basis both for the formation of secure parent–child bonds and comfortable peer interaction. The dialogues of depressed mothers with their infants and toddlers often may be less coordinated, "easy," and reciprocal. This may underlie children's increased risk for insecure attachments in which more prototypic aggressive, avoidant, and dependent patterns of relating to others first become established.

*Nurturance and Responsivity of the Caregiver.* In a study of depressed, schizophrenic, and well mothers and their children, Goodman and Brumley (1990) found maternal responsiveness and affectionate involvement to predict children's social functioning. They too suggest that maternal responsiveness may exert a positive influence by establishing the secure base needed by children to be more open, accepting, and responsive back toward their parents, and eventually toward peers and other adults. Parenting practices, and not diagnostic status per se, accounted for much of the child's intellectual and social competence in their study, supporting an interactional model for transmission of psychopathology.

Because depressed caregivers are sometimes unresponsive and unavailable, their children may be more likely to experience love withdrawal. Radke-Yarrow and Nottelmann (1989), in detailed observational analysis of mother–child interaction, have reported that depressed mothers show as much affection toward their children as well mothers do. This is consistent with findings from observations of Goodman and her colleagues and also with clinical observations that the depressed mother is not necessarily lacking in warmth and affection toward her child. But warmth, in conjunction with high expectations for interpersonally appropriate behavior, and the social withdrawal that accompanies depressive episodes, may make the love withdrawal (and psychological abandonment) of a depressed mother particularly salient. Their children may come to lack confidence in their abilities to regulate social interactions and, hence, experience uncertainty in relationships with others.

*Affective Climate of the Home.* Emotions that accompany depression (sadness, anxiety, guilt, and irritability) may influence parent–child interaction by creating a global, pervasive climate of distress (Radke-Yarrow & Kuczynski, 1983). Depressed mothers are likely to show dysphoric affect and lack of pleasure in interactions with children (Hops et al., 1987; Radke-Yarrow & Nottelmann, 1989). Close proximity to these emotions might be expected to lead to contagion of affect. This may serve both (a) to render the child vulnerable to emotion dysregulation, and (b) to create feelings of empathic distress and responsibility (guilt) for the caregiver's distress (Zahn-Waxler, Kochanska, Krupnick, & McKnew, 1990). Children also may, in turn, develop defense mechanisms for coping with these emotions.

Maternal depression often is part of a more global family climate of conflict and distress (Gotlib & Hooley, 1988; Radke-Yarrow & Kuczynski, 1983), and marital discord is very common in these families. Marital conflict is associated with behavior disturbances involving both overcontrol and undercontrol in children (Emery, 1982; Jouriles, Pfeffner, & O'Leary, 1988). These problems surface in children as early as the toddler period, are evidenced in their peer relations, and are most apparent for undercontrol or externalizing problems (i.e., aggressive, impulsive, uncontrolled behavior).

***Discipline and Control Practices.***    Depressed mothers have been described as harsh and critical (e.g., Belle, 1982; Webster-Stratton & Hammond, 1988). We examine here (a) the specific discipline and control methods used by depressed mothers, as well as (b) other ways in which their negativism and critical behavior may function to control child behavior. Depressed mothers, more than well mothers, make negative attributions about their children during mother–child interaction (Radke-Yarrow, Belmont, Nottlemann, & Bottomly, in press). In a study of mother–child interaction during structured laboratory tasks, Hammen et al. (1987) found that unipolar depressed mothers emitted high rates of criticism and off-task behaviors, and low levels of positive and productive behaviors. Depressed mothers report more use of anxiety- and guilt-arousing procedures (e.g., references to self-sacrifice), in conjunction with stated feelings of disappointment in their children (Susman, Trickett, Iannotti, Hollenbeck, & Zahn-Waxler, 1985). These findings were recently replicated by Hahn and Zahn-Waxler (1989), who found, in addition, more inconsistency, emphasis on achievement (e.g., high standards), and negative affect reported by depressed than well mothers.

It is as if the depressed mothers' self-critical patterns become transferred and directed toward the child during the course of disciplinary action and social interaction. This critical orientation also may be "transmitted" to offspring through modeling and imitation of a particular attributional style. Attributing negative events to internal, stable, and global causes ("It's my fault; I am responsible for everyone's problems") is characteristic of depressed individuals. Seligman et al. (1984) reported that mothers with such attributional styles had children with similar self-attributional patterns. Depressed mothers, more often than well mothers, talk with their preschool children about others' negative emotions, which may induce and amplify such feelings in offspring (Zahn-Waxler, Ridgeway, Denham, Usher, & Cole, in press). When such communications occur in the broader context of parental self-derision and child blame, their potency may be heightened with corresponding implications for the development of negative self-esteem. Children with self-concept problems are unlikely to fare well in interactions with other children.

Panaccione and Wahler (1986), in a home-based naturalistic observation of mother–child interaction, found an association between maternal depression and shouting, slapping, and other forms of disapproval directed toward the child. In home observations of low-income mothers and their year-old children, Lyons-Ruth, Zoll, Connell, and Grunebaum (1986) found that maternal depression was associated with covert hostility, interfering manipulation, and flattened affect. Overall, the studies suggest that these mothers may be at risk for behaving in a hostile, coercive manner toward their children.

Both power-assertive and (negative) psychological methods of discipline are more common, then, in depressed than well caregivers, but there are complexities that qualify this generalization. Kochanska, Kuczynski, Radke-Yarrow, and Welsh (1987) have found that depressed mothers, more than well mothers, sometimes choose less effortful conflict resolution strategies, either by enforcing obedience unilaterally or by withdrawing in the face of child resistance. Thus, their children may be being socialized to resolve interpersonal conflict through coercion or withdrawal rather than through negotiated, mutually agreed-on compromises. It seems unlikely that these parents *begin* with a value system about childrearing that actively sanctions the use of coercion; rather, the coercion or power assertion may result from anxiety over their inability effectively to control and regulate difficult interpersonal situations with their young children. In two different studies we have found that mothers with an affective disorder are no more likely than well mothers to endorse authoritarian control methods (Susman et al., 1985; Hahn & Zahn-Waxler, 1989). Goodman and Brumley (1990) recently reported that depressed mothers were observed to *avoid* punishment and discipline more than well mothers. Moreover, Kochanska, Kuczynski, and Maguire (1989) have reported that depressed mothers sometimes were *less* likely than well mothers to use direct commands with their toddlers and *more* likely to use explanations, whereas essentially the reverse was true when these same children were 5 years old.

Such longitudinal work provides a valuable perspective. Direct control strategies that are firm and clear, but not unduly harsh, may be more developmentally appropriate for young children. Psychological methods with greater verbal elaboration may be more age-appropriate to older children. If the mother of a very young child tries to minimize conflict by avoiding firmness and by relying too much on explanations that are difficult to understand, she may set the stage for protracted conflicts and struggles, and increase the likelihood of later coercion and withdrawal. The metacommunications given and received, with regard to reciprocity, control, and conflict resolution, may have broader implications for how the child resolves conflicts with playmates (e.g., negotiating vs. aggressing or withdrawing from the situation).

## Implications of Depressed Parenting for Children's Developing Peer Relations

Cumulatively, studies of depressed caregivers do identify disturbances in their affective relationships with offspring, their attempts to control child behavior, their social communication styles, the "roles" and behaviors that they model, and their relationships with their spouses. These socialization experiences might be expected to affect, indirectly, children's developing peer relations. Though parenting deficits described in this review were based on investigations of children across a large age range (infancy, preschool, elementary school), many of these studies include quite young children. Hence disturbances sometimes experienced early in the family system may generalize to children's later evolving relationships with peers in ways that compromise the quality of social interaction, relationship formation, friendship patterns, and the sturdy sense of self required for adaptive interpersonal functioning. Parental influence, however, will depend on the child's temperament, the type and severity of parental depression, and still other protective and risk factors. Moreover, studies are far from uniform in identifying detrimental effects of depressed parenting.

*Direct* influences, that is, the role the depressed parent plays in constructing, monitoring, and structuring the child's peer environment, have only recently been considered in research (Radke-Yarrow et al., 1988; Zahn-Waxler, Iannotti, Cummings, & Denham, 1990). Depression would also be expected to interfere with parents' active facilitation of their children's interactions with playmates. Depressed mothers may provide fewer opportunities for play and may have difficulty assuming a constructive managerial role during children's interactions (especially with regard to peer disputes). The social networks of these mothers may be more restricted and hence limiting for their children's involvements with others. We review next a recent study that examined direct, as well as indirect, influences of depressed parents on their children's peer interactions. The data is from a longitudinal research project in which children were seen during the toddler period and then again at the time of school entry (Zahn-Waxler, Iannotti, et al., 1990).

## PEER RELATIONS, PROBLEMS, AND SOCIALIZATION OF CHILDREN OF DEPRESSED MOTHERS

### Summary of Initial Research Questions and Methods

Two-year-old children's interactions with familiar peers were observed in two laboratory sessions, designed to stimulate and challenge the children (Cummings, Iannotti, & Zahn-Waxler, 1985). During these first two sessions, child behaviors that reflected a potential breakdown in patterns of reciprocity and mutual exchange—namely, aggressive, conflictual interactions—were measured. This included, for example, object struggles, physical aggression, out-of-control behavior. In a third observation session, the mother's childrearing practices during peer interactions were examined. This included ability to take the child's perspective, to teach the child *others'* perspectives, to show warmth, to encourage prosocial behavior, and to engage in modulated versus forceful control during peer interactions. In addition to these assessments of direct socialization, vis-à-vis peers, indirect maternal control influences were examined in a subsequent home visit, using the Block Q sort. Indirect measures included mothers' reports of more general use of rational guidance, authoritarian practices, protectiveness, inconsistency, and attempts to control by arousing guilt or anxiety. Children's aggressive behaviors then were examined in relation to mothers' childrearing behaviors during peer interactions in the third session and also in relation to mothers' general values and attitudes about childrearing according to the Q sort.

We were interested in (a) whether children of depressed and psychiatrically well mothers differed in their early patterns of aggression; (b) how depressed and well mothers responded to children differing in levels of aggression; and (c) if early child and maternal behaviors predicted child problem behaviors several years later. Problem behaviors at age 5 were measured using the Child Behavior Check List (CBCL), which assesses both externalizing and internalizing problems (Achenbach & Edelbrock, 1981). The Childhood Assessment Schedule (CAS), a psychiatric interview tapping symptoms in a variety of domains, was administered at age 6 (Hodges, McKnew, Cytryn, & Stern, 1982).

### Results and Interpretations

Both normative (e.g., object struggles, rough play) and maladaptive (e.g., dysregulated, out-of-control behavior) forms of toddler aggression were identified. Dysregulated aggression predicted externalizing problems reported by mothers when children were 5 years old. It also predicted children's reports of difficulties during the structured psychiatric interview at age 6. Problems were more frequent in children of depressed, rather than well, mothers, both in toddlers and at follow-up. Moreover, stability of problem behaviors over time was more evident for the depressed group. Early dysregulated, that is, maladaptive, aggression was a better predictor of later externalizing, than internalizing problems, but there was some evidence for the latter pattern as well.

Both direct and indirect childrearing practices were related to child outcomes: Negative influences were evident, but protective patterns were present as well. For a subgroup of depressed mothers who were likely to use direct, proactive approaches with their toddlers during peer interactions (and unlikely to endorse indirect negative practices), their children showed relatively few externalizing problems 3 years later. These children, in fact, appeared very similar to children of psychiatrically well mothers. The term *proactive* was used to characterize a maternal orientation that included anticipating the child's point of view; exerting modulated, respectful control; and providing structure and organization during children's interactions with each other when they had been asked to work together on a challenging task. This dimension of anticipatory, respectful guidance was derived from a principal components analysis of the observed childrearing practices.

Although this subgroup of children of proactive, depressed mothers did well at follow-up, there were still overall group differences with many children of depressed mothers showing more problems than children of well mothers. These different outcomes at follow-up may have been a function, in part, of how mothers of the relatively more aggressive children interacted with them when they were toddlers. For both groups, proactive childrearing behaviors (as previously defined) during peer interactions were linked to beneficial outcomes in the toddler period: Mothers who were engaged in those behaviors that appeared to have a scaffolding and regulating function had children who were less likely to aggress against their playmates. In addition, well mothers with aggressive toddlers were likely to encourage them to be prosocial (share, cooperate, help) and to use firm, sometimes forceful control. Well mothers who used rational guidance had toddlers who showed low levels of aggression. This pattern of childrearing behaviors may have helped their children to regulate aggressive impulses and hence to be at less risk for later problem behaviors. The pattern for depressed mothers differed. When they did engage in proactive approaches, their toddler-age children, as noted earlier, were less aggressive. However, when indirect negative childrearing practices were used by this group, they were linked to toddler aggression during peer interactions, particularly dysregulated aggression. Negative practices included inconsistency, protectiveness, regulation through constraint, affirmation of parental power, and anxiety- and guilt-arousal.

Both direct and indirect childrearing practices, then, were related to early child problem behaviors (and somewhat differently for well and depressed groups). In terms of long-term influences, childrearing practices observed directly were better predictors of later problem behaviors than indirect practices. Also, the beneficial effects of positive, proactive practices were more evident than the detrimental effects of negative, punitive practices (consistent with recent work by Pettit & Bates, 1989) in determining whether or not there were likely to be problems later in development. Finally, childrearing practices predicted later child outcomes most strongly for the depressed sample. Particularly encouraging were the findings that depressed mothers who were proactive in their rearing approaches during their young children's peer interactions (and who were unlikely to endorse more general, negative rearing attitudes and practices), had children with relatively few problems at follow-up. (See Zahn-Waxler, Iannotti, et al., 1990, for details concerning methods, measures, and statistical analysis.)

## Examination of Other Potential Socialization Influences

Still other characteristics of parents may impact on children's developing peer relations: they are not, strictly speaking, childrearing practices, yet are likely to play a role in socialization. Patterns of spouse selection, friendship choices, and personality characteristics of depressed women also help to characterize environments in which children are reared. Some data relevant to this issue are presented here. Several features of affective illness would suggest that these mothers may be less likely to interact with others and hence less likely to engage their children in activities that would facilitate early developing peer relations. We found that depressed mothers were significantly less likely to involve their 2-year-old children in formal or informal play groups with other children ($t[42] = 2.23, p < .05, M = .91_{WELL}$ & $M = .64_{DEPRESSED}$). Moreover, depressed mothers tended to associate with other depressed mothers (Zahn-Waxler, Iannotti et al., 1990), which may also help to define children's early play partners. Additional contextual aspects of the parenting environment that reflect different social-emotional and interpersonal climates within which children are reared are indicated in Table 11.1.

The SADS-L interview (Spitzer & Endicott, 1979) was given to the mother to assess depression when the child was 2 years old. It also probes for aspects of personality and relationships (e.g., introversion, quality of social relationships and friendships). When the child was 5 years old, the Beck Depression Inventory (BDI) was administered to mothers and fathers and marital conflict was assessed as well. In addition, mothers had been

TABLE 11.1
Social and Affective Contexts in Which Children
of Well and Depressed Mothers are Reared

|  | M Well | M Depressed | t | p |
|---|---|---|---|---|
| Introversion (2)* (SADS) | 2.75 | 3.67 | −2.78 | <.01 |
| Poor social relations (SADS) (2) | 2.06 | 2.73 | −2.15 | <.05 |
| Quality of maternal friendships (SADS) (2) | 2.56 | 2.53 | <1 | NS |
| Mother's frequency of contact (2) with her laboratory partner | 4.77 | 2.91 | 2.51 | <.025 |
| Marital conflict (5) | 16.41 | 18.40 | −1.85 | <.10 |
| Number of good friends (5) | 19.05 | 20.10 | <1 | NS |
| Number of best friends (5) | 3.29 | 3.00 | <1 | NS |
| Number of acquaintances (5) | 58.41 | 35.36 | 2.10 | <.05 |

*Numbers in parentheses refer to age of child when measure was taken. Total $N$s range from 31–44. (In a subset of the SADS interviews, questions were not asked about mothers' social relations, introversion, and quality of friendships.)

asked questions about their social networks (friendship and acquaintance-ship patterns), and the degree of familiarity of the mother with her labora-tory partner. (Children were observed with familiar peers, and typically the mothers were acquainted as well.) Mothers initially diagnosed as depressed when their children were toddlers, scored higher on the BDI 3 years later, suggesting an enduring quality to the depression of many of these women. In addition, and consistent with other research, their husbands were more likely to report depression than husbands of well women (Zahn-Waxler, Iannotti, et al., 1990).

Marital conflict was marginally higher in depressed than well families. In the initial psychiatric interview, the depressed women had reported substantially more introversion and problems in social relations, in addi-tion to depression. This combination of factors reflecting unhappiness with their spouses and an inward orientation also suggests that reaching out to others and establishing adaptive social connections will be difficult. There are likely to be corresponding implications for the social relations of their children as well as for themselves. The two groups of mothers did not differ on the number of good friends they reported, but the well mothers reported many more acquaintances, hence a larger social net-work. Well mothers were likely to be more intimately acquainted with their laboratory partner than were depressed mothers (see Table 11.1).

These more globally defined aspects of rearing and the affective en-vironment were examined in relation to problems in children at ages 5 and 6. For the total sample, marital conflict did not predict overall child problems, but it did relate to a specific measure of peer aggression (extracted from the externalizing items on the Achenbach), ($r[40] = .32, p < .05$). Children's self-reported problems with school adjustment on the CAS were predicted by poor social relations of the mother assessed several years earlier ($r[29] = .49, p < .005$). Children's self-reported problems with friends (CAS) were predicted by mother's depression at age 5 ($r[42] = .35, p < .025$) and marginally by the mother's own poor social relations when the child was a toddler ($r[29] = .33, p < .10$). The fewer good friends mothers had when their children were 5, the more likely their children were to report problems with friends at age 6 ($r[40] = -.34, p < .05$). Early participation in play groups was associated with fewer school adjustment problems at age 6 ($r[42] = -.29, p = .054$). Depressed mother–child dyads contributed more strongly to these patterns than the well group, although $N$s for analyses were small for some measures due to missing data.

## DISCUSSION

We have reviewed research on depressed women and their offspring to gain further understanding of how the socialization environment and parent–child relationship may impact on children's emerging social development. The children are known to be at greater risk for psychopathology, and problems with peers may presage some of their difficulties. Our own work indicates that some emotional problems present by school age date back to the first years of life. Moreover, they may be influenced, in part, by varied socialization practices that directly and indirectly impact on children's developing peer relations. We consider next some implications for theory, research, and practice that derive from the cumulative body of research on peer relations in offspring of depressed caregivers.

Children's uncontrolled and poorly regulated social exchanges with peers may emanate, in part, from still earlier problematic parent–child interactions in which regulated and constructively controlled, reciprocal exchanges are not well-achieved. Both our own research and that of others (reviewed earlier) indicate ways in which children of depressed parents may be at special risk for difficulty in achieving comfortable, mutually regulated interpersonal exchanges. Maccoby and Martin (1983) summarized research indicating that young children are more likely to comply with a parent if they perceive that they are participating in a reciprocal relationship. Crockenberg (1990) has argued that young children's propensities to comply or to engage in constructive noncompliance (i.e., self-assertion), as opposed to defiance, may be affected by the extent to which the mother's control strategies allow the child a degree of autonomy.

Pettit and Bates (1989) reported that proactive maternal involvement (anticipatory guidance and affectively positive, educative exchanges between mother and child), was related to few behavior problems in 4-year-olds. Their concept of proactive teaching is similar to our measures of anticipatory, respectful guidance, which were the best predictors of (reduction in) later problem behaviors. Cumulatively, such studies suggest the importance of positive caregiver behaviors in achieving reciprocal, mutually negotiated social interchanges, both in interactions with their own children and in facilitating peer social interactions. These patterns of reciprocity may reflect precursors of children's later adaptive social functioning. When depressed mothers engage in these practices, their children are at reduced risk for problem behaviors.

## The Role of the Global Family and Social Climate

Specific socialization practices, attitudes, and values occur within global family climates and broader social systems that also vary, and hence may impart different meanings to phenotypically similar parenting practices. Children with depressed mothers, as noted, are also likely to have depressed fathers, and marital tensions often predominate (Hops, Sherman, & Biglan, in press; Johnston, Gonzalez, & Campbell, 1987). Depressed women sometimes associate with other depressed women (and when they do, their observed direct rearing behaviors in peer interactions are less constructive [Zahn-Waxler, Iannotti, et al., 1990]). When the children of depressed mother dyads play together, this should increase the likelihood of developing poor social skills. Thus, an expanded "depressogenic" environment is more likely for these children and an early "drift to deviant peers" may be inadvertently established by some depressed caregivers. Depressed mothers' social networks are more constrained, and their self-absorption may prevent them from seeking out "corrective" activities (e.g., play groups) for their children. Our work suggests that problems in the caregivers' own social relationships with "peers" become reflected in children's social relations and friendship patterns.

## Are the Effects Unique to Depression?

Depression is just one of many conditions of parent and family dysfunction that influence children's social development. Parental maltreatment, for example (see Cicchetti, this volume), as well as other forms of parental problems, are also expected to produce interference. Depression coexists with other forms of psychiatric illness and related emotional problems (e.g., alcoholism, substance abuse, personality disorder, anxiety disorder, etc.). In future research it would be useful to explore whether different types (and subtypes) of psychopathology, in conjunction with particular childrearing practices, predict different types of problems in children over time. Such longitudinal studies would aid in understanding how emotional problems are perpetuated across generations—beginning in early family interactions and then extending into the child's expanding social world as significant connections with other persons, particularly peers, are forged. It is important to begin these tracings early in development. The toddler years represent a critical period of transition, with respect to self-development, individuation, and expansion of attachments and relationships beyond the family setting. Socialization experiences at this time thus assume special salience.

## Disentangling the Direction of Effects

On the basis of existing research, it remains difficult to determine fully the extent to which (a) depressed caregivers primarily contribute to emotional problems in their children and (b) constitutional problems in children make them draining and difficult to manage. Little is still known about how characteristics of children and depressed parents interact to produce coercive, dysregulated cycles. When poorly coordinated interpersonal exchanges, lacking in reciprocity and sensitivity to each other's needs and states, become repetitive, ritualized, and entrenched, they become possible harbingers of future problems. Primacy of effect of parent or child may differ in different families, with parental problems producing difficulties for children from some families, with the converse being true in other families. Regardless of how the coercive cycles are established, they do begin early and are likely to generalize to peer interactions well before that time in development more traditionally thought to represent a transition from the "world of family" to the "world of peers" (i.e., the early school years).

Genetic models of transmission of depression across generations focus on biological vulnerabilities of individuals and their offspring. It will be important to explore these predispositions in conjunction with psychosocial processes associated with intergenerational transmission patterns. Children of difficult temperament and who show poor affect regulation early in development will tax any parent's coping abilities—especially parents with limited emotional resources. Transactional models of development (e.g., Lewis, Feiring, McGuffog, & Jaskir, 1984; Sameroff

& Chandler, 1975) elaborate ways in which the combination of high rates of child symptoms and an unsupportive family environment are more likely to predict continuing problems than either one alone.

Patterson (1980) identified ways in which young children create adversive environments for caregivers. Aggressive children might be particularly likely to elicit symptoms of depression in caregivers who may come to feel helpless in trying to structure, organize, and regulate the child's behavior. Lytton (1990) has recently reviewed a large body of literature on child aggression that could be interpreted to indicate a "primacy of child" effect, that is, constitutional/genetic/biological factors play a primary role in determining a child's aggression. Parenting factors are acknowledged to matter, not so much in creating the aggression but as different ways of reacting to the aggression that make it more or less likely to continue. Although this position is debatable (Dodge, 1990; Wahler, 1990), it is evident that some children are particularly aggressive and difficult to manage. Some differences between children of depressed and well mothers are present very early, suggesting the role of temperament or possible prenatal and delivery problems (see review by Zuckerman & Beardslee, 1987). Not only do infants of depressed mothers show considerable negative affect, but they appear more difficult in interactions with unrelated mothers as well as their own (Field et al., 1988).

In our own work, even with children as young as 2 years, there is still a history of parent–child interaction and it is not possible to disentangle fully direction of influence. For example, we found that protectiveness in depressed mothers was associated with aggression in children. Protectiveness could represent a deeply ingrained philosophy of keeping the child away from situations and people that may cause trouble; or, it may result from real experiences with the child getting into trouble in ways that encourage isolation and protection. Because these children are too young to be associating with "troublemakers" by choice, and because the parents play such a primary role in arranging toddlers' early social interactions, a parent-to-child effect is plausible. Paradoxically, these caregivers may help to create some of the problems they attempt to avoid. Also, qualities of maternal depression likely to constrain the child's expanding social horizons (i.e., maternal introversion, poor social relations, limited social networks) could reflect personality characteristics established well before particular parent–child dynamics come into play.

Maternal depression sometimes may reflect pervasive inequities in societies and cultures that accord males more power and control. Circumstances that (a) fashion situations of unequality and dependency, (b) constrain and maintain women in relationships that are dismal, disappointing, and sometimes abusive, (c) expose women to many inescapable aversive encounters with their young children, yet (d) simultaneously hold caregivers responsible for molding the psyches and lives of their children, can indeed be demoralizing and depressing. Further work is needed to examine how multiple forces converge to be channeled through mothers in influencing child development. Particularly important here is the role of the father (or lack of it), his emotional well-being, his child-rearing practices, how he functions in the larger society, and how this is reflected in the family system. Work is also needed to determine why many depressed women are still able to function well as caregivers. Severity of depression appears to provide only a partial explanation.

## Undercontrol or Overcontrol?

In the NIMH study, the focus was more on problems of undercontrol (e.g., aggression, acting out) in children than problems of overcontrol (e.g., anxiety, withdrawal, depression). Both types of difficulties characterize children of depressed parents. Greater emphasis sometimes has been placed on internalizing problems, as these would appear to reflect a more direct pathway to later affective disorders. However, there are significant interdependencies and (causal) linkages between internalizing and externalizing patterns, and early aggression may be another pathway to later affective disturbances (e.g., Patterson, De Baryshe, & Ramsey, 1989; Pfeffer, 1986; Puig-Antich, 1982; Robbins, 1986; Serbin, Moskowitz, Schwartzman, & Ledingham, 1989; Zahn-Waxler, Iannotti, et al., 1990).

Goodman et al. (1991) have proposed that children of depressed mothers may alternate between being withdrawn or compliant (an over-controlled, internalizing pattern) and aggressive (an undercontrolled, externalizing pattern) in order to gain attention from an otherwise unavailable, inattentive, or self-absorbed mother. Research on interactions of infants with their depressed mothers does indicate that they become both withdrawn and distressed *and* more fussy (e.g., Field, 1984; Field et al., 1988; Tronick & Gianino, 1986). We offer an additional hypothesis. Not only may given children show both patterns, but also stress experienced in the parent–child interactions might exacerbate early differences in temperament. Shy, inhibited children may become even more withdrawn and avoidant if they have an anxious, depressed mother (Rosenbaum et al., 1988). Under similar conditions, more combative, assertive children may develop more intense, extreme aggression (Patterson, 1980). Both styles function to *control* or *regulate* the disorganization in children's environments and the asynchrony in interactions with caregivers. Thus, under conditions of intense stress, patterns of fight or flight may be activated differentially in different types of children.

To return to a central theme of this chapter, we propose that maladaptive patterns (both aggressive and avoidant) shown by children toward peers may evolve from failures to achieve coordinated reciprocal exchanges within the family setting during the early years of life. These behavior patterns, in turn, may lead to rejection, neglect, and unpopularity in the peer group. Direct and indirect parenting practices, as well as the global family climate and parental psychiatric problems, appear to contribute to the quality of children's peer relations early in development. As children become more isolated and/or become involved in deviant peer groups, the probability of developing serious and chronic behavior problems is likely to increase. The association between rejection by the normal peer group and antisocial behavior is well documented (also see Cantrell & Prinz, 1985; Dodge, Coie, & Brakke, 1982), as is the link between inadequate peer relations and the later development of psychopathology. Research on children with parents with serious emotional difficulties, like depression, provides one strategy for studying the etiology of child problem behaviors. Moreover, careful exploration of contributors to within-group variance may help to determine why only some children of depressed caregivers develop poor peer relations and/or serious psychiatric problems, as well as why different children develop different types of problems (e.g., conduct disorder or depression or both).

## Cognitive Biases and Attribution:
## One Possible Mediating Mechanism

Experimental studies of group formation indicate that aggressive behavior precedes peer rejection, rather than the reverse (Coie & Kupersmidt, 1983; Dodge, 1983). Aggressive children also tend to approach complex social situations with hostile attributional biases, that is, with expectations that their peers will have hostile intentions. Rejected children are also deficient in a number of social-cognitive skills, including peer group entry, perception of peer group norms, response to provocation, and interpretation of prosocial intentions (Dodge, 1986; Putallaz, 1983). Work by Goodman et al. (1991) illustrates how hostile attributional bias and related social-cognitive skills deficits may have origins in family dynamics. School-age children of depressed mothers were more likely than children of well mothers to misidentify nonhostile intentions as hostile (particularly prosocial intentions). In other research (Dodge, Murphy, & Buchsbaum, 1984), both rejected and neglected children were found to make hostile misattributions. This is consistent with the finding of Goodman et al. (1991), that children of depressed mothers who misattribute hostility were also both withdrawn and aggressive.

Goodman has hypothesized that misattributions of hostile intent to peers may reflect a generalized pattern of responding based on the nature of the home environment in which children of depressed mothers are reared. Such children may need to be alert to the possibility of hostility from their depressed mother that may occur unpredictably without warning. We hypothesize that there are multiple contributors to the increased likelihood of hostile attribution biases in children of depressed mothers. Such biases may be learned early and generalize from exposure to the conflict, anger, and discord that commonly characterize the marital relationships in these families. This explanation explicitly acknowledges the role of the father, as well as the relationship between spouses, in establishing suspicion, defensiveness, and anger in their children as they approach new social situations. That is, biases may reflect projection of children's own anger, resulting from feelings of resentment and a generalized sense of mistrust of others that occurs in a hostile and dysphoric family environment.

The tendency for children of depressed caregivers to misattribute *prosocial* intentions as hostile, that is, to misinterpret the kindness or benevolence of others as malevolent, is particularly intriguing. Early disturbances in family dynamics and relationship formation may influence both children's understanding and expressions of constructive and destructive behavior patterns. Extreme distress in the caregiver may lead to compliance and reduction of aggression in the short term (Hops et al., 1987). Similarly, it may lead to empathic overarousal, feelings of responsibility, and attempts to repair interactions by young children. This may sometimes create ambivalence, anger, alternation between overinvolvement and avoidance of others' needs, and lead, more generally, to distorted perceptions of circumstances of conflict and distress (Zahn-Waxler & Kochanska, 1990). When parents argue frequently, children as young as 2 years show a complex mixture of anger and distress, and they also try to intervene to stop the fight or comfort the perceived victim (Cummings, Zahn-Waxler, & Radke-Yarrow, 1981). When ministrations to the child's needs occur within a broader family climate of parental distress and disharmony, children are likely to become confused about the nature and meaning of others' cruel and kind behaviors. Distorted perceptions develop that may become reflected (a) in children's understanding of compassion and aggression, and (b) in their own prosocial and antisocial behavior patterns.

## Future Directions

An underlying assumption of this chapter is that early disturbances in environments where there is a depressed caregiver may result first in problems in parent–child relations, then in the child's peer relations, with implications for the development of psychopathology. Some caregivers do not develop depression until the child is older and friendship patterns have already become consolidated. For these children the influence of maternal depression on their social relations may differ in important ways. The preschool years represent a period of special risk as (a) mothers of young children are particularly vulnerable to depression, and (b) this is a critical period in development as children begin to expand their social worlds to include peers as well as family members. Further work is needed to explore how temperament and environment interact, as well as how different features of depressed parenting combine to created different outcomes for children.

The impoverished peer relations of many children of depressed caregivers suggests the need for early intervention programs that will facilitate children's developing social skills. Depressed mothers (or other family members) might be encouraged to seek out further play opportunities so that the children can develop the requisite skills for group interaction: This would allow children to develop experience engaging in mutually satisfying reciprocal exchanges, as alternatives to aggression and withdrawal. Child-care programs, play groups, and other recreational activities with other children could provide such opportunities. Parents could profit from specific information about ways to facilitate, monitor, and manage the child's environment during peer play. Such training might be accomplished by more sociable mothers whose active engagement in community life and activities has been shown to be associated with popularity and well-developed social skills in their children (Murray et al., 1983). For mothers whose depression is severe, their prevailing negative affect and self-absorption are likely to override efforts to create change. Physicians and pediatricians need to be informed about the ways in which depressed parenting interferes with the development of children's social skills, as they are in a unique position to communicate with the mothers (Zuckerman & Beardslee, 1987). These women often experience considerable guilt, helplessness, and inadequacy with regard both to their lives in general and to their families and children in particular. Thus, there are issues that would need to be broached with sensitivity. To ignore educating this population of caregivers (and others in a position to help them), however, helps to assure the continuation of problems in their offspring that then may become perpetuated across generations.

## REFERENCES

Achenbach, T., & Edelbrock, C. (1981). Behavioral problems and competencies reported by parents of normal and disturbed children aged 4 through 16. *Monographs of the Society for Research in Child Development, 46*(Serial No. 188).

Beardslee, W. R., Bemporad, J., Keller, M. B., & Klerman, G. (1983). Children of parents with major affective disorder: A review. *American Journal of Psychiatry, 140,* 825–832.

Belle, D. (1982). *Lives in stress: Women and depression.* Beverly Hills: Sage.

Billings, A. G., & Moos, R. (1985). Children of parents with unipolar depression: A controlled 1-year follow-up. *Journal of Abnormal Child Psychology, 14,* 149–166.

Blechman, E. A., McEnroe, M. J., Carella, E. T., & Audette, D. P. (1986). Childhood competence and depression. *Journal of Abnormal Child Psychology, 95,* 223–227.

Booth, C. L., Rose-Krasnor, L., & Rubin, K. H. (1989). *Preschool social skills and infant attachment security: Maternal and child effects.* Paper presented at the meeting of the Society for Research in Child Development, Kansas City, MO.

Cadoret, R. J. (1978). Evidence for genetic inheritance of primary affective disorder in adoptees. *American Journal of Psychiatry, 135,* 463–466.

Campbell, S. B. (1987). Parent-referred problem 3-year-olds: Developmental changes in symptoms. *Journal of Child Psychology and Psychiatry, 28*(6), 835–845.

Cantrell, V. L., & Prinz, R. J. (1985). Multiple predictors of rejected, neglected, and accepted children: Relation between sociometric status and behavioral characteristics. *Journal of Consulting and Clinical Psychology, 53,* 884–889.

Cicchetti, D., & Aber, J. L. (1986). Early precursors of later depression: An organizational perspective. In L. Lipsitt & C. Rovee-Collier (Eds.), *Advances in infancy* (pp. 87–137). Norwood, NJ: Ablex.

Coie, J. D., & Kupersmidt, J. P. (1983). A behavioral analysis of emerging social status in boys' groups. *Child Development, 54,* 1400–1416.

Crockenberg, S. (1990). Autonomy as competence in 2-year-olds: Maternal correlates of child compliance, noncompliance, and self-assertion. *Developmental Psychology, 26*(6), 961–971.

Cummings, E. M., Iannotti, R. J., & Zahn-Waxler, C. (1985). Influence of conflict between adults on the emotions and aggression of young children. *Developmental Psychology, 21,* 495–507.

Cummings, E. M., Zahn-Waxler, C., & Radke-Yarrow, M. (1981). Young children's responses to expressions of anger and affection by others in the family. *Child Development, 52,* 1274–1282.

Davenport, Y. B., Zahn-Waxler, C., Adland, M. L., & Mayfield, A. (1984). Early childrearing practices in families with a manic-depressive parent. *American Journal of Psychiatry, 141,* 230–235.

Denham, S., & Zahn-Waxler, C. (1989). *Social competence in young children's peer relations: Continuity and change from 2 to 5 years.* Paper presented at the meeting of the Society for Research in Child Development, Kansas City, MO.

Dodge, K. A. (1983). Behavioral antecedents of peer social status. *Child Development, 54,* 1386–1389.

Dodge, K. A. (1986). A social information processing model of social competence in children. In M. Perlmutter (Ed.), *Cognitive perspectives on children's social and behavioral development. The Minnesota symposium on child psychology, Vol. 18* (pp. 137–161). Hillsdale, NJ: Lawrence Erlbaum Associates.

Dodge, K. A. (1990). Nature versus nurture in childhood conduct disorder: It's time to ask a different question. *Developmental Psychology, 26*(5), 698–701.

Dodge, K. A., Coie, J. D., & Brakke, N. P. (1982). Behavior patterns of socially rejected and neglected preadolescents: The roles of social approach and aggression. *Journal of Abnormal Child Psychology, 10,* 389–410.

Dodge, K. A., Murphy, R. R., & Buchsbaum, K. (1984). The assessment of intention-cue, detection skills in children: Implications for developmental psychopathology. *Child Development, 55,* 163–173.

Downey, G., & Coyne, J. C. (1990). Children of depressed parents: An integrative review. *Psychological Bulletin, 108*(1), 50–76.

Emery, R. E. (1982). Interparental conflict and the children of discord and divorce. *Psychological Bulletin, 92,* 310–330.

Field, T. M. (1984). Early interactions between infants and their postpartum depressed mothers. *Infant Behavior and Development, 7,* 517–522.

Field, T., Healy, B., Goldstein, S., Perry, S., Bendell, D., Shamberg, S., Zimmerman, E., & Kuhn, G. (1988). Infants of depressed mothers show "depressed" behavior even with nondepressed adults. *Child Development, 59*(6), 1569–1579.

Forehand, R., & McCombs, A. (1988). Unraveling the antecedent-consequence conditions in maternal depression and adolescent functioning. *Behavioral Research and Therapy, 26*(5), 399–405.

Forehand, R., McCombs, A., & Brody, G. H. (1987). The relationship of parental depressive mood states to child functioning: An analysis by type of sample and area of child functioning. *Advances in Behavioral Research and Therapy, 9,* 1–20.

Goodman, S. H., Lynch, M. E., Brogan, D., & Fielding, B. (1991). *The development of social and emotional competence in children of depressed mothers.* Unpublished manuscript.

Goodman, S. H., & Brumley, H. E. (1990). Schizophrenia and depressed mothers: Relational deficits in parenting. *Developmental Psychology, 26*(1), 31–39.

Gotlib, I. H. (1982). Self-reinforcement and depression in interpersonal interaction: The role of performance level. *Journal of Abnormal Psychology, 91,* 3–13.

Gotlib, I. H., & Hooley, J. M. (1988). Depression and marital distress. In S. Duck (Ed.), *Handbook of personal relationships: Theory, research, and interventions* (pp. 543–570). Chichester: Wiley.

Grunebaum, H., Cohler, B., Kaufman, C., & Gallant, D. (1978). Children of depressed and schizophrenic mothers. *Child Psychiatry and Human Development, 8,* 219–225.

Hammen, C., Gordon, D., Burge, D., Adrian, C., Jaenicke, C. J., & Hirota, D. (1987). Maternal affective disorders, illness, and stress: Risk for children's psychopathology. *American Journal of Psychiatry, 144,* 736–741.

Hahn, J., & Zahn-Waxler, C. (1989). *Maternal depression and childrearing patterns as predictors of child behavior problems.* Unpublished manuscript.

Hartup, W. W. (1979). The social worlds of childhood. *American Psychologist, 34,* 944–950.

Hinchliffe, M., Hooper, D., & Roberts, F. J. (1978). *The melancholy marriage.* New York: Wiley.

Hodges, K., McKnew, D., Cytryn, L., & Stern, L. (1982). The Child Assessment Schedule (CAS) diagnostic interview: A report on reliability and validity. *Journal of American Academy of Child Psychiatry, 21,* 468–473.

Hokanson, J. E., Sacco, W. P., Blumberg, S. R., & Landrum, G. C. (1980). Interpersonal behavior of depressed individuals in a mixed-motive game. *Journal of Abnormal Psychology, 89,* 320–332.

Hops, H., Biglan, A., Sherman, L., Arthur, J., Friedman, L., & Osteen, V. (1987). Home observations of family interactions of depressed women. *Journal of Consulting and Clinical Psychology, 55,* 341–346.

Hops, H., Sherman, L., & Biglan, A. (in press). Maternal depression, marital discord, and children's behavior: A developmental prerspective. In G. R. Patterson (Ed.), *Depression and aggression: Two facets of family interaction.* Hillsdale, NJ: Lawrence Erlbaum Associates.

Jacobson, N., & Anderson, E. (1982). Interpersonal skill and depression in college students: An analysis of the timing of self-disclosures. *Behavior Therapy, 13,* 271–282.

Jaenicke, C., Hammen, C., Zupant, B., Hiroto, D., Gordon, D., Adrian, C., & Burger, D. (1987). Cognitive vulnerability in children at risk for depression. *Journal of Abnormal Child Psychology, 15*(4), 559–572.

Johnston, J. R., Gonzalez, R., & Campbell, L. (1987). Ongoing postdivorce conflict and child disturbance. *Journal of Abnormal Child Psychology, 15*(4), 493–509.

Jouriles, E. N., Pfeffner, L. J., & O'Leary, S. (1988). Marital conflict, parenting, and toddler conduct problems. *Journal of Abnormal Child Psychology, 16*(2), 197–206.

Kochanska, G., Kuczynski, L., & Maguire, M. (1989). Impact of diagnosed depression and self-reported mood on mothers' control strategies: A longitudinal study. *Journal of Abnormal Child Psychology, 17*(5), 493–511.

Kochanska, G., Kuczynski, L., Radke-Yarrow, M., & Welsh, J. D. (1987). Resolutions and control episodes between well and affectively ill mothers and their young child. *Journal of Abnormal Child Psychology, 15,* 441–456.

Ladd, G. W., & Golter, B. S. (1988). Parents' management of preschooler's peer relations: Is it related to children's social competence? *Developmental Psychology, 24,* 109–117.

Lewis, M., Feiring, C., McGuffog, C., & Jaskir, J. (1984). Predicting psychopathology in 6-year-olds from early social relations. *Child Development, 55,* 123–136.

Libet, J., & Lewinsohn, P. M. (1973). The concept of social skill with special reference to the behavior of depressed persons. *Journal of Consulting and Clinical Psychology, 40,* 304–312.

Lollis, S. P., & Ross, H. S. (1987, April). *Mothers' interventions in toddler–peer conflicts.* Presentation at the Society for Research in Child Development, Baltimore, MD.

Lyons-Ruth, K., Zoll, D., Connell, D., & Grunebaum, H. (1986). The depressed mother and her 1-year-old infant. Environment, interaction, attachment, and infant development. In E. Tronick & T. Field (Eds.), *Maternal depression and infant disturbance. New directions for child development, Vol. 34* (pp. 61–81). San Francisco: Jossey-Bass.

Lytton, H. (1990). Child and parent effects in boys' conduct disorder: A reinterpretation. *Developmental Psychology.*

Maccoby, E. E., & Martin, J. A. (1983). Socialization in the context of the family: Parent–child interaction. In P. H. Mussen (Ed.), *Handbook of child psychology, Vol. 4. Socialization, personality, and social development* (pp. 1–102). New York: Wiley.

MacDonald, K., & Parke, R. D. (1984). Bridging the gap: Parent–child play interaction and peer interactive competence. *Child Development, 55,* 1265–1277.

Murray, K., Webb, S., & Andrews, D. (1983, April). *The relationship between child and parental social competence.* Presentation at the Society for Research in Child Development, Detroit, MI.

Neale, J. M., & Weintraub, S. (1975). Children vulnerable to psychopathology: The Stoney Brook high-risk project. *Journal of Abnormal Child Psychology, 3,* 95–103.

Orvaschel, H., Weissman, M. M., & Kidd, K. (1980). Children and depression. The children of depressed parents; the childhood of depressed patients; depression in children. *Journal of Affective Disorders, 3,* 1–16.

Panaccione, V. F., & Wahler, R. G. (1986). Child behavior, maternal depression, and social coercion as factors in the quality of child care. *Journal of Abnormal Child Psychology, 14*(2), 263–278.

Parke, R. D., & Bhavnagri, N. P. (1989). Parents as managers of children's peer relationships. In D. Belle (Ed.), *Children's social networks and social supports* (pp. 241–259). New York: Wiley.

Patterson, G. (1980). Mothers: The unacknowledged victims. *Monographs of the Society for Research in Child Development, 45*(5, Serial No. 186).

Patterson, G. R., De Baryshe, B. D., & Ramsey, E. (1989). A developmental perspective on antisocial behavior. *American Psychologist, 44*(2), 329–335.

Pettit, G. S., & Bates, J. E. (1989). Family interaction patterns and children's behavior problems from infancy to 4 years. *Developmental Psychology, 25*(3), 413–420.

Pettit, G. S., Dodge, K. A., & Brown, M. M. (1988). Early family experience, social problem solving patterns, and children's social competence. *Child Development, 59,* 107–120.

Pfeffer, C. R. (1986). *The suicidal child.* New York: Guilford Press.

Piaget, J. (1965). *The moral judgment of the child.* Glencoe, IL: Free Press. (Original work published 1932)

Puig-Antich, J. (1982). Major depression and conduct disorder in prepuberty. *Journal of the American Academy of Child Psychiatry, 21,* 118–128.

Putallaz, M. (1983). Predicting children's sociometric status from their behavior. *Child Development, 54,* 1417–1426.

Putallaz, M. (1987). Maternal behavior and children's sociometric status. *Child Development, 58,* 324–340.

Radke-Yarrow, M., Belmont, B., Nottelmann, E., & Bottomly, L. (in press). Young children's self-conceptions: Origins in the natural discourse of depressed and normal mothers and their children. In D. Cicchetti & M. Beeghly (Eds.), *The self in transition: Infancy to childhood.* Chicago: University of Chicago Press.

Radke-Yarrow, M., Cummings, E. M., Kuczynski, L., & Chapman, M. (1985). Patterns of attachment in 2- and 3-year-olds in normal families and families with parental depression. *Child Development, 56,* 884–893.

Radke-Yarrow, M., & Kuczynski, L. (1983). Conceptions of environment in childrearing interactions. In D. Magnusson & V. L. Allen (Eds.), *Human development: An interactional perspective* (pp. 57–74). New York: Academic Press.

Radke-Yarrow, M., & Nottelmann, E. (1989). Parent–child similarities and differences: Affective development in children of well and depressed mothers. In S. Landesman (Chair), *Parent–child similarities and differences: A contextual perspective.* Symposium conducted at the meeting of the Society for Research in Child Development, Kansas City, MO.

Radke-Yarrow, M., Richters, J., & Wilson, W. E. (1988). Child development in a network of relationships. In R. Hinde & J. Stevenson-Hinde (Eds.), *Relationships within families: Mutual influences* (pp. 48–67). Oxford: Clarendon Press.

Robbins, L. N. (1986). The consequences of conduct disorder in girls. In D. Olweus, J. Block, & M. Radke-Yarrow (Eds.), *Development of antisocial and prosocial behavior: Research, theories and issues* (pp. 385–414). New York: Academic Press.

Roff, M., & Ricks, D. F. (1970). *Life history research in psychopathology, Vol. 1.* Minneapolis: University of Minnesota Press.

Rosenbaum, J. F., Biederman, J., Gersten, M., Hirshfeld, D. R., Memenger, S. R., Herman, J. B., Kagan, J., Reznick, S., Snidman, N. (1988). Behavioral inhibition in children of parents with panic disorder and agoraphobia. *Archives of General Psychiatry, 45*(5), 463–470.

Rubin, Z., & Sloman, J. (1984). How parents influence their children's friendships. In M. Lewis (Ed.), *Beyond the dyad* (pp. 223–250). New York: Plenum.

Sameroff, A. J., & Chandler, M. (1975). Reproductive risk and the continuum of caretaking casualty. In F. D. Horowitz (Ed.), *Review of child development research* (Vol. 4, pp. 187–244). Chicago: University of Chicago Press.

Seligman, M. E. P., Peterson, C., Kaslow, N., Tanenbaum, R., Alloy, L., & Abramson, L. (1984). Attributional style and depressive symptoms among children. *Journal of Abnormal Psychology, 93*(2), 235–238.

Serbin, L. A., Moskowitz, D. S., Schwartzman, A. E., & Ledingham, J. E. (1989). Aggressive, withdrawn, and aggressive/withdrawn children in adolescence: Into the next generation. In D. Peplar & K. Rubin (Eds.), *The development and treatment of childhood aggression* (pp. 55–70). Hillsdale, NJ: Lawrence Erlbaum Associates.

Spitzer, R. L., & Endicott, J. (1979). *Schedule for Affective Disorders and Schizophrenia—Lifetime version* (3rd ed.). New York: New York State Psychiatric Institute, Biometrics Research.

Susman, E. J., Trickett, P. K., Iannotti, R. J., Hollenbeck, B. E., & Zahn-Waxler, C. (1985). Childrearing patterns in depressed, abusive, and normal mothers. *American Journal of Orthopsychiatry, 55*(2), 237–251.

Trevarthen, C. (1989). Origins and directions for the concept of infant intersubjectivity. *Society for Research in Child Development Newsletter, Autumn*, pp. 1–4.

Tronick, E. Z., & Gianino, A. F. (1986). The transmission of maternal disturbance in the infant. In E. Z. Tronick & T. M. Field (Eds.), *Maternal depression and infant disturbance* (pp. 5–12). San Francisco: Jossey-Bass.

Vandell, D. L., & Wilson, K. S. (1987). Infants' interactions with mother, sibling, and peer: Contrasts and relations between interaction systems. *Child Development, 58*, 176–186.

Van Lieshout, C. (1987). *Peer competence and mother–child and child–child interactions in 1-year-olds*. Paper presented at the Biennial Meeting of the International Society for the Study of Behavioral Development, Tokyo.

Wahler, R. G. (1990). Who's driving the interactions? A commentary on "child and parent effects in boys' conduct disorder." *Developmental Psychology, 26*(5), 702–704.

Waters, E., Wippman, J., & Sroufe, L. A. (1979). Attachment, positive affect, and competence in the peer group: Two studies in construct validation. *Child Development, 50*, 821–829.

Webster-Stratton, C., & Hammond, M. (1988). Maternal depression and its relationship to life stress, perceptions of child behavior problems, parenting behaviors, and conduct problems. *Journal of Abnormal Child Psychology, 16*(3), 299–315.

Weintraub, S., Neale, J. M., & Liebert, D. E. (1975). Teacher ratings of children vulnerable to psychopathology. *American Journal of Orthopsychiatry, 45*, 838–845.

Weintraub, S., Prinz, R., & Neale, J. M. (1978). Peer evaluations of the competence of children vulnerable to psychopathology. *Journal of Abnormal Child Psychology, 4*, 461–473.

Weissman, M. M., & Paykel, E. S. (1974). *The depressed woman*. Chicago: University of Chicago Press.

Zahn-Waxler, C., Chapman, M., & Cummings, E. M. (1984). Cognitive and social development in infants and toddlers with a bipolar parent. *Child Psychiatry and Human Development, 15*(2), 75–85.

Zahn-Waxler, C., Cummings, E. M., McKnew, D. H., & Radke-Yarrow, M. (1984). Altruism, aggression, and social interactions in young children with a manic-depressive parent. *Child Development, 55*, 112–122.

Zahn-Waxler, C., Iannotti, R. J., Cummings, E. M., & Denham, S. (1990). Antecedents of problem behaviors in children of depressed mothers. *Development and Psychopathology, 2*, 271–291.

Zahn-Waxler, C., & Kochanska, G. (1990). The origins of guilt. In R. Thompson (Ed.), *Nebraska Symposium on Motivation, Socioemotional Development (1988)* (pp. 183–258). Lincoln, NE: University of Nebraska Press.

Zahn-Waxler, C., Kochanska, G., Krupnick, J., & McKnew, D. (1990). Patterns of guilt in children of depressed and well mothers. *Developmental Psychology, 26*(1), 51–59.

Zahn-Waxler, C., Mayfield, A., Radke-Yarrow, M., McKnew, D., Cytryn, L., & Davenport, Y. (1988). A follow-up investigation of offspring of parents with bipolar disorder. *American Journal of Psychiatry, 145*(4), 506–509.

Zahn-Waxler, C., Ridgeway, D., Denham, S., Usher, B., & Cole, P. (in press). Pictures of infants' emotions: A task for assessing mothers' and young children's verbal communications about affect. In R. Emde, J. Osofsky, & P. Butterfield (Eds.), Parental perception of infant emotions. *Clinical Infant Report Series*.

Zuckerman, B. S., & Beardslee, W. R. (1987). Maternal depression: A concern for pediatricians. *Pediatrics, 79*(1), 110–117.

# CHAPTER TWELVE

# An Organizational Perspective on Peer Relations in Maltreated Children

Dante Cicchetti
Michael Lynch
Susan Shonk
Jody Todd Manly
*Mt. Hope Family Center*
*University of Rochester*

In this chapter, we illustrate how a family context of child maltreatment may adversely influence the development of children's peer relationships. The family provides the context out of which peer relationships can emerge. An optimal familial environment includes a positive developmental history in each parent's family of origin, a harmonious contemporaneous marital relationship, and nurturant, sensitive, and predictable parent–child interactions (Belsky & Pensky, 1988; Caspi & Elder, 1988; Easterbrooks & Emde, 1988; Engfer, 1988; Main, Kaplan, & Cassidy, 1985; Sroufe & Fleeson, 1986, 1988). These conditions maximize the probability that children in such families will form secure attachment relationships with one or both caregivers (Belsky & Vondra, 1989; Cicchetti, 1990; Sroufe & Fleeson, 1988). This security reduces fear in novel situations and allows children to feel comfortable in exploring the environment.

One result of this is likely to be increased contacts with peers. Parents also can arrange interactions with peers for their children, thus setting up a social network in which children can participate. Finally, secure family relations where parents are emotionally supportive can promote successful peer relationships by fostering individuation and positive self-esteem (see Hartup, 1983, for a review of these findings). As Sroufe (1979, 1983) suggested, coherent ego development appears to mediate the quality of adaptation across family and peer social systems. Elicker and Sroufe (this volume) discuss relationship competence as a developmental and organizational construct. The manner in which young children adjust to the developmentally significant aspects of their attachment relationship with primary caregivers influences the organization of their adaptations to the tasks of later childhood, specifically those tasks connected to competent peer relationships.

Maltreating families, on the other hand, provide a context for peer interaction that is less than optimal (Garbarino & Gilliam, 1980; Wolfe, 1987). There is strong support for the notion that there are differences in the developmental ecologies of maltreating homes. Whereas these differences include the expected heightened conflict, control, and punitive discipline techniques (Parke & Collmer, 1975; Trickett & Kuczynski, 1986; Wolfe, 1985), or perhaps greater importance are the differences in the emotional climate of the homes and of expectations for and satisfaction with the child. For maltreating families, a picture emerges of worried parents with little enjoyment of parenting and little satisfaction with and expressed affection for the child, of isolation from the wider community, and of lack of encouragement for the development of autonomy and independence in the child while, nonetheless, holding high standards of achievement for the child (Trickett, Aber, Carlson, & Cicchetti, 1991; Trickett & Susman, 1988). These types of parental attitudes are likely to inhibit the development of competent peer relationships.

In a related vein, Belsky (1984; Belsky & Vondra, 1989) has proposed a process model of the determinants of parenting. Belsky stated that parental functioning is multiply determined by the personal psychological resources of parents, contextual sources of stress and support, and characteristics of the child. From existing research, we know that maltreating parents tend to have few psychological resources, higher rates of emotional disturbance (Cicchetti & Carlson, 1989; Wolfe, 1985), and that they tend to have limited sources of social support while often experiencing economic stress (Garbarino & Gilliam, 1980; Pelton, 1978; Wolfe, 1985, 1987). To the extent that maltreated children are behaviorally and emotionally difficult (even if such problems are largely the result of maltreatment per se), maltreated children themselves may contribute to the further breakdown of parental functioning (Cicchetti & Rizley, 1981). Based on the predictions of Belsky's model, the presence of each of these negative factors in maltreating families would exacerbate the probability of overall poor parenting. It is this poor parenting that most likely leads to difficulty in maltreated children's attachment relationships, with subsequent difficulties in peer relationships being mediated by faulty working models of attachment figures and of the self. In addition, children in maltreating families tend to experience a family history characterized by insecurity, fear, social isolation, and interpersonal loss (Carlson, Cicchetti, Barnett, & Braunwald, 1989b). Thus maltreated children may approach the world of peers with a basic mistrust. An assimilation of parental attitudes such as these are likely to inhibit the development of competent peer relationships. The patterns of maladaptation and incompetence that begin in the parent–child relationship may carry on to children's relationships with their peers.

Despite the disadvantages that characterize the lives of maltreated children, peer relationships and friendships may play an especially important role in promoting positive adaptation for maltreated children. In developmental research on normal populations, peer relationships have been found to exert significant influences throughout the lifespan. Many developmentally salient issues of social and emotional development are facilitated by children being introduced to the social world of peers (Hartup, 1983). Hartup (1983) discussed the processes of reinforcement, modeling, and conformity by which peers exert socializing influences on each other. Specific domains that have been examined for peer influences include the socialization of aggression, gender-typing, and the internalization of social standards.

The acquisition of social skills and the development of social competence occur through interactions with peers and friends (Dodge, 1983; Hartup, 1983). Specific skills and competencies that are acquired include strategies for peer group entry, playing, cooperation, problem solving, altruism, intimacy, and the expression and regulation of affect (Dodge, 1983; Hartup, 1986; Rieder & Cicchetti, 1989; Rubin, LeMare, & Lollis, 1990). Howes (1983) has suggested that social skills develop within the context of stable friendships. Thus it has been found that children with no friends or who have lost friends are less socially competent with peers (Howes, 1988).

Friendships, in particular, may be important for emotional development. Hartup (1983) suggested that involvement with peers is associated with "emotional security and an active orientation toward the environment" (p. 164). It is possible that children's stable, more intimate friendships may be serving as forms of emotional attachments (Ainsworth, 1989; Howes, 1988; see also Freud & Dann, 1951). There is some evidence that children experience separation distress upon losing a reciprocal friend (Field, 1984; Howes, 1988). Within the emotional climate of these close friendships, the regulation and expression of affect are important issues for children to manage.

It is believed that poor social skills and low popularity with peers put children at risk for later negative developmental outcomes. Poor peer relationships in childhood have been associated with juvenile delinquency and other types of behavior disorders (Hartup, 1983; James & Hesselbrock, 1978; Kohlberg, LaCrosse, & Ricks, 1972; Parker & Asher, 1987; Robins, 1966; Roff, Sells, & Golden, 1972; Rutter & Giller, 1983). One landmark study by Cowen and his colleagues (Cowen, Pederson, Babigian, Izzo, & Trost, 1973) demonstrates that the best predictor of mental health status in late adolescence was peer ratings from 11 years earlier. Recently researchers have concluded that childhood aggression and peer rejection are relatively stable and are good predictors of a number of negative outcomes including school dropout, criminality, delinquency, and psychological disturbance in adolescence and adulthood (Parker & Asher, 1987; Rubin & Mills, 1988; Rubin & Ross, 1988).

Of central importance, though, for the study of maltreated children's peer relationships is the view that family relationships and peer relationships interact "synergistically," as Hartup put it (1983). Both the comparative and human primate attachment literatures are filled with studies that show the links between parent–child and peer–peer relationships (cf. Arling & Harlow, 1967; Hartup, 1983). The primary findings are that positive, secure family relationships are associated with adaptive, competent peer relationships, whereas atypical, insecure family relationships are associated with less competent and sometimes maladaptive peer relationships (Sroufe, 1983; Sroufe & Fleeson, 1986; Troy & Sroufe, 1987). These latter findings are directly relevant for the study of maltreated children.

## Developmental Psychopathology

The discipline of developmental psychopathology can assist us in our investigation of maltreated children's peer relationships. The field of developmental psychopathology has been built upon the assumption that a developmental approach can be applied to any unit of behavior or domain of inquiry and to all populations, whether they are normal or atypical (Werner, 1948; see also Cicchetti, 1990; Kaplan, 1966, 1983). Researchers and theoreticians in this discipline emphasize that we can learn more about normal functioning by studying how developmental pathways go astray and become pathological, and, likewise, that we can learn more about pathology by understanding normal developmental pathways and trajectories (Cicchetti, 1984; Kaplan, 1966; Rutter, 1986). The field of developmental psychopathology takes a multidisciplinary perspective, suggesting that multiple domains of development be studied, including perceptual, cognitive, socioemotional, linguistic-representational, and biological processes (Achenbach, 1990; Cicchetti, 1984, 1989, 1990; Rutter & Garmezy, 1983). Concomitant with this perspective has been the acceptance of the view that a variety of factors play a role in the etiology, course, and sequelae of maladaptive and pathological development.

Accordingly, any consideration of atypical patterns of development must take into account the unique characteristics of the child, his or her age and stage–level of functioning, the experiences to which he or she has been exposed, and the stability of environmental conditions. Additionally, the characteristics of the caregiving environment, the compatibility of the child–caregiver dyad, the continuity of adaptive or maladaptive behavioral patterns, and the advances or lags in different behavioral and biological systems must be considered. This confluence of factors can be brought to bear upon the study of the nature and development of maltreated children's peer relationships.

## Organizational Perspective on Peer Relations

According to the organizational approach, development may be conceived as a series of qualitative reorganizations, among and within behavioral and biological systems, which take place by means of differentiation and hierarchical integration (Cicchetti & Schneider-Rosen, 1986). This orthogenetic principle (Werner, 1948) can explain the individual's continuous adaptation to the environment and how integrity of function may be maintained in the face of change. Continuity in functioning can be maintained via hierarchical integration despite rapid constitutional changes and biobehavioral shifts (Sackett, Sameroff, Cairns, & Suomi, 1981; Sroufe, 1979). Thus as Elicker and Sroufe (this volume) point out, we would predict continuity in relationship competence even though we do not expect to see behavioral continuity from parent–child interaction to peer interaction (see also Sroufe & Fleeson, 1988).

Normal development is defined in terms of a series of interlocking socioemotional, cognitive, social–cognitive, and representational competencies. Competence at one period of development, which tends to make the individual broadly adapted to his or her environment, prepares the way for the formation of competence at the next (Sroufe & Rutter, 1984). For example, the ability to form an emotional bond with a caretaker during infancy and the acquisition of symbolic and representational cognitive capacities may be among the prerequisite competencies for later social interaction skills with peers (Brownell, 1986; Howes, 1988; Sroufe, 1983). Social perspective taking and efficient information processing also may be among the skills required for competent peer interaction (Barahal, Waterman, & Martin, 1981; Dodge, 1986; Selman, 1976, 1980). Normal development, then, is marked by the integration of earlier competencies into later modes of functioning. It follows then that early adaptation tends to promote later adaptation and integration (cf. Erikson, 1950).

Pathological development, in contrast, may be conceived of as a lack of integration of the socioemotional, cognitive, social–cognitive, and representational competencies that are important to achieving adapta-

tion at a particular developmental level, or as an integration of pathological structures (Cicchetti & Schneider-Rosen, 1986; Kaplan, 1966; Sroufe,
1979). Because early structures often are incorporated into later structures, an early deviation or disturbance in functioning may ultimately lead
to the emergence of much larger future disturbances (Sroufe & Rutter,
1984). Thus, early negative consequences of child maltreatment—for example, impaired expression of affect and the formation of insecure attachment relationships with caretakers (Aber & Cicchetti, 1984)—may
be incorporated into the structures of maltreated children that are relevant to relating to peers. In this light, it becomes clear, too, how incompetent peer relationships may also be linked to later maladaptive and
pathological functioning.

The organizational perspective provides us with an excellent theoretical framework for conducting research on the role of the family and peer
relations in the socioemotional development of high-risk populations.
With its emphasis on the study of developing systems and on uncover-
ing the relation between normal and abnormal forms of ontogenesis, this
perspective allows us to investigate populations where differing patterns
of development may be expected as a consequence of the pervasive and
enduring influences that characterize the transaction between children
and their environment, as is the case with child maltreatment.

## The Role of Internal Working Models
## in Peer Relationships

Children's internal working models of attachment relationship figures provide an organizational construct around which we can come to a better
theoretical understanding of the processes that affect maltreated children's
peer relationships. Many researchers currently are proposing that internal working models may serve as mechanisms for the transmission of attachment across generations and relationships (Bretherton, 1985; Main
et al., 1985; Rutter, 1988; Sroufe & Fleeson, 1986, 1988). Working models
of specific relationships undoubtedly contain information that is unique
to that relationship; for example, expectations about how available the
other person is and how competent the self is in relation to that person.
But these specific models may also contribute information that is relevant to and part of more general models of relationships (Lynch, 1988).
It is possible, then, that internal representations of the parent–child relationship may provide the young child with general information and expectancies about other possible social partners and the self in relation
to those partners. If parents have been experienced (and are mentally
represented) as available and trustworthy, this information may be transmitted to a more general model of social relationships, with the result

being that children might expect others, namely peers, to be likewise available and trustworthy. Conversely, if children's experience of their relationship with their parents is represented in terms of unavailability and uncertainty, then children may have similar expectations for peer relationships.

Children's mental representations of themselves also may be relevant for the development of peer relationships. Ainsworth (1989), Bowlby (1969/1982), and Sroufe (1990) have stated that relationships are represented in terms of self and other; for each model of some "other" relationship figure, there is a corollary representation of the self. For example, if the mother is represented as available and caring, the child might have a model of himself as competent and worthy of love. Cummings and Cicchetti (1990) have shown that childrens' models of their depressed mothers may have a negative influence on their models of themselves. To the extent that these self models are stable and generalized to other relationship contexts, they could have an impact on the establishment of successful peer relationships.

Thus, the construct of internal working models may help us to understand better how the parent–child relationship environment may have an effect on children's peer relationships. Children's general models of self and other, derived in part from their working models of their attachment figures, may function to convey expectations of how other peers will act and react and how successful the self is likely to be in this broader social context.

## Models of Social Influence in Maltreated Children: Determinants of Peer Relations

In this section we discuss the social environments of maltreated children and how they may influence peer relationships. Mueller and Silverman (1989) proposed two models of influence on maltreated children's peer relationships. The first model is based on research conducted on the continuity of attachment and its sequelae. In addition to the role that children's internal working models of their attachment figures may have on children's peer relationships, there also has been considerable normative research conducted showing that the quality of attachment in infancy predicts to later social competence. Specifically, children who had secure attachments as infants tend, when toddlers, to engage in more reciprocal interactions, exhibit less negative and more positive affect with peers, show more empathy, have a more positive orientation, display greater sociability, employ a more flexible style to deal with negative peer interactions, use positive affect to initiate and sustain interactions, and receive higher ratings from both peers and teachers (LaFreniere & Sroufe,

1985; Lieberman, 1977; Pastor, 1981; Sroufe, 1983). In contrast, children with insecure attachments as infants tend to display the opposite pattern of social behaviors when they reach toddlerhood.

These findings from attachment research are relevant for the study of maltreated children because it has been demonstrated consistently that maltreated children are more likely to have insecure attachments than nonmaltreated children (Crittenden, 1988b; Egeland & Sroufe, 1981; Schneider-Rosen, Braunwald, Carlson, & Cicchetti, 1985). In normal children, specific patterns of insecurity have been related to different problems in peer relations. Children who had insecure–avoidant attachments as infants tended to exhibit more hostility and negative behavior toward peers and were more often rejected by them (LaFreniere & Sroufe, 1985; Sroufe, 1983). Children who had insecure–resistant attachments as infants tended to be more passive, withdrawn, and neglected by their peers (LaFreniere & Sroufe, 1985; Sroufe, 1983). A recent set of findings obtained in our laboratory is particularly intriguing in light of the potential link between attachment and later peer relationships. Carlson, Cicchetti, Barnett, and Braunwald (1989a) recently found that over 80% of maltreated infants could be classified as having "disorganized/disoriented" (Type D) attachments, a pattern in part characterized by approach/avoidance conflicts in the child upon reunion with the mother (Main & Solomon, 1986, 1990). Could this pattern be the groundwork for the approach/avoidance conflicts that George and Main (1979) observed in the peer relationships of their maltreated children?

The predominance of these disorganized/disoriented attachments in maltreated children may have direct implications for peer interaction. It is believed that the disorganization found in many maltreated children's attachments is related to both the inconsistent care and fear that are common elements of the experience of being maltreated (Carlson et al., 1989b; Cicchetti, Cummings, Greenberg, & Marvin, 1990). If fear is incorporated into children's more generalized models of relationship figures, it could lead to both "flight" and "fight" responses toward potential social partners. Specifically, it may contribute to maltreated children either avoiding peers or being aggressive toward them. Both of these types of response would be consistent with the alternate pathways toward peer rejection that Rubin's model predicts (Rubin & Lollis, 1988).

Maltreated children's sense of self may also have important influences on their ability to interact competently with peers. Bowlby (1969/1982) argued that internal models of self develop in parallel with working models of attachment figures. Knowing that maltreated children receive chronic insensitivity in their interactions with their parents (Aragona & Eyberg, 1981; Crittenden, 1981; Trickett & Susman, 1988) and that they are likely to experience insecure attachment relationships (Carlson et al.,

1989a; Crittenden, 1988b; Crittenden & Ainsworth, 1989; Egeland & Sroufe, 1981; Schneider-Rosen, et al., 1985), one would expect that maltreated children's sense of self might be impaired. Existing research supports this prediction with regard to maltreated children's self-concept and self-esteem.

In visual self-recognition experiments, maltreated children were more likely than comparison children to express either neutral or negative affect when viewing their rouge-marked images in the mirror (Schneider-Rosen & Cicchetti, 1984), possibly indicating an early precursor of a generalized low sense of self-worth. Research on variations in maltreated children's language performance has shown that maltreated toddlers talk less about themselves and produce less internal state language than do comparison toddlers (Cicchetti & Beeghly, 1987; Coster, Gersten, Beeghly, & Cicchetti, 1989). This impaired ability to talk about their own activities and feelings could be an obstacle for successful peer interaction. Finally, Vondra, Barnett, and Cicchetti (1989) found that young maltreated children (first to third grades) see themselves as being more competent and accepted than comparison children do, and also as more competent than their teachers believed them to be. It is possible that these young maltreated children's inflated self-perceptions may reflect unrealistic strategies to help them gain a sense of personal competence and control in home settings that are chaotic and uncontrollable. In fact, feelings of omnipotence and unrealistic idealization of the primary attachment figure may be an adaptive coping response to a sense of helplessness in one's environment (Cassidy, 1988; Costello, 1989). In contrast, Vondra and her colleagues found that older maltreated children (fourth to sixth grades) described themselves as less competent and accepted than comparison children did and in accordance with teacher ratings. It may be that these more mature children's ability to make social comparisons causes them to make more accurate appraisals of themselves than younger maltreated children. Feeling less competent and accepted in comparison to their peers may again impact on their ability to interact successfully with their peers.

Lewis (Lewis & Schaeffer, 1981) described an alternative model of social influence on peer relations that is based on social network theory. The main idea is that the availability of social contacts within a network of peers is helpful and necessary in order to gain relevant experience with peers and to develop interaction skills. Mueller and Silverman (1989) claimed that maltreating parents who do not facilitate secure attachments may also fail to provide their children with adequate experience with peers (cf. Lieberman, 1977). A second way in which maltreated children's relationship with their parents could influence their connection to a social network is through "generalized fear" (Mueller & Silverman, 1989).

A general fearfulness in maltreated children could lead them to shy away from contacts with peers, again possibly impeding them from acquiring necessary interactive skills (cf. Carlson et al., 1989b). Therefore, according to this social network model, it would be impaired social skills caused by a lack of contact and experience with peers that lead to disturbed peer relationships in maltreated children. Mueller and Silverman (1989) pointed out that maltreating parents tend to be isolated themselves and that this social isolation would in turn extend to their children (Garbarino & Gilliam, 1980; Wolfe, 1985, 1987).

The social environment of maltreated children is clearly a nonoptimal one. Maltreated children are likely to form an insecure attachment with their parent(s) and may, as well, have negative general working models of relationships and themselves in relationships. They may also have inadequate contact with a network of peers that inhibits the development of normal social skills. It should not be surprising, then, that initial research has found that maltreated children tend to have problematic peer relationships.

## Overview of Peer Relations in Maltreated Children

Only a handful of studies conducted have examined peer relations in maltreated children. To date, most studies on the peer relations of maltreated children have been conducted primarily with toddlers and preschoolers (Mueller & Silverman, 1989). The general findings from these studies suggest that maltreated toddlers evidence more disturbed patterns of interaction with peers than equivalent groups of nonmaltreated children. Maltreated children also tend to interact less with their peers and to exhibit less prosocial behavior than control children (Hoffman-Plotkin & Twentyman, 1984; Jacobson & Straker, 1982).

In their review of this literature, Mueller and Silverman (1989) identified two main themes that summarize the knowledge base on peer relations in maltreated children. One set of findings clearly indicates that maltreated children, especially physically abused children, tend to show heightened levels of physical and verbal aggression in their interactions with peers (George & Main, 1979; Herrenkohl & Herrenkohl, 1981; Hoffman-Plotkin & Twentyman, 1984). For example, Troy and Sroufe (1987) have reported how physically abused children may act in a verbally hostile fashion toward their nonmaltreated peer partners. More alarmingly, maltreated children were observed to respond with anger and aggression both to friendly overtures from their peers (Howes & Eldrege, 1985) and to signs of distress in other children (Howes & Espinosa, 1985; Main & George, 1985). In some instances, comforting and attacking behaviors were intermingled (Main & George, 1985). Howes and Espinosa

(1985), though, have found evidence that heightened aggressiveness and other problems with peers can be averted with treatment specifically aimed at these issues.

The second set of findings that Mueller and Silverman (1989) described is that there is a high degree of withdrawal from and avoidance of peer interactions in maltreated children when compared to nonmaltreated children for both toddlers and school-aged children (George & Main, 1979; Jacobson & Straker, 1982). Hoffman-Plotkin and Twentyman (1984) found that it was neglected children who tended to be more generally withdrawn from social interaction with peers. It appears that this social withdrawal may be an active strategy of avoidance on the part of maltreated children and not merely a passive orientation toward peer interaction (George & Main, 1979; Howes & Espinosa, 1985). In combination with the heightened aggressiveness found in some maltreated children, their social withdrawal may lead to increasing isolation and peer rejection.

This isolation and rejection may have serious developmental consequences for maltreated children. Rubin and his colleagues (Rubin, LeMare, & Lollis, 1990; Rubin & Lollis, 1988) proposed a model of peer rejection in which the active avoidance and increased aggression found in maltreated children could be part of two different developmental pathways, each with different possible sequelae. In one pathway, a combination of factors such as temperamental difficulty, insensitive parenting, and negative setting conditions lead to the development of hostile relationships. These hostile and possible aggressive relationships lead to rejection by the peer group. Being rejected may increase the child's hostility and eventually lead to the development of externalizing disorders. A second possible pathway to peer rejection begins with behavioral inhibition. These anxious, inhibited children react to the environment with increasing rates of withdrawal. Their deviance from age-appropriate social and emotional norms leads their peers to reject them. Such rejected children may respond with further withdrawal and the development of internalizing problems. These alternate developmental pathways provide a framework for understanding the peer interactions of maltreated children and their consequences. From the perspective of developmental psychopathology, it is possible to see that the experience of being maltreated can lead children along different pathways to peer rejection and isolation with the individual child's response to and integration of these issues leading to different developmental outcomes (cf. Aber, Allen, Carlson, & Cicchetti, 1989).

Howes and Espinosa (1985) found that maltreated children seem to have the most difficulty with unfamiliar peers. When placed in a new peer group, maltreated children demonstrated less social competence than nonmaltreated children. They exhibited fewer positive emotions, directed less behavior toward peers, initiated fewer interactions, and engaged in less complex play. This lack of social competence demonstrated with novel peers obviously would make it difficult for maltreated children to establish new peer relationships and friendship.

Overall, Mueller and Silverman (1989) concluded that the heightened aggressiveness, avoidance, and aberrant responses to both friendly overtures and distress in peers suggest that maltreated children are significantly unprepared to develop successful, positive peer relationships. Instead, contact with peers seems to elicit stressful reactions from maltreated children that decrease the likelihood of further interaction (Mueller & Silverman, 1989).

## Description of Our Research on the Peer Relations of Maltreated Children

According to the principles of the organizational perspective on development, in order to identify possible signs of incipient maladaptation or psychopathology in maltreated children, it is critical to assess their functioning across multiple contexts. Therefore, in designing our studies on the peer relations of maltreated children, we have incorporated this premise as a guiding principle. Because prior investigations have focused on examining the peer relations of maltreated children in controlled settings (e.g., research laboratories, day-care settings), we decided to obtain more naturalistic multicontextual assessments. In both school and daycamp environments, all measures were collected and coded by persons who were blind regarding experimental hypotheses and the maltreatment status of the children and adults. Children in all studies were between 5 and 12 years of age.

In addition, all of the maltreated children in our studies came from families that had been reported to the State Department of Social Services (DSS) or had voluntarily requested services for maltreatment issues. Each family had been screened in as an official maltreatment case under the criteria of the state law following a full investigation by the DSS. Each child's maltreatment status was further verified through an in-depth interview with the child's case worker. The interview was based on a checklist of incidents and behaviors indicative of the subtypes of maltreatment (e.g., physical abuse, sexual abuse, emotional mistreatment, neglect, etc.), developed and validated by Giovannoni and Becerra (1979). A similar checklist and description also was completed following a thorough investigation of the case records for each family. In addition, legal filings on the maltreatment group were checked at 6-month intervals in order to develop and validate a means of rating the severity and chronicity of the maltreatment.

These steps were taken in order to verify that all of our maltreating families had documented maltreatment histories. However, it is important to recognize that maltreatment is a heterogeneous problem: in symptom pattern or type of maltreatment, in etiology, in developmental sequelae, and in response to treatment (Cicchetti & Rizley, 1981). Because such children have different maltreatment experiences of varying severity at different developmental stages, they are expected to manifest diverse patterns of vulnerability (Cicchetti & Barnett, 1991; Cicchetti & Rizley, 1981). Additionally, subtypes of maltreatment, such as physical abuse and neglect, rarely occur in isolation because most maltreated children have experienced more than one subtype (Aber & Cicchetti, 1984; Cicchetti & Rizley, 1981; Erickson, Sroufe, & Egeland, 1985). Therefore, we were confronted with the decision of forcing a classification according to predominant subtype, or reducing our sample size drastically to include the small percentage of genuinely "pure" subtypes, which would not be representative of the majority of maltreated children. Instead we chose to obtain as much information as possible before making our maltreatment classifications on each case. As part of this process, we combined the detailed descriptions available from the DSS records with parental self-report measures. Although in this chapter we focus our analyses on maltreatment-comparison differences, in future reports we plan to incorporate a broad range of additional factors into our classification decision making including: frequency and chronicity of maltreatment; severity; developmental period(s) during which maltreatment occurred; differences in perpetrators; and nature of separation from caretakers, such as foster placements. Before these more fine-grained analyses are made, we believe it is necessary to determine what impact the experience of maltreatment has on child development above and beyond demographic characteristics such as socioeconomic status or life stressors.

Children from the lower socioeconomic strata were selected as the comparison group after a careful review of DSS reports on the demographic characteristics of families receiving preventive/protective services. We determined that children from families receiving Aid to Families with Dependent Children (AFDC) would constitute the best possible comparison group in a study of the developmental sequelae of child maltreatment because their families shared so many demographic features with the population of families of maltreated children served by the DSS (for instance, low parental education and low socioeconomic status, limited financial resources, and consequent dependency on public programs for basic income as well as health and social services, higher proportion of single-parent families, etc.). Therefore, over four fifths of the comparisons were receiving AFDC. Comprehensive demographic data were collected on all participating children and their families to insure that the maltreatment group and the comparison group were both representative of the service populations from which they were drawn and were comparable to each other in regard to major demographic characteristics. Clearly, both our maltreating and comparison families experience numerous socioeconomic stressors. However, great care was taken to define an appropriate comparison group to address questions concerning the effects of maltreatment over and above those effects attributable to risk factors associated with lower class status and welfare dependency.

Comparison families were recruited primarily through advertisements posted in local offices of the state Department of Public Welfare, and in neighborhood stores and laundromats. We also used door-to-door recruiting in low-income neighborhoods because we believe that personal contact is among the best means of outreach for these families who are often difficult to engage. The parents of all comparison families were screened by phone and later interviewed to check that the family had not been reported to the state as maltreating. Moreover, the DSS child abuse register was assessed to verify that none of the comparison families had ever been reported as maltreating. This registry was monitored at 6-month intervals in efforts to insure that none of the comparison families had been legally identified as maltreating during this interim period. All maltreating and comparison families participated in our research voluntarily and were financially reimbursed for their time.

### Results of Our Summer Daycamp and School Studies on Peer Relations

Our peer assessments were conducted in two principal settings: at summer camp and at school. We present the findings from our studies in these contexts in the following sections.

*Camp.*    In order to assess social interaction among peers in a naturalistic setting, we designed a summer daycamp program for children between the ages of 5 and 12. By employing a naturalistic yet structured environment where we can observe peer relationships being formed and study social dynamics within peer groups, we believe we have added an important dimension to the study of the peer relations of maltreated and nonmaltreated children.

The design of our camp proved to be optimal for studying peer relations for the following reasons:

1. The daycamp is a natural and ecologically valid setting in which to study and to observe the peer relations of maltreated children.

2. The continuity of interactions among children that are possible in a full week of camp are far superior to the sporadic interactions that would occur in a laboratory setting.

3. In a setting in which many children are present, affiliations will be more natural and intricate.

4. The camp setting allows for the provision of a wide range of activities, making the experience more fun for the children than laboratory interactions could possibly be, as well as increasing the range of assessments that are possible.

5. In the laboratory, one child's absence would make it virtually impossible to conduct validly the structured research measures. Because a greater number of children are present in the camp, the absence of a few children on a given weekday will not detract as greatly from the overall research protocol. Because of this enjoyable format, the camp setting maximizes attendance and participation in a population that is difficult to recruit and maintain (see Cicchetti & Todd Manly, 1990).

6. The camp setting provides an intense and comprehensive environment that allows for valid assessment of children's social adaptation using Q-sort and other counselor- and peer-nomination rating techniques.

The camp was designed so that each child belonged to a group of eight children of his or her own age and gender. The groups were equally divided into maltreated and nonmaltreated children, none of whom had known each other prior to attending the daycamp. Each group was staffed by three counselors, in order to provide considerable attention and support for each child, as well as to minimize the acting out that often occurs in this population (Aber & Cicchetti, 1984). The children attended a 1-week session during which they participated in a variety of activities. Data on peer relations was collected through interviews, videotaped structured and unstructured situations, and daily and weekly counselor ratings. In this chapter, we report the results of some of our self-report, interview, and peer and counselor ratings of the peer relations of maltreated children.

***Counselor and Peer Assessments.*** In our first camp, conducted over a 2-year period at Harvard University, 137 children attended (for a complete description of the Harvard camp, see Kaufman & Cicchetti, 1989). Half of the children had a history of maltreatment and the other children were matched low-income comparison children. The measures that were administered to the children during camp included California

Child Q-Sort ratings (Block & Block, 1969), counselor behavior ratings (Wright, 1983), and a peer sociometric interview (Coie & Dodge,
1983).

The California Child Q-Sort was completed by the camp counselors,
who had gotten to know the children in a variety of situations over the
course of their week-long session. The Q-sort method (Block, 1961; Block
& Block, 1980) is an ipsative procedure whereby scores are assigned to
100 personality or behavioral descriptive items by placing them in
categories ranging from the most characteristic to the most uncharacteris-
tic of the child. Among the advantages of utilizing the Q-sort with teachers
are that raters are unaware of the dimensions that will be derived from
their ratings and it helps to counter a social desirability response bias by
having raters sort items into a fixed distribution according to stringent
criteria. These sorted descriptions created a profile of the child that could
then be compared with prototypical profiles along the dimension of self-
esteem (Waters, Noyes, Vaughn, & Ricks, 1985).

The behavior rating questionnaire was completed by counselors during one activity, either structured or unstructured, each day. This nine-
item questionnaire was used to assess social behavior along the dimensions of prosocial, aggressive, and withdrawn behavior. Items were rated on a seven-point scale ranging from not at all descriptive to highly
descriptive of a child during the period rated.

The peer nomination measure was administered individually to all
camp children. They were asked to name the two children in their group
whom they would like to play with most, and the two they would like
to play with least. In addition, they were asked to name a child in their
group who best fit five behavioral descriptions depicting: (a) a cooperative child, (b) a disruptive child, (c) a shy child, (d) a fighter, and (e) a
leader. The total number of nominations a child received in each category
was then calculated.

The data from each of three measures was then collapsed to form the
following variables: Self-Esteem (Q-sort), Prosocial, Aggressive, and Withdrawn Behavior (Behavior Ratings), Peer Prosocial-Leadership and Aggressive–Disruptive factors (Peer Nomination). A multivariate analysis of
variance using these measures revealed that maltreated children differed
significantly from comparison children on the aggregate dimension of
peer competence ($p < .05$).

Further examination of the aspects of peer relations that differentiated the two groups revealed that, according to counselor ratings of the
children's behavior, maltreated children were found to exhibit significantly less prosocial behavior, such as cooperation, consideration of
others, and interest in group activities ($p < .05$). Additionally, Kaufman
and Cicchetti (1989) reported that maltreated children in the Harvard
camp exhibited significantly more withdrawn behavior than comparison

children, according to counselor ratings ($p < .01$). However, there were no differences on peer ratings of prosocial behavior or shyness.

In the Harvard sample, maltreated children were comparably impaired on measures of self-esteem and peer relations. Maltreated children's views of themselves and their competence may make it difficult for them to initiate and maintain adaptive peer relations. Their negative expectations and poor quality internal working models of attachment figures and of themselves increase the likelihood of unsuccessful peer interactions, which then may further diminish their self-esteem.

No significant between-group differences were found in the behavioral ratings or in the peer ratings of aggression in the Harvard camp; however, within the maltreated group, children who experienced a combination of physical abuse, neglect, and emotional abuse were seen by peers as more disruptive and more likely to start fights than any other peers. Thus, the children who were subjected to the most severe maltreatment were the most aggressive of the maltreated sample.

Another interesting finding to emerge from the Harvard camp was that children who received the lowest self-esteem ratings were more likely to be from families who received welfare than children who received high self-esteem ratings. Although the sample was drawn from a low socioeconomic population, gradations of poverty affected the children's outcome, independent of the effect of maltreatment (see also Aber & Allen, 1987; Trickett et al., 1991).

Our second camp, run through the Mt. Hope Family Center, University of Rochester, was based on the design of the Harvard camp. During the 3 years in which the Mt. Hope camp has been held, more than 250 children have attended, and 70% of the children have been followed longitudinally. Consequently, we have had the opportunity to conduct both cross-sectional and longitudinal investigations. In this chapter, we report the findings of a subset of children from this sample. Although many of the same constructs from the Harvard camp were assessed at the Mt. Hope camp, additional measures were utilized. For example, in addition to the Waters et al. (1985) self-esteem rating, a social competence rating from the Q-sort also was derived. Additionally, items characterizing hostility and anxiety were extracted to create child mega-items analogous to the adult mega-items devised by Kobak and Sceery (1988). Using a slightly modified set of variables, the Harvard findings were replicated in the Mt. Hope camp, in that children from maltreating families were found to have poorer peer relations in multivariate analyses of counselor and peer ratings of social competence ($p < .03$). The combination of counselor behavior ratings, Q-sorts, and peer sociometric nominations accounted for 20% of the variance in maltreatment status. (The means and standard deviations of the variables from both camps may be found in Tables 12.1 and 12.2.) (See Manly & Cicchetti, 1989.)

TABE 12.1
Mean Differences in Maltreated and Comparison Groups
Harvard Camp

| Group | Maltreated Children | | | Comparison Children | | |
|---|---|---|---|---|---|---|
| Measure | Mean | SD | N | Mean | SD | N |
| Q-Sort: | | | | | | |
|   Self-esteem | .13 | .35 | 70 | .28 | .30** | 67 |
| Behavior Ratings: | | | | | | |
|   Prosocial | 113 | 22 | 46 | 122 | 21* | 38 |
|   Aggression | 45 | 27 | 46 | 42 | 30 | 38 |
|   Withdrawn | 51 | 30 | 46 | 35 | 24* | 38 |
| Peer Nomination: | | | | | | |
|   Leader | −.57 | 1.1 | 70 | −.53 | 1.0 | 67 |
|   Disruptive | −.51 | 1.3 | 70 | −.64 | 1.1 | 67 |

*$p < .05$
**$p < .01$

In univariate analyses, maltreated children were rated by counselors as having significantly lower social competence ($p < .02$) than comparison children. Counselors also viewed the maltreated children as being more hostile ($p < .01$) and having lower self-esteem ($p < .03$) than comparison children. Peers also rated the maltreated children differently than comparison children. Maltreated children were viewed as more disrup-

TABLE 12.2
Mean Differences in Maltreated and Comparison Groups
Mt. Hope Camp

| Group | Maltreated Children | | | Comparison Children | | |
|---|---|---|---|---|---|---|
| Measure | Mean | SD | N | Mean | SD | N |
| Q-Sort: | | | | | | |
|   Self-esteem | .09 | .35 | 69 | .24 | .30* | 42 |
|   Social Competence | .10 | .39 | 69 | .28 | .33* | 42 |
|   Hostility | 5.10 | 1.50 | 69 | 4.30 | 1.40** | 42 |
|   Anxiety | 4.70 | .91 | 69 | 4.60 | .75 | 42 |
| Behavior Ratings: | | | | | | |
|   Aggression | 50.00 | 7.30 | 69 | 48.00 | 6.50 | 43 |
|   Withdrawn | 50.00 | 6.90 | 69 | 50.00 | 6.60 | 43 |
| Peer Nomination: | | | | | | |
|   Leader | .71 | .90 | 66 | 1.26 | 1.20* | 39 |
|   Disruptive | 1.22 | 1.73 | 66 | 0.50 | 1.03** | 39 |
|   Starts Fights | 1.23 | 1.69 | 66 | 0.52 | 1.10** | 39 |
|   Cooperative | 1.00 | 1.20 | 66 | .91 | 1.10 | 39 |

*$p < .05$
**$p < .01$

tive ($p < .02$), more likely to start fights ($p < .03$), and less likely to be leaders ($p < .02$).

In the Mt. Hope camp, behavioral differences were not found in peers' ratings of cooperative behavior. However, in multiple regression analyses using the variables found in Table 12.2, peer ratings of cooperation and leadership uniquely predicted maltreatment status. Thus, peers were able to identify specific qualities of interaction that differentiated maltreated children in a way that counselor ratings did not. If, as these data indicate, maltreated children are deficient in prosocial qualities that are identifiable by their peers, they are likely to be at a disadvantage in establishing and maintaining successful peer interactions.

Although no significant differences were found in behavioral observations of aggression in either the Harvard or Mt. Hope samples, more global ratings of hostility obtained in the Mt. Hope camp demonstrated that children from maltreating families were perceived by counselors as being significantly more hostile than were comparison children. Additionally, peers rated maltreated children as more disruptive to group activities and more likely to start fights than comparison children. It is possible that both maltreated and low-income comparison children exhibit high levels of aggressive behavior, but that the maltreated children may be the initiators of the conflict and the other children respond in kind when provoked. Further analyses of the videotapes of group processes will be conducted to test this hypothesis.

In the Mt. Hope sample, no differences were found on withdrawn behaviors or on anxiety ratings by counselors. Differences on peer ratings of shyness also did not emerge in either sample. The lack of findings in withdrawn behaviors contrasts with the significant differences obtained in the Harvard sample.

Taken together, the findings from the two camps provide considerable support for the hypothesis that being reared in a maltreating family, an extreme on the continuum of family dysfunction, has a deleterious impact on these children's ability to develop adaptive relationships outside of the family context. During latency years, these problematic relationships are manifested in the difficulty children experience in developing appropriate peer skills, an important stage-salient development task (Cicchetti & Schneider-Rosen, 1986; Elicker & Sroufe, this volume; Sroufe, 1979). Maltreated children were viewed by both adults and peers as being less socially competent, and, therefore, these children are likely to have greater difficulty initiating and maintaining other important relationships, making it difficult for them to have their interpersonal needs met either within or outside the family. The process by which these interpersonal difficulties develops needs further examination; however, as we have described earlier, research has documented that attachment relationships and the self system also are impaired in maltreated children (see Cicchetti, Beeghly, Carlson, & Toth, 1990).

***Maltreated Children's Reports of Relatedness to Their Peers.***
Within our summer camp studies, we have been able to assess children's relatedness to their peers using an adapted version of a measure developed by Wellborn and Connell (1986). The measure is designed to determine the degree to which an individual's need for relatedness—one of the three primary needs according to Connell (1990)—is being met by self-system processes. The measure contains 17 self-report items and allows for the assessment of relationship quality along two continuous dimensions that are believed to tap the internal working models of relationship figures. The two dimensions, labeled *emotional quality* and *psychological proximity seeking,* have been demonstrated to yield configurations that are consistent with attachment theory and research. Specifically, reports of higher emotional quality in a relationship tend to coincide with reports of a lower need for psychological proximity seeking in both normative and special populations (Lynch, 1988; Lynch & Wellborn, 1989).

With our maltreated and demographically matched nonmaltreated children, we assessed, during camp, the children's relationships to three categories of peers: (a) their classmates from the just-finished school year, (b) their best friend, and (c) the children in their group at camp (Lynch & Cicchetti, 1991). The measure of relatedness was administered for each of these peer relationships to a subset of the children in camp ($N$ = 215; 115 maltreated, 100 comparison) between the ages of 7 and 13. Our data confirmed previous normative findings on children's peer relatedness. For all three sets of peer relationships, and for both maltreated and nonmaltreated children, reports of higher emotional quality were correlated with reports of a lower need for psychological proximity seeking. Thus children who feel emotionally positive and secure with their peers tend to feel satisfied with how psychologically close they are to their peers. However, children who report feeling less positive and secure with their peers tend to wish they were closer to them.

Our data indicate that both maltreated and nonmaltreated children seem to have models of their peer relationships that are specific to the particular relationship, yet which share some variance among them. Multivariate analyses of variance (MANOVAs) revealed that the children's relatedness scores were significantly different for the three specific peer relationships, yet there were also significant correlations among the scores. This speaks to the formation of global and specific internal working models of relationships (Lynch, 1988). Children seem to form both models of *specific* peer relationships as well as more *general* models of peer relationships that may be based on some sort of summary of specific models.

This finding is in agreement with the attachment literature, specifically with the fact that the classification of children's attachments with different caretakers can be discordant (Bretherton, 1985). What this implies is that children can have distinct models of different caretakers, and of the self in relation to them. One set of models may be positive and the other set may be negative. An important point to address is the relative salience of different working models, especially as they contribute to more general models. It is possible that a negative model of one important relationship (e.g., one's relationship with the primary caretaker) may be salient enough to cause an individual's more general models of relationships to be negative, despite other working models of specific relationships that are positive. If such is the case, there would be strong implications for maltreated children's relationships.

Simple *t* tests revealed no differences between maltreated and non-maltreated children on either dimension of relatedness for the three sets of peer relationships. An examination of more specific patterns of children's relatedness to their *mothers,* however, showed some interesting effects on peer relationships.

Recently, we have identified in normative and maltreating samples five prototypical *patterns* of children's relatedness to their mothers (Lynch & Wellborn, 1989). The five patterns—*optimal, enmeshed, deprived, disengaged,* and *confused*—are based on configurations of scores from the emotional quality and psychological proximity seeking dimension to relatedness to mother. A MANOVA revealed a strong overall effect of mother–child patterns of relatedness on children's relationships with their peers. Children's relationships with all three sets of peers tended to show patterns of relatedness that were similar to their relationship with their mother. This finding is a strong statement of the linkage between family and peer relationships. For example, children with optimal patterns of relatedness to their mothers, characterized by relatively high levels of positive emotion and relatively low levels of psychological proximity seeking, tended to have optimal patterns and configurations of relatedness to their peers. It may be the case that the children's pattern of relating with their mothers is influencing their relationship *with* and the working model *of* their peers.

Further examination of these prototypical patterns of relatedness to mothers helped us to identify some interesting effects of maltreatment status on children's relationships with their peers. For children whom we identified as having one of the five prototypical patterns of relatedness to their mothers, maltreated children wanted to be closer to both their best friend and the children in camp significantly *more* than nonmaltreated children did. The pattern for wanting to be closer to their class-mates was in the same direction, but did not reach significance. This trend of wanting greater psychological closeness to peers is particularly true for maltreated children who reported having the most negative patterns of relatedness to their mothers; that is, those with *deprived* (low on emo-tional quality with mother, but high on wanting more psychological close-ness to mother), *disengaged* (low on emotional quality and no desire for closeness), and *confused* (high on reported emotional quality, but also not satisfied with existing closeness) patterns of relatedness. Thus maltreated children who are experiencing the most negative relationships with their mothers appear to want greater psychological closeness to their peers. These findings are similar to recent findings showing that maltreat-ed children also want to be closer to their teachers than nonmaltreated children do (Lynch & Wellborn, 1989). It appears as if maltreated chil-dren—especially those with the most negative relationships with their mothers—may be yearning to be close to some other significant relation-ship figures, perhaps in order to compensate for not feeling close to their own mothers. Peer relationships may be one way in which they attempt to satisfy this need for connectedness. However, with their peer relation-ships tending to be unsuccessful, maltreated children may be unable to satisfy this need.

***School.*** The parent–child relationship and the child's working model of self are not the only self-system domains jeopardized by the care-giving attitudes and behaviors of maltreating parents. For example, research has shown that abusive parents are higher than comparison par-ents on achievement orientation, and are also higher on control and the use of verbal prohibition (Trickett & Susman, 1988). Similarly, these par-ents provided less verbal reasoning, were less intellectually oriented, and were more dissatisfied with their children. This pattern of caregiving is consistent with Baumrind's (1967, 1968) descriptions of the authoritari-an parent, which is linked with less competence and lower school achieve-ment among children. The combination of a controlling environment and high performance demands also has been associated with the acquisition of an extrinsic motivational orientation toward task performance (Koest-ner, Ryan, Bernieri, & Holt, 1984; Lepper, 1981), and is viewed as exert-ing a negative influence on children's classroom functioning (Harter, 1981; Ryan, Connell, & Deci, 1985).

Independent investigators operating under disparate theoretical orien-tations have found that maltreated children exhibit more dependency on their teachers (Egeland, Sroufe, & Erickson, 1983), score lower on tests measuring cognitive maturity (Barahal, et al., 1981), and are rated by both parents and teachers as less ready to learn in school (Hoffman-Plotkin & Twentyman, 1984). To compound this negative transaction, the behavior problems that maltreated children manifest in school (Egeland et al., 1983) may lead to overcontrolling teaching styles that have been found to undermine an intrinsic motivational orientation in school (DeCharms, 1968; Deci, 1975). If this finding is confirmed with maltreated children, the risk that they will adopt an extrinsically motivated orientation towards their academic work will be exacerbated.

Clearly, the maltreated child is at multiple risk for poor school functioning, due to deficits in the self system that include low self-esteem, impaired perceptions of competence, and an extrinsic motivational orientation. As noted earlier, children's expectations about adult availability and responsivity are thought to develop in infancy and toddlerhood through interactions between children and their primary attachment figures. These expectations concerning the availability and predictability of adults are perpetuated through internal representational models of the self-in-relationships, which, in turn, may influence both the construction of new relationships and the ability to explore and to cope with the demands of unfamiliar and stressful situations such as the adaptation to school (Aber et al., 1989).

Studies of maltreated infants and toddlers (George & Main, 1979), and of maltreated preschool and early school-age children (Egeland et al., 1983) corroborate these hypotheses by suggesting the presence of impairments in maltreated children's relations with novel adults. As previously noted, in infancy and toddlerhood, physically abused children appear to experience greater approach/avoidance conflicts in relation to novel adults (Carlson et al., 1989a; Crittenden, 1988b; George & Main, 1979). In the preschool and early school-age years, maltreated children are especially dependent upon the social reinforcement of novel adults (Aber & Allen, 1987; Erickson, Sroufe, & Egeland, 1985). These findings underscore the possibility that impairments in maltreated children's relations with novel adults may affect their ability to negotiate entry into nursery school, kindergarten, and elementary school. Child characteristics such as excessive dependency on, wariness of, or avoidance of novel adults may interfere with a child's effective entry into school. Not surprisingly, these attributes are likely to exert a negative effect upon the formation of positive peer relations in the school setting.

To this end, the Mt. Hope Family Center began its longitudinal study on peer and academic competence in the Rochester city schools in the spring of 1987. All children assessed were between 6 and 12 years of age. The schools are a central setting for the negotiation of many stage-salient developmental issues for children. Teachers are able to provide valid assessments of children's functioning in social, emotional, and cognitive domains, given their professional training and their extensive interactions with the children at school. We are particularly interested in identifying the precursors of later maladaptation (e.g., conduct disorder, depression, substance abuse), which a disproportionate number of these children can be expected to manifest given the nature of their childrearing experiences. One domain of mastery that is salient for elementary school-aged children and which may predict subsequent dysfunction is social competence. Assessments of children's social competence, rated by teachers and by peers, have been shown to identify children accurately who are at risk for later maladaptive outcomes (e.g., Cowen, Pederson, Babigian, Izzo, & Trost, 1973).

Researchers are currently striving to move beyond simple descriptions of the incompetent child toward more precisely defining the processes underlying children's competent and incompetent functioning in social relationships. For example, Dodge and colleagues (Dodge & Murphy, 1984) have emphasized the need for identifying not only the socially incompetent child (i.e., the traditional approach), but also for delineating the specific social situations and tasks in which the incompetent behavior is manifest, and demarcating the situation-specific component skills deficits that underlie social incompetence in a particular child.

Theorists stress the importance of assessing social competence relative to the social context and the situational demands placed upon the child (e.g., Bandura, 1977). It is argued that socially competent and incompetent behaviors can be understood only as a response embedded within the child's social ecology, as contextual variables are thought likely to strongly influence the subsequently observed social behavior. Given such dependence on the social milieu, a child's relative competence or incompetence in his or her peer relationships may be better understood at the level of specific situations and skill deficits. Situation-specific analysis of social behaviors and the assessment of context-dependent skill deficits are critical to furthering our understanding of the aspects of social competence and incompetence that may differentiate groups of children at risk for maladaptive outcomes (Dodge et al., 1985). This approach also can be helpful in informing therapeutic interventions.

Therefore, a primary goal of our research in the schools has been to assess whether teachers rated maltreated children as showing more maladaptive/socially incompetent behavior than comparison children within the social environments of the school, classroom, and peer group. Further, if maltreated children are rated as less socially competent, on what dimensions of social competence and in what specific situations are these differences manifest? To address these questions, several measures of social competency were rated by the children's classroom teachers, including the *Taxonomy of Problematic Social Situations for Children* (TOPS) (Dodge et al., 1985), the *Children's Self-Efficacy for Peer Interaction Scale* (CSPI) (Wheeler & Ladd, 1982), the *Teacher's Checklist of Children's Peer Relationships* (TCCPR) (Richard & Dodge, 1982), and the *California Child Q-sort* ratings (Block & Block, 1969, 1980).

The TOPS provides teachers' ratings of children's social behavior in potentially conflictual situations with peers. Dodge and his colleagues (Dodge et al., 1985) empirically derived and subsequently evaluated this taxonomy of social situations that were identified by teachers as likely to be most problematic for elementary school-aged children (i.e., those most likely to lead to peer conflict). This measure allows us to go beyond merely identifying the socially incompetent child to a more detailed understanding of the specific social situations and the accompanying task that is difficult for the child with a delineation of the skills that are deficient. The teachers were asked to rate on a 1–5 Likert-type scale (1 = never to 5 = almost always) how much of a problem the specified situation is for the child and how likely he or she is to respond ineffectively or inappropriately in that situation.

Teachers also rated maltreated and comparison children on the 22-item CSPI (Wheeler & Ladd, 1982). On this measure of social behavior, teachers were asked to rate on a 1–4 scale (1 = hard to 4 = easy) the child's prosocial effectiveness in peer interactions based on their observations over the previous 3–4 months at school. The CSPI focuses on social self-efficacy, which is defined by Wheeler and Ladd as the "ability to enact prosocial, verbal persuasive skills in specific peer situations" (p. 796). The ability to influence the response of peers through verbal, socially appropriate means is argued by Wheeler and Ladd to be a potentially critical skill in gaining peer acceptance.

Whereas both the TOPS and the CSPI tap the competency of the child's social behavior, each addresses related yet distinct aspects of social competence. The TOPS focuses exclusively on situations that are potentially conflictual, and the CSPI depicts both conflictual social situations in which the goal of the child directly contradicts that of the peer (e.g., trying to persuade the peer to play a game that the peer does not like), and non-conflictual situations where there is no contradiction of goals between the child and his peer. The conflict/nonconflict situational distinction is grounded in Bandura's (1977) theory that self-efficacy is influenced by the context in which behavior is embedded, the skills demanded to effectively negotiate the interaction, and the perceived risk of the particular situation for the child in terms of negative outcomes. Wheeler and Ladd (1982) found that factor analyses supported the theoretical claim that the conflict/nonconflict dimension is one reacted to differentially by children in their interactions with peers.

The Teacher's Checklist of Children's Peer Relationships (TCCPR) is an 18-item measure that provides teachers' assessments of children's social relationships on such dimensions as popularity, peer acceptance, aggression, prosocial skills, and the general quality of the child's peer relationships all rated on 1–5 scales (1 = never true to 5 = almost always true).

The Q-sort descriptions of a particular child were then correlated with definitional sorts of constructs such as social competence, self-esteem, anxiety, and hostility to yield scores on these constructs for individual subjects.

Across these measures many significant differences between maltreated and nonmaltreated comparison children were found, highlighting the "at risk" status of maltreated children even in comparison to their lower socioeconomic agemates (Shonk & Cicchetti, 1989). Teachers consistently rated the 44 specified social situations on the TOPS as more problematic for maltreated than for comparison children, and the maltreated children as more likely to respond inappropriately in such situations. The comparison and maltreated groups significantly differed on the average score across all 44 TOPS items ($p < .001$). Standard deviations of the ratings within maltreated and comparison groups indicated that the variation in response was greater among the ratings of the maltreated group than among the controls.

Dodge et al. (1985) reported a six-factor solution for the 44-items of the TOPS. Utilizing these factor scores, multivariate and subsequent univariate analyses of variance were conducted to test for group differences. A marginally significant multivariate main effect of maltreatment status was found ($p < .08$), indicating that maltreated children were rated by teachers as generally less socially competent (i.e., more likely to respond inappropriately and ineffectively) in situations of peer conflict than were the comparison children. Significant univariate effects indicated that teachers rated social situations as significantly more problematic for maltreated as compared to control group children on five of the six factor scores (See Table 12.3). The largest difference in scores between the two groups was found for the factor score items depicting the child's response to provocation by peers. This is similar to the finding reported by Dodge et al. (1985) between socially rejected and adaptive children. Additionally, it is of interest that the only factor score that failed to differentiate the groups was the factor score tapping children's response to success.

Children's teacher-rated scores between the conflict and nonconflict dimensions of the CSPI were highly intercorrelated ($r = .67, p < .0001$). A marginally significant group difference was found for the average CSPI score across all items, with teachers of maltreated children tending to

TABLE 12.3
Teachers' Ratings of Children's Responses to Problematic Social Situations

| Factors[a] | Comparison[b] | Maltreated[c] | F | P's |
|---|---|---|---|---|
| Peer Group Entry | 2.54 | 2.92 | 8.29 | 0.004 |
| Peer Provocation | 2.95 | 3.39 | 9.18 | 0.003 |
| Response to Failure | 2.49 | 2.85 | 7.45 | 0.007 |
| Response to Success | 1.71 | 1.83 | 1.37 | 0.24 |
| Social Expectations | 2.00 | 2.26 | 7.64 | 0.006 |
| Teacher Expectations | 2.56 | 3.03 | 9.40 | 0.003 |

[a]The six factors were derived from Dodge, McClaskey, & Feldman (1985).
[b]The nonmaltreated, demographically matched comparison group means ($N = 92$).
[c]The maltreated group means ($N = 108$).

rate them as less socially effective ($p < .06$). A multivariate analysis of variance and subsequent univariates were conducted to test for significant group differences utilizing the average scores on the conflict and nonconflict dimensions. The multivariate main effect of status was not significant across the conflict and nonconflict dimensions. Although the average conflict item score failed to differentiate the maltreated and comparison groups, there was significant univariate main effect of status for the nonconflict average item score such that maltreated children were rated as significantly less socially competent at enacting persuasive verbal skills in nonconflictual situations with a peer ($p < .04$).

On the TCCPR, the *PEER RELATIONS* sum score failed to differentiate the maltreated and comparison groups. Additionally, maltreated and comparison children did not differ significantly on teacher-rated *AGGRESSION* sum scores. The lack of significant group differences on these dimensions may speak to the fact that both groups are at risk and above the median on rated relationship problems. Finally, maltreated children were rated by their teachers as possessing significantly less developed *PROSOCIAL SKILLS* in comparison to nonmaltreated controls ($p < .04$). This composite score includes understanding others' feelings, being aware of the effects of his or her behavior on others, and refraining from overimpulsive responding.

The results of univariate analyses of the Q-sort social competence score indicated that maltreated children were rated by teachers as significantly less socially competent than were their comparison, nonmaltreated agemates ($p < .02$). Q-sort correlations with the criteria sorts of self-esteem, hostility, and anxiety were also derived and indicated that maltreated children were rated by their teachers as having significantly lower self-esteem ($p < .01$), and as being significantly more anxious ($p < .005$) than comparison children. The Q-sort scores for hostility failed to discriminate maltreated and comparison children, similar to the lack of group differences in teachers' ratings of the children's overall level of aggression with peers. Again, this lack of significant findings may be indicative of the high-risk nature of the entire sample.

The contradictory pattern of group differences on $Q$-sorts of anxiety and hostility between camp and school is of interest. It may be the case that differences in the familiarity of the setting and of the demands placed on the children account for these differences. The camp setting is a relatively less-structured environment that may result in group differences in hostility versus the more structured setting of the classroom and its concomitant demands for performance on the child that may be more likely to produce group differences on aggregate dimensions of anxiety. These contradictory findings highlight the need for multiple assessments conducted across multiple contexts in order to afford a comprehensive understanding of children's functioning.

In summary, teachers' ratings of many aspects of social competence and personality functioning of maltreated and nonmaltreated comparison children provide empirical support for the longstanding hypotheses that early maltreatment experiences exert a significant, deleterious impact upon children's subsequent social adaptation and personality adjustment. On several levels of analysis, including social behaviors, social efficacy in conflict and nonconflict situations, quality of peer relationships, and personality and behavioral profiles, teachers evaluated maltreated children as significantly less competent in their social relationships, lower in self-esteem, and higher in anxiety than their comparison agemates. These findings support the causal chain that we have hypothesized from the caregiving environment to attachment and the subsequent effect of these factors on peer relations and adaptation outside of the home environment.

## Future Directions and Conclusions

One important direction for future research will be the development and validation of a nosology for classifying maltreatment experiences. As we previously mentioned, maltreatment encompasses a broad range of phenomena, which can have many different manifestations. Currently, however, there is no accepted system for classifying these diverse experiences. Each research group has its own methods, and the practices in legal and social work fields vary widely from state to state. As a result, the interpretation of research findings across laboratories and the assessment of the efficacy of treatment interventions is much more difficult. A comprehensive maltreatment classification system could provide researchers and professionals from different disciplines with a uniform method of assessing important information and communicating with one another. Such a system would enable investigators to determine the differential impact that a variety of maltreatment experiences has on different children at various points in their development. If a classification system was developed that could be implemented nationally, it would be extremely useful to researchers because it would enable them to be more standardized and uniform in making their maltreatment diagnoses. Moreover, the results of their studies could be compared more directly, leading to more clarity of interpretation across investigations. With better data and more information, it would then be possible to elucidate more clearly the processes by which maltreatment occurs and the differential consequences that various types of maltreatment exert on child development. Furthermore, more effective public policies and intervention strategies could be developed, implemented, and evaluated.

At the Mt. Hope Family Center, we have begun to develop a system for classifying DSS case records and official maltreatment reports (Cicchetti & Barnett, 1991). Our system involves classification along five dimensions: (a) subtypes; (b) severity; (c) frequency/chronicity; (d) developmental period(s) of occurrence; and (e) separations from caretakers. With regard to subtype, we have delineated five different subtypes of maltreatment: physical abuse, physical neglect, sexual abuse, emotional maltreatment, and moral/legal/educational maltreatment. We acknowledge that there can be considerable overlap between categories, and we are attempting to distinguish between subtypes while also identifying families in which multiple subtypes occur. Within each subtype of maltreatment, we have developed rating scales to address the severity of the maltreatment. The frequency and chronicity of the maltreatment is also an important variable because we expect that isolated or infrequent incidents of maltreatment could have a different impact on development than would a chronically maltreating environment. Another essential dimension in our nosology is the developmental period(s) during which the maltreatment occurred. Knowing the child's age and developmental stage provides important information for understanding not only the physical impact of the maltreatment, but also the psychological meaning for the child, the effect on the resolution of stage-salient developmental issues, and the manner in which the sequelae would be expressed (cf. Cicchetti, 1987). We also have assessed separations from caretakers, including foster placements, episodes of abandonment, residential treatment, and other separations, in order to identify their effect on children's attachment relationships and later adjustment.

We believe that these attachment relationships play an important role in later adjustment, particularly with peers. We suggested that children's representational models of parent–child relationships may affect their subsequent relationships with their peers. In particular, we believe that maltreated children's models of their attachment relationships may create a set of negative expectations—about how available and trustworthy others are and how competent and worthy the self is—that children bring with them to their relationships with their peers. These negative expectations would establish a maladaptive pattern of relating to peers that accounts for the typically poor peer relationships that maltreated children experience.

One would further expect that the *type* of maltreatment a child receives could have specific effects on that child's representational models and subsequent peer relationships. Crittenden has gathered some evidence that supports this claim (Crittenden, 1988a; Crittenden & Ainsworth, 1989). In her work investigating the relationships of maltreating and adequate families, she has found that families manifesting different forms of maltreatment exhibit correspondingly different distorted patterns of relationships and representational models of these relationships. Crittenden (1988a) proposed that physically abused children have representational models of relationships characterized by distrust, which causes them to behave in an inappropriately defensive or aggressive manner. Neglected children, on the other hand, have models defined by a lack of responsiveness from others and a lack of personal efficacy, which could lead them to put little effort into and withdraw from interpersonal relationships. Children who experience both abuse and neglect demonstrate both types of distortions in relationships, which may be manifested by a combination of acting-out behaviors and extreme inhibition and withdrawal. From Crittenden's data, one could generate hypotheses about the type of peer relationships specific maltreated children would have based on the representational models of their own maltreatment experience. For example, physically abused children may be overly aggressive with their peers, whereas neglected children may be withdrawn and isolated.

This type of hypothesis testing, however, is limited by our definition of maltreatment. Making predictions based on *type* of maltreatment is an initial attempt at specifying the possible sequelae of different forms of maltreatment. However, more accurate predictions can only be achieved by using a complete nosology of maltreatment that includes the important features that we discussed previously. Our future research should focus on how these different features of maltreatment influence, via representational models, maltreated children's peer relationships.

In this chapter, we have explored the effects of a history of maltreatment on the development of peer relations. By reporting multimodal assessments of child functioning obtained in daycamp and school settings, we discuss data that reveals impaired peer relations in children who have been maltreated. Of note is the fact that the maladaptive functioning of the maltreated children is a consistent finding that supersedes their membership in the lower socioeconomic strata.

Taken in tandem with our findings on the presence of insecure attachment relations and poor quality working models of the self in maltreated children, we are proposing a causal chain whereby these factors contribute to the development of impaired peer relations. Because the organizational perspective posits that unsuccessful negotiation of early stage salient tasks increases the likelihood of failure on subsequent issues (Cicchetti, 1987; Elicker & Sroufe, this volume), it is not surprising that the early familial histories of these children place them at heightened risk for difficulties throughout their lives (Cicchetti & Carlson, 1989). These findings have implications for future research, social policy, and intervention efforts directed toward reducing the plight of maltreated children.

From a research perspective, it is critical to conduct longitudinal assessments of the functioning of maltreated children that begin in toddlerhood (or as soon as the occurrence of maltreatment has been identified) and trace the negotiation of stage-salient issues throughout childhood and, optimally, into adolescence and adulthood. Experimental paradigms such as this will be necessary if the causal chain that we have hypothesized is to be verified. Equally important will be the identification of buffers that mitigate against the deleterious effects of maltreatment. In fact, positive peer relations may serve as a coping mechanism for promoting future adaptive functioning. However, the continued influence of a stressful family environment, coupled with the limits imposed by the social–cognitive reasoning and cognitive development of these children (Cicchetti & Carlson, 1989), suggests that support is likely to be required if this route is to be utilized successfully.

Because research has coalesced to reveal the adverse impact of child maltreatment on overall adaptation, we also believe that these data need to be conveyed to those involved in allocating monies for research and intervention for maltreated children. Unfortunately, far too few resources are available to identify adequately the long-term effects of maltreatment or to develop and test the efficacy of intervention efforts (Cicchetti, Toth, & Bush, 1988; Cicchetti, Toth, Bush, & Gillespie, 1988; Fantuzzo et al., 1988). We are hopeful that increased social awareness regarding the likelihood of severely maladaptive behavior emerging in maltreated children will result in increased resources for this important work.

Finally, the elucidation of the link between early attachment difficulties and subsequent developmental failures can provide important information for intervention efforts. Depending on where in the developmental sequence a maltreated child comes to the attention of mental health professionals, it may be possible to provide services that are specific to the failure of stage-salient issues (Cicchetti, Toth, & Bush,

1988). For example, a school-age abused child who is aggressive with peers most likely had a history of insecure attachment relations with his or her primary caregiver. Therefore, rather than only focusing on the current difficulties, work may need to be directed toward helping the child to modify his or her internal working models of relationships, the origins of which were developed in the maladaptive family context.

As we have shown, the peer difficulties of maltreated children reflect a complex sequence of events. Although in many ways the work reported in this chapter is the beginning of a vast body of research that will be necessary, we believe that it has provided a context within which to conceptualize future efforts.

## ACKNOWLEDGMENTS

We want to thank the many people who have assisted us in carrying out our studies on peer relations in maltreated children, including Douglas Barnett, Bonnie Bitran, Pam Block, Vicki Carlson, Janet Gillespie, Deborah Hay, Kevin Hennessy, Patty Hrusa, Joan Kaufman, Carol Kottmeier, Jennifer Larter, Diana Meisburger, Kurt Olsen, Gerald Rabideau, Pete Ragonese, and Miriam Wetzel. We wish to acknowledge the support of the A. L. Mailman Family Foundation, Inc., the Monroe County Department of Social Services, the National Institute of Mental Health, the Smith Richardson Foundation, Inc., the Spencer Foundation, and the Spunk Fund, Inc. We thank Sheree Toth for her helpful feedback and Victoria Gill and Donna Bowman for typing the manuscript.

## REFERENCES

Aber, J. L., & Allen, J. P. (1987). The effects of maltreatment on young children's socioemotional development: An attachment theory perspective. *Developmental Psychology, 23*, 406–414.

Aber, J. L., Allen, J., Carlson, V., & Cicchetti, D. (1989). The effects of maltreatment on development during early childhood: Recent studies and their theoretical, clinical, and policy implications. In D. Cicchetti & V. Carlson (Eds.), *Child maltreatment: Theory and research on the causes and consequences of child abuse and neglect* (pp. 579–619). New York: Cambridge University Press.

Aber, J. L., & Cicchetti, D. (1984). Socioemotional development in maltreated children: An empirical and theoretical analysis. In H. Fitzgerald, B. Lester, & M. Yogman (Eds.), *Theory and research in behavioral pediatrics* (Vol. II, pp. 147–205). New York: Plenum.

Achenbach, T. (1990). What is "developmental" about developmental psychopathology? In J. Rolf, A. Masten, D. Cicchetti, K. Nuechterlein, & S. Weintraub (Eds), *Risk and protective factors in the development of psychopathology* (pp. 29–48). New York: Cambridge University Press.

Ainsworth, M. (1989). Attachments beyond infancy. *American Psychologist, 44,* 709–716.

Aragona, J. A., & Eyberg, S. M. (1981). Neglected children: Mothers' report of child behavior problems and observed verbal behavior. *Child Development, 52,* 596–602.

Arling, G. L., & Harlow, H. F. (1967). Effects of social deprivation on maternal behavior of rhesus monkeys. *Journal of Comparative and Physiological Psychology, 64,* 371–377.

Bandura, A. (1977). Self-efficacy: Toward a unifying theory of behavioral change. *Psychological Review, 84,* 191–215.

Barahal, R., Waterman, J., & Martin, H. (1981). The social–cognitive development of abused children. *Journal of Consulting and Clinical Psychology, 49,* 508–516.

Baumrind, D. (1967). Child-care practices anteceding three patterns of preschool behavior. *Genetic Psychology Monographs, 75,* 43–88.

Baumrind, D. (1968). Authoritarian versus authoritative parental control. *Adolescence, 3,* 255–272.

Belsky, J. (1984). The determinants of parenting: A process model. *Child Development, 55,* 83–96.

Belsky, J., & Pensky, E. (1988). Developmental history, personality, and family relationships: Toward an emergent family system. In R. A. Hinde and J. Stevenson-Hinde (Eds.), *Relationships within families* (pp. 27–47). Oxford: Clarendon Press.

Belsky, J., & Vondra, J. (1989). Lessons from child abuse: The determinants of parenting. In D. Cicchetti & V. Carlson (Eds.), *Child maltreatment: Theory and research on the causes and consequences of child abuse and neglect* (pp. 153–202). New York: Cambridge University Press.

Block, J. (1961). *The Q-sort method in personality assessment and psychiatric research.* Springfield, IL: Thomas.

Block, J. H., & Block, J. (1969). *The California child Q-sort.* Berkeley, CA: Institute of Human Development, University of California at Berkeley.

Block, J. H., & Block, J. (1980). The role of ego-control and ego resiliency in the organization of behavior. In W. A. Collins (Ed.), *Minnesota symposia on child psychology,* Vol. 13 (pp. 39–101). Hillsdale, NJ: Lawrence Erlbaum Associates.

Bowlby, J. (1969/1982). *Attachment and loss (Vol. 1).* New York: Basic Books.

Bretherton, I. (1985). Attachment theory: Retrospect and prospect. In I. Bretherton & E. Waters (Eds.), Growing points of attachment theory and research. *Monographs of the Society for Research in Child Development, 50*(1–2, Serial No. 209).

Brownell, C. A. (1986). Convergent developments: Cognitive–developmental correlates of growth in infant/toddler peer skills. *Child Development, 57,* 275–286.

Carlson, V., Cicchetti, D., Barnett, D., & Braunwald, K. (1989a). Disorganized/disoriented attachment relationships in maltreated infants. *Developmental Psychology, 25,* 525–531.

Carlson, V., Cicchetti, D., Barnett, D., & Braunwald, K. (1989b). Finding order in disorganization: Lessons from research on maltreated infant's attachments to their caregivers. In D. Cicchetti & V. Carlson (Eds.), *Child maltreatment: Theory and research on the causes and consequences of child abuse and neglect* (pp. 494–528). New York: Cambridge University Press.

Caspi, A., & Elder, G. H., Jr. (1988). Emergent family patterns. The intergenerational construction of problem behaviour and relationships. In R. A. Hinde & J. Stevenson-Hinde (Eds.), *Relationships within families* (pp. 27–47). Oxford: Clarendon Press.

Cassidy, J. (1988). Child–mother attachment and the self in 6-year olds. *Child Development, 59,* 121–134.

Cicchetti, D. (1984). The emergence of developmental psychopathology. *Child Development, 55,* 1–7.

Cicchetti, D. (1987). Developmental psychopathology in infancy: Illustration from the study of maltreated youngsters. *Journal of Consulting and Clinical Psychology, 55,* 837–845.

Cicchetti, D. (1989). Developmental psychopathology: Some thoughts on its evolution. *Development and Psychopathology, 1,* 1–4.

Cicchetti, D. (1990). An historical perspective on the discipline of developmental psychopathology. In J. Rolf, A. Masten, D. Cicchetti, K. Nuechterlein, & S. Weintraub (Eds.), *Risk and protective factors in the development of psychopathology* (pp. 2–28). New York: Cambridge University Press.

Cicchetti, D., & Barnett, D. (1991). Toward the development of a scientific nosology of child maltreatment. In W. Grove & D. Cicchetti (Eds.), *Thinking clearly about psychology: Vol. 2. Personality and psychopathology* (pp. 346–377). Minneapolis: University of Minnesota Press.

Cicchetti, D., & Beeghly, M. (1987). Symbolic development in maltreated youngsters: An organizational perspective. *New Directions for Child Development, 36,* 5–29.

Cicchetti, D., Beeghly, M., Carlson, V., & Toth, S. (1990). The emergence of the self in atypical populations. In D. Cicchetti & M. Beeghly (Eds.), *The self in transition: Infancy to childhood* (pp. 309–344). Chicago: University of Chicago Press.

Cicchetti, D., & Carlson, V. (Eds.). (1989). *Child maltreatment: Theory and research on the causes and consequences of child abuse and neglect.* New York: Cambridge University Press.

Cicchetti, D., Cummings, M., Greenberg, M., & Marvin, R. (1990). An organizational perspective on attachment beyond infancy: Implications for theory, measurement, and research. In M. Greenberg, D. Cicchetti, & M. Cummings (Eds.), *Attachment during the preschool years* (pp. 3–49). Chicago: University of Chicago Press.

Cicchetti, D., & Rizley, R. (1981). Developmental perspectives on the etiology, intergenerational transmission, and sequelae of child maltreatment. *New Directions for Child Development, 11,* 31–55.

Cicchetti, D., & Schneider-Rosen, K. (1986). An organizational approach to childhood depression. In M. Rutter, C. Izard, & P. Read (Eds.), *Depression in young people. Clinical and developmental perspectives* (pp. 71–134). New York: Guilford.

Cicchetti, D., & Todd Manly, J. (1990). A personal perspective on conducting research with maltreating families: Problems and solutions. In G. Brody & I. Sigel (Eds.), *Family research journeys: Vol. 2: Families at risk* (pp. 87–133). New York: Academic Press.

Cicchetti, D., Toth, S., & Bush, M. (1988). Developmental psychopathology and incompetence in childhood: Suggestions for intervention. In B. Lahey & A. Kazdin (Eds.), *Advances in clinical child psychology* (pp. 1–71). New York: Plenum Press.

Cicchetti, D., Toth, S., Bush, M. A., & Gillespie, J. F. (1988). Stage-salient issues: A transactional model of intervention. *New Directions for Child Development, 39,* 123–145.

Coie, J. D., & Dodge, K. A. (1983). Continuities and changes in children's social status: A 5-year longitudinal study. *Merrill-Palmer Quarterly, 29,* 261–282.

Connell, J. P. (1990). Context, self, and action: A motivational analysis of self-system processes across the life span. In D. Cicchetti & M. Beeghly (Eds.), *The self in transition: Infancy to childhood* (pp. 61–97). Chicago: University of Chicago Press.

Costello, E. J. (1989). The utility of care: Behavioral decision analysis and the development of depression. *Development and Psychopathology, 1,* 69–89.

Coster, W. J., Gersten, M. S., Beeghly, M., & Cicchetti, D. (1989). Communicative functioning in maltreated toddlers. *Developmental Psychology, 25,* 1020–1029.

Cowen, E., Pederson, A., Babigian, H., Izzo, L., & Trost, M. (1973). Long-term follow-up of early detected children. *Journal of Consulting and Clinical Psychology, 41,* 438–446.

Crittenden, P. M. (1981). Abusing, neglecting, problematic, and adequate dyads: Differentiating by patterns of interaction. *Merrill-Palmer Quarterly, 27,* 201–208.

Crittenden, P. M. (1988a). Distorted patterns of relationship in maltreating families: The role of internal representational models. *Journal of Reproductive and Infant Psychology, 6,* 183–199.

Crittenden, P. M. (1988b). Relationships at risk. In J. Belsky & T. Nezworski (Eds.), *Clinical implications of attachment* (pp. 136–174). Hillsdale, NJ: Lawrence Erlbaum Associates.

Crittenden, P. M., & Ainsworth, M. (1989). Attachment and child abuse. In D. Cicchetti & V. Carlson (Eds.), *Child maltreatment: Theory and research on the causes and consequences of child abuse and neglect* (pp. 432–463). New York: Cambridge University Press.

Cummings, E. M., & Cicchetti, D. (1990). Attachment, depression, and the transmission of depression. In M. T. Greenberg, D. Cicchetti, & E. M. Cummings (Eds.), *Attachment during the preschool years* (pp. 339–372). Chicago: University of Chicago Press.

DeCharms, R. (1968). *Personal causation: The internal affective determinants of behavior.* New York: Academic Press.

Deci, E. L. (1975). *Intrinsic motivation.* New York: Plenum.

Dodge, K. A. (1983). Behavioral antecedents of peer status. *Child Development, 54,* 1386–1399.

Dodge, K. A. (1986). A social information processing model of social competence in children. In M. Perlmutter (Ed.), *Minnesota symposia on child psychology* (Vol. 18, pp. 77–125). Hillsdale, NJ: Lawrence Erlbaum Associates.

Dodge, K. A., McClaskey, C. L., & Feldman, E. (1985). Situational approach to the assessment of social competence in children. *Journal of Consulting and Clinical Psychology, 53(3),* 344–353.

Dodge, K. A., & Murphy, R. R. (1984). The assessment of social competence in adolescents. In P. Karoly & J. J. Steffan (Eds.), *Adolescent behavior disorders: Current perspectives* (pp. 61–96). Lexington, MA: D. C. Health.

Easterbrooks, M. A., & Emde, R. N. (1988). Marital and parent–child relationships: The role of affect in the family system. In R. A. Hinde and J. Stevenson-Hinde (Eds.), *Relationships within families* (pp. 83–103). Oxford: Clarendon Press.

Egeland, B., & Sroufe, L. A. (1981). Developmental sequelae of maltreatment in infancy. *New Directions for Child Development, 11,* 77–92.

Egeland, B., Sroufe, L. A., & Erickson, M. (1983). The developmental consequences of different patterns of maltreatment. *Journal of Child Abuse and Neglect, 7,* 459–469.

Engfer, F. (1988). The interrelatedness of marriage and the mother–child relationship. In R. A. Hinde & J. Stevenson-Hinde (Eds.), *Relationships within families* (pp. 104–118). Oxford: Clarendon Press.

Erickson, M. F., Sroufe, L. A., & Egeland, B. (1985). The relationship between quality of attachment and behavior problems in preschool in a high-risk sample. *Monographs of the Society for Research in Child Development, 50*(Serial No. 209).

Erikson, E. (1950). *Childhood and society.* New York: Norton.

Fantuzzo, J. W., Jurecic, L., Stovall, A., Hightower, D. A., Goins, C., & Schachtel, D. (1988). Effects of adult and peer initiations on the social behavior of withdrawn, maltreated preschool children. *Journal of Consulting and Clinical Psychology, 56,* 34–39.

Field, T. M. (1984). Separation stress of young children transferring to new schools. *Developmental Psychology, 20,* 786–792.

Freud, A., & Dann, S. (1951). An experiment in group upbringing. *The Psychoanalytic Study of the Child, 6,* 127–168.

Garbarino, J., & Gilliam, G. (1980). *Understanding abusive families.* Lexington, MA: Lexington Press.

George, C., & Main, M. (1979). Social interactions of young abused children: Approach, avoidance, and aggression. *Child Development, 50,* 306–318.

Giovannoni, J., & Becerra, R. M. (1979). *Defining child abuse.* New York: Free Press.

Harter, S. (1981). A model of intrinsic mastery motivation in children: Individual differences and developmental change. In A. Collins (Ed.), *Minnesota symposia on child psychology* (Vol. 14, pp. 215–255). Hillsdale, NJ: Lawrence Erlbaum Associates.

Hartup, W. (1983). Peer relations. In P. Mussen (Ed.), *Carmichael's manual of child psychology* (pp. 103–196). New York: Wiley.

Hartup, W. W. (1986). On relationships and development. In W. W. Hartup & Z. Rubin (Eds.), *Relationships and development* (pp. 1–26). Hillsdale, NJ: Lawrence Erlbaum Associates.

Herrenkohl, R. C., & Herrenkohl, E. C. (1981). Some antecedents and developmental consequences of child maltreatment. In R. Rizley & D. Cicchetti (Eds.), *Developmental perspectives on child maltreatment* (pp. 57–76). San Francisco: Jossey-Bass.

Hoffman-Plotkin, D., & Twentyman, C. (1984). A multimodal assessment of behavioral and cognitive deficits in abused and neglected preschoolers. *Child Development, 55,* 794–802.

Howes, C. (1983). Patterns of friendship. *Child Development, 54,* 1041–1053.

Howes, C. (1988). Peer interaction in young children. *Monographs of the Society for Research in Child Development, 53*(1, Serial No. 217).

Howes, C., & Eldredge, R. (1985). Responses to abused, neglected, and nonmaltreated children to the behaviors of their peers. *Journal of Applied Developmental Psychology, 6,* 261–270.

Howes, C., & Espinosa, M. P. (1985). The consequences of child abuse for the formation of relationships with peers. *Child Abuse and Neglect, 9,* 397–404.

Jacobson, R., & Straker, G. (1982). Peer group interaction of physically abused children. *Child Abuse and Neglect, 6,* 321–327.

James, C. L., & Hesselbrock, V. (1978). Problem children's adult adjustment predicted from teacher's ratings. *American Journal of Orthopsychiatry, 48,* 300–309.

Kaplan, B. (1966). The study of language in psychiatry: The comparative developmental approach and its application to symbolization and language in psychopathology. In S. Arieti (Ed.), *American handbook of psychiatry* (pp. 1046–1073). New York: Basic Books.

Kaplan, B. (1983). Genetic-dramatism: Old wine in new bottles. In S. Wapner & B. Kaplan (Eds.), *Toward a holistic developmental psychology* (pp. 53–74). Hillsdale, NJ: Lawrence Erlbaum Associates.

Kaufman, J., & Cicchetti, D. (1989). The effects of maltreatment on school-aged children's socioemotional development: Assessments in a day camp setting. *Developmental Psychology, 25,* 516–524.

Kobak, R., & Sceery, A. (1988). Attachment in later adolescence: Working models, affect regulation, and perceptions of self and others. *Child Development, 59,* 135–146.

Koestner, R., Ryan, R. M., Bernieri, F., & Holt, K. (1984). Setting limits on children's behavior: The differential effects of controlling versus informational styles on intrinsic motivation and creativity. *Journal of Personality, 52,* 233–248.

Kohlberg, L., LaCrosse, J., & Ricks, D. (1972). The predictability of adult mental health from child behavior. In B. Wolman (Ed.), *Manual of child psychopathology* (pp. 1217–1284). New York: Wiley.

LaFreniere, P., & Sroufe, L. A. (1985). Profiles of peer competence in the preschool: Interrelations between measures, influence of social ecology, and relation to attachment history. *Developmental Psychology, 21,* 56–69.

Lepper, M. R. (1981). Intrinsic and extrinsic motivation in children: Detrimental effects of superfluous social controls. In W. A. Collins (Ed.), *Minnesota symposia on child psychology Vol. 14. Aspects of the development of competence* (pp. 155–214). Hillsdale, NJ: Lawrence Erlbaum Associates.

Lewis, M. L., & Schaeffer, S. (1981). Peer behavior and mother–infant interaction in maltreated children. In M. L. Lewis & L. Rosenblum (Eds.), *The uncommon child* (pp. 193–223). New York: Plenum.

Lieberman, A. F. (1977). Preschoolers' competence with a peer: Relations with attachment and peer experience. *Child Development, 48,* 1277–1287.

Lynch, M. (1988). *Peer relationships as alternate types of attachments.* Unpublished manuscript, University of Rochester, Rochester, NY.

Lynch, M., & Cicchetti, D. (1991). Patterns of relatedness in maltreated and nonmaltreated children: Connections among multiple representational models. *Development and Psychopathology, 3,* 207–226.

Lynch, M., & Wellborn, J. G. (April, 1989). *Patterns of relatedness in maltreated and matched-control children: A look at mother–child relationships beyond infancy in high-risk groups.* Paper presented at the Biennial Meeting of the Society for Research in Child Development, Kansas City, MO.

Main, M., & George, C. (1985). Response of abused and disadvantaged toddlers to distress in agemates: A study in the day care setting. *Developmental Psychology, 21,* 407–412.

Main, M., Kaplan, N., & Cassidy, J. C. (1985). Security in infancy, childhood, and adulthood: A move to the level of representation. In I. Bretherton & E. Waters (Eds.), Growing points of attachment theory and research. *Monographs of the Society for Research in Child Development, 50*(1, 2, Serial No. 209).

Main, M., & Solomon, J. (1986). Discovery of a disorganized disoriented attachment pattern. In T. B. Brazelton & M. W. Yogman (Eds.), *Affective development in infancy* (pp. 95–124). Norwood, NJ: Ablex.

Main, M., & Solomon, J. (1990). Procedures for identifying infants as disorganized/disoriented during the Ainsworth Strange Situation. In M. Greenberg, D. Cicchetti, & M. Cummings (Eds.), *Attachment during the preschool years* (pp. 121–160). Chicago: University of Chicago Press.

Manly, J., & Cicchetti, D. (1989). *Peer relationships and social competence of maltreated children: Ratings in a summer daycamp setting.* Unpublished manuscript, University of Rochester.

Mueller, N., & Silverman, N. (1989). Peer relations in maltreated children. In D. Cicchetti & V. Carlson (Eds.), *Child maltreatment: Theory and research on the causes and consequences of child abuse and neglect* (pp. 529–578). New York: Cambridge University Press.

Parke, R. D., & Collmer, C. W. (1975). Child abuse: An interdisciplinary analysis. In E. Mavis Hetherington (Ed.), *Review of child development research* (Vol. V, pp. 509–590). Chicago: University of Chicago Press.

Parker, J. G., & Asher, S. R. (1987). Peer acceptance and later personal adjustment: Are low-accepted children "at risk"? *Psychological Bulletin, 102,* 357–389.

Pastor, D. L. (1981). The quality of mother–infant attachment and its relationships to toddlers' initial sociability with peers. *Developmental Psychology, 17,* 326–335.

Pelton, L. (1978). Child abuse and neglect: The myth of classlessness. *American Journal of Orthopsychiatry, 48,* 608–617.

Richard, B. A., & Dodge, K. A. (1982). Social maladjustment and problem solving in school-aged children. *Journal of Consulting and Clinical Psychology, 50*(2), 226–233.

Rieder, C., & Cicchetti, D. (1989). Organizational perspective on cognitive control functioning and cognitive–affective balance in maltreated children. *Developmental Psychology, 25,* 382–393.

Robins, L. N. (1966). *Deviant children grown up.* Baltimore: Williams & Wilkens.

Roff, M., Sells, B., & Golden, M. M. (1972). *Social adjustment and personality development in children.* Minneapolis: University of Minnesota Press.

Rubin, K. H., LeMare, L., & Lollis, S. (1990). Social withdrawal in childhood: Developmental pathways to peer rejection. In S. R. Asher & J. D. Coie (Eds.), *Peer rejection in childhood* (pp. 217–249). New York: Cambridge University Press.

Rubin, K. H., & Lollis, S. P. (1988). Beyond attachment: Possible origins and consequences of social withdrawal in childhood. In J. Belsky & T. Nezworski (Eds.), *Clinical implications of attachment* (pp. 219–252). Hillsdale, NJ: Lawrence Erlbaum Associates.

Rubin, K. H., & Mills, R. S. L. (1988). The many faces of social isolation in childhood. *Journal of Consulting and Clinical Psychology, 56,* 916–924.

Rubin, K. H., & Ross, H. S. (1988). Toward the study of social competence, social status, and social relations. In C. Howes (Ed.), Peer interaction in young children. *Monographs of the Society for Research in Child Development, 53*(1, Serial No. 217).

Rutter, M. (1986). Child psychiatry: The interface between clinical and developmental research. *Psychological Medicine, 16,* 151–169.

Rutter, M. (1988). Functions and consequences of relationships: Some psychopathological considerations. In R. A. Hinde & J. Stevenson-Hinde (Eds.), *Relationships within families* (pp. 27–47). Oxford: Clarendon Press.

Rutter, M., & Garmezy, N. (1983). Developmental psychopathology. In P. Mussen (Ed.), *Handbook of child psychology* (Vol. IV, pp. 775–911). New York: Wiley.

Rutter, M., & Giller, H. (1983). *Juvenile delinquency: Trends and perspectives.* Harmondsworth, England: Penguin.

Ryan, R. M., Connell, J. P., & Deci, E. L. (1985). A motivational analysis of self-determination and self-regulation in education. In C. Ames & P. E. Ames (Eds.), *Research on motivation in education: The classroom milieu* (pp. 13–51). New York: Academic Press.

Sackett, G., Sameroff, A., Cairns, R., & Suomi, S. (1981). Continuity in behavioral development: Theoretical and empirical issues. In K. Immelmann, G. Garlow, L. Petrinovich, & M. Main (Eds.), *Behavioral development* (pp. 23–57). Cambridge: Cambridge University Press.

Schneider-Rosen, K., Braunwald, K., Carlson, V., & Cicchetti, D. (1985). Current perspectives in attachment theory: Illustration from the study of maltreated infants. In I. Bretherton & E. Waters (Eds.), Growing points of attachment theory and research. *Monographs of the Society for Research in Child Development, 50* (Serial No. 209), 194–210.

Schneider-Rosen, K., & Cicchetti, D. (1984). The relationship between affect and cognition in maltreated infants: Quality of attachment and the development of visual self-recognition. *Child Development, 55,* 648–658.

Selman, R. (1976). Social cognitive understanding. In T. Lickona (Ed.), *Moral development and behavior* (pp. 299–316). New York: Holt, Rinehart, & Winston.

Selman, R. (1980). *The growth of interpersonal understanding: Developmental and clinical analyses.* New York: Academic Press.

Shonk, S., & Cicchetti, D. (1989). *Teachers' ratings of the social competence and peer relationships of maltreated children.* Manuscript in preparation.

Sroufe, L. A. (1979). The coherence of individual development. *American Psychologist, 34,* 834–841.

Sroufe, L. A. (1983). Infant–caregiver attachment and patterns of adaptation in preschool: The roots of maladaptation and competence. In M. Perlmutter (Ed.), *Minnesota symposia on child psychology: Vol. 16* (pp. 41–83). Minneapolis: University of Minnesota Press.

Sroufe, L. A. (1990). An organizational perspective on the self. In D. Cicchetti & M. Beeghly (Eds.), *The self in transition: Infancy to childhood* (pp. 281–307). Chicago: University of Chicago Press.

Sroufe, L. A., & Fleeson, J. (1986). Attachment and the construction of relationships. In W. Hartup & Z. Rubin (Eds.), *Relationships and development* (pp. 51–71). Hillsdale, NJ: Lawrence Erlbaum Associates.

Sroufe, L. A., & Fleeson, J. (1988). The coherence of family relationships. In R. A. Hinde and J. Stevenson-Hinde (Eds.), *Relationships within families* (pp. 27–47). Oxford: Clarendon Press.

Sroufe, L. A., & Rutter, M. (1984). The domain of developmental psychopathology. *Child Development, 55,* 17–29.

Trickett, P. K., Aber, J. L., Carlson, V., & Cicchetti, D. (1991). The relationship of socioeconomic status to the etiology and developmental sequelae of physical child abuse. *Developmental Psychology, 27,* 148–158.

Trickett, P. K., & Kuczynski, L. (1986). Children's misbehaviors and parental discipline in abusive and nonabusive families. *Developmental Psychology, 22,* 115–123.

Trickett, P. K., & Susman, E. J. (1988). Parental perceptions of childrearing practices in physically abusive and nonabusive families. *Developmental Psychology, 24,* 270–276.

Troy, M., & Sroufe, L. A. (1987). Victimization among preschoolers: The role of attachment relationship history. *Journal of the American Academy of Child Psychiatry, 26,* 166–172.

Vondra, J., Barnett, D., & Cicchetti, D. (1989). Perceived and actual competence among maltreated and comparison school children. *Development and Psychopathology, 1,* 237–255.

Waters, E., Noyes, D., Vaughn, B., & Ricks, M. (1985). *Q*-sort definitions of social competence and self-esteem: Discriminant validity of related constructs in theory and data. *Developmental Psychology, 21,* 508–522.

Wellborn, J. G., & Connell, J. P. (1986). *Manual for the Rochester assessment package for schools.* Rochester, NY: University of Rochester.

Werner, H. (1948). *Comparative psychology of mental development.* New York: International Universities Press.

Wheeler, V. A., & Ladd, G. W. (1982). Assessment of children's self-efficacy for social interactions with peers. *Developmental Psychology, 18,* 795–805.

Wolfe, D. A. (1985). Child-abusive parents: An empirical review and analysis. *Psychological Bulletin, 97,* 462–482.

Wolfe, D. A. (1987). *Child abuse.* Newbury Park, CA: Sage.

Wright, J. (1983). *The structure and perception of behavioral consistency.* Unpublished doctoral dissertation, Stanford University.

# CHAPTER THIRTEEN

# Family Economic Circumstances, Life Transitions, and Children's Peer Relations

Charlotte J. Patterson
Pamela C. Griesler
Nancy A. Vaden
*University of Virginia*

Janis B. Kupersmidt
*University of North Carolina at Chapel Hill*

A growing consensus has emerged in recent years about the importance of associations between difficulties in peer relations during childhood, on the one hand, and negative life outcomes, on the other (Kohlberg, LaCrosse, & Ricks, 1972; Kupersmidt, Coie, & Dodge, 1990; Parker & Asher, 1987). Children who are disliked or rejected by their peers appear to be more vulnerable than other children to a broad range of psychosocial problems during adolescence and adulthood. For example, Parker and Asher (1987) reviewed evidence demonstrating connections between childhood peer acceptance and later school dropout rates, criminality, and psychopathology, and concluded that there are significant associations in each of the three areas. Although relatively little is known at present about pathways through which such associations may occur, there is considerable consensus that peer rejection is an important variable for research on developmental psychopathology to consider (Cicchetti, 1984; Garmezy, 1987; Rutter, 1987; Sroufe & Rutter, 1984).

Whereas the behavioral correlates and long-term outcomes associated with peer rejection during childhood have been widely studied (Coie, Dodge, & Kupersmidt, 1990; Hartup, 1983; Parker & Asher, 1987), relatively little is known about factors that may predispose children to be rejected by their peers. Rejected children are likely to display more aggressive, disruptive behavior than other children (Coie, Dodge, & Coppotelli, 1982), and such behavior is likely to lead to rejection among peers (Coie & Kupersmidt, 1983; Dodge, 1983); particular behavioral styles thus appear to be antecedents of peer rejection. Certain personal characteristics such as intelligence and attractiveness also seem to be related to peer acceptance (Hartup, 1983). Less is known, however, about other factors that may increase children's vulnerability to rejection by peers.

Primary among other factors that would seem relevant to children's vulnerability to peer rejection are the experiences encountered by children in their families. In addition to contributions in the present volume, research on family variables and children's peer relations has recently been reviewed by a number of investigators (Cohn, Patterson, & Christopoulos, 1991; Parke, MacDonald, Beitel, & Bhavnagri, 1988; Parke, et al., 1989; Putallaz & Heflin, 1990; Rubin & Lollis, 1988). Despite some dissenting voices (Lamb & Nash, 1989), there is general agreement that research has demonstrated connections between the quality of parent–child relations and peer relations during childhood.

The preponderance of research evidence has shown, for example, that quality of infant–mother attachment relationships is associated with social competence throughout the first 10 years of life (see also Elicker, Englund, & Sroufe, this volume). At the same time, related studies have found that parental warmth and involvement are associated with children's social acceptance among peers (Putallaz & Heflin, 1990). Parents in their roles as managers and supervisors of children's social lives also seem to have influences on peer relations; particularly for younger children, parents who initiate social contacts with peers and who effectively supervise their children's peer interactions are more likely to have children who are popular among their peers (Ladd, Muth Profilet, & Hart, this volume). There is little doubt that significant connections do exist between family interactions and relationships, on the one hand, and peer relations on the other (Cohn et al., 1991).

Linkages between family interaction and children's peer relations, though increasingly well documented, would be better understood if they could be grounded in the ecological contexts (Bronfenbrenner, 1979) in which they occur. Relatively little work has focused on the social, cultural, or economic contexts of family relations, as these may affect peer relations (Cohn et al., 1991). In addition to the need for greater understanding of chronic or enduring conditions that affect social development, there is also a relative dearth of information about the ways in which acute life events influence children's peer relations. We need to understand more clearly the ways in which ecological factors such as chronic life circumstances and acute life events affect the development of peer relationships during childhood.

Existing research on family and peer relations among children also tends to focus on a relatively limited set of assessments of peer relations; in addition, most studies involve assessments of only one aspect of peer relations (Cohn et al., 1991). For instance, research with preschool children has placed considerable emphasis on observational measures of peer interaction, but has devoted less attention to sociometric techniques for examining social acceptance. In research with older children, these emphases tend to be reversed. Relatively little research with children at any age has explored links between individual differences in family and peer relations that rely on more than one kind of assessment of peer relations. It would be helpful to broaden studies of peer relations to include the formation and maintenance of friendships, the influence of social networks of peers, and companionship with peers during activities outside of school, as well as behavior with and acceptance among peers at school.

In short, a review of available information on family–peer linkages during childhood suggests a need for more information about the kinds of life circumstances that are likely to facilitate favorable peer relations. In such work, peer relations ought to be construed broadly, to include acceptance and popularity versus rejection among peers, specific friendship relationships, and companionship while engaged in out-of-school activities. Our research conducted in the context of the Charlottesville Longitudinal Study has been designed to address some of these concerns.

In this chapter, we present some initial results from our research documenting linkages between ecological contexts and children's peer relations, then discuss possible pathways through which such linkages may occur. Before describing our findings, however, we first provide a brief overview of the Charlottesville Longitudinal Study, from which our findings are drawn.

## CHARLOTTESVILLE LONGITUDINAL STUDY

The Charlottesville Longitudinal Study (CLS) was designed to study psychosocial risk and resilience in a large, relatively unselected group of school children. The main aims of our overall project have been to develop a comprehensive program to identify children who are at social and/or academic risk, to provide and evaluate approaches to invention with these children, and to study the predictive causes, concurrent correlates, and longitudinal outcomes of risk status among children. Principal research-related aims of the study have been to further understanding of the personal, familial, community, and cultural contexts and consequences of social and academic risk among children; and to identify and explore conditions under which children may continue to develop normally even when subject to heightened risk. Given the focus of the present chapter, only material relevant to the first of these two research aims is presented here.

## Setting

The study took place in the public schools of Charlottesville, Virginia, with annual assessment in each of the 4 years of the study (1986–1989). The population of the city of Charlottesville was approximately 41,000 during the period of the study, and the population of the surrounding county of Albemarle was about 62,000. Thus, while growing at a rate of about 1% per year, the population of city and county together was hovering just above 100,000 during the time that CLS data were being collected (Knapp, Chesser, Olsen, & Barnes, 1989).

Unemployment in Charlottesville was very low during this period (Knapp et al., 1989). In 1986, for example, the unemployment rate was 7.0% for the United States as a whole, 5.0% for the Commonwealth of Virginia, and only 3.6% for the city of Charlottesville.

On the other hand, average weekly wages in Charlottesville for 1987 were only $316 per week (Knapp et al., 1989). For that year, the federal poverty threshold for a family of four was $11,611 (U. S. Bureau of the Census, 1989). A Charlottesville worker receiving average wages while working full-time for 50 weeks per year in 1987 would thus have earned $15,800, or only 136% of the federal poverty threshold for a family of four.

These figures suggest, and Census Bureau figures confirm, that many families were living at or below the poverty line. Of the 13 census tracts in the city of Charlottesville, 6 were considered poverty areas in the 1980 census (i.e., at least 20% of the population below the poverty line), and of these, two were considered extreme poverty areas (i.e., at least 40% of the population below the poverty line) (U. S. Bureau of the Census, 1982).

Overall, then, the study took place in a small Southern city, at a time of stable population, low unemployment, and relative prosperity. Despite these conditions, however, many families lived in poverty.

## Sample

The CLS employed a cohort-longitudinal design to follow a large, heterogeneous group of students in the Charlottesville Public Schools over 4 years. In the spring of 1986, when the study began, the three cohorts of children were in second, third, and fourth grades; and their modal ages were 8, 9, and 10 years, respectively. An additional cohort of second graders was added in 1987 and followed in 1988 (when most were in third grade), but our resources did not allow testing of this group in 1989. No effects of grade were found for analyses reported in this chapter, so effects associated with cohorts are not discussed further here. Unless otherwise noted, all data presented here are from 1986, the first year of the CLS.

In the spring of 1986, there were 1,153 students who were listed as enrolled in regular education classes for the second, third, or fourth grades of the Charlottesville Public Schools. Due to lack of parental permission, incomplete questionnaires, or school absence on the day of testing, however, some children who were enrolled did not participate fully in the study. For assessments based on peer nominations, scores could be derived even for students who were themselves absent on the day of testing; for these assessments, we collected data for 1,042 students. For self-report assessments, however, we could collect data only for students who had attended school on the day of testing; for these assessments, we collected data from 933 students. Due to incomplete data (e.g., from teacher absences on the day of testing, or from shortened testing periods in some cases), and the need to drop some children from some analyses (see the following), precise numbers of children for each analysis reported here range from 866 to 1,042. Regardless of the manner in which the response rate is calculated, however, our sample represents at least 75% of the population from which it was drawn.

The sample of students we studied was heterogeneous in several respects. In terms of household composition, 1986 school records revealed that 62% of the children lived in two-parent homes, 34% lived in mother-headed one-parent homes, and 4% lived in some other type of household. School records also revealed that, in ethnic terms, 64% of the children were classified as White, 33% as Black, and 3% as belonging to other ethnic groups. In terms of income level, 34% of the children were reported by teachers to be receiving free or reduced-price lunch, or some other form of public assistance.

## Materials and Procedures

In each year of the CLS, core assessments focused on three areas of children's competence at school: conduct, academic achievement, and peer relations (Patterson, Kupersmidt, & Vaden, 1990). Because many of the findings described in the following are drawn from them, we describe some of the assessments of peer relations here.

Group sociometric testing was conducted in each participating classroom by an adult experimenter and one or two aides, according to procedures outlined by Coie et al. (1982). Children were presented with an alphabetized list of children in their grade (for third and fourth graders) or class (for second graders) and were asked to nominate three children whom they liked most and three whom they liked least.

While the sociometric testing was conducted in his or her classroom, each teacher was individually interviewed in a separate room. For the teacher interviews, the interviewer read each item aloud and recorded the teacher's responses. Most important among the teacher interview items for our present purposes, teachers were asked to identify children in their classes who came from low-income families (defined as those receiving free or reduced-price school lunches and/or other forms of public assistance; see Patterson, Kupersmidt, & Vaden, 1990).

Coding of the sociometric data was accomplished using the criteria and procedures developed by Coie et al., (1982). Standardized liked-most and liked-least scores were computed to derive values for a child's social preference among peers (i.e., the difference between standardized liked-most and standardized liked-least nominations); these were then restandardized to yield the social preference scores used as an index of children's popularity among peers. Children whose standardized social preference scores were less than $-1.00$, standardized liked-most scores were less than 0, and standardized liked-least scores were greater than 0, were classified as sociometrically rejected; for present purposes, all others were classified as not rejected.

## Teacher Reports of Low Family Income

Because assessments of family income level were central to many of our findings, we explored the reliability and validity of teacher reports of family income levels. The fact that siblings generally share the same home environment suggested a way of checking reliability. Sibling pairs were identified in the sample, and teacher reports of low family income were then compared for the two siblings. Because none of the sibling pairs were in the same classroom, these two reports were always provided by two different teachers. There were 73 sibling pairs for whom teacher reports about family income level were available; of these, 61, or 84%, had the same score (kappa = .67) (Patterson, Kupersmidt, & Vaden, 1990). Thus, teacher reports about low family income showed satisfactory reliability.

A check on the validity of teacher reports was possible for the data from the 1988 year. We collected teacher reports in 1988 exactly as we had during the previous years of the study. We also had access to official school records for 1988, showing which children received free or reduced-price lunches. A comparison of the two sources of information revealed that they were in exact agreement in 85% of the cases (kappa = .68). Thus, the teacher reports showed satisfactory correspondence with school records.

## INITIAL FINDINGS FROM
## THE CHARLOTTESVILLE LONGITUDINAL STUDY

We begin our consideration of ecological influences on children's peer relations by examining similarities among siblings in the CLS sample. Encouraged by our finding of significant commonality, we then describe results of a study of family background variables, acute life stress, and peer rejection during childhood. Following up on major results of this work, we then report the results of further studies designed to clarify connections between low family income and children's peer relations. Taken together, results of these initial studies reveal the significance of associations between economic adversity and children's difficulties in peer relations.

### Extent of Similarity Among Siblings

If differences between families are important influences on the development of children's relationships with their peers, then peer relations among siblings in the same family should be similar (Rowe, 1989). Siblings growing up in the same household generally share family characteristics such as ethnicity and economic resources. When families experience stressful life events or transitions such as divorce or separation of parents or geographic relocations, these experiences are generally also shared by siblings. In addition, of course, siblings share, on the average, half of their genetic endowment. To the extent that factors that are shared influence the development of peer relations among children, then, one should see resemblances among siblings.

To evaluate this hypothesis, and to assess the extent of between-family differences in our sample, we assessed correlations among indexes of peer relations among siblings (Vaden, Bloom, Griesler, Kupersmidt, & Patterson, 1989). We identified sibling pairs in the CLS using a two-step procedure. First, demographic information was taken from the children's school records, and potential sibling pairs were identified as those children whose last names, parents' names, and home addresses were the same. Next, school registration cards (on which names of siblings had been listed by parents) were checked to verify sibling status. Only sibling pairs that were identified in both steps were retained for purposes of the present research. Twin pairs were identified as siblings who shared the same date of birth; there were too few twin pairs to allow separate analyses, however, so they were excluded from the sample for the present purposes. In families where there were more than two siblings in the sample, the two oldest siblings were selected for further analysis. The resulting sample of 76 pairs of children thus comprised a sample of nontwin siblings.

As expected, we found that assessments of siblings' peer relationships were correlated to a significant degree (Vaden et al., 1989). For example, we found correlations of .44 for standardized social preference scores of siblings. The number of peer nominations received by children as companions in activities was also significantly correlated for siblings, especially for activities at home ($r = .31$) and for activities in the neighborhood ($r = .35$). Although these results certainly leave room for within-family differences, they are consistent with earlier findings for social preference (Roff, Sells, & Golden, 1972), and they are valuable in revealing the moderate size of between-family differences in children's peer relationships. We turn now to the question of what kinds of between-family differences might be most important.

## Family Background, Life Events, and Peer Rejection in Childhood

In our first study of family background, life events, and children's peer relations (Patterson, Vaden, & Kupersmidt, 1991), we distinguished between enduring or chronic conditions, on the one hand, and acute life events or transitions, on the other. For instance, among the enduring conditions of family life that may be related to children's peer experiences, we considered especially single parenting and family economic hardship. Among life events or transitions, we considered especially death of a parent, parental divorce, and residential mobility. Although no precise line separates relatively enduring conditions from briefer events or transitions, the two categories were helpful in identifying factors in a child's family life that might be connected to peer relations.

A substantial body of evidence now exists to demonstrate associations between children's enduring experiences in the family and peer acceptance in both preschool and elementary school (Cohn, 1990; Cohn et al., 1991; MacDonald & Parke, 1984; Putallaz, 1987; Roopnarine & Adams, 1987). Behavioral styles associated with peer rejection have also been found to be associated with characteristics of family backgrounds such as low income, single parenting, and parental unemployment (Cowen, Weissberg, & Guare, 1984; Hetherington, 1988; Hetherington, Cox, & Cox, 1979; Hetherington, Stanley-Hagan, & Anderson, 1989; Rutter, 1979; Shaw & Emery, 1988). Because children nominated by teachers as showing behavior problems often receive low liking ratings from peers (Ledingham, 1981), many of these family background factors may be related to peer rejection.

In addition to background information about enduring family circumstances, we also wanted to explore the potential role of acute stressors in affecting children's peer relations. Connections between stressful life events and psychological maladjustment among children have been widely studied (Compas, 1987; Johnson, 1986). For example, Sterling, Cowen, Weissberg, Lotyczewski, and Boike (1985) found an association between teacher-reported life stress and children's school adjustment. Cowen and his colleagues reported that children who had recently experienced significant negative life events were more likely to be referred to a school mental health program than those who had not. Life events that occurred relatively frequently included parental separation or divorce, remarriage of a parent, death in the family, serious illness in the family, and a new person in the home. Many of the behaviors characterizing maladjustment and leading to referral in the Cowen studies have also been found in other research to characterize the behavior of children rejected by their peers (Coie et al., 1990).

Taken together, these data suggest the potential contributions of family background and recent life events to peer rejection in childhood. Indeed, Elkins (1958) and Roff et al. (1972) found that children from low-income homes were not as well accepted among their peers as other children. These authors did not, however, study peer rejection as a specific phenomenon. Little is known about the ways in which combinations of chronic and acute stressors may affect children's peer relations. Cumulative effects of multiple stressors on children's behavior have been reported (Masten, et al., 1988; Rutter, 1979, 1987; Shaw & Emery, 1988), but studies of peer relations have not addressed this issue.

We thus wanted to explore connections between chronic family adversity and stressful life events on the one hand, and peer relations on the other, with an eye to evaluating possible cumulative effects of multiple stressors. To accomplish these aims, we (Patterson, Vaden, & Kupersmidt, 1991) studied children's peer status as a function of family background and life events as assessed using both teacher ratings (Study 1) and parent reports (Study 2), and we focused especially on peer rejection as an index of difficulties in peer relations.

In the first study, we assessed family background and life events using an adaptation of materials developed by Cowen et al. (1984). Each classroom teacher completed a checklist, indicating whether or not various family background characteristics were true and whether or not various life events had occurred for each child in his or her class. Four family background characteristics were included in the study: economic difficulty, biological mother not living in child's home, biological father not living in child's home, and child lacks education stimulation in the home. Scores for the family background scale were calculated by summing each child's scores for each of these four items, and could thus vary between 0 and 4.

The four life event items were: death of a family member, serious illness in the family, child transferred schools, and parental separation or divorce. To be marked, the event should have occurred within the previous 12 months. Scores for the life events scale were calculated by summing each child's scores for each of the four items; the possible range was thus from 0 to 4.

Preliminary analyses revealed that, as expected, the correlation between family background and life event scale scores was small but highly significant, $r = .19, p < .001$; teachers reported that children with many family background factors were also more likely to have experienced many life events. Consistent with earlier findings (Elkins, 1958, Roff et al., 1972), there were also small but significant relationships between children's standardized social preference and the scale scores for family background, $r = .25, p < .001$. The same association also held for life events, $r = .17, p < .001$. Children who were scored as having many family background variables and many life events were less well liked by their peers than other children.

With these initial results in hand, we wanted also to examine possible connections between children's family background, life events, and their rejection by peers at school. To this end, we calculated the probability of peer rejection among children for whom teachers reported different numbers of family background and/or life event items. These calculations allowed us to focus specifically on the degree to which family background and life events might be related to difficulties in peer relations.

The likelihood of rejection by peers (Coie et al., 1982) among children who were reported by teachers as experiencing different numbers of family background factors is shown in Fig. 13.1. As expected, the probability of peer rejection was strongly related to family background; children reported to have experienced three or more family background factors were three times as likely to be rejected by peers as those with none.

We also calculated the probability of peer rejection associated with each individual family background item; these figures are shown in Table 13.1. As expected, the probability of peer rejection was higher for children rated by teachers as living in low-income homes, homes without biological mother or father, and in homes lacking in educational stimulation.

The likelihood of rejection by peers among children who were reported by teachers as having experienced different numbers of stressful life events during the preceding year is shown in Fig. 13.2. As expected, the probability of peer rejection was strongly related to recent life events. Children reported to have experienced one life event were twice as likely, and those reported to have experienced two life events were more than

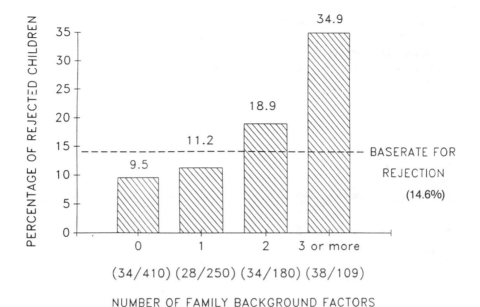

FIG. 13.1.   Percentages of children rejected by peers as a function of number of family background factors reported by teachers (from Patterson, Vaden, & Kupersmidt, 1991, Study 1).

TABLE 3.1
Percent of Children Classified as Sociometrically Rejected
as a Fuction of Family Background Variables and Recent Life Events
Reported by Teachers

| | Was family background item or life event reported by teacher? | | Fisher Exact |
|---|---|---|---|
| | No | Yes | p < |
| Family Background | | | |
| Biological mother not in home | 14.0 | 25.5 | .05 |
| Biological father not in home | 11.7 | 19.2 | .01 |
| Lacks educational stimulatiom at home | 11.2 | 30.7 | .01 |
| Low income home | 10.3 | 21.8 | .01 |
| Recent Life Events | | | |
| Illness in family | 14.4 | 23.3 | ns |
| Death of family member | 14.2 | 26.5 | .10 |
| Child transferred schools | 12.6 | 24.8 | .01 |
| Separation or divorce of parents | 13.2 | 35.5 | .01 |

*Note.* From Patterson, Vaden, and Kupersmidt, 1991, Study 1.

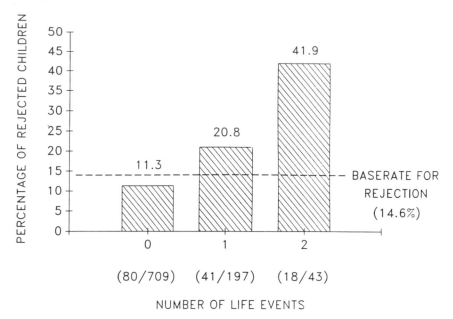

FIG. 13.2.   Percentages of children rejected by peers as a function of number of recent life events reported by teachers (from Patterson, Vaden, & Kupersmidt, 1991, Study 1).

three times as likely to be rejected by peers as those who had experienced none.

We also calculated the probability of peer rejection given teacher reports of specific life events and peer rejection; these figures are shown in Table 13.1. Although results for all four items are in the same direction, in only two cases is the probability of rejection significantly elevated. Children who were reported by teachers to have transferred schools or to have experienced parental separation and/or divorce were more likely than other children to be rejected by peers.

We also examined the likelihood of rejection by peers as a joint function of both family background and life events scores. In particular, we wanted to assess whether there were cumulative effects of family background and life events when considered together. Categorical modeling analysis revealed that the likelihood of peer rejection was strongly related both to family background and to life events. The interaction term was not significant. We conclude that the joint contributions of family background and life events were additive in this context.

The probability of rejection by peers as a function of the numbers of family background and life events items reported for each child is shown in Fig. 13.3. Within each level of family background, the probability of

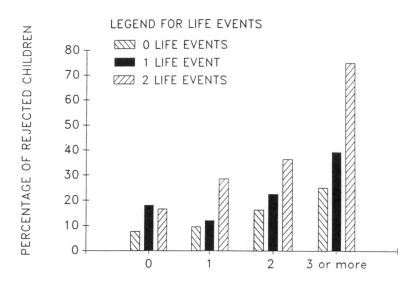

FIG. 13.3.   Percentages of chldren rejected by peers as a function of family background and recent life events reported by teachers (from Patterson, Vaden, & Kupersmidt, 1991, Study 1).

peer rejection was markedly higher for those who experienced acute life stresses. As expected, children for whom teachers reported no chronic family background or acute life event stresses had the lowest, and children for whom teachers reported three family background and two life event items had the highest probability of rejection. As compared to those in the former group, children in the latter group were thus almost 10 times more likely to be rejected by their peers at school.

Our results showed, then, that children described by their teachers as coming from environments characterized by continuing family adversity and as experiencing many recent life events were rejected by their peers more often than other children. The probability of rejection by peers rose from about 8% among children for whom teachers reported neither chronic family background nor acute life event stressors to about 35% among children for whom teachers reported three or more family background factors, and to about 42% among those for whom teachers reported two recent life events. Among those for whom teachers reported both three or more chronic family background and two acute life event stressors, the probability of rejection by peers was fully 75%. The probability of rejection by peers was thus considerably elevated among children subjected to high levels of chronic and acute life stresses.

Although these results are clearly consistent with the body of literature on acute and chronic stressors during childhood, a potential limitation of the methodology was its reliance on teacher reports of family
background and life events. Teacher reports were collected late in the
school year, after teachers had spent several months working with the
children. It is clear, however, that teachers may not be aware of all significant events or conditions that affect the lives of children in their classes. As a result, teacher reports may have been conservative estimates of
the incidence of family background factors and recent life events. Alternatively, teachers may have been more aware of the family situations of
children who presented classroom management problems for them, and
hence have reported more items for these children. In either case, we
thought that evidence from other sources about family background and
life events would be a valuable addition to the findings we have already
described.

To provide such information, we (Patterson, Vaden, & Kupersmidt,
1991) conducted a second study. Working with the same sample of children, we collected information from school registration cards that had
been filled out for each child by a parent or guardian at the beginning
of the school year. Using this information, we then calculated probabili-
ties of peer rejection as a function of family background variables and
life events reported by parents.

For several reasons, information provided by parents should be seen
as supplementing rather than duplicating data from teachers reports. First,
not all information was available from both sources. Even when information was available from both sources on the same topic, however, there
were often differences in the precise form of the data available from each
source. For example, teachers had been asked to report whether a child
had experienced a parental separation and/or divorce within the previous year whereas parents were simply asked to record whether the child's
biological parents were currently separated or divorced. In addition, parents and teachers provided information at different times of the year; parents generally filled out registration cards in the fall, whereas teacher
interviews were conducted during the following spring. Within the limits
of available information, however, we expected that results would parallel
those for teacher reports.

From the registration cards, we coded four items relevant to chronic
family background conditions for each child. These were: the person or
persons that each child lived with, whether or not the child lived in one
of several designated low-income housing areas, employment status of
parent or parents, and whether or not there was a telephone in the child's
home. We also coded two items relevant to life events experienced by
each child. These were: whether either biological parent had died, and

TABLE 13.2
Percent of Children Classified as Sociometrically Rejected
as a Function of Family Background Variables and Recent Life Events
Reported by Parents

| | Was family background item or life event reported by parent? | | Fisher Exact |
| --- | --- | --- | --- |
| | No | Yes | p < |
| Family Background | | | |
| Child does not live with both biological parents | 12.1 | 18.3 | .05 |
| Child lives in public housing for low income families | 13.3 | 22.9 | .01 |
| No parent living in child's home is employed | 13.5 | 24.0 | .01 |
| No telephone in child's home | 13.1 | 24.4 | .01 |
| Life Events | | | |
| At least one biological parent has died | 14.7 | 17.2 | ns |
| Biological parents have separated or divorced | 13.5 | 18.8 | .10 |

Note. From Patterson, Vaden, and Kupersmidt, 1991, Study 2.

whether the biological parents had separated or divorced. In cases where a parental separation, divorce, or death had occurred, the records did not indicate how recently the events had occurred.

To assess possible connections between children's family backgrounds and rejection by peers, we compared the probability of rejection given that any of the four family background items was present or absent. As can be seen in Table 13.2, the probability of rejection by peers was significantly higher for children who were not living with both biological parents, who were living in low-income housing, who had no parent who was employed, and who had no telephone in the home.

We also wanted to assess possible cumulative effects of the presence of multiple family background variables. To create a chronic family adversity scale for use in such analyses, we scored one point for each of the following variables reported for each child: not living with both biological parents, living in low-income housing, no parent employed, no telephone at home. Scores on this scale ranged from 0 (least adversity) to 4 (most adversity). As shown in Fig. 13.4, the probability of rejection by peers was significantly related to degree of chronic family adversity. Children who come from homes experiencing multiple chronic adversities were more likely than others to be rejected by peers.

To assess possible associations between life events and rejection by peers, we compared the probability of rejection given that either of the

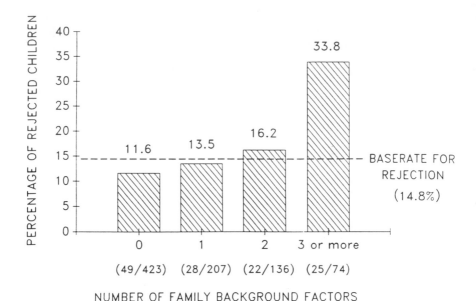

FIG. 13.4.    Percentages of children rejected by peers as a function of number of family background factors and recent life events reported by parents (from Patterson, Vaden, & Kupersmidt, 1991, Study 2).

two life events had been reported. As can be seen in Table 13.2, the probability of rejection by peers was not significantly higher for children who had experienced the death of a parent. As expected, however, the probability of rejection tended to be higher for children whose biological parents had separated or divorced.

To summarize the overall results, then, our main finding was that children from families subject to multiple chronic adversities were more likely than other children to be rejected by their peers at school. Whether assessed using teacher ratings or parent reports, variables related to low family income were significantly related to peer rejection. Further, the impact of multiple chronic adversities appeared to be cumulative; the greater the number of adversities, the greater a child's likelihood of being rejected by peers. These results are consistent with the literature on chronic adversity and behavior problems of children (Rutter, 1979; Rutter & Garmezy, 1983; Slaughter, 1988), and they extend these findings by showing that peer relations are also affected.

Our results showed that children whose biological parents had separated or divorced were more likely than other children to be rejected by peers at school. This pattern was significant in Study 1, in which teachers reported separations or divorces that had taken place during the previous 12 months, and approached significance in Study 2, in which parents reported any separation or divorce, without regard to timing of these events. These results fit well with the literature suggesting that non-normative life events such as divorce disrupt both children's behavior and their peer relations (Hetherington, 1988; Hetherington et al., 1979, 1989).

In summary, then, we found that children growing up in certain kinds of home environments were more likely than others to be rejected by peers. The probability of rejection by peers was markedly higher for children who were subjected to relatively high levels of chronic and acute life stresses. In particular, chronic stress associated with low family income, and acute stress associated with parental separation or divorce, contributed significantly to children's risk of peer rejection.

## Economic Hardship and Children's Popularity Among Peers

Our results thus far have suggested the importance of low income, divorce, and single parenting as risk factors for difficulties in children's peer relations. In the next study, we (Patterson, Kupersmidt, & Vaden, 1990) focused more specifically on issues related to chronic stress associated with economic adversity.

One of the difficulties in interpretation of findings like those just reported is that the likelihood of experiencing any particular risk factor is not independent of the probability of experiencing others. For instance, poverty, ethnicity, and the likelihood of growing up in mother-headed single-parent homes are themselves interrelated (Edelman, 1985, 1987, Glick, 1988; Laosa, 1988; Slaughter, 1988). Of children growing up in the United States today, about 1 in 5 lives in a home that is below the federally defined poverty line; of Black children, however, almost half live in poverty. Similarly, female-headed households are disproportionately represented among the poor; almost half of female-headed families are below the poverty line. Black children are also more likely than White children to grow up in female-headed homes; for example, about half of all Black children are born to single mothers (Laosa, 1988). In short, Black children in this country are more likely than White children to grow up in low-income, mother-headed single-parent homes (Edelman, 1985, 1987; Glick, 1988; Laosa, 1988; Slaughter, 1988).

These national trends were mirrored in our sample. As expected on the basis of national figures, household composition, income level, and ethnicity were strongly related in the CLS sample. For example, children from single-parent homes were three times as likely as those from two-parent homes, and Black children were twice as likely as White children, to come from low-income homes. In addition, Black children were twice as likely as White children to live with only one parent. The net result of these trends is shown in Fig. 13.5, which shows that the probability of low family income in the CLS sample ranged from 11% for White children growing up in two-parent homes to 73.5% for Black children growing up in one-parent homes.

Simple analyses assessing the predictive value of any of these variables are thus very likely to be confounded by the effects of the other variables as well. For example, the greater incidence of behavior problems among children living in single-parent homes (Rutter & Garmezy, 1983) could result at least in part from the facts that mother-headed single-parent families are more likely than other families to have low incomes, and that children growing up in low-income homes are more likely than other children to have behavior problems (Emery, 1988). To assess the predictive value of variables such as these relative to one another, a multifactorial approach is clearly needed (Hofferth, 1985).

In addition to the influence of family income, ethnicity, and household composition, another important predictor of many areas of social competence is gender. Gender differences in behavior problems have been widely reported, with boys exhibiting more behavior problems during the childhood years (Rutter & Garmezy, 1983). Boys are also more likely than girls to show serious disturbances of peer relations during childhood (Coie et al., 1982; Hartup, 1983). In addition, boys appear to suffer more adverse effects of economic deprivation and single-parent rearing than do girls (Elder, 1979; Hetherington et al., 1989).

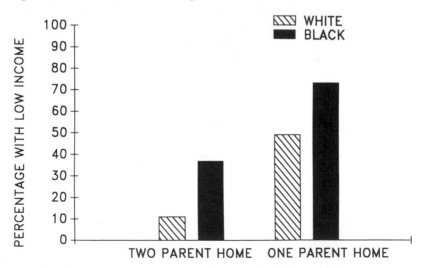

FIG 13.5. Percentage of children from low income homes as a function of ethnicity and household composition (from Patterson, Kupersmidt, & Vaden, 1990.

To assess the contributions of income level, gender, ethnicity, and household composition to prediction of children's competence at school, we (Patterson, Kupersmidt, & Vaden, 1990) studied three indices of children's school-based competence: peer relations, assessed via sociometric nominations; conduct, assessed via teacher ratings of classroom behavior; and academic achievement, assessed via scores on standardized achievement tests among children in the CLS. Given the focus of the present chapter, however, we report here only the results for peer relations.

We collected information about each child's gender, ethnicity, and household composition from school records. We coded ethnicity as White, Black, or other; as there were too few children in the "other" category to allow statistical analyses in the present framework, we dropped them for these analyses. Household composition was coded as living with both parents, with mother only, or other; again, as there were too few children in the "other" category, we dropped them for these analyses.

Taking into account the intercorrelations among independent variables, our major questions focused on the relative contributions of each of the four predictor variables to prediction of child social competence. To examine this issue, a simultaneous (standard) regression analysis was conducted, using income level, gender, ethnicity, household composition, and their interactions as independent variables. The dependent measure was each child's standardized social preference score.

Results showed that income level was the best predictor, followed by gender; both were significant at $p < .001$. There were no significant effects for ethnicity or household composition, nor were there any significant interactions. Boys and children from low-income homes were less well liked by their peers at school than were other children. This result is presented in Fig. 13.6.

Another way to look at these data is to examine them in categorical terms, examining the probability of rejection by peers as a function of the four predictor variables. Results here also showed that gender and family income level were the best predictors. Boys and children from low-income homes were more likely to be rejected by their peers than were other children (see Fig. 13.7). Again, there were no other main effects or interactions.

These results underline the importance of associations between low-family income and children's difficulties in peer relations. Even after controlling for ethnicity and for household composition, family income was still a significant predictor of children's popularity among peers. Consistent with results reported by Dishion (1990a) and by Roff et al. (1972) about peer acceptance, children from low-income homes were also more likely to be rejected by peers at school.

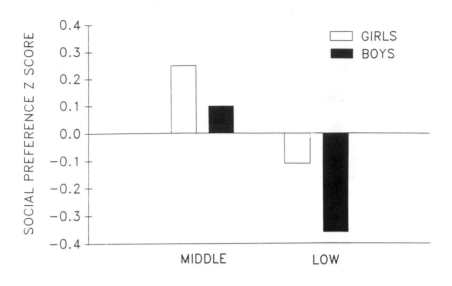

FIG. 13.6.   Average social preference Z scores as a function of gender and family income level (data from Patterson, Kupersmidt, & Vaden, 1990).

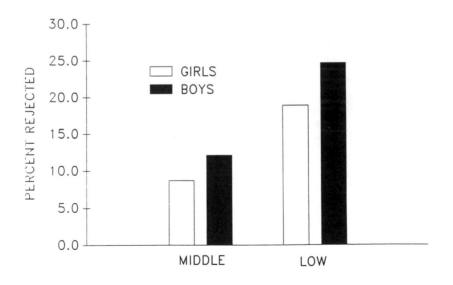

FIG. 13.7.   Percentages of children rejected by peers as a function of gender and family income level (data from Patterson, Vaden, & Kupersmidt, 1991).

One possible alternative interpretation of these results might focus on the potential confounding of family income and neighborhood of residence. Low-income families often live in low-income neighborhoods; the nature of opportunities for peer interaction may be different in these neighborhoods than in more affluent ones. It is possible, then, that the effects of family income as reported are actually attributable to the neighborhoods rather than to the families in which children are growing up.

To explore this possibility, we (Kupersmidt, Griesler, DeRosier, Patterson, & Davis, 1990) classified the neighborhoods in which children lived into low- or middle-income neighborhoods, using information from the 1980 U. S. Census (U. S. Bureau of the Census, 1982). Each child was thus classified as living in either a low- or middle-income family and— independently—as living in either a low- or a middle-income neighborhood. Using these classifications, we compared connections among family income level, neighborhood income level, and children's peer relations. To provide sufficient numbers of children in all cells of the design, we used data from the second year of the CLS (i.e., 1987), in which an additional grade cohort of children had been tested, for these analyses.

Results of these analyses clearly revealed that it was family income level rather than neighborhood income level that was associated with peer rejection. After considering family background, the income level of a child's neighborhood of residence did not have a significant impact on peer rejection. Children growing up in low-income families were, however, more likely than other children to be rejected by peers. In short, these results confirm the importance of economic hardship as a predictor of the quality of children's peer relations.

## Economic Hardship and Children's Peer Companionship Outside of School

Having established connections between economic disadvantage and children's popularity among their peers at school, we were also interested in studying possible connections between economic circumstances and other aspects of children's peer interactions, especially as these might occur outside of school. To this end, we also conducted a study of connections between economic hardship and the extent of children's peer companionship in activities outside of school (Patterson, Vaden, Griesler, & Kupersmidt, 1991).

Our previous work on peer companionship (Kupersmidt, Griesler, & Patterson, 1990), had revealed that, relative to other children of the same age, unpopular (i.e., rejected and neglected) children had fewer peer companions, and were socially isolated in a wider range of activities with same-aged peers outside of school. Taking into account our finding that economically disadvantaged children are more likely than other children to be unpopular among peers at school, and assuming that interpersonal attraction is a major determinant of companionship, we expected children from low-income homes to experience less peer companionship than other children in activities outside of school.

Using our Activity Playmate Checklist (Kupersmidt, Griesler, & Patterson, 1990), we explored the extent of children's same-aged peer companionship in seven different activities. The activities were: playing together on the playground, riding the school bus together or walking to and from school together, playing together in the neighborhood, taking lessons or playing on teams together, talking on the telephone, playing at home together, and eating meals at home together. On the Activity Playmate Checklist, children were asked to nominate all the children with whom they participated in each of the seven activities, from seven identical rosters of children in the same grade (or same class, for second graders). From these nominations, we calculated scores for self-reported companionship, peer-reported companionship, and number of reciprocated votes for companionship in each of the seven activities. We also calculated the number of activities in which each child was socially isolated from peers (i.e., had no reciprocated votes).

As before, we sought to disentangle the contributions of income level, ethnicity, household composition, and gender to the prediction of children's peer relations. To this end, we examined the peer companionship variables in multivariate analyses of variance for the three principal dependent measures, and in a univariate analysis of variance for the number of activities in which each child was socially isolated from peers.

Results confirmed the significance of economic disadvantage as a predictor of children's peer companionship. Children from low-income homes received fewer reciprocated nominations as companions in activities than did those from more affluent homes. In addition, as shown in Fig. 13.8, children from low-income homes were socially isolated (i.e., had no reciprocated votes for companionship) in a larger number of activities outside of school than other children. Independent of the contributions of other variables, then, economic disadvantage was associated with a relative lack of peer companionship in activities outside of school.

Differences in peer companionship associated with economic disadvantage were most pronounced for activities taking place in the home. Children from low-income homes had fewer reciprocated votes for peer companionship for all three in-home activities (viz., talking on the telephone, playing at home, and eating meals at home). The connection between income level and companionship was not entirely limited to activities taking place in the home, however, as low-income children also had fewer reciprocated nominations for companionship when playing on

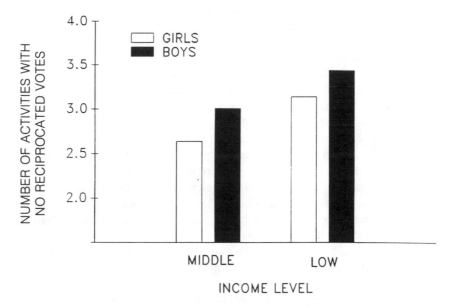

FIG. 13.8. Average number of activities for which children had no reciprocated votes as a function of gender and family income level (from Patterson, Vaden, Griesler, & Kupersmidt, 1991).

the playground. The differences on two of the three other out-of-home
activities, though not significant, were also in the same direction.

Consistent with results from our earlier study of popularity among
peers (Patterson, Kupersmidt, & Vaden, 1990), gender was also a significant predictor of the extent of children's peer companionship. Boys had
fewer reciprocated votes for companionship in activities and were socially isolated (i.e., had *no* reciprocated votes) in more activities than girls.
Ethnicity and household composition were not, however, significantly
related to peer companionship in our sample.

In summary, results of this work emphasize the significance of connections among gender, economic conditions, and the nature of children's
relations with peers. Consistent with earlier reports that boys and children from low-income homes are less well liked (Patterson, Vaden, &
Kupersmidt, 1990; Roff et al., 1972) and more likely to be rejected by
their peers at school (Patterson, Vaden, & Kupersmidt, 1991), our findings suggested that boys and children from low-income homes were also
less likely to experience the companionship of same-aged peers outside
of school.

As we had done for peer popularity, we also examined the possibility
that these results arose from a confounding of family and neighborhood
income levels (Kupersmidt, Griesler, DeRosier, et al., 1990). Assuming

that low-income families are more likely to reside in low-income neighborhoods, and that opportunities for peer companionship are likely to vary as a function of neighborhood characteristics that are associated with income levels, we wanted to evaluate the possibility that connections between peer companionship and family economic circumstances were attributable mainly to neighborhood rather than to family variables. To provide sufficient numbers of children in all cells of the design, we again used data from the second year of the project (i.e., 1987), in which an additional grade cohort of children had been tested, for these analyses.

Results showed that, for the most part, connections between family background and peer companionship were not the result of neighborhood influences (Kupersmidt, Griesler, De Rosier, et al., 1990). Neighborhood income level had no significant effect on the number of reciprocated votes for peer companionship in out-of-home activities. For in-home activities, both family and neighborhood variables had significant effects on numbers of reciprocated votes; children living in middle-income families and middle-income neighborhoods had larger numbers of reciprocated votes for peer companionship during in-home activities. There was also a significant family-by-neighborhood interaction, which revealed that neighborhood differences in peer companionship during in-home activities occurred for White children in middle-income homes, but not for other children. White children from middle-income homes in middle-income neighborhoods had significantly more reciprocated votes for peer companionship during in-home activities than did White children from middle-income homes in low-income neighborhoods; neighborhood of residence did not significantly affect peer companionship at home among other children. Overall, then, middle-income neighborhoods were associated with greater peer companionship during in-home activities for White children, but neighborhoods had no significant effect on peer companionship for other groups of children or for other activities.

In summary, our results suggest that both children's popularity among peers and their companionship from peers are linked to family economic circumstances. In our studies, children from low-income homes were less popular (Patterson, Kupersmidt, & Vaden, 1990), more likely to be rejected (Patterson, Vaden, & Kupersmidt, 1991), and had less companionship from peers outside of school (Patterson, Vaden, Griesler, & Kupersmidt, 1991). The extent to which this pattern extends also to other aspects of peer relations (e.g., children's dyadic friendships), or indeed to other types of social relationships (e.g., those with parents, teachers, and other significant adults) is as yet unknown. At the present time, however, our data suggest that children growing up in low-income homes have less favorable experiences with peers than children in more economically advantaged circumstances.

## HYPOTHESES ABOUT MEDIATING VARIABLES

To the extent that links have been established between family economic circumstances and children's peer relations, it is of interest to explore some of the ways in which these connections may arise. In this section, we discuss four major groups of hypotheses about how such linkages take place: the life transition, family interaction, genetic influence, and the person–environment fit hypotheses. We assume that mediating variables might themselves exert influence in any of a number of different ways (e.g., by affecting children's psychological states and/or their behavior with peers). Given the dearth of direct evidence, however, we do not speculate at any length about these possibilities here.

Although we discuss each group of hypotheses separately, they need not be seen as mutually exclusive. The existing research literature is too sparse at this time to sustain definitive conclusions. It seems likely, however, that all of the processes described in the following may play at least some role in mediating associations between family economic circumstances and children's peer relations.

### Life Transition Hypotheses

One cluster of hypotheses about links between family economic circumstances and children's peer relations focuses on the possible mediating role of life transitions. In this view, effects of family economic disadvantage on children's peer relations occur because families experiencing economic hardships are also more likely to experience life events, disruptions, and transitions, and these have negative effects on children's peer relations. With roots in traditions of research on acute life stress, social support, and mental health (Compas, 1987; Dohrenwend & Dohrenwend, 1974, 1981; Johnson, 1986), this group of hypotheses might include a number of specific possibilities.

One well-known version of this hypothesis is that effects of chronic and acute stressors are cumulative. This hypothesis suggests, for example, that children in low-income families who also experience acute life events or transitions would be more vulnerable to negative outcomes than low-income children who did not experience acute stress. Although cumulative effects of multiple stressors have been reported (Masten et al., 1988; Rutter, 1979, 1987; Shaw & Emery, 1988), the existing evidence has focused mainly on child behavior problems as the outcome measure.

As described earlier, we found support for the cumulative stressors hypothesis, using data from the CLS, and examining peer rejection as the outcome measure (Patterson, Vaden, & Kupersmidt, 1991). Consistent with findings for adults (Dohrenwend & Dohrenwend, 1974, 1981), we found that children from families experiencing economic hardship were also significantly more likely to have experienced acute life events and transitions. Those who experienced high levels of both chronic and acute stress were more likely to be rejected by peers than were other children. Associations between cumulative stress and other aspects of children's peer relations remain, however, to be studied.

Through what process or processes do associations such as these emerge? One possibility is that life events have a direct influence on children's emotional states, that these affect behavior, and that, in turn, children's behavior influences the qualities of their peer relations. Of course, stressful life events also affect parental emotions and behaviors in ways that have an impact on children. In addition, the occurrence of some life events (e.g., parental divorce) may contribute to the probability that others (e.g., residential mobility) will also occur. Connections among these and other factors are likely to be complex.

In summary, little evidence is available about different versions of the life transition hypothesis, as they might bear on associations between economic adversity and children's peer relations. The extent to which acute life stress may overshadow other variables is, for instance, not yet clear. We also need to know more about the impact of life events and transitions on children's peer relations over time, and about the pathways through which such effects may occur.

## Family Interaction Hypotheses

A second group of hypotheses about links between family economic circumstances and children's peer relations suggests that connections result from differences in social interactions among family members, in social relationships among family members, and/or in family processes. In this view, effects of family economic disadvantage on children's peer relations occur because interactions, relationships, and family processes are different in low-income families than in other families, and these differences lead to differences in children's peer relations. With its roots in a long tradition of social science research on poverty and social class (Auletta, 1982; Gecas, 1979; Harrington, 1962; Moynihan, 1968; Wilson, 1987), this family of hypotheses has many variant forms.

One of the most influential ideas in this area is that the quality of children's attachment relationships with their principal caregiver influences the quality of their relationships with peers (Cohn, 1990; Cohn et al, 1991; Elicker et al., this volume; Mueller & Silverman, 1989; Rubin & Lollis, 1988). Indeed, some of the most compelling evidence that the quality of children's peer relations is a reflection of the underlying quality of the parent–child relationship has been inspired by formulations of attachment theory (Ainsworth, Blehar, Waters, & Wall, 1978; Bowlby, 1988; Sroufe & Fleeson, 1986). Individual differences in the caregiver's responsivity and sensitivity to infants' needs are thought to influence later relationships outside the family because parents who are responsive to their infant's cues are able to provide the baby with a secure base from which to explore the environment. A child who is encouraged to develop autonomy but who can feel confident that his or her emotional needs will be met will be more likely to approach peer relations with a sense of confidence and self-efficacy (Mueller & Silverman, 1989).

At the same time, a child's interactional history with the parent shapes his or her expectations about how others will respond. More specifically, children who have formed secure attachment relationships develop a "working model" or image of the parent as responsive, and of themselves as worthy of love (Elicker et al., this volume). As compared to children with insecure attachment relationships, securely attached children are thus thought to be more likely to have positive expectations about how peers will respond to them and more likely to elicit positive responses from other children.

Considerable evidence has accumulated in support of the idea that quality of attachment relationships is predictive of children's peer relationships (Cohn et al., 1991; Elicker et al., this volume). Longitudinal studies have consistently demonstrated connections between the quality of infant–parent attachment relationships and the quality of children's social interactions with peers throughout the first 10 years of life (Erickson, Sroufe, & Egeland, 1985; Grossman & Grossman, in press; LaFreniere & Sroufe, 1985). Cross-sectional studies of attachment and children's peer relations have also shown that children with secure attachment relationships are likely to have more favorable peer relations (Cohn, 1990; Park & Waters, 1989).

In the present context, differences in children's peer relations attributable to family economic hardship could be mediated by differences in children's attachment relationships with parents (Rubin & Lollis, 1988). The evidence suggests that insecure attachment relationships are more common among low-income than among middle income-families (Ainsworth, et al., 1978; Vaughn, Egeland, & Sroufe, 1979; Waters, Vaughn, & Egeland, 1980). It is thus possible that higher numbers of insecure attachment relationships among children from low-income homes result in greater difficulties in peer relations for these children. To the extent that this is true, linkages would most likely be mediated by differences between low- and middle-income families in the nature of parent–child interactions.

Whereas attachment hypotheses focus on relationships, a related set of hypotheses focuses on qualities of social interaction in the family as influences on children's peer relations (Putallaz & Heflin, 1990; Parke et al., 1988; Parke et al., 1989). Much of the research on family interactions and peer relations has focused on two dimensions of parent behavior with their children: warmth and control (Maccoby & Martin, 1983). Warmth has generally referred to parental behaviors such as praise, encouragement, physical affection, and approval, whereas control has most often referred to consistent enforcement of rules together with age-appropriate demands on the child. Baumrind's (1973, 1989) research has shown that preschool children of parents high on warmth and control (whom she called "authoritative") were consistently more socially confident and skilled with their peers than were children whose parents acted in other ways. Similar results have been reported by Hinde and Tamplin (1983), Putallaz (1987), and Attili (1989).

Do differences in parent–child interaction mediate differences in children's peer relations as a function of economic disadvantage? Experimental work in laboratory settings has shown that when parents are mentally preoccupied, they become less responsive in interaction with their young children (Zussman, 1980). Based on home observations, Patterson (1982) has reported that mothers under stress were more likely than other mothers to use negativistic disapproval with their children. Social class differences in childrearing practices consistent with these ideas have also been reported (Gecas, 1979; Kohn, 1959, 1963). These findings suggest that parents experiencing economic hardship and its attendant concerns are less likely to show authoritative patterns of interaction with their children.

Consistent with such suggestions, studies of families suffering severe economic losses during the Great Depression of the 1930s revealed many changes in interaction patterns among family members. Heavy loss of income increased both marital conflict (Liker & Elder, 1983) and fathers' likelihood of using arbitrary or punitive disciplinary techniques (Elder, Liker, & Cross, 1984; Elder, Van Nguyen, & Caspi, 1985). Effects of these changes were mediated by many factors, including age and gender of the offspring, but the available evidence showed only inconsistent effects on children's peer relations (Elder, 1974). These results might be attributed to the widespread nature of economic difficulties in the country at that time, or they might relate to other factors; the evidence is not sufficient to allow clear conclusions on this point.

Contemporary studies of the effects of parental unemployment or recent family economic crises on children and families have also revealed a variety of effects (Flanagan, 1990; Lempers, Clark-Lempers, & Simons, 1989; McLoyd, 1989; Slaughter, 1988). For example, Flanagan (1990) has reported that adolescents in families with recent parental unemployment describe greater conflict with parents than do their peers in families with steady employment. In a study of economic hardship in families affected by a downturn in the agricultural economy of the Midwestern United States during the early 1980s, Lempers et al., (1989) found that family economic stress was associated with depressive feelings among adolescents, and that this connection was mediated in part by adolescent reports of less nurturance and more inconsistent discipline from parents. Effects of such changes for peer relationships of the children and adolescents who are involved remain, however, to be explored.

Another version of the parent–child interaction hypothesis focuses on the role of parents as managers of their children's peer relations, monitoring and supervising children's activities (Ladd et al., this volume; Parke et al., 1988, 1989). The evidence suggests that appropriate parental monitoring and supervision of peer relations can be helpful in sustaining positive interactions among peers (Ladd & Golter, 1988; Ladd, Hart, Wadsworth, & Golter, 1988; Parke & Bhavnagri, 1989; Parke et al., 1989). Conversely, lack of appropriate discipline, monitoring, and supervision is associated with antisocial behavior and rejection by peers (Dishion, 1990a, 1990b; Patterson, Kupersmidt, & Griesler, 1990; Patterson & Stouthammer-Loeber, 1984).

Do differences in parental supervision and monitoring underlie differences in children's peer relations as a function of economic disadvantage? One approach to this question is to focus on parental involvement with their children's educational activities, as monitoring and supervision of children's activities presumably form at least a portion of what highly involved parents do. Consistent with the family interaction hypothesis, teacher ratings of parental involvement in children's education are higher for children from middle-income than for those from low-income families (Stevenson & Baker, 1987).

To explore the hypothesis that low parent involvement is related to disturbances in peer relations, we (Kupersmidt, DeRosier, Patterson, & Griesler, 1990) compared teacher ratings of parent involvement and family income level as predictors of peer popularity among children in the CLS sample. Consistent with Stevenson and Baker's (1987) results, we found that parent involvement was rated higher among children from middle-income than among those from low-income homes. Most interesting, however, from the standpoint of the family interaction hypothesis, our results showed that parent involvement was the best predictor of popularity among peers at school; effects of income level were not significant after parental involvement had been taken into account.

These findings are clearly consistent with the hypothesis that effects of low income on children's peer relations are mediated by the nature of parent–child interactions. The generality of this finding across different aspects of children's peer relations remains to be assessed, and the specific nature of parent–child interactions responsible for the results remain to be specified. The result is nevertheless a promising step toward understanding of the ways in which patterns of interaction within families may affect children's relationships with peers.

Also of potential interest when considering ways in which economic factors and patterns of family interaction may be related to children's peer relations is the extent to which parents are able to provide for children's basic health and medical needs. Although not usually considered under the rubric of research on parent–child interaction, it is clear that competent care for children involves provision for basic needs such as nutrition, exercise, rest, and medical care. To the extent that children from economically disadvantaged homes are more likely to be malnourished, restless, sleepy, or ill (McLoyd, 1989; Physician Task Force on Hunger in America, 1985), these conditions will surely affect their behavior and relations with peers. As yet, however, little in the way of research evidence is available to document ways in which such variables may influence children's relationships with their peers.

In summary, there are a number of ways in which relationships and interactions in the family might be thought to mediate the connections between economic disadvantage and children's peer relations. Although there is good reason to believe that such mediating linkages may occur, there is as yet relatively little direct evidence to document the existence of specific links.

## Genetic Hypotheses

Another group of hypotheses about links between family economic circumstances and children's peer relations suggests that the connections result at least in part from genetic factors. In this view, connections between family economic hardship and children's peer relations occur because family members share some genetic characteristics and these are related both to family economic conditions and to children's relationships with peers. With its roots in research and theory on human behavior genetics (Goldsmith, 1983, Plomin, 1989; Plomin & Daniels, 1987; Scarr & McCartney, 1983), this family of hypotheses presents a number of possibilities, most of which have yet to be addressed in the empirical literature.

As Rowe (1989) has suggested, results of research on peer relations among siblings and twins suggest the existence of significant genetic commonalities in children's peer relations. For instance, Roff et al. (1972) reported significant correlations between peer-rated popularity scores that ranged from about .30 for nontwin siblings up to about .70 for identical twins. The fact that identical twins' peer status scores were more highly correlated than those for nontwin siblings suggests the possibility that genetic factors might account for some or even most of the similarity in peer relations among family members.

There are a number of avenues through which hereditary influences might occur. For instance, physical attractiveness has long been recognized as a correlate of children's popularity among peers (Hartup, 1983). Although children growing up in low-income families may be at a disadvantage in matters of grooming (Elder, 1974), genetic influences are also important influences on children's physical appearance. Scores on popular tests of intelligence are related to peer acceptance during childhood (Hartup, 1983), and there may be genetic influences here as well. Further research using the techniques of behavior genetics might disentangle genetic and environmental sources of variation in children's peer relations (Rowe, 1989), but few conclusions can be drawn on the basis of existing research.

### Hypotheses About Person–Environment Fit

Another group of hypotheses about links between family economic circumstances and children's peer relations suggests that connections result not from characteristics of the person alone, nor from characteristics of the environment alone, but from characteristics of the fit between people and the environments in which they live. In this view, effects of family economic disadvantage on children's peer relations occur at least in part because many of the institutional (e.g., school) settings in which children meet and spend time with other children embody normative values of the dominant culture, and children from low-income homes may not fit very easily into such environments. With roots in traditions of research on person–environment fit within the areas of personality and developmental psychology (e.g., Ekehammer, 1974; Endler & Magnusson, 1976; Magnusson & Allen, 1983), this family of hypotheses has as yet been little studied, but it could take a variety of forms.

As an illustration of the person–environment fit concept as it relates to peer status among children, consider findings from a study by Wright, Giammarino, and Parad (1986). Studying behavior and popularity among boys attending a summer camp for disturbed children, they compared popularity as a joint function of boys' own behavior *and* of the modal pattern of behavior among other children in their group. The major finding was that aggressive children were less well liked when they were placed in groups composed of nonaggressive children than when they were placed in groups composed of children who were also aggressive. Similarly, withdrawn children were less well liked when placed in a group of aggressive children than when placed with other withdrawn children. In other words, when children were placed in a peer environment that did not match their own behavioral tendencies, they were more likely to encounter difficulties with peers. Wright et al. (1986) argued that, out of his or her element, a child was more likely to be regarded as a "misfit" and to be disliked by peers.

Extrapolating from the work of Wright et al. (1986), one might consider the possibility that children from low-income families are at a social disadvantage when enrolled in schools that draw the majority of their students from middle-income homes. Normative values of the dominant American middle class culture celebrate individual academic achievement and economic success (Bellah, Madsen, Sullivan, Swidler, & Tipton, 1985). Because it is more difficult for children from low-income homes to feel successful in these ways, it may also be more difficult for them to "fit in" and be accepted by their peers at school.

It is possible that children from low-income homes are more popular among peers and have better peer relations when they attend schools in which they are the majority rather than the minority of students. If so, then at least some of the associations between family income level and children's peer relations as described may turn out to be related more strongly to context than to characteristics of children or their families. None of these possibilities has, to our knowledge, been addressed in empirical research to date; further research will be necessary in order to clarify these issues.

## Summary and Directions for Research

Overall, the evidence suggests that children's experiences with peers are associated with family economic circumstances. We and others have found that children from low-income homes are less popular among peers than those from middle-income homes (Dishion, 1990a; Elkins, 1958; Patterson, Kupersmidt, & Vaden, 1990; Roff et al., 1972). We have also reported that children from low-income homes are more likely to be rejected by peers (Patterson, Vaden, & Kupersmidt, 1991), less likely to have peer companionship, and more likely to be socially isolated in activities outside of school (Patterson, Vaden, Griesler, & Kupersmidt, 1991).

The relatively more negative peer experiences of children from low-income homes may be helpful in understanding linkages among economic circumstances, peer relations, and mental health. Difficulties in childhood peer relations have been shown to predict negative life outcomes such as school dropout, delinquency, and psychopathology (Parker & Asher, 1987). The greater vulnerability of low-income populations to most mental health difficulties is also well known (Dohrenwend & Dohrenwend, 1974, 1981). It is thus possible that difficulties in peer relations during childhood may be one important mediator of social class differences in mental health. Further research will be necessary, however, before this possibility can be evaluated.

In this chapter, we have presented initial cross-sectional findings from the first year of the CLS about linkages between family income and children's peer relations. As Featherman and his colleagues (Featherman, Spenner, & Tsunematsu, 1988) have pointed out, though, family income and social class are often dynamic contextual features of the contexts of child development. In particular, many families move into and out of poverty as a function of family formation and dissolution. The effects of such shifts are not, however, well understood. Future research in this area should, where possible, study associations between varying family economic circumstances and children's peer relations over time.

We have discussed a number of different clusters of hypotheses to account for the associations we observed between family economic adversity and children's peer relations. These included hypotheses about increased stressful life transitions; difficulties in family interactions, relationships, and processes; genetic hypotheses; and hypotheses about person–environment fit. Any or all of these proposed links might take effect through their influences on children's psychological states and/or behavioral tendencies. Little direct evidence about such mediating linkages is available, however, and exploration of the possibilities remains an important task for future research.

Our findings also suggested that important life transitions were associated with difficulties in children's peer relations. Consistent with previous findings (Hetherington, 1988; Hetherington, et al., 1979; Hetherington, et al., 1989), we found that parental divorce and separation were significantly associated with peer rejection among children in the CLS sample (Patterson, Vaden, & Kupersmidt, 1991). As has been found in studies of children's behavior problems (Masten et al., 1988; Rutter, 1979, 1987; Shaw & Emery, 1988), relations between chronic and acute life stresses and peer rejection appeared to be cumulative; the more chronic and acute stressors to which children had been subjected, the greater the risk of peer rejection. These results suggest that particularly significant problems in peer relations are likely to be faced by children growing up in highly stressful circumstances (cf. Cicchetti, Lynch, Shonk, & Manly, this volume; Zahn-Waxler, Denham, Iannotti, & Cummings, this volume).

We have emphasized associations between family economic circumstances and children's peer relations, and in so doing, we have focused on differences between families. Also deserving of attention, however, are differences within families in the responses of different family members to economic disadvantage. A number of writers have pointed to the variety and range of responses to economic adversity (Elder, 1974; Garmezy, 1987; Rutter, 1987; Werner & Smith, 1982), and others have argued for the importance of within-family differences in socialization and development (Plomin & Daniels, 1987; Rowe, 1989). It will be important for future research to explore factors underlying resilience and successful coping in the face of economic adversity among children and families.

If, as Perloff (1990) has argued, "poverty is the most important social issue of our time" (p. 7), then increasing our knowledge about social and psychological concomitants of economic hardship among children is an important task for developmental psychologists to undertake. As we have described, connections between family economic hardship and children's peer relations are beginning to be identified. Related studies using CLS data (Patterson, Kupersmidt, & Vaden, 1990) have revealed associations between low family income level and children's difficulties in conduct and in academic achievement that are as large or larger than the ones discussed here, and these results are consistent with those reported by other investigators (McLoyd, 1990). Though ably documented for the period of the Great Depression (Elder, 1974), the impact of economic hardship during childhood on concurrent adjustment and on development during adolescence and adulthood is in need of further study in our own historical time.

## ACKNOWLEDGMENTS

Work described here was supported in part by a grant from the W. Alton Jones Foundation and by a cooperative agreement between the United States Department of Education and the University of Virginia. We wish to thank Dr. Vincent Cibbarelli and the staff and students of the Charlottesville Public Schools for their cooperation, as well as the numerous others whose diligent efforts made it possible to collect and analyze the data on which our studies are based.

## REFERENCES

Ainsworth, M., Blehar, M.,Waters, E., & Wall, S. (1978). *Patterns of attachment*. Hillsdale, N J: Lawrence Erlbaum Associates.

Attili, G. (1989). Social competence versus emotional security: The link between home relationships and behavior problems at school. In B. H. Schneider, G. Attili, J. Nadel, & R. P. Weissberg (Eds.), *Social competence in developmental perspective*, (pp. 293–311). London: Kluwer.

Auletta, K. (1982). *The underclass*. New York: Random House.

Baumrind, D. (1973). The development of instrumental competence through socialization. In A. D. Pick (Ed.), *Minnesota symposium of child psychology*, (Vol. 7, 3–46). Minneapolis: University of Minnesota Press.

Baumrind, D. (1989). Rearing competent children. In W. Damon (Ed.), *Child development today and tomorrow*, (pp. 349–378). San Francisco: Jossey-Bass.

Bellah, R. N., Madsen, R., Sullivan, W. M., Swidler, A., & Tipton, S. M. (1985). *Habits of the heart: Individualism and commitment in American life*. Berkeley, CA: University of California Press.

Bowlby, J. (1988). *A secure base: Parent–child attachment and healthy human development*. New York: Basic Books.

Bronfenbrenner, U. (1979). *The ecology of human development: Experiments by nature and design*. Cambridge, MA: Harvard University Press.

Cicchetti, D. (1984). The emergence of developmental psychopathology. *Child Development, 55,* 1–7.

Cohn, D. A. (1990). Child–mother attachment of 6-year-olds and social competence at school. *Child Development, 61,* 152–162.

Cohn, D. A., Patterson, C. J., & Christopoulos, C. (1991). The family and children's peer relations. *Journal of Social and Personal Relationships, 8,* 315–346.

Coie, J. D., Dodge, K. A., & Coppotelli, H. (1982). Dimensions and types of social status in the school: A cross-age comparison. *Developmental Psychology, 18,* 557–570.

Coie, J. D., Dodge, K. A., & Kupersmidt, J. B. (1990). Peer group behavior and social status. In S. R. Asher & J. D. Coie (Eds.), *Peer rejection in childhood*, (pp. 17–59). New York: Cambridge University Press.

Coie, J. D., & Kupersmidt, J. B. (1983). A behavioral analysis of emerging social status in boys' groups. *Child Development, 54,* 1400–1416.

Compas, B. E. (1987). Stress and life events during childhood and adolescence. *Clinical Psychology Review, 7,* 275–302.

Cowen, E. L., Weissberg, R. P., & Guare, J. (1984). Differentiating attributes of children referred to a school mental health program. *Journal of Abnormal Child Psychology, 12,* 397–410.

Dishion, T. J. (1990a). The family ecology of boys' peer relations in middle childhood. *Child Development, 61,* 874–892.

Dishion, T. J. (1990b). The peer context of troublesome child and adolescent behavior. In P. E. Leone (Ed.), *Understanding troubled and troubling youth: A multidisciplinary perspective*. Beverly Hills, CA: Sage.

Dodge, K. A. (1983). Behavioral antecedents of peer social status. *Child Development, 54,* 1386–1399.

Dohrenwend, B. S., & Dohrenwend, B. P. (1974). *Stressful life events: Their nature and effects*. New York: Wiley.

Dohrenwend, B. P., & Dohrenwend, B. S. (1981). Socioenvironmental factors, stress, and psychopathology. *American Journal of Community Psychology, 9,* 128–164.

Edelman, M. W. (1985). The sea is so wide and my boat is so small: Problems facing Black children today. In H. P. McAdoo & J. L. McAdoo (Eds.), *Black children: Social, educational, and parental environments*, (pp. 72–82). Beverly Hills, CA: Sage.

Edelman, M. W. (1987). *Families in peril: An agenda for social change*. Cambridge, MA: Harvard University Press.

Ekehammer, B. (1974). Interactionism in personality from a historical perspective. *Psychological Bulletin, 81,* 1026–1048.

Elder, G. H., Jr. (1974). *Children of the Great Depression*. Chicago: University of Chicago Press.

Elder, G. H., Jr. (1979). Historical change in life patterns and personality. In P. B. Baltes & O. G. Brim (Eds.), *Lifespan development and behavior*. (Vol. 2, pp. 117–159). New York: Academic Press.

Elder, G. H., Jr., Liker, J, & Cross, C. (1984). Parent–child behavior in the Great Depression: Life course and intergenerational influences. In P. Baltes & O. Brim (Eds.), *Life span development and behavior*, (Vol. 6, pp. 109–158). New York: Academic Press.

Elder, G. H., Jr., Van Nguyen, T., & Caspi, A. (1985). Linking family hardship to children's lives. *Child Development, 56,* 361–375.

Elkins, D. (1958). Some factors related to the choice status of 90 eighth grade children in a school society. *Genetic Psychology Monographs, 58,* 207–272.

Emery, R. E. (1988). *Marriage, divorce, and children's adjustment*. Beverly Hills: Sage.

Endler, N. S., & Magnusson, D. (1976). Toward an interactional psychology of personality. *Psychological Bulletin, 83*, 956–979.

Erickson, M. F., Sroufe, L. A., & Egeland, B. (1985). The relationship between quality of attachment and behavior problems in a high-risk sample. In I. Bretherton & E. Waters (Eds.), Growing points in attachment theory and research. *Monographs of the Society for Research in Child Development, 50*, (1–2, Serial No. 209).

Featherman, D. L., Spenner, K. I., & Tsunematsu, N. (1988). Class and the socialization of children: Constancy, change, or irrelevance? In E. M. Hetherington, R. M. Lerner, & M. Perlmutter (Eds.), *Child development in life-span perspective*, (pp. 67–90). Hillsdale, NJ: Lawrence Erlbaum Associates.

Flanagan, C. A. (1990). Changes in family work status: Effects on parent–adolescent decision making. *Child Development, 61*, 163–177.

Garmezy, N. (1987). Stress, competence, and development. *American Journal of Orthopsychiatry, 57*, 159–174.

Gecas, V. (1979). The influence of social class on socialization. In W. R. Burr, R. Hill, F. I. Nye, & I. L. Reiss (Eds.), *Contemporary theories about the family*, (Vol. 1, pp. 365–404). New York: Free Press.

Glick, P. C. (1988). Demographic pictures of black families. In H. P. McAdoo & J. L. McAdoo (Eds.), *Black children: Social, educational, and parental environments*, (pp. 111–132). Beverly Hills, CA: Sage.

Goldsmith, H. H. (1983). Genetic influences on personality from infancy to adulthood. *Child Development, 54*, 331–335.

Grossman, K. E., & Grossman, K. (in press). Attachment quality as an organizer of emotional and behavioral responses. In P. Marris, J. Stevenson-Hinde, & C. Parkes (Eds.), *Attachment across the life cycle*. New York: Rutledge.

Harrington, M. (1962). *The other America: Poverty in the United States*. New York: Macmillan.

Hartup, W. W. (1983). The peer system. In E. M. Hetherington (Ed.), *Handbook of child psychology: Socialization, personality, and social development*, (pp 103–196). New York: Wiley.

Hetherington, E. M. (1988). Parents, children, and siblings: Six years after divorce. In R. A. Hinde & J. Stevenson-Hinde (Eds.), *Relationships within families: Mutual influences*, (pp. 311–331). Oxford, England: Oxford University Press.

Hetherington, E. M., Cox, M., & Cox, R. (1979). Play and social interaction in children following divorce. *Journal of Social Issues, 35*, 26–49.

Hetherington, E. M., Stanley-Hagan, M., & Anderson, E. R. (1989). Marital transitions: A child's perspective. *American Psychologist, 44*, 303–312.

Hinde, R., & Tamplin, A. (1983). Relations between mother–child interaction and behavior in preschool. *British Journal of Developmental Psychology, 1*, 231–257.

Hofferth, S. L. (1985). Children's life course: Family structure and living arrangements in cohort perspective. In G. H. Elder (Ed.), *Life course dynamics: Trajectories and transitions* (pp. 75–112). Ithaca, NY: Cornell University Press.

Johnson, J. H. (1986). *Life events as stressors in childhood and adolescence*. Beverly Hills, CA: Sage.

Knapp, J. L., Chesser, D. E., Olsen, E. R., & Barnes, G. E. (1989). *An economic profile of the Charlottesville Metropolitan Statistical Area*. Charlottesville, VA: University of Virginia Center for Public Service.

Kohlberg, L., LaCrosse, J., & Ricks, D. (1972). The predictability of adult mental health from childhood behavior. In B. B. Wolman (Ed.), *Manual of child psychopathology*, (pp. 1217–1284). New York: McGraw-Hill.

Kohn, M. L. (1959). Social class and the exercise of parental authority. *American Sociological Review, 24*, 352–366.

Kohn, M. L. (1963). Social class and parent–child relationships: An interpretation. *American Journal of Sociology, 68*, 471–480.

Kupersmidt, J. B., Coie, J. D., & Dodge, K. A. (1990). Predicting disorder from peer social problems. In S. R. Asher & J. D. Coie (Eds.), *Peer rejection in childhood* (pp. 274–305) New York: Cambridge University Press.

Kupersmidt, J. B., DeRosier, M. E., Patterson, C. J., & Griesler, P. C. (1990). Parental involvement and children's peer relationships, behavior, self-concept, and academic adjustment. Unpublished manuscript, University of North Carolina at Chapel Hill, Department of Psychology.

Kupersmidt, J. B., Griesler, P. C., DeRosier, M. E., Patterson, C. J., & Davis, P. W. (1990). Family and neighborhood influences on social and behavioral adjustment. Unpublished manuscript, University of North Carolina at Chapel Hill, Department of Psychology.

Kupersmidt, J. B., Griesler, P. C., & Patterson, C. J. (1990). Sociometric status, aggression, and affiliation patterns of peers. Unpublished manuscript, University of North Carolina at Chapel Hill, Department of Psychology.

Ladd, G. W., & Golter, B. S. (1988). Parents' management of preschoolers' peer relations: Is it related to social competence? *Developmental Psychology, 24*, 109–117.

Ladd, G. W., Hart, C. H., Wadsworth, E. M., & Golter, B. (1988). Preschoolers' peer networks in nonschool settings: Relationships to family characteristics and school adjustment. In J. Antrobus, M. Hammer, & S. Salzinger (Eds.), *Social networks of children, adolescents, and college students*, (pp. 61–92). Hillsdale, NJ: Lawrence Erlbaum Associates.

LaFreniere, P., & Sroufe, L. A. (1985). Profiles of peer competence in the preschool: Interrelations between measures, influence of social ecology, and relation to attachment history. *Developmental Psychology, 21*, 56–68.

Lamb, M. E., & Nash, A. (1989). Infant–mother attachment, sociability, and peer competence. In T. J. Berndt & G. W. Ladd (Eds.), *Peer relationships in child development* (pp. 219–245). New York: Wiley.

Laosa, L. M. (1988). Ethnicity and single parenting in the United States. In E. M. Hetherington & J. D. Arasteh (Eds.), *Impact of divorce, single parenting, and stepparenting on children* (pp. 23–49). Hillsdale, NJ: Lawrence Erlbaum Associates.

Ledingham, J. E. (1981). Developmental patterns of aggressive and withdrawn behavior in childhood: A possible method for identifying preschizophrenics. *Journal of Abnormal Child Psychology, 9*, 1–22.

Lempers, J., Clark-Lempers, D., & Simons, R. L. (1989). Economic hardship, parenting and distress in adolescence. *Child Development, 60*, 25–39.

Liker, J. K., & Elder, G. H., Jr. (1983). Economic hardship and marital relations in the 1930s. *American Sociological Review, 48*, 343–359.

Maccoby, E. E., & Martin, J. (1983). Socialization in the context of the family: Parent–child interaction. In E. M. Hetherington (Ed.), *Handbook of child psychology: Vol. 4. Socialization, personality, and social development* (pp. 1–101). New York: Wiley.

MacDonald, K. B., & Parke, R. D. (1984). Bridging the gap: Parent–child play interaction and interactive competence. *Child Development, 55*, 1265–1277.

Magnusson, D., & Allen, V. (Eds.). (1983). *Human development: An interactional perspective*. New York: Academic Press.

Masten, A. S., Garmezy, N., Tellegen, A., Pellegrini, D. S., Larkin, K., & Larsen, A. (1988). Competence and stress in school children: The moderating effects of individual and family qualities. *Journal of Child Psychology and Psychiatry, 29*, 745–764.

McLoyd, V. (1989). Socialization and development in a changing economy: The effects of paternal job and income loss on children. *American Psychologist, 44,* 293–302.

McLoyd, V. (1990). The impact of economic hardship on Black families and children: Psychological distress, parenting, and socioemotional development. *Child Development, 61,* 311–346.

Moynihan, D. P. (Ed.). (1968). *On understanding poverty: Perspectives from the social sciences.* New York: Basic Books.

Mueller, E., & Silverman, N. (1989). Peer relations in maltreated children. In D. Cicchetti & V. Carlson (Eds.), *Child maltreatment* (pp. 529–578). New York: Cambridge University Press.

Park, D., & Waters, E. (1989). Security of attachment and preschool friendships. *Child Development, 60,* 1076–1081.

Parke, R. D., & Bhavnagri, N. (1989). Parents as managers of children's peer relationships. In D. Belle (Ed.), *Children's social networks and social support* (pp. 241–259). New York: Wiley.

Parke, R. D., MacDonald, K. B., Beitel, A., & Bhavnagri, N. (1988). The role of the family in the development of peer relationships. In R. D. Peters & R. J. McMahan (Eds.), *Marriages and families: Behavioral treatments and processes* (pp. 17–44). New York: Brunner-Mazel.

Parke, R. D., MacDonald, K. B., Burks, V. M., Carson, J., Bhavnagri, N., Barth, J. M., & Beitel, A. (1989). Family and peer systems: In search of linkages. In K. Kreppner & R. M. Lerner (Eds.), *Family systems and life span development* (pp. 65–92). Hillsdale, NJ: Lawrence Erlbaum Associates.

Parker, J., & Asher, S. R. (1987). Peer acceptance and later personal adjustment: Are low accepted children "at risk"? *Psychological Bulletin, 102,* 357–389.

Patterson, C. J., Kupersmidt, J. B., & Griesler, P. C. (1990). Children's perceptions of self and of relationships with others as a function of sociometric status. *Child Development, 61,* 1335–1349.

Patterson, C. J., Kupersmidt, J. B., & Vaden, N. A. (1990). Income level, gender, ethnicity, and household composition as predictors of children's school-based competence. *Child Development, 61,* 485–494.

Patterson, C. J., Vaden, N. A., Griesler, P. C., & Kupersmidt, J. B. (1991). Income level, gender, ethnicity, and household composition as predictors of children's peer companionship outside of school. *Journal of Applied Developmental Psychology, 12,* 447–465.

Patterson, C.J., Vaden, N. A., & Kupersmidt, J. B. (1991). Family background, recent life events, and peer rejection during childhood. *Journal of Social and Personal Relationships, 8,* 347–361.

Patterson, G. R. (1982). *Coercive family process.* Eugene, OR: Castalia.

Patterson, G. R., & Stouthammer-Loeber, M. (1984). The correlation of family management practices and delinquency. *Child Development, 55,* 1299–1306.

Perloff, R. (1990). Examining the psychological correlates of poverty: Toward advancing psychology in the public interest. *Advancing the Public Interest,* II (No. 2), 7.

Physician Task Force on Hunger in America. (1985). *Hunger in America: The growing epidemic.* Middletown, CT: Wesleyan University Press.

Plomin, R. (1989). Environment and genes: Determinants of behavior. *American Psychologist, 44,* 105–111.

Plomin, R., & Daniels, D. (1987). Why are children in the same family so different from one another? *Behavioral and Brain Sciences, 10,* 1–60.

Putallaz, M. (1987). Maternal behavior and children's sociometric status. *Child Development, 58,* 324–340.

Putallaz, M., & Heflin, A. H. (1990). Parent–child interaction. In S. R. Asher & J. D. Coie (Eds.), *Peer rejection in childhood*, (pp. 189–216). New York: Cambridge University Press.

Roff, M., Sells, S. B., & Golden, M. M. (1972). *Social adjustment and personality development in children*. Minneapolis: University of Minnesota Press.

Roopnarine, J. L., & Adams, G. R. (1987). The interactional teaching patterns of mothers and fathers with their popular, moderately popular, or unpopular children. *Journal of Abnormal Child Psychology, 15*, 125–136.

Rowe, D. (1989). Families and peers: Another look at the nature/nurture question. In G. W. Ladd & T. J. Berndt (Eds.), *Peer relationships in child development* (pp. 274–299). New York: Wiley.

Rubin, K. H., & Lollis, S. (1988). Peer relationships, social skills, and infant attachment: A continuity model. In J. Belsky (Ed.), *Clinical implications of infant attachment* (pp. 219– 252). Hillsdale, NJ: Lawrence Erlbaum Associates.

Rutter, M. (1979). Protective factors in children's responses to stress and disadvantage. In M. W. Kent & J. E. Rolf (Eds.), *Primary prevention of psychopathology*. Vol. III. *Social competence in children* (pp. 49–74). Hanover, NH: University Press of New England.

Rutter, M. (1987). Psychosocial resilience and protective mechanisms. *American Journal of Orthopsychiatry, 57*, 316–331.

Rutter, M., & Garmezy, N. (1983). Developmental psychopathology. In E. M. Hetherington (Ed.), *Handbook of child psychology: Socialization, personality, and social development* (pp. 775–911). New York: Wiley.

Scarr, S., & McCartney, K. (1983). How people make their own environments: A theory of genotype-environment effects. *Child Development, 54*, 424–435.

Shaw, D. S., & Emery, R. E. (1988). Chronic family adversity and school-age children's maladjustment. *Journal of the American Academy of Child and Adolescent Psychiatry, 27*, 200–206.

Slaughter, D. (Ed.). (1988). *Black children and poverty: A developmental perspective. New Directions in Child Development, No. 42*. San Francisco: Jossey-Bass.

Sroufe, L. A., & Fleeson, J. (1986). Attachment and the construction of relationships. In W. W. Hartup & Z. Rubin (Eds.), *Relationships and development* (pp. 51–71). New York: Cambridge University Press.

Sroufe, L. A., & Rutter, M. (1984). The domain of developmental psychopathology. *Child Development, 55*, 173–189.

Sterling, S., Cowen, E. L., Weissberg, R. P., Lotyczewski, B. S., & Boike, M. (1985). Recent stressful life events and young children's school adjustment. *American Journal of Community Psychology, 13*, 87–99.

Stevenson, D. L., & Baker, D. P. (1987). The family–school relation and the child's school performance. *Child Development, 58*, 1348–1357.

United States Bureau of the Census. (1982). *U. S. census of population and housing: 1980 census tracts*. Washington, DC: U. S. Government Printing Office.

United States Bureau of the Census. (1989). *Money income and poverty in the United States, 1988* (Current Population Reports, Series P-60, No. 166, Advance data from the March 1989 Current Population Survey). Washington, DC: United States Government Printing Office.

Vaden, N. A., Bloom, M., Griesler, P. C., Kupersmidt, J. B., & Patterson, C. J. (April, 1989). *Subjective and objective assessments of peer acceptance and behavior among siblings in elementary school*. Paper presented at the Society for Research in Child Development, Kansas City, MO.

Vaughn, B. E., Egeland, B., & Sroufe, L. A. (1979). Individual differences in infant–mother attachment at 12 and 18 months: Stability and change in families under stress. *Child Development, 50*, 971–975.

Waters, E., Vaughn, B. E., & Egeland, B. R. (1980). Individual differences in infant–mother attachment relationships at one: Antecedents in neonatal behavior in an urban, economically, disadvantaged sample. *Child Development, 51*, 208–216.

Werner, E., & Smith, R. (1982). *Vulnerable but invincible: A study of resilient children*. New York: McGraw-Hill.

Wilson, W. J. (1987). *The truly disadvantaged: The inner city, the underclass, and public policy*. Chicago: University of Chicago Press.

Wright, J., Giammarino, M., & Parad, H. W. (1986). Social status in small groups: Individual–group similarity and the social "misfit." *Journal of Personality and Social Psychology, 50*, 523–536.

Zussman, J. (1980). Situational determinants of parental behavior: Effects of compelling cognitive activity. *Child Development, 51*, 792–800.

# CHAPTER FOURTEEN

# Epilogue:
# Remaining Issues and Future Trends
# in the Study of Family–Peer Relationships

Ross D. Parke
*University of California, Riverside*

A variety of issues remain to be addressed in the field and in this final chapter, we underscore some of these directions for future research.

## Multiple Pathways Between Family and Peer Systems

First, family and peer systems are linked in multiple ways. In several chapters throughout the volume, illustrations of the myriad of ways in which family and peer systems are linked have been examined. Indirect and direct pathways (Parke et al., 1989) between family and peers have been illustrated in this volume. Indirect pathways describe the impact of relationships among family members as well as the cognitive and behavioral processes that evolve from these interactions. Several examples of how relationships between family members can directly influence subsequent peer relationships have been provided. In their respective chapters, Elicker, Englund, and Sroufe underscore the long-term implications of attachment for peer functioning, whereas Parke and his colleagues focus on the importance of different types of family interaction patterns. Direct pathways involve parental efforts to promote and manage children's experiences with peers. These include a variety of parental roles such as designers, mediators, supervisors, and consultants (Ladd & Coleman, in press). Several contributors to this volume (Ladd et al., and Lollis & Ross) indicate the progress that has been gained in our understanding of these direct modes of parental influence.

425

Although further work is clearly needed in exploring both of these pathways, little effort has been made to explore how the strategies represented by them operate in combination to produce their impact on peer outcomes. This array of socialization strategies that is available to parents can be viewed as analogous to a "cafeteria model" in which various combinations of items can be chosen or ignored in variously sized portions. Are there family typologies in which different combinations are evident across families? If so, are these stable across time? Some parents may spend relatively little time in interaction but provide multiple opportunities for contact with peers. In contrast, other parents may be highly involved with their children in family settings but limit their children's peer contacts. Some parents may invest heavily in teaching their children social skills and other parents may regard peer social skills as best acquired in interactions with other children. Do all combinations produce equally socially competent children, or are some "ingredients" in this mix more important than others? Do different combinations produce different, but equally well-adjusted children—in recognition of the fact that developmental adaptations may be achieved through multiple pathways? Can heavy investment in one set of strategies compensate for limited utilization of another mode of influence? For example, Howes (1990) has found that a high-quality relationship with a day-care provider can, in part, compensate for an insecure attachment relationship with a primary caregiver in the home.

What are the determinants of these patterns or combinations of strategies? Developmental level of the child clearly influences these patterns. Parent–child relationships are clearly primary in infancy and early childhood, and variations in parental provision of opportunities become more salient as the child develops. Other direct strategies, such as supervision, change with age; younger children benefit more from this type of parental support than do older children (Bhavnagri & Parke, 1991). Similarly, monitoring shows developmental shifts and becomes more important in adolescence. Perhaps the "sensitive" parent shifts his or her style of intervention across development. Instead of functioning as an initiator and arranger, as children develop, parents probably function in less public roles. For example, they may function as problem solvers or coaches, but often *before* confronting a new social context, or assist the child to solve a problem that arises with another child. As the child reaches adolescence, monitoring is a more likely form of parental management (Patterson & Stouthamer-Loeber, 1984). Parent gender is a further factor that influences utilization of different strategies. Whereas both mothers and fathers serve as interactive partners and attachment figures, evidence suggests that mothers and fathers differ in their utilization of direct influence strategies. Mothers serve as managers of children's social lives by arranging contacts between their children and peers to a greater degree than fathers (Ladd & Golter, 1988).

## Nature of Linking Processes

The search for linking processes has only begun, and much more work is needed to specify the nature of the mechanisms and how these change with age. Several candidates were suggested by the contributors, but more work is needed before we can begin to understand how children transfer lessons learned in either the family or the peer group across these contexts. Attachment theories suggest the role of working models as mediating mechanisms. How these develop, the nature of the dimensions that characterize these "models," and their structure and organization all need further specification. Do children develop several models in light of the independence of mother– and father–child relationships (Main & Weston, 1981) or are experiences fused in additive or multiplicative ways into single models?

How do these "models" change across time either as a function of peer experience or from changes in familial relationships? For example, Thompson, Lamb, and Estes (1982) found that shifts in family circumstances (e.g., job loss, divorce), in turn may influence parent–child attachment relationships, with secure attachments shifting to insecure relationships. What implications do these shifts in attachment relationships have for children's "working models" and their relationships with peers?

The recent work of Puttalaz, Costanzo, and Smith (1991) concerning the role of parental recollections of their own childhood peer experiences as a predictor of their own children's peer relations raises interesting questions concerning the relative degree of specificity of content of working models that may prove useful in this area. Is it advantageous to explore parental working models of attachment—a general measure—versus a more specific index of their working models of peer relationships?

Alternative types of cognitive models beyond working models merit consideration, as well. A great deal of attention has been devoted to the role of children's social information-processing models (Dodge, 1986; Ladd & Crick, 1989) in understanding the processes underlying variations in peer relationships, and less attention has been given to the origins of these social information-processing differences in the family. Little progress has been made in understanding the ways in which these cognitive models develop in the context of family. Do similar sets of processes guide parental decision making about social situations? Are parental social information-processing models related to similar processes in their children? Do parents have similar ways of solving family and adult peer issues, or do they have different approaches to these two sets of issues? Do parents approach peer situations involving their child differently than they approach other types of problem situations? Answers to these types of questions would begin to reveal patterns of similarities and differences across adults and children and provide a clearer picture of the nature of representational models of social behavior across the peer and family systems (Burks & Parke, 1991).

Moreover, application of existing theoretical models that have proven heuristic value in the peers domain (e.g., Dodge, 1986) to the family context would be useful. These existing models also provide guidelines concerning specific dimensions (e.g., strategies, goals, expectations, anticipated consequences) that could be fruitfully applied to furthering our understanding of family-based information processing. Progress may be made by adoption of a common set of dimensions across the two systems, rather than separate dimensions for family and peer contexts (Burks & Parke, 1991).

Finally, recent work on beliefs could be usefully extended from parents (Goodnow & Collins, 1990) to children. To date, we know little about children's views of the issues raised in this volume. Progress is being made in the mapping of children's working models (Sroufe & Fleeson, 1986) but this work needs to be complemented by research on children's views of the appropriateness of different types of parental discipline and management. For example, when do children view it as inappropriate for parents to initiate contacts on their behalf? A better understanding of the culturally determined developmental norms as viewed through the eyes of children would be a helpful addition to research agenda in this area.

Emotional regulatory processes have also been suggested as candidates to explain the links between family and peer systems. As Parke et al. (this volume) note, more work needs to be done in terms of both specification of the aspects of emotional regulation that merit consideration and the role of the family in the socialization of these emotional processes. Finally, a fusion between models that focus on cognitive processes and models that champion emotional processes would be of value. It is clear that both cognitive and emotional processes play important roles in this area. Moreover, it is evident that there is room for emotional variables in cognitive models as well as vice versa. For example, theories of working models within the attachment tradition clearly emphasize the role of emotion within relationships (Sroufe & Fleeson, 1986). Similarly, information processing (Dodge, 1991) as well as attribution theorists (Grych & Fincham, 1990) have stressed the importance of including emotions in their theories. On the other side, emotion-oriented researchers are increasingly recognizing the role that cognition plays in their theories (Parke et al., this volume). The main obstacle to a better fusion of these two classes of variables is the development of theoretical language and measurement systems that will allow a dialogue across different theoretical paradigms.

## Levels of Analysis

Greater attention needs to be paid to the level of analysis involved in measurement of the family and peer group. In spite of the efforts to describe various levels of analysis (Kreppner, 1989; Parke, 1988) such as individual, dyad, triad, and group, little work has reflected these distinctions. To date, our focus has been on individual characteristics of parents (e.g., their directiveness, warmth, etc.), although these are often measured in dyadic interactional contexts. Attachment theorists are more likely to measure relationship qualities (e.g., mother–infant relationship). Few studies have assessed the nature of family interaction in triadic contexts or have treated the family as the unit of analysis in their explorations of family–peer links. This is not only merely a mechanical exercise, but it represents an important set of distinctions that carry implications for the types of learning that may take place. The question that we need to address is whether children's experience in dyadic, triadic, or familial interactions differ in meaningful ways that, in turn, will impact their relationships with peers.

It is important to begin to identify the particular levels of family (e.g., individual, dyadic, family) that, in turn, relate to levels of peer functioning. Do the same levels of analysis within the family predict to similar levels on the peers' side? Youngblade and Belsky (1991) have suggested that attachment relationships, for example, which allow opportunities to learn how to handle intimacy and closeness, will be better predictors of friendship relationships—the parallel form of relationship across systems—than other types of peer indices, such as group or sociometric measures. Similarly, do family experiences that teach cooperation and coordination in the execution of household work (Goodnow, 1988) alter children's behavior in peer work group settings?

## Direction of Influence: Toward a Transactional Model

The issue of direction of influence needs more attention in future studies. Although it is implicitly assumed that the family is "influencing" the children's peer relationships, the correlational nature of the vast majority of the evidence presented in this volume suggests that the direction of causality may run from child to parent. (See Dodge, 1990; Lytton, 1990; and Wahler, 1990, for a discussion of this issue.) Attempts to establish direction of causality are interesting, yet it is likely that transactional models (Sameroff & Chandler, 1975) in which parents and children mutually influence each other across time will prove most useful for guiding subsequent research in this area. Van Aken (1991) has recently provided empirical support for the utility of transactional models in this area. In the final analysis, it is no longer an issue of whether influence is bidirectional, but how the relative degree of influence changes across age and context.

Another form of this issue concerns the question of whether families influence peer systems or vice versa. To a very large degree, the underlying assumption is that the flow of influence moves from family to peer system. Whereas this may be a reasonable assumption in the case of young children, it is less tenable as the child develops and consolidates his or her relationships with others outside the home. The mapping of the ways in which peers influence families across development is an understudied task, but it is a necessary step if we are to achieve a full appreciation of the links between these domains.

To begin this mapping process, we consider possible ways in which this influence could take place. It is useful to distinguish various levels of analysis. At the individual level, the child may acquire new attitudes and/or behaviors as a consequence of peer group interactions that may alter their relationships in the family. Although it is common to assume that these behaviors may often be negative (e.g., aggression), it is feasible to view this as a potentially positive process as well. The child may acquire more sophisticated social skills or more desirable behaviors (e.g., sharing and prosocial behavior), which, in turn, may improve their family relationships. At the level of the dyad, the child may develop relationships with peers that begin to rival the family-based relationships and lead to increased time spent in peer activities to the detriment of the family relationship. In the case of family transitions such as divorce, children, especially adolescents, become more peer-oriented, often at the expense of family ties (Hetherington, 1989). At the group level, the peer group may in extreme cases replace the family in terms of loyalty and commitment. Studies of gangs (Horowitz, 1982) suggest that this transfer of loyalty may occur; in these cases, the peer gang becomes a second or substitute family. Clearly, this transfer process has potentially deleterious effects on the original family unit. At the same time, it is recognized that family–peer conflict is often exaggerated and, in general, there is a high degree of agreement between children and their parents (Douvan & Adelson, 1966; Youniss & Smollar, 1989).

## Beyond Sociometric Status

Our focus has been almost exclusively on peer sociometric assessments as our index of peer group adaptation. This is obviously a useful measure backed by a lengthy history of research, but are there other measures on the peers' side of the equation that need to be explored? This measure provides a portrait of how the individual child is perceived by his peer group. However, other ways of measuring peer relationships are possible and merit consideration. The most obvious are dyadic friendship relationships, which are, to a degree, independent from a child's sociometric status. Several researchers have distinguished the concept of *friend* from the more inclusive concept of *peer* (e.g., Bukowski & Hoza, 1989; Cochran, this volume; Furman & Robbins, 1985; Ladd, 1989). Other types of relationships can be distinguished as well. Play or work partners in school settings may not have the intensity and intimacy of friendships but do represent another type of peer–peer dyadic relationship that needs to be considered. Group level activities characterize a great deal of peer interaction, such as informal play groups, structured team activities, and formal work groups. Successful adaptation in these types of group settings may require different types of skills than are required for either friendship relationships or for social status. Such skills as adhering to one's role and coordinating individual actions with other group members' behavior in terms of timing, competence, and appropriateness, are all required to be a successful group participant. The types of roles that one achieves within a group, whether as leader or follower, are other aspects of peer group functioning that need to be examined.

## Gender of Child: Beyond a Psychology of Boys

Progress in this area is likely to proceed more quickly if we develop a better theory of gender differences. Our understanding of boys' peer relationships in general (Asher & Coie, 1990) and our insights concerning how families and peer systems relate to one another are better developed for boys than for girls. Some studies focus only on boys (MacDonald, 1987) or are able to explain boys' behavior as a function of family variables better than girls' (e.g., Krappman, Oswald, & von Salisch, 1991; Ladd & Golter, 1988; MacDonald & Parke, 1984). Are we measuring the wrong aspects of girls' social relationships? In light of recent evidence (Asher & Williams, in press; French, 1990) that the behavioral correlates of sociometric rejection differ for boys and girls, this is a distinct possibility. Does parental influence assume different forms in the case of boys' and girls' social relations with peers? Are we measuring boys and girls at the wrong developmental periods? Some evidence suggests that during adolescence when girls are negotiating cross-sex relationships, the impact of familial relationships, especially father–daughter ties, may be particularly salient (Hetherington, 1972). It is clear that more attention needs to be given to the ways in which girls and boys are differentially socialized into peer relationships. In turn, the inclusion of *both* mothers and fathers in future studies of this gender issue is critical if we are going to improve our ability to understand girls as well as boys.

## Towards an Ecology of Family–Peer Relationships

Neither family nor peer relationships exist in social vacuums, but rather need to be viewed within their ecological niches. A number of contributors to this volume have illustrated the importance of an ecological orientation to this problem. The Cochran et al. (this volume) work on social networks, as well as the Patterson et al. (this volume) work on family economic circumstances both underscore the value of this perspective. A useful direction for future research is to explore in further detail how neighborhood characteristics alter family–peer relationships. An increasingly sophisticated approach to the assessment of neighborhoods (e.g., Eliot & Huizinga, 1990) makes new research on this issue an exciting avenue to explore (Cupp, Spitzer, Isley-Paradise, Bentley, & Parke, 1992). As Sameroff (in press) has shown, often our well-accepted assumptions are challenged when an ecological viewpoint is adopted. In his work, Sameroff found that parents in high risk neighborhoods who use "authoritarian" parenting strategies were more effective than parents who employed "authoritative" strategies in keeping their adolescents out of trouble. It is clear that families may need to behave differently in order to adapt to the demands of different neighborhood characteristics.

## Variations in Family–Peer Relationships

One of the lessons derived from this volume is that greater attention needs to be given to issues of generalizability. This issue assumes several forms.

*Historical Continuity.* Is it appropriate to assume that family–peer relationships can be accounted for by the same set of principles in different historical periods? Probably not! However, we still know relatively little about the nature of this historical variation. Historical analyses can serve several functions (Elder, Modell, & Parke, 1992). First, history can provide unique opportunities to assess the generalizability of our explanatory principles in different historical periods. Historical variations such as war, famine, or economic depression represent important and powerful natural experiments that permit opportunities for theory and model testing, often under conditions that are much more drastic than developmental researchers could either ethically or practically engineer or produce in the laboratory or in the field. Tracing how shifts or turns in family organization alter peer group relationships would be an interesting and profitable enterprise. For example, during wartime, the increased degree of father absence accompanied by a higher percentage of mothers in the workplace and children in day care provides unique opportunities to assess family–peer relationships. Cross-time comparisons between earlier periods and the present era in which day-care enrollment are high would provide interesting insights concerning how the historical period conditioned family–peer relationships.

*Cultural Continuity.*   Just as history provides us with naturally occurring variations, so do cross-cultural contexts provide opportunities for exploring the boundary conditions of our theories. Developmental psychologists increasingly recognize that culture shapes the nature, timing, and rate of social development. This recognition is part of our shift away from endorsement of a positivistic assumption that psychological laws of development are applicable universally (Parke, 1989). At a minimum, the necessity of examining the assumption by replicating findings in other cultural contexts is increasingly common, whereas in stronger form it is assumed that culture organizes behavioral patterns in fundamentally unique ways (see Rogoff, 1990; Whiting & Edwards, 1988).

Variations in family organization and structure that are evident in different societies represent one point of departure. Do extended family arrangements produce different peer relationships than do nuclear family types? Different role arrangements for household members provide opportunities to examine variations in mother versus father contributions to peer socialization. Similarly, how do variations in child caregiver roles in the family condition peer relationships? Are peer relationships different in cultures where older siblings are required to assume caregiving responsibility for younger siblings? In turn, are subsequent peer relationships different as a consequence of siblings versus parents as the primary socialization agent? How do variations in the organization of peer groups change across cultures? Are they largely informal or is contact between agemates limited to formal settings? Are groups limited to single-age groups or do they involve multiple ages in single groups?

How is the family's role modified by other institutions? The role that parents play may shift if organizing peer contacts varies considerably as a function of schooling. In cultures with no formal schooling, parental involvement in peer group activities may assume a more major role than in cultures where school attendance is normative.

Cross-cultural studies provide interesting ways of examining the impact of parental cognitions, such as perceptions, attitudes, and beliefs (Goodnow & Collins, 1990) on peer relationships. Cultures vary in their assumptions about the relative importance of peer relationships, the assumed competence of children to manage these types of relationships at different ages, and the role that parents play in the promotion and maintenance of the relationships. Cross-cultural studies offer important opportunities to replicate and extend earlier work in this area.

## Uniqueness of Models of Family–Peer Linkage

Another issue that needs to be addressed is the uniqueness of the models that have been developed to account for family–peer relationships. Are these models specific and limited to peer relationships or do they have utility in understanding other types of social relationships such as marital or later parental roles? Alternatively, do we need separate models to account for family relationships with other institutions such as schools? Multisetting and multirelationship studies are needed to answer this issue of the heuristic value of these current models for links between families and other types of relationships and institutions.

## Intervention

Intervention efforts can be undertaken for several reasons. Although the goal is generally to improve the social life of the target child, another central reason for intervention is to provide a test of a theoretical position.

In considering intervention, several issues merit consideration, including the target of the intervention, the context of the program, and the strategy involved. In terms of target, it has been fashionable to focus on the child as the target of the intervention. This is a useful strategy in this area as a way of examining how changes in children's behavior in the peer context can modify family relationships. This is a beginning step in unraveling the direction of influence issue and in particular to see how shifts in peer functioning can alter feedback on family relationships.

Second, the parent can be the target of intervention, whereby techniques of discipline, beliefs, and knowledge are systematically modified and, in turn, the impact on (a) parent–child relationships are examined, and (b) children's peer relationships are scrutinized to determine if shifts in fact have occurred. Patterson's (1982) work is an example of this type of strategy.

Interventions can also be targeted at the level of the neighborhood. For example, increasing safety or improving access to play spaces for children may, in turn, alter parental actions on behalf of their children. In this case, the shifts occur in terms of "opportunity structures" (Cochran et al., this volume) that are available to parents who, in turn, permit their children access to these resources. This type of intervention could be viewed as a modification of parental gate keeping, by reorganizing the availability of resources. A variety of other interventions at the level of the community such as increased day care for young children could be viewed within this framework.

Little attention has been paid to the types of strategies that might be used to modify parental behavior. The history of success of coaching and modeling strategies (Ladd, 1983) suggests that similar techniques could be employed with parents as the intervention agents.

Other types of interventions involve targeting not the individuals, but the links across contexts. There are programs (Epstein, 1989) that provide opportunities for parents to become more involved in the activities of the institutions, such as schools in which the children participate through such mechanisms as notes to parents concerning school activities and student progress. Parent–teacher conferences provide opportunities for parents to become more aware of not only their child's behavior in these settings, but may increase the parental sense of efficacy in terms of their ability to modify or alter their children's behavior in these extrafamilial settings.

Another strategy involves increasing parental awareness of the importance of peer relationships through media campaigns, such as TV spots, that show not only the important role of peer relationships but also heighten parental awareness of the ways that they can influence these outcomes.

## Conclusion

A variety of problems remain, but as the chapters in this volume illustrate, substantial progress, both conceptually and methodologically, has been made in recent years. By continuing this search for the family's role in the emergence and management of peer relationships, not only will our understanding increase, but we will be in a better position to improve the social lives of children through research-based interventions. It is our hope that this volume has moved us closer to the achievement of both of these goals.

## ACKNOWLEDGMENT

Preparation of this chapter was supported in part by National Science Foundation Grant BNS 8919391 to Ross D. Parke.

## REFERENCES

Asher, S., & Coie, J. (Eds.) (1990). *Peer rejection in childhood.* New York: Cambridge University Press.

Asher, S., & Williams, G. (in press). New approaches to identifying rejected children in school settings. *Child Development.*

Bhavnagri, N., & Parke, R. D. (1991). Parents as direct facilitators of children's peer relationships: Effects of age of child and sex of parent. *Journal of Personal and Social Relationships, 8,* 423–440.

Bukowski, W. M., & Hoza, B. (1989). Popularity and friendship: Issues in theory, measurement, and outcome. In T. Berndt & G. Ladd (Eds.), *Peer relationships in child development* (pp. 15–45). New York: Wiley.

Burks, V., & Parke, R. D. (1991, July). *Parental and child representations of social relationships.* Symposium presentation at the International Society for the Study of Behavioral Development, Minneapolis, MN.

Cupp, R., Spitzer, S., Isley-Paradise, S., Bentley, B., & Parke, R. D. (1992, June). *Children's social acceptance: The role of parents' perceptions of the neighborhood.* Paper presented at the annual meeting of the American Psychological Society, San Diego, CA.

Dodge, K. A. (1986). A social information-processing model of social competence in children. In M. Perlmutter (Ed.), *Minnesota symposia on child psychology* (Vol. 18, pp. 77–126). Minneapolis: University of Minnesota Press.

Dodge, K. A. (1990). Nature versus nurture in childhood conduct disorders: It is time to ask a different question. *Developmental Psychology, 26,* 698–701.

Dodge, K. A. (1991). Emotion and social information processing. In J. Garber & K. A. Dodge (Eds.), *The development of emotion regulation and dysregulation* (pp. 159–181). New York: Cambridge University Press.

Douvan, E., & Adelson, J. (1966). *The adolescent experience.* New York: Wiley.

Elder, G. H., Jr., Modell, J., & Parke, R. D. (1992). *Children in time and place.* New York: Cambridge University Press.

Eliot, D. S., & Huizinga, D. (1990). *The mediating effects of the social structure in high risk neighborhoods.* Paper presented at the Annual Meeting of the American Sociological Association, Washington, DC.

Epstein, J. L. (1989). The selection of friends: Changes across the grades and in different school environments. In T. Berndt & G. Ladd (Eds.), *Peer relationships in child development* (pp. 158–187). New York: Wiley.

French, D. (1990). Heterogeneity of rejected girls. *Child Development, 61,* 2028–2031.

Furman, W. J., & Robbins, P. (1985). What's the point? Issues in the selections of treatment objectives. In B. Schneider, K. Rubin, & J. Ledingham, (Eds.), *Children's peer relationships: Issues in assessment and intervention* (pp. 41–54). New York: Springer-Verlag.

Goodnow, J. J. (1988). Children's household work: Its nature and function. *Psychological Bulletin, 103,* 5–26.

Goodnow, J. J., & Collins, W. A. (1990). *Development according to parents: The nature, sources, and consequences of parents' ideas.* Hillsdale, NJ: Lawrence Erlbaum Associates.

Grych, J. H., & Fincham, F. D. (1990). Marital conflict and children's adjustment: A cognitive-contextual framework. *Psychological Bulletin, 108,* 267–290.

Hetherington, E. M. (1972). Effects of father absence on personality development of adolescent girls. *Developmental Psychology, 7,* 303–326.

Hetherington, E. M. (1989). Coping with family transitions: Winners, losers, and survivors. *Child Development, 60,* 1–18.

Horowitz, R. (1982). Adult delinquent gangs in a Chicano community: Masked intimacy and marginality. *Urban Life, 13,* 3–26.

Howes, C. (1990). Can the age of entry into child care and the quality of child care predict adjustment in kindergarten? *Developmental Psychology, 26,* 292–303.

Krappman, L., Oswald, H., & von Salisch, M. (1991, July). *Parents' effective and ineffective strategies of supporting their 10-year-old child's peer activities.* Symposium presentation at the International Society for the Study of Behavioral Development, Minneapolis, MN.

Kreppner, K. (1989). Linking infant development-in-context research to the investigation of life-span development. In K. Kreppner & R. Lerner (Eds.), *Family systems and life-span development* (pp. 33–64). Hillsdale, NJ: Lawrence Erlbaum Associates.

Ladd, G. W. (1983). Social networks of popular, average, and rejected children in school settings. *Merrill-Palmer Quarterly, 29,* 283–307.

Ladd, G. W. (1989). Toward a further understanding of peer relationships and their contributions to child development. In T. Berndt & G. Ladd (Eds.), *Peer relationships in child development* (pp. 1–11). New York: Wiley.

Ladd, G. W., & Coleman, C. (in press). Young children's peer relationships: Forms, features, and functions. In B. Spodek (Ed.), *Handbook of research on the education of young children* (2nd ed.). New York: Macmillan.

Ladd, G. W., & Crick, N. R. (1989). Probing the psychological environment. Children's cognitions, perceptions, and feelings in the peer culture. In M. Maehr & C. Ames (Eds.), *Advances in motivation and achievement: Motivation enhancing environments* (Vol. 6, pp. 1–44). Greenwich, CT: JAI.

Ladd, G. W., & Golter, B. S. (1988). Parents' management of preschoolers' peer relations: Is it related to children's social competence? *Developmental Psychology, 24,* 109–117.

Lytton, H. (1990). Child and parent effects in boys' conduct disorder: A reinterpretation. *Developmental Psychology, 26,* 683–697.

MacDonald, K. (1987). Parent–child physical play with rejected, neglected, and popular boys. *Developmental Psychology, 23,* 705–711.

MacDonald, K., & Parke, R. D. (1984). Bridging the gap: Parent–child play interaction and peer interactive competence. *Child Development, 55,* 1265–1277.

Main, M., & Weston, D. (1981). The quality of the toddler's relationship to mother and father: Related to conflict behavior and readiness to establish new relationships. *Child Development, 52,* 932–940.

Parke, R. D. (1988). Families in life-span perspective: A multilevel developmental approach. In E. Hetherington, R. Lerner, & M. Perlmutter (Eds.), *Child development in life-span perspective* (pp. 159–190). Hillsdale, NJ: Lawrence Erlbaum Associates.

Parke, R. D. (1989). Social development in infancy: A 25-year perspective. In H. W. Reese (Ed.), *Advances in child development and behavior* (Vol. 21, pp. 1–48). Orlando, FL: Academic Press.

Parke, R. D., MacDonald, K., Burks, V., Carson, J., Bhavnagri, N., Barth, J., & Beitel, A. (1989). Family and peer systems: In search of the linkages. In K. Kreppner & R. M. Lerner (Eds.), *Family systems and life-span development* (pp. 65–92). Hillsdale, NJ: Lawrence Erlbaum Associates.

Patterson, G. R. (1982). *A social learning approach: Coercive family processes.* Eugene, OR: Castilla.

Patterson, G. R., & Stouthamer-Loeber, M. (1984). The correlation of family management and delinquency. *Child Development, 55,* 1299–1307.

Puttalaz, M., Constanzo, P. R., & Smith, R. (1991). Maternal recollections of childhood peer relationships: Implications for their children's social competence. *Journal of Social and Personal Relationships, 8,* 403–422.

Rogoff, B. (1990). *Apprenticeship in thinking: Cognitive development in social context.* New York: Oxford University Press.

Sameroff, A. J. (in press). Cross levels: Metaphors for cross-systems relationships. In R. D. Parke & S. Kellam (Eds.), *Exploring family relationships with other social contexts.* Hillsdale, NJ: Lawrence Erlbaum Associates.

Sameroff, A. J., & Chandler, M. J. (1975). Reproduction risk and the continuum of caregiving casualty. In F. D. Horowitz (Ed.), *Review of child development research* (Vol. 4, pp. 187–244). Chicago: University of Chicago Press.

Sroufe, L. A., & Fleeson, J. (1986). Attachment and the construction of relationships. In W. W. Hartup & Z. Rubin (Eds.), *Relationships and development* (pp. 51–72). Hillsdale, NJ: Lawrence Erlbaum Associates.

Thompson, R. A., Lamb, M. E., & Estes, D. (1982). Stability of infant–mother attachment at 12 and 18 months: Stability and change in families under stress. *Child Development, 53,* 144–148.

Van Aken, M. A. G. (1991). *Competent development in a transactional perspective: A longitudinal study.* Unpublished doctoral dissertation, Catholic University, Nijmegen, The Netherlands.

Wahler, R. G. (1990). Who is driving the interactions? *Developmental Psychology, 26,* 702–704.

Whiting, B. B., & Edwards, C. P. (1988). *Children of different worlds.* Cambridge, MA: Harvard University Press.

Youngblade, L., & Belsky, J. (1991, April). *Predicting 5-year-olds' relationships with close friends from antecedent parent–child relationships: A soft modeling approach.* Paper presented at the Biennial Meeting of the Society for Research in Child Development, Seattle, WA.

Youniss, J., & Smollar, J. (1989). Adolescents' interpersonal relationships in social context. In T. Berndt & G. Ladd (Eds.), *Peer relationships in child development* (pp. 300–316). New York: Wiley.

# Author Index

## H

# Subject Index